OXFORD STUDIES IN ROMAN SOCIETY AND LAW

General Editors

PAUL DU PLESSIS   THOMAS A. J. MCGINN

OXFORD STUDIES IN ROMAN SOCIETY AND LAW

The aim of this monograph series is to create an interdisciplinary forum devoted to the interaction between legal history and ancient history, in the context of the study of Roman law. Focusing on the relationship of law to society, the volumes will cover the most significant periods of Roman law (up to the death of Justinian in 565) so as to provide a balanced view of growth, decline, and resurgence. Most importantly, the series will provoke general debate over the extent to which legal rules should be examined in light of the society which produced them in order to understand their purpose and efficacy.

Security and Credit in Roman Law

The historical evolution of pignus *and* hypotheca

HENDRIK L. E. VERHAGEN

OXFORD
UNIVERSITY PRESS

OXFORD
UNIVERSITY PRESS

Great Clarendon Street, Oxford, OX2 6DP,
United Kingdom

Oxford University Press is a department of the University of Oxford.
It furthers the University's objective of excellence in research, scholarship,
and education by publishing worldwide. Oxford is a registered trade mark of
Oxford University Press in the UK and in certain other countries

First Edition published in 2022

Published in the United States of America by Oxford University Press
198 Madison Avenue, New York, NY 10016, United States of America

British Library Cataloguing in Publication Data
Data available

Library of Congress Control Number: 2022931816

ISBN 978-0-19-969583-6

DOI: 10.1093/oso/9780199695836.001.0001

Voor Marie-José, Eva, en Laura

Acknowledgments

Family, friends and colleagues have helped and supported me over the years: I am immensely grateful to all of them. For this book I would like to thank a number of persons specifically. My home country, the Netherlands, has a great Romanist tradition, which is continued by a range of bright young scholars. I am very grateful to some of them for their comments of chapters of my book: Vincent van Hoof, Elsemieke Daalder, Rian Bobbink, and Quintijn Mauer. I am thankful to my daughter Laura for checking citations of the *Corpus iuris civilis* and to Vincent Hunink for his advice on some of the translations from Latin. I would like to thank two colleagues at the faculty of law of the Radboud University for their encouragement over the years: Corjo Jansen and Ben Schuijling. I would also like to express my thanks to those who have given useful comments in earlier publications, on which this book is partly based: Giuseppe Dari-Mattiacci, Dennis Kehoe, Jaap den Hollander, and Willem Zwalve. A special word of thanks goes to Peter Richerson, who kindly read the sections on social and cultural evolution. I am extremely grateful to the anonymous reviewers of this book, not only for their comments on specific points but even more so for the very useful suggestions for enhancing the presentation of the material contained in this book. I also would like to express my thanks to the editors of the series *Roman Studies in Law and Society*, Paul du Plessis and Thomas McGinn, for their guidance. I remember with great respect Felix Wubbe, Robert Feenstra, and Hans Ankum. The latter read and corrected all my preliminary studies on *pignus* and *hypotheca* and encouraged the writing of this book.

I am fortunate to have spent my entire professional life in stimulating and diverse working environments. My career started at the Department of Roman law of the Radboud University, chaired by Paul Nève, where the seeds for my interest in Roman law were sown. In the Financial Markets Group of Clifford Chance Amsterdam, I learned much about law and finance in action. Within the Department of Private Law of the Faculty of Law of the Radboud University, for a long time chaired by Bas Kortmann and now by Steven Bartels, I have always had absolute freedom to pursue any legal subject, past or present, that I was interested in. At the same university I also enjoy the privilege of being a member of the Ancient and Medieval History Department of the Faculty of Arts chaired by Olivier Hekster. I would like to thank Charlotte Loveridge, Henry Clarke and Jamie Mortimer at Oxford University Press, who have patiently encouraged and supported my book. Janet Walker and Thomas Deva skilfully edited the manuscript for publication, and Ian Macavoy corrected the proofs.

Many years ago my wife Marie-José first took me to the *Mercati di Traiano* in Rome, where the idea for this book was born. Ever since she has been an inspiring, sensible and caring travelling companion on the long and adventurous road which led to the present book. I dedicate this book to her and to our daughters Eva and Laura, without whose loving support it could not have been written.

Rick Verhagen

Contents

Abbreviations

C.	Codex of Justinian[1]
C.Th.	Theodosian Code[2]
D.	Digest of Justinian[3]
Gai. *Inst.*	Gaius, *Institutiones*[4]
TPSulp	*Tabulae Pompeianae Sulpiciorum*[5]

Other abbreviations for inscriptions, papyri, and other legal texts are taken from Kaser 1971. Abbreviations of Latin and Greek authors are taken from Simon Hornblower, Antony Spawforth, and Esther Eidinow (eds), *The Oxford Classical Dictionary* (4th edn, Oxford: Oxford University Press, 2012).[6]

[1] P. Krüger (ed.), *Corpus iuris civilis, Codex Justinianus*, vol. II, Berlin: Weidmann 1905. English translations of Codex texts are taken from B.W. Frier (ed.), *The Codex of Justinian*, 3 vols, Cambridge, Cambridge University Press 2016 and have occasionally been slightly amended.

[2] Th. Mommsen and P. M. Meyer (eds), *Codex Theodosianus*, 3 vols, 3rd edn, Berlin: Weidmann 1962.

[3] P. Krüger (ed.), *Corpus iuris civilis, Digesta*, vol. I, Berlin: Weidmann 1905. Translations of Digest texts are taken from A. Watson (ed.), *The Digest of Justinian*, 4 vols, Philadelphia, PA: University of Pennsylvania Press 1998, and adapted where I preferred a different translation.

[4] *The Institutes of Gaius*. Translated with an introduction by W.M. Gordon and O.F. Robinson. With the Latin text of Seckel and Kuebler, Duckworth: London 1988.

[5] There are two excellent editions of the 'archive of the Sulpicii': G. Camodeca, *Tabulae Pompeianae Sulpiciorum, Edizione critica dell'archivio puteolano dei Sulpicii*, Rome: Quasar 1999; J. G. Wolf, *Neue Rechtsurkunden aus Pompeji, Tabulae Pompeianae Novae*, 2nd ed., Darmstadt: WBG 2012. The texts and references in this book are taken from Camodeca's edition (TPSulp), omitting some of the epigraphic symbols from the Latin texts.

[6] Translations are taken from the Loeb Classical Library (LCL) unless indicated otherwise.

Introduction

In 40 AD a borrower from the Campanian port city Puteoli declared to his creditor:

> If on the Ides of May I shall not give, pay or satisfy the above-mentioned 20,000 sesterces, then you will be authorised to sell at auction the grain in question under the terms of the pledge. If it shall fetch more, you shall return everything which remains to me; if it shall fetch less, I will give the difference to you or your heir.[1]

Two hundred years later, this contractual clause had evolved into a mandatory rule of law, which almost 2,000 years later is still included in most (if not all) Western codifications.[2] Where the debtor fails to pay his debt in time, the creditor shall be authorized to sell the charged objects and shall be liable to pay any surplus proceeds (*superfluum*) to the debtor. What we see here is an example of how a contractual practice can trigger an evolutionary process leading to the formation of a legal rule. This is the main subject of this book, for which the classical Roman law of real security has been taken as a specific illustrative theme.[3] Much variety in law is generated by transactional practices, which are designed by legal practitioners in order to meet the economic demands of their clients.[4] These transactional 'legal variants' provide input to the legal system and may trigger legal change when they become the subject of litigation or (less frequently in Rome) legislation.[5] There is no other legal institution than *pignus* and *hypotheca* where the formative effect of legal practice can be so clearly observed.[6]

[1] TPSulp 79. Original Latin text on p. 137.
[2] For example, art. 2346 French civil code, § 1228 German civil code, art. 2796 and 2797 Italian civil code and art. 3:250 Dutch civil code.
[3] Inspired by Frier 1980: xvii.
[4] For the purpose of this book 'transactional practices' are contractual clauses, entire contracts, or multi-contractual constructions (e.g., a pledge agreement combined with a rental agreement), which are regularly used within a population.
[5] But see Constantine's constitution outlawing forfeiture clauses (C. 8.34.3) discussed in section 11.5.
[6] Kaser 1976: 172; Kaser 1982: 218.

Security and Credit in Roman Law: The historical evolution of pignus *and* hypotheca. Hendrik L. E. Verhagen, Oxford University Press. © Hendrik L. E. Verhagen 2022. DOI: 10.1093/oso/9780199695836.003.0001

Much law finds its origin not in parliaments, justice departments, imperial chanceries, or court rooms, but in contractual and other (e.g., testamentary) transactional practices.[7] As one of the founders of the sociology of law, Eugen Ehrlich, observed, transaction documents are 'levers of legal development'.[8] This book outlines the legal history of *pignus* and *hypotheca* in terms of an iterative relationship between transactional lawyers drafting legal transactions *and* jurists deploying their analytical skills and practical insights in order to accommodate new transactional practices into the Roman legal system. Legal rules which find their origin in transactional practices may have come into existence under the pressure of the particular interests of certain parties (e.g., bankers) having a stronger bargaining power and may be supported by jurists who were members of a particular class.[9] Legislation can correct or supplement the results of spontaneous evolution triggered by transactional practices, by imposing certain duties upon 'stronger' parties (e.g., to sell charged property and pay the surplus to the debtor) or invalidating certain transactional practices (e.g., forfeiture clauses) in order to protect structurally weaker parties. This is what happened in the Roman empire. In the late classical period, although the law of real security did remain by and large creditor-friendly, the imperial chancery increasingly interfered with it in order to provide a considerable degree of protection to debtors. This aspect of legal evolution will not be ignored in this book.[10]

Archive of the Sulpicii, Digest, and Codex

In this book, the evolution of the Roman law of real security, well-known through the legal sources (in particular Justinian's Digest and Codex), will be reconstructed, while matching it with actual banking practices, in particular the secured lending transactions documented in the archive of the Sulpicii (TPSulp). From the Digest and the Codex the legal framework of the law of real security can be reconstructed. The problem is that we do not always know exactly to what extent the law in the books accurately reflects the law in

[7] Luhmann 2004: 236–43. See also Luhmann 2004: 104, 130, 163, 401. For Roman law, see in particular Manigk 1939. For *pignus* specifically, see Kaser 1982: 155; Kaser 1976: 171–2. For Roman contract law, see Jakab 2006 (with references to Mitteis, Rabel, Nörr, Wolff, and others); Meissel 2011 (*societas*).

[8] Ehrlich 1913: 5 ('*Hebel der Rechtsentwicklung*').

[9] Hayek 2013: 85. Hayek mentions the law on the relations between landlord and tenant and creditor and debtor.

[10] See in particular section 11.2.

action. 'The writings of the jurists and imperial constitutions in general show us legal practice only through the lens of juristic abstraction and reflection.'[11] It is true that court rooms are the ultimate testing grounds for the validity of legal transactions, but only a few of them reach these grounds. By focusing on actual transactions one gets a better view of how legal institutions were used by participants in the Roman economy in everyday situations. Ultimately, documents reflecting actual transactions provide the real basis for identifying the economic and social conditions of private law institutions and their functioning in practice.[12]

The documents of the Sulpicii archive give us a much more detailed picture of the economic and social setting of legal transactions than the Digest or the Codex. Although in contrast with the 'law of the emperors' and the 'law of the jurists' contained in the Codex and the Digest they are not formal sources of law, they do demonstrate how these normative sources were actually applied in practice. This collection of documents provides a unique and fascinating insight into the daily practice of a family of financiers (the Sulpicii) active in the Roman empire of the first century AD.[13] The tablets included in the Sulpicii archive demonstrate that Roman law was not a purely intellectual construct of members of the elite, but rather that the Roman legal system—in all its complexity—was actually applied in financial and commercial practice, even by relatively small bankers such as the Sulpicii.[14] The archive of the Sulpicii not only provides us with specific examples of transaction documents—loans, guarantees, pledges, auction announcements—they also enable us to reconstruct how various legal institutions (e.g., *mutuum*, *stipulatio*, *pignus*, and *fideiussio*) were linked to each other in practice. The archive even contains 'client files', consisting of legal documents which allow us to follow a client–bank relationship over a period of several years.[15] More generally, the documents in the archive are connected, in the sense that they were part of the same business operation. The fact that the environment of the Sulpicii archive was Campania and not Rome does not detract from its significance for Roman law at all. It is beyond doubt that the documents of the Sulpicii archive

[11] Kunkel 1973: 197 (translated by Metzger 2005: 2). In the same sense Schulz 1936: 16. This is not wholly true, as there are many fragments to be found in the Digest which do give realistic accounts of actual transactional practices. Johnston 2022: 30–3.

[12] Wieacker 1988: 82. See also Crook 1996: 35–6.

[13] In the two complete editions of these documents (Camodeca 1999 and Wolf 2012) they are called the *Tabulae Pompeianae Sulpiciorum* (TPSulp) and *Tabulae Pompeianae Novae* (TPN), respectively. They are sometimes also referred to as the 'Murecine tablets', after the locality near Pompeii where archaeologists found them. Most of these documents were, however, executed in Puteoli, where the Sulpicii operated their banking business before they moved to Pompeii.

[14] Wolf 2010: 126. See also Crook 1996: 34.

[15] For instance, the file C. Novius Eunus discussed in section 6.2.

are representative of a much wider area (including Rome itself).[16] The form (*tabulae ceratae*, diptychs/triptychs), style (chirographs, *testationes*), and content (e.g., *mutuum cum stipulatione*) of these documents, are found not only in the other Campanian (Pompeii, Herculaneum) tablets but also in writing tablets from Dacia, Frisia, and in the recently published writing tablets from Roman London.[17]

Evolution of Pignus and Hypotheca: *Ius Civile*, *Ius Honorarium*, and *Ius Novum*

If we look at the forms of pledge which originated during the first half of the classical period, we can see that the *ius honorarium* recognized new transactional practices and thus contributed decisively to the evolution of the Roman law of real security. The *ius honorarium* created the path for the evolution of Roman law from a static law for an agrarian society primarily based on land tenure and personal relationships, to a more dynamic law facilitating the free circulation of goods and the availability of credit. The law of pledge is one of the most important examples of this.[18] The Roman law of pledge is to a large extent the product of the *ius honorarium* and its interactions with commercial and financial practices. The right of pledge evolved from a simple possessory pledge of a single tangible asset into a highly versatile security interest, which could be granted as a non-possessory pledge, by way of a multiple pledge, over basically all types of assets (including intangibles) and even as a floating charge over an entire dynamic portfolio of assets.

During the course of the classical period limitations were placed on the parties' ability to structure their legal relationships themselves. The first limitation was that at some stage the creditor became obliged by operation of law to pay back the surplus to the debtor. This obligation may have followed from the *bona fides*, a *ius civile* concept with roots in the *ius honorarium*. From the second century AD onwards the imperial rescript practice, in particular that of the Severan emperors, began to interfere with the law of real security. The late classical Roman concepts and rules protecting the debtor were not part of the *ius honorarium* but rather of imperial law (*ius novum*). However, even here it can still be observed that the most important late classical rules on

[16] Meyer 2004: 127. Several of the agreements to appear in court (*vadimonia*) concern the appearance before the praetor in the Forum of Augustus in Rome (TPSulp 13–15).

[17] Tomlin 2016. On chirographs in Roman law, see Verhagen 2018 (with further references).

[18] Wieacker 1988: 474–5.

enforcement—prescribing sale of the charged property and a duty for the creditor to pay the surplus back to the debtor—find their origin in transactional practices, as we encounter powers of sale coupled with provisions on surplus already in documents dating from the first century AD. The law of pledge at the end of the classical period, which was largely taken over in the *Corpus iuris civilis* and later received in the European *ius commune*, has therefore evolved in different 'strata' of the legal system: *ius civile*, *ius honorarium*, and *ius novum*.

Scope and Structure of this Book

The scope of this book is largely confined to the classical Roman law of the Principate.[19] Classical Roman law knew two forms of real security: *pignus/hypotheca* and *fiducia* (*cum creditore*). In this book, I have not been able to give *fiducia* the more elaborate treatment that I originally planned, although there are still many references to it. Also, a comparison with personal security (e.g., *fideiussio*) has been omitted, although again there will be occasional references to this form of security.[20] In my contribution to the second volume of *Roman Law and Economics* the effectiveness of the Roman law of real security is discussed more elaborately than here (including publicity and its alternatives).[21] The developments in post-classical law are (with a few exceptions) not discussed in this book: *Deo volente* they will be reviewed in future publications. In this book I concentrate on those issues which are directly concerned with its main theme: legal rules and institutions connected with *pignus* and *hypotheca* which find their origin in transactional practices.

The first three chapters of this book lay the groundwork for a detailed account of the evolutionary history of *pignus* and *hypotheca*. In chapter 1 there are general observations on the co-evolution of Roman law and economy, with reference to social systems theory and socio-cultural evolution theory. Chapter 2 gives an outline of the specific institutional mechanisms for the evolution of Roman private law in the Principate, including the formulary procedure and the edictal system, and reviews the role of the jurists. Chapter 3

[19] See, however, chapter 4, mainly devoted to the origins of *pignus* and its remedies in the law of the Republic. For imperial constitutions references are up to (and including) Constantine.

[20] See in particular Pellecchi 2018: 457–63, 469–73, and passim. See also Chemain 2015: 148–51 and passim.

[21] Verhagen 2020. See, however, sections 11.5 (publicity) and 12.3 (effectiveness). All my publications included in the Bibliography are preliminary studies for this book. Accordingly, texts from these publications have been reused (usually heavily reworked) in this book.

discusses the economic environment of the law of real security, in particular in the context of secured lending and the rental markets. The origins of *pignus* and *fiducia* and its remedies in the Republic will be discussed in chapter 4. The evolutionary trajectories of *pignus* and *hypotheca* in the first two centuries AD will largely be charted in chapters 5 and 6, which map the evolution of *pignus* from a forfeiture pledge to a pledge enforceable by sale (chapter 5), as well as the evolution of *hypotheca* and its ancestors as a non-possessory pledge that could be granted *nuda conventione* (chapter 6). In subsequent chapters, dealing with the Nerva–Antonine age, we look at variants of the 'contractual' pledge: multiple pledges (chapter 7), *pignus nominis* and *antichresis* (chapter 8), and the general pledge (chapter 9). In chapters 10 and 11 developments in the Severan age will be discussed, with a focus on the emergence and evolution of 'pledge-like' preferential rights of the Roman treasury and publicity (chapter 10), and the execution of charged assets (chapter 11). Did the evolutionary trajectories mapped in the preceding chapters result in a law that was well-adapted to its economic environment and could it have contributed to economic growth in the Roman empire? In chapter 12 the outcome of the largely (but certainly not completely) spontaneous evolution of the Roman law of real security will be assessed. The order of this book is largely chronological, the chronology usually being determined by the time of origin of a new variant of *pignus*. The chronology will, however, not always be strictly maintained: on many occasions we will look forward to future developments, while discussions of the emergence of new variations will often be preceded by a brief glance back at their ancestors in the past.[22]

Terminology

In the sources the term '*pignus*' ('pledge') is often used as the generic term for possessory and non-possessory pledges, while the term '*hypotheca*' usually (but by no means always) denotes non-possessory pledges specifically.[23] In this book, however, the term '*hypotheca*' will be reserved for non-possessory pledges. The term 'charged property' (*res obligata*) will be used as a general term for all property which serves as collateral, by way of *pignus* and *hypotheca*, *fiducia cum creditore*, and fiscal pledges (privileges). I will use both

22 No exceptions to the chronology are made when later texts from the Digest or Codex are used to reconstruct the Roman law of earlier periods, where these texts can plausibly be regarded as reflecting that law.

23 Section 6.5.

'*fiducia cum creditore*' and '*fiducia*' in order to designate a fiduciary transfer of ownership for security purposes. The debtor who has granted a right of pledge will usually be simply referred to as the 'debtor' and the creditor to whom it has been granted as the 'creditor'.[24] However, in particular where it is important to distinguish these parties from other debtors and ('ordinary', non-secured) creditors, I will use the terms 'pledge debtor' and 'pledge creditor'. I will sometimes use the adjective 'conventional' in order to refer to a right of pledge that is based on a pledge agreement (*conventio pignoris*) governed by private law. The conventional pledge is thus contrasted with pledges arising by operation of law (e.g., in favour of the fiscus) and security governed by public law. The body of legal rules concerning *pignus*, *hypotheca*, and *fiducia cum creditore* will usually be referred as the 'law of real security' or 'law of secured credit', while the rules governing *pignus* and *hypotheca* specifically will be referred to as the 'law of pledge' or 'law of *pignus* and *hypotheca*'.

[24] Although there were certainly Roman women acting as creditors and debtors (e.g., Poppaea Note and Dicidia Margaris in the *Mancipatio Pompeiana* (p. 115–17), the female pawnbroker Faustilla in Pompeii (p. 70), and the women appearing in the Sulpicii archive), most of the Romans granting and taking credit would have been male. For this reason, I have used masculine pronouns throughout this book, unless it appears from the context that the person is female.

1

Co-evolution of Law and Economy

1.1 Introduction

A general methodological problem of legal history is 'whether it is the law that influences patterns of social or economic behaviour or it that is shaped by them'.[1] Can this be explained in terms of cause or effect? The answer is that it must be explained in terms of reciprocal cause and effect.[2] Legal change is unquestionably influenced by socio-economic factors, although in modern scholarship there is still much controversy on the degree and nature of this influence.[3] At the same time there can be no mistake that socio-economic patterns of behaviour are influenced by law. The state even tries—both in the present and (to a lesser extent) in antiquity—to influence these patterns through legislation, although not always successfully. The interactions between law and society, in the past and the present, are an exciting area of scientific research.[4] One of the main purposes of the science of legal history is to explain how *legal* institutions interacted—synchronically (functioning of law) and diachronically (evolution of law)—with other parts of society in the past. Economic theories of law—Law and Economics (L&E) and New Institutional Economics (NIE)—are valuable for analysing the functioning of law in its economic environment.[5] Social systems theory, into which evolutionary theory is integrated, can provide a new perspective for legal historians interested in long-term historical processes of legal change and continuity. The use of social systems theory, evolutionary theory, and economic theories of law, however, is far from generally accepted in legal history. Care has therefore been taken to assure that the results reached by my legal-historical research can also stand up without the prop of any metajuridical perspectives: they only place them in a more varied light, revealing patterns that otherwise would perhaps have remained hidden from view. In this chapter, after having

[1] Johnston 2022: 33. [2] Cf. for the Roman law of real security, Schulz 1951: 403.
[3] See, e.g., Cotterrell's (2006: 110) discussion of Alan Watson's view that '[t]here is no necessary correlation between the law and the society in which it operates' (Watson 2007: 26).
[4] For Roman law and society, see Pölönen 2016. [5] Section 12.2.

Security and Credit in Roman Law: The historical evolution of pignus *and* hypotheca. Hendrik L. E. Verhagen, Oxford University Press. © Hendrik L. E. Verhagen 2022. DOI: 10.1093/oso/9780199695836.003.0002

looked at legal evolution from the perspectives of systems theory (section 1.2) and socio-cultural evolution theory (section 1.3), I will carry out a closer examination of how Roman law co-evolved with the Roman economy (section 1.4). This chapter will conclude with a brief review of the economic functions of *pignus* and *hypotheca* (section 1.5).

1.2 A Systems Perspective

Wieacker has observed that the *ius civile* developed into a 'subsystem' (*Teilsystem*) within the Roman political, social, and cultural order, in particular through the unique phenomenon of Roman jurisprudence. Legal history demonstrates that there is an interdependence between the subsystem and the system as a whole (*Gesammtsystem*). On the one hand, the conscious experiences and intentions of the jurists and the judicial and legislative institutions were conditioned by 'reality as a whole' (*Gesammtwirklichkeit*). On the other hand, the legal subsystem has changed this reality through its legislation, its law developed by the magistrates, and its jurisprudence.[6] The division of society into subsystems (e.g., law, economy, politics, religion) is fundamental to the theory of social systems developed by the German sociologist (and lawyer) Niklas Luhmann.[7] Social systems theory analyses the operations, structures, and evolution of the subsystems of society and the relationships between them. To answer the question whether Luhmann's social systems theory can successfully be applied to (ancient and modern) society as a whole is far beyond my expertise. From the perspective of the legal system I can only say that it provides a useful interpretative scheme for analysing the interactions between law and economy in any society, both ancient and modern, in which the legal system can be regarded as a separate subsystem. Above all, social systems theory provides a good model for analysing how the origin and evolution of legal rules and institutions are often triggered by economic circumstances,[8] while at the same time they are conditioned by the internal structure of the legal system.

[6] Wieacker 1977: 358.

[7] The two major works on autopoietic legal systems are Luhmann 2004 (original German edition 1995) and Teubner 1993 (original German edition 1989). In this book the expression '(social) systems theory' will refer to Luhmann's theory and theories building on Luhmann (e.g., Teubner, Amstutz, Deakin).

[8] Pugliese 1966: 162–3.

Law as a subsystem of society

Lawyers usually think of a legal *system* in terms of a coherent, well-ordered, and hierarchical set of interacting principles, concepts, and rules.[9] Thus Kaser's introduction to Roman law states that a system which is clearly governed by logical principles and is adapted to the needs of legal education can only be found for the first time in Gaius's Institutes, with its subdivision into *personae*, *res*, and *actiones*.[10] Luhmann operates with an entirely different understanding of a legal system.

> But we do not use 'system' like some lawyers who mean by it a context of coordinated rules. We mean by 'system' a context of factually enacted operations, which have to be communicated because they are social operations, whatever defines them—and in addition to that—have to be communicated as a legal communication. This means, however, that the basic distinction is not to be found in a typology of norms or of values but in a distinction between system and environment.[11]

According to Luhmann, a legal system consists of communications, which can be found not only in the traditional sources of law (legislation, court decisions, legal opinions, etc.) but also in private transactions (e.g., contracts, conveyances, testaments). These legal communications are processed within a self-referential legal system, through procedures internal to that system.[12] In functionally differentiated societies, the interactions between the legal system and its environment—which is composed of other subsystems, such as the economy and the political system—are determined by the 'autopoietic' (i.e., self-producing) nature of the legal system. Autopoietic systems have their own internal structure and processes, creating, modifying, and extinguishing their own elements.[13] This so-called *operative closure* 'implies that the law produces by itself all the distinctions and concepts which it uses'.[14]

The ways in which operative closure is achieved within a social (sub)system are different, depending on the differing functions and codes of that system. The function of law is the stabilization of normative expectations: the law

[9] Fögen 2005: 90.
[10] Kaser, Knütel, and Lohsse 2021: 34–5. See also Kaser 1986: 84–6; Wieacker 1988: 51–2. For an in-depth account of different conceptions of legal 'systems', see Vesting 2018a: 39–84.
[11] Luhmann 2004: 78.
[12] Luhmann 2004: 80–1.
[13] Luhmann 2004: 70, 73, and passim.
[14] Luhmann 2004: 70.

indicates what people may expect that ought to occur.[15] This function is, however, also performed by other institutions and subsystems, such as tradition, morality, politics, and religion. What distinguishes legal communications from other social communications, and what makes law an autonomous subsystem of society, is that they are concerned with law's code. Law performs its function by coding patterns of facts by means of a *binary code* that is unique to law: legal/illegal (*Recht/Unrecht*).[16] Which fact patterns constitute legally relevant events is determined by the legal system itself: only communications that are concerned with the legal/illegal code belong to the legal system.[17] The application of the legal system's code takes place through *conditional programmes*. A legally relevant fact pattern which is in conformity with the legal system's norms is coded with a positive value (legal), while a fact that infringes a legal norm is coded negatively (illegal). The 'jurisdiction' which administers justice by applying the code 'legal' and 'illegal' to individual cases is a matter internal to the legal system.[18] An autopoietic legal system only responds to that part of its environment that is selected in accordance with its own legal concepts, rules, and procedures, and the form of response is determined by the legal system itself, not by its environment.[19]

Roman jurisprudence as an autonomous discipline

The theory of autopoietic legal systems can be regarded as a reformulation of the doctrine of the autonomy of law.[20] Can Roman law be regarded as an autonomous legal system? In Roman society it was the law which first differentiated itself from the 'primordial soup of societal communications' and

[15] Luhmann 2004: 153. See also Hayek 2013: 96–8.

[16] Luhmann 2004: 98–103. Luhmann's concept of law's only code has been criticized for 'not [doing]...justice to the richness or texture of legal communication' and to be based on (perhaps obsolete) thinking in information theory and artificial intelligence. Baxter 1987: 2069. See also Vesting 2018a: 70–4. However, the Roman formulary procedure did operate with a binary code. The binary code was 'condemnation to pay/dismissal' (section 2.3), which can be regarded as the Roman procedural expression of the legal/illegal code. But even if one disagrees with Luhmann about the function of law and law's binary code, the concept of conditional programmes remains a useful one for analysing the operation and evolution of legal rules (section 2.3).

[17] 'If the question arises whether something is legal or illegal, the communication belongs to the legal system, and if not then not' (Luhmann 1991: 1428).

[18] Luhmann 2004: 183.

[19] In a similar sense for Rome, Bretone 2006: 29 and Bürge 1999: 25.

[20] On the autonomy of law from the angle of systems theory, see Luhmann 2004: 95–7. For a critical review of Luhmann's conception of the autonomy of law, see Lempert 1988. For a nuanced approach to the autonomy of Roman law, see Du Plessis, Ando, and Tuori (2016: 4–6) and Pölönen (2016: 15). For the autonomy of law in the Western legal tradition, with reference to Luhmann, see Jansen 2019.

created, maintained, and developed its own separate language.[21] Once rules are no longer defined by divine revelation (as in Rome where rules were 'interpreted' originally by the priests)[22] or social custom but are produced by distinctly legal acts (legislation, judgments, legal opinions), they become part of an 'internal reproductive cycle'.[23] In Rome this resulted in an increasing legal complexity, requiring the existence of a corresponding expertise: the emergence of jurists as specialists in the law. The jurists developed legal knowledge (jurisprudence), resulting 'in abstractions, which rendered the law and its self-referential concepts independent of plain facts and made a law-centered evolution possible'.[24]

The following observation by Luhmann applies to the works of the late republican and classical jurists:

> The specification of the way in which arguments refer to legal materials in the legal system is the true carrier of the evolution of the legal system and the breakthrough to an autonomous legal culture, which can even be differentiated from morals, common sense, and the everyday use of words.[25]

It was in the Rome of the late Republic that jurisprudence, for the first time in human history, became an autonomous discipline, distinguishing between legal precepts and religious, social, and moral ones.[26] Roman jurists would primarily search for values which could justify legal solutions within the legal system itself and they were careful to separate these solutions from extra-legal factors which determined or influenced them.[27] For the jurists, legal rules had become 'a distinct cognitive field, replete with its own figures of thought'.[28] The jurists developed a new ontology, constituted by a limited number of forms—possession, ownership, usufruct, pledge, sale, partnership, obligation, etc.—which 'established itself as the motor of any development of *ius*'.[29] This corresponded not only to the needs of an autonomous jurisprudence in relation to other disciplines but also to the 'fundamental limits of the law' which the jurists recognized in their opinions.[30] It was not only the jurists

[21] Fögen 2003: 209.

[22] On the development of Roman law in the early Republic through the '*interpretatio*' by the *pontifices*, see Jolowicz and Nicholas 1972: 88–97.

[23] Teubner 1988: 224.

[24] Luhmann 2004: 249. In a similar sense, Frier 1989–1990.

[25] Luhmann 2004: 248. In a similar manner, for Roman law, Fögen 2003: 209.

[26] Pugliese 1966: 186–7. See also Pölönen 2016: 9.

[27] Pugliese 1966: 186–7.

[28] Frier 1989: 280.

[29] Schiavone 2012: 202. See also Bretone 2006: 112–3; Ando 2015.

[30] Pugliese 1966: 187.

themselves who regarded law as autonomous: the autonomy of the law was a 'fundamental belief within Roman society'.[31]

The 'isolation' of Roman law

A well-known observation by Schulz is: '[t]his isolation of private law had its disadvantages, but except in isolation private law could not have been elaborated in its classical purity'.[32] The 'isolation' of Roman law should, however, not be taken to its extreme. Like other members of the Roman intelligentsia, the Roman jurists were strongly influenced by Greek philosophy in their elaborations of legal concepts, distinctions, and principles, although their practical sense prevented them from engaging in unproductive theorizations.[33] The jurists would sometimes even interpret existing legal rules, or adopt new ones, with express reference to extra-legal evaluations: moral ones (e.g., *pietas*, *humanitas*, *aequitas*, *affectio*, and *verecundia*) or more practical ones (e.g., *utilitas*).[34] The Roman jurists were in continuous contact with financial and commercial practice. One of the core tasks of the Roman jurists was *cavere*, which included advising parties on drafting contracts, conveyances, and other transactions.[35] Also in their legal opinions we find many references to commercial and financial transactions, which they often treat with profound 'economic' insights.[36] The achievement of the late republican jurists was to create 'a law of markedly liberal temper, freed from archaism and oriented to the needs of commerce'.[37] In an important contribution on the autonomy of Roman law Pugliese prefers not to speak about the 'isolation' of Roman law.[38] It is true that the Roman jurists deliberately separated law from religion, ethics, and custom. At the same time, Pugliese observes, it is plausible (or we can assume by way of conjecture) that many institutions of

[31] Bretone 2006: 29.

[32] Schulz 1953: 84. More recently, Schiavone (2012: 29) observes that 'law would have been unable to perform its task had it not succeeded in establishing itself as an autonomous and literally untouchable space, determined by its own criteria' (Schiavone 2012: 291). See also Schiavone 2012: 200 and Fögen 2003: 212.

[33] Kaser, Knütel, and Lohsse 2021: 4–5. See also Wieacker 1988: 618–62. For an overview of the influence of Greek philosophy on classical Roman law, see Giltaij 2016. See also p. 197 (Labeo).

[34] For a discussion of the use of these extra-legal evaluations in the legal reasoning of Papinian, see Wolf 2013. See on *utilitas* also section 12.2.

[35] Wieacker 1988: 557–60.

[36] See section 12.2. For valuable studies on how the Roman law on tenant's pledges was influenced by socio-economic considerations, see Frier 1980: 105–35 and Du Plessis 2010.

[37] Frier 1989: 275.

[38] Pugliese 1966: 186. See also Bretone 2006: 29; Kirov 2005: 14–15.

the *ius gentium*, *ius honorarium*, and even *ius civile* have originated for socio-economic reasons. Without the economic activities taking place in the Roman world during the many centuries of its history these institutions would not have come into existence, or would have had a profoundly different structure.[39]

Operative closure must, therefore, 'not be misunderstood as isolation'.[40] The legal system is not only operatively closed but also *cognitively open* to the external environment.[41] The evolution of Roman law was triggered by 'irritations' coming from the other subsystems of Roman society, such as the Roman economy.[42] However, the legal system has its own filters which select the elements of the environment that are allowed to resonate within the system.[43] The specific legal consequences of these resonations are also determined within the legal system. Luhmann has identified processes which trigger and channel irritations between operatively closed subsystems and determine the degree of resonance of a particular subsystem.[44] The most important mechanism is that of 'structural coupling'.

Structural coupling between law and economy: property and contract

Operations of the economic system may be coupled with operations of the legal system and vice versa. For instance, a payment can be both an element of the economic system (exchange of value) and the legal system (discharge of an obligation). Coupling mechanisms are *structural* couplings 'if a system presupposes certain features of its environment on an ongoing basis and relies on them structurally'.[45] An important form of structural coupling in Rome, between the political system and the legal system, was the state office of the praetor.[46] Although for Roman private law it is less important (but certainly not irrelevant), of great significance for contemporary societies is the structural

[39] Pugliese 1966: 162–3. See also section 1.4.

[40] Luhmann 2004: 80.

[41] 'Notwithstanding his insistence on "legal closure", I argue, Luhmann emphasizes at the same time the possibilities and conditions of law's "openness"' (Baxter 1987: 1995). See also Teubner 1988: 2.

[42] Pugliese 1966: 163; Wieacker 1977: 358. See also section 1.4.

[43] In Roman law, these filters were the conditions of the conditional programmes contained in forms of action (*formulae*). Section 2.3.

[44] Baxter 2013: 171.

[45] Luhmann 2004: 382.

[46] Luhmann 2004: 140. More generally, for its enforcement the legal system will often be dependent upon the political system (Luhmann 2004: 162).

coupling of law and politics through legislation.[47] The development of Roman private law into a more complex legal system 'took place in conjunction with those legal concepts which lend themselves to a structural coupling of the legal system and the economic system, namely property and contract'.[48] *Property* rights play a crucial role in economies, ancient and modern.[49] As it is the legal system which determines who has property rights and the economic value of property rights depends on the legal remedies protecting them, there is a structural coupling here.[50] In economies where the exchange value of property is predominant, *contract* is the second principal form of structural coupling between legal and economic systems. Most operations of the economic system take the form of contracts: exchanges (e.g., contracts of sale), services (e.g., contracts of employment), and credit operations (loans). One of the interesting features of the Roman law of real security is that it combines both structural couplings between law and economy. This is reflected in the prominent place of the *conventio pignoris* in the form of action for the *actio Serviana*, which is an *actio in rem*. In other words, a *property* interest (*pignus* and *hypotheca*) could be created by means of a *contract*. The central thesis of this book will be that the fact that the pledge agreement (*conventio pignoris*) was a central element in the *formula* of the *actio Serviana* allowed contracting parties to adjust security interests to their economic needs, by inserting in the security documents clauses on non-possessory security, second-ranking security, security over receivables, the use of pledged property by the creditor (*antichresis*), and general security. Thus the pledge agreement functioned as a structural coupling between the Roman financial world and the law of real security.

Mechanisms of structural coupling operate slowly and carefully: they do not lead to instantaneous 'one-to-one' responses of the legal system to communications from the economic system. This means that the legal system can seriously lag behind economic developments. Luhmann observes that structural coupling between the economic and the legal systems proceeds 'at an extremely cautious pace, which does not immediately give in to pressure from problems, but first gains experience and tries minute variations in its own system'.[51] A good example of this in the Roman law of real security is the multiple pledge, which—via a transitional stage—was only recognized in the second half of the second century AD.[52]

[47] Luhmann 2004: 140.
[48] Luhmann 2004: 250.
[49] Hodgson 2015: 101–11.
[50] Baxter 2013: 178.
[51] Luhmann 2004: 401.
[52] See chapter 7.

Systems, individuals, and culture

The use of the concept of 'social (sub)systems' is often rejected because it 'rests on a highly reified notion of societies'.[53] According to US legal historian Robert Gordon the legal system is *not* a 'secondary specialized subsystem of society, being worked on by social change and working back on it'.[54] But even some of Luhmann's sternest critics admit that regarding law as an autopoietic subsystem of society provides a useful model or metaphor.[55] In the scientific reconstruction of reality the concepts of systems and subsystems can be usefully employed as 'cross-cutting slices' which are made on the basis of theories, models and metaphors and which allow us to examine causal relationships.[56] The focus in this book on the evolution of legal institutions means 'abstracting away a great many social ties, and retaining only the links that make up long transmission chains'.[57] In this sense, legal institutions are also deliberately reified in this book. However, even in institutional legal history, we cannot neglect how individuals can be responsible for the consequences of legal systems.[58] The thinking and actions of transacting parties, individual jurists, praetors, and emperors may be conditioned by their religious beliefs, position in society, economic rationality, and other non-legal factors.[59] Even when the conditions included in a conditional programme (e.g., a Roman *formula*) are framed in purely legal terms (as they usually are), this does not exclude that in deciding whether or not a given fact pattern could be subsumed under these conditions non-legal values endorsed by individual jurists, praetors, judges or emperors played a role.

For its effectiveness the legal system is dependent on the culture of the society to which it applies.[60] Without using cultural accomplishments the law cannot effectively co-ordinate the actions of individuals and bring order to society. In many respects cultural factors have an impact on the functioning and evolution of legal rules and institutions.[61] Although the embeddedness of law in culture and society is not at all incompatible with a systems-theoretical

[53] Sanderson 2007: 286, 301.

[54] Gordon 2012: 202. In social systems theory the legal system is *not* regarded as a *secondary* subsystem: no subsystem has causal priority. See also section 1.3 *in fine*.

[55] Lempert 1988: 188–99; Cotterrell 2001: 97, 99.

[56] Jansen 2010: 229.

[57] Morin 2016: 21 (with respect to cultural traditions).

[58] Cotterrell 2001: 95 ('responsible for the consequences of social systems').

[59] Pugliese 1966: 163. Wieacker 1977: 358. See section 12.2 on 'economic' considerations by the jurists.

[60] From the perspective of NIE, see Voigt 2019: 3.

[61] Vesting 2018a: 5–6.

analysis, there is a risk that when one focuses on the subsystem of law one loses sight of the interplay of legal rules with religious, economic, and socio-cultural norms and behaviour.[62] One example of how the 'formal rules' on secured credit were supplemented by 'informal constraints' is the deterrent effect of social norms and religious concepts (oaths) for pledging someone else's property or not disclosing earlier charges.[63] Also, the evolution of Roman law was influenced by cultural factors. With the Romans, 'the belief system underlying the institutional matrix [deterring] radical change' was particularly strong.[64] This belief system had a significant impact on the evolution of Roman law. The Romans were extremely reluctant to discard existing institutions, religious, political, legal, or otherwise. Thus, the introduction of new forms of personal security like the *fideiussio* was—in classical law—not accompanied by discarding the more ancient forms (*sponsio* and *fidepromissio*), which were left to wither away gradually.[65] When it became possible to charge *res mancipi* by way of *pignus* or *hypotheca*, *fiducia cum creditore* continued to exist and was only gradually ousted by its more efficient competitors.[66] We should, however, be careful with equating the traditionalist mindset of Romans generally with a lack of innovative spirit with the Roman jurists.[67] They did introduce many legal innovations but would usually try to do so by modifying existing legal institutions (e.g., *mancipatio*) rather than creating entirely new ones.[68] When this was not possible, existing institutional elements were used to build a new institution. This recombination of existing institutional elements can be observed in the Roman practice of the pledge and lease back (section 6.7), in the extension of the *ius offerendi et succedendi* to novation (section 7.4), and in the adapted action granted to a creditor to whom a claim had been pledged (section 8.3) or an independent right of *antichresis* had been granted (section 8.4).

1.3 An Evolutionary Perspective

Many of (ancient and modern) society's complex structures have evolved independently from the conscious planning of individuals or the co-ordinated actions of groups in society. Law is no exception. In this section I will outline

[62] Cotterrell 2001: 95.
[63] Section 10.5. For creditor–debtor relationships, see Verboven 2002; Ioannatou 2004.
[64] North 2005: 77. [65] Zimmermann 1990: 120–1. [66] Section 6.7.
[67] Nörr 2003, vol. II: 1385–409.
[68] For institutions in general, see Greif 2006: 194–5; Deakin 2003: 40; Granovetter 2017: 177.

how an evolutionary perspective on legal change (and continuity) can enrich legal-historical research methods and provide an instructive analytical framework for the interactions over time between law and other subsystems of society. The largest value for legal history of an evolutionary approach lies perhaps in the questions it raises. How are legal variants created? By private parties designing new types of contractual clauses? By praetors adapting forms of action in litigation, by imperial chanceries drafting new constitutions, by jurists contemplating alternative solutions in their writings, by the reception of foreign legal institutions (legal transplants), by new legislation? Why is a legal variant adopted by transacting parties or judicial or legislative authorities? To reduce transaction costs, under social pressures from dominant groups, because it fits into existing normative structures? How is a selected legal variation stabilized? By codification, in the praetor's edict, through legal dogmatics, by a doctrine of precedent for imperial rescripts? Are resemblances between legal institutions from different legal systems (e.g., Greek and Roman law) the outcome of convergent evolution due to similar environmental selection pressures, homologous descent (common historical origin), or lateral diffusion (e.g., expansion of Roman law after the *Constitutio Antoniniana*)?[69] Can an evolution towards efficiency or complexity be detected in Roman private law? How can a highly complex body of rules such as the Roman law of real security have evolved without a 'grand design' by a legislator? These are important questions for a science of legal history that (varying on the great evolutionary biologist Ernst Mayr) not only wants to discover the facts but also wants to know how the law changed and why.[70]

Intentionally created and evolutionary perspectives

Economists have developed two perspectives on institutional change: the *intentionally created* perspective and the *evolutionary* perspective.[71] The intentionally created perspective holds that forward-looking individuals deliberately create institutions, in order to serve various functions, and it deals with the responses to these functions. Transaction costs analysis, which postulates that economic actors tend to choose those forms of transactions

[69] On the general applicability of Roman law throughout the empire after the *Constitutio Antoniniana* (212 AD), see Alonso 2020.

[70] 'The searching human mind is not satisfied merely to discover the facts. We also want to know how things happened and why' (Mayr 2002: 73). See also Frier 1986: 888.

[71] Greif 2006: 153–6.

that minimize transaction costs, plays an important role in this perspective.[72] Evolutionary institutionalism, by way of contrast, views institutions as patterns of behaviour which are the result of unintentional consequences of 'interactions among individuals with limited rationality'.[73] Greif perceives a gap between these two perspectives:[74] the role which human intentionality plays in socio-cultural selection processes is incompatible with the 'blind' processes of Darwinism.[75]

It appears, however, that within contemporary social evolutionary theory the intentionally created perspective is integrated. Richerson and Boyd observe:

> Darwinian tools help us build linkages between phenomena at different levels as given problems require. Individuals seem to be hapless prisoners of their institutions because, in the short run, individual decisions don't have much effect on institutions. But, in the long run, accumulated over many decisions, individual decisions have a profound effect on institutions. Evolutionary theory gets right the basis structure of the relationship between individuals and the collective properties of their societies.[76]

The same perspective is chosen in this book for legal history. No one has constructed the formulary procedure or drafted the praetor's edict from scratch: they are the result of long-term incremental evolutionary processes. As Schulz observed in respect of the *formulae* for the *bonei fidei iudicia*: 'these *formulae* were gradually developed and were not framed by one man according to a comprehensive plan'.[77] Nevertheless, generations of Roman jurists have shaped legal evolution by consciously assimilating contractual innovations into the existing legal framework and incrementally building up a complex body of legal rules. Sometimes individuals jurists were even responsible for dramatic accelerations of legal evolution. The first 'evolutionary leap' for *pignus*—the introduction of the *actio Serviana*—was taken in the first century BC by Servius Sulpicius Rufus.[78] But Servius did not start from scratch either.

[72] Greif 2006: 7, 154. [73] Greif 2006: 7, 155. [74] Greif 2006: 7, 156.

[75] North 2005: 65–6; Greif 2006: 12. For a rebuttal, see Hodgson and Knudsen 2010: 48–50.

[76] Richerson and Boyd 2005: 247: 'Darwinian tools were *invented* to integrate levels.'

[77] Schulz 1951: 36. In similar terms Hayek: 2013: 65; Luhmann: 2004: 252. See also Luhmann 2012: 261, 307; Schulz 1951: 59; Deakin 2003: 14; Richerson and Boyd 2005: 253; Sanderson 2007: 301. In a similar sense already Cic., *Rep.* 2.1.2 and (much) later moral philosophers of the Scottish enlightenment, including Adam Smith ('invisible hand') (Den Hollander 2014: 244–5).

[78] Section 4.5. The second 'evolutionary leap' took place when Julian recognized that a right of pledge could be created 'by mere agreement' (*nuda conventione*) and (possibly) extended the scope of the *actio Serviana* to all rights of pledge. See sections 6.5 (*nuda conventione*) and 6.6 (*actio Serviana*).

The origin and content of the *actio Serviana* may have been closely connected to the *interdictum Salvianum* and, in any case, will have built upon existing transactional practices (e.g., Cato's pledge templates).[79] Moreover, even a great mind like Servius could not have planned the evolutionary path the *actio Serviana* would take in the three centuries following its creation, enforcing multiple pledges, pledges of claims, and even 'floating' charges over all the debtor's assets. The Roman law of pledge is 'far too complex for even the most gifted innovator to create from scratch'.[80] A good evolutionary theory of legal change can provide a balanced account of legal evolution as a combination of unplanned and incremental processes and the intentional acts of individuals.

Evolution of law

The available sources for legal history have, according to Luhmann, not been sufficiently evaluated from a theoretical perspective.[81] This can only be achieved through concepts of evolutionary theory.[82] The evolutionary analysis of law is an integral part of Luhmann's social systems theory in order to describe how legal systems adjust to changing conditions.[83] Thus, building upon Luhmann, Deakin formulates an evolutionary theory of legal change which is based on three related propositions.

> The first is that legal evolution is *cumulative*: incremental mutations in legal forms, when coupled with the selective effect of environmental pressures, can give rise to complex, multifunctional legal institutions. Secondly, legal forms are *adaptive* without being optimal. They reflect an internal dynamic of change which is shaped by historical conditions, rather than predestined convergence on a single, uniquely efficient form or 'evolutionary peak'. Thirdly, legal evolution operates through a process analogous to *inheritance* in the biological sphere, which involves the vertical transmission of stored information.[84]

[79] Sections 4.2–4.5. [80] Richerson and Boyd 2005: 53 (for social institutions generally).

[81] Luhmann 2004: 230. See also Vesting 2018a: 152–3. For similar approaches to legal evolution, see Teubner 1988, Deakin 2011 and 2013, Amstutz 2001. For Roman law, see Fögen 2003: 16–7, 209–12; Kirov 2005: 14–5; Steinhauer 2007.

[82] For a very positive appreciation of Luhmann's contribution to this field, see Zumbansen and Calliess 2011: 5.

[83] Luhmann 2004: 231.

[84] Deakin 2003: 4.

The fundamental thesis of evolutionary social scientists (including lawyers and economists) is that not only living organisms are subject to Darwin's 'descent with modification' but also social, economic, and cultural phenomena such as languages, scientific theories, organizations, and legal institutions.[85] This generalized Darwinism is not all about biological metaphors and analogies.[86] Socio-cultural evolutionary scholars have identified specific evolutionary processes in the social and cultural world, in which human intentionality does plays an important role.[87] One of the evolutionary processes which is different in socio-cultural evolution is *biased transmission*: based on their content, people adopt some cultural variants rather than others according to their own cultural and cognitive biases.[88] Like natural selection, biased transmission is a culling process ('a process of selective retention'),[89] but it is not identical to it. Biased transmission is dependent on human preferences, choices, and desires, whereas in most forms of natural selection the fitness of genes depends on their effect of reproduction independent of human intentionality.[90] Very different from its biological counterpart and crucial for social and legal evolution is *guided variation*: the changes that are transmitted are not random but the result of adaptive modifications which are deliberately made by humans.[91] Biased transmission and guided variation together are 'decision-making forces', which are based on learning rules and are likely to be subject to many of the same psychological mechanisms. The main difference is that unlike biased transmission, guided variation itself is not a culling process.[92]

What exactly is the nature of the information which is the object of processes of legal evolution? Dawkins has coined the term 'replicators' in order to designate the packages of information that are changed and transmitted in

[85] Dawkins 1991: 128; Dennett 1996: 136; Richerson and Boyd 2005: 60, 154; Hodgson and Knudsen 2010: vii, 23; Jablonka and Lamb 2014: 11–42. For the evolutionary analysis of law, see Luhmann 2004: 230–73; Teubner 1988. See also the contributions to Zumbansen and Calliess 2011 (with further references) and Vesting 2018a: 139–69. For evolutionary approaches by eighteenth- and nineteenth-century lawyers, see Stein 1980; Wieacker 1973 and Behrends 1993 (Jhering); Rabban 2013 (Maine, Holmes, and many other US and English legal scholars).

[86] Hodgson and Knudsen 2010: 223. In the same sense, Luhmann, 2004: 231; Deakin 2003: 3; Richerson and Boyd 2005: 242. See also Popper 1973: 261.

[87] Richerson and Boyd 2005: 51, 115–20; Jablonka and Lamb 2014: 201; Luhmann 2012: 305. The terms 'social', 'cultural', and 'socio-cultural' evolution are used interchangeably.

[88] Richerson and Boyd 2005: 51, 68–72, 115–20. See also Luhmann 2012: 305; Mesoudi 2011: 57, 82–3; Jablonka and Lamb 2014: 201. See also section 2.4.

[89] Richerson and Boyd 2005: 79.

[90] Richerson and Boyd 2005: 79, 116. See also Jablonka and Lamb 2014: 216.

[91] Richerson and Boyd 2005: 69, 116–7. 'The system is a little like an imaginary genetic system in which mutations tend to be fitness enhancing rather than random' (Richerson and Boyd 2005: 116).

[92] Richerson and Boyd 2005: 116.

evolutionary processes.[93] These replicators are often regarded as 'miniscule, genelike particles that are faithfully replicated during cultural transmission' (e.g., memes).[94] Richerson and Boyd observe, however, that what they call *cultural variants* sometimes are 'somewhat genelike, while at other times they decidedly are not'. They must be gene-like to the extent that they carry cultural information, but 'this can be accomplished in most un-genelike ways'.[95] Darwin himself had a very un-gene-like picture of inheritance but this did not matter because evolutionary processes 'are tolerant of how heritable variation is maintained'.[96] Nevertheless, in law we do have replicators that would even satisfy the strict demands of 'universal Darwinists' such as Hodgson and Knudsen. In order to define replicators they refer to biologist Ernst Mayr, who characterizes replicators as programmes.[97] The programme-like character of legal rules appears to make them suitable candidates for being legal replicators. In late republican and classical Roman law legal evolution takes place by the creation or modification of conditional programmes encapsulated in forms of action (*formulae*).[98] A legal institution can be regarded as the aggregate of the legal rules which determine the development of legal relationships of a certain type (e.g., sale, partnership, *pignus*, *hypotheca*, and *fiducia*). Evolutionary sequences of variation, selection, and replication may change conditional programmes contained in legal rules, so that the legal institutions to which they apply acquire different traits: this is evolution of law.

A proper theory of legal evolution

The right method for building a theory of legal evolution is, at this stage, neither deductive nor aimed at logical correctness in the use of Darwinian evolutionary concepts.[99] We first have to find out exactly how processes of variation, selection, and inheritance operate within legal systems. After microevolutionary processes operative in law have been identified and analysed, it could then be tested whether they can be generalized and are logically compatible with the Darwinism elaborated by evolutionary social scientists.[100] This is not a

[93] Dawkins 1991: 128; Hodgson and Knudsen, 2010: ix, 24. Laor and Jablonka 2013: 296 consider the 'adherence to notions of genotype and phenotype in the cultural realm…misplaced'.

[94] Richerson and Boyd 2005: 80. For memes, see Dennett 2017: 224–33. For memetic approaches to legal evolution, see Balkin 1998 and Deakin 2003.

[95] Richerson and Boyd 2005: 81. See also Jablonka and Lamb 2014: 202–8.

[96] Richerson and Boyd 2005: 81.

[97] Hodgson and Knudsen 2010: 230–1.

[98] See section 2.3.

[99] See in particular Amstutz 2001: 167–210. See also Hayek 2013: 23.

[100] In a similar sense, Deakin 2011: 673.

task I have set for myself in this book. My evolutionary approach boils down to historical narratives of how legal evolution consists of long-term *cumulative* and *adaptive* processes, involving mechanisms which can be labelled as 'variation', 'selection', and 'inheritance'. For the purpose of this book I use the following working definitions of these mechanisms. A legal *variation* (or *variant*) is a modified (including differently interpreted) copy of an existing legal rule, form of action (*formula*), or legal institution (e.g., new variant of pledge).[101] There is *selection* if a judicial (praetor, *iudex*, emperor), legislative, or other legally recognized authority (e.g., jurist with *ius respondendi*) recognizes the variation as positive law,[102] either incidentally (e.g., *actio in factum*) or structurally. In the latter case there is *stabilization* ('inheritance': replication, retention, transmission): a legal variant remains part of positive law and will thus continue to determine the legal consequences of future legal relationships. Although certainly in Rome 'doctrinal structures' did have a stabilization function,[103] there were also other important stabilization mechanisms, such as the praetor's edict, legislation, and a doctrine of precedent in imperial constitutions.[104]

From systems theory I accept that although legal evolution may be triggered by the economic environment, the legal system itself determines whether this takes place and in what form. The operative closure of the legal system therefore limits its capacity for legal change, while at the same time it contributes to its stability.[105] The functional differentiation of society into autopoietic subsystems entails that within an evolving society an independent evolution of law is possible. From the perspective of the legal system this means that the economy may produce 'irritations', which are processed by evolutionary mechanisms operating *within* the legal system.[106] From the perspective of the economic system, this co-evolution entails that legal changes (e.g., legislation enacted to regulate prices) can have economic effects, but these effects are determined by economic 'laws' rather than by the legal system. The evolution of law cannot, therefore, be treated as simply mirroring the evolution of certain other parts of society (e.g., politics, economy,

[101] Luhmann 2004: 247–8: 'Variation attended to the mutation of law (which is largely unsuccessful but occasionally can be confirmed). Without it, no evolutionary changes would be possible.'

[102] Luhmann 2004: 248: 'Selection attends to the task of defining which opinion is in accordance with the legal system.'

[103] Teubner 1988: 228; Luhmann 2004: 340.

[104] For variation, selection and stabilization mechanisms in Roman law, see in particular chapter 2.

[105] Teubner 1988: 231.

[106] Deakin 2011: 675; Teubner 1988: 228; Vesting 2018a: 152.

religion).[107] This also has the consequence that system-specific time frames develop. The legal system may be 'out of synch' with the economy and only give in to economic selection pressures after a long time (e.g., multiple pledge).[108]

Evolutionary functionalism: evolutionism

A formidable critique on evolutionary, systems, and economic perspectives on legal history comes from Gordon. In his *Critical Legal Histories* (1984), Gordon's purpose was to 'describe and critique a grand theory', which he calls 'evolutionary functionalism'.[109] In Gordon's perception this theory has two components. The first—'evolutionary'—part is 'that there is a process of social development common to most "advanced" or "dynamic" societies, culminating in modernity'.[110] What Gordon calls 'evolutionary' is called 'evolutionist' by socio-cultural evolutionary scholars and is firmly rejected in modern evolutionary analyses of social and legal change.[111] There is neither a universal sequence of stages of legal change nor is there a 'predestined convergence on a single, uniquely efficient form or "evolutionary peak"'.[112] In an important contribution on law, economics, and evolutionary theory, Roe observes: 'economic evolution selects out for extinction very inefficient results, and efficient results tend to survive'.[113] This evolution-to-efficiency paradigm must be used with care (as Roe readily admits).[114] As a conjecture one can maintain that it is plausible that grossly inefficient legal institutions are unlikely to survive. At the same time one must realize that legal evolution is conditioned by the operative closure of the legal system and heavily dependent upon historical contingencies and other factors (e.g., governmental policies, religion, culture), which may prevent the most efficient outcome being reached.[115] It therefore will not do, for instance, to simply say that because *fiducia* lost the struggle for existence against *pignus* and *hypotheca* it must have been less

[107] Vesting 2018a: 152–3; Teubner 1988: 232. See also Amstutz 2001: 103; Tamahana 2017: 113.

[108] See section 7.2. However, Bürge (1979: 148) observes that precisely because of the entanglement of the right of pledge with the economy, it was subject to relatively rapid changes.

[109] See Gordon 2012: 200. In Gordon 2012 he reflects on Gordon 1984. For a rebuttal of Gordon's critique, see in particular Teubner 1988: 226–8.

[110] Gordon 2012: 200–1.

[111] Sanderson 2007: 2.

[112] Deakin 2003: 4. For an excellent and succinct discussion of the misunderstandings of the concept of legal evolution, see Teubner, 1988: 225–8. For a similar rebuttal of the criticisms of socio-cultural evolution theory generally, see Hodgson and Knudsen 2010: 13–23; Mesoudi 2011: 131–3; Hayek 2013: 23–4. For a more elaborate review, see Sanderson 2007.

[113] Roe 1996: 641.

[114] Roe 1996: 642–3.

[115] Kehoe, Ratzan, and Yiftach 2015: 13.

efficient. This may ultimately very well have been the reason, but this does not discharge the researcher from the obligation to search for specific historical factors which may have contributed to the demise of *fiducia*.[116] One cannot assume that within a legal system there is an intrinsic trend toward efficiency (or complexity). This is something that detailed legal-historical research has to prove or falsify for each legal institution and each legal system.

Legal evolution is a historical process, which for each legal system is a unique one. The evolutionary process is, also in autonomous (autopoietic) legal systems, to a large extent one of intermittent adaptation triggered by the law's environment. If environments differ (as they always do), legal evolution will be different as well.[117] But all this is not to say that no regularities—evolutionary trends—can be discerned.[118] A basic fact of comparative law is that in societies with similar socio-economic structures similar legal institutions emerge.[119] Thus, legal systems operating in modern free market economies all have individual ownership rights, freedom of contract, limited liability companies, and real security rights, irrespective of whether they belong to the common law or the civil law tradition.[120] The many exceptions to this statistical law demonstrate, however, that evolving legal systems must have a 'higher potential of autonomy' than purely economic theories of legal evolution predict.[121] With economic historian Joel Mokyr, I believe that an evolutionary approach 'places the analysis between the extremes of a materialist analysis that regards historical outcomes as inexorable and foreordained and a nihilist approach that sees nothing but randomness everywhere'.[122]

Evolutionary functionalism: functionalism

The second—'functionalist'—part of evolutionary functionalism identified by Gordon is that legal systems can be viewed as providing 'adaptive responses'

[116] Section 4.6.

[117] On the generality of evolutionary analysis and the specificity of historical analysis see Richerson and Boyd 2005: 245–8; Morris 2015: 11–3; Lewens 2015: 160–1, 183; Mokyr 2017: 9, 22–33. See also Popper 1973: 270.

[118] See Richerson and Boyd 2005: 60, 96; Jablonka and Lamb 2014: 223; Sanderson 2007: 276.

[119] Zweigert and Kötz 1998: 40.

[120] Some of these legal institutions are legal transplants (e.g., the Dutch United East India Company (*VOC*) served as a model for English companies). The laws of real security of common law and civil law jurisdictions seem to have evolved independently, but still share many features. See Verhagen 2013b.

[121] Teubner 1988, 229. For a selection of articles on the 'efficient evolution' of Anglo-American common law, see Rubin 2007.

[122] Mokyr 2017: 32. See also Richerson and Boyd 2005: 246–8; Bresson 2016: 22.

to social needs; law as a 'dependent variable'.[123] It is, however, according to him inherently impossible to establish strong causal links between economic needs and legal responses to these needs. Gordon observes that:

> saying things like 'the negligence principle' or 'property rights in land' were preconditions to, or even just very favorable legal environments for, economic growth, ignored the basic insight of Legal Realism—the myriad ways in which legal doctrines can be interpreted and differentially applied or ignored or worked around on the way to enforcement.[124]

Gordon's criticism in statements like this is to a large extent certainly justified. In particular, economic analyses on the contribution of 'property rights' to economic growth in past societies sometimes suffer from generalizations which are either too general to be meaningful or not supported by historical evidence.[125] The autonomous nature of the legal system entails that a purely adaptionist approach, in which the law always and immediately responds by adopting rules that serve economic needs, is inappropriate.[126] Moreover, certainly in relation to ancient societies, it is often already very difficult or impossible to establish correlations, let alone to prove that correlation and causation coincide. Compared with the sources that are available for contemporary laws, and even compared with those concerning medieval and early modern laws, data allowing us to do so are scarce.[127] Where correlations between economic change and legal evolution do appear to exist, causal links can often only be made plausible.

What *can* be proven, however, is that in many instances legal evolution is triggered by transactional practices. Certainly if realistic assumptions can be made in respect of the economic rationality of the transacting parties (or their legal counsel),[128] the identification of transactional practices will allow us to make plausible inferences about the law responding to economic needs. The findings of detailed empirical economic analyses of contemporary collateral laws can then be applied to Roman law in order to examine whether the accommodation of transactional practices into the existing legal framework did create a favourable legal environment for economic growth. Above all, 'crude functionalist accounts' of the origin and evolution of legal institutions can be avoided by 'studying the dynamics of how the institution was created

[123] Gordon 2012: 201. [124] Gordon 2012: 203.
[125] Arruñada 2012: 21–4; Boldizzoni 2011: 28; Granovetter 2017: 65–6.
[126] Greif 2006: 381–2. [127] Donahue, foreword to Frier 1980: xiii. [128] Section 12.2.

over time'.[129] This is precisely the purpose of the detailed historical accounts on the origin and evolution of the variants of pledge in this book.

Evaluation

Even at this stage, where no unified evolutionary synthesis of social and legal evolution exists, it may still be useful to employ the 'evolutionary algorithm'[130] of variation, selection, and inheritance (stabilization) to organize one's thoughts about the co-evolution of law, economy, and other subsystems of society.[131] Although I do not assume (however plausible this may be) that these evolutionary processes are truly Darwinian, this will not prevent me from tapping into the 'collective wisdom' of evolutionary social scientists whenever I think this is possible and useful.[132] There is much to learn from evolutionary approaches developed for other areas of the socio-cultural domain.[133] In one of their joint contributions on evolutionary theory and history, historian Joseph Fracchia and evolutionary biologist Richard Lewontin ask sceptically: 'What constitutes an evolutionary process as opposed to a "merely" historical one? What explanatory work is done by claiming that culture has evolved?'[134] The answer is that legal evolution is something other than merely legal change: it is—in the words of Frier—'adaptation in response to external stimuli'.[135] Although I accept that to a certain extent my evolutionary approach consists of a borrowed set of metaphors and analogies, it is more than that.[136] Triggered by their economic, political, or religious environment, legal institutions originate or change: they become more (or less) complex, display enhanced (or decreased) adaptedness, or disappear.[137] These are real evolutionary processes operating within legal systems.[138] Most legal institutions 'did not emerge in one single step, but are the result of cumulative historical processes'.[139] Legal evolution is (like cultural evolution) 'an instance of

129 Granovetter 2017: 6–7. 130 Dennett 1996. 131 Basalla 1988: vii.
132 Richerson and Boyd 2005: 248. 133 Renn 2020: 17.
134 Fracchia and Lewontin 1999: 57.
135 Frier 1986: 888. Cf. Smith, Gabora, and Gardner-O'Kearny 2018: 84.
136 Cf. Popper 1973: 261.
137 Roman jurisprudence developed in accordance with, what Popper (1973: 261) calls, a 'largely Darwinian theory of growth of knowledge'. For Roman jurisprudence, see Capogrossi Colognesi 2014: 333.
138 Richerson and Boyd 2005: 4; Smith, Gabora, and Gardner-O'Keary 2018: 85.
139 Jablonka and Lamb 2014: 222, with regard to 'complex cultural practices'.

general evolution, in the full, nontrivial sense of cumulative, adaptive, open-ended change'.[140] Legal evolution is an evolutionary process in its own right.

1.4 Co-evolution of Roman Law and Economy

In respect of one of the fundamental questions of legal history—*why* and *how* legal systems change?—Bruce Frier observes: '"Why" refers to the initial impulses and the motives for legal change; "how" refers to the factors conditioning the form that legal change takes.'[141] The answer to the second part of the question ('how') is largely to be found within the legal system itself. The Roman jurists, praetors, and emperors would primarily try to fill perceived gaps in the law in a manner which was consistent with the existing legal framework.[142] The evolution of Roman law can, therefore, not be treated as simply mirroring the evolution of the Roman economy.[143] At the same time, however, without 'irritations' from its economic environment there would not have been sufficient stimuli for the evolution of Roman law to its classical state. The answer to the first part of the question ('why') is, therefore, largely to be found in the legal system's environment, in particular the economy. Moreover, the legal system may have contributed to the functioning of the economic system by offering a differentiated and versatile set of principles and rules, allowing the law effectively to deal with the complexity of its economic environment.[144] From a legal perspective we can learn a lot about the evolution of law by studying the economy. From an economic perspective, by studying law, we can also learn something about the nature of the economy. Thus the sophistication of the Roman law of secured credit does shed light on the alleged 'primitive' nature of the Roman economy.

Roman law in a weakly cultivated economic environment?

In her *Römische Rechtsgeschichten*, Marie-Theres Fögen holds that as a system Roman law was 'a lonely highly cultivated plant in the midst of a systemically

[140] Smith, Gabora, and Gardner-O'Kearny 2018: 84. [141] Frier 1986: 888.

[142] Frier 1986: 888–9.

[143] Similar views are expressed (for modern legal systems) by Teubner 1988: 232; Amstutz 2001: 103; Tamahana 2017: 113; Vesting 2018a: 152–3.

[144] The legal system offers 'cognitive resources which, in their turn facilitate economic transactions' (Deakin 2011: 119).

weakly cultivated environment'.[145] Fögen observes that Roman law was only moderately cognitively open in relation to economic manifestations. The legal system came up with the contract of sale when money was invented and with the maritime loan when Roman ships began sailing the Mediterranean, but otherwise, there were no demands from the economy, because there was no Roman economy. There were economic relationships within the family, and there was a social structure: both were protected by the law in the form of principles and rules on inheritance, tutelage, adoption, and dowry. The evolution of Roman law presumably was made possible by the fact that for a long time a co-evolution between the law and other social subsystems failed to happen. The law was, Fögen observes, largely exempted from labour-intensive, irritating interactions and couplings in need of attention. From a safe house, guarding it from criticism, hostilities and reproaches, the law could self-referentially specify itself almost autistically. Fögen is right where she observes that the image of a 'safe house' was particularly appropriate for the relationship between law and politics. The political system could have used the law as an instrument to realize political purposes, which it only incidentally did, and even have dominated it, which—certainly in the law of property and the law of contract—it failed to do (even after the codification of the praetor's edict and the distinct change of the imperial rescript practice under Hadrian).[146] As far as the co-evolution of law and economy is concerned, however, Fögen seriously underestimates the nature and significance of the Roman economy and the 'irritations' which it must have caused for the legal system.[147]

Roman economy as a subsystem of society?

Fögen's perception of the Roman economy has a respectable pedigree. For more than a century the Roman economy is the object of the so-called Bücher/Meyer Controversy between 'primitivists' and 'modernists'. The original version of the primitivist doctrine, as forwarded by Karl Bücher in 1893, holds that the Roman economy was a 'very simple, small-scale, closed household economy aimed at self sufficiency and engaged only in very limited

[145] Fögen 2003: 212. In restating Fögen's position I follow the original German text closely.

[146] Schiavone 2012: 200.

[147] The criticism given here in no way detracts from my deep admiration for Fögen's inspiring book.

exchanges with other households'.[148] This is in stark contrast to the modernist view of the Roman economy, as originally defended by Eduard Meyer, pursuant to which the Roman economy was very similar to the economies of early modern Europe but only was much smaller. In the twentieth century the controversy continued, although on neither side would one still fully adhere to the original positions.[149]

In *The Social and Economic History of the Roman Empire*, Rostovtzeff collected an enormous amount of archaeological, epigraphical, numismatic, and other empirical data, which led him to believe that the Roman economy did not fit in the primitivist model of Bücher. In a book review Rostovtzeff made the following—often quoted—remark: 'I am certain that the differences with respect to the modern economy were only quantitative, not qualitative'.[150] According to Rostovtzeff, 'the main source of large fortunes' was commerce. The law of secured credit played a significant role in generating wealth: 'Money acquired by commerce was increased by lending it out mostly on mortgage, and it was invested in land.' Commercial exchanges were significant and not confined to small local circles, but took place within a 'world economy'.[151] In *The Ancient Economy*, Finley adopted an entirely different model. Finley denied that the ancient economies of Greece and Rome were subject to modern economic principles and played down the role of commerce and finance.[152] The Greeks and Romans 'lacked the concept of an economy' as well as 'the conceptual elements which together constitute what we would call "the economy"'. They did of course farm, manufacture, sell, lend and borrow money, and write about these activities, but they did not 'combine these particular activities conceptually into a unit, in Parsonian terms into "a differentiated sub-system of society"'.[153] This was not merely 'an intellectual failing', but rather 'the consequence of the structure of ancient society'.[154] The most fundamental concept of a modern economy, that of the market, was absent from Roman society. There was no labour market, money market, etc., in which individuals were active whose preferences can be analysed with modern investment models.[155] According to Finley, the justification for using

[148] Morris 1999: ix. For references to Bücher (including to English translations), see Schiavone 2000: 226–7.

[149] Schiavone 2000: 51.

[150] Rostovtzeff 1932: 335 (translation Schiavone 2000: 239).

[151] Rostovtzeff 1957: 153.

[152] For an important and very critical review, see Frederiksen 1975. For an account of how the position of Finley (who 'was not a theoretician') was influenced by Max Weber (and to a lesser extent Polanyi), see Bresson 2016: 8–15.

[153] Finley 1999: 21, with reference to Parsons and Smelser 1956.

[154] Finley 1999: 21.

[155] Finley 1999: 23. For an entirely different view, see Temin 2013: 1–11 and passim.

the term 'ancient economy' can only be found in 'reasons which have little or nothing to do with the economy'. For this reason, one has 'to seek different concepts and different models, appropriate to the ancient economy, not (or not necessarily) to ours'.[156] Even if Finley's minimalist interpretation of the Roman economy is right and one cannot speak of a Roman economic subsystem, this does not prevent us from using systems theory to analyse the interactions between the differentiated legal system with its (undifferentiated) environment.[157] Certainly when one's prime interest is in how the evolution of Roman law was influenced by 'economic' factors, it does not matter whether or not these factors are produced within a differentiated economic subsystem of the legal system's environment. What matters is that Roman law can be regarded as a legal system (in the Luhmannian sense), which is both cognitively open and operatively closed at the same time. This provides the analytical framework for examining how the evolution of Roman law was influenced by factors coming from its (economic or other) environment.

A legal perspective

Although many contemporary historians of the Roman economy profess to distance themselves from it,[158] in reality it would appear that the Bücher/Meyer controversy is still alive.[159] The school of thought which in the *Oxford Handbook of Roman Studies* is considered as the most influential still has primitivist connotations. It considers the Roman economy as 'a highly localized, fragmented, and largely agrarian economy that sustained a thin veneer of coerced transfers and trade in luxuries and a network of towns that were dominated by landowning elites'.[160] A modernist stance has been taken by economist Peter Temin, who recognizes that not all transactions were market exchanges and that even a substantial part of economic activity would be carried on within Roman households. Temin does not deny that markets are embedded in society, but this does not prevent him from concluding that the Roman economy was a market economy, albeit not 'the market economy of

[156] Finley 1999: 27.

[157] Bresson (2016: 14) criticizes Finley's 'refusal to describe the ancient economy as an integrated system'.

[158] Bang 2008: 19–36; Andreau 2010: 13–26.

[159] See also Schiavone 2000: 46; Bang 2008: 20; Andreau 2010: 22.

[160] Scheidel 2010: 593.

elementary textbooks'. Rather the Roman economy was like that of other advanced agricultural economies, such as those of seventeenth- and eighteenth-century England and the Dutch Republic.[161]

A legal perspective points towards a more modernist orientation. According to Schiavone the Roman economy was characterized by 'dual equilibria', formed by an 'archaic' and 'advanced' form of economy.[162] In the archaic period economic relationships were clearly 'Finleyan': 'In every transaction, a bundle of expectations and interests comes into play that could never be reduced to pure economic quantification'.[163] However, where according to Finley nothing fundamentally changed in the period from 700 BC to 250 AD, Schiavone holds that if one looks at the mature Roman imperial economic system the picture drastically changes. After the second Punic war economic developments were set in motion which led to several 'areas of innovation, from which there was no turning back'.[164] There was a noticeable increase in trade, both regional and interregional, accompanied by the formation of 'new social classes with specifically mercantile interests' and the 'accumulation of a substantial amount of commercial capital'.[165] This increase in trade had a substantial impact on the institutions of the Republic, in particular resulting in the creation of the office of the *praetor peregrinus*, which developed a body of legal rules applicable to commercial transactions with non-Romans (to whom the *ius civile* did not apply). Many legal innovations in Roman contract law—in particular the consensual contracts—find their origin in commercial transactions entered into via Mediterranean trade circuits between Romans and foreigners. They were submitted to the *praetor peregrinus*, who granted new actions to enforce these transactions. At a later stage these new contractual forms were also recognized by the *praetor urbanus* and incorporated into the law for the Roman citizens (*ius civile*).[166] The law of pledge, although it did not evolve under the jurisdiction of the *praetor peregrinus*, must also be counted among the 'areas of innovation' coming into existence in response to the economic developments taking place after the second Punic war. As we will see in chapter 4, Rome's 'Economic Revolution' was accompanied by the emergence of almost all the specific remedies that

[161] Temin 2013: 8.

[162] Schiavone 2000: 66. Cf. also Camodeca 2003: 96 (endorsed by Andreau 2003: 281) who holds that Roman economic and financial life was a mixture of 'modern' and 'archaic' elements and that it was precisely this which gave the Roman economy its distinctive nature.

[163] Schiavone 2000: 56. [164] Schiavone 2000: 56.

[165] Schiavone 2000: 56. See also chapter 3.

[166] Schiavone 2000: 56. Recently De Ligt (2020: 88–9) has pointed out that before 242 BC there was only one praetor, who must have dealt with Roman and foreign litigating parties.

became available for pledge creditors or pledge debtors: *interdictum Salvianum*, *interdictum de migrando*, and, most importantly, the *actio Serviana*. Here also these legal innovations were preceded by transactional practices, as shown in Cato's *De agricultura*, some of which may have Hellenistic origins.

According to Richerson and Boyd, 'adaptionist reasoning can be run "backward"—we can predict past environments from present behaviour'.[167] Likewise, evolutionary reasoning can be used to predict past economic environments from past legal institutions. Thus evolutionary reasoning can shed light—from a legal angle—on the Bücher/Meyer Controversy. Certainly classical Roman law did offer a legal framework sophisticated enough for a market economy in which finance plays an important role.[168] If that is so, one wonders how likely it is that an empire with a primitive, 'Finleyan' economy would develop a highly versatile and differentiated law of secured credit? More generally, if one accepts that the legal system—albeit in its own 'autopoietic' way—responds to impulses from its economic environment, it would seem highly unlikely that a 'thin veneer of coerced transfers and trade in luxuries' would provide sufficient stimuli for the evolution of the complex Roman private law of the late Republic and the Principate.[169]

1.5 Roman Law of Real Security

When the rules for the taking and enforcement of security are 'cumbersome, inefficient and awkward', security may lose its essential economic function of mitigating risk for lenders.[170] This is the condition of the Roman law of real security according to a widely shared view in modern literature on Roman law.[171] It is often added that flaws in real security were not a major problem, since personal security (guarantees, suretyships) was far more important in ancient Rome than real security.[172] But in the archive of the Sulpicii we see that in ordinary commercial relationships personal security was used for

[167] Richerson and Boyd 2005: 229. [168] Section 12.2.

[169] In a similar sense, with reference to the Roman law of sale Crook (1996: 35–6). See also for commercial law generally, Johnston 2022: 133.

[170] Fleisig 2008: 90.

[171] To mention only one example: Koops (2010: 36) considers the Roman system of real security 'without any doubt' one of the least successful parts of Roman law. See also Schulz 1951: 403 ('poor'). For positive assessments of the Roman law of real security, see Krämer 2007: 1–6; Terpstra 2008: 356–60.

[172] Schulz 1951: 405. In a similar sense, Zimmermann 1990: 115–6. More nuanced Kaser 1971: 457; Kaser, Knütel, and Lohsse 2021: 228; Johnston 2022: 112–14.

small loans and real security for larger ones.[173] It is also hard to believe that the Roman law of real security was relatively insignificant when so many opinions of the jurists and imperial constitutions on *pignus*, *hypotheca*, and *fiducia* have survived.[174] The Roman law of security was highly sophisticated and versatile, allowing multiple charges, non-possessory security, and even floating charges. Since legal systems often adapt in reaction to impulses from their economic environment, the complexity of the Roman law of real security would suggest that *pignus* and *fiducia* did play a significant role in the Roman economy. In chapter 12 it will be shown that this role was generally a positive one. Its main weakness was lack of publicity, and even this weakness has often been exaggerated in modern literature.

Risk reduction

In their groundbreaking *Yale Law Journal* article Jackson and Kronman observed that '[t]o a considerable extent, the value of a security interest depends on the degree to which it insulates the secured party from the claims of the debtor's other creditors'.[175] The primary economic function of security is therefore *risk reduction* for the creditor.[176] In case of secured loans the risk concerned is that of non-payment of principal and interest at the agreed time. The more this risk is reduced by taking security, the greater its value will be to the creditor. The risk manifests itself in particular when the debtor is insolvent. In that event creditors are likely to receive only a small portion of their claims, since the liquidation proceeds of the debtor's assets are usually significantly less than the aggregate amount of his debts. Under the principle of *pari passu* or *paritas creditorum* ('equality of creditors'), all creditors receive distributions proportionate to their claims. Real security, however, creates a separate

[173] Gröschler 2008: 303–5; Krämer 2007: 182. In Kaser, Knütel, and Lohsse (2021: 228) it is noted that, although at the beginning of the Principate personal security was still preferred, in the second century AD real security had developed into the most significant form of security. The archive of the Sulpicii would suggest that this development had already taken place in the first century AD. This is confirmed by Chemain 2015: 377–86. In the papyri of Roman Egypt personal security is rare throughout the Principate (Lerouxel 2016: 246).

[174] In the Digest a whole book (D. 20) and a large title (D. 13.7) are devoted to real security (*pignus* and *hypotheca*), while also the Codex contains a large number of rescripts and other imperial constitutions dealing with these legal institutions (C. 4.24; C. 8.13–8.34). Also elsewhere in the Digest and Codex there are many fragments on *pignus* and *hypotheca*. The large number of legal texts on *pignus* and *hypotheca* only implies that these legal institutions were not as insignificant as they are often professed to be in modern textbooks, but in itself that is no proof of their economic efficiency.

[175] Jackson and Kronman 1979: 1143.

[176] Röver 1999: 108.

class of creditors, with preferential rights to the proceeds of specific assets (the charged assets). Thus, a secured creditor who has obtained a security interest on one or more of the debtor's assets is not affected by this *pari passu* principle. In other words, where the law allows a creditor to obtain effective security, this will considerably reduce the risk that he will suffer losses when the loan is not fully repaid at the agreed time. The corresponding benefit for debtors granting security is that they may obtain credit in a manner (amount, term) which otherwise would not be available to them or only at higher costs (interest). Also, in ancient Rome the primary reason for taking security cannot have been anything else than maximizing the lender's prospects for recovery, and so it is likely to have facilitated the borrower's access to credit.[177]

Depersonalizing credit relationships: impersonal exchange

In economic studies it is often emphasized that economic development is facilitated by legal and other social institutions that support impersonal exchange.[178] The Roman law of real security may have facilitated impersonal exchange in financial transactions and may thus have contributed to economic growth in the Roman empire. In particular Verboven, however, has demonstrated that highly personalized relationships based on *amicitia* ('friendship') played an important role in the Roman economy. *Amicitia* was not merely a relationship based on mutual affection and altruism, it could also involve the exchange of money, goods, and services. In many cases, the exchange aspect was even the *raison d'être* of the *amicitia* relationship. In financial transactions *amicitia* entailed that one friend helped out another, by providing interest-free loans or at low(er) interest.[179] Also productive loans at higher interest (but still on more favourable terms) were preferably obtained from friends. *Amicitia* would provide the lender with an extra guarantee that repayment would take place, while it would protect the debtor from excessive

[177] See also Pellecchi (2018: 476), who also mentions the avoidance of social costs attached to the use of personal security. Harris (2011: 230) mentions Cic., *Att.* 16.6.3 as an example of a borrower's differential treatment of secured and unsecured debt. The Sulpicii archive unfortunately does not contain documents mentioning interest rates (although they must have calculated interest). In particular for Roman Egypt there is relatively much evidence for the enhancement of borrowing capacity by real security. See Lerouxel 2015, who does, however, not discuss whether the interest rate for secured loans was substantially lower than for unsecured loans.

[178] Arruñada 2012: 17 and Arruñada 2020: 247. For Rome, see Kay 2014: 110. Haselmann, Pistor, and Vig (2010: 551) observe that a strong collateral regime offers a 'substitute for cultural and local knowledge' to foreign banks as lenders in emerging markets.

[179] Verboven 2002: 116.

interest rates and allow him to count on more leniency when unable to repay the loan in time.[180] However, if *amicitia* was as pervasive in the financial world as Verboven claims it to be, one wonders how the substantial evidence for real security can be explained.[181] Precisely real security enables a lender to provide credit outside the circle of his relatives, friends, and their dependants. The law of real security may have provided a mechanism of bringing lenders and borrowers together who otherwise would not have engaged in credit transactions. The lender's lack of information as to the borrower's creditworthiness is much less a concern when the value of the collateral will be sufficient to cover the debt.[182] The Roman law of real security may have facilitated impersonal exchange in financial transactions and may thus have contributed to economic growth in the Roman empire. To put it differently, the existence of a large body of fragments in the Digest and the Codex on real security at least suggests that many credit relationships were depersonalized.[183]

Zero-sum game or redistribution of wealth to secured creditors?

From a macroeconomic perspective, the most important advantage of the microeconomic function of risk reduction is that it increases available credit, which leads to higher investment, increased production, and ultimately a higher gross domestic product.[184] A fundamental objection, however, which has been raised against the efficiency of real security is that secured credit involves a zero-sum game: interest rate savings for debtors granting security are wiped out by corresponding interest rate increases for debtors unable to offer security.[185] So-called redistributive theories even hold that the benefit of lower interest rates is acquired at the expense of non-secured creditors, who will receive less in the insolvency of a debtor who has granted security rights

[180] Verboven 2002: 170–4.

[181] Terpstra (2013: 29) observes: 'if indeed *amicitia* and *clientela* were all-important in business, it is simply not visible in the Murecine documents'. This in itself, however, does not falsify Verboven's thesis. The very nature of *amicitia* makes it unlikely to find references to it in legal documents.

[182] For Roman Egypt, see Lerouxel 2012: 960–3. According to Kay (2014: 110) there are two ways around the problem of the lender's lack of information as to the borrower's creditworthiness: using a financial broker (with information) introducing the borrower to the lender, and deposit banking. In the latter case the lender takes a credit risk on the banker rather than on the ultimate borrower, while the banker's expertise is in evaluating the creditworthiness of persons. Kay does not mention, however, real security as another way of remedying the lender's lack of information.

[183] On the other hand, rights of pledge were also created in highly personalized contexts, such as between husband and wife (e.g., Paul. D. 20.6.11) and between brothers (e.g., Pap. D. 20.4.3.2). See also section 3.3.

[184] Röver 1999: 109–10.

[185] Schwartz 1984.

to one or more other creditors. The growing empirical literature on the use of secured credit, however, refutes these redistributive theories and demonstrates that, as Armour states, 'secured credit is, on the whole, socially beneficial, and that such benefits are highly likely to outweigh the social costs of any transaction motivated by redistribution'.[186] Armour argues that granting security, by facilitating monitoring and bonding, reduces the probability of the debtor engaging in risky wealth-reducing transactions and thus increases the value of *all* creditors' claims.[187]

Some years ago it was argued that, in the more than thirty years of debate since the Jackson/Kronman article, 'a comprehensive justification of secured commercial credit on efficiency grounds is unproven and perhaps not provable'.[188] However, legal history seems to provide strong indications that security is efficient. As McCormack has put it:

> an inefficiency conclusion would go against the grain of history. Security devices are widespread and pervasive not only in the modern industrialized world but also in ancient societies, and one might ask the rhetorical question: why does secured credit persist for so long if it is inefficient?[189]

This conclusion is supported by quantitative research, which underscores 'the importance of laws relating to the pledgeability of assets as a driver of credit supply'.[190]

[186] Armour 2008: 11–2. [187] Armour 2008: 7–8. [188] McCall 2009: 11.
[189] McCormack 2004: 26.
[190] Haselmann, Pistor, and Vig 2010: 567. See chapter 12.

2

Mechanisms of Legal Evolution

2.1 Introduction

The evolution of Roman law largely took place within the institutional framework of the formulary procedure and the edictal system. The responses by the legal system to economic events were channelled through the structural coupling of law and economy by means of contract. Transactional 'legal variants' provided inputs to the legal system and had the potential of triggering legal change when they became the subject of litigation (section 2.2). The formulary procedure was much more sensitive to legal innovations than its predecessor, the *legisactio* procedure (section 2.3). By interpreting existing conditions of the conditional programmes encapsulated in the forms of action (*formulae*), or by incidentally changing or adding conditions, Roman law could respond to new transactional practices. For a substantial part of the classical period, the praetor's edict provided an effective mechanism of stabilizing legal innovations. As early as in the course of the Republic this resulted in the emergence of a second body of law alongside the *ius civile*: the *ius honorarium* (section 2.4). After the codification of the praetor's edict (*Edictum perpetuum*) under emperor Hadrian, the imperial chancery became the most important institutional agency for legal change, which resulted in a third body of law: *ius novum*. In particular, the Severan chancery sometimes curbed the spontaneous evolution of the law through contractual practices by placing limitations on party autonomy in order to protect debtors.

The intellectual framework for all these mechanisms of legal evolution was formed by Roman jurisprudence (section 2.5). The Roman jurists would be materially responsible for the content of the praetor's edict. They would introduce contractual innovations and in litigation they would advise the litigating parties, the praetor, and the *iudex*. The lines of evolution of Roman law are largely drawn by an iterative relationship between transactional lawyers (and later also practitioners without much legal training) drafting legal transactions *and* the jurists deploying their analytical skills and practical

Security and Credit in Roman Law: The historical evolution of pignus *and* hypotheca. Hendrik L. E. Verhagen, Oxford University Press. © Hendrik L. E. Verhagen 2022. DOI: 10.1093/oso/9780199695836.003.0003

insights in order to accommodate new transactional practices into the Roman legal system.[1]

2.2 Transactional Practices as Levers of Legal Evolution

From its earliest history Roman law has allowed parties to shape the content of their legal relationships themselves (*stipulatio*, *mancipatio*). In practice, this 'private self-shaping' would—certainly in the Republic—be carried out by the jurists (originally: the priests). They would have drafted *stipulationes* and *mancipationes* which reflected the economic or other needs (e.g., inheritance planning) of transacting parties. The jurists will also have been instrumental in accommodating Greek-Hellenistic transactional practices into the Roman legal system. The outcome of evolutionary culling processes working on transactional practices may have influenced which practices would be subject to litigation and had the potential of triggering legal change. Some transactional practices became so common that they were deemed to be agreed and sometimes even evolved into rules of objective law (e.g., a licence to sell). Transactional practices were 'levers of legal evolution'.[2] This is true for large areas of Roman private law, but there is no other legal institution than *pignus* and *hypotheca* where the formative effect of legal practice can be so clearly observed.[3] The structural coupling between law and economy through the pledge agreement (*conventio pignoris*) was what made the evolution of *pignus* and *hypotheca* into highly versatile security interests possible.[4]

Private self-shaping in Roman law

Where in the fifth century BC the law of the Twelve Tables was enacted, the legal institutions mentioned therein were already existing ones. They were not created by the Roman legislator, but were the product of civil and commercial practices of the preceding centuries. The law of the Twelve Tables did not introduce these legal institutions, but assumes their pre-existence.[5] In fact, archaic Roman law knew only two types of legal transactions (*negotia*): *stipulatio* and *mancipatio*. They could be enforced with the *legis actio*

[1] The expression 'iterative relationship' is borrowed from Armour 2004: 28.
[2] Ehrlich 1913: 5 (for legal history generally).
[3] Kaser 1976: 172; Kaser 1982: 218.
[4] On *structural coupling*, see section 1.2.
[5] Manigk 1939: 268–9.

sacramenti in personam (*stipulatio*) and the *legis actio sacramenti in rem* (*mancipatio*), respectively. This scantiness and formality of legal institutions did not entail that archaic law lacked flexibility.[6] The structure of these *negotia* allowed individuals to use them for many different purposes. Thus the contract of *stipulatio* was 'an empty vessel that could be filled with every content'.[7] Provided that the parties used the prescribed question-and-answer format, they could basically make any lawful agreement a valid and enforceable contract. This substantial flexibility (adaptability) must have been the reason for the longevity of the *stipulatio*, which continued to be used by Romans until well after the classical period. Its ancient origin did not detract from (or perhaps even contributed to) its popularity among the Romans of the Principate.

But also the *mancipatio*, usually associated with legal areas (law of property, family law) where party autonomy does not prevail, gave much room to transacting parties to determine themselves the content of their legal relationship. The law of the Twelve Tables (tab. VI 1) provided: '*cum nexum faciet mancipiumque, uti lingua nuncupassit, ita ius esto*'.[8] This can be read as a legislative authorization for private 'self-shaping'.[9] The declarations pronounced during the *mancipatio* ceremony (*nuncupationes*) made it so versatile.[10] They enabled jurists to design variations of the original *mancipatio*, in order to meet new demands from society. The *mancipatio* could be used not only as a genuine sale but also for many other purposes. The *mancipatio* came to be used, often in combination with *fiducia*, for the formal release of debts (*solutio per aes et libram*), marriage (*co-emptio*), testament (*mancipatio familiae*), release from paternal power (*emancipatio*), and adoption (*adoptio*).[11] Most importantly, the *mancipatio* evolved into a general method of conveyance for *res mancipi* and became an essential component for the granting of security by way of *fiducia cum creditore*. The *pactum fiduciae* would enable the parties to further specify the legal consequences of the fiduciary transfer (e.g., creditor's right of sale coupled with a duty to return any surplus).[12] In Cato's pledge templates the *conventio pignoris* had a similar function for *pignus*,[13] a function which it continued to have during the entire classical period.[14]

[6] Fiori 2016: 583. [7] Fiori 2014: 33; Fiori 2016: 583.

[8] 'When he shall perform *nexum* and *mancipium*, as his tongue has pronounced, so is there to be a source of rights' (translation Crawford 1996: 654). Fiori 2016: 582–3.

[9] Manigk 1909: 2290. [10] Watson 1971: 61. On *nuncupationes* and *fiducia*, see Bellocci 1979.

[11] Noordraven 1999: 42–123. [12] Section 4.6. [13] Sections 4.2 and 4.3.

[14] Chapters 5–9 and 11.

Standard form contracts

In a time when there was hardly any dispositive law supplementing the terms of the parties' contracts, there was much room for party autonomy, allowing transacting parties themselves to determine the substance of their legal relationships. This is why transaction templates providing model documents for individual legal transactions were so important, not only in the time they were actually used by transacting parties but later also for the jurists as a treasure trove for designing dispositive rules.[15] In the Roman Empire (and beyond) contract templates and standard form contractual clauses were widespread in space and show a large degree of continuity in time.[16] As early as the time of the Republic, template collections circulated, often stemming from the Greek world. From the republican period we have the standard form pledging clauses recommended by Cato, which may have been derived from an earlier collection of templates possibly of Greek origin.[17] The loan and pledge agreements, auction announcements, and procedural documents in the Sulpicii archive were clearly based on standard form templates drafted by local jurists or copied from Rome or elsewhere.[18] Contractual licences to sell are common throughout the whole of the classical period in virtually identical format.[19] Documents recording *fiducia cum creditore* from Campania (Pompeii, Herculaneum, Puteoli) and Baetica (Spain) show strong similarities in structure and content. The *Formula Baetica* is particularly interesting. The text of this *mancipatio 'fidi fiduciae causa'* and the accompanying *pactum fiduciae* is engraved on a bronze tablet.[20] This bronze tablet was probably affixed to a wall of the office of a professional scribe or banker and must have served as a template for specific transfers of ownership by way of security.[21] It contained fictitious names of the parties and the land transferred as collateral and included several optional clauses (e.g., on secured debts) to adapt it to individual transactions. In 1885, an engraved stone was found in Rome near the *Porta Salaria*—the so-called *lex horreorum Caesaris*—which provides that all the goods stored by customers in the warehouse shall be pledged to the *horrearius* in order to secure payment of the storage fees.[22] Innumerable individual rights of pledge will have been created pursuant to these 'general terms

[15] Von Lübtow 1957: 232–3; Wieacker 1961: 108.

[16] For Greek practice, see Wolff 1978: 5 and passim. On Roman books of precedents for contracts and wills, see Schulz 1953: 90.

[17] Krämer 2007: 144. Section 4.2. [18] Camodeca 2003: 80. [19] Sections 5.3 and 5.4.

[20] For a photograph, see Bruns and Gradenwitz 1912: XXIII. [21] Wenger 1953: 757–8.

[22] FIRA III, nr. 145. See Du Plessis 2012: 176–7 and 187 (with further references). For a photograph of one of these tables, see Bruns and Gradenwitz 1912: XX.

and conditions'. Also in the Digest we find evidence of persistent transactional practices relating to secured credit. Thus Pomponius refers to the clause 'commonly added to pledges' that the debtor shall be liable for any deficit in the sale proceeds of the pledged property.[23] In his commentary on the *formula hypothecaria* Gaius refers to 'the clause commonly inserted in deeds' that beside the property specially hypothecated the debtor's present and future remaining assets will also be charged.[24] The same jurist mentions the widespread practice of debtors making declarations to creditors on whether the pledged property was already charged.[25] There is an opinion from Ulpian on the 'every day' ('*cottidie*') practice of constructing non-possessory charges by using *precarium*.[26] In a constitution by Alexander Severus from AD 223, the licence to sell is referred to as a 'common pact' ('*pactum vulgare*').[27] From the classical period many more examples can be given, such as transactional practices in relation to multiple pledges and to the executing creditor's exclusion of liability for eviction.[28]

Evolution of transactional practices

In particular, standard form contracts and standard clauses can be subject to evolutionary processes: there may be different versions of templates circulating for particular types of legal transactions (variation), certain versions may be preferred over others by transacting parties (selection) and templates often show a large degree of continuity (stabilization). My conjecture is that in private law an important evolutionary force is that people tend to select those transactional practices that they (or their legal advisers) think best suit their needs. Where those choices are made rationally,[29] those transactional practices which are better adapted to their socio-economic environment are most likely to be reproduced. In this sense a kind of 'natural' selection (or biased transmission) takes place.[30] When, however, certain transactional practices are no longer used in practice, they will no longer provide input to the legal system, which may result in the corresponding legal rules or institutions becoming obsolete. In evolutionary theory this is called 'subset selection':[31]

[23] Paul. (Pomp.) D. 20.5.9.1 ('*quod in pignoribus dandis adici solet*'). Section 5.4.
[24] Gai. D. 20.1.15.1 ('*[illa conventio] quae cottidie inseri solet cautionibus*'). Section 9.3.
[25] Gai. D. 20.1.15.2 ('*solent pati*'). Section 7.2.
[26] Ulp. D. 43.26.6.4.
[27] Alex. C. 4.24.4.
[28] Chapter 7 (multiple pledges) and section 10.5 (eviction).
[29] See section 12.2.
[30] See also section 1.3.
[31] Mayr 2002: 125.

the less adapted species becomes extinct.[32] Transactional practices may thus be subject to evolutionary culling processes, whose outcomes may determine which practices will be subject to litigation (or sometimes legislation) and can trigger legal change. From a causational perspective it may look as if selection completely takes place in the economic environment of the legal system. The proper analysis is, however, that ultimately the legislator or judicial authorities (in Rome: praetor, imperial chancery, jurisprudence) select which legal variants will count as law.

What mechanisms exactly cause certain transactional practices to be transmitted more frequently than others? The research of Boyd and Richerson and others has shown that people's choices to prefer one cultural element over the other often follow certain identifiable patterns. The concept of what they call 'biases' can be usefully applied to the transmission of legal variants in the form of transactional practices. *Direct bias* means that certain authorities function as 'an information cost-saving device who have great influence on others' cultural beliefs', such as priests.[33] This form of bias must have been instrumental for the evolution of Roman law. Certainly in the Republic private individuals would turn to the jurists in order to ask for advice on how to draft contracts, wills, and other legal transactions. There is *content-based bias* where the choice for a particular cultural variant is made 'because of the inherent qualities and content of this variant'.[34] Throughout the classical period transacting parties—often advised (or using templates designed) by jurists—would prefer contractual clauses which best suited their financial or commercial needs. Mathematical models of social evolution demonstrate that when it is difficult to determine which variant is the best, 'selection favors heavy reliance on imitating others'.[35] This is *model-based bias* (*imitation*).[36] For instance, templates used by reputable bankers may have been copied by other lenders in order to document their credit transactions. Also from a transaction costs perspective imitation can be an effective strategy; rather than spending money on legal advisers, one simply copies templates designed by (or at the expense of) others. A similar bias is *frequency dependence bias*, which also involves imitation. 'Translated' to the legal domain this bias means that individuals tend to choose those transactional practices which the majority of people around

32 Hodgson and Knudsen 2010: 94.

33 Mokyr 2017: 49. Biases are conveniently classified by Mokyr 2017: 48–56, on which this account is based.

34 Mokyr 2017: 48.

35 Richerson and Boyd 2005: 118, 161.

36 Mokyr 2017: 51.

them employ.[37] Again this saves on information costs: others have already tested the new legal variant and considered it useful.[38] It could also lower bargaining costs.

From express to implied term to statutory rule

One important economic function of the law is 'to leave ultimate economic decisions to the parties, but to create institutions that clarify their choices, especially to default rules applicable when the express contract is silent'.[39] These supplemental (dispositive) rules will often lower transaction costs as they will not have to be negotiated by the parties.[40] Supplemental legal rules ideally reflect what economically rational parties would have agreed had they chosen to write their intentions down in their contract. This is precisely what happened in the Roman law of secured transactions: contractual clauses which were common practice at the beginning of the classical period evolved into (supplemental or mandatory) rules in late classical law. Certain pledge agreements may have become so typical in certain situations that in the absence of express wording they were deemed also to have been made.[41] For urban tenancies tenant's pledges of *invecta et illata* were so common that they were deemed to have been tacitly agreed.[42] In respect of *invecta et illata* brought into rural premises, however, an express agreement continued to be required.[43] The reason for this may have been that the *invecta et illata* of a tenant farmer were too important to be impliedly pledged: the tenant's livelihood would depend on them.[44] Where the nature of the property, which was pledged in order to secure loans, entailed that it would be used and/or yielded fruit (living accommodation, slaves, agricultural land) and the creditor was granted possession of it, it would be presumed not only that the creditor would be entitled to use it but also that the value of the use or the fruit would be deducted from principal and/or interest.[45]

The evolutionary sequence often is: (1) express agreement, (2) implied agreement, (3) legal rule. We can observe this in the evolution of the creditor's power of sale. The epigraphic sources show that in the first century AD express

[37] Mokyr 2017: 52.
[38] Mokyr 2017: 52. [39] Frier and Kehoe 2007: 124.
[40] Frier and Kehoe 2007: 124: 'such default rules can lower bargaining costs considerably, since parties need not bother to negotiate terms allocating risks they may well deem remote'.
[41] Kaser 1982: 206.
[42] For example, Nerat. D. 20.2.4 pr.; Pomp. D. 20.2.7 pr.; Ulp. D. 20.2.6; Paul. D. 2.14.4 pr.
[43] Van den Bergh 2009: 160–1. [44] Van den Bergh 2009: 161–2.
[45] Manigk 1910: 51–5; Kaser 1982: 208. See p. 261–2.

licences to sell were common (stage 1).[46] Pomp. D. 13.7.5 appears to indicate that during Pomponius's time (second century AD) the creditor was impliedly authorized to sell the property (stage 2).[47] For the third century AD Ulpian D. 13.7.4 makes clear that a licence to sell was no longer based on (express or implied) consent, but was inherent to the right of pledge (stage 3).[48] There is in many (if not all) legal systems a thin (and not always clear) line between implied agreements and supplemental rules of law which apply irrespective of the parties' intentions. In Rome certainly, it is often impossible to distinguish between *pacta tacita* and dispositive rules of unwritten law.[49] The 'statutory' pledges arising by operation of law for the benefit of the imperial treasury have evolved from 'tacit' pledges, which in their turn evolved from express contractual provisions on pledge.[50] In many cases, the construction adopted in the sources that general pledges were impliedly agreed with the fiscal debtor was a pure fiction.

Hellenistic transactional practices

In the nineteenth century, Dernburg took the view that the use by the jurists of the Greek loan words *hypotheca*, *hyperocha*, and *antichresis* demonstrate a continuous influence of the Greek right of pledge on its Roman equivalent.[51] For a long time this position was very influential among Romanists, until scholars like Manigk brought forward that most jurists do not use these words borrowed from the Greek or use them only occasionally. It is therefore no longer thought that there was a pervasive influence of Greek law(s).[52] However, it may not be a coincidence that in the Roman law of real security many expressions are derived from Greek.[53] Rome's expansion into the Hellenistic economic world, with its highly differentiated business institutions, trade systems, and forms of credit, was the decisive factor for the evolution of the archaic, strictly Roman *ius civile* to a 'world law' of the Mediterranean.[54] Hellenistic influences rather concerned the imitation of business

[46] Section 5.3. [47] Section 5.7.

[48] Kaser 1975: 319; Biscardi 1976: 161 ('*elemento essenziale*'). Section 11.2.

[49] Kaser 1982: 206. As Kaser (1982: 289 n 289) rightly stresses, we are not dealing with rights regulated by the Roman state or by imperial constitutions. We are rather dealing with 'jurists' law developed from stereotypical agreements, derived through interpretation from their content and function.

[50] Kaser 1982: 2. Section 10.2. [51] Dernburg 1860: 67.

[52] The other extreme, that every *hypotheca* in the Digest is a post-classical (but pre-Byzantine) interpolation (Schulz 1951: 409), has also been abandoned. For a detailed discussion, see Manigk 1916: 364–411. See also pp. 201–3.

[53] Kaser 1976: 203.

[54] Wieacker 1988: 349. See also Schiavone 2000: 56.

practices than the reception of Greek laws.[55] For all variants of pledge discussed in this book it has been suggested that they have Greek-Hellenistic ancestors: pledge of *invecta et illata*, multiple pledge, conventional general pledge, statutory general pledge, *antichresis*, conditional sale, and the 'Gordian' lien.[56]

Ideally this book would have contained more detailed comparative accounts of *pignus, hypotheca,* and security interests of other ancient laws. Nevertheless, on many occasions references are made to possible Greek-Hellenistic origins or influences on Roman law. The focus on classical Roman law also entails that any suggestion of how the Roman law of real security could have contributed to economic growth in the Roman empire must be qualified by the fact that Roman law did not apply to every credit transaction concluded within its boundaries, not even after the *Constitutio Antoniniana* of 212 AD.[57] However, in the writings of jurists such as Scaevola and Marcianus we encounter rights of pledge which were granted over assets situated in the eastern part of the Roman empire. Gaius and Marcianus even wrote monographs on the *formula hypothecaria*: their consistent use of the Greek loan word *hypotheca(ria)* may be explained by their connections with the eastern part of the Roman empire.[58] From this part of the empire many papyri have survived, recording grantings of real security which were similar to those used in the Western empire:[59] even where these documents were not governed by Roman law, they reflect transactional practices that were commonly used throughout the Roman empire and which may have contributed to economic growth in the Roman empire in a manner similar to their Western counterparts.

2.3 Formulary Procedure

Different normative expectations of individuals continuously cause legal disputes, in both the past and today. From the multitude of varying and

[55] Wieacker 1988: 349.

[56] See, e.g., Krämer 2007: 144 (*invecta et illata*); Biscardi 1969 (multiple pledge); Bobbink and Mauer 2019: 28 (*antichresis*); Frezza 1963: 171 (conventional general pledge); Wieacker 1939 (fiscal general pledges).

[57] The fundamental work is Mitteis's *Reichsrecht und Volksrecht* (1891). See the contributions collected in Czajkowski and Eckhardt 2020. On the influence of the *Constitutio Antoniniana* on transactional practices in the Eastern empire, see Alonso 2020. See also Johnston 2022: 10–14.

[58] More than half of the texts using *hypotheca* are from Marcian (Manigk 1916: 362–3). See section 6.5.

[59] For instance, P. Vindob. L 135 (Egypt) and TPSulp 55 are both from the first century AD and both document a possessory pledge of objects made of precious metals.

conflicting normative expectations, which cannot all be met at the same time, selection mechanisms have to choose which to count as law. Thus, legal proceedings constitute a continuous process of trial and error contributing to the evolution of law.[60] Not only in modern societies but also in Rome these selection mechanisms are institutionalized in formal legal proceedings, such as the *legisactio* and *formula* procedures. The older *legisactio* procedure was much less capable of adapting Roman law to socio-economic change than the more flexible formulary procedure.[61] The latter procedure, which was the most important one for the Principate, enabled the praetors (assisted by the jurists in their *consilium*) to recognize new legal variants in individual cases. The selection of legal variants largely took place in the formulary procedure, which was highly sensitive to variations. The conditions of the conditional programmes included in the *formulae* could be changed in order to adapt the law to new transactional practices and changes in the law's environment.

From *legisactio* to *formula*

The most important type of civil proceedings in the late Republic and the Principate was the formulary procedure: *litigare per formulas*.[62] This procedure originated in the last quarter of the second century BC, a period in which Roman economic and social life drastically changed. Its predecessor, the *legisactio* procedure,[63] could 'never have met the needs of the emerging Roman empire'.[64] The forms of action of the extremely formalistic *legis actiones* were limited to a small number of cases that could be reduced to *leges*. These *legis actiones* were laid down in unchangeable and oral forms of action and were only available for Roman citizens. In legal systems operating with oral communications, stability will need to be achieved by means other than writing, in particular by fixed rituals.[65] The Roman *legisactio* procedure was oral and operated with ritualistic forms of action, whose fixed wording had to be strictly observed.[66] The forms of action were limited in number and scope, a position which remained unaltered for centuries. As Fögen lucidly

[60] Hayek 2013: 96–8. See also Luhmann 2004: 24.

[61] See, however, section 2.2, on the *mancipatio* and *stipulatio* (both enforceable with *legis actiones*) as instruments of 'private self-shaping'.

[62] For example, Gai. *Inst.* 4.30.

[63] For example, Gai. *Inst.* 4.30 (*legis actiones*).

[64] Nicholas 1962: 21. [65] Fögen 2003: 82.

[66] This detracts from Goody's observation that 'there is greater flexibility in the oral context' (Goody 1986: 136).

observes, the fixed wordings of the *legis actiones* restricted 'the entrance of life to the law'.[67] The formulary procedure granted life much wider access to the law.[68] The forms of action of the formulary procedure did not need their foundation in a *lex*. They could be adapted to the circumstances of the case, were in writing, and were also available to *peregrini*.[69] The formulary procedure was, however, not a radical innovation but—according to Wieacker—rather an 'organic developmental stage' of the *legisactio* procedure.[70] Features which the formulary procedure did at least borrow from the *legisactio* procedure were the operating with forms of action and the division of the procedure in two stages (praetor and *iudex*). Legislation seems to have significantly contributed to the supersession of the formulary procedure at the expense of the *legisactio* procedure.[71]

As Nicholas observes, the formulary system 'is remarkable for its simplicity, economy, and adaptability. By the use of a small number of typical "parts" or elements, the essentials of any dispute could be concisely and clearly expressed.'[72] It is no wonder then that the rigid *legisactio* procedure was largely ousted by the more flexible formulary procedure.[73] The new procedure gave a large freedom of assessment to judicial magistrates in adapting Roman law to socio-economic developments and enabled the creative force of the jurists to unfold.[74]

Actiones in factum and *actiones utiles*

Where the fact pattern on which the claimant sought redress in formulary proceedings could not be subsumed under an existing *formula* in the praetor's edict—not even by reinterpretation of concepts included as conditions of existing forms of action—the praetor could simply deny the claimant's action (*denegatio actionis*). In that case a negative selection took place: the praetor decided not to enforce a legal variant which would have accommodated the

[67] Fögen 2003: 140.

[68] For the role of writing in the functioning and evolution of Roman law, see Moatti 2015: 99–102; 126–31. See also Luhmann 2004: 234–43; Fögen 2003: 82–4, 132–43; Kirov 2005: 64–7; Vesting 2018a: 161–5; Vesting 2018b: 225–49.

[69] Wieacker 1961: 101.

[70] Wieacker 1961: 103–4. See also Jolowicz and Nicholas 1972: 220. According to Kaser and Hackl (1996: 157) it was an independent creation, which cannot be simply explained as a derivative of the *legisactio* procedure.

[71] *Lex Aebutia* (second half of second century BC); *leges Iuliae de iudiciorum privatorum* (17 BC). Jolowicz and Nicholas 1972: 218–25; Kaser and Hackl 1996: 159–62.

[72] Nicholas 1962: 20.

[73] See in particular Kaser and Hackl 1996: 153–62. See also Jolowicz and Nicholas 1972: 218–25.

[74] Kaser and Hackl 1996: 151–2.

claimant. Where, on the other hand, the praetor was willing to enforce a new legal variant he could grant an 'action on the facts' (*actio in factum*). A *formula* would be devised—presumably by the jurist acting as counsel for the claimant or as *consilium* to the praetor—which was specifically tailored for the individual facts of the case.[75] The praetor could even add an entirely new action to his edict. In many cases these newly standardized actions would then bear the name of the praetor who first consolidated them in his edict.[76] But even after they were stabilized in the edict, they would still be regarded as *in factum concepta*. Thus all the actions which were based on the *conventio pignoris*—the *actio Serviana* and the *actiones pigneraticiae* (*directa* and *contraria*)—did have *formulae in factum conceptae*.[77] The praetor could also incidentally change the scope of an existing action, by amending the *formula* and grant an analogous action.[78] The expression '*actio utilis*' was used where a condition of an existing *formula* was changed or deleted, in order to accommodate new cases. Thus, in the late classical period an *actio Serviana utilis* was granted to the creditor, where future assets had been pledged. In the adapted *formula* of this action the condition that the pledged assets were owned (*in bonis*) by the debtor *at the time of conclusion* of the pledge agreement was modified, so that also assets which were afterwards acquired would be charged.[79] Such a change could also be drastic, such as when the *actio Serviana* was adapted in order to enforce pledge agreements pursuant to which receivables were pledged.[80]

Luhmann observes that consistency 'does not require a reflection on the unity of the system or orientation by a sense of the system as a whole'.[81] One can also attempt to reach consistency by solving similar cases in a similar manner. This is what common law courts have been doing for centuries. The adaptation of an existing form of action by the praetor to a new situation would involve this kind of consistency. In particular here one could find support for the proposition that it is 'the need for consistency in its internal operations, and not its alignment with the economy or the political system, that above all drives the workings of the legal system and defines its "efficiency"'.[82]

[75] Kaser and Hackl 1996: 238.

[76] Kaser and Hackl 1996: 237. This was different for the *actio Serviana*, which was probably named after Servius Sulpicius Rufus. The latter did not introduce this action in his capacity of praetor, but may have recommended it to a praetor for inclusion in his annual edict.

[77] While the *intentio* of *actiones civiles* would usually refer to the subjective right (e.g., ownership) on which the claim was based (e.g., *si paret hominem ex iure Quiritium Auli Agerii esse*), the *intentio* of an *actio in factum* would state the facts supporting the claim (Kaser and Hackl 1996: 329).

[78] Kaser and Hackl 1996: 329–33. [79] Section 9.4. [80] Section 8.3.

[81] Luhmann 2004: 258.

[82] Deakin 2011: 675. Luhmann, interestingly, observes that the legal system can deal with a larger variety of cases if it 'relaxes strict requirements as to the consistency of legal decisions'. Luhmann 2004: 269.

Formula as conditional programme

A decisive factor for the evolution of Roman law as an autonomous system was the role played by the praetor in instructing judges on how to make their decisions. These instructions, which were documented and passed on in edicts, were cast in the form of—what Luhmann calls—'conditional programmes'. The concept of the conditional programme is 'one of the great evolutionary achievements of social development'.[83] Luhmann mentions the Roman *formula* as a classical example of a conditional programme.

> Only conditional programmes can instruct the continuous linking of self-reference and external reference; only conditional programmes provide the system's orientation to and from its environment with a form which is cognitive and at the same time which can be evaluated deductively in the system. The formal Roman process began with the instruction: 'si *paret*....'[84]

It is through its conditional programmes that the legal system responds to communications from the other subsystems of society (e.g., economy). They contain the conditions on which it depends whether (and which) legal consequences must be attached to fact patterns which are within the scope of the legal system. A conditional programme has an 'if *a* then *b*' structure: *if* conditions a_1, a_2, and a_x occur, *then* the legal consequence shall be *b*.[85] Whenever concrete fact patterns meet these conditions the legal consequence shall be the same. Although they may borrow the values from other subsystems, the 'filters' included in the conditional programmes—that is, the conditions a_1, a_2, and a_x—determine whether the defendant would be condemned or dismissed. This allowed the Roman legal system to respond to other subsystems, but only where its conditional programmes were capable of recognizing events of these other systems as legally relevant facts, by subsuming them under the conditions of a *formula*. Under the influence of societal circumstances (e.g., new transactional practices) conditional programmes may change over time, by changing the conditions or by giving them a new interpretation. Legal evolution takes place by creating, modifying, or deleting conditional programmes

[83] Luhmann 2004: 197.

[84] Luhmann 2004: 196. The words 'formal Roman process' are an unfortunate translation of '*Formularprozeß*' (= formulary procedure) in Luhmann 1993: 195.

[85] Luhmann 1988: 24. I have employed a_x in order to indicate that the number of conditions may vary between different forms of action/conditional programmes. The *formula* of the *actio Serviana* has six conditions (a_1–a_6). See section 6.6.

encapsulated in forms of action, legislation, legal opinions, and judgments.[86] The concept of the conditional programme appears to be very useful for analysing the evolution of the Roman law of real security, which to a large extent took place by interpreting or modifying the conditional programme comprised in the *formula* of the *actio Serviana* (the *actio* with which a creditor could enforce his right of pledge both against the debtor and against third parties).

Conditional programmes and legal institutions

A criticism on reducing law to conditional programmes is that it neglects legal forms which cannot be fitted into the 'conditional scheme'.[87] In particular, it has been said not to give sufficient weight to the importance of the concept of 'legal institution' as a complex of connected legal rules.[88] It is true that many of the legal characteristics of *pignus* and *hypotheca* are not expressly mentioned in the *formula* of the *actio Serviana* but are to be found in jurists' opinions and imperial constitutions interpreting this form of action. Thus, the conditions of the *actio Serviana* (e.g., *in bonis*, *solutio*, and *satisfactio*) have given rise to a complex body of rules of substantive law, which together with those on *fiducia cum creditore* constitute (what we now call) the Roman law of real security. To employ the concept of a conditional programme as an analytical tool is by no means irreconcilable with considering legal institutions as the prime focus of legal-historical research. The focus can be on how a particular conditional programme changed over time or on how a particular legal institution (e.g., *pignus* and *hypotheca*) evolved in a particular period. For the action-based Roman private law, the latter (legal institution) will in most cases make the first (conditional programme) necessary. The conditional programme expressed in a *formula* can be regarded as the procedural expression of a number of more specific rules of substantive law relating to the validity or enforceability of contracts, rights *in rem*, or other legal relationships. Although the jurists did discuss *pignus* and *hypotheca* in terms of

[86] Luhmann 2004: 217.

[87] In his monograph on literary form criticism and Roman law, David Daube distinguishes between Roman legislation which has been drafted in the form of a conditional clause ('if so and so has occurred') and in the form of a relative clause ('whoever does so and so'). The conditional clause is typically edictal and used by praetors and aediles. Legislation using the relative clause can generally also be reformulated in the conditional clause (Daube 1956: 5–6).

[88] Vesting 2018a: 25.

substantive law, they often also spoke in terms of actions.[89] This intimate connection between substance and procedure in Roman law is nicely illustrated by Gaius in D. 9.4.27 pr.: 'for it is not a pledge what cannot be recovered' ('*nullum enim pignus est, cuius persecutio negatur*'). In other words, there cannot be a substantive right (*pignus*) where there is no action (*actio Serviana*). Therefore, although this book primarily looks at (the evolution of) *pignus* and *hypotheca* as a legal institution, it does so—in imitation of the Roman jurists—with intermittent references to the conditional programme encapsulated in the *formula* of the *actio Serviana*.

2.4 Praetor's Edict, *Ius Honorarium*, and *Ius Novum*

The incidental adaptation by the praetor of a standard form of action would only result in structural legal change if there were stabilization mechanisms causing the change to be conserved and remain accessible. In modern Western legal systems, either codification (civil law systems) or a doctrine of binding precedent for case law (common law systems) are the most important stabilization mechanisms.[90] In the Principate neither a general codification of private law was enacted, nor was there published case law subject to a doctrine of precedent. When subsequent praetors granted an adapted action on the basis of similar fact patterns as the original one, the jurists would—certainly in the last two centuries BC—have recommended that they be included in the edict as a new standard *formula*. In the edict the praetor would then give a standardized description of the fact patterns in respect of which an action would be granted, accompanied by the relevant form of action (*formula*). What is unique about Roman law is that the praetor's edict, 'that masterpiece of republican jurisprudence',[91] combined the stability and predictability of a codification, with the adaptability of case law. The *ius honorarium* was the product of this combination. After the fixation of the praetor's edict under Hadrian, the adaptive capacity of this source of law was significantly reduced. The imperial chancery, however, took over the role of the praetor in adapting Roman law to new needs of Roman society. This resulted in a new body of rules, which in modern literature is referred to as '*ius novum*'.

[89] See, e.g., Lab. D. 20.6.14; Jul. D. 13.7.29; Ulp. D. 13.7.11.1; Ulp. (Marcell.) D. 18.2.4.3; Marci. D. 20.1.13.4.

[90] A classic study on the sources of law in Roman, English, French, and German law, is Dawson 1968.

[91] Schulz 1951: 127.

Praetor's edict: stability and adaptability

At the beginning of his one-year term in office, the *praetor urbanus* would issue an edict, which was made accessible to the public by placing an *album* (texts written in black with red rubrics against a white background) on the forum.[92] In the praetor's edict it was indicated in which circumstances he would be prepared to grant an action (*iudicium dabo*) in formulary proceedings. The praetor's edict would also contain an elaborate list of the forms of action (*formulae*) which a claimant should use in litigation, often accompanied by standard form defences (*exceptiones*) and counter-defences (*replicationes*). Although formally each year the new praetor enacted a new edict, in practice the great majority of *formulae* included in such edict would be copied from the edict of his predecessor. The Romans even used a special term for the unaltered part of the edict: 'handed-down edicts' (*edicta translaticia*).[93] The praetors were generally not trained as lawyers and at the beginning of their one-year term in office there would not have been sufficient time to elaborate an entirely new praetor's edict.[94] Only the jurists in the praetor's *consilium* were capable of securing the continuity of the praetor's edict.[95] The legal rules to be found in successive edicts by the praetor were either identical to their predecessors or only incidentally modified. This ensured a stability of normative expectations which is essential for a well-functioning legal system. Stability was, however, combined with adaptability.[96] The law could be adapted, because the praetor could insert new remedies in his edict, including those granted in rulings (*decreta*) by his predecessor outside the latter's edict during his time in office, or amend existing ones.[97] The structure of the praetor's edict clearly shows that it is the product of incremental evolution.[98] Schulz reflects that Mommsen called the edictal order a 'disorder' and observes that 'certainly it is anything but a masterpiece of systematization'.[99] An example of this disorder is the place of the *actio Serviana* in the praetor's edict.[100]

[92] Mantovani 2016: 28–9.

[93] Cic., *Verr.* 1.114. Schiller 1978: 412. The term '*edictum*' was (in single form) used to refer to 'the' (annual) edict of the praetor, but could also refer to the individual 'chapters' (e.g., *edictum de pactis*) included in the annual edict.

[94] Kaser 1976: 210–1.

[95] Kaser 1976: 211.

[96] Wieacker 1961: 91.

[97] Schiller 1978: 412.

[98] Jolowicz and Nicholas 1972: 357. For the evolution of the praetor's edict, see in particular Kelly 1966b; Watson 1970; Watson 1974: 31–60; Wieacker 1988: 462-70; Kirov 2005: 136–57.

[99] Schulz 1953: 151.

[100] Section 4.5.

The praetor's edict and evolution of classical law

The most formative period of the praetor's edict was probably the second and first century BC.[101] By the end of the Republic most praetorian remedies had already been included in the edict and the creation of new remedies was a rare occasion during the Principate. If new clauses were added to the edict, it was usually to implement legislation (*senatus consulta* and *leges*).[102] This did not mean, however, that in classical Roman law the possibility of edictal changes of law was completely cut off. Thus, the prevailing opinion among modern Romanists (to which I do not necessarily subscribe) is that the scope of the *actio Serviana* was only extended from tenant's pledges to pledges in general at the time of (and perhaps even by) Julian.[103] In addition, there are indications that another pledge remedy—the creditor's contractual *actio pigneraticia (contraria)*—did not yet exist in early classical law, and must therefore have been introduced into the edict in the classical period.[104]

Even the fixation of the praetor's edict under Hadrian still left room for praetorian innovations. Kelly notes that because it is likely that in the one hundred and fifty years before the codification of the *Edictum perpetuum* very little new material had been added to the edict, 'it would be quite wrong to suppose that its final edition by Salvius Julianus under Hadrian brought to an end an era of continuous productivity'.[105] In cases not provided for in the *Edictum perpetuum* there would still be room for innovation by the praetor, albeit curtailed by the existing edictal framework. Their fixation in the praetor's edict was no obstacle for jurisprudence to develop variations of existing rules by using innovative interpretations.[106] Moreover, *actiones utiles* and *actiones in factum* could still be granted. In fact, we will see that under the regime of the *Edictum perpetuum* many of the most significant changes of the law of pledge took place. New transactional practices were positively sanctioned by the praetors, by granting adapted versions of the *actio Serviana*. The contractual *actiones pigneraticiae in ius conceptae* even originated after the codification of the praetor's edict and were stabilized as extra-edictal actions.[107]

[101] Kelly 1966a: 88–9; Schiavone 2012: 358; De Ligt 2020: 97.
[102] Jolowicz and Nicholas 1972: 356. [103] Section 4.5. [104] Section 6.6.
[105] Kelly 1966a: 88. [106] Fögen 2005: 97. [107] Kaser 1982: 98. See section 6.6.

Ius honorarium and '*ius novum*'

The interventions by the praetors (and the *aediles curules* for market sales) resulted in a second body of law existing alongside the traditional *ius civile*.[108] This *ius honorarium* was largely responsible for Roman law developing from a static law for an agrarian society primarily based on land tenure and personal relationships, to a more dynamic law facilitating the free circulation of goods and the availability of credit.[109] The Roman law of pledge is to a large extent the product of the *ius honorarium* and its interactions with commercial and financial practices. The landlord's pledge on *invecta et illata*, the non-possessory pledge, the creditor's right to sell the pledged assets, the creditor's obligation to pay any surplus proceeds back to the debtor, multiple security rights, the charge of receivables, the antichretic pledge, and the general pledge all find their origin in transactional practices. These transactional practices were recognized by the praetor, by inventing, interpreting and adapting remedies—in particular the praetorian *actio Serviana*—in order to give effect to the new arrangements put before him. The law of pledge was largely developed through transactional practices which were recognized by the *ius honorarium*. The *ius honorarium* ultimately allowed a right *in rem* (*hypotheca*) to be created merely by way of an informal agreement: *nuda conventione*, as Julian and Ulpian state.[110] It is precisely the fact that it was largely a creation of the *ius honorarium*—being less strict than the *ius civile*—that made it possible that a wide-ranging right *in rem* evolved that could be created without formalities or the transfer of possession.

In the late classical period important changes occurred, most importantly through imperial intervention. In particular, the imperial chancery of the Severans made significant contributions to the development of Roman law, which leads Coriat to speak of the '*ius novum Severianum*'. Coriat builds upon a theory advanced by others (including Biondi and Schiller) that late imperial law constituted a 'third stratum' in the history of the sources of classical Roman law.[111] This *ius novum* was largely developed by the imperial rescript practice. Not only Roman officials but also individual citizens could petition the emperor for an answer on a question of law. This could take place during legal proceedings, but also in preparation for legal proceedings or precisely in order to avoid them. Although formally not a statute or judgment, a rescript

[108] See recently, De Ligt 2020. [109] Wieacker 1988: 474–5.

[110] Jul. D. 41.3.33.4; Jul. D. 41.3.33.5; Ulp. D. 13.7.1 pr. Section 6.5.

[111] Coriat 1997: 170–1.

was 'an authoritative ruling on the law'.[112] To the extent that they were concerned purely with matters of law, rescripts were regarded as having general force, and were used by the jurists as legal precedents.[113] As such, rescripts not only could be invoked by persons who had petitioned for the rescript but could be relied upon by anyone.[114] It may not be a coincidence that the rescripts practice, and more generally imperial constitutions, really started to influence Roman law with emperor Hadrian, the same emperor who ordered Julian to codify the *Edictum perpetuum*.[115] This may be the main reason why imperial law took over the leading role from the *ius honorarium* in reforming Roman law. Legal change was no longer the product of a joint effort of magistrates and independent jurists. Law-making became, at least formally, more firmly in the hands of the imperial state and much law can be found in constitutions and *senatus consulta* drawn up in the imperial chancery.[116] There was, however, a large degree of continuity between the *ius honorarium* and the *ius novum*. The imperial chancery used 'praetorian techniques' in order to fill lacunae in the praetorian edict and to adapt Roman law to the needs of society. Like the praetors before them, although rescripts were supposed to be statements concerning existing law, the chancery actually innovated the law by introducing new rules and institutions in the legal system, without disturbing its coherence.[117] Also in another sense, there was continuity: the jurists continued to be materially responsible for interpreting and changing the law.

2.5 The Roman Jurists

It is almost impossible to overstate the significance of the Roman jurists for the evolution of Roman law.[118] They would advise transacting parties on how to draft their agreements, litigating parties on choosing the right remedies, the praetor on the content of his annual edict and on granting remedies in individual proceedings, the *iudex* on how to apply the conditional programme recorded in the *litis contestatio*, and the emperor on issuing rescripts and other imperial constitutions. In the last two centuries of the Republic and for the whole of the Principate the Roman jurists were materially responsible for

112 Honoré 1994: 38.
113 Honoré 1994: 41–2. See, e.g., Marci. D. 20.1.16.9 (discussed section 11.4) and Tryph. D. 20.5.12 pr.
114 Honoré 1994: 36.
115 Honoré 1994: 13, 15; Coriat 1997: 170. For a more negative view, see Peachin 1996: 204–7.
116 Coriat 1997: 170.
117 Jolowicz and Nicholas 1972: 357; Honoré 1994: 41; Coriat 1997: 549–50.
118 Dawson 1968: 107.

the stability and change of Roman law.[119] In particular in the Republic, they used their authority with 'the conscious purpose of defending the law from petrification and sterilization'.[120] The jurists (rather than the legislator or the courts) were the 'effective determiners' of the law.[121] This is why legislation was only incidentally used for reforming Roman private law. Although their freedom to change the forms of action became more limited in the Principate, the jurists still were the instigators of legal innovation. Even after the codification of the praetor's edict, the Roman jurists continued to be materially responsible for the capacity of the legal system to maintain itself over time in a changing environment. In the imperial chancery they would draft rescripts and other constitutions, although in the Severan period some emperors did occasionally personally intervene against the opinions of their jurists.[122] As we will see in chapters 5 to 11, the elaboration of the law of *pignus* and *hypotheca* was largely the work of Roman jurisprudence.

Cavere

One of the core tasks of the Roman jurists, in addition to advising the parties on forms of action in litigation (*agere*) and giving legal opinions (*respondere*), was *cavere*. Certainly in the Republic they would draft individual transactions (contracts, wills, conveyances, etc.) and template documents, and advise the parties which templates to choose and how to comply with the required formalities.[123] However, at the end of the Republic and during the empire, when commercial intercourse was intensive and Roman law covered a large geographical area, the prominent jurists would no longer be actively engaged in drafting transaction documents, but more with giving legal opinions (*responsa*). One cannot exclude that the great jurists whose writings were included in the Digest were occasionally involved in designing new contractual clauses. But usually, the everyday drafting of contracts and other legal transactions would be the responsibility of local jurists of lower standing or in the hands of professional scribes (*tabelliones*) without much legal expertise.[124]

[119] According to De Ligt (2020: 98) in the final centuries of the Republic the *praetors* used their edictal powers for introducing legal innovations, while in the Principate the *jurists* adapted and extended the law 'through creative interpretation'. The praetorian innovations in the Republic would also have been masterminded by the jurists.

[120] Schulz 1953: 60. [121] Frier 1989–1990: 279–80.

[122] See in particular Coriat 1997: 560–7. One example could be Marci. D. 20.1.16.9, discussed in section 11.4.

[123] Wieacker 1988: 557–60. [124] Schulz 1953: 109–11, 155; Nörr 2003: 273.

For the transactions preserved in the archive of the Sulpicii, Camodeca observes that they were based on templates which were the product of local cautelary legal practice.[125] In Roman Egypt new legal templates or formulas were not the work of jurists but were designed by documentary scribes who were capable of adapting them to the commercial and financial needs of the transacting parties. Rupprecht warns us that 'the role played by these scribes in furthering private economic activity should not be underestimated' and gives the example of the development of the *hypallagma* as a less strict form of real security than the older *hypothéke*.[126]

Respondere

The emergence of the so-called *ius respondendi*—the privilege of certain jurists to give opinions which were binding on judges—may be linked to the decline in praetorian standards of which the first signs appear in the early Principate.[127] As early as during the Republic, *iudices* would be under a moral compulsion to follow the advice of the jurists. But where jurists would give their advice *ex auctoritate Augusti*, this compulsion 'would be not just moral and qualified, but political and absolute'.[128] In his treatise on legal history, *Enchiridion*, Pomponius devotes a large passage to the *ius respondendi* and declares that 'it was the deified Augustus who, in order to enhance the authority of the law, first established that opinions might be given under his authority'.[129] Pomponius also refers to a rescript by emperor Hadrian 'on an occasion when some men of praetorian rank were petitioning him for permission to grant opinions'. Hadrian responded favourably to this petition and 'said that this was by custom not merely begged for but earned and that he would accordingly be delighted if whoever had faith in himself would prepare himself for giving opinions to the people at large'. Pomponius mentions that 'to Sabinus the concession was granted by Tiberius Caesar that he might give opinions to the people at large'. The second main classical source for the *ius respondendi* is Gaius's Institutes.[130]

> **Gai. *Inst.* 1.7** Responsa prudentium sunt sententiae et opiniones eorum, quibus permissum est iura condere. quorum omnium si in unum sententiae

[125] Camodeca 2003: 76.
[126] Rupprecht 2014: 21.
[127] Kelly 1966a: 89, 95.
[128] Kelly 1966a: 97.
[129] Pomp. D. 1.2.2.49.
[130] A similar text is Just. *Inst.* 1.2.8.

> concurrunt, id, quod ita sentiunt, legis uicem optinet; si uero dissentiunt, iudici licet quam uelit sententiam sequi; idque rescripto diui Hadriani significatur.
>
> Juristic answers are the opinions and advice of those entrusted with the task of building up the law. If the opinions of all of them agree on a point, what they thus hold has the status of a statute; if, however, they disagree, a judge may follow which opinion he wishes. This is made known in a rescript of the Emperor Hadrian.

Like Pomponius, Gaius refers to a rescript by Hadrian, which rules that the *communis opinio* of those jurists who have been allowed to *iura condere* is a binding source of law. Only if on a particular question of law there is no unanimity is the *iudex* free to decide which opinion to follow. Pomponius and Gaius seem clear enough. However, for various reasons (corruption of Pomponius's text; Gaius's text is not on *ius respondendi* but on *communis opinio*; there is no mention in other sources) part of modern literature holds that the existence of the *ius respondendi* cannot be reasonably assumed.[131] But even if it did not exist, the interpretation and elaboration by the jurists of the formal sources of law (e.g., *leges,* praetor's edict, and imperial constitutions) would normally be followed in the Roman courts. To give but one of many examples: in a constitution from 223 AD Alexander Severus says that, although the produce of pledged land is (in the absence of an express term in the pledge agreement) impliedly pledged, 'nevertheless no jurist has held (*nulli prudentium placuit*) that land purchased with the money derived from such produce is also included for the same purpose' (Alex. C. 8.14.3). If not binding authority, the writings of the jurists would in any case have constituted persuasive authority (even for Roman emperors).[132]

In his *History of Roman Legal Science,* Schulz observes that '[t]he heroic age of creative geniuses and daring pioneers had passed away with the Republic'.[133] For the law of *pignus* and *hypotheca* this observation does not do justice to the contribution of the classical jurists. It is true, most of the remedies for pledge (*interdictum Salvianum, interdictum de migrando, actio pigneraticia directa,* and, most importantly, *actio Serviana*) were created by the republican jurists. However, *hypotheca,* multiple pledge, *ius offerendi et succedendi, pignus nominis,* and the general pledge were all the result of the classical jurists

[131] For an extensive discussion of the interpretations of the Pomponius and Gaius fragments, see Tuori 2007: 71–134.

[132] This is not to say that the emperor would always follow the opinions of the jurists.

[133] Schulz 1953: 99.

applying their creative powers to the accommodation of transactional practices. Much of these variants of *pignus* required adaptations of the standard form of action of the *actio Serviana*, which would have been impossible without the expertise of the jurists. They were often part of the emperor's *consilium* or members of the imperial chancery. For instance, in the second century AD, Julian had been a member of the emperor's *consilium*, tribune of the plebs, praetor, prefect of the treasury, consul, and provincial governor.[134] It was at the request of emperor Hadrian that Julian drafted the *Edictum perpetuum*. In the third century AD, both Papinian and Ulpian were, among other things, *procurator a libellis* and praetorian prefect.[135] One thing did not change, however: the impartiality of their legal opinions. Also in the Principate it was expected from the jurists that they acted as legal experts, whose task it was to give an objective statement of the law.[136] They were not supposed to represent the interests of one particular party or the state, even though during the course of the Principate they increasingly earned their income from giving legal advice to magistrates and citizens, or were (like Julian, Papinian, and Ulpian) engaged by the emperor in high positions within the imperial administration. The emperor might be tempted to appoint certain jurists who were particularly loyal to him and who would give legal opinions that supported certain results preferred by him in individual cases. At the same time, however, the emperor would be careful to avoid criticisms of the professional body of jurists or from public opinion.[137]

Litigation, praetor's edict, and imperial chancery

In individual litigation, the jurists would advise the litigating parties in choosing the right action and other remedies, advise the praetor in granting these remedies, provide their advocates with legal 'ammunition', and counsel the *iudex* in applying the actions and remedies to the case at hand.[138] The individual forms of action as well as the praetor's edict as a whole were the creation of the jurists.[139] The forms of action included in the praetor's edict were

[134] Peachin 2016: 164. [135] Peachin 2016: 164. [136] Liebs 2010: 9.

[137] Liebs 2010: 10. Both Papinian and Ulpian were murdered, however, as a result of imperial palace conspiracies (Schiavone 2012: 398).

[138] Lehne 2014. It is impossible to answer the question whether in contributing to the design of new *formulae* the jurists acted as counsel to the litigating parties or as *consilium* to the praetor. Kaser and Hackl 1996: 237.

[139] There is an abundance of literature of this. I refer only to Schulz 1953: 49–53, 60–1, 99–100, 111–8, 124–9.

largely written in a highly technical and very concise language confined to the essential elements of the remedy concerned. This language was devised by the jurists for the jurists: it was their task to interpret this language, apply it to concrete cases, and generally to secure its accessibility to the public. In the framing and maintenance of the forms of action the jurists of the late Republic and the early Principate used their 'highest creative powers'.[140] The jurists had, already at the time of the late Republic, developed from mere 'expert witnesses' on the content of the law to the 'effective determiners of law'.[141] In the Principate, when most standard forms of action had more or less become settled, the drafting of forms of action in individual cases would have been routinely performed by 'lesser' jurists or scribes.[142] The first ranking jurists mainly 'determined' the law in their legal opinions and (from Hadrian) in the imperial chancery. On those rare occasions in the classical period where a new action (e.g., *actio pigneraticia contraria*) was created outside the praetor's edict, or the scope of an existing one was significantly changed (e.g., *actio Serviana utilis*), the jurists would have been materially responsible for this.

After the codification of the praetor's edict the jurists would largely be responsible for the substance of the imperial *ius novum*. Before Hadrian they would advise the praetor in compiling the edict; after Hadrian they would prepare the rescripts and other constitutions. The 'codification' of rescripts only took off under Diocletian, whose rescripts were often more directed at stabilizing the law than reforming it.[143] Moreover, rescripts carried out the same function as the unanimous opinions of authoritative jurists, which (since Hadrian) were binding for judges on questions of law.[144] Although in this period the balance between jurisprudence and imperial politics tipped in favour of the latter, the jurists would remain instrumental in answering questions of law and formulating new legal rules.[145]

[140] Kaser and Hackl 1996: 308. [141] Frier 1989–1990: 279–80. [142] Schulz 1953: 112.
[143] Schulz 1953: 153, 287. [144] Honoré 1994: 39. [145] Schiavone 2012: 384–9.

3

Economic Environment

3.1 Introduction

Throughout history the financial world proves to be a stimulating environment in complex societies for the origin and evolution of legal institutions. For ancient Rome one could think of *constitutum debiti*, *receptum argentarii*, set-off, and, most importantly, real security. It would, however, be a mistake to associate *pignus*, *hypotheca*, and *fiducia cum creditore* exclusively with commercial lending by banks. Agriculture was the most important sector of the economic environment and it is no coincidence that it was this sector that triggered important developments in the law of real security. Specific late republican legal remedies for *pignus*—the *interdictum Salvianum* and (perhaps) the *actio Serviana*—were designed specifically for security granted to owners of agricultural estates by tenant farmers. Another republican legal remedy, the *interdictum de migrando*, demonstrates that real security was also important for the law of landlord and tenant in an urban context, both for living accommodation and for commercial real estate (e.g., *tabernae*).[1] Real security was even frequently granted within the context of family relationships, for example to secure dowries, and in order to secure (tax and other) claims by the state. Nevertheless, although the other contexts will not be ignored, in this book the emphasis will be on how the law of *pignus* and *hypotheca* evolved in the context of commercial lending. Between the end of the third century and the middle of the first century BC, a 'remarkable qualitative change in the structure of the Roman economy' took place.[2] Not only was there a shift in agriculture towards commercialization and specialization but there was also a substantial increase in trade and commerce.[3] These economic changes were accompanied by the development of financial

[1] Frier 1980: 105–35; Du Plessis 2007. [2] Kay 2014: 2.

[3] On investment farming and agricultural exploitation, see Kay 2014: 131–88; on trade, see Kay 2014: 189–213; on credit and banking, see Kay 2014: 107–28. By the mid-third century BC, manufacturing and commerce were significant in the city of Rome (De Ligt 2020: 93).

Security and Credit in Roman Law: The historical evolution of pignus *and* hypotheca. Hendrik L. E. Verhagen, Oxford University Press. © Hendrik L. E. Verhagen 2022. DOI: 10.1093/oso/9780199695836.003.0004

intermediation and increased availability of credit.[4] From this time and during the whole of the Principate, 'irritations' produced by the financial sector were significant stimuli for the evolution of the Roman law of real security. In this chapter, we will first look at the role of bankers and elite financiers in the Roman credit markets (section 3.2) and various forms of credit will be reviewed (consumptive, productive, and secured credit: section 3.3). Subsequently an overview will be given of several categories of valuable capital goods for important sectors of the Roman economy (agriculture, urban economy, maritime trade), which were financed and served as collateral (section 3.4). As will be shown at the end of this chapter, real security was significant not only for secured lending but also for the rural and urban rental markets (section 3.5).

3.2 Elite Financiers and Bankers

In the Roman empire there were several categories of persons who regularly lent money, either as a professional activity or by way of investment.[5] The most general category of 'financiers' operating in the last century of the Republic and the first two centuries of the Principate can be divided into several subcategories, depending on factors such as the nature of their activities, their social class and lifestyle, and their financial means.[6] The most important distinction is that between members of the aristocracy and wealthy plebeians who lent money (elite financiers) on the one hand, and professional bankers on the other.[7] The share of elite financiers in the credit market is likely to have been substantial and according to some historians even larger than that of banks.[8] For a period of at least four centuries bankers did, however, play a significant role in the Roman economy. Already in the sixties and fifties BC 'there was a liquid and sophisticated market for lending and borrowing money on a very significant scale'.[9] In these credit markets bankers played a leading part, as is illustrated by the growth of the number of bankers on the place for international commerce Delos.[10] For bankers it was common practice to take security for both consumptive and productive credit. For loans

[4] Kay 2014: 2, 4. [5] See recently Andreau 2020b.

[6] Andreau 1999: 3; Ioannatou 2006: 164–72; Kay 2014: 235–6. [7] Andreau 2010: 145.

[8] This is not a unique characteristic of ancient economies. For renaissance Florence, see Goldthwaite 2009: 409.

[9] Kay 2014: 194. [10] Kay 2014: 213.

granted between members of the elite, real security would have been less common: these credit relationships would have been subject to social norms (*amicitia*) and personal security (suretyship) would frequently be taken.[11] Indirectly, however, the Roman law of real security would also have been relevant for elite financiers, in particular where they would give money to intermediaries (e.g., freedmen or slaves) who would use it to grant secured credit to non-elite borrowers.

Elite financiers

In Rome, lending money at interest with the intention of making a profit (*faeneratio*) was associated with *avaritia* and was held in ill-repute.[12] The modern depiction of the overwhelming importance of agriculture for investment by the wealthy aristocracy risks obscuring the relevance of other sectors of investment, such as the exploitation of natural resources *and* finance.[13] Members of the elite did invest part of their wealth by lending it at interest, including to professional lenders (*faeneratores*) who would use these loans to fund their lending activities in the commercial credit markets. The subcategory of elite financiers consisted of members of the senatorial class, *equites*, and wealthy citizens of plebeian extraction, who—besides granting loans for political and other non-commercial purposes—invested part of their wealth in interest-bearing loans.[14] They would often lend large sums of money and spent considerable time and effort in doing so, but were not acting in a professional capacity. This is not to say that members of the upper classes would never be professional bankers. In his correspondence with Atticus, Cicero mentions on three occasions a financier who may have been an upper-class merchant banker with a banking establishment of considerable size.[15] This Castricius not only lent substantial amounts of money at interest against (personal and real) security[16] but seems to have been actively engaged in (slave?)

[11] On *amicitia* and lending, see Verboven 2002: 116–82 and Ioannatou 2006: 229–307. Nevertheless, as Pellecchi (2018: 460) observes, in one of Martial's epigrams (Mart. 12.25) real security over land was asked by the lender within the context of an *amicitia* relationship.

[12] Verboven 2002: 171–2; Ioannatou 2006: 50–5; Rathbone and Temin 2008: 389.

[13] Kay 2014: 332 (for the second century BC).

[14] On upper-class women as lenders and borrowers, see Ioannatou 2006: 30–3.

[15] Ioannatou 2006: 349.

[16] In Cic., *Att.* 27.5 (LCL 7: 156–7) from 59 BC, Cicero mentions that he shall 'correct the Castricius mistake' in respect of his brother Quintus by increasing the amount in his books. Ioannatou's (2006: 347) hypothesis is that Castricius had lent money to Quintus for which Cicero stood as surety.

trade himself.[17] Members of the elite would, besides lending at interest, also carry out other activities nowadays associated with banks. They would sometimes act as intermediaries in bringing together lenders and borrowers and assist with carrying out payments between different regions of the empire.[18] Although many loan agreements will have been entered into between members of the same class (e.g., members of the elite), transactions could also cross social boundaries.[19] This would certainly be the case where a patron would lend money to a client, or when a politician would turn to professional lenders (*faeneratores*) for obtaining credit. But also elite financiers would invest their fortune by providing loans to *faeneratores*, who would lend these on to Romans of the lower classes. Cicero had entered into such a relation with banker Cluvius from Puteoli (who on his death left him a substantial part of his estate).[20] The economic position of these elite financiers would sometimes be similar to that of a shareholder in a modern bank, providing capital to slaves, freedmen, or independent persons in order to set up a bank.[21]

Roman banks

Did the Roman empire have banks or bankers? Modern scholars have been blamed for using modern concepts of banking in discussing Roman 'banks', thereby obscuring the specific functions of ancient banks.[22] However, if a banker is defined as someone who manages 'an undertaking the business of which is to take deposits or other repayable funds from the public and to grant credits for its own account',[23] than Rome certainly did have bankers. And if a bank is an organization within which several persons co-operate on a continuous basis to carry out these activities, Rome certainly had banks too. In particular, the *argentarii* received deposits from their clients and used the money to grant loans to other clients. They often did so in collaboration with others, whether by way of partnerships (*societas*), or by using slaves, or a combination of both.[24] At one time six persons were active in the Sulpicii bank:

[17] See also p. 148. Ioannatou 2006: 347 n 212. TPSulp 24 and 64 mention two other Castricii.
[18] Andreau 2010: 146. [19] Harris 2011: 237–8. [20] Verboven 2002: 129.
[21] Ioannatou 2006: 167. [22] Von Reden 2010: 114; Bürge 1987: 508: Lerouxel 2016: 212.
[23] Article 4.1(1) of Regulation (EU) no 575/2013 of the European Parliament and of the Council of 26 June 2013 on prudential requirements for credit institutions and investment firms. For Roman banks, see also Andreau 1999: 2; Temin 2013: 157, 179; Kay 2014: 329.
[24] For jurists' opinions on banking partnerships, see Pap. D. 17.2.82; Pap. D. 45.2.9 pr.; Ulp. D. 17.2.52.5; Paul. D. 2.14.25 pr.; Paul. D. 2.14.27 pr. (referring to the early classical jurists Proculus and Labeo), and Paul. D. 4.8.34 pr. See on these texts Meissel 2004: 155–74. On the organization of

Faustus, Cinnamus, and four slaves actively involved in the bank's business.[25] It is likely that other slaves would have been used for other, more minor tasks (e.g., as scribes).[26] Even when one adds a third element to the definition of banks, that of executing payment orders on behalf of clients, one can still speak of Roman banks. There is good evidence of *argentarii* and other bankers administering accounts and carrying out payment orders for their clients.[27] The characterization of an institution as a 'bank' did not have the same legal consequences as today. In particular, no banking supervision rules or a central bank existed for Roman banks. This is not to say that there were no legal regulations specifically for certain bankers (in particular: *argentarii*).[28]

The share of Roman banks in the credit markets was smaller than today, although differences of opinion exist in modern literature. Andreau, for instance, endorses a rather minimalist view and thinks that elite financiers were—in quantitative terms—much more important than banks.[29] This would certainly have been the case during some financial crises which occasionally confronted the Roman economy. The credit crisis of 88 BC and other economic and monetary problems may have resulted in a dwindling number of bankers (*argentarii*) and a reduction of their balance sheets.[30] In the second half of the third century AD, bankers even temporarily completely disappear from the scene.[31] But outside these periods of financial crises banks did play a significant role in the credit market.[32] Rathbone and Temin emphasize that banks seem to have been involved in all important sectors of the Roman economy. 'Even if the modal Roman bank was small, Roman banking was big business.'[33] They do not deny that members of the elite lent on a large scale,

banks, see in particular Cerami and Petrucci 2010: 164–90. On the employment of slaves in banks, see Andreau 1999: 64–70.

[25] The above is based on Wolf 2012: 26–7. See also Verboven 2008: 222. A Dacian writing tablet from 28 March 167 AD records a partnership set up for moneylending (FIRA III, nr. 157). However, because the duration of this *societas* was less than four months one cannot realistically call it a bank.

[26] Verboven 2008: 222.

[27] See Gröschler 1997. See also Rathbone and Temin 2008: 397–8. For a different view see Wolf 2010: 195–6.

[28] See in particular Cerami and Petrucci 2010: 109–63, 191–220. Probably in the second century AD an edict on the disclosure of bank accounts (*edictum de rationibus argentariis edendis*) was enacted (Lenel 1927: 62–4). On bankers' legal duty to disclose, see, e.g., Ulp. D. 2.13.6.3.

[29] Andreau 2020a. [30] Kay 2014: 333.

[31] Andreau 1999: 33–4; Harris 2011: 251.

[32] Rathbone and Temin 2008: 407; Harris 2011: 236–44; Lerouxel 2016: 209. For the second century BC, see Kay 2014: 329 and passim.

[33] Rathbone and Temin 2008: 407. According to Kay (2014: 213) the Mithridatic wars may have been the cause why no large corporate banks emerged in the Roman Republic. Mithradates offered a remittance of 50 per cent. of their debts to borrowers who killed their Roman or Italian creditors. This may even have contributed to the temporary disappearance of *argentarii* from the sources.

but they conclude that much of the lending and borrowing by the elite was routed through banks.[34] When in 33 AD emperor Tiberius tried to rescue the Roman credit market by injecting 100 million sesterces as loans, these loans were granted through banks (*mensae*).[35] They also facilitated non-cash payments between parties and between different regions of the empire. They granted overdraft facilities to their clients by carrying out payment instructions on behalf of their customers, even when this was not backed by sufficient funds in the customer's account.[36] They were an 'alternative to social financial networks' existing between members of the elite or others (e.g., patronage relationships).[37]

The bank of the Sulpicii

In the Sulpicii archive we encounter, according to Camodeca, grand maritime commerce on a Mediterranean scale, with its cosmopolitan world of *peregrini*, oriental goods and its entrepreneurial slaves and freedmen: 'Trimalchio's world'.[38] The Sulpicii took part in financing maritime commerce in Puteoli, although the scale was rather modest. The Sulpicii were not a major bank. The loans they provided are small compared with the loans granted by elite financiers like Seneca, but certainly not insignificant: HS 12,000 (TPSulp 57), HS 18,000 (TPSulp 31), HS 20,000 (TPSulp 53, 54 and 58), HS 26,000 (TPSulp 85), and HS 50,000 (TPSulp 72).[39] In addition, there is a document in which Cinnamus declares to have received on behalf of his patron Faustus an amount of 130,000 sesterces.[40] Also contained in the Sulpicii archive is a document which may refer to a *fiducia cum creditore* for an amount of 120,000 sesterces.[41] There are also more than five *vadimonia* concerning amounts over 50,000 sesterces. The annual turnover of the Sulpicii must have been hundreds of thousands of sesterces and accordingly their annual profits must have been tens of thousands of sesterces.[42] The profitability of their bank may

[34] Rathbone and Temin 2008: 417. [35] Tac., *Ann.* 6.17.3. See Andreau 1987: 66.
[36] Von Reden 2010: 121. [37] Von Reden 2010: 117.
[38] Camodeca 2003: 71. Also Wolf (2012: 27) notices the similarity of the Sulpicii with Trimalchio, the (fictional) contemporary banker in the Puteoli of Petronius's Satyricon. On the Sulpicii bank, see in particular Jones 2006: 11–161; Jaschke 2010: 185–220. See also Andreau 1999: 71–9; Terpstra 2013: 11–23; Bransbourg 2014; Lerouxel 2016: 214–32.
[39] See table 2 in Jones 2006: 70–1. HS is modern shorthand for values in sesterces.
[40] TPSulp 74. Wolf (TPN 112) reads 50,000 sesterces. The nature of the underlying debt remains unclear.
[41] TPSulp 49. [42] Verboven 2008: 221.

have enabled the 'last' generation Sulpicii to purchase the valuable building in Pompeii in which the archive was found almost 1,900 years after it had been stored there before the cataclysmic eruption of Mount Vesuvius.

Accepting loans for funding purposes belongs to the core activities of a bank. The Sulpicii partly funded their bank by accepting loans from elite financiers. In the Sulpicii archive there are several documents showing the involvement of the imperial *familia* and the senatorial aristocracy.[43] From the imperial perspective this may have been prompted by a desire to make profitable investments in one of the empire's commercial maritime centres. The motivation behind these loans may have been to support the trade in Alexandrian grain, with a view to the *annona publica* in Rome.[44] One of the largest IOUs (HS 94,000) in the archive of the Sulpicii is executed by Gaius Sulpicius Cinnamus in favour of a slave of emperor Claudius (TPSulp 69).[45] This could be an indication that the Sulpicii bank (at least partly) was funded by accepting loans from the imperial family, for the purpose of lending it on to its clients.[46] Lerouxel even goes so far as concluding that one of the main functions of the Sulpicii bank was to link 'two universes': the commercial world and the imperial court.[47] The Sulpicii can also be characterized as true financial intermediaries in the sense that they did carry out activities for third parties, by bringing together lenders and borrowers, and by managing loans provided by third parties. The Sulpicii may also have been *coactores argentarii*, who besides arranging new loans also collected outstanding debts on behalf of their clients. This may explain the presence of several documents in the archive to which none of the Sulpicii is a party.[48]

3.3 Consumptive, Productive, and Secured Credit

The majority of texts in the Digest and Codex do not provide us much context (if any at all) about the identity of the creditor and debtor, the purpose of the

[43] Imperial family: TPSulp 45, 51 and 52 (= file C. Novius Eunus); TPSulp 67, 68, 94 and 95. Senatorial class: TPSulp 54, 73 and 109.

[44] Camodeca 2003: 86–7. See also Rathbone and Temin 2008: 388.

[45] On imperial slaves in the archive of the Sulpicii, see Lerouxel 2016: 220–1, 230–2.

[46] Lerouxel 2016: 216–7.

[47] Lerouxel 2016: 224. However, the money received from the imperial slave had to be repaid already after one month and ten days, so this may very well have concerned a short-term cash deposit for reasons other than funding the Sulpicii bank. Jones (2006: 65) considers it likely that the cash was deposited in order to pay shippers and merchants of overseas goods destined for the imperial household.

[48] For example, TPSulp 51, 52, and 55.

secured debt, or the nature of the collateral. They refer to the pledged objects in neutral terms, such as 'thing(s)' (*res*),[49] 'pledges' (*pignora*) and/or 'hypothecs' (*hypothecae*),[50] or 'charged object' (*res obligata*).[51] Creditors and debtors are usually referred to as *debitor* and *creditor* and the secured debt (if mentioned at all) with words such as 'money' (*pecunia*),[52] 'principal' (*sors*),[53] and 'indebtedness' (*debitum*).[54] I would hypothesize, however, that in the great majority of texts in which these words are used, the secured debts arose under loan agreements, certainly where the same text also refers to interest (*usuris*). In some texts we find more details about the nature of the collateral. In addition to texts on generic pledges (*invecta et illata*, *grex*, *taberna*) and maritime loans, we have a small number of texts on other objects, such as leather bags (Scaev. D. 13.7.43.1), marble plates (Scaev. D. 20.4.21.1), and precious metals and minerals (e.g., Scaev. D. 32.33.2). There are many texts in the Digest and Codex which expressly state that the pledged objects are land, buildings, or slaves. From most texts it cannot be deduced whether the acquisition of these valuable objects was financed by the loans they secured, but there are some interesting exceptions. We have literary evidence of secured credit granted by professional and non-professional lenders (including the imperial treasury), ranging from small short-term consumptive loans to large long-term productive ones.[55]

Consumptive credit

The hypothesis of Finley is that, as in ancient Greece, there was not much productive credit in Rome. Money was borrowed for consumptive rather than for commercial purposes.[56] To be sure, there is plenty of evidence in the legal and epigraphic sources on consumer credit, often secured by pledges of jewellery, precious metals, or valuable cloth(es). Literary texts illustrate that taking up consumptive credit from bankers against collateral was a vital part of the

49 For example, Pap. D. 20.1.1 pr.

50 For example, Pap. D. 20.1.2: '*pignora vel hypothecas*' ('pledged or hypothecated goods').

51 For example, Gai. D. 20.1.15.2.

52 For example, Pomp. D. 13.7.3; Ulp. D. 13.7.9.1.

53 Pomp. D. 13.7.8.5, which beside principal also mentions other debts such as interest ('*usuras*') and expenses made for the pledged property ('*impensae*').

54 For example, Marci. D. 20.1.13.5.

55 See also Pellecchi 2018: 463 (mentioning also long-term loans from *kalendarii*).

56 Finley 1999: 141–2. Finley regards maritime loans as 'an insurance policy rather than as a form of credit'. Andreau 1999: 28–9 and Ioannatou 2006: 57–60 also think that productive credit was relatively rare.

imperial Roman economy.[57] In Pro P. Sestio, Cicero contemptuously refers to a fellow citizen whose 'books were even often pledged for wine'.[58] In one of his epigrams Martial ridicules someone who pledged his ring to a banker for a small loan to finance a dinner.[59] That these literary texts reflect reality is shown by graffiti from Pompeii. In the house of A. Granius Romanus there are graffiti recording loans for which jewellery and clothes were pledged to the female pawnbroker Faustilla. One of the graffiti reads:

> **CIL IV, 8203** Idibus Iul(i)is inaures pos(i)tas ad Faustilla(m) pro (denariis) II usura(m) deduxit aeris a(ssem) ex sum(ma) XXX.
>
> On the Ides of July gold earrings were placed with Faustilla; for two denarii she has deducted one copper *as* from a total of 30.

This inscription states that the interest is 'deducted' from the principal sum, which appears to refer to the practice of charging interest by deducting it from the money actually paid out by way of *mutuum*.[60] For another loan by the same Faustilla, with a principal amount of 50 denarii, a traveller's cloak (*paenula*) and a small cloak (*palliolum*) were pledged. Here we seem to be dealing with small pawnbrokers granting short-term (weeks, months) credit for consumer purposes against pledges. In these cases the pledges are likely to have been possessory ones. The graffiti use the verb *ponere* (in CIL IV, 8203: '*pos(i)tas*'): in the jurists' writings the expression *pignori ponere* almost always refers to a possessory pledge.[61] From Roman Egypt we also have epigraphic evidence of what presumably was a consumptive loan secured by a possessory pledge of valuables. In P. Vindob. L 135, cavalryman L. Caecilius Secundus declares to owe another soldier, C. Pompeius, 400 imperial and Ptolomaic

[57] Pellecchi 2018: 463. Ioannatou 2006 has several accounts on lenders granting secured credit from the writings of Cicero, including the security granted by Cicero's brother Quintus to Castricius (Ioannatou 2006: 346–9, 372, 395).

[58] Cic., *Sest.* 51, 110: '*libelli etiam saepe pro vino oppignerabantur*'.

[59] Mart. 2.57.7 See also Bürge 1987: 479–80.

[60] The same practice may have been used by the Sulpicii. The loan transactions in the archive are all structured as a *mutuum cum stipulatione* (e.g., in TPSulp 51 and 52). The stipulation would have added value, where the borrower used it for promising to pay interest (e.g., Mod. D. 22.1.41.2), which would not be actionable on the basis of *mutuum*. In the Sulpicii archive, however, the *stipulatio* is never used—at least not expressly—for promising interest: the *stipulatio* is for the same principal amount as owed pursuant to *mutuum*. Nevertheless, the purpose of the *mutuum cum stipulatione* might also here have been to grant loans against interest. This could be achieved by making the interest payable immediately when the loan was granted and deduct it from the money actually paid out by way of *mutuum*. Pursuant to the *stipulatio* the full amount could then still be recovered. See Verhagen 2018: 271–3 (with further references).

[61] Paul. (Alf.) D. 12.6.36; Pap. D. 13.7.27; Scaev. D. 32.33.2; Ulp. D. 13.7.27; Sev.-Ant. C. 8.16.2. In Scaevola D. 32.38 pr., however, to 'place' lands as a pledge ('*pignori ponere*') seems to refer to pledges generally.

drachmas against a pledge of 'a helmet inlaid with silver, a silvered insigne and a silver scabbard for a dagger adorned with ivory'.[62] The purpose of this loan is not stated, but as the loan was between two soldiers it is likely to have been a consumptive one. In the Digest and Codex there are texts concerning the pledge of jewellery,[63] pearls,[64] (bare or wrought) gold[65] or silver,[66] silverware,[67] or other valuables.[68] These objects are typically assets serving as collateral for consumptive loans, with the exception of bare gold and silver (which may also have been used as collateral for productive credit).[69]

Productive credit

There is much evidence in the legal sources of productive credit as well, even if one only mainly looks (as I have done) to the evidence of secured credit.[70] Not only did the Romans take over the Greek maritime loan: in the archive of the Sulpicii and in the Digest we encounter secured credit granted to grain merchants, marble dealers, cloth merchants, oil sellers, and shipowners.[71] There are strong indications that a significant part of the loans in the Sulpicii archive were productive in the sense that they facilitated production and commerce.[72] This is what one would expect in case of bankers who were active in the commercial hub that was Puteoli in the first century AD. In particular, the loans to grain traders, secured by a pledge on wheat and other foodstuffs (TPSulp 51, 52, and 79) and the loan to (presumably) a clothes merchant, secured by a pledge of precious cloth or clothing ('*purpuras laconicas*': TPSulp 83 and 84) must have involved productive credit.[73] There are also *testationes* in the archive that appear to concern the auction of slaves who

62 '*dr(achmas) Aug(ustas) et Pt(olemaicas) CCCC ob pignera cassidem inargentatam et insigne inargentatum et vaginam pugionis argenteum subiecto eboreo*'. Harrauer and Seider 1979.

63 For example, Scaev. D. 32.33.2.

64 For example, Afr. D. 30.108.13 and Ulp. D. 44.4.4.8.

65 Ulp. D. 13.7.1.2; Ulp. 13.7.1.11; Ulp. D. 13.7.27; Ulp D. 13.7.36 pr.; Paul. D. 47.2.20 pr.; Diocl.-Max. C. 4.2.8.

66 Alex. C. 4.24.5.

67 Pap. D. 33.10.9.2.

68 Gai. D. 37.9.5.1 ('*pretiosis*').

69 TPsulp 55 is on the pledge of bare silver, securing a loan of HS 5,000 to Publius Vergilius Ampliatus.

70 Cicero (Cic., *Sull.* 58; Cic., *Fam.* V.17) distinguishes between loans contracted '*libidine*' and '*negotii gerendi studio*'. See Ioannatou 2006: 53–4.

71 In Petronius's Satyricon (38) one of Trimalchio's guests tells how a Gaius Julius Proculius had set up the business of an undertaker (*libitinarius*) with his freedmen. However, the business did not go well, so that Proculius was forced to borrow heavily against real security ('I don't think that even his hair is free from mortgage'). On productive loans, see also Andreau 2020b: 98–102.

72 Temin and Rathbone 2008: 405. See also Camodeca 2003: 81.

73 See also Camodeca 2003: 81–2; Lerouxel 2016: 221–4.

were charged (*fiducia*) in order to secure productive loans to slave traders.[74] In all these cases, productive credit was secured by real security over the type of assets which the borrower used for his business.

The same pattern can be detected in many examples of productive credit in the Digest. One example of secured productive credit is Scaev. D. 20.1.34 pr., concerning a pledge of the floating stock of a shop (*taberna*). Although the purpose of the secured credit is not mentioned, this is likely to have been to finance the purchase of new merchandise.[75] In another text from Scaevola (D. 13.7.43.1) the grain merchant Titius borrowed money from Gaius Seius against a pledge of leather bags: again the purpose of the loan is likely to have been the purchase of new grain. In D. 14.5.8 Paul discusses the liability of a master for certain acts of a slave who had been appointed in order to 'provide loans and to accept pledges'[76] and who seems to have been the (sole) manager of a bank financing the grain trade.[77] Ulp. D. 14.3.13 pr. is not concerned with secured credit. This text does, however, demonstrate how the master's liability for money borrowed by his slave, who was authorized to manage an olive oil trade in Arles, could depend on the productive nature of the loan. In particular, where it could not be proven by the lender that the slave had also been expressly authorized to take up loans, the master could still be liable if it could be demonstrated that the money was borrowed in order to finance the merchandise. Also in relation to maritime trade we can find many examples of loans with a commercial purpose.[78] A right of *pignus* could also secure commercial sellers' credit. Ulp. D. 14.3.5.15 deals with the scope of the *actio institoria* in relation to a slave who was an *institor* of an olive oil business. Ulpian declares that the owner of this 'slave/manager' shall be liable with the *actio institoria* when the manager has accepted a pledge for payment of the purchase price but refuses to return the charged object when the purchase price has been fully paid.[79]

Secured credit in banking and other contexts

Secured credit would often be provided by bankers and other professional moneylenders. Faustilla probably earned her living as a pawnbroker in Pompeii. In secured lending transactions evidenced by the archive of the

[74] Lerouxel 2016: 223, 253. [75] See also Scaev. D. 20.4.21.1.

[76] '*Mutuis pecuniis dandis et pignoribus accipiendis*'.

[77] See also Afr. D. 12.1.41. [78] See section 3.4.

[79] See also other texts from the Digest and Codex listed in Pellecchi 2018: 467 n 98.

Sulpicii the Puteolean bankers acted as lenders to whom real security (*pignus* or *fiducia*) had been granted.[80] In other transactions in the archive, the secured lenders may have been private citizens, but these secured loans were negotiated and/or monitored by the Sulpicii as financial intermediaries.[81] In some Digest texts we also encounter security granted in order to secure the debts owed to professional financiers.[82] Ulpian D. 2.13.6.3 records an opinion by Labeo on the taking of pledges by bankers, in which he says that pledges are not recorded in the ledgers of a banker (*argentarius*) and for that reason, an *argentarius* cannot be forced to disclose the pledge. This text indicates that in Labeo's time, bankers would habitually receive pledges from their debtors.[83] In Scaev. D. 13.7.43.1, grain merchant Titius borrowed money from Gaius Seius, who received a possessory pledge of leather bags. These bags were requisitioned by an officer of the *officio annonae* while they were stored in the *horreum* of Gaius Seius himself. This creditor may therefore very well have been a merchant financier both operating and financing grain trading.[84] There may also have been professional collateral *givers*: Gai. D. 13.7.12 refers to persons 'who do usually borrow money against pledges'.

It would be a mistake, however, to associate *pignus*, *hypotheca*, and *fiducia* exclusively with commercial lending by bankers. The Roman law of real security also played a significant role in renting out rural and urban real estate, as will be elaborated in section 3.5.[85] Loans with which members of the senatorial class funded the purchase of agricultural or urban real estate would often be taken from family and friends and would normally not be secured.[86] But real security was sometimes agreed between relatives. Suetonius reports that Vespasianus (when still a senator and consul) borrowed money from his brother Sabinus, in order to fund his participation as a limited partner in a partnership.[87] This loan between brothers was secured by Vespasianus

[80] TPSulp 79 is the only secured loan in the archive where one of the Sulpicii himself acted as lender. The archive does, however, contain a relatively large number of announcements of the execution sale of slaves, real estate, and cloth pledged or mancipated by way of *fiducia cum creditore* to one of the Sulpicii. See TPSulp 83, 84, 85, 87, 90, 91, 92 and 93.

[81] TPSulp 51, 52 and 55. See also TPSulp 81.

[82] Pellecchi 2018: 459.

[83] Manigk 1904: 36.

[84] Morley (2008: 588) considers the Sulpicii the exception to the scantiness of the 'evidence for the existence of "merchant financiers" both operating and financing trade'. The archive contains little evidence, however, of the Sulpicii being seriously involved in any operating trade. There are two documents which could possibly be placed in this context: TPSulp 66 and TPSulp 101. Verboven (2008: 221) assumes that both contracts are contracts of sale, but this is not certain. See also Ulp. D. 4.9.1.7, discussed p. 192.

[85] Pellecchi 2018: 467–9. For a list of Digest and Codex texts on pledges securing loans and tenant's pledges, see Pellecchi 2018: 467 n 96 (loans) and n 97 (leases of agricultural or urban real estate).

[86] Ioannatou 2006: 207–11.

[87] Seut., *Vesp.* 4.6.

charging all his land to his brother ('*omnia praedia fratri obligaret*').[88] This loan was granted in order to finance investments and the secured credit relationship was not different from one that would have been entered into at arm's length.[89] Security was granted in the context of family and other personal relationships, between husband and wife (Paul. D. 20.6.11), between heirs (Pap. D. 20.4.3.2), and between a warden and his pupil (Scaev. D. 20.4.21), on a much larger scale, it seems, than today. In Pap. D. 33.1.9 a pledge was granted over a *fundus* in order to secure legacies to the testator's freedmen in the form of annual payments. Moreover, Romans would also borrow from the state and these loans would need to be secured.[90] For instance, we know that Marcus Antonius (before he was emperor) charged certain of his assets in favour of the state and ran the risk that they would be sold if the loan could not be repaid.[91] Vice versa, Roman moneylenders did also provide high interest loans to cities in the East, for which they demanded public property as collateral.[92]

3.4 Capital Goods as Collateral

Capital goods and related assets were used as collateral in financing important sectors of the Roman economy: agriculture, urban production, and retail and maritime trade. The investment in capital goods used in these sectors will have strongly stimulated economic growth.[93] The most valuable categories of assets would have been slaves and (even more so) immovable property. In a slave-based economy slaves would be valuable human resources, although there would be large differences in value between unskilled workers and well-trained or educated specialists.[94] Most of the wealth in the ancient world, however, was locked up in land, so that flexible rules connected with charging land could unlock this wealth as collateral for credit. In the archive of the Sulpicii auction announcements concerning charged real estate and slaves

[88] On the granting of pledge in testaments, see, e.g., Pap. D. 33.1.9 and Paul. D. 34.1.12.

[89] Ioannatou 2006: 282.

[90] See Pellecchi 2018: 461–2, who refers to Ulp. D. 22.1.33 pr. See also chapter 10 on fiscal pledges, which would secure not only tax debts but also loans from the imperial treasury.

[91] Ioannatou: 2006: 210. [92] Kay 2014: 195. [93] Broekaert and Zuiderhoek 2020: 99.

[94] I have found twenty-seven texts in title 13.7 and book 20 of the Digest and titles C. 4.24 and C. 8.13–34 of the Codex, which expressly mention slaves, such as Pomp. D. 13.7.8 pr. and 1; Gai. D. 20.1.15 pr.; Afr. D. 13.7.31; Scaev. D. 20.1.34.1; Marcell. D. 20.1.27; Pap. D. 20.1.1.1; Marci. D. 20.1.13.1; Ulp. D. 20.1.21.1; Paul. D. 20.1.29.1; Alex. C. 4.24.2; Sev.-Ant. C. 8.25.1; Diocl.-Max. C. 8.13.26.

figure prominently.[95] In this section we will focus on the financing of land and other capital goods which were owned by borrowing farmers, merchants, manufacturers, craftsmen, and shopkeepers. Recent research has suggested that this must have been rare. Broekaert and Zuiderhoek present the working hypothesis that gaining access to fixed assets, ships, and heavy equipment in rural and urban production would have been 'extraordinary difficult for ordinary Romans who were not in some way attached to an elite household'.[96] In particular, the large number of texts in the Digest and Codex on loans secured by real estate suggests that more Roman entrepreneurs were owners of these capital goods than Broekaert and Zuiderhoek seemingly expect to have been the case.

Agriculture

Farms and farmland

The most valuable capital goods for agriculture would be farmland and buildings (farmhouses, stables, barns). I have comprehensively examined the sections of the Digest (title 13.7 and book 20) and the Codex (C. 4.24 and C. 8.13–34) specifically on pledge and have found more than sixty fragments which expressly mention pledges of *land* (usually *fundus*, *praedium*, *ager*) and buildings.[97] From most of these texts the relationship between the loan and the charged real estate cannot be reconstructed: it remains unclear whether the borrowed funds were applied to purchase the real estate, whether the real estate was rural or urban, and what its nature was (farmland, farm building, living accommodation, commercial real estate).[98] One difficult question concerns the extent to which real estate was used as security in loans for productive purposes, rather than for acquisition finance or for loans to meet

[95] TPSulp 85 (slaves), 87 (slaves), 88 (*fundi*), 90–3 (slaves).

[96] Broekaert and Zuiderhoek 2020: 136–8.

[97] Examples from the Digest are Pomp. D. 13.7.8 pr.; Pap. D. 20.1.1.2; Scaev. D. 13.7.43 pr.; Marcell. D. 13.7.34; Ulp. D. 13.7.15; Marci. D. 20.1.16 pr.; Paul. D. 20.4.17; Mod. D. 20.6.9 pr. Examples from the Codex: Alex. C. 4.24.3; Sev.-Ant. C. 8.13.4; Ant. C. 8.13.6; Alex. C. 8.14.3; Diocl.-Max. C. 8.15.6. As a sample I also reviewed books 1–10 of the Digest, which rendered twelve texts on immovable property (e.g., Ulp. (Jul.) D. 6.1.39.1; Ulp. (Jul.) D. 10.3.6.8; Ulp. (Jul.) D. 10.3.6.9; Mod. D. 10.3.17) and eleven texts on slaves (e.g., Paul. D. 9.4.22.1 and 2; Pomp. D. 10.4.3.12 and Pap. 10.2.31).

[98] Both *ager* and *fundus* refer to land. The difference between *ager* and *fundus* is that the latter term presupposes the presence of buildings (Du Plessis 2012: 142). Flor. D. 50.16.211: '*ager cum aedificio fundus dicitur*'. However, in addition, the term *praedium* refers to land with buildings on it (Du Plessis 2012: 146). A relatively small number of texts expressly mention buildings, such as Lab. D. 20.1.35 (*insula*); Pap. D. 20.2.1 (*insula*); Ulp. D. 20.1.20 (*aedificium*); Paul. D. 20.1.29.2 (*domus*); Marci. D. 20.1.11.1 (*fundus, aedes*). From the Codex: e.g., Alex. C. 4.24.2 (*domus*); Sev.-Ant. C. 8.15.1 (*domus*), Alex. C. 4.24.7 (*fundus* and *domus*); Alex. C. 8.27.4 (*villa*); Diocl.-Max. C. 8.15.6 (*praedium*).

immediate needs for cash. The sources do not allow for a straightforward answer to this question. For instance, TPSulp 88 evidences the announcement of the auction of three *fundi*, which were charged by way of *fiducia cum creditore*. The loan must have been for a significant amount and may have been a productive one, but the fragmentary preservation of the document prevents us from making firm conclusions. In particular, where farms were charged in order to secure loans, it is likely that in many (if not most) cases the money would have been borrowed in order to finance the agricultural enterprise.

Operative farm: *fundus cum instrumento*

In modern historical literature the *fundus* is regarded as a territorial (topographical) unit, an economic unit, or a combination of both.[99] As a *territorial* unit the *fundus* is generally understood as an agricultural plot of land, which (by *assignatio*) had been partitioned from the *ager publicus* and ultimately became the object of private 'ownership' as a cadastral registration based on *census* lists.[100] In particular, in the agricultural writings (e.g., Cato, Varro, and Columella) the notion of *fundus* was conceived as an *economic* unit: a fully operative farm, whose assets constituted a unity. A range of slaves and movable assets were permanently connected with the operation of a *fundus* as an economic unit.[101] These movable assets were called *instrumentum* and would include slave workers, livestock, agricultural tools, and storage devices. For legacies of a *fundus cum instrumento*, a large number of legal opinions have been collected in Title 33.7 of the Digest on whether or not certain assets are part of the *instrumentum*.[102] However, I have not been able to find one text in the Digest or Codex expressly dealing with the granting of a pledge over a *fundus cum instrumento*. But that does not necessarily mean that this did not happen in practice. In fact, in one of the few surviving epigraphic sources on charging land (*Formula Baetica*), we do appear to encounter the granting of

[99] De Neeve 1984b: 3–19.

[100] Steinwenter 1943: 10–1. The *fundus* was named after its first private owner and as such registered in the *forma*. De Pachtère adds to this that while the *forma* only recorded the original partition of the ground to the first 'owner', later owners of the *fundus* were registered in tables which were executed for the purpose of the *census*. De Pachtère 1920: 67. See also Veyne 1957. By the end of the second century BC most of the arable *ager publicus* had come into private hands or was controlled by some town (Kay 2014: 184). On the *ager publicus*, see Roselaar 2010.

[101] Broekaert and Zuiderhoek 2020: 101.

[102] See in particular the elaborate Ulp. D. 33.7.12, taken from Ulpian's Sabinus commentary, containing forty-seven fragments (many from late Republican or early classical jurists such as Servius Sulpicius Rufus, Alfenus, Labeo, Pegasus, Cassius). See Steinwenter 1943: 12. Mentxaka (1986: 70) and Du Plessis (2012: 144) point out that it must be assumed that what counted as *instrumentum* would have been dictated by the type of property and the purpose for which it was used.

security over a *fundus cum instrumento* (although another term is used).[103] Alternatively, the scope of the pledged assets of an operating farm could be defined by making use of the ancient and much-used concept of *invecta et illata*.[104] The late classical jurist Modestinus mentions a transaction in which the debtor granted a pledge not only over several pieces of land but also over the slaves working on the land from time to time, and this is likely to have been common.[105] From the second century AD we have Gai. D. 20.1.15 pr., which says that 'future assets can be hypothecated, for example, unharvested crops, offspring of a female slave, and the young of animals once born'. In other words, the products of both agriculture and stock rearing, and the children of slaves, could be pledged in order to secure credit granted to a farmer.[106] From the second half of the second century AD, farms as an economic unit could be pledged by way of a general 'all assets' pledge.[107]

Urban production, services, and retail

Tabernae

The Roman urban economy of the late Republic and the Principate was a '*taberna* economy'.[108] *Tabernae* were primarily used for commercial services: as shops for retail business, for moneylending (*taberna argentaria*) and money-changing, as workshops (e.g., *taberna ferraria*: smithy), as accommodation for providing services (e.g., barbers, doctors, and fullers), and as bars and inns.[109] Would the users of these *tabernae* have been able to offer them as collateral in order to finance the purchase of stock, inventory, tools, raw materials, etc.? In the Digest there are texts discussing the pledge of a '*taberna*'. In one of these texts (Scaev. D. 20.1.34 pr.) it is not the building structure itself which is pledged but the inventory of the *taberna*. In another text from the same jurist (Scaev. D. 20.1.34.1) the borrower had written a letter (in Greek) to the lender: 'I have borrowed fifty from you and asked you to accept a pledge instead of a surety. You well know that my *taberna* and slaves are bound to no one but you, and you have trusted me as the honest man I am.' Here '*taberna*' may have concerned the building itself, although again it equally could have referred to the merchandise in the shop.

103 Section 9.2 (p. 277). 104 Scaev. D. 20.1.32 (see section 9.2).
105 Mod. 20.1.26.2 (Wagner 1968: 117–20).
106 Pomp. D. 20.2.7 pr. (products of the pledged farmland); Scaev. D. 20.1.32 (animals born at the farm). See also Marci. D. 20.1.13 pr. on the pledge of a herd (section 9.2).
107 See section 9.3. 108 See section 3.4. 109 Holleran 2017: 153–9.

The granting of a pledge of a *taberna* as a building would only have been effective if the debtor had owned it. *Tabernae* were structures typically consisting of ground-floor rooms opening directly onto the street (or portico or arcade), which, after opening hours, could be closed with wooden shutters placed in grooved thresholds.[110] They were often part of larger building complexes (e.g., Trajan's Markets in Rome), which one would expect to be mostly publicly owned, certainly when they were connected to a *forum* or public bath complexes. But there were certainly *tabernae* which were situated on land and in buildings which were privately owned. In Rome, Pompeii, Puteoli, and other cities, the ground floors of apartment blocks (*insulae*) and private houses often had *tabernae*.[111] This would, however, still make it legally impossible to pledge an individual *taberna*, because—as part of a larger building—it was not a separate piece of property.[112] These *tabernae* would often form part of the real estate investment portfolio of wealthy members of the elite, who let them—often via middlemen—to third parties.[113] But occasionally *tabernae* were (small) separate buildings, consisting of the store itself and an adjoining 'living room',[114] which were situated on land owned by their operators.[115] Thus in Scaev. D. 32.38.5 the object of a legacy is a '*praediolum cum taberna*'.[116] Such a small plot of land with a *taberna* would be susceptible to a pledge, if it were owned by the shopkeeper, innkeeper, or craftsman. Moreover, it is also conceivable that such persons would pledge their right of *superficies* (i.e., the right to have a building on someone else's land, including public land).[117] In D. 33.7.7 Scaevola opines on a legacy of a *taberna* with a living room ('*tabernam cum caenaculo*'), which was situated in an apartment block (*insula*). Because Roman law did not recognize co-ownership rights of individual apartements, the object of the legacy must have been a right to live in (*habitatio*) and make use of the *taberna*.[118] It is conceivable that such right could also be pledged to a third party. After all, a right of usufruct could also be pledged.[119]

110 Holleran 2017: 144.

111 Flohr 2013. See for instance the plan of the House of the Faun in Pompeii in Beard 2008: 29 and the House of the Tragic Poet in Beard 2008: 83. For Puteoli, see Jaschke 2010: 50.

112 Frezza 1963: 176.

113 Frier 1978; Flohr and Wilson 2017: 15. See section 3.4.

114 Some *tabernae* also had back rooms or mezzanine floors, where the shopkeeper and his family would have their living quarters. See Beard 2008: 108–9, mentioning a (now disappeared) notice attached to a house in Pompeii for accommodation to let, among which '*tabernae cum pergulis suis*' ('with mezzanines'). See also Scaev. D. 33.7.7.

115 Wagner 1982: 396–7.

116 See also Scaev. D. 32.35.2: '*fundum Satranum, qui est in regione Niphana, cum taberna*'.

117 Wagner 1982: 398–9; Sturm 1993a: 35–7.

118 Kaser 1971: 454.

119 Marci. (Pap.) D. 20.1.11.2.

Larger production facilities

Where *tabernae* were used as workshops, these would be small production or service facilities in which only a limited number of persons would be working. Most small-scale workshops in Pompeii would be run by two to three workers.[120] There is also archaeological evidence for larger production facilities, such as a bakery employing at least five persons. In Rome and Ostia we even find large-scale facilities, such as a fullery employing fifty or more persons.[121] These large facilities, which did not have shops or living quarters, had been constructed for the purpose of investment in the urban production economy.[122] In these production facilities, heavy equipment (e.g., millstones, ovens, furnaces, presses), tools, and raw materials would be located.[123] These large facilities and their inventory would require substantial capital. In the majority of cases these large production facilities would be owned by elite members, towns, or the state and they would be rented by the producers.[124] It would have been beyond the financial means of most merchants and craftsmen to own large commercial and productive facilities and accordingly, this category of real estate would often not be available as collateral for productive credit. One cannot exclude the possibility, however, that some of these facilities were owned by the manufacturers themselves, who could then use them as collateral for loans from bankers or other financiers. Moreover, it is certainly possible that elite investors in commercial real estate would leverage their investments by using borrowed money in order to finance its acquisition.[125] These investors may have charged the purchased investment real estate to their financiers. The rights of pledge of these 'acquisition secured creditors' would even enjoy 'super priority' over other security interests.[126]

Maritime trade

Financing ships

Also for maritime trade there is evidence of loans which were secured by capital goods typically used for this sector of the Roman economy.[127] Plutarch

[120] Broekaert and Zuiderhoek 2020: 129.
[121] Broekaert and Zuiderhoek 2020: 129.
[122] Broekaert and Zuiderhoek 2020: 130.
[123] Broekaert and Zuiderhoek 2020: 130.
[124] Broekaert and Zuiderhoek 2020: 131.
[125] We have seen (p. 73–4) that Vespasianus borrowed money from his brother Sabinus, in order to fund his participation as a limited partner in a partnership. This example shows that borrowed money was used to fund investments.
[126] Section 12.3 (n 5).
[127] On maritime loans financing cargoes, see sections 3.4 and 6.7.

describes how Cato financed a society of shipowners and merchants which, with fifty ships, was of considerable size even for modern standards.[128] Cato's innovation (according to Plutarch) was that in order to spread risk, he financed the society as a whole, rather than its individual partners. This society is likely to have existed for several years, with complex accounts and annual renewals for the coming sailing season.[129] There is evidence for the existence of these shipowner and merchant partnerships in the Principate as well.[130] Rathbone suggests that 'it was the unprecedented scale of trade in the Roman world that encouraged formation of these *societates*'.[131] We do not know whether Cato only financed the purchase of the shipped cargoes or also the acquisition of the ships.

From Roman Egypt there is evidence of the so-called *misthoprasia* (*μισθοπρασία*), which was a kind of long-term financial lease of ships entered into between maritime carriers and financiers. Rathbone notes that there is only one clear allusion to the *misthoprasia* in the Digest.[132] Ulp. D. 14.1.1.15 says that for the purposes of the *actio exercitoria* the *exercitor* 'either may be the owner (*dominus*) of the ship, or has leased it from the owner for a lump sum (*aversio*) for a set period or for ever (*in perpetuum*)'.[133] There are, anyhow, only a few texts in the Digest and Codex on loans for financing the construction, purchase, fitting out, or repair of ships, and for the maintenance of the crew.[134] Rathbone thinks that the reason for this is that in the Western empire many, if not most, shipowners used their own resources, whether or not they were pooled with those of partners, in order to purchase these relatively cheap capital goods. He argues that the cargoes were much more valuable than the ships themselves.[135] Broekaert and Zuiderhoek have recently questioned this conclusion. They argue that even for ships with limited tonnage, more capital was required than was previously thought.[136] The capital required for medium-sized and larger ships would only be available to wealthy members of the elite, persons financially supported by elite members, or by pooled finances.[137] Moreover, they stress that Rathbone's model only takes the costs of acquiring ships into account, while the operating costs should not be underestimated.[138]

[128] The figure of fifty may be exaggerated, but it still would have been a large society. See also Rathbone 2003: 214 n 62.
[129] Rathbone 2003: 214. [130] See Paul. D. 22.2.6.
[131] Rathbone 2003: 215. [132] Rathbone 2003: 206. [133] Translated by Rathbone.
[134] Paul. D. 42.5.26; Marci. D. 42.5.34; Ulp. D. 20.4.5 and Ulp. D. 20.4.6.
[135] Rathbone 2003: 199 and 211. [136] Broekaert and Zuiderhoek 2020: 121.
[137] Broekaert and Zuiderhoek 2020: 124. [138] Broekaert and Zuiderhoek 2020: 112.

But all this does not exclude that of the many texts in the Digest and Codex on secured loans, which do not disclose the purpose of the loan, the nature of the charged property or the identity of the parties, some were on the acquisition finance of ships. Besides, it may not be without significance that the few Digest texts on loans for the purpose of acquiring or operating ships all grant the lenders a preferential position (*privilegium*).[139] Such intervention in the general rules on ranking would have been motivated by the recognition that third-party finance of ships was of significant interest for Roman society. In conclusion, although quantitatively speaking there is not much evidence in the transmitted sources for the finance of the acquisition and operation of ships, definitely not by bankers, it certainly was not without significance in the Roman economy.

Maritime loans

Loans for purchasing the merchandise to be shipped are more frequently attested in the Roman legal sources, as well as in epigraphic and literary sources from the Greek-Hellenistic world.[140] This does provide some support to Rathbone's view that cargoes, rather than ship owning, attracted finance by third parties.[141] Maritime loans were the principal source for financing international commerce in antiquity.[142] The maritime loan is known under various names in the Roman legal sources. The classical sources use expressions like *mutua pecunia nautica*,[143] which may have been derived from the Greek *δάνειον ναυτικόν*, *pecunia traiecticia* ('travelling money'), and *pecunia usuris maritimis*.[144] Mod. D. 22.2.1 defines *pecunia traiecticia* as '*ea pecunia est quae trans mare vehitur*' ('money which is transported overseas'). The term chosen by the *Compilatores*, *fenus nauticum*, came to be used relatively late, at the time of Diocletian.[145] The maritime loan would finance a single seaborne round trip, more precisely the merchant's purchase of the outward cargo and the carriage costs. The proceeds of the outward cargo would be used to purchase the return cargo.[146] Characteristically for this type of loan, the borrower

139 Ulp. D. 20.4.5 and Ulp. D. 20.4.6. For a lucid analysis of texts dealing with credit *ad armandam vel reficiendam navem*, see Pellecchi 2018: 498–504.

140 Loans for the purchase of the merchandise to be shipped are discussed in Ulp. D. 14.1.1.8–11 and Afr. D. 14.1.7. For maritime loans see also section 6.3.

141 Rathbone 2003: 199.

142 Chevreau 2008: 43.

143 Scaev. D. 45.1.122.1.

144 Paul. D. 22.2.6. See Chevreau 2008: 40–3.

145 Diocl. and Max. C. 4.33.4. Cf. the titles *De nautico fenore* of D. 22.2 and C. 4.33.

146 Rathbone 2003: 212. Maritime loans in Greek practice were for either the outward voyage or for the whole round trip (Chevreau 2008: 38).

did not have to repay the loan when the cargo did not arrive intact at its port of destination. As Paul writes in D. 22.2.7, the lender would typically agree with the borrower as follows: 'I lend ten as a maritime loan on terms that I recover capital and interest at a certain rate if the ship is safe'. The lender rather than the borrower would bear the risk of shipwreck and other perils of the sea. In modern terms the maritime loan provided both credit and insurance.[147] Because of the large amounts of the loans and the high degree of risk for the lender, the statutory maximum rate of interest (12 per cent) did not apply to maritime loans.[148] For the same reason, maritime loans would be secured by a pledge of the cargo and (if the borrower owned it) the ship.[149]

3.5 Rural and Urban Tenancy

In many parts of the Roman empire the economy changed in an unprecedented way in the last two centuries of the Republic, from an economy driven by small-scale agriculture to an economy in which small farms were gradually replaced by larger agricultural estates devoted to commercial production and owned by absentee elite 'investment farmers'.[150] This may have differed from region to region: archaeological surveys show that smaller farms continued to exist and that larger agricultural estates were concentrated on the prime coastal and river valley areas.[151] The process of change would have been a gradual one, rather than a 'single dramatic displacement of the small farmer by elite landowners'.[152] In any case, in the late Republic and during the whole of the Principate, members of the Roman elite were the empire's largest landowners. Around 100 BC the tenancy of farmland by tenant-farmers (*coloni*) became economically more significant than farming by farm owners. Large landowners would also invest in other capital goods, such as farm buildings, olive presses, and wine presses, which would be part of the objects which were put at the disposal of tenant-farmers.[153] Another sector of the Roman economy in which members of the elite invested their wealth were the markets for

[147] Sirks 2002: 145; Bresson 2016: 284.

[148] All interest rates mentioned in this book are *per annum*, unless stated otherwise. In the classical period there were no statutory limits for *usurae maritimae* ('maritime interests') (cf. PS 2.14.3), although in practice interest rates from 22.5 to 30 per cent would normally be agreed. Bresson 2016: 283; Chevreau 2010: 195–6.

[149] In section 6.3 we will look closer at these pledges.

[150] Kay 2014: 173.

[151] Kay 2014: 173, 186.

[152] Kay 2014: 186.

[153] Broekaert and Zuiderhoek 2020: 107.

urban living accommodation and commercial real estate.[154] The rental income from all these investments would be protected by the Roman law of real security, in the form of tenant's pledges of *invecta et illata*.

Rural real estate

Given the immense importance of agriculture for the Roman economy it is not surprising that we are reasonably well informed about objects that would serve as collateral for contracts connected with the exploitation and finance of farms and other agricultural enterprises. In c. 146 of Cato's *De agricultura*, the pledged assets are generically defined as 'all that which is brought into the estate' ('*quae in fundo inlata erunt*'). This includes oil-pressing equipment; several types of vessels, bowls, and pots; large carts; ploughs and ploughshares; yokes and harnesses; spades, shovels, and rakes; oil and wine jars; a donkey-mill; a hand-mill, and a 'Spanish' mill.[155] For other transactions Cato recommends taking a pledge over cattle and slaves (c. 149) and slave-shepherds (c. 150).

There are not many details in the jurists' writings on the objects covered by tenant's pledges of *invecta et illata*. The classical sources on tenant's pledges of farms usually suffice with using the generic term *invecta et illata* (or variations thereof), without providing much detail on the specific types of objects covered by this concept.[156] In many cases the landlord would provide not only the land and its buildings but also heavy equipment such as olive presses, wine presses, and storage devices (e.g., *dolia*). The jurists mention as *invecta et illata*: slaves permanently working on the farm (e.g., Jul. D. 43.33.1), products of the pledged farmland (Pomp. D. 20.2.7 pr.), and animals born at the farm (Scaev. D. 20.1.32).[157] In the jurists' writings there is much more detailed casuistry on the question of whether or not certain assets are subject to a legacy of the *instrumentum* of a *fundus*. The notion of *instrumentum* denoted the range of movable assets which were permanently connected with the operation of a *fundus* as an economic unit.[158] Many of the objects that were

[154] Frier 1980: 105–35; Du Plessis 2007. See also Pellecchi 2018: 468.

[155] Cato, *Agr.*, c. 10.

[156] Afr. D. 47.2.62 does not mention a pledge of *invecta et illata*, but mentions the common practice ('*ut adsolet*') of expressly pledging the fruits (*fructus*) of the land (*fundus*) in order to secure the payment of rentals.

[157] According to Broekaert and Zuiderhoek (2020: 106) the Roman jurists 'seem mostly to have a moderately well-to-do tenant in mind, someone who did indeed have the resources to bring his own tools, cattle, and slaves to the farm'.

[158] See also pp. 76–7 and 275–7.

part of the *instrumentum* are likely also to have been *invecta et illata*.[159] There is, however, not a complete coincidence between the two concepts. Thus in his commentary on the praetor's edict, Ulpian examines 'what the lessor of a farm (*fundus*) customarily provides to his tenant-farmer under the heading of "*instrumentum*"'.[160] Ulpian refers to a letter from Neratius to Aristo from which it appears that the tenant must be provided with storage jars, a press and grinder fitted with ropes, cauldrons for washing olives, and storage jars for wine. In other words, unless the parties had expressly agreed otherwise, part of the *instrumentum* must be provided by the landlord and was therefore normally not part of *invecta et illata* (which would be owned by the tenant-farmer).[161]

Urban real estate

One would normally expect relatively poor Romans to live in rented city dwellings. In that case, their furniture, household equipment and other objects situated in the rented premises would be pledged as *invecta et illata* to their landlords, from the end of the first century AD even in the absence of an express pledge agreement by way of tacit pledge.[162] But also Romans of the wealthier classes would often live in rented accommodation.[163] The great length of Roman urban leases, which would normally extend to multiple years,[164] meant that the aggregate of rentals payable to the landlord could amount to large sums. In this case, the *invecta et illata* could consist of valuable objects (expensive furniture, statues, paintings, books) and even slaves (e.g., Paul. D. 20.2.9), so that the collateral would have a considerable commercial worth.[165]

According to Frier, the considerable development of the law on tenant's pledges shows that landlords must have relied almost exclusively on taking preferential recourse against *invecta et illata*.[166] In *Landlords and Tenants in Imperial Rome*, Frier's conclusion (for urban tenancies) is:

159 Mentxaka 1986: 98.

160 Ulp. D. 19.2.19.2.

161 As Broekaert and Zuiderhoek (2020: 102) point out (with reference to Plin., *Ep.* 3.19.7) it could also be agreed between the parties that the landlord would provide the tenant with slaves.

162 Ner. D. 20.2.4 pr. Frier 1980: 107. According to Ulp. D. 19.2.13.11 and Val.-Gal. C. 4.65.16, when a tenant remains in the rented property beyond the agreed term, he must be deemed to have re-rented the premises and the tenant's pledge continues to secure the payment of the rentals for the new period. Frier 1980: 165–7.

163 Frier 1980: 39–47.

164 Frier 1980: 105.

165 Frier 1980: 134.

166 Frier 1980: 134. Again, there is much more detail in the jurists' writings on what the legacy of the *instrumentum* of living accommodation comprises. See in particular Ulp. D. 33.7.12 (with many references to early classical jurists) and other texts of Title 33.7 of the Digest.

> The evenness and clarity of it, its responsiveness to the varied claims of the parties to the pledge, above all its drive toward legal control of the situation, all of these characteristics display the consequence of deep and sustained thought by the jurists. Indeed, in perhaps no other area of Roman lease law are the principal interests of Roman landlords and tenants so precisely articulated over so long a period of time.[167]

The economic significance of tenant's pledges concerning urban tenancies also lies in the exploitation of commercial real estate by members of the elite. Already by the second century BC, Pompeii experienced an 'economic boom', as evidenced by the large-scale construction of *tabernae* (shops and workshops) on its main streets.[168] A middle-sized city (7,500–13,000 inhabitants) such as Pompeii had 900 shops.[169] The omnipresence of *tabernae* in the Roman empire is interpreted by modern historians as reflecting the nature of the Roman urban economy. Rome has been characterized as a 'city of shops, its people a nation of shopkeepers'[170] and the Roman urban economy as a '*taberna* economy'.[171] According to Flohr, the *taberna* was the 'quintessential commercial facility in the Roman world'.[172] *Tabernae* were also used as small production or service facilities, such as smithies, carpentries, and leatherworking facilities.[173] The wealthy elite clearly made investments in the urban '*taberna* economy'.[174] They invested their capital in profitable works of economic infrastructure, not only in farms but also in commercial urban properties.[175] Thus Cicero's real estate portfolio included not only farms and rural villas but also *tabernae* in Puteoli.[176] The elite would actively manage their urban real estate portfolio and change strategies in order to enhance profitability in a similar manner as the agronomists recommended for rural real estate.[177] In one of his letters to Atticus, Cicero writes that on the advice and instigation of Vestorius, a building scheme was planned in order to restore his collapsed or cracked *tabernae* in Puteoli, 'which should turn this loss into a source of profit'.[178] Income would be generated by letting the *tabernae* to shopkeepers, innkeepers, and craftsmen, whose goods present in *tabernae* would be pledged as *invecta et illata* to Cicero or his agents. Indeed, following their reconstruction Cicero's *tabernae* would render 80,000 sesterces a year, which he hoped to increase to 100,000.[179]

167 Frier 1980: 135. 168 Robinson 2017: 247–53. 169 Flohr and Wilson 2017: 13.
170 Purcell 1994: 659. 171 Mayer 2012: 61–74. 172 Flohr 2013.
173 Broekaert and Zuiderhoek 2020: 130. 174 Robinson 2017: 248.
175 Broekaert and Zuiderhoek 2020: 132. 176 Cic., *Att.* 14.9.1–2. Robinson 2017: 244.
177 Robinson 2017: 253–5. 178 Cic., *Att.* 14.9.1–2 (translation Robinson 2017: 244).
179 Cic., *Att.* 14.9.3, discussed by Frier 1978 and Robinson 2017: 255.

The capital needed to construct, fit out, and maintain large-scale production facilities would be substantial, which makes it likely that they would mostly be owned by towns or the Roman state, or have been part of commercial real estate investment portfolios of the wealthy elite. Manufacturers would pay substantial rents for these capital goods and these rents would be secured by pledges of all the manufacturer's slaves, equipment, and raw materials located in the facility. In the archive of the Sulpicii we find pledges of goods stored in warehouses concerning considerable quantities of grain and other agricultural produce.[180] This is not surprising, given the fact that in the first century AD, Puteoli was the most important port for the import of food and other goods for Rome.[181] Grain and other agricultural produce would be transported overseas from Alexandria or Sicily to Puteoli, reloaded into smaller ships for Ostia[182] and from there transported up river (Tiber) to Rome.[183] *Horrea* were therefore of crucial importance for the Roman economy and even for Roman society in general (food for Rome). Privately owned warehouses would also be a considerable source of rental income.[184] The goods stored in these warehouses would serve as collateral for this income (unless they were specifically pledged to third parties).[185]

[180] On the management of warehouses, see Aubert 2016: 623–31. See also Rickman 1971 and recently Van Oyen 2020.

[181] Terpstra 2013: 51. More detailed, Jaschke 2010: 92–157.

[182] Jones 2006: 96.

[183] See Sirks 2010.

[184] Candy 2020: 63.

[185] See section 6.2.

4
Origins

4.1 Introduction

The two centuries from 300 to 100 BC are 'the darkest period of Roman law'.[1] For the period before 300 BC we have the (reconstruction of the) Law of the Twelve Tables and for the period after 100 BC, in particular, the writings of Cicero provide a wealth of information on Roman law. But for *pignus* and *hypotheca* even these sources do not yield much.[2] But fortunately there are other sources from the Republic from which we can extract data concerning the early evolution of *pignus*. The 'Catonian pledges' are ancestors of a form of pledge that later was crucial for the evolution of a full-fledged right of pledge: the tenant's pledge of *invecta et illata* (sections 4.2 and 4.3). In a sense one could even say that many features of the fully evolved right of pledge of the classical period find their origins here (or in the templates used by Cato himself): an early and important example of transactional practices with formative effect. For the first century BC the sources again are scarce, although precisely in this final period of the republican age decisive events took place for the evolution of *pignus*. For the first time in the history of Roman law specific legal remedies were developed for *pignus* in late republican law. One of these remedies was the *interdictum Salvianum*, which was a prohibitory interdict that gave the landlord permission to remove pledged assets from the leased farm or land (section 4.4).[3] The *interdictum de migrando* is an early example of a remedy which protected the debtor (tenant) against abuse by the landlord of his right to lock out the tenant. Not long after the introduction of these interdicts, the *actio Serviana* was included in the praetor's edict, perhaps originally exclusively for tenant's pledges, so that in the first century BC at least this form of pledge had evolved into a full-fledged right *in rem* (section 4.5).

[1] Watson 1971: 3.

[2] For the first century BC Cicero does not give us much information on *pignus*, other than occasional references to *hypotheca* and forfeiture in a Hellenistic environment. See section 5.2. For the reconstruction of the *actio fiduciae* Cicero's writings are important: see Noordraven 1999: 286–339; Bertoldi 2012: 24–30.

[3] Krämer 2007: 198.

Security and Credit in Roman Law: The historical evolution of pignus *and* hypotheca. Hendrik L. E. Verhagen, Oxford University Press. DOI: 10.1093/oso/9780199695836.003.0005

In republican law a second form of real security originated: *fiducia cum creditore*. Where Gaius writes that '*fiducia* is entered into with a creditor by way of right of pledge', this may be an echo from an earlier period in which *fiducia* was regarded as a species of the genus of *pignus*.[4] In any case, because of their functional identity, *pignus* and *fiducia* gave rise to similar legal problems for which the classical jurists found similar solutions. Therefore, although this book is on the evolution of *pignus* and *hypotheca*, *fiducia* cannot be ignored. At the end of this chapter, I will not only look at the origin and early evolution of *fiducia cum creditore* in the Republic (section 4.6) but also outline its historical and structural relationships with *pignus* in the classical period (section 4.7).

4.2 Cato's *De agricultura*

One of the most informative sources for the Roman agricultural economy of the second century BC *and* for the early history of *pignus* is *De agricultura*, written by Marcus Porcius Cato 'the Elder' (234–149 BC). *De agricultura* was written around the middle of the second century BC (ca. 160 BC).[5] Rome's military conquests (in which Cato had participated as a soldier) and the establishment of its empire resulted in an enormous accumulation of capital in the form of slaves, land, precious metals, and tax revenues.[6] The world of Cato's *De agricultura* is that of investment farming (the 'villa system') in which the wealthy elite played an important part.[7] *De agricultura* contains many practical recommendations to investment farmers. Among these recommendations are a number of contractual terms which they could use for the exploitation of their farms and lands. Some of these recommendations can be regarded as early evidence for the recognition of consensual contracts in Roman law. But most interesting for the purposes of this book are Cato's 'pledge templates'. In these texts *pignus* gets much sharper contours than in earlier sources (e.g., *Foedus Cassianum*)[8] and contemporary literary texts (Plautus, Terentius). We are very fortunate that this work provides us with

[4] Gai. *Inst.* 2.60 ('*fiducia contrahitur... cum creditore pignoris iure*'). Kaser 1982: 108.

[5] De Iuliis 2017: 77. [6] Kay 2014: 1. [7] Kay 2014: 132.

[8] The Treaty of Cassius (*Foedus Cassianum*), concluded between the Roman Republic and the Latin League in 493 BC, contained a clause providing: '*Si quid pignoris nanciscitur sibi habeto.*' It cannot be proven, however, that the '*pignus*' of the *Foedus Cassianum* was an ancestor of the right of *pignus* of later Roman private law. It could equally have referred to hostages. La Rosa 1977:16–9; Schanbacher 2010: 404–5; De Iuliis 2017: 13–9.

detailed accounts of actual transactional practices in relation to *pignus*.[9] It is possible that Cato, who also was an experienced legal expert in his time (Cicero: '*iuris civilis omnium peritissimus*'),[10] derived the pledge templates from earlier collections of templates, possibly of Greek origin.[11] In any case, it is beyond doubt that Cato did not create new law, but relied on existing legal practices which originated in an earlier period.[12]

Cato's pledge templates: olives, grapes, and wine (c. 146–148)

In c. 146 of *De agricultura* there are several recommendations to a landowner for creating rights of pledge in connection with the commercial exploitation of his olive yards. In c. 147 and c. 148 these recommendations are extended to the sale of grapes on the vine and the sale of wine in barrels.

De agricultura, c. 146 starts with a sample of an actual announcement of an auction of the olives yet to be harvested on a particular estate: 'Olives for sale on the tree on the Venafrum estate.' The highest bidder at auction for the right to harvest the olives is granted a period of ten months from the first of November to pay the purchase price. This is the first debt which is owed by the purchaser to the landowner. In addition, the purchaser shall be liable for the payment of the workers who were employed for harvesting and pressing the olives.[13] These workers may already have been instructed by the landowner before the auction or they may have been hired by the purchaser afterwards.[14] In both cases the landowner had a commercial interest in the payment of their wages so that he could rely on these workers (or their supervisor) for future crops. It must be for this reason that Cato recommends that the owner or his manager shall obtain a formal promise from the purchaser, in the form of a *stipulatio,* that all amounts (including the wages) shall be paid and that a guarantee (which at Cato's time must have been a *sponsio*) shall be

[9] For a detailed discussion of the Catonian pledge, see De Iuliis 2017: 77–109, with many references. For a legal-historical account of the *villa catoniana*, see Capogrossi Colognesi 2012: 139–65.

[10] Cic., *De or.* 1.171. See also the jurist Pomponius in D. 1.2.2.38, who reports that works on law survived from Cato. It seems to be the prevailing opinion among modern Romanists that Cato was an expert on Roman law, but see Wieacker 1988: 538–9. For a convincing refutation of Wieacker, see Braukmann 2008: 104–5.

[11] Krämer 2007: 144.

[12] Manigk 1916b: 354.

[13] In Cato, *Agr.*, c. 144 and 145, Cato gives recommendations for the terms of contracts entered into by the landowner or the purchaser of the crop for the gathering (c. 144) and milling (c. 145) of the olives. Cato mentions a number of fifty gatherers and pickers (c. 144).

[14] Von Lübtow 1957: 304–7; Krämer 2007: 152 n 30.

tolled from a third party.[15] Cato advises the landowner that, until such guarantee is given, a right of pledge is granted to him by the purchaser.

> Donicum solutum erit aut ita satis datum erit, quae in fundo inlata erunt, pigneri sunto; ne quid eorum de fundo deportato; si quid deportaverit, domini esto.
>
> Until payment is made, or such satisfaction has been given, all that which is brought into the estate shall serve as a pledge, and none of these shall be removed from the estate; whatever is so removed shall belong to the owner.[16]

The owner shall, Cato adds, also have the right to pay the wages (when the purchaser fails to do so) and the owner's right of reimbursement for these expenditures shall also be secured by right of pledge. Presumably this right of pledge also secured the owner's contractual right (as recommended by Cato) to a fair price for presses, tools, ladders, and other objects, which the owner made available to the purchaser but were not returned in the same good condition (unless broken because of age).

In c. 146 of *De agricultura* the pledged assets are generically defined as 'all that which is brought into the estate' ('*quae in fundo inlata erunt*'). The objects of security shall be everything which the purchaser of the olives brings onto the estate in order to harvest and process the olives. Elsewhere Cato gives an inventory for a farm with olive yards, which gives us a more detailed picture of the objects that would be pledged pursuant to c. 146. This list includes oil-pressing equipment; several types of vessels, bowls, and pots; large carts, ploughs and ploughshares; yokes and harnesses; spades, shovels, and rakes; oil and wine jars; a donkey-mill, a hand-mill, and a 'Spanish' mill ('*hispaniensis unas*').[17] Where olives on the tree have been sold, it is likely that, in particular, the smaller movable objects on the list and (perhaps) the animals and slaves would belong to the purchaser of the crop and would accordingly be charged with the pledge. The oil-pressing equipment may have been owned by the landowner (as the provision in c. 146 on the purchaser's duty to pay a fair price for non-returned equipment shows), but could also have been brought into the estate by the purchaser of the crops.[18] In order to ensure that the landowner could effectively take full possession of these objects when the

[15] Von Lübtow 1957: 308.
[16] LCL 238: 130–3. I have altered the translation.
[17] Cato, *Agr.*, c. 10.
[18] From Cato, *Agr.*, c. 145 it appears that when the owner of the land made a contract for the milling of the olives, the miller may be responsible for setting up the mill.

purchaser failed to pay the secured debt, Cato's templates provide that they shall be forfeited to the landowner if they are removed from the land: '*si quid deportaverit, domini esto*'.[19]

Cato's pledge templates: winter pasturage (c. 149)

In c. 149 of *De agricultura* we find other recommendations for taking security for certain contracts. This section deals with the temporary 'sale' of (the right to use) winter pasturages. This form of 'sale' would later evolve into a contract of lease (*locatio conductio*).[20] From March to August the landowner would use these pasturages himself, but in the winter, they would be 'leased' to the owners of herds (who in the summer would use pasturages higher up in the mountains). The terms of the contract should, according to Cato, include an indication of the property, the duration of the contract (maximum period: 1 September–1 March) and the reservation of certain rights of use for the landowner himself.[21] Cato then advises that all damage done to the owner by the purchaser or his herdsmen or cattle, or to the purchaser by the owner or his servants or cattle, shall be settled according to the decision of a good man ('*viri boni arbitratu*'). The text of c. 149 again concludes with advice to take a pledge, in this case on cattle and slaves.

> Donicum pecuniam <solverit aut>[22] satisfecerit aut delegarit, pecus et familia, quae illic erit, pigneri sunto. Si quid de iis rebus controversiae erit, Romae iudicium fiat.
>
> Until <he shall have paid> the money or shall have given satisfaction or shall have delegated, all herds and servants that shall be there shall serve as a pledge; and if there arises any dispute over such matters, let the decision be made at Rome.

A comparison with c. 146 would suggest that, in any case, the pledge of the herds and servants shall secure the landowner's claim for payment of the 'purchase price'.[23] However, like (presumably) the landowner's right to compensation for damaged presses, tools, and ladders in c. 146, this right of pledge may

[19] On this so-called deportation clause, see section 4.3.
[20] See section 4.3.
[21] Von Lübtow 1957: 343.
[22] This conjecture has been added because '*pecuniam satisfecerit*' would not be meaningful. Also c. 146 and c. 150 mention both *solutio* and *satisfactio*. Krämer 2007: 146 n 8.
[23] Von Lübtow 1957: 344.

also have secured the owner's right to compensation for damage to his property inflicted by the purchaser. It is also not entirely clear how the reference to dispute resolution in Rome must be understood. In Cato's time the *praetor urbanus* could send delegates (*praefecti iure dicundo*) to the countryside. The parties could, however, also expressly agree to submit their disputes in Rome. This is what the jurisdiction clause in c. 149 purports to achieve.[24] But is this jurisdiction clause exclusively concerned with the right of *pignus*, or does it extend to all the contractual clauses mentioned in c. 149, including the assessment of damages by a *vir bonus*? The separate reference to the decision of a *vir bonus* for the assessment of damages seems to be to a person other than the praetor and *iudex* in Rome, which would seem to make the first interpretation (exclusively *pignus*) the more plausible one.[25]

Cato's pledge templates: sheep (c. 150)

The final template provided by Cato is concerned with a contract pursuant to which the landowner grants someone else the right to all the products of sheep (milk, wool, and lambs) for a certain period of time.[26] This person is alternatively referred to in the text as 'purchaser' (*emptor*) and as 'tenant' (*conductor*): I shall refer to him as 'contractor'. One part of the landowner's reimbursement consists of payment in kind (specified amounts of milk and cheese) and another consisting of cash payment. The contractor shall auction the wool and the lambs, and the amounts of cash owed by him are dependent upon the prices reached at auction, with the landowner's share to be agreed in individual transactions. The contractor is given credit by the landowner for a period of ten months after the auction date. When the credit period expires, the 'collector' (*coactor*) used by the contractor at auction shall pay the landowner's share in the purchase price directly to the landowner.[27] For the last two months of this period the contractor shall provide one of his slaves in order to herd the sheep. This slave shall serve as collateral until the owner is

[24] Von Lübtow 1957: 345.

[25] Von Lübtow (1957: 345) adopts the second interpretation: all the clauses mentioned in c. 149. De Iuliis (2017: 65 n 185, 103–5) considers, in my view rightly, the hypothesis that litigation in Rome would—in relation to *pignus*—have concerned a prohibitory interdict the most plausible one.

[26] Von Lübtow 1957: 347.

[27] This is another case of delegation (as more generally provided for in Cato, *Agr.*, c. 149). The '*coactor*' is not the *coactor argentarius* of later times who not only collected money raised at auction, but also provided loans to the purchasers at auction (Andreau 1987: 147–55).

paid or until a formal guarantee has been provided. In c. 150 Cato recommends the following pledge agreement:

> Donec domino satisfecerit aut solverit, pignori esto.
>
> He (the shepherd) shall serve as a pledge until he (the contractor) shall have satisfied or paid the owner.

As in c. 149, the right of pledge secures the payment of the landowner's remuneration, ceases to exist in case of payment or the issue of a formal guarantee, is to be created over *res mancipi* (slave) and is not accompanied by a 'deportation clause'. There is no provision for dispute resolution in Rome.

4.3 Legal Aspects of the Catonian Pledges

The origins of *pignus*, both etymological and as a legal institution, are obscure.[28] Exactly when conventional *pignus* did acquire legal status is therefore impossible to say, but this is likely to have taken place relatively early, in any case before the second century BC.[29] From the Comedies of Plautus and Terentius we can infer that *pignus* at this time was already a well-known and established legal institution, but not much more.[30] It is from Cato's *De agricultura* that more specific information on the state of *pignus* in the second century BC can be extracted. In this treatise we first encounter the structural coupling between law and economy that made the adaptation of the Roman law of pledge to the economy possible: the *conventio pignoris*. In a sense one could even say that many features of the fully evolved right of pledge of the classical period find their origins here (or in the templates used by Cato himself): an early and important example of transactional practices with formative effect. *De agricultura* describes an ancestor of the tenant's pledge of

[28] Kaser 1982: 255. In his commentary on the Law of the Twelve Tables the second-century AD jurist Gaius says that *pignus* comes from *pugnus*, which means 'fist'. It was so called, according to Gaius in D. 50.16.238.2, because pledged assets are delivered 'by hand' ('*Pignus appellatum a pugno, quia res, quae pignori dantur, manu traduntur*'). Although this etymological explanation by Gaius is often dismissed as naïve (e.g., Kaser, Knütel, and Lohsse 2021: 230), it may have an element of truth in it. For, one possible etymology that has been suggested is *peg-no* to *pangō* (to insert, fix). The etymological origins of *pignus* and *pugnus* may be related: proto-Indo-European *pewǵ-*, *peuk-* (prick, punch). De Vaan 2008, sub voce *pignus, -eris/-oris*. See also La Rosa 1977: 12.

[29] La Rosa 1977: 10. On the earliest appearances of *pignus* in the Latin sources, see De Iuliis 2017: 13–9.

[30] See, however, Schanbacher (2006: 59–61), who derives from Plautus's *Pseudolus* and *Truculentus* that *pignus* already existed as a non-possessory pledge in the second century BC.

invecta et illata, contains a clause on forfeiture of the pledged property, and refers to the discharge of pledge by way of *satisfactio*. These are all traits which rights of pledge continue to carry for much (or the whole) of the classical period.[31] The Catonian pledges could even be characterized as representing a preliminary or intermediate stage of a non-possessory pledge (*hypotheca*).[32]

Commercial agriculture in the late Republic

The 'Catonian pledge' attests to a remarkable evolution of the institution of *pignus*: on a technical level the pledge of *invecta et illata* is much more elaborate than the simple possessory pledge that could be created by giving possession of a valuable object to the creditor.[33] According to La Rosa this evolution was determined by the need to satisfy the demands of a modest rural economy. The entire estate of tenant-farmers (*coloni*) consisted of a few tools, animals, and slaves and that was the only collateral they could offer, and they could not arrange for someone to stand as surety for their debts.[34] The situations dealt with by Cato, however, concern forms of agriculture which were capital intensive and do not represent a 'modest' rural economy at all. The Catonian pledge existed in a time that Roman agriculture underwent drastic changes and—in many parts of the newly created empire—small farms were replaced by larger agricultural estates devoted to commercial production and owned by absentee elite 'investment farmers'.[35] This form of agriculture was capital intensive and required that the aristocratic investment farmers provided credit to their tenants or purchasers of olives, grapes, wine, and (the produce of) sheep. In *Rome's Economic Revolution* Kay observes that '[t]he cultivation of grapes and olives in the second century [BC] represented an intensive system of agriculture directed towards the large scale commercialization of produce requiring complex processing'.[36] Wine and olives were now introduced as cash crops and slave labour was intensively used to cultivate these crops.[37] The tenancy of farmland by *coloni*, which was of great significance for the evolution of the Roman law of pledge, became economically

[31] The tenant's pledge of *invecta et illata* continues to exist in the whole classical period, while *satisfactio* remains a condition of the *actio Serviana* of this whole period (section 6.6). In the course of the second century AD *pignus* evolved from a forfeiture pledge to a pledge enforceable by sale, although forfeiture could still be agreed (section 5.6).

[32] Rabel 1971: 229–30; Manigk 1941: 1246–7; von Lübtow 1957: 309–10; Kaser 1982: 6; Krämer 2007: 143. See section 6.4.

[33] La Rosa 1977: 32.

[34] La Rosa 1977: 33–4.

[35] Kay 2014: 173.

[36] Kay 2014: 147–8.

[37] Morel 2007: 506.

significant from around 100 BC, after Cato wrote *De agricultura*. In particular, in many regions of Italy, stock rearing was a profitable form of commercial farming and a source of investment for the Roman elite.[38] Commercial agriculture was, therefore, more diversified than appears from *De agricultura*.

Ancestor of tenant's pledge of *invecta et illata*

Cato's pledge templates can be regarded as ancestors of the tenant's pledge over *invecta et illata*, which, as we will see later, played a crucial role in the evolution of *pignus* and *hypotheca*.[39] In classical law the tenant's pledge presupposed that the creditor (landlord) and debtor (tenant) had entered into a contract of *locatio conductio*. The contracts giving rise to the secured obligations in Cato's pledge templates are, however, regarded by Cato as contracts of sale. In c. 146, for instance, the debtor is presented as a purchaser (*emptor*) of the olives on the tree,[40] rather than as a tenant of the olive yard. Also under classical law it would have been possible to sell olives and grapes as future crops.[41] The fact that the commercial arrangements recorded in c. 146, c. 147, and c. 148 also allow the purchaser to use the land for a certain period of time in order to produce the oil, and the wine on the land does not in itself exclude the characterization as a true sale. When we look at the 'sale' of winter pasturage, however, it becomes clear that Cato is also advising on legal arrangements which under later law would be leases of land (*locatio conductio*): this really is a form of tenancy.[42] Cato had modelled his contract templates on the granting of public land.[43] The '*emptio venditio*' of public land is unlikely to have been a true sale in the sense of a contract aimed at transferring ownership of the land to the 'purchaser'.[44] In the second century BC the lease of land and other property was not yet regarded as a form of *locatio conductio*.[45] The 'sale' of winter pasturage is exactly the same as what classical jurists regarded as a lease of land (*locatio conductio*), so that the pledge

38 Kay 2014: 148.   39 Kaser 1971: 464 n 15.

40 Cato, *Agr.*, c. 146 also uses '*emerit*' (shall purchase).

41 See in particular Pomp. D. 18.1.8 pr. See Zimmermann 1990: 246.

42 Cato, *Agr.*, c. 150 alternatively refers to the tenant as *emptor* and *conductor*. See La Rosa 1987: 283–4.

43 Von Lübtow 1957: 237, 241–54; Krämer 2007: 153–4.

44 Gai. *Inst.* 3.145 still mentions the lease of public land as a borderline case of *emptio venditio* and *locatio conductio*.

45 In Cato's time *locatio conductio* would be confined to contracts of employment and other contracts for 'hiring' labour. See, e.g., Cato, *Agr.*, c. 144 and 145.

recommended by Cato in c. 149 can be regarded as an ancestor of the tenant's pledge on *invecta et illata*.[46]

In his important study on the private tenancy of farmland De Neeve disagrees with the view endorsed by many Romanists that the Catonian pledges are the ancestors of the tenant's pledges, which were later sanctioned by the *interdictum Salvianum*.[47] The scope of the *interdictum Salvianum* was—according to Gai. *Inst.* 4.147—confined to contracts between a landowner and a *colonus*, for the use of the land on which the latter—as farmer—conducted his agricultural enterprise. According to De Neeve, the jurists were very precise as to where they used the word *colonus*: it was only used for a farmer who leased the farm's land (and buildings) from the landowner.[48] The *interdictum Salvianum* was intended for rights of pledge securing the debts of *coloni* and not for the arrangements discussed by Cato.[49] This is, according to De Neeve, no coincidence. The tenancy of farmland by tenant-farmers (*coloni*) became economically significant from around 100 BC, many decades after Cato wrote *De agricultura*. The *interdictum Salvianum* can be regarded as the law's response to this. The reason why it was precisely here that the law responded in order to protect landowners was that the rented lands were not within their physical control. This was different in case of the contracts discussed by Cato, where the 'purchasers' or 'tenants' carried out their activities on lands which were supervised by (or on behalf of) the landowner.[50] The olives, grapes, and sheep (c. 146–148, 150) would be situated on the owner's plantation, while winter pasturages (c. 149) would either border the landowner's estate or at least be very close to it. The latter is demonstrated by Cato's mention of the landowner's right to graze his own animals and his right of way on the winter pasturages.[51] In these cases it will not have been difficult for the landowner to seize the pledged objects and take recourse against them.[52] However, even if none of Cato's contracts would have been within the scope of the *interdictum Salvianum*, the right of pledge securing these contracts can still be regarded as an ancestor of the tenant's pledge of *invecta et illata*. Labeo's opinion in D. 20.6.14 confirms this. The words '*ut invecta importata pignori essent, donec*

[46] See also Krämer 2007: 152–7; Braukmann 2008: 102 n 88.

[47] On the *interdictum Salvianum*, see section 4.4.

[48] De Neeve 1984: 51–2, with reference to Alf. D. 19.2.30.4 (*villa*); Gai. D. 19.2.25.3 (*opera rustica, villa*); Scaev. D. 7.1.58 pr. (*ager*); Paul. D. 19.2.24.2 (*fundus*); Ulp. D. 19.2.19.2 (*fundus*); Ulp. D. 33.7.12.3 (*ager*).

[49] De Neeve 1984: 53. See also La Rosa 1987: 283–4. Krämer holds a similar view, but also concludes that substantially the fact patterns discussed by Cato correspond with what would be characterized in classical law as tenancy of agricultural land (German: *Pacht*). Krämer 2007: 152.

[50] De Neeve 1984: 53, 97–100.

[51] De Neeve 1984: 97 n 151.

[52] De Neeve 1984: 97–100.

merces tibi soluta aut satisfactum esset' in D. 20.6.14 seem to echo *De agricultura* c. 146: '*donicum solutum erit aut ita satis datum erit, quae in fundo inlata erunt, pigneri sunto*'.[53] These words must either have been derived from Cato, or at least have a common ancestor. In both cases we are dealing with generic pledges on all present and future property brought on the land, which would terminate upon repayment or the offering of alternative (personal) security.

Satisfactio

In Lenel's reconstruction of the *formula* of the classical *actio Serviana*, a negative condition is included: 'that this money has not been paid nor otherwise satisfaction has been given for this claim'.[54] This 'satisfaction clause' has ancient origins, which may very well lie in transactional practices. We already come across it in the Catonian pledge templates.[55] Cato's *De agricultura* c. 150 provides that the right of pledge shall exist for as long as the creditor has not been satisfied or paid ('*satisfecerit aut solverit*') by the debtor. At the time of the Catonian pledge templates, this *satisfactio* would take place when a guarantee (surety) would be executed in favour of the creditor in the form of a *sponsio*. Satisfaction is even mentioned before payment: the right of pledge shall exist until a formal guarantee has been given by a surety or the debt has been paid. This is an indication that at Cato's time, personal security in the form of *sponsio* was still preferred over real security. The harsh rules on the execution against the person (here: the surety), which originally could cost the surety his life or freedom and later his entire estate, would cause a surety to monitor the solvency of the debtor closely. The economic function of monitoring would thus not (exclusively) be performed by the creditor himself but (also) by the surety. Moreover, the fact that someone was prepared to assume the (high) risk of standing surety would send positive signals to creditors about the debtor's economic and ethical qualities.[56]

In later epigraphic sources we also encounter the satisfaction clause. For example, a marble tablet found near Rome in 1885 contains the following words:

> Quae in his horreis invecta inlata [erunt pignori erunt horreario, si quis pro pensionib]us satis ei [non fece]rit.[57]

[53] See also Ulp. D. 13.7.9.3 and Afr. D. 20.4.9 pr.
[54] Lenel 1927: 494–5.
[55] See Marino 2018: 39–46.
[56] Von Lübtow 1957: 339–41.
[57] FIRA III, nr. 145a.

> Whatever shall be introduced and brought in the warehouses shall be pledged to the warehouseman, if he shall not have given satisfaction for the rents.[58]

In one of his opinions, Labeo confirms the accessory nature of the right of pledge for early classical law (Lab. D. 20.6.14). The tenant's pledge of *invecta et illata* automatically ceases to exist—without anything like an express release being necessary—when the secured debt is paid or the creditor has otherwise been satisfied. Moreover, it shows that *satisfactio* consisted of replacing real security (tenant's pledge) with personal security (*fideiussio*). We find exactly the same construction with Cato's *De agricultura*, which makes it likely that this was a well-settled transactional practice. For the whole of the classical period the satisfaction clause remained an integral part of the *formula* of the *actio Serviana*: we still find it with late classical jurists.[59] Thus, a direct evolutionary line can be drawn between transactional practices from the second century BC and the mature Roman law of the third century AD.

Pignus of *res mancipi*?

In modern Romanist literature it has been argued that Cato merely gave recommendations on taking real security and expected the parties to use the appropriate legal instruments to give effect to these recommendations.[60] This leaves open the possibility that the 'pledges' of c. 149 and 150, which concerned *res mancipi*, would have been in the form of a *mancipatio fiduciae causa*. It is more likely, however, that at Cato's time *pignus stricto sensu* (i.e., *not* including *fiducia*) was possible in respect of *res mancipi*. In Plautus's *Pseudolus*, Calidorus complains to his slave Pseudolus that 'he can find credit nowhere' and asks his slave for a loan of one drachma just for one day. The slave answers: 'Hardly, I think, even if I offer myself as a pledge (*si me opponam pignori*).'[61] The term *pignus* is here probably not used as a generic term for real security (as in Gai. *Inst.* 2.60) but appears to designate *pignus* specifically. In texts from the Digest the expression *pignori ponere* is relatively often used in order to refer to the granting of a (usually possessory) pledge.

[58] FIRA III, nr. 145c adds '*solutio* to *satisfactio*: *[Quae in his horreis i]nvecta inla[ta importata erunt, horreario pig]nori erunt d[onec satis ei factum non sit aut pensi]o solvatur*'. See also TPSulp 79: '*de[dero] sol[vero] satisve facero*'.

[59] Section 6.6.

[60] Krämer 2007: 351–2.

[61] '*Vix hercle, opinor, [est] si me opponam pignori*'. Plaut., *Pseud.*, LCL 260: 250–1.

For instance, in Paul. (Alf.) D. 12.6.36 a slave had (without his master's knowledge) lent a plate to someone, who 'placed it as a pledge' (*pignori eam posuit*) and then disappeared.[62] Therefore, it is plausible that by Cato's time, in the second century BC, *res mancipi* could be charged by way of *pignus*. Originally, like in Greek law, *pignus* may not have entailed that the creditor could directly enforce the pledge against third parties.[63] It merely meant that the property was encumbered in the sense that the creditor, in case of default by the debtor, could attach the property and take recourse against it as provided in the *conventio pignoris*. The *conventio pignoris* was a proprietary disposition, originally aimed at making the object of pledge itself exclusively 'liable' for recourse by the creditor. This is a proprietary effect, in the sense that it is attached to the property itself rather than to the person of the debtor.[64] It is certainly possible that the *conventio pignoris* may originally also have had this proprietary effect in respect of *res mancipi*.[65]

A right of *pignus* on *res mancipi* may have put the creditor in a less strong position than under a *fiducia cum creditore*, in particular where he would have wanted to recover charged *res mancipi* (e.g., runaway slaves) from third parties in possession. For this reason, in practice creditors would often have preferred a *mancipatio* by way of *fiducia*, so that the creditor—as owner—would have had the *legis actio sacramento in rem* or *rei vindicatio* at his disposal. However, in respect of short-term credit and generically defined collateral (as in c. 149), *mancipationes* may not have been practical and the creditor would have settled for *pignus*.

Cato's pledges as ancestor of *hypotheca*

The Catonian pledges can be characterized as a hybrid institution with possessory and non-possessory elements.[66] A common characteristic with a non-possessory pledge is that the debtor had physical control over the pledged assets and could continue to use them (on the creditor's estate). At the same time the pledged assets were to some extent also under the control of the creditor (landowner), in the sense that they were situated on land or in

[62] See also Pap. D. 13.7.27 ('*ut pignori apud alium creditorem poneret*'); Scaev. D. 32.33.2 ('*ornamentum pignori positum*'); Scaev. D. 32.38 pr. ('*pignori ponere*'); Ulp. D. 13.7.27 ('*ut pignori apud alium creditorem poneret*'). See also Sev.-Ant. C. 8.16.2 ('*pignori posuit*').

[63] Kaser 1982: 156.

[64] Kaser (1982: 156) calls this '*rechtliche Sachbindung*'.

[65] See also section 6.4 (consensual *pignoris capio*).

[66] Rabel 1971: 229–30; Manigk 1941: 1246–7; von Lübtow 1957: 309–10; Kaser 1982: 6; Krämer 2007: 143.

buildings which he owned and possessed. De Neeve has pointed out that a difference between the tenant's pledges of the classical period and the Catonian pledges is that in the latter case, the landowner or his manager would still be present on the estate.[67] This would make the possessory elements of the Catonian pledges stronger than those of the tenant's pledges of classical law. Moreover, unlike a pure non-possessory pledge (*hypotheca*), this form of pledge was not created *nuda conventione* but required that the pledged assets were brought into the estate.[68] Although the 'primitive phase' of the *traditio,* with its immediate transfer of possession to the creditor, was overcome, this could be regarded as equivalent to a *datio pignoris.*[69] The *inductio* on the estate would have conferred possession upon the creditor, so that he could have used the possessory interdicts against persons threatening to interfere with the pledged assets. It would also have conferred ownership upon the creditor where the debtor would fail to discharge the secured debt. Likewise, Kaser suggests that the deportation clause can be regarded as a 'fiktive *traditio ex iusta causa*'.[70] As soon as a pledged object was removed from the land its ownership would transfer to the landowner, as if it had been delivered to him. In respect of *res nec mancipi,* such as olives (c. 146), grapes (c. 147), and wine (c. 148), such *traditio* would confer full ownership upon the creditor. In relation to *res mancipi,* however, a deportation clause acting as a 'fictitious *traditio*' could not have this effect because here the transfer of full (quiritarian) ownership would require a *mancipatio* or *in iure cessio*. This could explain why Cato does not include a deportation clause in respect of the *res mancipi* pledged in c. 149 (cattle and slaves) and c. 150 (slave).[71]

4.4 *Interdictum de Migrando* and *Interdictum Salvianum*

It is in the context of the tenant's pledge that—for the first time—specific remedies for *pignus* were designed by the praetor and the jurists advising him.

[67] De Neeve 1984: 97–100.

[68] Rabel (1971: 230) observed that this form of pledge instead on possession was based on fixating the movable assets on the estate. See also Krämer 2007: 197 (referring to Gai. D. 20.4.11.2) and De Iuliis 2017: 133 (who observes that the 'relative' *conventio pignoris* was not yet sufficient for the formation of the '*vincolo reale*'). See also Pomp. D. 20.2.7.1 and Ulp. D. 43.32.1.5.

[69] Giuffrè 1992: 115.

[70] Kaser 1982: 145.

[71] Krämer (2007: 351) argues that Kaser's theory that the deportation clause served to make the pledge enforceable against third parties in possession cannot explain the 'asymmetry' existing between c. 146 on the one hand and c. 149 and 150 on the other. Why do we only encounter the deportation clause in c. 146 (and c. 147 and c. 148 by cross-reference) and not in c. 149 (winter pasturage) and c. 150 (flock of sheep)? This 'asymmetry' can, however, be explained by the nature of the pledged assets: *res nec mancipi* in c. 146–8 and *res mancipi* in c. 149–50.

One of these remedies—the *interdictum Salvianum*—originated in a period in which the tenancy of farmland by tenant-farmers (*coloni*) had become economically significant. Likewise, the *interdictum de migrando* originated in a period in which the population of the city of Rome may have grown to a million inhabitants and in which the rental market for urban housing must have been of a substantial size. The '*taberna* economy' of Rome and other cities would have been accompanied by a significant market for letting commercial real estate. The references in the *formulae* of these interdicts to things which were brought on the premises ('*invecta importata*': e.g., Lab. D. 20.6.14) or born or made there ('*ibi nata factave*': e.g., Ulp. D. 43.32.1 pr.) will have been taken from transaction documents.[72] The *interdictum Salvianum* and *interdictum de migrando* can thus be regarded as the law's responses to economic developments, triggered by transactional practices. Where the *interdictum Salvianum* reinforced the creditor's right of pledge in case of farm tenancies, the *interdictum de migrando* protected the debtor against the creditor's abuse of his pledge in case of urban tenancies.[73]

Right of lock-out

With respect to the renting of urban tenancies, the landlord would have the right to lock out (*perclusio*) the tenant. The landlord therefore did not need an interdict or action in order to take possession of the pledged assets. This self-help remedy was not based on any statute but can be regarded as based upon customary law and may already have existed at the time of Cato. The fact that the pledged objects were situated in a building owned and possessed (through his tenants) by the landlord may explain why no special legal remedy was deemed necessary. The *interdictum de migrando*, which was created in order to prevent abuse of this right to lock out, demonstrates that this self-help remedy predates the introduction of this interdict.[74] An opinion of the early

[72] Kaser 1986: 322. The sources use the following words: *inducta (et/vel) illata* (Nerat. D. 20.2.4 pr.; Pomp. D. 20.2.7.1; Alex. C. 4.65.5); *invecta (et) illata* (Paul. D. 2.14.4; Ulp. D. 11.7.14.1; Ulp. D. 13.7.11.5; Marci. (Pomp.) D. 20.2.2; Ulp. (Nerat.) D. 20.2.3; Ulp. D. 20.2.6); *invecta* (Marci. D. 20.2.5 pr.; Ulp. D. 43.33.2). Labeo D. 20.6.14 uses '*invecta importata*' (first sentence) and '*illata*' (second sentence). Ulpian's citation in D. 43.32.1 pr. of the *formula* of the *interdictum de migrando* mentions '*introducta importata ibi nata factave*'. This last phrase was used in a case discussed by Scaev. D. 20.1.32 concerning a loan secured by a pledge of 'whatever was brought on the pledged land or there arose or was produced' ('*quaecumque in praedia pignori data inducta invecta importata ibi nata paratave essent*').

[73] Frier has demonstrated that the Roman law of urban leasehold, including lock-out and the tenant's pledge of furnishings, reflects 'the structure and preexisting social institutions or practices of the rental market' (Frier 1980: 198).

[74] On the *interdictum de migrando*, see Frier 1980: 105–35; Krämer 2007: 122–42; Du Plessis 2007.

classical jurist Marcus Cocceius Nerva (consul before 24 AD) on the landlord's right of lock-out is recalled in D. 20.2.9. Paul writes that 'the jurist Nerva was mocked for holding that we can free slaves detained for rent by pointing at them through the window'. Why was Nerva mocked?[75] Was this because he failed to see that manumission of a slave was a formal act which could not be performed simply by pointing at the slave in question, or should Nerva have advised that the tenant should go the praetor and ask for the *interdictum de migrando*?[76]

Interdictum de migrando

It is very likely that the *interdictum de migrando* was introduced in the latter part of the first century BC, but the precise moment is unknown. This must, in any case, have taken place before the reign of Augustus (27 BC), because Labeo commented upon it.[77] The interdict's scope was confined to urban tenancies and was introduced to prevent abuse by the landlord of his right to lock out the defendant.[78] The praetor would order the landlord to release assets which were not within the scope of the tenant's pledge or because the rent had been fully paid. As such it is an early example of 'legislative' intervention in order to protect debtors granting security.[79] This is interesting, also given the fact that—as we will see in later chapters—in the late Republic and much of the classical period the praetor was mainly concerned with expanding the scope of the legal institution of *pignus* and its remedies. Here the praetor fixed the exact scope of an already existing remedy.[80] In the late classical period the *interdictum de migrando* had lost much of its practical significance because there was a more effective procedure available, which may explain why so few texts on this interdict are included in the Digest.[81]

[75] Frier 1980: 120 n 148: 'The tone of cold ridicule is remarkable.'

[76] Du Plessis 2010: 51. The most plausible reason is, in my view, that it should have been clear to Nerva that after lock-out the tenant did no longer have the legal power to manumit pledged slaves (section 9.7). According to Wagner (1974: 167) Nerva's opinion shows how 'tactile-plastic' the early classical jurists' perception of the *perclusio* was and how intimately the restriction of the tenant's power to manumit pledged slaves was connected with this factual exclusion from the dwelling.

[77] Frier 1980: 106–7. Paul. (Lab.) D. 43.32.1.4. According to Du Plessis (2007: 243) it was introduced somewhere between 150 and 27 BC, possibly based on an earlier model for agricultural tenancies.

[78] Ulp. D. 43.32.1.1: 'it is not available to a tenant of agricultural land'.

[79] According to Frier (1980: 105–35), the law on tenant's pledges was developed with a view to protecting upper-class tenants. For a different view, see Wubbe 1960: 183.

[80] La Rosa 1987: 287. [81] Du Plessis 2012: 134.

The *formula* of this interdict (which assumes that the asset pledged as *invecta et illata* is a male slave (*homo*)) has been preserved in a late classical fragment:

> **D. 43.32.1 pr.** *Ulpianus libro septuagensimo tertio ad edictum.* Praetor ait: 'Si is homo, quo de agitur, non est ex his rebus, de quibus inter te et actorem convenit, ut, quae in eam habitationem qua de agitur introducta importata ibi nata factave essent, ea pignori tibi pro mercede eius habitationis essent, sive ex his rebus est et ea merces tibi soluta eove nomine satisfactum est aut per te stat, quo minus solvatur: ita, quo minus ei, qui eum pignoris nomine induxit, inde abducere liceat, vim fieri veto.'
>
> The praetor says: 'If the person in question is not one of the objects included in the agreement between you and the plaintiff, according to which things introduced or imported into the dwelling in question, or born or made there, should be a pledge to you for the rent of the dwelling; or if he is included among those things but the rent has been paid to you, or satisfaction given, or if it is your fault that payment has not been made, I forbid the use of force so as to prevent the person who brought him in by way of pledge from taking him away from there.'[82]

The point of reference of the interdict is a pledge agreement in which the landlord and tenant have agreed that assets introduced or imported into the rented premises, or born or made there, are pledged for the rent. Whenever the situation is outside the scope of such agreement, the praetor shall order the landlord to allow the tenant to take away assets which are situated on the premises. Thus, where a slave who happens to be in a rented house at the moment the landlord locks out the tenant clearly was not meant to be pledged (e.g., because he did not live on the premises and was normally employed elsewhere), he has to be released by the landlord.[83] When the rent has been paid, the landlord must allow the tenant to take away all his assets which are present on the premises at the end of the lease.

In one of the earliest recorded opinions on *pignus* we find further refinements on the relationship between the interdict and the rent owed by the tenant. In Paul. D. 43.32.1.4 Labeo deals with the question of whether the mere fact

[82] I have taken over the adaptations of the Watson translation by Du Plessis 2012: 132, with the exception of '*pignori(s)*', which I have translated as 'pledge' (rather than 'hypothec') and '*quo minus solvatur*', which I have translated as 'payment has not been made' (rather than 'security has not been given'). See also the translation in Frier 1980: 228.

[83] For example, Scaev. D. 20.1.32.

that the rent is not due, does entail that the tenant can invoke the *interdictum de migrando*. According to Labeo this is not the case. Thus the interdict does not apply when the rent is not yet due, unless the tenant is prepared to pay all the future rent in advance. Since tenant's pledges 'are given as security for the entire lease', it follows, according to Labeo, that the interdict can only be granted if the lease is for a definite period and all the rent for that period has been paid. This is only different—as appears from the *formula*—when other security (in particular: personal security) has been given. Also when there is 'creditor's default' (*mora creditoris*), in particular where the landlord refuses to accept payment of the rentals, the tenant can invoke the *interdictum de migrando*.

Interdictum Salvianum

In practice it would normally be relatively easy to lock out a tenant from a rented house or apartment. In case of farms and agricultural land this would often be more difficult. In any case, the right to lock out the tenant did not exist in respect of tenant-farmers (*coloni*). Here, relatively late, a new remedy needed to be invented, pursuant to which the landlord could take possession of *invecta et illata*. This new remedy was the *interdictum Salvianum*. It would allow the landlord to take actual possession of the tenant's assets, so as to prevent the tenant from removing them from the premises or for taking recourse against them by way of execution sale. In his Institutes, Gaius gives the following description of the *interdictum Salvianum*.

> **Gai. *Inst.* 4.147.** Interdictum quoque, quod appellatur Salvianum, apiscendae possessionis causa comparatum est, eoque utitur dominus fundi de rebus coloni, quas is pro mercedibus fundi pignori futuras pepigisset.
>
> The interdict known as Salvian is also for obtaining possession. This is used by a landowner to obtain things pledged by his tenant for future rents.

We do not know exactly when the *interdictum Salvianum* originated. Cato does not refer to it: the *interdictum Salvianum* is unlikely to already have existed when *De agricultura* was written.[84] In modern literature its origin is

[84] La Rosa 1987: 286. Krämer (2007: 170–1) considers it possible that already at Cato's time the *interdictum Salvianum* existed.

said to lie in the second half of the first century BC, not long before the *actio Serviana* was introduced.[85] In the Digest only a few fragments on the *interdictum Salvianum* have been preserved.[86]

In modern literature it is highly controversial whether the *interdictum Salvianum* could only be invoked against the tenant, or whether the landlord could also use it against third parties who were about to remove pledged objects from the land or who were already in possession.[87] If the scope of the *interdictum Salvianum* was confined to the contractual relationship between landlord and tenant, for farm tenancies it would have had the same function as the *perclusio* for urban tenancies, the difference being that the interdict was a legal remedy while *perclusio* was a self-help one.[88] There is a constitution by emperor Gordian from 238 AD which does indeed state that this interdict can only be invoked against 'the tenant or debtor'.[89] In the Digest title D. 43.33 (*De Salviano interdicto*) there is, however, an opinion by Julian which implies that the *interdictum Salvianum utile* could be instituted against the purchaser of a pledged object.

> **D. 43.33.1 pr.** *Iulianus libro quadragensimo nono digestorum.* Si colonus ancillam in fundo pignoris nomine duxerit et eam vendiderit, quod apud emptorem ex ea natum est, eius adprehendendi gratia utile interdictum reddi oportet.
>
> If a tenant brings a female slave on the farm by way of pledge and sells her, then to acquire possession of what is born to her when she is with the buyer, an adapted interdict (*utilis*) should be granted.

Where a female slave, who had been subject to a pledge of *invecta et illata*, was sold and delivered by the tenant, the purchaser could be ordered with the adapted version of the interdict to give back a child born to the slave at the purchaser's. Why would Julian have granted the *interdictum Salvianum utile* rather than the *interdictum Salvianum* itself? The most plausible way of reconciling Julian D. 43.33.1 pr. and Gord. C. 8.9.1 is to hold that the imperial constitution is on the *interdictum Salvianum* itself, while Julian's opinion is

[85] Frier (1985: 93) refers to a Salvius as the urban praetor who introduced the *interdictum Salvianum* in 76 BC, while Kelly (1966b: 347) suggests a praetor with that name in 74 BC. Kaser (1982: 8 n 40) rightly notes that the question requires further research.

[86] Jul. D. 43.33.1; Ulp. D. 43.33.2; Paul. D. 43.1.2.2. See also Gai. *Inst.* 4.147; Gord. C. 8.9.1; PS 5.6.16.

[87] For a detailed review of literature, see Krämer 2007: 52–121. On the *interdictum Salvianum*, see De Iuliis 2017: 157–255.

[88] Krämer 2007: 198.

[89] Gord. C. 8.9.1 ('*adversus conductorem debitoremve*').

on the derivative *interdictum Salvianum utile*. The *interdictum Salvianum directum* operated *inter partes*, while the *interdictum Salvianum utile* worked *erga omnes*.[90]

4.5 Origin of the *Actio Serviana*

One cannot exclude that the *actio Serviana* originally was closely connected to the *interdictum Salvianum* and was confined to tenant's pledges, certainly if the interdict operated *inter partes* only. It may have been the famous jurist Servius Sulpicius Rufus who—in the first century BC—strengthened the transactional practice of pledging *invecta et illata*, by creating a new action with which the assets could be recovered from third parties. At the latest, in Hadrian's *Edictum perpetuum* the standard form of action for tenant's pledges would have been replaced with the generalized *formula*.[91] As a general *edictal* action available to all pledge creditors, the *actio Serviana* may thus have been introduced by Julian in the second century AD, when he drafted the *Edictum perpetuum*. Alternatively, as put forward by Magdelain, the generalized *actio Serviana* may have found its edictal basis in the *edictum de pactis* by the first century BC, as the action with which the *conventio pignoris* could be enforced against both the debtor and third parties. The most plausible interpretation is that the *actio Serviana* indeed originated in the first century BC as a general remedy, but found its place in a separate edict in the praetor's edict alongside the *actio Publiciana*.[92]

Invecta et illata

The creditor with a possessory pledge may, already in Cato's time, have been entitled to request the granting of possessory interdicts by which others were restrained from interfering with his possession of the pledged property and

[90] Krämer 2007: 75–82, 114–5, 344.

[91] For example, Schulz 1951: 408; Kaser 1971: 472; De Iuliis 2017: 141–54; Kaser, Knütel, and Lohsse 2021: 237.

[92] The *actio Serviana* is known in the sources by various other names. The term *actio pigneraticia (in rem)* is used in Marcell. D. 44.2.19; Scaev. D. 13.7.43 pr.; Ulp. D. 10.3.7.12; Ulp. 10.4.3.3; Paul. D. 12.6.13 pr.; Diocl.-Max. C. 8.15.5. For other references, see Kaser 1982: 153 n 91. The term *actio hypothecaria* probably was used in legal writings in conjunction with the term *hypotheca*, which originated in the eastern part of the Roman empire (section 6.5).

institute the *actio furti*.[93] Hanard has even argued that the jurisdiction clause in c. 149 of Cato's *De agricultura* attests the oldest appearance of (what he calls) the action *de rebus coloni*, which later served as the prototype for the *actio Serviana*.[94] For the tenant's pledge of *invecta et illata* the element of physical control was lacking, which may explain why the *actio Serviana* may have originally been created for this type of pledge only. The non-possessory nature of tenant's pledges may have entailed a greater need for creating a legal remedy which would allow the landlord to recover possession from third parties than for ordinary possessory pledges, certainly if the *interdictum Salvianum* only operated *inter partes*. One cannot rule out, therefore, that the *actio Serviana* originally was introduced for tenant's pledges only. Servius Sulpicius Rufus was responsible for much of the Roman law of urban leasehold,[95] so that it is certainly not impossible that it was this great jurist who did create the *actio Serviana* specifically for tenant's pledges.

An argument supporting the hypothesis that the scope of the *actio Serviana* was originally confined to tenant's pledges is that in three texts from the *Corpus iuris civilis*, the general pledge remedy is called *actio quasi Serviana*, although only one of these texts is from the classical period. Gai. D. 16.1.13.1 speaks of '*quasi serviana quae et hypothecaria vocatur*'. The reference to *quasi serviana* has been explained as it being an extension of the actual *actio Serviana*, the latter's scope being confined to tenant's pledges. There are other possible explanations, however, for the term *actio quasi Serviana*. Gaius may have used *quasi* because of the fact that his opinion concerned an adapted version (*utilis*) of the *actio Serviana*, or because he was commenting on the provincial edict and therefore not on the actual *actio Serviana* of the edict of the *praetor urbanus*.[96] Before Gaius, the expression *quasi serviana* is never attested, not even in texts clearly dealing with other pledges than tenant's pledges.[97] Neither did the addition *quasi* become commonplace after Gaius. The only other texts in the *Corpus iuris civilis* in which we find it are from Justinian's Institutes.[98] This work from the sixth century AD was based on Gaius's Institutes and the use of *actio quasi Serviana* could be explained by the author's reverence for his predecessor Gaius. Therefore, neither the occur-

93 See also Biscardi 1961: 99; von Lübtow 1957: 310; Krämer 2007: 161. See also Diósdi 1970: 119 (*actio furti*); De Iuliis 2017: 98–109 ('*tutela interdittale "in rem"*'). Krämer (2007: 170–1) considers it possible that already at Cato's time the *interdictum Salvianum* existed as a counterpart to the possessory interdicts.

94 Hanard 1994: 243–5.

95 Frier 1980: 107 n 118.

96 Wagner 1968: 23; Sirks 2019: 332.

97 Jul. D. 13.7.28 pr.; Pomp. D. 21.2.34.2; Afr. D. 16.1.17.1.

98 Just. *Inst.* 4.6.7 and 4.6.31.

rence of the expression *actio quasi Serviana* in Gai. D. 16.1.3.1 nor that in Just. *Inst.* 4.6.7 and 4.6.31 are decisive proof for the hypothesis that the scope of the *actio Serviana* was originally restricted to tenant's pledges.[99]

Pre-Julian Digest texts

The main argument in modern literature in favour of the relatively late evolution of the *actio Serviana* into a general remedy is that there are no sources mentioning the *actio Serviana* as a general pledge remedy from before Julian.[100] It is risky, however, to attach too much value to statistical data of this kind.[101] The absence of the *actio Serviana* in the early classical jurists' writings may also simply be a consequence of the relatively limited number of early classical texts (in general and on *pignus* specifically) which have survived in the Digest. For instance, the *interdictum Salvianum* (which undoubtedly was introduced in the first century BC) is also not mentioned in Digest texts from Julian's predecessors. The only remedy specifically available for *pignus* (*invecta et illata*) that is mentioned *expressis verbis* by the early classical jurists is the *interdictum de migrando*.[102] There are, moreover, Digest texts from before Julian which could be interpreted as assuming the existence of a general *actio Serviana* or an adapted action granted to pledge creditors other than landlords: in particular Octavenus's opinion in Marci. D. 20.3.1.2.[103] Emperor Augustus had issued an edict which provided that any purchase—from a seller not in possession—of property which was the object of litigation (*res litigiosa*) was void.[104] When the purchaser would institute the *rei vindicatio* against the possessor, the latter could raise the *exceptio rei litigiosae*. In D. 20.3.1.2 Marcian mentions the opinion of Octavenus that the scope of this exception should be extended to situations where *res litigiosae* were pledged. The pledged property was land, so that it could not have concerned a tenant's pledge of *invecta et illata*. This could be regarded as an indication that the *actio Serviana* as a general remedy was recognized before Julian.[105]

[99] For a different view, see Krämer 2007: 41.

[100] The reference by Celsus in Ulp. D. 20.1.14 to '*persequi pignora*' must be to the *actio Serviana* sanctioning a tenant's pledge.

[101] Wubbe and Pichonnaz 2003: 219.

[102] For example, Paul. (Lab.) D. 43.32.1.4.

[103] The other text is Cels. D. 46.3.69. See Krämer 2007: 291–8.

[104] *Fragmenta de iure fisci*, Fol. I, nr. 8, FIRA II, 628. See also Gai. *Inst.* 4.117; Ulp. D. 44.6.1 and 2; Sev.-Ant. C. 8.36.1. See Kaser and Hackl: 1996: 298.

[105] In this sense firmly, Manigk 1904: 42. More carefully, Krämer 2007: 293–8. It has also been argued that Octavenus wrote *after* the *Edictum perpetuum* (with the generalized *actio Serviana*) was codified, but this is not the prevailing opinion in modern literature (Krämer 2007: 295–6).

Octavenus was active around the turn from the first to the second century AD.[106] The case on which he gave his opinion must have been one in which a pledge was created by a debtor who was not in possession of the pledged land. The Augustan edict—as extended to pledge—would apply to situations in which A would grant a pledge to B, while the pledged property was in the possession of C and the subject matter of litigation between A and C. B would then try to obtain possession by instituting an *actio in rem* against C, against which C could invoke the *exceptio rei litigiosae*. This *actio in rem* must have been either the *actio Serviana*, or—in any case—an adapted version thereof. The security over the land could also have been by way of *fiducia*, but then it would be odd that Marcian included it in a comment on the *actio Serviana* (*hypothecaria*).[107]

In section 6.4 three late republican or early classical texts will be reviewed which appear to recognize a non-possessory pledge long before Julian. One would expect the creditors to whom these rights of pledge were granted to have had either the *actio Serviana* or an adapted version (*actio in factum*, *actio utilis*) at their disposal in order to recover these assets from third parties in possession.[108] Even if the *actio Serviana* was originally confined to tenant's pledges, then perhaps already in the period shortly after its introduction it was extended (through *actiones in factum* or *utiles*) to other forms of pledge.[109] This may have resulted in the *actio Serviana* having been included in the praetor's edict as a general pledge remedy by the beginning of the classical period.[110]

Actio Serviana within scope of *edictum de pactis*?

More than fifty years ago the French legal historian André Magdelain developed an elegant theory which supported the conclusion that the general *actio Serviana* originated in the late Republic and that its central element by that time was the *conventio pignoris*. Magdelain's point of departure is the fact that the praetor's edict contained an *edictum de pactis*.[111] According to the classical jurists this *edictum de pactis* had a limited scope, which was confined to the

[106] Kunkel 1967: 150–1.

[107] Krämer (2007: 297–8) considers it a distinct possibility that D. 20.3.1.2 originally was on *fiducia*, but needs a lot of conjecture to reach this conclusion.

[108] Krämer 2007: 248, 354.

[109] Schulz 1951: 408; Kaser 1971: 472.

[110] Ankum, van Gessel-de Roo, and Pool 1987: 370.

[111] For a recent discussion of the relationship between the *edictum de pactis* and the *pactum vendendi* and the *pactum commissorium*, see Perani 2021: 53-82.

so-called *exceptio pacti conventi*. This defence could be used when instituting an action that would be in violation of an additional agreement (*pactum adiectum*) or of a promise made in relation to an existing contract (e.g., *pactum de non petendo*).[112] It would be odd, however, if the ambitious promise to enforce *pacta conventa* would as a matter of positive law always have had this limited scope. Moreover, a separate edict on defences would be an anomaly.[113] The original purpose of the edict on pacts must have been to make agreements enforceable, which did not fit into one of the pigeonholes of the types of contracts (*stipulatio*, *mutuum*, etc.) recognized by the *ius civile* or sanctioned elsewhere in the praetor's edict. For these reasons Magdelain argues that as the right of pledge was created pursuant to a *pactum conventum*, it would originally have been within the scope of the *edictum de pactis*.[114] Accordingly, a special edict was not necessary for the action with which this *pactum conventum*—the *conventio pignoris*—could be enforced: the *actio Serviana*. In contrast with these special edicts (in which the praetor's promise was immediately followed by the form of action), the general edict was separated from the actions which were based on it. Because of its connection with the *interdictum Salvianum*, the *formula* of the *actio Serviana* found its place in the praetor's edict immediately after this interdict.[115] If Magdelain's hypothesis could be proven it would have far-reaching implications for the time of origin of the *actio Serviana* as the general pledge remedy.

Magdelain's theory, if true, would also explain the anomalies that the *actio Serviana* did not have an introductory edict and that it was part of the same edict as an interdict. In Lenel's reconstruction of the *Edictum perpetuum* § 265 on the *interdictum Salvianum*, is immediately followed by § 266 on the *actio Serviana*.[116] Combining the *formulae* of an interdict and an action, two fundamentally different remedies, is an anomaly.[117] Another anomaly is that in Lenel's reconstruction the *actio Serviana* does not have an introductory edict. Lenel justifies this by the fact that no trace of an introductory edict can be found in the sources.[118] Again, this is problematic as there is no doubt that this action is a creation by the praetor and thus part of the *ius honorarium*. While actions belonging to the *ius civile* did not need an introductory edict,

[112] Ulp. D. 2.14.7.4; Gai. *Inst.* 4.122. Zimmermann 1990: 508–9.

[113] Magdelain 1958: 77; Wubbe 2003: 205.

[114] See also my discussion of Lab. D. 20.1.35 in section 6.4.

[115] Magdelain 1958: 118–20. Wagner 1968: 52–3 considers this interpretation highly likely. Magdelain's theory on the *edictum de pactis* has later found support in Schiavone 2012: 322, 324.

[116] Lenel 1927: 490–5. [117] Magdelain 1958: 115.

[118] Lenel 1927: 493. He also points out that the monographs by Gaius and Marcianus on *pignus* are entitled '*ad formulam hypothecariam*' rather than '*ad edictum hypothecarium*'.

because they were long recognized and did not need the praetor's support, actions belonging to the *ius honorarium* did. Kaser has argued that the *interdictum Salvianum* itself functioned as the introduction of the subsequent *formula* of the *actio Serviana*. This explanation is rightly rejected by Magdelain, and later by Wubbe and Pichonnaz as '*une thèse en soi si peu convaincante*'.[119]

Separate edict for *actio Serviana*

Inspired by Magdelain's writings, Wubbe and Pichonnaz developed a theory on the origin of the *actio Serviana* which, on balance, I consider the most plausible one.[120] They argue that the *actio Serviana* is closely related to the *actio Publiciana* and was introduced in the same period in the first century BC, during the transition from the *legisactio* procedure to the formulary procedure.[121] Wubbe and Pichonnaz suggest that the praetor's edict included a separate edict for the *actio Serviana*, which could be reconstructed as follows:

> Si quis rem propter pecuniam debitam sibi obligatam petet iudicium dabo.
>
> If someone claims that something has been charged to him for money owed I will grant an action.[122]

This edict could have found its place in the praetor's edict alongside the *actio Publiciana*, in a section entitled by Lenel: XV—*De his quae cuiusque in bonis sunt*.[123] The replacement of the *legisactio* procedure with the formulary procedure and the ensuing differentiation of *fiducia* as full and absolute ownership and *pignus* as a subordinate real right (*ius in re aliena*) had the consequence that the pledge creditor did no longer have a specific *actio in rem* in order to recover pledged objects from third parties in possession. While in case of *fiducia* the creditor would have the ownership-based *rei vindicatio* to recover the property from third parties, for the creditor to whom a

[119] Wubbe and Pichonnaz 2003: 210 ('a proposition in itself so unpersuasive').

[120] For a discussion of Magdelain, including the remarks he made in a seminar with the authors in July 1991, see Wubbe and Pichonnaz 2003: 203–10.

[121] Although not provable, Ankum, Van Gessel-de Roo, and Pool (1987: 370) consider it likely that the *actio Serviana* was already at the beginning of the classical period included in the praetor's edict as a general pledge remedy.

[122] Wubbe and Pichonnaz 2003: 215.

[123] Wubbe 2003: 374–5.

right of *pignus* was granted the *ius civile* no longer offered an action.[124] The general *legis actio sacramento in rem* was not superseded by a more specific '*vindicatio pignoris*'.[125] In a number of late classical texts the *actio Serviana* is called *vindicatio pignoris* or referred to in terms of *(pignus) vindicare*.[126] The term *vindicatio*, however, which is normally used for actions based on the ancient *ius civile* (*rei vindicatio, vindicatio servitutis, vindicatio ususfructus*), here denotes the praetorian *actio Serviana*. The use of this 'civilian' term may be a reflection of the fact that *pignus* itself finds its origin in the ancient *ius civile* rather than in the *ius honorarium*. Even the praetorian *actio Serviana* can thus be regarded as the historical descendant of an action rooted in the *ius civile*: the *legis actio sacremento in rem*. All *actiones in rem* ultimately derive not from newly created law by the praetor but from long-standing institutions of the *ius civile*. [127]

In the *legisactio* procedure the judge had to decide whether the claimant had to be regarded as owner in relation to the defendant (relative ownership), while in the formulary procedure the judge had to decide whether the claimant was the owner vis-à-vis the whole world (absolute ownership). For possessors in good faith who were in the process of usucapting a thing, this entailed that there was no longer an *actio in rem* available to them. The gap thus left was filled by introducing the *actio Publiciana*, which again allowed the judge to decide whether the claimant had to be regarded as the owner in his relationship with the defendant. The *actio Serviana* did provide a 'relative protection' of the same kind. When the property had been pledged by someone who was not the civilian owner but a *bona fide* possessor on the way to *usucapio*, the *actio Serviana* could be instituted against any possessor of the property, with the exception of the civilian owner and his successors.[128] The right of pledge was a relative right, which was not enforceable against certain superior title holders.[129] Operating like this is characteristic of praetorian law

[124] Kaser (1986: 330) suggests that as long as the *actio Serviana* (or its non-edictal extensions) were not available, pledge creditors would settle for the 'though rudimentary but still practicable operation' of the *legis actio sacramento in rem*.

[125] Kaser 1986: 324–5.

[126] Scaev. D. 13.7.43 pr.; Paul. D. 20.1.28; Paul. D. 20.1.29 pr.; Marci. D. 20.1.16.3; Marci. D. 20.4.12 pr.; Gord. C. 8.25.4; Diocl.-Max. C. 4.10.7 pr.; Diocl.-Max. C. 4.24.10.2; Diocl.-Max. C. 8.31.2.

[127] Kaser 1986: 321. Kaser 1986: 345, with reference to Selb 1982: 345.

[128] Wubbe and Pichonnaz 2003: 218–27; Verhagen 2014.

[129] Wubbe 1960: 73, 175–6. As Sirks (2019) has recently convincingly argued, where the expression *in bonis esse* was used in the *formula* of the *actio Serviana* (or an adapted version: *actio quasi Serviana* or *actio hypothecaria*) included in the provincial edict, it would also have included the protected possession of provincial land. The most appropriate understanding of *in bonis esse* would therefore be *bona fide possessio ex iusta causa*. This would include not only the usucaptor *a domino* and *a non domino* (Wieacker 1962: 69; Verhagen 2014: 986–8) but also the exclusive entitlement to provincial land. Sirks 2019: 333.

and both the *actio Publiciana* and the *actio Serviana* are typical examples of it.[130] For usucaptors a praetor named Publicius created the *actio Publiciana*, which was modelled after the *rei vindicatio*. Around the same time (ca. 50 BC) the famous jurist Servius Sulpicius Rufus invented a related remedy for the creditor with a right of pledge: the *actio Serviana*.[131] It is tempting to think that this brilliant jurist—Cicero's deeply admired friend—who 'laid down a basic structure that would not be much altered by the jurisprudence of subsequent centuries',[132] was responsible for one of the last and most significant legal innovations from the late Republic. Would this organizer of Roman law into a 'new logical and systematic framework'[133] have settled for an *actio Serviana* with a limited scope (*invecta et illata*) rather than recognizing a general pledge remedy analogous to the *actio Publiciana*?[134]

4.6 *Pignus* and *Fiducia*: Common Origin

Under Roman law, *res mancipi* (land subject to Roman ownership, slaves, and beasts of draft and burden) were transferred—through a *mancipatio*—as security to a creditor by way of *fiducia cum creditore*.[135] It may very well have been that originally—entirely parallel to the transfer of ownership—*res mancipi* were given as collateral through *mancipatio* or *in iure cessio* (*fiducia cum creditore*), while for *res nec mancipi* a *traditio* would suffice (*pignus*). Where Gaius writes that '*fiducia* is entered into with a creditor by way of right of pledge' ('*fiducia contrahitur... cum creditore pignoris iure*') this may be an echo from an earlier period in which *fiducia* was regarded as a species of the genus of *pignus* (Gai. *Inst.* 2.60).[136] *Pignus* and *fiducia* may even have a common ancestor in some form of security ownership. There is, in any case, a remarkable structural similarity between *pignus* and *fiducia cum creditore*. Therefore, although this book is on the evolution of *pignus* and *hypotheca*, *fiducia* cannot be ignored. We will first look at the origin and early evolution of *fiducia cum creditore*. We will then examine the structural similarity between the two forms of real security. At the end of this section we will

[130] See also Kaser 1982: 28, 155–6; Kaser 1986: 365.
[131] Kaser 1982: 260; Kaser 1986: 329.
[132] Capogrossi Colognesi 2014: 147.
[133] Capogrossi Colognesi 2014: 147.
[134] On Servius Sulpicius Rufus, see also Schiavone 2012: 245–69.
[135] A transfer in court by way of *in iure cessio* was also possible, though it is likely to have been relatively rare: Gai. *Inst.* 2.25. See also Noordraven 1999: 154–5.
[136] Kaser 1982: 108. Contra Noordraven 1999: 36.

discuss the concept of 'functionally divided' ownership and the remarkable institution of *usureceptio*.

Origin of *fiducia*

Originally, the *mancipatio* by way of *fiducia* was the transfer of ownership by one person to a befriended other person (the *fiduciarius*), so that the latter could manage the first's property for a certain period of time (e.g., during his absence for military service). In this early stage—which may even precede the Law of the Twelve Tables (450 BC)—it is likely that there was no actionable agreement at all.[137] The *fiduciarius* was under a moral duty, and not under a legally enforceable obligation, to exercise his right of ownership for the benefit of the original owner and to 're-mancipate' the object of *fiducia* once the purpose of the fiduciary agreement had been realized.[138] Later, when the *actio fiduciae* had come into existence, a condemnation of the *fiduciarius* for neglecting his fiduciary duties would result in *infamia*.[139] An 'infamous' Roman would no longer be eligible for higher offices and *infamia* would result in certain procedural disabilities. This may be a remnant of an earlier period, in which *fiducia* was merely sanctioned by the threat of sacral and censorial penalties.[140] In the second century BC the praetor would grant the debtor an action for reconveyance of the charged object after the debt had been discharged.[141] This *actio fiduciae* was not based on the ancient *ius civile*. The basis for this action would have been the *fides*, which was recognized in the Republic as a non-statutory source of liability, beside the *ius civile* and the *ius honorarium*.[142] In classical law this *actio fiduciae* became a *bonae fidei iudicium* and as such it became part of the *ius civile*.[143]

Although the use of *fiducia* as a security interest may have earlier origins, it may really have taken off at the time of the Punic wars. Frequent and long-term absence from farms because of military service may have resulted in lower profitability of farmland and increased the need for credit for farmers. The availability of cheap corn from Sicily and elsewhere may have forced

[137] Noordraven 1999: 1, 188.

[138] According to Noordraven, there was no remedy available to the debtor in the *legisactio* procedure: the *actio fiduciae* was only recognized in the formulary procedure. Noordraven 1999: 297.

[139] Gai. *Inst.* 4.182. [140] Kaser 1971: 47; Noordraven 1999: 2.

[141] Noordraven 1999: 1. [142] Kaser 1982: 100–1.

[143] According to Wieacker, Kaser and Hackl, and others, all *bonae fidei iudicia* originated in the *ius honorarium*. Wieacker 1988: 457–8; Kaser and Hackl 1996: 327.

Roman farmers to change to other crops (olives) and products (wine) or to cattle breeding. The investments needed for this may have forced small farmers to obtain credit from lenders against collateral.[144] *Fiducia* had the advantage that valuable assets (land, slaves, horses, and cattle) could be offered as collateral, while the borrowing farmers could continue to use these assets on their farms. The *mancipatio* (or *in iure cessio*) needed for *fiducia* did not require the transfer of possession to the creditor.[145]

Fiducia cum creditore: epigraphic evidence

In the Sulpicii archive there are two groups of documents, all drawn up in the same format, relating to the auction of *res mancipi* which had been mancipated by way of *fiducia cum creditore*.[146] Although these documents are not records of the actual *mancipatio* and *pactum fiduciae* (which have not been preserved in the archive), they do expressly refer to the core of a transfer by way of security: the *mancipatio* by way of *fiducia* for a nominal amount. Thus TPSulp 90 reads: '*Mulier Fortunata, quam Marcia Aucta C(aio) Sulpicio Oniro fideì fiduciae causa HS n(ummo) I mancipasse diceretur*.' From elsewhere in Campania and from Baetica (Spain) we have documents evidencing such transfers which are remarkably similar.[147] It is quite likely that a *mancipatio fiduciae causa* in the late Republic would already have had a similar (dual) structure and content. The chirographs or *testationes* executed for *fiducia cum creditore* in Puteoli may very well have looked like the so-called *Mancipatio Pompeiana* of AD 61.

> Poppaea Prisci liberta Note iuravit pueros Simplicem et Petrinum, sive ea mancipia alis nominib[us] sunt sua esse seque possidere, neque ea mancipia [-] ali ulli obligata esse neque sibi cum ul<l>o com[munia] esse eaque mancipia singula sestertis nu[mmis sin]gulis Dicidia Margaris emit ob seste[rtios n(ummos) ∞ LD et] mancipio accepit de Popp<a>ea Prisc[i liberta Note] tutore auctore D. Caprasio A[mpliato] libripende in si[ngu]la P. C[- an] testat{us} in singula [-].

[144] Noordraven 1999: 8.

[145] See also section 6.7 on the practice of 'charge and lease back'.

[146] TPSulp 85, 87, 90–3. TPSulp 88 is concerned with the auction of real estate, but the document is only partially preserved and does not reveal whether it had been charged by way of *fiducia cum creditore*. Camodeca 1999: 196 assumes that this was the case.

[147] Noordraven 1999: 128.

[Dicidia Margaris cum] Popp<a>ea Prisci li[b(erta) Note pactum conventum fecit] uti<que> ea manc[ipia sumtu inpensa periculoque eius sint supra haec inter se convenerunt pactaeque... inter se sunt.

Actum Pompeis IX Kal.... L. Iunio Caesennio Paeto P. Calvisio Rusone cos.].

[Pactum conventum. quae mancipia hodie mihi ven]didi[sti, ita tibi heredive tuo (?) restituentur ut antea pecunia quam], m[u]t[uam] pro duobu[s mancipiis tibi hodie (?) dedi, o]mnis mihi <h>ere[dive meo solvatur vel ad me ut rede] at usu ve[ni]at. Si ea pecu[nia omnis mihi heredive meo] k(alendis) Novem(bribus) primis solu[ta non erit ut mihi heredive meo liceat] ea mancip[ia q(uibus) d(e) a(gitur) i]dibus D[ecembr(ibus) primis pecunia praesenti] Pompeis in foro luce palam [vendere - neve] tibi eg[o] neve heres me[us teneamur nisi proptere]a si minus de dolo malo ea ve[nditione redactum esse...] tatur.

Si quo minoris e[a] mancipia q(uibus) d(e) a(gitur) venie[rint in sortis vi]cem d[e]bebun[t]u[r] mihi herediv[e meo quae reliqua erunt. quod si pluris] ea mancipia q(uibus) d(e) a(gitur) veni[erint id quod superfluum erit reddetur tibi h]ered[ive tuo -] ea pecunia [-]. utique ea mancipia sumtu inp[e]nsa peri[culoque tuo sint] id mihi tecum convenit e[t pacta tecum sum.

Dicidi] a Margaris Popp<a>ea [P]risci lib(erta) Note tuto[re D. Caprasio Ampliato] supra h<a>ec inter eas conveneru[nt pactaeque -] inter se sunt.

Ac[t(um)] Pompeis IX k[al. -] L. Iunio Caesennio [Paeto] P. Calvisio Rusone cos.

Poppaea Note, freedwoman of Priscus, swore that the boys Simplex and Petrinus, or if these slaves are (known) by other names, are hers and that she possesses them and that these slaves [-] are not charged to any other person and that they are not (held) in common with anyone, and Dicidia Margaris bought these slaves individually with a single sesterce for [1,450] sesterces and accepted (them) by mancipation from Poppaea Note freedwoman of Priscus, with her tutor D. Caprasius Ampliatus as *auctor*, P. C[-] (acting as) *libripens* for the single (nummus), [-] (acting as) *antetestatus* for the single (*nummus*) [-.

Dicidia Margaris made a *pactum conventum* with Poppaea Note, freedwoman of Priscus, that these slaves would be at her assumed expense and danger, about these things they agreed amongst themselves and they made a pact... among themselves.

Done at Pompeii on the ninth day before the kalends of—when L. Junius Caesennius Paetus and P. Calvisius Ruso were consuls.

Pactum conventum. Those slaves who today you have sold to me thus, let them be restored to you or your heir when that previous money, which today

I gave to you as a loan for the two slaves is all paid back to me or my heir or when it returns to me as it happens. If all that money shall not have been paid back to me or my heir by the first kalends of November, be it permitted to me or my heir to sell for cash these slaves whom this matter concerns on the first ides of December, at Pompeii in the forum by day openly and let neither me nor my heir be held unless on this account, if less is returned from this sale on account of malicious fraud.

If these slaves whom this matter concerns shall have sold for some lesser amount, let that which shall be left over be repaid to me or my heir in repayment of the remaining (debt). But if these slaves whom this matter concerns shall have sold for more, let that which shall be extra be returned to you or your heir [-] this money [-]. And that these slaves shall be at your assumed expense and danger, this is agreed by me with you and I have made a pact with you.

Dicidia Margaris Poppaea Note, freedwoman of Priscus with her tutor D. Capracius Ampliatus amongst these things they agreed amongst themselves and made a pact between themselves.

Done at Pompeii on the ninth day before the kalends [of -] when L. Junius Caesennius Paetus and P. Calvisius Ruso were consuls.[148]

This document has many interesting features: sale for one sesterce, licence to sell for the creditor, reference to sale at auction, obligation for the creditor to return the surplus, the debtor's continuing liability for the deficit. For that reason it has been reproduced completely; we will return to it on several occasions in this book.

Dual structure of *fiducia* and *pignus*

The *Mancipatio Pompeiana* and other epigraphic sources show that there is a remarkable structural similarity between *pignus* and *fiducia*.

	object	**agreement**	**disposition**	***actio in personam***	***actio in rem***
fiducia	*res mancipi*	*pactum fiduciae*	*mancipatio*	*actio fiduciae*	*rei vindicatio*
pignus	*res nec mancipi*	*conventio pignoris*	*traditio*	*actio pigneraticia*	*actio Serviana*

[148] Latin text and translation (with amendments) taken from Meyer 2004: 141-2. Meyer's Latin text is based on FIRA III, nr. 91, with minor restorations by Meyer. See also Noordraven 1999: 126, 248.

Both legal institutions have a dual structure, consisting of a contractual component (*pactum fiduciae* and *conventio pignoris*), in which the creditor and debtor set out their mutual rights and obligations in relation to the charged property, and a proprietary component (*mancipatio* and *traditio*), a disposition aimed at conferring a real (*in rem*) security interest upon the creditor.[149] The obligation of the creditor to return the charged property upon payment of the secured debt was sanctioned by *actiones in personam*: the *actio fiduciae* and the *actio pigneraticia (directa)*, respectively. The proprietary component is reflected in the availability of an *actio in rem* for the creditor with which the charged object could be recovered from both the debtor and third parties in possession: the *rei vindicatio* (*fiducia*) and the *actio Serviana* (*pignus*), respectively. In the case of *fiducia cum creditore*, the *mancipatio* resulted in an immediate transfer of ownership of the charged object to the creditor. In the case of *pignus*, the *traditio* may originally—analogous to *fiducia*—also have conferred some form of ownership upon the creditor.

In respect of the exact relationship between the *pactum fiduciae* and the *mancipatio*, different views have been put forward in modern literature. The *Mancipatio Pompeiana* has been used in modern literature as an argument in support of the view that the *mancipatio* and the *pactum fiduciae* must be neatly separated.[150] The *mancipatio* only served to convey ownership of the charged property. It is the *pactum fiduciae* that defined the legal relationship between debtor and creditor with respect to the mancipated property and which turned the creditor's ownership into a security interest.[151] A second view, however, is that the fiduciary nature of the legal relationship between debtor and creditor was a legal consequence of the *mancipatio* itself.[152] The fact that in all but one of the classical epigraphic sources of the *fiducia cum creditore* this phrase is used could indicate that the words *fidi fiduciae causa* did have a specific legal meaning. The *Mancipatio Pompeiana*, however, which does not include this phrase, is a strong indication that, in any case, the use of the exact words *fidi fiduciae causa* was not a formal requirement for the creditor's obligation to return the property.[153] The third view holds that *mancipatio*

[149] On the *pactum fiduciae* as a contract in (late) classical law, see Fercia 2012. See also Noordraven 1999: 138–43.

[150] Kaser 1971: 47.

[151] In this sense Magdelain 1958: 101–3; Kaser 1982: 234 n 7; Noordraven 1999: 132–8; Bertoldi 2012: 72–4. See also my discussion of Pap. D. 33.10.9.2 in section 4.7.

[152] In this sense Manigk 1909: 2291; Burdese 1949: 9–10; Watson 1962; Wubbe 1967: 507 n 16; Biscardi 1976: 43; Dunand 2000: 119.

[153] Unlike the auction documents in the TPSulp and the *Formula Baetica*, the *Mancipatio Pompeiana* does not contain the phrase '*(fidei) fiduciae causa*'. Recently, it has been argued that the 1,450 sesterces do represent the purchase price. This would then demonstrate that the *Mancipatio*

and *pactum fiduciae* constitute an inseparable unity consisting of two elements, which as such is governed by the *fides*. Pursuant to this *fides*, the creditor's obligation to re-mancipate is enforceable with the *actio fiduciae* granted to the debtor.[154] The general fiduciary nature of the transfer of ownership is expressed in the *mancipatio* itself, while the *pactum fiduciae* makes clear what the purpose (management, security, etc.) of the fiduciary transfer is.[155] An attractive side of the third view is, on the one hand, that like the first view, it substantiates the idea that the creditor's ownership was conditioned by its fiduciary nature. On the other hand, as in the second view, it regards the *pactum fiduciae* as indispensable for the *actio fiduciae*, which makes the *actio fiduciae* the counterpart of the *actio pigneraticia (directa)* and thus fits well with the structural similarity of *fiducia* and *pignus*.

Functionally divided ownership and *usureceptio*

Throughout his academic career Kaser has insistently argued that originally Roman law endorsed neither an absolute nor a unitary concept of ownership.[156] As a preliminary or early stage of ownership there only existed one undifferentiated proprietary interest.[157] In archaic Roman law ownership and subordinated real rights (*iura in re aliena*) were not neatly separated and several 'ownership rights' could coexist simultaneously in respect of the same object.[158] These ownership rights could be attributed to different persons, in order to grant (what in later law would be) usufructs, servitudes, *or* rights of pledge.[159] When a debtor charged his or her property as collateral, ownership was originally *functionally divided* between debtor and creditor. Both parties would have a right of ownership that was restricted by the exercise of its corresponding functions.[160] Thus, as long as the secured debt was not discharged, the debtor would be deprived of his or her right to transfer the pledged

Pompeiana is a genuine contract of sale, which is entered into for security purposes and thus was a functional alternative to the *fiducia cum creditore*. Marra 2017. I find it very hard to believe that the *Mancipatio Pompeiana* is not a *fiducia cum creditore*.

154 In this sense Bellocci (1983: 162, 214) and perhaps previously Erbe (1940: 5–6).

155 Lambrini 2016: 218–9.

156 For example, Kaser 1982: 25–6, 55–6, 72–3. Similar views have been adopted by von Lübtow 1957: 318–21 and Wubbe 2003: 22–5, 239. The concept of functionally divided ownership for *fiducia* and *pignus* in archaic and pre-classical Roman law is rejected by Diósdi 1970: 116–20. Also critical are Krämer 2007: 194–206 and Perani 2021: 293-7. More positive is Braukmann 2008: 95–7.

157 Kaser 1982: 72–3.

158 Kaser 1982: 22–5, 239.

159 Kaser 1982: 28. For a detailed account of the emergence of *iura in re aliena*, see Giuffrè 1992: 114–224.

160 Diósdi 1970: 107.

property and in the event of default this right could be exercised by the creditor. The creditor would acquire a redeemable (and thus temporary) 'security ownership', while the debtor retained a right of ownership for the 'remainder'. In the event of default the creditor's security ownership would convert into full ownership (forfeiture). One remaining trace in classical law of this functional division is the *usureceptio fiduciae*.[161]

The *usureceptio fiduciae* is a very old institution possibly dating back to the time of the Twelve Tables.[162] Under this special form of *usucapio* the debtor in possession of the object of *fiducia* regained civil ownership of it after one year, also in respect of land (where the general *usucapio* term was two years). Gaius says that *usureceptio* only takes place when, during the time the secured debt has not yet been discharged, the debtor neither rents the property from the creditor nor holds it as bailee (*precarium*).[163] Apparently it was felt that where he consented to a non-possessory *fiducia* the creditor should not, before the debt was discharged, lose ownership as a consequence of the 'lighter' *usureceptio* rules.[164] For the majority of cases, therefore, *usureceptio* is not as odd as it may initially seem. The creditor could prevent *usureceptio* from taking place by allowing the debtor to use the object of *fiducia* pursuant to *locatio conductio* or *precarium*. When the secured debt was discharged the *locatio conductio* or *precarium* would automatically terminate, which would only then trigger the *usureceptio* mechanism.[165] Here *usureceptio* would even have the advantage for the creditor and debtor of dispensing with the necessity of a formal re-mancipation. The debtor would, after discharge of the secured debt, automatically reacquire civilian ownership of the collateral after one year. During that year the debtor would have the position of a praetorian owner and would have the *actio Publiciana* (or an analogous action) at his or her disposal for recovering the property from third parties.[166] The law was adapted to the economically most efficient solution, by giving debtors the

[161] Section 4.7. [162] Noordraven 1999: 188.

[163] Gai. *Inst.* 2.60. For *pignus* the same transactional practice was used in the classical period (section 6.7).

[164] Kaser 1982: 169–70. A more technical explanation would be that *precarium* and *locatio conductio* indicated that the debtor did not have the intention to possess for himself (*animus possidendi*), so that the possession which was required for *usucapio* was not present (Serrao 2008: 357). See also Noordraven 1999: 197.

[165] Kaser 1982: 169; Wubbe 2003: 9. The situation is very similar to a *traditio brevi manu* and is perhaps even identical to it.

[166] The *formula* of the *actio Publiciana* reads as follows: '*si quem hominem* A^s A^s *bona fide emit et is ei traditus est*...'. Lenel 1927: 171. Although some extensions (to other contracts than sale) may have taken place, it could be that to include *usureceptio* cases within the scope of the direct action would have gone one step too far. In that event an *actio in factum* or *actio utilis* would have been granted, which was modelled after the *actio Publiciana*.

right to use the collateral while at the same time protecting creditors against the adverse consequences of an ancient legal institution (*usureceptio*). One feature of *usureceptio* that *is* peculiar, however, is that if the debtor had taken away the property from the creditor's premises without the latter's permission, it could lead to loss of ownership on the side of the creditor *before* the secured debt had been discharged. Several explanations have been offered in modern literature for this peculiarity, including the one offered by Wubbe that *usureceptio* reflects that the debtor was in some respects still regarded as the owner of the charged property.[167]

4.7 *Pignus*, *Hypotheca*, and *Fiducia*: Parallel and Divergent Evolution

Although by the end of the Republic, *pignus* and *fiducia* had evolved into separate species of real security, possible traces of their common origin could still be found in the classical period. As we will see throughout this book, in classical law *pignus* and *fiducia* did often evolve along parallel lines. The functional similarity between *pignus* and *fiducia* created similar problems, for which the jurists found similar solutions.[168] It would not have been sensible had the legal consequences of two legal institutions, which performed the same function in the economy, differed too much.[169] Nevertheless, despite the fact that several evolutionary lines of *pignus*, *hypotheca*, and *fiducia* ran parallel courses, there were also important divergences, which had the effect that ultimately *fiducia* lost the struggle for existence against *pignus* and *hypotheca*. Originally *fiducia* may have had the practical advantage that farmers could offer their farm, land, and cattle as non-possessory collateral to lenders.[170] This advantage disappeared when a pledge could be created as a non-possessory *hypotheca*.[171] This could even take place 'by mere contract' (*nuda conventione*), while *fiducia* continued to require a formalistic *mancipatio*. Also in other respects in the second and third century AD, *pignus* and *hypotheca* acquired certain traits which made them superior to *fiducia*.

[167] Wubbe 2003: 22–5, 239. [168] Kaser 1982: 107–25. [169] Noordraven 1999: 35.
[170] Noordraven 1999: 8. [171] See also Pellecchi 2018: 477–9.

Pignus of *res mancipi* and *fiducia* of *res nec mancipi*

My original hypothesis was that originally *res mancipi* were always provided as collateral by way of *fiducia* and *res nec mancipi* by way of *pignus*, and that this continued to be the case in early classical law.[172] Thus, in the archive of the Sulpicii and in other epigraphic sources *res mancipi* are consistently charged by way of *fiducia* and *res nec mancipi* by way of *pignus*. However, we have seen that it is conceivable that already at Cato's time *res mancipi* were pledged.[173] Moreover, it appears that at the time of the Sulpicii *res mancipi* could also be charged by way of *pignus*. This is because in the Digest there are several texts, including on tenant's pledges of *invecta et illata*,[174] which by the time of early classical jurists seem to be dealing with a right of *pignus* granted over land or slaves.[175] Therefore, assets charged by way of *pignus* apparently could include *res mancipi*, which refutes the hypothesis that still in the early classical period *res mancipi* were always charged by way of *fiducia*. There can be no doubt that at the beginning of the second century AD it had even become common practice to grant right of pledge over *res mancipi*.

Charging *res nec mancipi* by way of *fiducia*, on the other hand, must have been rare, if it ever occurred at all. The best candidate for a Digest text which may originally have concerned a *fiducia cum creditore* in respect of *res nec mancipi* is from Papinian.

> **D. 33.10.9.2.** *Papinianus libro septimo responsorum*. Supellectili sua omni legata acceptum argentum pignori non continebitur, quia supellectilem suam legavit, utique si non in usu creditoris id argentum voluntate debitoris fuit, sed propositum propter contractus fidem ac restituendae rei vinculum.
>
> In a legacy of all a man's furniture, silver accepted as a pledge will not be included. Because he legated his own furniture, especially if the silver was not used, with the debtor's consent, by the creditor, but set aside with a view to the (good) faith of the contract and his obligation to restore the thing.

It is unlikely that this text originally dealt with *pignus*. It would have been self-evident that a legacy of furniture would not include the assets which had been pledged to the testator.[176] The question whether charged property would be

[172] Verhagen 2011a: 8–9. [173] See pp. 98–9. [174] Paul (Nerva) D. 20.2.9.

[175] Paul (Nerva) D. 20.2.9; Paul (Cass.) D. 41.3.4.21; Lab. D. 20.1.35; Marci. (Octav.) D. 20.3.1.2; Iav. D. 41.3.16; Pomp. (Sab./Atil.) D. 13.7.6 pr.

[176] There is, however, another text in which the question is addressed whether pledged property was part of a legacy. In D. 32.101 pr., Scaevola's opinion did concern a forfeiture pledge, pursuant to

included in a legacy is only a sensible one when it was owned by the testator. This text implies that if the debtor had allowed the creditor (testator) to use the silverware, it would have been part of the legacy, which only could be the case if the silverware was owned by the creditor. The most plausible interpretation of this fragment therefore is that it originally must have been on *fiducia*.[177] This interpretation makes D. 33.10.9.2 a peculiar text because *fiducia* is normally associated with *res mancipi*, while silverware obviously is not. The transfer to the creditor may have been by way of *in iure cessio* (which could be used for *res nec mancipi* also), perhaps as part of a larger collection of assets. It is even conceivable that this text constitutes evidence of the fact that in the second century AD, *res nec mancipi* were sometimes fiduciarily transferred through a *traditio*, certainly if one assumes that the fiduciary nature of the creditor's ownership is not a consequence of the *mancipatio* but of the *pactum fiduciae*.[178] Although the creditor is the owner of the silverware, the legacy is interpreted as excluding this fiduciary property, certainly when the creditor was not allowed to use it. In other words, the creditor's ownership is conditioned by its fiduciary nature, as expressed in the *pactum fiduciae*.[179]

Traces of functionally divided ownership

The writings of the early classical jurists demonstrate that by the end of the Republic, *pignus* had already acquired its typical characteristics, which were now considerably different from those of *fiducia*. Where for much of the Republic Kaser's theory of functionally divided ownership is plausible, at the beginning of the classical period it certainly no longer applied (as Kaser would be ready to admit). As a consequence of the *mancipatio*, the creditor acquired *dominium ex iure Quiritium* (civilian ownership) of the object of *fiducia*. The debtor was left with merely a personal claim for reconveyance of the property after the secured debt had been paid: the *actio fiduciae*. From the perspective of property law, the debtor's position was therefore fundamentally

which the creditor would upon the debtor's default acquire ownership of the pledged property. The difference, however, between Scaev. D. 32.101 pr. and Pap. D. 33.10.9.2, is that in Papinian's case the debtor apparently was not in default, because the creditor was still under a duty to return the silverware. It is therefore less plausible to explain Pap. D. 33.10.9.2 in terms of a forfeiture pledge.

177 Noordraven 1999: 162–3.

178 See pp. 118–19. Wubbe (2003: 237) notices that, although theoretically a *traditio fiduciae causa* would appear to have been possible, there is no trace of it, either in the writings of the jurists or in the epigraphic sources. Pap. D. 33.10.9.2 might be the exception.

179 Verhagen 2014: 145–6.

different from that in case of *pignus*. In the latter case, the debtor remained the (civilian or praetorian) owner of the charged property: the creditor merely acquired a subordinate right on someone else's property (*ius in re aliena*). Unlike *fiducia*, the right of *pignus* was an accessory right, whose existence was dependent upon the secured debt (Lab. D. 20.6.14), and upon discharge of the secured debt the right of pledge automatically ceased to exist.[180]

The most significant enduring remnant of the old conception of functionally divided ownership was that in case of a possessory pledge the creditor, although now formally a holder for someone else (*Fremdbesitzer*), would for several purposes still be regarded as *possessor*. The debtor only possessed for the purposes of *usucapio*, while for all other purposes (in particular, the possessory interdicts) the creditor was treated as having possession.[181] One could call this functionally divided *possession*.[182] But we can detect traces of the old functional division in other features of classical *pignus*.[183] For a long time in the classical period, after the granting of a right of pledge, the debtor's powers of disposition were still seriously limited.[184] The debtor could no longer set free pledged slaves, could not transfer the pledged property to third parties, would commit *furtum* if he would secretly take away (his own!) pledged property from the creditor, and would not be able to create multiple pledges simultaneously existing over the same pledged property.[185]

Joint treatment in jurists' writings and imperial constitutions

It has been argued by Kreller that *pignus* and *fiducia* were subject to the same edict.[186] Although Kaser has convincingly demonstrated that this is not plausible, he also holds that certain of Keller's premises are correct and do shed light on the relationship between *pignus* and *fiducia*.[187] Where Gaius says that *fiducia cum creditore* is entered into 'by way of right of pledge' ('*pignoris iure*'), this indicates that these two institutions are not merely similar but that *fiducia* can even be regarded as a species of the genus of *pignus* in a wider sense.[188] This is recognized by other jurists and many of the legal opinions in the Digest

[180] For example, Ulp. D. 20.6.6 pr. [181] Iav. D. 41.3.16; Paul. D. 41.2.1.15.

[182] Kaser 1956: 353–4. In Paul. D. 41.2.1.15 Julian's opinion is restated that the pledged object is possessed by the debtor for one reason only: *usucapio*.

[183] For a more elaborate discussion of 'ownership-like' characteristics of *pignus* and 'pledge-like' characteristics of *fiducia cum creditore*, see Verhagen 2013b.

[184] When the pledged asset was in the possession of the creditor it would be practically impossible to dispose of the assets by way of *mancipatio, in iure cessio*, or *traditio* anyhow. Kaser 1982: 29.

[185] Kaser 1986: 330–45. [186] Kreller 1942. [187] Kaser 1982: 108.

[188] Kaser 1982: 108.

can be related to both *pignus* and *fiducia*.[189] In many respects *pignus* and *fiducia* were treated similarly by the jurists and the emperors, such as in respect of the necessity of secured debts being for the payment of money, the treatment of interest, *antichresis*, and the liability for expenditures.[190] Also, the enforcement of the security would be subject to the same rules: the creditor's authority to sell, obligation to return the surplus, and duty of care (e.g., announcement of auctions), the debtor's liability for eviction, and the creditor's right to request forfeiture from the emperor (*impetratio dominii*).[191]

In the Digest and Codex one will not find fragments expressly dealing with *pignus* and *fiducia* jointly: all references to *fiducia* have been systematically removed by the compilers of the *Corpus iuris civilis*. In other pre-Justinian sources, however, the *Pauli Sententiae* in particular, there are some fragments expressly treating *pignus* and *fiducia* on an equal footing and which reflect classical law.[192] Also, in the Digest and Codex there will be texts which were interpolated and which do reflect common principles for *pignus* and *fiducia*.[193] In particular in introductory works, a joint treatment of *pignus* and *fiducia* would seem plausible. Besides, one cannot exclude that sometimes a jurist deliberately used an analogy with *fiducia* in order to substantiate a conclusion for *pignus*, or vice versa. One can also not exclude the possibility that a legal ruling in an imperial constitution, which endorsed a general principle, was intended to apply to both *pignus* and *fiducia*.[194] Accordingly, both in the Digest and Codex several fragments can be identified in which the Roman jurists from whose writings they are derived must have both *pignus* and *fiducia* in mind.[195] Important examples of the parallel evolution of transactional practices in relation to *pignus* and *fiducia* are the licence to sell (*pactum de vendendo*), the 'charge and lease back', and the *pactum antichreticum*.[196]

Struggle for existence between *pignus* and *fiducia*

For a long time the *mancipatio (fiducia)* may have offered much comfort to secured creditors: it would confer quiritarian ownership upon them and the prescribed

[189] Kaser 1982: 109. [190] Kaser 1982: 133. [191] Kaser 1982: 115.

[192] *Pignus* and *fiducia* are jointly referred to in PS 1.9.8; 2.13.4; 2.17.15; 3.6.16; 5.1.1; and 5.26.4. See also C.Th. 15.14.9. See Kaser 1982: 118 and Noordraven 1999: 35.

[193] For example, Pomp. D. 13.7.6 pr., discussed at pp. 160–3.

[194] Kaser 1982: 120. Also an indeterminate question addressed to a jurist could have provoked such a treatment by the jurist.

[195] For example, Pap. D. 13.7.42; Pap. D. 20.1.2; Ulp. D. 13.7.13 pr.; Diocl.-Max. C. 8.27.20. See Kaser 1982: 339–45. See also Noordraven 1999: 36–41; Bertoldi 2012: 184–5.

[196] Sections 5.3-5.7, 6.7, and 8.4.

formalities would reduce the risk that their debtors would give someone else's property as security. However, by the end of the Republic *mancipatio* probably had lost much of its publicity function, when Rome from a small agrarian community around the Palatine had developed into a metropolitan city with hundreds of thousands of inhabitants.[197] The formalities of the *mancipatio* may have become a burden rather than a benefit. The spread of Roman law throughout the empire, especially in the West, where so many cities were either *municipia* with Latin rights or *coloniae* (sometimes with the *ius Italicum*), the requirement that land, slaves, cattle, and horses be treated differently from other property as *res mancipi* must often have been burdensome.[198] For *pignus* and *hypotheca* the inability to grant multiple charges was gradually overcome, initially by granting the second pledge conditionally upon discharge of the first pledge.[199] A *mancipatio*, however, could not take place conditionally, so that this obstacle for multiple charges was never removed. Also, in other respects *pignus* and *hypotheca* acquired new traits. From the second century AD onwards, only *pignus* and *hypotheca* could be created over future assets, over receivables, and by way of 'floating charge' over a fluctuating fund of mixed assets (real estate, movable property, and receivables).[200] In other words, in this period *pignus* and *hypotheca* had acquired certain traits which made this form of real security superior to *fiducia*.

Legal institutions that are no longer used in practice, because they are less adapted to their economic environment, may fall into disuse, or even be abolished by the law makers. This ultimately happened to *fiducia*, although not until after the end of the classical period.[201] The story is well known. At the time of Justinian *fiducia* had become obsolete. In order to adapt legal opinions and imperial constitutions to their new environment, references to *fiducia* were replaced with references to its functional equivalents. This means that certain texts from the Digest or Codex which now refer to *pignus* or *hypotheca* were originally on *fiducia cum creditore*. The most systematic and influential attempt to chart these interpolations was that by Lenel, who identified more than fifty Digest fragments which were originally dealing with *fiducia*.[202] Since then almost seventy Digest fragments have been added to this group, as

197 Section 10.5.

198 See, however, Eckhardt (2020: 423–8) on wax tablets from second-century AD Dacia evidencing *mancipationes* (between *peregrini*) of sold slaves.

199 See pp. 224–7.

200 See chapters 7 (multiple pledge), 8 (pledge of claims), and 9 (general pledge).

201 Bertoldi 2012: 201–8.

202 Lenel 1927: 291–5.

well as almost twenty texts from the Codex.[203] In addition, there are several references on *fiducia cum creditore* in other collections of legal texts, such as the *Pauli Sententiae*, as well as in literary sources.[204] Last but not least, we are fortunate to have epigraphic sources recording *fiducia cum creditore*. Of preeminent importance are the specimens of *fiducia cum creditore* recorded in documents found in Pompeii, Herculaneum, Puteoli, and Baetica.[205]

[203] Bertoldi (2012: 14–5 n 29 and 30) lists the texts identified by Lenel and in subsequent literature. See also Erbe 1940: 191–207; Noordraven 1999: 17–41.

[204] For example, PS. 1.9.8; 2.13.1–7; 2.17.15; 3.6.16; 3.6.69; 5.1.1; 5.26.4. Literary sources: e.g., Cic., *Off.* 3.15.61 and 3.17.70; Cic., *Fam.* 7.12.2; Cic., *Caec.* 3.7 12–14. See Noordraven 1999: 17–41.

[205] FIRA, nrs 91 (Pompeii) and 92 (Baetica); TH 61 (Herculaneum); TPSulp 85, 87, 90–3 (Puteoli).

5

From Forfeiture to Sale

5.1 Introduction

In societies with a '*Naturalwirtschaft*' (subsistence economy) and an archaic legal system, the object given as collateral usually serves as an alternative to the performance promised by the debtor (substitution pledge). If the debtor fails to pay the secured debt, the creditor acquires unconditional ownership of the collateral instead. Roman law was no exception (section 5.2). There was originally no duty for the creditor to sell the charged property in public, nor was he obliged to account for the surplus where the value of the charged property exceeded the amount of the secured debt. This may have been a relic of the archaic idea of forfeiture as a penalty for the failure to repay the secured debt. The downside for creditors was that forfeiture of the charged property would extinguish the secured debt, also where the value of the charged property was less. In a monetary economy, such as the Roman economy of the Principate, the enforcement of a pledge by way of sale achieves a much more finely tuned method of execution than forfeiture.[1] In such an economy, lenders are normally not interested in obtaining ownership of the charged object as such: they want to liquidate it as soon as possible, in order to be able to take recourse against the proceeds and satisfy their claims. In case of a shortfall they want to recover it from the debtor, while the latter would like to lay his hands on any surplus proceeds. In the Sulpicii archive there is a document evidencing a transactional practice in the first century AD purporting to achieve this: TPSulp 79 (section 5.3). In addition to a licence to sell, TPSulp 79 also contains an express provision that any surplus of the proceeds of a sale (*superfluum*) would be paid to the debtor, while the debtor would remain liable for any deficit (*reliquum*): the 'surplus/deficit clause' (section 5.4). This transactional practice can be regarded as the common ancestor of the pledges enforceable by sale in modern civil law jurisdictions. The express licence to sell may, in addition, also have had the purpose

[1] Manigk 1916: 355.

Security and Credit in Roman Law: The historical evolution of pignus *and* hypotheca. Hendrik L. E. Verhagen, Oxford University Press. © Hendrik L. E. Verhagen 2022. DOI: 10.1093/oso/9780199695836.003.0006

of specifying the modalities of an execution sale: time, place, and price (section 5.5).[2]

In the second century AD, *pignus* and *hypotheca* evolved to be true security interests. Although in the first decades of this century the creditor's power of sale may still have been based upon forfeiture (section 5.6), it came to be regarded as a power to alienate someone else's (i.e., the debtor's) property (section 5.7). The right of pledge attributed preferential rights of recourse to the creditor for exactly the amount of the secured debt: nothing more, nothing less. What had started as a transactional practice in the first century AD (or before)—the licence to sell coupled with the surplus/deficit clause—evolved in the second century AD into a rule of law. This evolution from *Verfallpfand* (forfeiture) to *Verkaufspfand* (sale) set new evolutionary processes in motion which ultimately led to the differentiated and versatile security interest that *pignus* was to become in high and late classical law.

5.2 Forfeiture

The question of whether the original form of pledge in Roman law was a forfeiture pledge has caused fierce controversy in modern literature.[3] According to Kaser, the forfeiture pledge can be regarded as a command of legal logic determined by the purpose of real security: if someone places an object at the disposal of someone else to secure the fulfilment of his debt, he should regain the object when the debt is settled; if the latter has not been effected, the other person may retain the object (as owner). The debtor has forfeited his right to the object (and any surplus value included therein) by failing to pay his debt.[4] A comparison with Hellenistic laws, Roman public law, and *fiducia cum creditore* makes it plausible that the Roman pledge originally was a forfeiture pledge (*Verfallpfand*) and continued to be so in the first century AD. According to others (e.g., Wacke, Noordraven, Perani), however, the early classical Roman pledge was nothing more than a right of retention, which merely gave the creditor the right to refuse to release the pledged object to the debtor in case of default. *Pignus* was a possessory right, originally only

[2] In this book I use the term 'execution sale' in order to designate a sale (whether or not at auction) of charged property by a secured creditor (*pignus*, *hypotheca*, *fiducia cum creditore*, fiscal pledge or privilege), which has the purpose of taking recourse against the proceeds of the sale in order to (wholly or partly) discharge the secured debt.

[3] For a review of the forfeiture clause in pledges (*lex commissoria*) in the *ius commune* and the European codifications, see Verhagen 2011b.

[4] Kaser 1982: 14.

protected by possessory interdicts, which functioned as a psychological pressure tool. The creditor could only take recourse against the pledged object if the parties had explicitly agreed that the creditor was authorized to sell the pledged object (*pactum de vendendo*), or that the object would be forfeited to the creditor (*lex commissoria*).[5] In this section the arguments raised for and against the pledge as a forfeiture in literature will be assessed on their merits.

Hellenistic forfeiture pledges

At the end of the Republic the Romans were well aware of the existence of forfeiture pledges in the Greek world. The forfeiture of charged real estate was even a source of wealth for Roman *equites* acting as moneylenders in the provinces.[6] From Cicero we have an account of a Hellenistic forfeiture pledge. In a letter from 51–50 BC to Atticus he writes:

> Philocles Alabandensis hypothekas Cluvio dedit. Eae commissae sunt. Velim cures ut aut de hypothecis decedat easque procuratoribus Cluvi tradat aut pecuniam solvat.
>
> Philocles of Alabanda has given Cluvius hypothecs. These are forfeited. I should be grateful if you would see that he either gives up the hypothecated properties and delivers them to Cluvius's agents or else pays the money.[7]

Philocles had granted non-possessory security over local pieces of land in Alabanda (Caria in Asia Minor) to Cluvius. Philocles must have failed to repay one or more loans in time because the security had become enforceable. Cicero asked Thermus, the propraetor of Asia, to take care of the interests of Philocles, by seeing to it that he either gave up the possession of the charged properties or else paid the money owed. So apparently, the properties had been forfeited ('*commissae*'), but debtor Philocles was still in a position to redeem the security. If Philocles failed to do so, Cluvius would have a right to possession and the charged properties would be definitively forfeited to him.[8]

[5] Wacke 1998. In the same sense, Biscardi 1976: 157–75; Noordraven 1999: 23–4, 231–43; Braukmann 2008: 50–5; Perani 2021: 70–5, 134–6.

[6] Kay 2014: 190.

[7] Cic., *Fam.* 13.56, LCL 216: 54–5.

[8] See also Cic., *Flacc.* 21, 51 ('*fiduciam commissam*'). This text appears to be dealing with real security granted in accordance with Greek law, pursuant to which the charged property is forfeited to the creditor upon default. But here Cicero does not use the word '*hypothekas*' but '*fiducia(m)*', which suggests that he considered this form of security to be more similar to *fiducia* than *pignus*. See

We are dealing with a non-possessory ('*hypothekas*', '*hypothecis*') forfeiture pledge.[9]

In modern literature it has been argued that no arguments can be derived from the comparison between the development of law in Rome and in other ancient legal systems, specifically in Greece, in order to substantiate the existence of a forfeiture pledge in republican and early classical law.[10] A Greek influence on the Roman law of real security, however, cannot a priori be excluded.[11] In fact, as we will see throughout this book, Greek-Hellenistic influences are conceivable for maritime loans, *hypotheca*, multiple pledge, *antichresis*, the general pledge, fiscal pledges, and the conditional sale of pledged property. Irrespective of this, there would not necessarily have been any Greek influence in pre-classical and early classical law. It is also possible to assume a parallel evolution of law. A basic fact of comparative law is that in societies with similar socio-economic structures similar legal institutions emerge.[12] The comparison with Greek law does not in itself provide conclusive proof for the existence of a forfeiture pledge, but makes it plausible that the Roman pledge originated as a forfeiture. 'In its early form, security is always substitution, a forfeit'.[13] We can see this in ancient Greek laws, in early medieval Germanic laws, and later also in high- and late-medieval customary laws (including English law).[14] Fiscal pledges and other charges arising by operation of law in favour of public bodies may also have evolved from forfeiture charges to rights of recourse enforceable by sale. Thus, the *subsignatio praediorum* was enforced by selling the charged property in public, but forfeiture may also have been possible.[15] The *lex portorii provinciae Asiae* (AD 62) provides that after a grace period of thirty days, the charged property shall be forfeited to the person entitled to collect the taxes. This tax creditor would then be free to sell the forfeited property as owner and retain the entire proceeds.[16] We will see that also for conventional pledges, the forfeiture pledge is the ancestor of the pledge enforceable by sale: the creditor's power of sale was originally based upon forfeiture.

Noordraven 1999: 157 and, in particular, Bertoldi 2012: 47–50. The Greek form of security may have been the *πρᾶσις ἐπὶ λύσει* (Bertoldi 2012: 48).

9 Manigk 1916: 356–7. 10 Wacke 1998: 176–7.

11 Wieacker 1988: 300–4. See also Krämer 2007: 175–6. Schanbacher (2006: 69–70) even asserts that the Roman pledge is a legal institution taken from Greece.

12 Zweigert and Kötz 1998: 40. There are, of course, many exceptions to this statistical law.

13 Finley 1953: 266.

14 See the references in Krämer 2007: 173 n 3; Verhagen 2011a: 12 (Merovingian law, medieval Dutch laws) and Verhagen 2013b: 150–1 (English law). See also Levy 1951: 215 (West Roman vulgar law). See also Kaser 1982: 13; Manigk 1916: 355; Manigk 1941: 1257–8. For a comparison with Greek law, including also subsequent Greek-Hellenistic laws, see also Schanbacher 2006; Krämer 2007: 172–6.

15 Van Gessel 2003: 97. 16 Klingenberg 1992: 361.

Lex commissoria

One of Cato's templates expressly provides that the pledged tools shall be forfeited to the landowner if they are removed from the land: '*si quid deportaverit, domino esto*'.[17] This clause is a strong indication that upon the debtor's failure to pay the secured debt, the pledged objects were also forfeited to the creditor.[18] Cato had a profound knowledge of Roman law and of agricultural management and was a financier of a complex maritime venture: surely he would also have recommended an express forfeiture clause if—as a matter of law—the creditor would have nothing more than a possessory lien (right of retention), the hypothetical alternative to a forfeiture pledge.[19] The purpose of the deportation clause was to ensure that the removal of pledged assets would have the same consequence as payment default: forfeiture.

Although for Roman law epigraphic evidence is lacking, in the late Republic and early Principate pledge agreements presumably did frequently contain a forfeiture clause: a *lex commissoria*.[20] Classical Roman law knew two variations of the *lex commissoria*.[21] The first one was the transfer of sold property under the resolutive condition of non-payment of the purchase price. The second variation can be characterized as the transfer of ownership of pledged property under the suspensive condition of non-payment of the secured debt. The Latin term '*lex commissoria*' has been suspected to be post-classical in respect of *pignus*,[22] although in respect of the seller's right to recover the sold thing as owner it is attested by classical sources.[23]

Dernburg has reconstructed the *lex commissoria* in a pledge agreement as follows:

> If the money is not paid on the day on which it falls due, the land shall become the creditor's.[24]

[17] Cato, *Agr.*, c. 146. See sections 4.2 and 4.3.

[18] Contra, Wacke 1998: 173.

[19] Krämer 2007: 178.

[20] '*Lex*' here means 'clause' (not: 'law' or 'statute'), while '*commissoria*' derives from '*committere*', which can be translated as 'to mature', 'to fall to', or 'to forfeit'. E.g. Paul. D. 3.5.12 ('*ne praedia in publicum committerentur*'); Afr. D. 16.1.17.2 ('*quod fundus communis in publicum committeretur*'). Both are concerned with forfeiture of real estate to the state for failure to pay public claims. See Klingenberg 1992: 369–71. Cicero (Cic., *Fam.* 13.56) writes about charged properties which '*commissae sunt*'. See also Peters 1973: 166 n 106.

[21] For a comparison, see Peters 1973: 165–8.

[22] Levy 1951: 189; Peters 1973: 168.

[23] For example, Ulp. D. 18.3.3.

[24] '*si pecunia intra diem soluta non sit, fundus creditoris esto*'. Dernburg 1864: 276. On *lex commissoria* (*pactum commissorium*), see Perani 2021: 65–70.

One might refer to this clause as an *express* forfeiture clause: the *conventio pignoris* would state that upon the debtor's failure to pay the creditor would acquire ownership of the pledged property, without there being a different legal basis (e.g., sale) other than the clause itself necessary to this effect.[25] There is not much evidence of these express forfeiture clauses in the *Corpus iuris civilis*. Perhaps classical writings and constitutions that concerned express forfeiture clauses were omitted on purpose because they were invalid on account of Constantine's constitution of 320/326 AD,[26] or because a *traditio pignoris causa* already implied forfeiture. There is more evidence, mainly from the second and third century AD, of what one could call constructive forfeiture arrangements: contractual arrangements which achieve the same legal result as a *lex commissoria* (i.e., acquisition of ownership by the creditor upon default), but employ other legal institutions (in particular sale and *datio in solutum*) to achieve this result.[27]

Fiducia cum creditore and *pignus*

In the Sulpicii archive there are two groups of documents, all drawn up in the same format, relating to the auction of *res mancipi*, which have been mancipated by way of *fiducia cum creditore*.[28] The *pacta fiduciae* accompanying the *mancipationes* to the Sulpicii or their clients would have expressed that if the debtor failed to repay the secured debt in time then the creditor's duty to reconvey the charged property would be extinguished.[29] The creditor's ownership would then enable him to transfer the charged slaves and land to purchasers at auction. Therefore, in early classical law, in *fiducia cum creditore* upon the debtor's failure to pay a creditor retained ownership of the charged *res mancipi* without there being a clause necessary to this effect.[30]

Noordraven observes that a simple right of retention is implausible and forfeiture of the charged property to the creditor is the only meaningful

[25] Kaser 1982: 17. The *lex commissoria* would be the *iusta causa* for a *traditio pignoris causa*.

[26] C. 8.34.3. See section 11.5. According to Kaser (1950: 564) and Levy (1956: 188–9), express forfeiture clauses never existed. 'Forfeiture clauses' instead entailed that in case of an event of default the creditor was entitled to acquire ownership of the pledged property by way of purchase. See also sections 5.6 and 11.4.

[27] See sections 11.3 and 11.4. See also section 5.6, on Scaev. D. 32.101 pr. and Scaev. D. 18.1.18 pr.

[28] TPSulp 85, 87, 90–3. TPSulp 88 is concerned with the auction of real estate, but the document is only partially preserved and does not reveal whether it had been charged by way of *fiducia cum creditore*. Camodeca 1999: 196 assumes that this was the case.

[29] See the licence to sell in the *pactum conventum* of the *Mancipatio Pompeiana* on pp. 116–17.

[30] Noordraven 1999: 287, 294. The function of the licence to sell in the *pactum fiduciae* will be explained in sections 5.3–5.5.

completion of the *fiducia cum creditore*.[31] But it is also the only meaningful completion of *pignus*. I find it difficult to imagine that in the first century AD, in the absence of an express *lex commissoria* (as in TPSulp 51, 52, and 55) the position of a creditor with a right of pledge over *res nec mancipi* was much weaker than that of a creditor to whom *res mancipi* were transferred by way of *fiducia cum creditore*. Throughout the classical period the same rules (e.g., on proscription, mandatory sale, surplus, and *impetratio dominii*) applied to the enforcement of *pignus* and *fiducia cum creditore*. This makes it rather unlikely that in regard to the realization of real security over *res nec mancipi* (*pignus*), the creditor would merely have a right to detain the pledged property. The most plausible interpretation is that also in case of *pignus* the creditor's ownership upon forfeiture would have enabled him to sell the pledged assets at auction.

Traditio pignoris causa

In classical law, *pignus* and *fiducia* were in principle dealt with in a similar manner by the jurists. This would only be different where the position of the parties under property law required a different approach.[32] But isn't that precisely the case here? In case of *fiducia*, at the time of default by the debtor the creditor already owned the property, as a consequence of the *mancipatio* on 'day 1' of the transaction.[33] In case of *pignus*, however, in classical law ownership did not transfer to the creditor on day 1. How can one explain that in *pignus* the creditor did acquire ownership of pledged property in case of default?[34] If one assumes (which I do) that the acquisition of the pledged property by the creditor must comply with the same requirements as those applicable to the transfer of *res nec mancipi* in general,[35] one will have to construct a *traditio* in this respect. This is not too difficult. In early classical law the physical delivery of a pledged object to the creditor would have been equivalent to, or may actually have been, a *traditio* aimed at the conditional transfer of ownership.[36] In other words, the *datio pignoris* was equivalent to a *traditio*, which took place by way of conditional payment (*pro soluto*).[37]

[31] Noordraven 1999: 236–9. [32] Kaser 1982: 114–15; Noordraven 1999: 35.
[33] E.g., Paul. D. 20.5.13 (reconstructed text in Perani 2021: 219–20).
[34] Noordraven 1999: 23–4; Perani 2021: 75–6. [35] Noordraven 1999: 23.
[36] In the same sense Kaser 1982: 24, 72–4. On *pignus* and *traditio* in republican law, see De Iuliis 2017: 31–41.
[37] Manigk 1941: 1251; Kaser 1982: 14, 18; Krämer 2007: 188–9. See also Perani 2021: 81–91.

If upon the granting of the pledge the creditor was given actual control over the pledged property,[38] the transfer of possession required for *traditio* was present and all requirements for the transfer of *res nec mancipi* were met.[39]

In many texts the creation of a possessory pledge is described in terms of *tradere* or *traditio.*[40] There are even opinions by Julian and his pupil Africanus which speak of a *traditio* taking place *pignoris causa.*[41] Whenever these texts on *pignus* speak of *traditio*, this is, in my view, a genuine *traditio* in the legal sense.[42] For certain purposes this *traditio* did result in the creditor having *possessio* as a matter of law. From a legal perspective the creditor's possession differed significantly from that of someone to whom possession had been transferred pursuant to a contract of sale, donation, dowry, or other 'title' for the transfer of ownership. The creditor's lack of will to possess as owner entailed that the creditor possessed on behalf of someone else.[43] This 'natural' (*naturaliter*) possession did, however, have legal consequences.[44] In D. 41.3.16, Iavolenus describes what one could call functionally divided possession:[45] 'one who gives a pledge possesses only for the purposes of *usucapio* but, for all other purposes, the one who accepts (the pledge) possesses'.[46] In particular, the creditor to whom a possessory pledge had been granted would, for the purposes of the interdicts, be treated as a possessor. The creditor could rely on the possessory interdicts against persons who interfered with his possession of the pledged property. This could be justified by the general idea that until the secured debt has been discharged, the creditor's interest in the pledged

[38] In TPSulp 51 a non-possessory pledge was established, which was converted into a possessory pledge in TPSulp 52: the pledge creditor entered into a lease agreement with the operator of a warehouse in which the pledged goods were stored. This construction resembles a *traditio longa manu*. See section 6.2.

[39] In the same sense Kaser 1982: 24, 72; Krämer 2007: 188–9. Where *res mancipi* came to be pledged, even then this *traditio* would be effective: it would make the creditor bonitary owner and (through *usucapio*) quiritarian owner after one (movables) or two (immovables) years. Burdese 1949: 207; Kaser 1982: 17, 48, 74, 114; Krämer 2007: 188–9.

[40] For example, Macer D. 2.8.15.2. See also Sev.-Ant. C. 7.8.3 ('*qui pignoris iure specialiter traditi vel obligati sunt*').

[41] Jul. D. 41.2.36 and D. 44.7.16; Afr. D. 23.3.50.1. See also Ulp. D. 32.68 pr.: '*ex causa pignoris nactus est*'. According to Noordraven (1999: 17–9, 56–9, 218–9) these texts may originally have been dealing with *fiducia*.

[42] See also De Iuliis 2017: 40–1; Perani 2021: 299. Contra Noordraven 1999: 218–9 n 17 (who argues that *traditio* here only has a colloquial meaning).

[43] Gai. D. 6.2.13.1; Paul. D. 41.3.13 pr.; Paul. D. 9.4.22.1; Macer D. 2.8.15.2.

[44] Ulp. D. 10.4.3.15.

[45] Kaser 1956: 353–4.

[46] '*qui pignori dedit, ad usucapionem tantum possidet, quod ad reliquas omnes causas pertinet, qui accepit possidet*'. In Paul. D. 41.2.1.15, Julian's opinion is restated that the pledged object is possessed by the debtor for one reason only: *usucapio*. From other writings by Julian it appears, however, that not for *all* other purposes the creditor's possession has the same legal consequences as *possessio civilis*. Thus, Jul. D. 41.1.37 pr. says that even though possession of a pledged slave is with the creditor, the latter will not acquire possession of things delivered to the slave.

property is more significant than the debtor's.[47] Another trace of this idea is that initially both the debtor and the creditor could institute the *actio furti*: the creditor for the amount of the secured debt and the debtor for the surplus value.[48] It is, therefore, not at all strange that the jurists frequently use the words *tradere* and *traditio* when they are dealing with a possessory pledge. This would be even less strange if one accepts that the *traditio*'s original purpose was to confer ownership upon the creditor, upon the debtor's failure to pay (forfeiture).

5.3 Licence to Sell and Forfeiture

In modern literature it is assumed that in the early Principate the method of recourse was provided for by the parties themselves, by means of either a forfeiture clause (*lex commissoria*) or an express licence to sell (*pactum de vendendo, pactum vendendi*).[49] One of the pledges included in the archive of the Sulpicii, TPSulp 79, does contain a *pactum de vendendo*. If the parties did not include such licence to sell, one would—in this view—expect a forfeiture clause.[50] The other pledge agreements of the Sulpicii archive (TPSulp 51, 52, and 55), however, do not have a *lex commissoria*. The rights of pledge evidenced by these documents would—without these clauses—have been nothing more than rights of retention: 'pledge-liens'.[51] It is, however, not very plausible that the creditor of TPSulp 51 and 52, who had obtained a pledge over a total of 73 tonnes of agricultural goods and was able to exact from the debtor that a non-possessory pledge later be converted into a possessory one,[52] would settle for a lien in the absence of a licence to sell. Such a creditor would, if a lien were the only alternative, have insisted on either a *lex commissoria* or on a *pactum de vendendo*. From the whole archive of the Sulpicii it appears that they knew their law well. One would not expect them to accept (for themselves or their clients) such weak form of security for loans which (for their standards) were for considerable amounts.

47 Kaser 1982: 259.

48 This changed in late classical law, where the creditor's liability for *custodia* entailed that in case of a possessory pledge he would be exclusively entitled to the *actio furti*.

49 Kaser 1982: 15, 72–3. See now Perani 2021. For the different expressions used in the classical sources, see Perani 2021: 101–17. E.g., Paul. D. 20.3.3 (*pactum de pignore vendendo*).

50 Abatino 2012: 314, hesitantly suggests that '*arrabo*' in TPSulp 51 could allude to an implicit *lex commissoria*.

51 For the pledges in the Sulpicii archive, see Gröschler 2008: 316–9; Wacke 1998: 168–202. For a different interpretation, Krämer 2007: 181–4; Verhagen 2011a.

52 See section 6.2.

TPSulp 79

From 40 AD we have epigraphic evidence of a contractual clause providing that the creditor shall have the right to sell the pledged property. This document reproduced below is part of one of the client files from the archive of the Sulpicii: the file L. Marius Iucundus.

TPSulp 79 (scriptura exterior)
C(aio) Laecanio Basso Q(uinto) Terentio Cull[eone] co(n)s(ulibus),
ìdibus Mart[ii]s.
L(ucius) Ma[rius Didae l(ibertus) Iucundus scripsi me dedisse C(aio) Sulpicio]
Fa[usto pignoris nomine triti]ci alexan[drini modium]
millia [decem et tri]a, quae sunt posita in [pr]aedis Do[miti]=
ae Lepidae [h]orreis Barbatianis superioribus [horreo]
XXVI, ob HS vigintì millia nu[mmum, quae per chiro]=
graphum scripsi me ei debere [---].
Si idibus Maìs primis ea HS ((I)) [((]I)), q(uae) s(upra) s(cripta) s(unt), non de[dero] sol[vero]
satisve fecero, tum liceat tibì id triticu[m, quo d(e) agitur,]
sub [p]raecone de condicione pig[nor]is? quo [de ag(itur) vendere].
[Si pluris venier]it, tu omne quod superesse[t] reddas [mihi he]=
[redive meo; si] quo minoris venierit, id ego reddam tibì
heredive tuo. Utique id triticum, quo de agitur,
omnì periculo esset meo heredisve meì: haec
mihì tecum ita convenerunt pactusque sum.
Actum Puteolis

Under the consuls Gaius Laecanius Bassus and Quintus Terentius Culleo,
on the Ides of March (15 March 40)
I, Lucius Marius Iucundus, freedman of Dida, have written that I have given to Gaius Sulpicius Faustus as a pledge 13,000 modii of Alexandrian grain, which is stored on the lands of Domitia Lepida in the upper Barbatian Warehouse of Domitia Lepida in storeroom 26,
for the 20,000 sesterces, which I have written in a chirograph to owe him.
If on the Ides of May (15 May 40) I shall not give, pay
or satisfy the abovementioned 20,000 sesterces, then you will be authorised to sell at auction the grain in question under the terms of the pledge.

> If it shall fetch more, you shall return everything which remains to me or my heir; if it shall fetch less, I will give the difference to you or your heir.
> We have agreed and I have undertaken
> that the risk for the grain in question is for me or my heir.
> Done in Puteoli.

In TPSulp 79, Lucius Marius Iucundus grants a pledge over grain to one of the Sulpicii (Faustus) in order to secure a loan of 20,000 sesterces. The express licence to sell in this document is expressed in terms of '*liceat... vendere*'. Likewise, the sources in the Digest speak of the creditor having the faculty (rather than the obligation) to sell.[53]

In *fiducia cum creditore* the creditor had, as a result of his right of ownership, the legal power to dispose of the charged property.[54] Nevertheless, the epigraphic sources show that in *fiducia* too the creditor is explicitly granted a licence to sell.[55] This shows that the fact that the creditor would (upon forfeiture) own the charged property did not make a licence to sell redundant, at least not according to the transacting parties. Noordraven holds the view—which by his own account is different from almost every other modern author—that a *pactum de vendendo* in *fiducia* did not read *ut vendere liceret* but *ut venderet*.[56] In substance the clause therefore reflects that the charged property had to be sold by the creditor and he was not allowed to retain title to it. This, according to Noordraven, is also the best explanation from a dogmatic point of view: after all, the creditor—as owner—already had the power of sale.[57] Bertoldi observes, however, that it will have differed from case to case whether there was an obligation or a licence to sell.[58] The added value of a licence to sell in *fiducia cum creditore* was that it expressed that the creditor would not violate his fiduciary duty to reconvey where he would sell upon the debtor's failure to pay.[59] Therefore, also in case of *fiducia* a licence to sell is not irreconcilable with the creditor's ownership.

[53] The following texts use *vendere licere*: Lab. D. 20.1.35; Scaev. D. 44.3.14.5; Scaev. D. 46.1.63; Paul. D. 20.3.3; Ulp. D. 13.7.4 and Ulp. D. 13.7.6 pr. In the same sense Gai. *Inst.* 2.64 and Alex. C. 4.24.4. Pap. D. 20.5.4 speaks of exercising a '*vendendi pignoris potestas*'.

[54] Noordraven 1999: 244.

[55] This can be found, for example, in the *Mancipatio Pompeiana*. See pp. 116–17.

[56] Noordraven 1999: 244. [57] Noordraven 1999: 244. [58] Bertoldi 2012: 81.

[59] In section 5.4 I will argue that the so-called 'surplus/deficit clause' explains how forfeiture can be reconciled with granting a licence to sell to the pledge creditor.

Why no licence to sell?

The other pledge agreements of the Sulpicii archive (TPSulp 51, 52, and 55) do not have any provisions for the method of recourse. In TPSulp 51, 52, and 55 the creditors were not the Sulpicii bankers themselves but ordinary citizens who (presumably) did not act as professional moneylenders. Could the absence of a licence to sell have been caused by their lack of experience in legal matters? This is unlikely. These lenders may very well simply have used templates provided by the Sulpicii. TPSulp 51 and 52 document a transaction that may have been arranged by the same Gaius Sulpicius Faustus who appears as creditor in TPSulp 79.[60] These documents show a profound knowledge of Roman law, which makes it highly unlikely that a licence to sell was omitted because of a lack of legal skills of the person(s) responsible for the drafting of TPSulp 51, 52, and 55.[61] One could simply regard the inclusion of a licence to sell in TPSulp 79 as the manifestation of a phenomenon that is also encountered in contemporary practice: the parties explicitly reaffirm in their contract the powers already conferred on them by law.[62] Thus in a constitution by Alexander Severus from AD 223 the licence to sell is referred to as a 'common pact' ('*pactum vulgare*'),[63] which shows that even in a time in which it had long been established that the creditor would have a right of sale by operation of law the parties still used to include an express licence to sell in their pledge agreement. But in the archive of the Sulpicii, the licence to sell was *not* a 'common pact': it was included in only one of the four pledge agreements contained in the archive (TPSulp 79). It is remarkable that in TPSulp 79, while in respect of the granting of the pledge itself the creditor is (like in TPSulp 51, 52, and 55) addressed in the third person ('*dedisse C Sulpicio Fa(usto)*'), in the licence to sell this is changed to the second person ('*liceat tibi... vendere*'). This suggests that the licence to sell was not part of the original template and was inserted incidentally. This in its turn is a strong indication that an express licence to sell was not standard practice for the Sulpicii. It has been suggested that the express licence to sell was inserted in TPSulp 79 because an earlier transaction with debtor C. Novius Eunus had been problematic and the Sulpicii now wanted to make absolutely sure that they could auction the pledged goods immediately upon an event of default.[64] The wish

[60] He was one of the *signatores* of TPSulp 51.
[61] See also Krämer 2007: 183.
[62] Krämer 2007: 183.
[63] Alex. C. 4.24.4.
[64] Bransbourg 2014: 132.

to enforce immediately upon default may indeed have been a motivation for inserting a licence to sell in the pledge agreement.[65]

Implied licence to sell?

At the time of the Sulpicii the enforcement of pledge by way of sale was a well-settled practice. It could be argued that the mere fact that the other pledge agreements in the Sulpicii archive (TPSulp 51, 52, and 55) do not contain an express licence to sell does not justify the conclusion that the parties did not have such licence in mind. After all, the right to sell would give the creditor an effective means of securing payment of the debts owed to him. In particular, Chevreau takes the position that by the time of the Sulpicii, in the first century AD, a licence to sell was implied in pledge agreements.[66] In TPSulp 67 and 68 C. Novius Eunus promises to pay remaining amounts (1,150 and 1,250 sesterces, respectively) which were still unpaid under transactions previously entered into. Chevreau argues that these amounts were still due under the secured loans documented in TPSulp 51 and 52.[67] The lender must have sold the pledged assets, upon which it became clear what amount was still owed by the borrower. Such execution sale must have taken place pursuant to an implied licence to sell, because TPSulp 51 and 52 do not contain an express right of sale. For various reasons this argumentation is not entirely convincing. First of all, it is not very likely that there would be a deficit (*reliquum*) after the assets pledged pursuant to TPSulp 51 and 52 had been sold in order to discharge the amount due under these documents. The value of the pledged assets (30,000 sesterces) far exceeded the amount of the secured debt (13,000 sesterces).[68] Moreover, as Camodeca notices, it cannot be proven that TPSulp 67 and 68 are concerned with the final settlement of the loans recorded in TPSulp 51 and 52 merely on the basis that these documents were part of the same archive.[69] Other loans may have been concluded in the period between 2 July 37 AD (TPSulp 52) and 29 August 38 AD (TPSulp 67). In fact, in TPSulp 68 C. Novius Eunus promises to pay the net amount (1,250 sesterces) remaining after *all* the credits and debits had been balanced ('*nummos reliquos ratione omni putata*') upon termination of the entire credit relationship.[70]

[65] Section 5.5. [66] Chevreau 2010.
[67] TPSulp 51 and 52 are reproduced in section 6.2. [68] Camodeca 1999: 140.
[69] Camodeca 1999: 167. [70] Camodeca 1999: 167.

This may be boilerplate, but it may also reflect that the final settlement of TPSulp 67 and 68 concerned more transactions than TPSulp 51 and 52.[71]

For the first century AD Chevreau's conclusion that a licence to sell was deemed to be agreed in every pledge agreement is too bold. It is true that, although few early classical texts on *pignus* have come down to us, the enforcement of *pignus* by way of sale is well attested in jurists' writings from this period. There is even a legal opinion from the late republican period on it. In Ulp. D. 47.10.15.32, Servius Sulpicius Rufus expresses the view that someone who makes an announcement of the auction of 'pledged' property, while such pledge had not actually been granted by the person in question, is liable with the *actio iniuriarum* for defamation.[72] This is an important fragment, as it demonstrates that already in the late Republic a creditor would take recourse against the pledged property by auctioning it.[73] This right could, however, have been granted expressly: this is particularly clear in opinions from Labeo and (possibly) Sabinus. In Lab. D. 20.1.35 the words '*ex pacto convento licuit vendere*' are a reference to the *conventio pignoris* giving the creditor the right to sell the pledged property.[74] If the opinion discussed in Pomp. D. 13.7.6 pr. could be attributed to Sabinus, it would also be an early opinion in the Digest on the express licence to sell.[75] Looking at the Digest, one cannot but conclude that—at the earliest—only from the second century AD there is a basis in the legal sources for an implied licence to sell.[76]

Power of sale and forfeiture

In a sense, however, an implied power of sale did exist in the first century AD. The *datio pignoris*, which in TPSulp 45 was effected by the creditor renting the storage units where the goods pledged in TPSulp 52 were stored[77] and in TPSulp 55 by handing over the silver to the creditor, was aimed at a conditional transfer. If there would be an event of default under the loan agreement, the pledged goods would be forfeited to the creditor, enabling him to sell and transfer the pledged goods at auction. In this sense a *datio pignoris* did imply

[71] A good case has been made for TPSulp 67 and 68 being stipulations for the payment of interest which was due under TPSulp 51 and 52. See Bransbourg 2014: 128–30.

[72] This is the first mention in the Digest of a pledge enforced by sale. Bertoldi (2012: 15 n 30) lists this text as being interpolated and concerning *fiducia*. Noordraven 1999 does not mention this text.

[73] See also Paul. D. 20.4.13 discussing the views of Nerva and Proculus on the distribution of the sales proceeds of a tenant's pledge between the old and new owner of a leased building.

[74] In Pap. D. 20.4.3.2 an agreement allowing one party to sell the other's property when a certain obligation is not performed is characterized as an agreement to pledge that property.

[75] This text will be discussed in section 5.6. [76] See section 5.7. [77] See section 6.2.

a power of sale. In late republican and early classical Roman law, as in Greek-Hellenistic law, the power of sale resulted from the right of ownership that the creditor had acquired after forfeiture of the charged object.[78] Once the creditor had become the owner of the pledged property, he could decide either to keep it, or to sell it in order to settle the secured debt. The 'categorical separation' (Manigk) of the *Verkaufspfand* from the *Verfallpfand*, which later took place in Roman law (as witnessed by Gai. *Inst.* 2.64 and Scaev. D. 44.3.14.5), is specifically Roman.[79] In Hellenistic laws the licence to sell would always remain an ancillary agreement to the forfeiture pledge.[80] We can see this in the maritime loan from Muziris from mid-second century AD.[81] The parties have agreed that upon the debtor's failure to pay, ownership of the pledged property shall pass to the creditor. It is expressly provided that thereupon the creditor is absolutely free to do with it as a he pleases: rehypothecate it, or sell it at the then prevailing market price.[82] The coupling of forfeiture and sale would also have been a feature of a Roman pledge in the first century AD.

The hypothesis that the creditor's power of sale is based on forfeiture of the pledged object is supported by the fact that the auction announcements in the Sulpicii archive always provide a precise definition of the legal status of the slaves, land or other goods to be auctioned.[83] It looks very much as if the auction announcements showed the core contents of the documents through which real security (*pignus* or *fiducia*) was established.[84] The description of a *fiducia cum creditore* in the auction announcement of TPSulp 87 contains all the essential elements of a *mancipatio fiduciae causa*.[85] The reference to the pledge in TPSulp 83 is brief,[86] but so are the pledging clauses from the Sulpicii archive, such as TPSulp 55.[87] None of these auction announcements mentions a licence to sell, which one would have expected if the creditor were authorized to sell only if he were granted such a licence. Apparently, an explicit licence to

[78] I will use the expression 'power of sale' as a shorthand expression for the creditor's contractual right to sell the pledged property coupled with the power to transfer ownership to the purchaser at an execution sale. However, the expressions 'licence to sell' and 'right to sell' will also be used.

[79] See section 5.7. [80] Manigk 1941: 1269; Taubenschlag 1955: 279.

[81] See Rathbone 2003: 220–2.

[82] Schuster 2005: 107–8, 113–20. For text and translation of the Muziris papyrus (P. Vindob. G 40822), see De Romanis 2020: 14–30.

[83] On the auction announcements in the Sulpicii archive, see Costabile 1992 and Romeo 2006.

[84] In the same sense Cerami and Petrucci 2010: 130–1.

[85] '*testa[t]us est mancipia* [list of slaves conveyed], *quae mancipia M(arcus) Egnatius Suavis C(aio) Sulpicio Cinnamo fidei fiduciae caussa [HS n(ummo) I pro HS X]XVI obligasse* [*dicitur*] . . .'.

[86] '*purpuras laconicas reliquas, quas L(ucius) Marius Agathemer C(aio) Sulpicio Cinnamo pignori dedisse dicitur*'.

[87] '*P(ublius) [V]ergilius Ampliatus sc[ripsi me] dedisse Sex(to) Granio Num[enio] pignori argentum p(ondo) X[---]*'.

sell was not regarded as necessary in the relevant trade circles.[88] Fiscal pledges and other charges arising by operation of law in favour of public bodies may also have evolved from forfeiture charges to rights of recourse enforceable by sale.[89]

Forfeiture and over-collateralization

In TPSulp 51 and 52 the Puteolean *mercator frumentarius* Gaius Novius Eunus acts as debtor of a loan and as grantor of a pledge with regard to a stock of agricultural products which were stored for him in the 'Bassian Public Warehouses of Puteoli'. In modern literature it is inferred from TPSulp 51 and 52 that a forfeiture pledge could not have existed in the first century AD.[90] A decisive argument against the existence of a forfeiture pledge lies, in this view, in the particularly high value of the pledged goods. The debt for which the pledge was granted concerned a total amount of 13,000 sesterces, whilst the value of the pledged goods is estimated to be at least 30,000 sesterces.[91] It is deemed implausible that a merchant like C. Novius Eunus, who is said to have had a high degree of creditworthiness (he was, after all, the owner of a stock of wheat and legumes with a value of 30,000 sesterces), would accept that in such a situation the pledged goods would be forfeited to his creditor.[92] I am not convinced at all by this line of reasoning. The value of a person's assets says nothing in itself about a person's creditworthiness; his or her liabilities may be such that his or her creditworthiness is low. The conversion of a non-possessory pledge into a possessory one, which took place after an additional loan of 3,000 sesterces was granted (TPSulp 52),[93] rather suggests that creditor Evenus Primianus (or his slave-manager Hesychus) did not rely in blind faith on the creditworthiness of his debtor C. Novius Eunus. After all, when this borrower requested for additional credit of 3,000 sesterces, the lender wished to strengthen his position by this conversion. Also, the other documents contained in the file suggest that this grain merchant, C. Novius Eunus, was anything but creditworthy.[94]

[88] In the same sense Krämer 2007: 183. [89] Section 5.2. [90] Gröschler 2008: 316–9.

[91] Gröschler assumes Camodeca's (1999: 140) estimate of the value of the wheat of 30,000 sesterces (surplus value: 17,000 sesterces). Other estimates range from HS 2 to HS 12 per *modius*. See, in particular, Rathbone 2009: 303–10. Even with a price of HS 2 per *modius* the surplus value would still be 13,000 sesterces.

[92] Gröschler 2008: 316–19. [93] See section 6.2. [94] See Bransbourg 2014: 131–2.

There is a much better explanation for the surplus value of the pledged objects in TPSulp 51 and 52.[95] In modern finance transactions a large *debt to collateral ratio* is often negotiated. In doing so, the lender seeks to ensure that in case of default, the debt can be fully satisfied out of the collateral. A substantial surplus value creates a buffer for situations where the value of the collateral is reduced (e.g., falling prices, damage) or part thereof is sold by the debtor to third parties. The surplus value furthermore leaves room for additional credit on the basis of the existing collateral. There is no reason to doubt that the same motives also played a role in classical Rome or Puteoli.[96] The pledge of TSulp 51 was first granted for a loan of 10,000 sesterces, while the surplus value made it possible that the same collateral could also serve as security for an additional loan of 3,000 sesterces shortly thereafter.[97] The high value of the goods pledged in TPSulp 51 and 52 therefore does not provide conclusive evidence against forfeiture at all.

Pledge-lien as a viable alternative?

A hypothetical alternative to the forfeiture pledge would be a pledge that gives the creditor a mere right of retention. In TPSulp 51 and 52 there was a considerable surplus value, so that in the insolvency of the debtor there would have been a strong incentive for the *bonorum emptor* to repay the secured debt. Such a pledge-lien would not, however, have enabled a secured creditor to take recourse outside (often long-winded) collective execution proceedings.[98] Time is of the essence, as TPSulp 79 illustrates, in particular in the case of pledged goods with volatile prices (such as grain).[99] Creditors would like to take matters into their own hands in taking recourse against pledged assets by selling them at their earliest convenience. It is not for nothing that we find so many auction announcements in respect of charged property in the archive of the Sulpicii. A 'pledge-lien' could conceivably in some cases have worked in practice, if the creditor would be entitled to use the pledged objects (e.g., slaves, livestock, land, houses) or apply their fruits by way of amortization or interest. However, such 'antichretic' pledges are attested in Roman legal sources not earlier than the third century AD and may not yet have existed in

[95] In TPSulp 55 silver is pledged. The specification of the weight of the silver is no longer completely legible (Camodeca 1999: 146).

[96] Lerouxel (2008: 189) points to TPSulp 106, in which the creditor had to compete with the tax authorities. A high surplus value ensures that even then enough would remain for the creditor.

[97] In the same sense Camodeca 1999: 140. [98] See section 12.3. [99] See section 5.5.

the Western Roman empire of the first century AD.[100] Moreover, an antichretic pledge would also not have benefited the creditor in TPSulp 51 and 52, where the pledged goods (grain, chickpeas, lentils, etc.) could not be used without consuming them, nor did they produce fruits which could reduce the amount due under the loan or serve as interest. On the contrary, in TPSulp 51 and 52 they were perishable goods, whose value would gradually dissipate. In case of well-stored wheat this could take years, but retaining the goods for a lengthy period of time could lead to considerable storage costs for the creditor. These were minimal in TPSulp 45 (HS 1 per month), but in another rental agreement (TPSulp 46) a monthly rent of HS 100 had to be paid for storing the pledged goods, which was equivalent to 0.5 per cent per month over the amount of the loan. The creditor and the debtor will possibly have agreed in relation to TPSulp 45 that the actual storage costs were to be borne by the debtor.[101] If, however, the debtor is no longer able to pay off his debts due to insolvency, the creditor will have to bear the actual storage costs in order to maintain his right of retention.

In conclusion, a pledge-lien would not have been a viable alternative for the secured credit transactions documented in the Sulpicii archive.

5.4 The Surplus/Deficit Clause

From the first and second century AD we have epigraphic evidence of express authorizations in security documents allowing the creditor to sell the charged object in case of a payment default. In practice, such licence to sell was always accompanied by a contractual provision to the effect that in case of such a sale, the creditor would be liable to return the surplus to the debtor and the debtor would be liable for any deficit ('surplus/deficit clause').[102] The whole arrangement of a licence to sell coupled with a surplus/deficit clause was at the creditor's discretion. In other words, the creditor was not obliged to sell and only if he chose to do so would he be liable for any surplus. This raises an important question. Why would the creditor in respect of a forfeiture pledge demand that he *may* sell? After all, if the pledged property would be forfeited,

100 See section 8.4.

101 In the same sense Wolf and Crook 1989: 21. Camodeca (1999: 123) explains the symbolic rental price by the fact that lessor Cypaerus was the *patronus* of Eunus and had an interest in the transaction of his *libertus*.

102 Scaev. D. 46.1.63 couples a licence to sell only with a clause on the debtor's liability for the *reliquum* after the sale by the creditor.

the creditor could—as owner—do anything he liked with the property, including selling it.[103] In a pledge as lien the licence to sell would have added value as it gives him a power that he otherwise would not have. There is therefore potentially a good argument against the hypothesis of a forfeiture pledge—an argument which eventually does not prove to be decisive either. The surplus/deficit clause provides the key for unlocking the meaning of the practice of granting a licence to sell to a creditor who would become the owner of the pledged property upon forfeiture.

Ersatzpfand (substitution pledge)

Not only in TPSulp 79, but also in other documents (*Mancipatio Pompeiana* and *Formula Baetica*) from the first century AD the licence to sell is coupled with a surplus/deficit clause.[104] This is an indication that in the first century AD no binding rule of law existed from which it already arose that the creditor would be liable for the surplus and the debtor for the deficit. This is consistent with what we know about the time of origin of the duty to pay the surplus or deficit arising by operation of law.[105] The appearance of the surplus/deficit-clause in the epigraphic sources shows that in the first century AD the pledge was effectively still an '*Ersatzpfand*', pursuant to which the secured debt would be substituted with the charged property. The licence to sell coupled with a surplus/deficit clause was intended to evade the adverse consequence of this.

In the law of Athens and the law of Greco-Roman Egypt, forfeiture pledges were accompanied by clauses providing that the debtor remained liable for the *reliquum*. The maritime loan (ca. 340 BC) quoted in the Demosthenic speech *Against Lacritus* provides with respect to the pledged amphoras that if payment is not made within the agreed time, the creditors will have the right to sell the amphoras at the going rate. To this it is added that if the sale proceeds are less than the amount of the secured debt, the debtor shall remain liable for the deficit with all his remaining assets.[106] Five centuries later, in the Muziris papyrus (mid-second century AD), we find another example of this. The parties have agreed that upon the debtor's failure to pay, ownership of the

[103] Wacke 1998: 184–5.

[104] The *Formula Baetica* could also be from the second century AD. According to Camodeca (1999: 176) TPSulp 77 is a confirmation by the debtor that he had received the *superfluum* (HS 4,300) which remained after the auction of a slave who had been fiduciarily transferred.

[105] Kaser 1982: 75–8. See section 5.7.

[106] Against Lacritus, 35.10–14 (translation taken from Bresson 2016: 282).

pledged property shall pass to the creditor and that thereupon the creditor shall be authorized (*inter alia*) to sell it at the then prevailing market price. At the end of the pledge agreement, the debtor declares that he shall be liable for any shortfall.[107] In republican and early classical Roman law it will have been the same. Kunkel claims to have identified an early ancestor of the non-possessory pledge, which he calls the 'substitution pledge' (*Ersatzpfand*) or 'estimation pledge' (*Ästimationspfand*).[108] This arrangement entailed that the parties agreed that if the debtor failed to pay the secured debt, the creditor shall have the right to take a specified object as an alternative to the payment. The value of this object has (at the time the transaction was concluded) been estimated by the parties to be more or less equal to the secured debt, hence the term 'estimation pledge'. The pledged object completely substituted the creditor's claim for payment. The creditor did not have to account for any surplus value, nor was the debtor liable for an undervalue of the pledged object.[109] There is too little evidence for Kunkel's substitute pledge in order to assume that it actually existed. There are, however, certain elements which are plausible. In particular, the substitution of the secured debt with the pledged object may explain the early classical transactional practice of combining a contractual licence to sell for the creditor with a clause providing that the debtor shall be liable for any shortfall of the proceeds of the sale (while the creditor shall pay the surplus to the debtor). The purpose of such surplus/deficit clauses would be to shift the economic risk of the pledged object from the creditor back to the debtor.

We can still see traces of the original idea of substitution in the second and third centuries AD. From Pomponius there is an opinion saying that 'the clause commonly included in pledging that, to the extent that the object of pledge yields too little return at sale, the debtor must pay the remainder, is superfluous as it is also the situation by operation of law without this addition'.[110] Pomponius's opinion still echoes the transactional practice of the surplus/deficit clause (which may have continued to be used in the practice of his time), but clearly shows liability for the remainder now arises by operation of law.[111] At the end of the third century AD the imperial chancery still considered it necessary to rule that the creditor had an *actio in personam* against

[107] Schuster 2005: 107–8, 113–20. Text and translation of the forfeiture clause, licence to sell, and deficit clause in P. Vindob. G 40822, De Romanis 2020: 14–7.

[108] See section 6.4, discussing Lab. D. 20.1.35.

[109] Kunkel 1973: 164.

[110] Paul. (Pomp.) D. 20.5.9.1 ('*quod in pignoribus dandis adici solet, ut, quo minus pignus venisset, reliquum debitor redderet, supervacuum est, quia ipso iure ita se res habet etiam non adiecto eo*').

[111] Manigk 1941: 1259. See also Gai. D. 12.1.28; Scaev. D. 46.1.63.

the debtor for the remainder after the proceeds of sale had been applied to the secured debt.[112] This would not have been necessary if in the past the law had not been otherwise.[113]

Risks for creditors and debtors

In republican and early classical law the creditor was entitled to any surplus value present in the charged property. This may have been a relic of the archaic idea of forfeiture as a penalty for the failure to repay the secured debt.[114] For a long time the Roman law of secured credit reflected the economically dominant position of lenders.[115] Only where, as a corollary to a licence to sell, a surplus/deficit clause had been agreed *and* the creditor did actually exercise his right of sale, would the creditor be obliged to pay the surplus value to the debtor. Without such a clause, the charged object completely replaced the claim as such, irrespective of whether it was worth more or less. This could turn out very well for the creditor. In a letter to Atticus from 45 BC Cicero sets out how his brother Quintus had granted security to banker Castricius over a number of slaves.[116] The aggregate value of these slaves undoubtedly being much higher than the amount of the secured debt, Castricius had indicated that he preferred taking possession of the slaves over payment of the secured debt. Castricius, who may have been what we now call a merchant banker, seemingly not only had his (security) interest as creditor in mind but may here even more have been motivated by the commercial value of the slaves.[117] This appeared inequitable to Cicero: '*non mihi videtur esse aequum*'.[118] Certainly where Quintus had not defaulted under the loan, a definitive appropriation by Castricius of the charged slaves would even be in violation of his fiduciary duty to reconvey the slaves after repayment of the loan. From a later letter it appears that the matter was probably settled through the mediation of L. Egnatius Rufus.[119] What this affair does show is that in case of a large surplus value, forfeiture and substitution would be attractive for a secured creditor.

112 Diocl.-Max. C. 4.10.10.

113 Manigk 1941: 1258.

114 Kaser 1982: 211. See also Klingenberg 1992: 366, discussing the possible 'penal' element of forfeiture in relation to fiscal pledges.

115 Kaser 1982: 211.

116 The slaves were in all likelihood charged by way of *fiducia cum creditore*. In Cic., *Att.* 270.2 Cicero refers to them as Castricius's slaves ('*mancipiis Castricianis*'). Ioannatou 2006: 346–9.

117 Ioannatou 2006: 348, 395.

118 Cic., *Att.* 267.3.

119 Cic., *Att.* 270.2. Ioannatou 2006: 372.

This could, however, also work against the creditor. Cassius Dio reports how in the credit crisis which ravaged the Roman real estate market in 49–48 BC, creditors would not be satisfied with debtors giving up their charged real estate but rather insisted on receiving payment in bare silver. In early classical law forfeiture of the charged object was probably constructed as the result of a conditional *traditio pignoris causa* taking place by way of payment (*pro soluto*).[120] The debt was repaid by delivering another performance than initially agreed on, also when its value was lower than the original debt. If there was an undervalue, it would therefore have benefited the creditor to negotiate that in case of default he could sell the collateral, recover his claim from the proceeds, and take recourse against the other goods of the debtor for any remaining deficit. In all likelihood this was the main motivation for the creditor to insist on the *vendere licere* clause: to avoid the consequences of substituting the secured debt with an object worth less.[121] The surplus/deficit clause coupled with the licence to sell would allow lenders to take recourse for the shortfall against the debtor's other assets. Particularly for solvent debtors, this would be a strong incentive for avoiding deliberately defaulting under a secured loan in a depressed market.

Coupling of licence to sell and surplus/deficit clause

The fact that in practice a surplus/deficit clause was always coupled with a licence to sell can be explained by the fact that a deficit or surplus only manifests itself in a sale of the charged assets. The assumption, however, that the surplus/deficit clause has emerged simultaneously with the licence to sell has been opposed in modern literature: the argument is contested that the creditor sought to protect himself from a deficit through this clause. It would suggest that objects with an undervalue were used as collateral on a regular basis. This is considered to be unlikely: a sensible creditor would never accept that.[122] The appearance of a surplus/deficit clause in the epigraphic sources indicates, however, that in the first century AD parties did take into account the possibility of an undervalue. For this liability to pay the *reliquum*, third parties were made surety.[123] This shows that deficit clauses were not meaningless boilerplate, but that undervalue was a real concern. In Pomp. D. 13.7.6 pr.

[120] Manigk 1941: 1248–9; von Lübtow 1957: 314–37; Kaser 1982: 14, 18. See section 5.2.

[121] In the same sense for *pignus* and *fiducia*, Manigk 1941: 1256, 1257, 1260. See also Kunkel 1973: 153; Krämer 2007: 180; Hofstetter 1999: 228.

[122] Noordraven 1999: 247.

[123] See, e.g., Pap. D. 46.1.52 pr.

a case was submitted to (possibly) Sabinus and Atilicinus in which the value of real estate (pledged or transferred by fiduciary agreement) was at risk of falling sharply in the near future.[124] Like in present day secured lending, it must also have occurred in classical Rome that objects were found to have an undervalue at the time of execution. There may have been a variety of reasons for this: a decline in market price (e.g., Pomp. D. 13.7.6 pr.), an incorrect assessment by the creditor, damage or destruction of the pledged object (e.g., Pap. D. 46.1.52: collapsed building), or a compulsory sale that generates less than an ordinary one. Consequently, this undervalue does not need to exist, or does not need to be apparent, at the time of taking out the loan, but may have manifested itself later. In a text from the second century AD (Scaev. D. 46.1.63), it was expressly agreed that if the proceeds of the pledged assets would be less than the amount of the secured debt, the debtor would pay the difference to the creditor. There can be no doubt that creditors in classical Rome were aware of this risk and sought to safeguard themselves against it by means of a surplus/deficit clause.

It is obviously also possible that a surplus/deficit clause was included with the *mutual* intention of effectuating a balanced distribution of the enforcement proceeds which, without a clause agreed by the parties, would not occur by operation of law. In other words, the clause was intended to protect the creditor in case of an undervalue and the debtor in case of a surplus value. The parties wanted to create an exact match between the amount of the secured debt and the execution proceeds to which the creditor was entitled. In modern literature this is used as an argument against forfeiture. Certainly where surplus value was likely, creditors would never have agreed to a licence to sell as long as the alternative of a forfeiture pledge was available to them.[125] This representation is too simple. There will undoubtedly have been cases where a creditor with a great deal of bargaining power insisted on a forfeiture pledge, without the obligation to pay the *superfluum*. But there will also certainly have been cases where there was a more balanced distribution of bargaining power between the parties, resulting in a licence to sell linked to a surplus/deficit clause. Admittedly, the licence to sell did not imply an obligation to sell, so that the creditor still had the liberty not to sell. But if the creditor chose to sell, he was under a contractual obligation to restore the

[124] Hofstetter (1999: 229) rightly counters Noordraven, arguing that the parties at the time of granting of the security right do not yet know the value of the collateral at the time of sale.

[125] Noordraven 1999: 24; Wacke 1998: 184–5.

superfluum to the debtor. If by the first century AD a public auction had become the normal method of exercising recourse in *pignus* and *fiducia*,[126] the debtor would in most cases have been protected by a surplus/deficit clause.

Conclusion

The archive of the Sulpicii provides a fascinating portrait of the reality of Roman law. Nonetheless, this historical reality is, in regard to the execution of real security in the first century AD, not easily retrievable. Based on the sources available to us, one can only find ways to approach this reality. It can therefore not entirely be excluded that in the first century AD the creditor, in the event that the parties had agreed neither on a licence to sell nor on a forfeiture clause, was merely authorized to retain possession of the pledged goods. It is unlikely, however, that in the first century AD creditors such as those of the *Tabulae Pompeianae Sulpiciorum* would be satisfied with merely a right of retention. The most plausible interpretation of the pledge agreements in the archive of the Sulpicii is that the Roman pledge in the first century AD was still a forfeiture pledge. The creditor's ownership of the forfeited property would have enabled him to sell and transfer it to the highest bidder at auction. The hypothesis that in the first century AD, *pignus* was a forfeiture pledge is not refuted by the presence of contractual licences to sell in the epigraphic sources in the first century AD. The surplus/deficit clause provides the key for unlocking the meaning of this practice. Creditors would not be prepared to grant secured credit which would leave them exposed to the risk of an undervalue of the collateral. By auctioning the property such shortfall would manifest itself and the creditor could then hold the debtor liable for the deficit.[127] The debtor's contractual right to the surplus was a side effect of this. This whole arrangement was entirely optional for the creditor.[128] In the first century AD a public auction was the normal method of realising real security (*pignus* as well as *fiducia*). Therefore, particularly where a liquid market existed for the objects concerned (e.g., slaves, real estate, cloth, and wheat), in the majority of cases borrowers would receive any surplus proceeds.[129] In fact,

[126] See section 5.5. [127] See Verhagen 2011a: 40–5. Contra Noordraven 1999: 246–7.

[128] TPSulp 79: '*liceat... vendere*'.

[129] The archive of the Sulpicii contains documents referring to the auctioning of the following objects of security: cloth (TPSulp 83–4); land (TPSulp 88); slaves (TPSulp 90–2; TPSulp 85; TPSulp 87a).

one would then in actual practice already have a pledge similar to the one functioning in contemporary codifications: the secured creditor takes recourse against the collateral by means of a public auction, subject to the obligation to pay the debtor the surplus resulting from the execution sale. In transactional practices of the first century AD an equilibrium was reached between the interests of secured creditors and debtors that over centuries (and even millennia) proved to be extremely stable.[130]

5.5 Functions of Licence to Sell: Modalities of Sale

It is thought unlikely for the early Republic that there was a pledge enforceable by sale, because in those days the Roman economy was too underdeveloped to allow for recourse by means of a public auction.[131] From a later period (160–150 BC), however, we have Cato's *De agricultura* recommending that farmers sell olive oil, wine, and grain at auction and containing templates for such sales (the so-called *leges venditionis*). The *Tabulae Pompeianae Sulpiciorum* show that, in any case, a well-organized practice of public auctioning did exist in the first century AD, through which effective recourse could be taken against the charged objects.[132] In the first century AD the pledged property would in the event of default still be forfeited to the creditor. The ownership thus acquired by the creditor would enable him to sell the pledged property at auction (or otherwise). Given the popularity of auctions for selling property, also other than by way of execution, the right of pledge effectively had become a pledge enforceable by sale. A licence to sell could then have added value, where it was used to specify the modalities of sale. In TPSulp 79 one of the functions of the licence to sell may very well have been to enable the creditor to sell the pledged goods immediately upon the debtor's failure to repay the loan on the agreed date, without the need to observe a period of thirty days. In addition, in other respects a contractual licence to sell could be used to specify the modalities of an execution sale, such as the place and conditions of the auction.

[130] Verhagen 2011b. [131] Kaser 1982: 15.

[132] Noordraven 1999: 247; Lerouxel 2008: 189. On auctions (*auctiones*) in classical law and the role played by bankers, see Cerami and Petrucci 2010: 126–42. For legal aspects of auctions, see Ankum 1972. For a discussion of the documents relating to auctions in the TPSulp, see Costabile 1992; Noordraven 1999: 247–59; Romeo 2006; Petrucci 2008: 277–300; Lerouxel 2016: 259–67.

The public auction practice in the first century AD

Auctions were actually a frequently utilized method of sale in Rome, both 'voluntary' as well as 'involuntary' (execution) auctions.[133] In the Sulpicii archive we find quite a large number of documents relating to the auction of charged assets (slaves, cloth, and immovable property).[134] It may very well be the case that by the first century AD, public auction had already become the normal method of realizing real security (*pignus* as well as *fiducia*), particularly in the case of goods for which a liquid market existed (agricultural produce, slaves, real estate, and cattle). The relatively large number of auction announcements found in the archive of the Sulpicii is an indication that creditors often chose to order a public auction for objects pledged or transferred by way of *fiducia cum creditore*. This gave maximum publicity to execution sales, so that more potential buyers were reached, which would generally result in higher proceeds.[135] These auction proceeds would normally reflect the market value of the collateral: where a surplus/deficit clause had been agreed (as in TPSulp 79) this could also benefit debtors.[136] Selling at auction would also entail that a wide diversity of assets could be sold effectively, even where the secured creditor did not have particular knowledge of the market for the type of assets concerned.[137] We also know that there were many bankers in the Roman empire specializing in providing credit to bidders at auction (*argentarii*).[138] The Sulpicii may have belonged to this category, which would mean that enforcing security by way of auction would be familiar to them.[139] TPSulp 82 demonstrates, according to Camodeca, that the Sulpicii provided credit at auctions.[140] This is a receipt of the proceeds of a sale at an auction organized by C. Sulpicius Cinnamus, who, as such, typically acted as a banker who was professionally involved with auctions.[141]

[133] Cerami and Petrucci 2010: 127; Noordraven 1999: 247; Lerouxel 2008: 189. On the role of bankers in Roman auctions, see also Petrucci 2008.

[134] TPSulp 83–5, 87, 89, and 90–2.

[135] Lerouxel 2016: 260; Pellecchi 2018: 475.

[136] Lerouxel (2016: 261) also observes that auctions have a '*légitimité supérieure*' and prevent the creditor from colluding with a purchaser in selling the charged property at a relatively low price and then repurchasing the property at the same (or only marginally higher) price. Modern experiences show that by selling at auction, disputes between debtors and creditors are avoided and this reduces transaction costs (Lerouxel 2016: 261–2). It should be noted, however, that—in contrast with modern laws—selling *at auction* never became mandatory in classical Roman law.

[137] This is noted by Lerouxel (2016: 260), with reference to the Sulpicii. However, one would think that bankers in Puteoli would be well aware of the markets for the types of assets (grain and other foodstuffs, slaves, real estate, and precious metals) that they accepted as collateral.

[138] Andreau 1999: 38–9.

[139] Pellecchi 2018: 475.

[140] Camodeca 2003: 74, followed by Gröschler 1997: 62–6.

[141] Camodeca 1999: 188.

Proscriptio and *denuntiatio* in the Sulpicii archive

In the Sulpicii archive there are two groups of documents, all drawn up in the same format, relating to the auction of *res mancipi* which had been mancipated by way of *fiducia cum creditore*. The same template has obviously been used for all of these documents (although there are minor differences) and they are evidence of a well-settled standardized practice.[142] These *testationes* all record that a notice had been fixed to a column in the Sextian Portico of Augustus, stating that charged slaves or real estate would come up for sale on a certain date. The auctions themselves always took place on the forum before the Caesonian Chaldicium in Puteoli on market days (*nundinae*): Thursdays between 8 a.m. and 9 a.m.[143] The creditor on whose instruction the charged assets were auctioned apparently considered it important that it could later be proven that these announcements had taken place.

In the archive of the Sulpicii there is one document (a diptych/*testatio*) evidencing the *proscriptio* of the auction of *pledged* goods.[144]

TPSulp 83 (*scriptura interior*)
Tì(berio) Claudio C[aesare Aug(usto) V]
L(ucio) [A]ntistio Carminio Vetere co(n)s(ulibus)
VIII ìdus Sept(embres).
Putiolis in porticu Aug(usti) Sextiana
ìn parastatica libellus f«i»xus fuit, ìn quo scriptum erat ìd quod ìnfra scriptum est:
Purpuras laconicas reliquas,
quas L(ucius) Marius Agathemer
C(aio) Sulpicio Cinnamo pignorì
dedisse dicitur,
venib(unt) V ìdus Sept(embres) primas

Under the consuls Tiberius Claudius Caesar, for the fifth time,
and Lucius Antistius Carmius Vetus
on the eighth day before the Ides of September (6 September 51)
At Puteoli in the Sextian Portico of Augustus,

[142] Romeo 2006: 211; Wolf 2012: 111.

[143] According to Costabile (1992: 77), this would secure that the auction of charged property would take place at one of the busiest hours of the market day.

[144] Also, TPSulp 84 has an identical content and bears the same date as TPSulp 83. The only difference is that the name of the second consul is now Lucius Calventius (Camodeca 1999: 190).

> there has been fixed to a column a notice in which was written
> what appears below:
> The residual Laconian purple,
> which Lucius Marius Agathemer
> is said to have given as pledge to Gaius Sulpicius Cinnamus,
> will come up for sale on the fifth day before the next Ides of September
> (9 September 51)[145]

The fact that the announcements of auctions were so well documented are a strong indication that non-observance of the procedure could have legal consequences for the creditor.[146] The interval between *proscriptio* and auction is always thirty days,[147] which is the same term that is applicable to the *proscriptio* in collective execution proceedings.[148] It may very well be that the execution of assets charged by way of *fiducia cum creditore* or *pignus* was governed by the same customary rules as would apply to a general execution. The thirty-day term gave the debtor the opportunity to check whether the conditions for maximizing the proceeds of the sale were satisfied and possibly allowing more time to come to an arrangement with the creditor.[149]

Legal basis of duty to announce execution sale

Custom may have demanded the observance of certain formalities for the execution of charged assets, which guaranteed that the highest possible price would be realized and on the best possible terms.[150] These formalities were the announcement (*proscriptio*) of the sale to the 'spender crowd', accompanied by a notification (*denuntiatio*) of the intended sale to the debtor. It is not inconceivable that at the time of the Sulpicii, creditors were under a legal duty to observe these formalities. For an early witness of a *proscriptio* of the sale of pledged goods, see Servius in Ulp. D. 47.10.15.32, where he notes that someone who publicly announces that he will sell someone's property ('*pignus*

[145] Translation based (with some changes) on Jones 2006: 84.

[146] Noordraven 1999: 253. Romeo (2006: 211) observes that the *testationes* attest a procedure which has been formalized through custom, but in respect of which there is no lack of traces of recognition by jurisprudence (which is, however, from a much later period).

[147] Romeo 2006: 214. Although TPSulp 83 itself is dated 6 September AD 51, according to Camoda the *proscriptio* of this pledge started at 10 August AD 51. Apparently, Camodeca assumes that the thirty-day term, which is consistently applied in the archive to the *proscriptio* of the auctions of slaves transferred by way of *fiducia cum creditore*, also applied to *pignus*.

[148] According to Bertoldi (2012: 85) the execution of assets charged by way of *fiducia cum creditore* would take place in the same manner as general execution.

[149] Romeo 2006: 221. [150] Dernburg 1864: 134–5.

proscripserit venditurus') as if given in pledge, shall be liable for defamation with the *actio iniuriarum*.[151] The *lex portorii provinciae Asiae* imposes a grace period of thirty days, which appears to presuppose that here also *proscriptio* and *denuntiatio* were required. This tax creditor would only then be free to sell the forfeited property as the owner and then retain the proceeds.[152] For *pignus* there are several imperial constitutions in which the creditor's duties in respect of *proscriptio* and *denuntiatio* are said to derive from the *bona fides*:[153] *proscriptio* and *denuntiatio* together constitute the *solemniter vendere* of Alexander Severus's constitution of 225 AD on the execution of charged property.[154] But these constitutions are from a much later period. At the time of the Sulpicii the *formula* of the debtor's *actio pigneraticia (directa)* would not yet have contained the words *ex fide bona*.[155] There are, however, jurists' opinions which, relatively early, assume a duty of care for the creditor in the exercise of his right of sale. Thus, in Pomp. D. 13.7.6 pr. Atilicinus assumes that a creditor was under a legal duty of care, which entailed that sometimes he was obliged to sell. Although this view is rejected by Pomponius, it shows that it is not inconceivable that already in the first century AD a creditor did have a duty of care, which also entailed that he was legally bound to announce a sale of pledged property.[156]

TPSulp 79: 'time is of the essence' and other modalities of sale

The function of the licence to sell in TPSulp 79 may very well have been to avoid the observance of a thirty-day term for the announcement of an execution sale.[157] The loan agreement between the Sulpicii bank and Lucius Marius Iucundus (TPSulp 53), which was secured by TPSulp 79, says nothing about when the borrowed sum must be repaid. However, because TPSulp 53 is dated 13 March 40 and TPSulp 79 provides that the lender shall have the right to sell the pledged goods if the borrower has not repaid the loan on 15 May 40, we know that the term of the loan was two months. The secured loan transaction between the Sulpicii and Iucundus was entered into in mid-March, that

[151] Bertoldi (2012: 15 n 30) lists D. 47.10.15.32 as being interpolated and concerning *fiducia*. Noordraven does not mention this text.

[152] Klingenberg 1992: 361. [153] Alex. C. 8.27.4; Diocl.-Max. C. 8.27.9.

[154] Alex. C. 8.27.4. Romeo 2006: 222. [155] See pp. 209–10.

[156] Pomp. D. 13.7.6 pr. could, however, originally have been concerned with *fiducia* (section 5.6). See also Iav. D. 47.2.74 reproduced in section 5.6: premature execution leads to liability for theft.

[157] This seems to have been the case in the Hellenistic part of the Roman empire. In Cic., *Fam.* 13.56 Cicero describes how Philocles, who had granted security over land in Caria (Asia Minor), had already defaulted in the repayment of the loan(s), but was still in a position to redeem the security.

is more than two months before the first ships of the grain fleet from Alexandria would arrive in Puteoli at the beginning of June.[158] If Iucundus failed to repay the loan on the agreed date, there might still be time for the Sulpicii bank to sell the grain at a good price before the Alexandrian grain fleet arrived and prices would drop.[159] Time was of the essence. In Scaev. D. 46.1.63, it was agreed that the creditor would have the right to sell the pledged jewellery within a certain time if the loan were not repaid on first demand. The purpose of this clause may have been a waiver of the creditor's duty to notify the debtor of an intended execution sale and to announce the auction thirty days in advance. The purpose of the licence to sell in TPSulp 79 may have been exactly the same.

In TPSulp 79 a function of the licence to sell may, therefore, very well have been to enable the creditor to sell the pledged goods immediately upon the debtor's failure to repay the loan on the agreed date, without the need to observe a period of thirty days. A contractual licence to sell would also have added value if it was used to specify other modalities of sale. For instance, Pomp. D. 13.7.8.3 concerns a secured loan for three years, which was repayable in three annual instalments. The lender was granted a right of pledge 'subject to a pact that I shall have power to sell if the money is not paid, each part on its proper day'.[160] The purpose of this licence to sell is to leave no doubt that if the debtor failed to pay the first or second instalment, the creditor was already authorized to sell. These clauses were all for the benefit of creditors. There must, however, also have been debtors with substantial bargaining power. Another text by Pomponius (D. 13.7.5) discusses a *pactum de vendendo*, providing that sale by the creditor shall only take place subject to certain conditions (e.g., price, and location). In the *Formula Baetica* the creditor was expressly given the liberty to sell only some of the slaves who had been charged. The pledge agreement between Gaius Sulpicius Cinnamus and Lucius Marius Agathemer, which gave rise to the auction of 'residual Laconian purple' ('*purpuras laconicas reliquas*'), may have contained a similar clause.[161] The only specification of the manner of sale itself in TPSulp 79 is that it shall take place (literally translated) 'by an auctioneer subject to the condition' ('*sub [p]raecone de condicione*'). This means that, in any case, the creditor was

[158] Jones 2006: 101. [159] Camodeca 1999: 183; Jones 2006: 101; Krämer 2007: 184.

[160] '*Si annua bima trima die triginta stipulatus acceperim pignus pactusque sim, ut nisi sua quaque die pecunia soluta esset, vendere eam mihi liceret*'.

[161] TPSulp 83 (Camodeca 1999: 189). See also Pomp. D. 13.7.8.1 ('*reliqua mancipia*'). An interesting alternative interpretation is given by Jones (2006: 85), who points out that Agathemer may have been a 'remnant dealer' (*centonarius*), who specialized in trading in off-cuts which were left over when new garments were cut out from lengths of cloth or which were saved from worn-out clothes.

authorized to sell at auction, subject to one or more auctioning conditions whose content have not been transmitted. This could be a reference to conditions governing the sale of pledges at auction generally, it may also have concerned the terms of payment of the purchase price.[162]

5.6 Forfeiture in the Second Century AD

From the second century AD we have some Digest texts, with a Hellenistic background, from which it can be derived that in this period forfeiture was still the default rule. Moreover, in the western part of the Roman empire it continued to be possible to agree, whether or not in the form of a conditional sale or *datio in solutum*, that in the event of default, ownership of the pledged object would transfer to the creditor.[163] One cannot entirely exclude the possibility that in this period the creditor would, in the absence of a *pactum de vendendo* or *lex commissoria*, merely have a right of retention. But this is as implausible for the second century AD as it is for the time of the Sulpicii. The most plausible interpretation is that in the second century AD the creditor would also, in the absence of an express *pactum de vendendo*, have a right to sell the pledged assets. A licence to sell would either have been an implied condition in every *conventio pignoris* or the pledged object must still have forfeited to the creditor. In this section we will focus on forfeiture and its hypothetical alternative (retention), and in the next section on the implied licence to sell and surplus and deficit. It is impossible, however, to determine when exactly in the second century AD the Roman pledge ceased to be a forfeiture pledge and became a pledge enforceable by sale.

Iav. D. 47.2.74: against forfeiture (I)?

From Julian's teacher Iavolenus there is an opinion in which this jurist says that when the creditor sells the pledged property without an agreement to sell, he shall be liable to the debtor with the *actio furti*.

[162] Camodeca tentatively reads '*de condicione pig[nor]is*' (TPSulp 79). Wolf's edition reads, '*DE CONDICIONE*... *vendere*', (TPN 69). In TPSulp 90, 91, and 92 '*sub praecone*' is followed by '*pecunia praesenti*'.

[163] Sections 11.3 and 11.4.

> **D. 47.2.74.** *Iavolenus libro quinto decimo ex Cassio.* Si is, qui pignori rem accepit, cum de vendendo pignore nihil convenisset, vendidit, aut ante, quam dies venditionis veniret pecunia non soluta, id fecit: furti se obligat.
>
> If he, who has accepted a thing as pledge, when nothing has been agreed about the sale of the pledge, sells, or, the money remaining unpaid, does so before the time of sale, he then makes himself liable for theft.

The first part of this opinion, if authentic, is difficult to reconcile with the hypothesis that still, in the second century AD, and also in the absence of a *lex commissoria*, the creditor became the owner of the pledged property and as such would have acquired a power of sale.[164] For how can an owner be liable for the theft of his own property?[165] Not much later, Pomponius says in D. 13.7.5 that a sale by the creditor only constitutes a *furtum* when the parties have agreed that no sale shall take place.[166] How can this difference be explained? Iav. D. 47.2.74 could represent a transitory stage in which *pignus* was no longer a forfeiture pledge and the creditor would have needed either a *lex commissoria* or a *pactum de vendendo* in order to take recourse against the pledged property.[167] Perhaps it is in this transitory stage that, where neither forfeiture nor sale had been expressly agreed, the creditor merely had a right of retention. This transitory stage, if it existed at all, must have been relatively short, for it follows from Pomp. D. 13.7.5 that without an express contractual selling restriction, the creditor was impliedly authorized to sell the property.[168]

Iav. D. 47.2.74 could possibly also be read as saying that also in the absence of a *pactum de vendendo*, the creditor could sell the pledged property by way of execution, but only after first having notified the debtor.[169] From the late classical period there is a text from Ulpian which says that when there is an agreement precluding the creditor from selling the pledged property, the selling creditor is not liable (for theft) 'where the debtor has been given three warnings to pay and has failed to respond'.[170] This part of the fragment has been suspected of being an interpolation. Nevertheless, as Krämer has argued, it may represent a 'historical nucleus' in that where no express licence to sell

[164] Manigk 1941: 1265.

[165] This is, however, not uncommon: also, where a debtor/owner would secretly take away from the creditor property pledged by way of possessory pledge this would constitute *furtum*. See Ankum 1979–1980.

[166] Liebs (1997:147) dates Pomponius's *Ex Sabino* (from which D. 13.7.5 is taken) after the codification of the *Edictum perpetuum* (131 AD) and before Julian's *Digestorum libri XC* (153–160 AD).

[167] See Kaser 1982: 229; Schanbacher 2002a: 648; Krämer 2007: 184; Perani 2021: 71–2.

[168] In section 5.7 we will look closer at the implied licence to sell.

[169] See section 5.5.

[170] Ulp. D. 13.7.4.

has been agreed, the creditor must warn the debtor that his failure to pay will result in an execution sale.[171] In other words, the first part of Iav. D. 47.2.74 could have been concerned with cases where the creditor sold the pledged property without first having warned the debtor.[172] In any case, Iav. D. 47.2.74 is an isolated text from which no firm conclusions on the nature of *pignus* as a forfeiture pledge in the second century AD can be drawn.

Pomp. D. 13.7.6 pr.: against forfeiture (II)?

There is an opinion by Pomponius which is regarded in modern literature (Noordraven) as evidence against the existence of a forfeiture pledge in classical law. Lenel and many other authors following in his footsteps hold the view that this text relates to *fiducia*.[173] The first sentence of this text can probably be attributed to *Sabinus*, which would make Lenel's interpretation consistent with the assumption that in the time of Sabinus (first century AD) *res mancipi* normally served as collateral security by way of a *fiducia cum creditore*.[174] By contrast, Noordraven takes the view that it here entails a *pignus* fragment. After all, in *fiducia*, the creditor, as owner, already had the power to dispose and, therefore, the licence to sell would not have been made in his interest, especially not if there was a surplus value.[175] The following will show that I do not consider this argument to be valid. It might nonetheless be appropriate to say that Pomponius's opinion, in substance, applies to both *fiducia* and *pignus*.[176]

> **D. 13.7.6 pr.** *Pomponius libro trigensimo quinto ad Sabinum.* Quamvis convenerit, ut fundum pigneraticium tibi vendere liceret, nihilo magis cogendus es vendere, licet solvendo non sit is qui pignus dederit, quia tua causa id caveatur. Sed Atilicinus ex causa cogendum creditorem esse ad vendendum dicit: quid enim si multo minus sit quod debeatur et hodie pluris venire possit pignus quam postea? Melius autem est dici eum, qui dederit pignus,

[171] Krämer 2007: 183–4 n 51. Krämer also cites PS 2.5.1: '*Creditor si simpliciter sibi pignus depositum distrahere velit, ter ante denuntiare debitor suo debet*'. See also section 5.5 on TPSulp 79 and the executing creditor's duty to observe a thirty-day term for the announcement of an execution sale.

[172] See also Paul. (Arist.) D. 20.3.3 (section 5.7): only in case of a deliberate omission by the parties did the creditor not have a power of sale.

[173] Lenel 1889, vol. II: 146. For an elaborate analysis of Pomp. D. 13.7.6 pr. see Perani 2021: 269–87. See also the references in Krämer 2007: 186 n 61.

[174] See also Krämer 2007: 188. [175] Noordraven 1999: 24.

[176] See also Kaser 1982: 212 n 104; Hofstetter 1999: 227. See also Perani 2021: 275–8 (*pignus*).

> posse vendere et accepta pecunia solvere id quod debeatur, ita tamen, ut creditor necessitatem habeat ostendere rem pigneratam, si mobilis sit, prius idonea cautela a debitore pro indemnitate ei praestanda. Invitum enim creditorem cogi vendere satis inhumanum est.
>
> Even though there is an agreement that you may sell an estate which has been pledged, that does not make it any more possible to compel you to sell, even if the grantor of the pledge is insolvent. For the term is inserted in your own interest. Yet Atilicinus says that on special facts the creditor can be compelled to a sale. For what if the debt is much less, and the pledge can now be sold for more than later on? It is better to say that he who granted the pledge can sell and use the money he gets to pay off the debt to the extent that the creditor should be compelled to display the thing if it is movable, subject to the debtor's first giving good security for indemnifying him. For making the creditor sell against this will is quite inhuman.

Pomponius shares (what presumably is) Sabinus's opinion that a licence to sell does not entail an obligation to sell, not even where the debtor is insolvent. Atilicinus, on the other hand, holds the view that in certain circumstances an obligation to sell does exist, for example, if the value of the pledged property is much higher than the amount of the debt, and it can be sold for more now than in the future. In this case, too, Pomponius still does not want to assume an obligation to sell but believes it to be a better solution that in the case that the surplus value is at risk of turning into an undervalue (for which the debtor would be liable), the creditor should co-operate in a sale by the debtor. The creditor is hereby held to show the pledged (movable) property to potential buyers. The debtor is then, however, obliged to provide alternative security in case he fails to use the sale proceeds for repaying his debt to the creditor.[177,178]

On the basis of a combination of three premises, Noordraven infers from D. 13.7.6 pr. that, in the absence of a licence to sell, the creditor merely had a right of retention. These premises are:

[177] In the same sense Kaser 1982: 77. According to Hofstetter (1999: 231–2), this refers instead to damage to an object which occurs while the potential buyer has taken away the object. This would then also explain why Pomponius only assumes an 'obligation to show' for movable goods. However, could this rather not be explained by the fact that in the high classical and late classical period there was often a possessory pledge for movable goods and a *hypotheca* for immovable property?

[178] In Marci. D. 20.6.8.10, it is recommended that (before the actual sale) the creditor shall obtain an undertaking (*cautio*) from the purchaser that he shall pay the purchase price (up to the amount of the secured debt) to the creditor.

1. There was a surplus value (s): the value (v) of the property was higher than the amount of the debt (d) ($v > d$, where $s = v - d$).[179]
2. A licence to sell is according to Pomponius intended to benefit the creditor.
3. A licence to sell would *not* benefit the creditor if, in the *absence* of such licence, the pledged property would be forfeited to him.

In case charged property with surplus value would be forfeited, the creditor would gain: a claim worth d would then be substituted with an object worth v (with $v > d$).[180] Where, on the other hand, the creditor would exercise his licence to sell, as a result of the surplus/deficit clause he would only get d. In other words, under a licence to sell the creditor would be worse off (d) than under a forfeiture pledge (v). In case of a sale, the creditor would miss out on the opportunity to pocket the surplus proceeds, so that the licence to sell would *not* benefit him. This means, according to Noordraven, that the text assumes that in the absence of a licence to sell, the property is *not* transferred to the creditor by way of forfeiture. For only then would the creditor benefit from the licence to sell: he would get d rather than nothing at all. Therefore only the possibility of a right of retention remains.[181] This conclusion is wrong, because one assumption on which it based is wrong: the assumption that the exercise of the licence to sell *must* benefit the creditor. Sabinus meant when he referred to '*quia tua causa id caveatur*' no more than that a licence to sell does not entail an *obligation* to sell, precisely because the creditor has made this clause in his own interest. What he does *not* express or imply is that exercising this power always *leads* or *must lead* to a beneficial outcome for the creditor. This is for the creditor himself to assess at the time of accepting the pledge, and for the future to tell when the property is sold.

Neither Sabinus nor Pomponius have expressed direct views as to what the legal consequence was when the creditor chose not to exercise the licence to sell—retention or forfeiture. Could it be argued that apparently in Pomp. D. 13.7.6 pr. the debtor's failure to repay the secured debt did not result in forfeiture, because Pomponius recommends that the debtor sells the property himself? This presupposes that the debtor owns the pledged property, which would seem to be irreconcilable with forfeiture to the creditor. However, if

[179] Variables v, d, and s are all positive values. The (simple) arithmetic is mine.

[180] $v = d + s$, because $s = v - d$.

[181] Noordraven 1999: 22–4. See now also Perani 2021: 176–8. Other analyses of Pomp. D. 13.7.6 pr., which are more consistent with my own interpretation, can be found in Hofstetter 1999: 226–32 and Krämer 2007: 186–8. See also Kaser 1982: 77.

Pomponius's opinion were on *fiducia cum creditore*, which is a distinct possibility, then the same problem would arise. For this problem *Pauli Sententiae* 2.13.3 offers a solution: (i) the debtor sells the object to a third party; (ii) the debtor pays the creditor from the purchase price; (iii) the creditor reconveys (by way of *mancipatio*) the object to the debtor; and (iv) the debtor mancipates the object to the third party/buyer. It can certainly not be ruled out that Pomponius had this construction in mind, either for *fiducia* or for *pignus* (with *traditiones* rather than *mancipationes*). The most plausible interpretation in the light of the foregoing is that the creditor need not accept that in case of default the object of security is permanently forfeited to him, without the possibility of holding the debtor liable for a deficit (*reliquum*). If there were an undervalue at the time of default, the creditor could then proceed to sell: a deficit in the proceeds of the execution was therewith established and the creditor could recover the deficit from the other goods of the debtor.[182] This was the aim of the *vendere liceret* clause.[183]

Pledge as lien

What would have been the creditor's position in the absence of a *pactum de vendendo* or a *lex commissoria* in the second century AD? A hypothetical alternative to the forfeiture pledge would be a pledge that gives the creditor a mere right of retention, combined with a *preferential right* in respect of the distribution of the proceeds of the execution. According to Kaser, this hypothesis is refuted by the reality under Roman enforcement law: in the *venditio bonorum* (which was the prevailing method of collective execution in the second century AD) there was no room for a preferential ranking of the pledge creditor.[184] In some cases, however, the creditor with a pledge-lien could have had a *de facto* preference, in particular where there was a substantial surplus value in the pledged goods. It would then be economically sensible for the *bonorum emptor* to pay the pledge creditor the amount of the secured debt, so that the pledged goods could be included in the *venditio bonorum*. In D. 13.7.8.1, Pomponius deals with a case where a number of slaves were

[182] Apparently, the value of the goods was rather volatile: a sharp decrease in prices was imminent.

[183] In the same sense Hofstetter 1999: 226; Krämer 2007: 187. From another opinion by Pomponius it appears that in the second century AD the debtor would remain liable for the deficit by operation of law (Paul. (Pomp.) D. 20.5.9.1). However, such a deficit could only be proven when the pledged property was actually sold.

[184] Kaser 1982: 14.

pledged and the creditor had sold some at given prices and expressly undertaken to be liable for their eviction. Pomponius holds that even when the secured debt could be satisfied from the proceeds of the sale, the creditor could detain the other slaves until the debtor had undertaken to indemnify him against his liability under his promise against eviction. This shows that a right of retention was regarded as a pressure tool by the Roman jurists (although only where the right of pledge itself had ceased to exist).[185] When a *pactum antichreticum* had been agreed, the creditor would also be entitled to apply the (civil or natural) fruits of the pledged property for amortisation of principal and payment of interest.[186] From a later period, we have an example of antichretic rights which would only accrue to the creditor on default.[187] The value of the fruits gathered by the creditor would then be deducted from the secured debt.[188]

Therefore, it is not inconceivable that a pledge-lien could have worked in certain cases where the parties failed to agree a *pactum de vendendo* or a *lex commissoria*. Such a pledge-lien would not, however, have complied with one of the main prerequisites for an effective law of real security. It would not have enabled a secured creditor to take immediate recourse outside (often long-winded) collective execution proceedings.[189] Moreover, an antichretic pledge would also not have benefited the creditor in cases where the pledged goods could not be used without consuming them (e.g. foodstuffs in TPSulp 51 and 52), or did not produce fruits which could reduce the amount due under the loan or serve as interest (e.g., precious metals). The only viable alternative to a forfeiture pledge would be a pledge enforceable by sale, also where no express licence to sell had been agreed.[190]

Forfeiture in the Eastern empire

In the eastern provinces of the Roman empire, forfeiture continued to be common in the second century AD, as two opinions by the jurist Q. Cervidius Scaevola illustrate.[191] In D. 32.101 pr., Scaevola discusses a case where

[185] This is also attested by the occasional use of clauses precluding the creditor from selling the pledged property (e.g., Pomp. D. 13.7.5) and from other texts in which the creditor is granted a right of retention as a 'supplement' to his right of pledge, such as Pomp. D. 13.7.8 pr. (right of retention for necessary expenses (e.g., medical expenses for pledged slaves or repair of pledged buildings) made by creditor); C. 8.26.1.2 (Gordian lien).

[186] Section 8.4. [187] Pap. D. 20.1.1.3. [188] Ulp. D. 36.4.5.21. See Bobbink 2021: 28–30.

[189] pp. 382–3. [190] Kaser 1982: 21–2. See section 5.7.

[191] For example, P.Oxy. XVII 2134, 21 (Oxyrhynchus, 170 AD). Mauer 2022: 70–1. According to Schanbacher (2002a: 649–50, 653–7) the express forfeiture clause even prevailed in the third to fourth centuries AD, until it was prohibited by Constantine.

someone left a number of plots of land (*praedia*) situated in Syria to his native town. In a codicil, he referred to 'all the places which I possess in Syria with all the cattle, slaves, fruits, stores, and equipment that are in them' (original in Greek). The question was raised whether this legacy also covered plots of land which had been pledged to the testator. Scaevola's answer was that that would not be the case, 'provided that they had not been included in his patrimony, which generally happens when the debtor fails to pay'.[192] Therefore, pledged property which *had* forfeited to the creditor would be part of the legacy. This can hardly be interpreted otherwise than that—at least in second-century AD Syria—forfeiture of pledged property was still common.

In another opinion by Scaevola (D. 18.1.81 pr.), Titius had borrowed money against interest. In order to secure the loan, he had pledged plots of land (*praedia*) and requested Lucius to stand as surety (*fideiussor*). Titius promised Lucius that he would 'liberate' him within three years, presumably by repaying the secured debt or offering alternative security to the lender. It was also agreed between Titius and Lucius that if Titius failed to liberate him, and Lucius would have to pay the secured debt to the lender, the pledged assets should then be considered to have been sold to Lucius ('*empta haberet... praedia*'). According to Scaevola, a valid conditional sale agreement exists, unless the parties actually intended to establish a pledge in favour of Lucius. Such a pledge would have been a forfeiture pledge, possibly of Greek-Hellenistic origin.[193] The conditional sale is treated here as an alternative to pledge: upon the debtor's failure to discharge the surety, the latter would become the owner of the land formerly pledged to the creditor, pursuant to either a conditional sale *or* a forfeiture pledge. The continuing existence of the forfeiture pledge is confirmed in jurists' opinions (Scaevola) rendered as a matter of Roman law.[194] These opinions are rendered in a Hellenistic context, but they could be an indication that also in the Roman West forfeiture continued to be the rule where no licence to sell had been agreed.

5.7 From Substitution to Security

There can be no doubt that in the second century AD, express licences to sell, which were coupled with a surplus/deficit clause, were still widely used. Less

[192] On D. 32.101 pr., see Mauer 2022: 70–1.

[193] For an elaborate analysis of the Greek-Hellenistic background of this 'forfeiture arrangement with purchase fiction', see Schanbacher 2002b. See also Kaser (1982: 74 n 91), who does not mention the Greek-Hellenistic background of the pledge.

[194] A similar text by Ulpian is D. 32.68 pr. Bertoldi mentions it as one of the texts that were identified by Lenel as concerning *fiducia*. Neither Noordraven 1999 nor Burdese 1949 mention D. 32.68 pr.

certain, but still plausible, is that in this period the creditor was, in the absence of an express licence to sell, also impliedly authorized to sell the pledged property (although perhaps still based on forfeiture).[195] It is only from the late classical period that the transmitted legal sources unequivocally indicate that the creditor is entitled by operation of law to sell pledged objects and that the creditor is obliged by operation of law to pay the *superfluum* to the debtor. There are, however, also jurists' opinions already from the second century AD from which it could be derived that the creditor may have become obliged by law to pay the surplus to the debtor. In particular, the writings of Pomponius suggest that this was the case.[196] This same jurist certainly makes clear that the debtor would be liable for any deficit remaining after the sale of pledged assets, and would be liable also in the absence of a clause to that effect. The most plausible interpretation is that in the course of the second century AD, the right of pledge evolved into a true security interest, with the creditor having the right to sell the pledged objects and to take recourse against their proceeds for the amount of the secured debt: nothing more, nothing less. Thus, already in the second century AD, an equilibrium may have been reached by *operation of law* in which the interests of creditors and debtors were more or less balanced.

From forfeiture to sale

Finley is one of the few historians of the ancient economy who has fully recognized the importance of real security.[197] He even devoted a whole book to real security on land in classical Athens. In its preface he wrote: 'since security is the external link between land, the basic form of wealth in the Greek economy, and credit, a full examination of this bond appeared essential as a prelude to the larger work on business practices'.[198] In respect of the evolution from forfeiture to sale Finley observed:

> In its early form, security is always substitution, a forfeit. X owes Y something, an object, money, a performance, which he does not render, and Y accepts a substitute—land for money—in full satisfaction of X's obligation to him. Athenian security practice remained on that level right down to the

195 Manigk 1941: 1254, 1259; Kaser 1982: 12–7.
196 Kaser 1982: 75-8. Noordraven 1999: 247.
197 But fortunately not the only one: see recently in particular Lerouxel 2016. See also Terpstra 2008.
198 Finley 1952: vii. See also Schulz 1951: 405.

> Roman conquest, and perhaps for centuries thereafter. Occasional exceptions were made when the two parties had special reasons for introducing them, but the original conception continued unbroken. Collateral security involves economic thinking of quite another order. The security now becomes a guarantee of payment, not a substitute; default entails not simple forfeit but compulsory sale and a division of the proceeds according to the respective monetary values of the debt and the property. Between substitution and collateral there lies a profound economic transformation.[199]

According to Finley, the cause of this 'profound economic transformation' lies outside the law of security and has everything to do with the growing importance of credit. Credit providers are not interested in obtaining ownership of the charged object as such: they want to liquidate it as soon as possible, in order to be able to take recourse against the proceeds and satisfy their claims. At the same time, debtors wish to lay their hands on the surplus value of the collateral they provided. In a monetary economy the enforcement of a pledge by way of sale achieves a much more finely tuned method of execution than forfeiture.[200] This method was already comprised in transactional practices of the first century AD and may have been provided for by Roman law itself in the second century AD.[201]

The sale of pledged assets did not, however, always yield economically optimal results, as is attested by Plinius the Younger. In a letter to Calvisius Rufus (written 97–102 AD), Plinius asks for advice on the purchase of an agricultural estate adjoining one of his own estates. After listing a number of advantages (e.g., economy of scale) and disadvantages (e.g., no spread of risk), Plinius comes to (what he himself calls) his main point. 'The last owner, on more than one occasion, sold up the tenants' possessions, so that he temporarily reduced their arrears but weakened their resources for the future, and consequently their debts mounted up again.'[202] This passage illustrates that the Romans realized that an eagerness to sell the tenant's pledged objects can be a bad long-term economic strategy. The secured debt is temporarily reduced, but so is the tenant's earning capacity and his solvency in the future.

[199] Finley 1953: 266. [200] Manigk 1916: 355.

[201] Also, in the late Republic, pledges were enforced through execution sale, as Servius attests in Ulp. D. 47.10.15.32. A 'compulsory sale' was only provided for in the imperial constitutions of the third century AD (Alex. C. 8.34.1) and even by this time, alternative execution methods were still available (e.g., conditional sale to creditor against market value: Marci. D. 20.1.16.9). See chapter 11.

[202] Plin., *Ep.* 3.19.6, LCL 55: 229–31. Pliny himself granted remissions to tenants who were unable to pay the rent and introduced a sharecrop-arrangement for tenants who were still in arrears after five years. See Broekaert and Zuiderhoek 2020:102 n 7 (with reference to Plin., *Ep.* 9.37).

Certainly in times of economic troubles, scarcity of tenants, and diminishing returns from land, Plinius considers it to be a better strategy to ensure that tenants continue to be able to work the land and even to provide them with the means to do so (give them a 'good type of slave'). The sale of pledged assets may also fail to yield economically optimal results in times of high inflation or depressed markets.[203]

Legal basis of creditor's power of sale: authorization by debtor

In the course of the second century AD, the legal basis for the creditor's ability to transfer the pledged objects to a purchaser after an execution sale changed.[204] We have seen that this basis was originally the creditor's ownership after forfeiture had taken place.[205] In the second half of the second century AD this no longer appears to have been the case, certainly not where a licence to sell had been expressly agreed. Julian says in D. 18.1.39 pr. that where the debtor repurchases the pledged property from the creditor, he is a purchaser of his own property. In Julian's case, the debtor must have failed to repay the secured debt, which triggered the creditor's power of sale. This would seem to indicate that in Julian's time a power of sale was no longer based upon forfeiture: had this been the case then the debtor would have purchased the *creditor's* property.[206] A main witness of such an ownership-independent power of sale is Gai. *Inst.* 2.64.

> **Gai. *Inst.* 2.64.** item creditor *pignus* ex pactione (alienare potest), quamvis eius ea res non sit. sed hoc forsitan ideo videatur fieri, quod voluntate debitoris intellegitur pignus alienari, qui olim pactus est, ut liceret creditori pignus vendere, si pecunia non solvatur.
>
> Again a creditor has the power to alienate a pledge pursuant to agreement, although the thing is not his. But here perhaps this happens, because it is understood that the pledge is alienated with the debtor's will, who has previously agreed that the creditor shall be authorized to sell the pledge if the money is not paid.

[203] See sections 11.3–11.5.

[204] Perani 2021 was published too late to be taken into account other than incidentally.

[205] Section 5.3.

[206] Flor. D. 13.7.35.1 (ownership remains with debtor); Pap. D. 13.7.40 pr. (debtor cannot buy his own property from creditor); Paul. (Jul.) D. 47.2.67 pr. (creditor cannot institute the *actio furti* as owner).

Gaius mentions the transfer of the pledged object by the creditor pursuant to a contractual licence to sell as an example of a situation where someone other than the owner can alienate property. This jurist somewhat hesitantly suggests that the transfer of ownership might perhaps be based on the owner's consent. Gaius's contemporary Scaevola expresses no doubts at all. Where it has been agreed that upon failure to pay the creditor shall be authorized to sell ('*convenerit, nisi pecuniam solvisses, licere ex pacto pignus vendere*'), the creditor can sell the property even when later the actual sale takes place against the debtor's will. The reason is that 'if you have not paid the money, you are then treated as having acquiesced in the sale at the time when you entered into the contract' ('*iam enim illo in tempore, quo contrahebas, videri concessisse venditioni, si pecuniam non intulisses*').[207]

According to Kaser, the idea that an owner can, at the time of granting the pledge, conditionally authorize someone else to transfer ownership demonstrates advanced legal thinking, which can only be reached in a legal system's mature state.[208] My view is that this idea is more associated with a transitory state. Originally, the creditor's power of sale was based upon forfeiture, then on the debtor's consent (Gai. *Inst.* 2.64; Scaev. D. 44.3.14.5), and finally upon a power of sale which is an attribute of the right of pledge itself (Ulp. D. 13.7.4).[209] The 'fundamental detachment' of the *Verkaufspfand* (sale) from the *Verfallpfand* (forfeiture), which took place in the second century AD, is specifically Roman. In Greek-Hellenistic laws, the licence to sell would always remain an ancillary agreement to the forfeiture pledge.[210]

Licence to sell

There is evidence from the second century AD, as we shall see later in this section, that the creditor's power of sale did not have to be expressly agreed. There are, however, many legal opinions from this period which were seemingly rendered on the assumption that a *pactum de vendendo* had been expressly agreed. From the early second century AD, here is an opinion by Aristo, which was recorded by Paul.

[207] Scaev. D. 44.3.14.5. See also Ulp. D. 41.1.46 and Paul. D. 20.6.10.1.

[208] Kaser 1982: 72. See now Perani 2021: 225–52.

[209] See section 11.4.

[210] Manigk 1941: 1269. Also Taubenschlag 1955: 279.

> **D. 20.3.3.** *Paulus libro tertio quaestionum.* Aristo Neratio Prisco scripsit:... Denique si antiquior creditor de pignore vendendo cum debitore pactum interposuit, posterior autem creditor de distrahendo omisit non per oblivionem, sed cum hoc ageretur, ne posset vendere, videamus, an dici possit huc usque transire ad eum ius prioris, ut distrahere *pignus* huic liceat. Quod admittendum existimo: saepe enim quod quis ex sua persona non habet, hoc per extraneum habere potest.
>
> Writing to Neratius Priscus, Aristo said:... Further, if the first creditor made an agreement with the debtor that the pledged property might be sold, and the second creditor failed to agree on sale, not because he forgot but because it was intended that he could not sell, we must see whether the right of the first passes to him, so that he can sell. I think he can. It often happens that a person can acquire via a stranger something which he does not have in right of his own person.

In the second secured loan discussed by Aristo, a *pactum de vendendo* was deliberately omitted because it was the parties' intention that the second creditor should not have a power of sale. Aristo's opinion could be interpreted as saying that where the parties simply forgot to include an express licence to sell, it could still be implied in the pledge agreement. This is also what Pomponius and other jurists after him hold: the parties' articulated intention that the creditor shall not be authorized to sell must be respected as a matter of law. But where no such intention existed, the creditor does have the right to sell the pledged property upon default.

In a legal opinion on the valuation of a share in a jointly owned farm, which (the share) had been pledged by one of the co-owners, Julian reportedly said that 'the arbitrator appointed to divide common property should reduce the valuation of the share in view of the fact that the creditor is able to sell it under the pact' ('*quod ex pacto vendere eam rem creditor potest*').[211] In another opinion, however, Julian routinely speaks of the sale (with an *in diem addictio*) of pledged property without mentioning a *pactum de vendendo*.[212] This could indicate that a licence to sell was so common that it was deemed to be agreed. After all, in Julian's time even the granting of a right of pledge itself was in certain cases presumed to have taken place impliedly (*invecta et illata*).[213] A particularly relevant opinion is D. 13.7.8.4, taken from book 35 of

[211] Ulp. D. 10.3.6.8.
[212] So Ulp. (Jul.) D. 13.7.13 pr. See also, e.g., Scaev. D. 36.1.80.15 and Scaev. D. 46.1.62.
[213] Nerat. D. 20.2.4 pr.

Pomponius's commentary on Sabinus. The first sentence says that 'a *pactum de vendendo pignore* should be framed *in rem* so as to reach everyone'.[214] This sentence probably reflects the opinion of Sabinus, who obviously considered it important to ensure that the creditor's heirs would have the right to sell the charged property. Pomponius adds that even if it only mentioned the name of the creditor, his heir would still be able to sell.[215] This could be interpreted as, according to Pomponius, that a power of sale was implied in the *conventio pignoris*, so that it was not necessary to frame the licence to sell *in rem* (i.e., as not being granted to the original creditor personally). Another text from Pomponius's Sabinus commentary does support this interpretation.

> D. 13.7.5. *Pomponius libro nono decimo ad Sabinum*. Idque iuris est, sive omnino fuerint pacti, ne veneat, sive in summa aut condicione aut loco contra pactionem factum sit.
>
> The same rule applies whether there is an absolute pact against sale or an infringement only of an agreement as to amount, condition, or place.

The transaction practice, existing at the time of Pomponius's commentary, that the parties would expressly agree that no sale shall take place, implies that without such contractual prohibition, the creditor was authorized to sell the property. For what would otherwise be the reason for such pact?[216] From the third century AD there are imperial constitutions that still mention the sale of pledged objects taking place pursuant to a contractual licence to sell.[217] This demonstrates that the existence of a practice of express licences to sell does not exclude that also without such provisions the creditor would be entitled to sell.

Reliquum and *superfluum*

From Pomponius there is an opinion saying that the standard clause commonly inserted in pledge agreements, providing that the debtor is liable for

[214] According to Lenel this text was concerned with *fiducia*. See also Burdese 1949: 40–7. According to Kaser 1982: 76 n 103 its substance applies to both *fiducia* and *pignus*. Noordraven (1999: 283) holds that Lenel's conclusion was based on the wrong assumption that book 35 of Pomponius's *ad Sabinum* was concerned with *fiducia*.

[215] See also Pomp. D. 13.7.8.5, holding that when pledged property can be sold pursuant to a pact, it can be exercised not only for the principal sum but also for interest accrued and expenses.

[216] In the same sense Kaser 1982: 21. Also a text like Marcell. D. 20.1.27 appears to presuppose that the creditor was impliedly authorized to sell the pledged property upon default.

[217] Gord. C. 8.27.8: '*legem venditionis exercuit*'. The reference to *lex* is to a contractual clause, not to legislation.

the deficit, is superfluous, as it is also the situation by operation of law.[218] So, apparently, at the time of Pomponius's commentary, *pignus* was no longer a 'substitution pledge'. The *datio pignoris* had ceased to be a *datio in solutum*. The right of *pignus* had evolved into a proper security interest, which is aimed at a complete repayment of the secured debt.[219] Where the proceeds of an execution sale were insufficient to do so the debtor remained liable for the *reliquum*. From Pomponius and Scaevola we know that in the second half of the second century AD the express licence to sell was in practice still coupled with a surplus/deficit clause.[220] These texts show that, although from a legal perspective this was no longer necessary, creditors were still adamant that any shortfall could be recovered from the debtor. As D. 46.1.63 clearly illustrates, this shortfall manifests itself when the pledged property is actually sold.

> **D. 46.1.63.** *Scaevola libro sexto responsorum.* Inter creditricem et debitorem pactum intercesserat, ut, si centum, quae mutua dederit, ubi primum petita fuissent, non solverentur, ornamenta pignori data intra certum tempus liceret ei vendere et si quo minoris venissent, quodque sortis vel usurarum nomine deberetur, id creditrici redderetur, et fideiussor acceptus est: quaesitum est, an fideiussor in universam summam obligari potuerit. Respondit secundum ea quae proponerentur teneri fideiussorem in id, quod minus ex pignoribus venditis redactum esset.
>
> It was agreed between a (female) creditor and her debtor that if the hundred which she advanced were not repaid when first asked for, it would be lawful for her to sell ornaments given in pledge within a certain period and that any shortfall on the sale and what was due as interest should be rendered to her; a surety was also taken; the question was whether the surety would be liable in full. His answer was that on the facts stated, the surety would be liable for the deficiency on the sale of the pledges.

The fact that at the time of Pomponius, the debtor was liable for the deficit by operation of law might already be an indication that also the creditor's liability for the surplus arose by operation of law. The other writings of Pomponius also seem to indicate that in the second century AD, the creditor was obliged to pay the surplus to the debtor. In D. 13.7.6.1 Pomponius says that where the creditor has sold the pledged land for a higher amount than the secured debt and has lent the surplus against interest to a third party, or has used the

[218] Pomponius's opinion is restated in Paul. D. 20.5.9.1.

[219] Manigk 1941: 1254, 1259.

[220] Paul. (Pomp.) D. 20.5.9.1; Scaev. D. 46.1.63.

surplus proceeds himself, he must pay interest to the debtor. Where, on the other hand, he has safekept the money he does not have to pay interest.[221] All this presupposes that the debtor was entitled to the *superfluum*.[222] The same Pomponius also holds (as reported by Marci. D. 20.1.13.2) that in case of a *pignus nominis* the creditor, once the pledged claim is realized, must set it off against his own claim.[223] This reference to set-off would again appear to indicate that if the amount of the pledged claim exceeded that of the secured debt, the creditor was obliged by operation of law to pay the surplus to the debtor. In Afr. D. 30.108.13, someone had pledged pearls to his creditor, Titius. Later, he made his son heir and disinherited his daughter and asked the same Titius to be his trustee: 'I request you, Titius, and charge on you as a *fideicommissum* that you sell the pearls I left you as a pledge and after deduction of all that is due to you deliver all the residue to my daughter.' Although the sale does not seem to have been an execution sale, the arrangement does reflect that the debtor is entitled to the surplus. It could also be argued that the pledge of the *superfluum* to a second pledge creditor, as first attested in Gai D. 20.1.15.2,[224] lends support to the existence of the creditor's duty to pay the surplus already in high classical law because granting a right of pledge of the *superfluum* seems to presuppose that the debtor was entitled to dispose of it.

[221] In D. 13.7.7 Paul adds that where the creditor returns the money too late, he is liable to pay default interest.

[222] See also Pomp. D. 46.3.26: 'If the creditor should sell pledged land and recover what was due to him, the debtor will be released.'

[223] See section 8.3. [224] See sections 7.2 and 7.3.

6

From *Pignus* to *Hypotheca*

6.1 Introduction

The archive of the Sulpicii provides evidence for an ancestor of another 'modern' variant of pledge. It seems that *pignus* already could exist as a non-possessory security right long before the second-century AD jurist, Julian, who is the author of the earliest legal opinions on the *hypotheca* granted *nuda conventione*. The archive of the Sulpicii provides epigraphic evidence of a transactional practice of granting possessory and non-possessory pledges over goods stored in a warehouse, which took place without a transfer of physical possession (section 6.2). Also, the practice of granting of what were effectively non-possessory pledges in order to secure maritime loans may have its roots in late republican or early classical legal practices (section 6.3). From long before Julian, texts have been preserved in the Digest which can be regarded as witnesses of ancestors of the high and late classical *hypotheca* (section 6.4).

The transfer of possession through *traditio* would have originally served as a mode of transferring ownership to a creditor upon default (forfeiture). However, when it came to be accepted in the second century AD that the exercise of the creditor's power of sale did not require him to be the owner, the *traditio* was no longer needed for this purpose. Thus, indirectly, the recognition of the creditor's independent power of sale may have paved the way for the pledge created 'by mere agreement'(section 6.5). This *hypotheca* granted *nuda conventione* was the outcome of a long evolutionary process triggered by transactional practices. Julian's main role may have been that he 'codified' the generalized *formula* of the *actio Serviana*. The fact that it appeared from the *Edictum perpetuum* that a right of pledge could be granted by mere agreement layed down a firm basis for future developments of the law of real security: the multiple pledge, *pignus nominis*, and the general pledge are all pledges which were granted *nuda conventione*. Not only in the personal (*in personam*) *actiones pigneraticiae* but also in the *formula* of the *actio Serviana* in the *Edictum perpetuum*, the *conventio pignoris* was the central element. This

Security and Credit in Roman Law: The historical evolution of pignus *and* hypotheca. Hendrik L. E. Verhagen, Oxford University Press. © Hendrik L. E. Verhagen 2022. DOI: 10.1093/oso/9780199695836.003.0007

enabled contracting parties to adjust real security interests to their economic needs (section 6.6).

High and late classical legal sources still attest to the continuing use of certain transactional practices with a 'diluted' possessory element, which may already have been employed before the *Edictum perpetuum* was codified: pledge and lease-back and the handing over of title documents (section 6.7).

6.2 Possessory and Non-possesory Pledges in the Sulpicii Archive

Where large quantities of agricultural goods (e.g., grain, olives, and wine) were to be pledged, the sheer volume of the pledged assets might create logistical difficulties if, in order to create a right of pledge, they were to be handed over to the creditor and be stored by him. The pledges of goods stored in warehouses discussed in this section concern considerable quantities of grain and other agricultural produce: 47 tonnes of grain and 26 tonnes of legumes and other foodstuffs in TPSulp 51 and 52 and 87 tonnes of grain in TPSulp 79. TPSulp 51 appears to evidence a non-possessory pledge, which in TPSulp 52 is converted into a possessory one. One cannot entirely exclude the possibility that the original (non-possessory) pledge (TPSulp 51) was not valid and enforceable at the time it was made and that, when they realized this, the parties decided to create a possessory pledge (TSPsulp 45 and 52). From the whole archive of the Sulpicii it appears, however, that they knew their law well,[1] so one would not expect them to accept (for themselves or their customers) invalid security for loans which were for considerable amounts. What is certain, in any case, is that already by the first century AD a possessory pledge of bulk goods stored in a warehouse operated by a third party could be created without the need for a physical movement of these assets. The creditor could be given 'legal control' over the pledged objects by means of a rental agreement with the warehouse operator. In this sense we are already dealing with a right of pledge created merely by contract(s). The warehouse pledges can, therefore, be regarded as possessory pledges with a 'diluted' *traditio*. Therefore, even if TPSulp 51 would not evidence a non-possessory pledge, warehouse pledges certainly belong to the line of ancestors of the non-possessory *hypotheca* of the second century AD.

[1] Terpstra 2013: 26–7. Terpstra mentions TPSulp 43, which records a contract of sale of a slave and which provides that the sale shall be governed by 'the other provisions in the edict of the curule aediles of this year, which are written and included . . . in keeping with the *formula* in the way that is customary'. See also TPSulp 42 and 44.

File C. Novius Eunus (TPSulp 51, 52, and 45)

A typical example of a secured credit transaction from the Sulpicii archive is the 'file C. Novius Eunus', a series of five documents all concerning one and the same credit relationship, which was arranged and managed by the Sulpicii. The grain trader Gaius Novius Eunus borrowed 10,000 sesterces from Evenus Primianus, against what appears to be a non-possessory pledge. The purpose of this loan has not been expressed, but it may have been taken in order to repay a maritime loan with which the purchase of the pledged goods had been financed, or in order to buy more grain in anticipation of higher grain prices later in season. The loan was entered into in June, at a time when the new season's shipments of grain from Alexandria (or elsewhere) would have arrived in Puteoli. Grain prices would be low and Eunus could have speculated that they would rise later in the season. With the profits made from future sales, the loan (plus interest) could be repaid and the pledged wheat and other foodstuffs would also become available for sale at a higher profit.[2] If all this would not go according to plan and Eunus would fail to repay the 10,000 sesterces, the lender, Evenus Primianus (or the Sulpicii on his behalf), could sell the pledged goods at auction and take recourse against the proceeds.

We encounter pledges of goods stored in warehouses in the archive of the Sulpicii as well as in several Digest texts. From a later period, we have two opinions by Scaevola, which, as they so often do, give us a good insight into Roman law in action. In Scaevola D. 13.7.43.1, grain merchant Titius borrowed money from Gaius Seius and received a possessory pledge of leather bags. These bags were requisitioned by the *officio annonae* for the distribution of grain while they were stored by Gaius Seius in a warehouse. The *horreum* mentioned in the text probably wasn't the creditor's own warehouse but that of a professional warehouse operator.[3] Another case discussed by Scaevola is D. 20.4.21.1, regarding a marble dealer who had granted a right of pledge over marble slabs to the lender who had financed the purchase of the marble.[4] The slabs were stored in an imperial warehouse rented by the borrower. The construction may have been the same as that used by the Sulpicii in TPSulp 45

[2] Jones 2006: 96; Jaschke 2010: 197; Bransbourg 2014: 130–1.

[3] When the creditor managed to get them back, the bags had suffered tear and wear. According to Scaevola, creditor Seius was not liable for the wear and tear. Diocl.-Max. C. 4.24.9 concerns goods which were deposited in public granaries and which are most likely charged by way of non-possessory pledge.

[4] Ulpian D. 10.4.5 pr. records an opinion by Celsus and seems to be dealing with a possessory pledge, pursuant to which the pledged goods are stored in a warehouse on the creditor's behalf.

and 46: the creditor rented the space in the warehouse formerly rented by the debtor.[5]

TPSulp 51: non-possessory pledge

The first document in the file C. Novius Eunus is TPSulp 51, which I shall describe in more detail than the other documents from the archive. TPSulp 51 is a virtually intact triptych of which both the *scriptura interior* and *exterior* have been preserved. The *scriptura interior* was written by its author Gaius Novius Eunus in vulgar Latin. This authentic version of this chirograph has many grammatical and spelling mistakes. The *index* and the *scriptura exterior* are reproduced in this section. At the bottom of the last page (side 3) of the *scriptura interior* there are traces of a seal, which is likely to have been that of C. Novius Eunus. Side 4 of the triptych has a groove (*sulcus*) with the remains of six seals adjoined by the names of the *signatores* written in ink. The name of Gaius Novius Eunus is recorded twice (alongside the first and the last seal). The other seals are those of witnesses. One of these witnesses was Gaius Sulpicius Faustus, who may have acted as a financial intermediary for this credit transaction. This may explain why TPSulp 51 is part of the archive, which is confirmed by the fact that it is based on the same template as used by the Sulpicii themselves.[6]

TPSulp 51 (*margines* and *scriptura exterior*)

Chirographum C(aii) Nov || ii Euni HS X mutuorum

Put(eolis) XIV k(alendas) Ìul(ias) || Proculo et Nigrìno co(n)s(ulibus).
Cn(aeo) Acerronio Proculo C(aio) Petronio Pontìo Nigrìno co(n)s(ulibus),
quartum kalendas Ìulias.
C(aius) Novius Eunús scrìpsi me accepisse mútua ab Eueno
Tì(berii) Caesaris Augustì liberto Primiano apsente per
Hesychum servum eìus et debere eì sestertium
decem mìllia nummum, quae eì reddam cum petìerit,
et ea HS X m(ilia) n(ummum), q(uae) s(upra) s(cripta) s(unt), p(roba)
r(ecte) d(ari) stipulátus est
Hesychus Euenì Tì(berii) Caesaris Augustì l(iberti) Prìmianì
servus, spopondì ego C(aius) Novius Eunús; proque
iìs séstertiìs decem m[ill]ibus nummum dedì

[5] See also Du Plessis 2012: 183–4.

[6] Jones 2006: 93 presumes that Evenus held an account with the Sulpicii bank, from which his business manager (*institor*) Hesychus was authorized to draw funds.

eì pignoris arrabonisve nomine tritìcì Alexandrìnì
modium septem mìllia '[plu]s minus' et ciceris farris monocopì
lentis ìn saccìs duc[en]tìs [mod]ium quattuor mìllia p(lus) m(inus),
quae omnia reposita habeo penes me ìn horreìs
Bassianìs publicìs Pu[teo]lanorum, quae ab omnì vì
perìculo meo esse fat[e]or.
Act(um) Puteolìs.

Chirograph of C. Novius Eunus on 10,000 borrowed sesterces

Puteoli, on the 14th day before the Kalends of July under the consuls Proculus and Nigrinus (28 June 37).[7]
During the consulship of Gnaeus Acceronius Proculus and Gaius Petronius Pontius Nigrinus,
on the 4th day before the Calends of July.
I, Gaius Novius Eunus, have written that I have received a loan from Euenus Primianus, freedman of Tiberius Caesar Augustus, in his absence through Hesychus his slave. And that I owe him 10,000 sesterces in cash,
which I shall give him back, when he so requires.
And that these aforementioned 10,000 sesterces are to be duly paid in good coin has been stipulated by
Hesychus, slave of Euenus Primianus, freedman of Tiberius Caesar Augustus,
and I, Gaius Novius Eunus, have promised. For
these 10,000 sesterces I have given him
as pledge or *arrabo*[8] 7,000 *modii* of Alexandrian wheat,
more or less, and 200 sacks of chickpeas, flour, *monocopi*
and lentils, 4,000 *modii*, more or less,
all of which I keep with me in the Bassian Public Granaries of the Puteolans,
which I admit is at my risk for all danger.
Done in Puteoli.[9]

In TPSulp 51 the debtor C. Novius Eunus declares, in respect of the wheat and two hundred sacks of other foodstuffs which were pledged in order to secure

[7] The date of the *scriptura interior* (*XIV k. Iul*: 18 June) is confirmed by the same date of the *index*. Nevertheless, according to Camodeca one cannot rule out entirely that the date of the *scriptura exterior* (*IV k. Iul*: 28 June) is the date on which the document was executed.

[8] In the hendyadis *pignoris arrabonisve*, the colloquial term *arrabo*, a lexical borrowing from Greek (*ἀρραβών*), is probably used in order to clarify the meaning of the document to Greek merchants. Krämer 2007: 27–8. For an elaborate analysis of *arrabo* in TPSulp 51, see Abatino 2012.

[9] Translation taken (with changes) from Abatino 2012: 313 n 7.

the initial loan of 10,000 sesterces: 'all of which I keep with me' in the 'Bassian' public warehouses of Puteoli.[10] The words '*penes me*' ('with me') already suggest that the debtor was still in control of the pledged goods. Two other documents from the file C. Novius Eunus make it even more plausible that we are actually dealing with such non-possessory pledge: TPSulp 52 and 45.

TPSulp 52 and 45: possessory pledge

In TPSulp 51, 7,000 *modii* of wheat were given in pledge. Camodeca assumes that the minimum price of wheat was three sesterces per *modius*.[11] Therefore, the value of the wheat was at least 21,000 sesterces.[12] The value of the other goods mentioned in TPSulp 51 has been estimated at approximately 9,000 sesterces. Therefore, the total of the collateral in TPSulp 51 is to be estimated at a value of at least 30,000 sesterces, while the loan was for 10,000 sesterces only.[13] This means that there was a considerable surplus value of at least 20,000 sesterces.[14] This over-collateralization left plenty of room for C. Novius Eunus to obtain an additional loan on the basis of the same collateral. This is what happened in TPSulp 52.

TPSulp 52 (*margines* and *scriptura interior*)

Chirographum C(aii) No || vìi Euni HS ∞ ∞ ∞ mutuor(um)
praeter alia HS X || ob pignus triticì.

C(aio) Cessasare Germanico Aug(usto)
Tì(berio) Claudio Germanico co(n)s(ulibus),
VI nonas Ìulias. C(aius) Novius Eunus
scripssi me accepisse muta ab
Hessco Eunni Tì(berii) Cessaris Augustì
l(iberti) Primiani ser(vo) et
debere eì sestertia tra milia
nummu, pret(er) alia HS X n(ummum)
que alio chirographo meo
eìdem debo, et ea sestertia

[10] The *horrea Bassiana publica* were named after a certain Bass(i)us, who must have donated or bequeathed the building complex to the city of Puteoli. It must have had at least three levels, because it had a middle level. Its actual location is unknown (Jaschke 2010: 54–5).

[11] Camodeca 1999: 140. Other estimates range from 2 to 12 sesterces per *modius*. I will use Camodeca's estimate, but occasionally indicate the implications of higher or lower estimates in the footnotes.

[12] Camodeca 1999: 140. With a price of HS 2 per *mod.* the value of the wheat would be HS 14,000.

[13] Gröschler 2008: 318. With a price of HS 2 per *mod.*: HS 23,000.

[14] Even with price of HS 2 per *mod.* the surplus value would still be HS 13,000.

tra milia num(mum) nummu,
q(uae) s(upra) s(cripta) s(unt), p(roba) r(ecte) recete dari
stipulatus ets Hessucus Eunì
Tì(berii) Cessaris Augustì l(iberti) Primiani
ser(vus) spepodi ego C(aius) Novius Eunus,
in qua ominis suma dedì eì
pignoris tridigi Alxadrini modi=
um septe mila, quot est possit[um]
in horeìs Bassianìs puplicis Putola[nor(um)]
medis horeo duode[cimo], et sacos ducen[t]=
os lentis c[ice]r[is · ·] + issi monocopì
et faris in quibus sunt modium
quator milia, qui sunt possiti in
ìsdem horeìs, que ominia ab ominì
vi priculo meo est, fator.
Actum Putolis.

Chirograph of C. Novius Eunus on HS 3,000 borrowed
in addition to the other HS 10,000 against pledge of wheat.

Under the consuls Gaius Caesar Germanicus Augustus and
Tiberius Claudius Germanicus
on the sixth day before the Nones of July (2 July 37). I, Gaius Novius Eunus,
wrote that I received as a loan from
Hesychus, the slave of Evenus Primianus, the freedman of Tiberius Caesar
Augustus, and owe him 3,000 sesterces
in cash, in addition to the other 10,000 sesterces in cash
which by my other chirograph
I owe him. And that these
3,000 sesterces in cash,
which are written above, will be duly given in good coin
has been stipulated by Hesychus, the slave of
Evenus Primianus, the freedman of Tiberius Caesar Augustus
and I, Gaius Novius Eunus, have promised to do so.
And for the whole sum I gave him
as a pledge 7,000 modii of Alexandrian
wheat, which is stored
in the Bassian Public Granaries of the Puteolans,
in the middle level in grainstall 12, and 200 sacks

of lentils, chickpeas, monocopi,
and flour, which hold 4,000 modii, which are placed
in the same grain-stalls, which I
admit is at my risk for all danger.
Done in Puteoli.

When this additional loan of 3,000 sesterces was granted, the same wheat as already pledged in TPSulp 51 was now pledged again to secure the total debt of 13,000 sesterces. This time, however, in TPSulp 52 Novius Eunus does *not* declare that the wheat was stored 'with me'. From another document (TPSulp 45) it becomes clear why.

TPSulp 45 (*margines* and *scriptura exterior*)

Chir[ograp]hum Diogne || ti C(aii) Novii Cypaeri servi
co[ndu]ctionis hor || rei XII in Bassianis
in quo triticum est || p[i]gnori accept(um) a C(aio) Novio Euno.

C(aio) Caesare Germanico Augusto
Tì(berio) Claudio Nerone Germanico co(n)s(ulibus),
sextum nonas Ìulias. Dìognetus C(aii) Novì
Cypaerì servus scripsi ìussu Cypaerì dominì
meì coram ipso me locasse Hesycho
Tì(berii) Ìulì Augustì l(iberti) Euenì ser(vo) horreum
duodecimum ìn horreìs Bassianìs publicis
Puteolanorum mediìs, ìn quo repositum
est triticum Alexandrinum, quod pignorì
accepit hac dìe a C(aio) Novio Euno, ìtem
in iìsdem horreìs {horreìs} ìmìs ìnter
columnia, ubì repositos habet saccos ~~du~~
legumìnum ducentos, quos pignorì accepit ab
eodem Euno.
Ex k(alendis) Ìulìs ìn menses singulos sestertiìs singulis n[u]m(mis).
Act(um) P[u]t(eolis).

Chirograph of Diognetes slave of Gaius Novius Cypaerus
for the lease of storeroom 12 of the Bassian (Public Granaries)
in which is wheat accepted as a pledge from Gaius Novius Eunus.

Under the consuls Gaius Caesar Germanicus Augustus and
Tiberius Claudius Germanicus

> on the sixth day before the Nones of July (2 July 37). I Diognetus, slave of
> Gaius Novius Cypaerus, have written on the order of my master Cypaerus,
> in his presence, that I have rented to Hesychus,
> the slave of Evenus, the freedman of Tiberius Julius Augustus, the twelfth
> granary in the middle level of the Bassian Public Granaries of the
> Puteolans, in which is stored
> Alexandrian wheat which he accepted today as a pledge
> from Gaius Novius Eunus. Also
> the spaces between the columns in the lower level of the same granaries,
> where he has 200 sacks of
> vegetables, which he has accepted as a pledge from
> the same Eunus.
> From the Kalends of July for 1 sesterce in cash per month.
> Done in Puteoli.

The creditor rented the space in the warehouses where the pledged wheat, chickpeas, and other foodstuffs were stored,[15] for a nominal amount of one sesterce per month, thus effectively bringing the pledged objects under his control.[16] What must have happened here is that the pledge, which was originally created as a non-possessory pledge (TPSulp 51), is now converted into a possessory one (TPSulp 52 and TPSulp 45).[17] The motivation behind this conversion is not expressed, but is likely to have been that the creditor wished to strengthen his position. Bringing the pledged wheat (etc.) under his control would entail that the creditor could be sure that as long as there was sufficient wheat in the storeroom rented by him, the execution proceeds would be sufficient to repay the loans. The creditor's possession may also have had legal advantages; in particular if the *actio Serviana* was not yet available to all pledge creditors, the creditor's possession would at least give him the protection of the possessory interdicts. The possession of the pledged goods would also be crucial for a sale at auction by way of execution: there would be no need to institute legal proceedings against the debtor or third parties in

[15] See Du Plessis 2012: 175–89 on rental agreements between *horrearii* and their customers.

[16] This will be discussed more elaborately shortly with reference to the file L. Marius Iucundus.

[17] See Krämer 2007: 300–38. Strictly speaking, from a legal perspective, TPSulp 52 probably does not represent a conversion of the original pledge. The right of pledge granted in TPSulp 51 was granted for a loan of 10,000 sesterces. The accessory nature of the right of pledge entails that for new secured debt a new right of pledge must be granted (unless the original pledge was also granted for future obligations, which was not the case in TPSulp 51).

possession.[18] This effective control—analogous (or perhaps identical) to the *traditio* of *res nec mancipi*—may even have functioned as a conditional transfer of ownership of the pledged objects in case of default (forfeiture), which would have enabled the creditor to sell and transfer these to third parties.[19]

File Lucius Marius Iucundus

Another client file in the archive is formed by TPSulp 46, 53, and 79, concerning the Puteolean *mercator frumentarius* L. Marius Iucundus, this time with one of the Sulpicii acting as creditor. In TPSulp 53 Iucundus declares to have borrowed 20,000 sesterces from Gaius Sulpicius Faustus. In another triptych/chirograph (TPSulp 79) Iucundus declares that in order to secure this loan he has 'given as a pledge' ('*dedisse pignoris nomine*') Alexandrian grain, which is stored in store room 26 of the upper Barbatian Warehouse of Domitia Lepida.[20] That this is a possessory pledge appears from TPSulp 46, which records a rental agreement pursuant to which that same storeroom of the Barbatian Warehouse is let to Gaius Sulpicius Faustus.

TPSulp 46 (*margines* and *scriptura exterior*)

[Chirographum Nardi P(ublii) Anni Seleuci ser(vi)]
con[ductionis (?) h]orr[ei] XXVI [- - -] P(ublio) Annio [Seleuco - - -].

C(aio) Laecanio Basso Q(uinto) Ter[en]tio Culleone co(n)s(ulibus),
III ì[du]s Martias.
Nardus P(ublii) Annì Seleucì servus sc[ri]psì coram et iussu
Sel[eu]cì dominì meì, [q]uod is negaret se litteras
scire, m[e] locasse C(aio) Sulpicio Fausto horreum
vicensimum et sexstum, quod est in praedis Domì=
tiae L[e]pidae B[a]rbatianis superioribus, in quo reposì=
tum est triticì Alexandrinì millia mod[iu]m
decem et tria, [quae] admetietur dominus meus
cum s[er]vis [sui]s, m[er]c[ed]e in mensibus singulis

[18] Pellecchi 2018: 472. [19] See section 5.2.

[20] TPSulp 79 is reproduced below. Domitia Lepida was the aunt of Nero and mother-in-law of Claudius. She may have inherited the 'Barbatian' warehouse from her first husband M. Valerius Messalla Barbatus, after whose family the warehouse was named. Domitia also owned real estate in Rome, Calabria, and Africa (Jones 2006: 101 and Jaschke 2010: 55). There are no archeological remains to which the *horrea Barbatiana* have been linked (Jaschke 2010: 54).

sestertis centenis nummis.

Actum Puteolis.

Chirograph of Nardus, slave of Publius Annius Seleucus for the lease of storeroom 26... Publius Annius Seleucus.

Under the consuls Gaius Laecanius Bassus and Quintus Terentius Culleo
on the third day before the Ides of March (13 March 40).[21]
I, Nardus, slave of Publius Annius Seleucus, have written in the presence and
on the order of my master Seleucus, because he denied to be able to write,
to have let to Gaius Sulpicus Faustus storeroom
26 which is on the lands of Domitia
Lepida in the upper Barbatian Warehouse, in which are stored
13, 000 modii of Alexandrian grain,
which my master will measure out
with his slaves, with 100 sesterces
in cash each month as rent.

Done in Puteoli.

This rental agreement, for a monthly rate of one hundred sesterces, is executed as a triptych/chirograph by Nardus, a slave, who acts on the order and in the presence of the *horrearius* P. Annius Seleucus (who professed to be unable to write). Unlike in TPsulp 45, this time the rent of the warehouse is not for the nominal amount of one sesterce per month. The rent agreed in TPSulp 46 (HS 100 per month) equals 6 per cent per annum of interest on the borrowed sum. The burden of the rent will in one way or another (e.g., in a separate stipulation or an informal agreement) have been passed on by Faustus to Iucundus.[22]

It is likely that storeroom 26 was originally rented by the debtor Iucundus[23] and that this original lease was replaced by the lease with Faustus. This operation is equivalent to a *traditio* of the pledged grain from debtor to creditor. In the Digest we find texts on the *traditio* of goods stored elsewhere by way of sale. According to these texts, a *traditio* of goods which have been stored in a warehouse or wine cellar can take place by the seller handing over the keys of these repositories to the buyer.[24] One would think that a possessory pledge could be created in exactly the same manner. Because delivery of the keys

[21] In Wolf's edition of TPN 87 (= TPSulp 46) the date cannot be reconstructed, but in Camodeca's edition it is 13 March 40.

[22] Jones 2006: 101.

[23] Camodeca 1999: 126.

[24] Pap. D. 18.1.74 ('*mercium in horreis*'); Paul. D. 41.2.1.21 ('*cellae vinariae*'); Gai. D. 41.1.9.6 ('*merces in horreo repositas*'). See also Alex. C. 4.48.2.1 ('*universam [amphorarum], quod in horreis erat*

would give access to the goods, it was 'probably regarded as sufficiently analogous to touching or moving to have the effect of giving possession'.[25] Whether storeroom 26 was locked and whether the keys were handed over to Faustus, we do not know.[26] This may very well not have been the case. In the other lease agreement of the archive (TPSulp 45), part of the pledged objects were stored in 'the spaces between the columns in the lower level of the same granaries, where he has two hundred sacks of vegetables': this is unlikely to have been a closed-off space which could be locked.[27] But the lease agreement with Seleucus (through his slave Nardus) would also have given Faustus control over the stored goods. It would entail that the staff of the Barbatian warehouse would no longer allow Iucundus (or anyone else) to take away the stored grain without the permission of Faustus.[28]

TPSulp 79: a non-possessory pledge?

In Camodeca's edition the date of the rental agreement in TPSulp 46 reads 13 March 40, the same date as the loan agreement (TPSulp 53), but two days before the pledge agreement (TPSulp 79) was entered into. Camodeca offers a plausible explanation, by suggesting that these two days were necessary in order to enable the warehousemen to weigh and determine the exact quantity of the grain so that the value of the collateral could be determined.[29] But Camodeca admits that the date is uncertain: it might also have read 15 March 40, the same date as the deed of pledge.[30] This is, in any case, more plausible than Krämer's suggestion that the lease agreement was dated 15 May 40. The latter date would fit nicely with Krämer's thesis that non-possessory pledges were already recognized at the time of the Sulpicii. The pledge granted by Iucundus on 15 March 40 (TPSulp 79) would then have been granted as a non-possessory pledge. Only when the loan was not repaid on 15 May 40 and Iucundus was in default, did Faustus take possession of the pledged grain by

positum'). Pap. D. 18.1.74 requires that the keys are handed over in the proximity ('*apud*') of the warehouse.

25 Gordon 1970: 59.

26 Jakab 2014: 334 deduces from the fact that the quantity was not specified that storeroom 12 was a separate and locked room.

27 Klinck 2015: 63.

28 See also (but more hesitant) Klinck 2015: 62–3.

29 Camodeca 1999: 126. See also Jones 2006: 101.

30 TPSulp 46 does not state the term of the lease, but this will at least have been the same as the term of the loan recorded in TPSulp 79 (two months). However, when Iucundus failed to repay the loan, the lease is likely to have continued until the pledged grain was auctioned and delivered to the purchaser at auction.

entering into the lease agreement, in preparation of auctioning it by way of execution.[31] An argument in favour of Krämer's interpretation is that in contrast with TPSulp 45 ('wheat accepted as a pledge from Gaius Novius Eunus'), no mention at all is made in TPSulp 46 of the fact that the lease agreement is entered into by C. Sulpicius Faustus for the custody of goods pledged to him. This might indicate that the goods were already forfeited to the creditor and that they were stored in anticipation of auction. On the other hand, one of the freedmen of *horrearius* (P. Annius Seleucus) had acted as a witness to the loan agreement between Faustus and Iucundus, which suggests that the warehouse was already involved with this secured loan transaction on 'day 1', in anticipation of the lease agreement to be concluded a few days later.[32] All in all, the file L. Marius Iucundus cannot be used as strong evidence for the existence of non-possessory pledges in the first half of the first century AD.

Warehouse operator's pledge on *invecta et illata*

Horrea were of crucial importance for Roman society.[33] In Puteoli the role of warehouse operators may not have been confined to organizing the storage of goods but could also have extended to financial intermediation in bringing together lenders and borrowers.[34] In the archive of the Sulpicii we encounter several *horrearii* who were connected to the parties to the loan agreement. In the file C. Novius Eunus, the rental of the storage unit is for a nominal amount of one sesterce per month (TPSulp 45). This suggests that there must have been some (commercial or personal) relationship between the warehouse operator and the lender or borrower. In fact, we know that C. Novius Eunus was the freedman (*libertus*) of *horrearius* C. Novius Cypaerus,[35] who also acted as witness to TPSulp 52.[36] In the file L. Marius Iucundus, one of the freedmen of the *horrearius* acted as a witness to the loan agreement between Gaius Sulpicius Faustus and L. Marius Iucundus (TPSulp 53).

Privately owned warehouses would be a considerable source of rental income for their owners.[37] The goods stored in these warehouses would serve as collateral for this income. The *leges horreorum* provide (*inter alia*) that

[31] Cf. Paul. (Alf.) D. 13.7.30 and Ulp. D. 47.2.56, discussed in section 6.4.

[32] Camodeca 1999: 142. [33] See Van Oyen 2020. [34] Lerouxel 2016: 249–50.

[35] TPSulp 45: 'Gaius Novius Eunus, freedman of Cypaerus' ('*C. Novii Cypaeri liberti Euni*'). Jones (2006: 96) even considers it likely that Cypaerus had a partner's share in his freedman Eunus's grain trade business.

[36] Camodeca 1999: 142. [37] Candy 2020: 63.

(unless other security has been granted) all the goods stored by customers in the warehouse shall be pledged to the warehouse operator in order to secure payment of the storage fees.[38] Let us suppose that a similar announcement was made at the entrance of the Bassian (TPSulp 45, 51, and 52) and Barbatian (TPSulp 46 and 79) warehouses. Which rights of pledge would then prevail, the pledges of the warehouse operators pursuant to the *leges horreorum* or those of the lenders renting the storage units from the *horrearii*? From the second century AD the lenders would, if the tenant's pledges came into existence earlier, have a second ranking security interest. In the first century AD, however, they would not even have that. For a long time, the granting of a pledge would deprive the debtor of his power to create other rights of pledge over the same pledged asset.[39] In other words, *if* the warehouse operator did have a prior tenant's pledge, the rights of pledge purported to be granted in TPSulp 51, 52, and 79 would have been invalid. Again, it is difficult to imagine that the Sulpicii would have accepted (for themselves or their clients) an invalid pledge. Each of the warehouse operators may very well have had a pledge over the wheat under the original leases with the borrowers, but this pledge will either have ceased to exist upon termination of this lease and payment of the rentals, or the warehouse operators will have waived their pledges in co-operating with the leases to the lenders.[40]

6.3 Maritime Loans

Transport by sea was of the greatest importance for the Roman economy because it was the fastest form of transport. Grain and Laconian purple from Alexandria, slaves from Delos, and marble from Greece, would all be transported by ship to Puteoli and from there be carried on smaller ships to Rome.[41] At the same time, maritime trade was a risky business because of perils at sea and pirates.[42] The maritime loan not only financed this hazardous enterprise but also functioned as insurance. This is because a maritime loan only had to be repaid if the financed cargo arrived safely and in good time at its port of destination. As a compensation for this high risk, the interest rates for maritime

[38] FIRA III, no. 145. [39] Section 7.2. [40] See also Scaev. D. 20.4.21.

[41] Jones 2006: 24–5. For grain from Alexandria, see TPSulp 51, 52, and 79. For Laconian purple ('*purpuras laconicas*'), see TPSulp 83. According to Jones (2006: 85), although the purple dye was produced in Laconia from shellfish from seas surrounding the island of Cythera, the purple cloth or garments arriving in Puteoli are more likely to have been made in Alexandria. This city was a major centre of textile production and had strong trading links with Puteoli.

[42] Chevreau 2008: 37.

loans were much higher than those of ordinary loans. These high rates of interest would increase the credit risk which the lender took on the borrower. For this reason, it was common that the financed cargo would be pledged to the lender and, if the borrower owned the ship, the ship and its gear as well.[43] In most cases this pledge must have been either a non-possessory pledge, or at least a pledge with a diluted possessory element. As such, pledges granted in the late Republic and early Principate in order to secure maritime loans can be regarded as ancestors of the Roman non-possessory pledge.[44]

Greek origins

The origins of the maritime loan secured by a pledge of the cargo lie in the ancient Greek economy. Demosthenes's record of a maritime loan agreement (c. 340 BC) in *Against Lacritus* has elaborate provisions on the pledge of a cargo of wine amphoras, which were to be purchased during the voyage.[45] After the ship left the harbour, the pledged cargo would be out of the lender's physical control and only the document evidencing the maritime loan would remain in his possession.[46] In fact, as the traditional Greek possessory rights of pledge could not satisfy the needs of maritime trade, it is a plausible presumption that the development of maritime trade did have a decisive influence on the origin of the ὑποθήκη (*hypothéke*) as a form of non-possessory security.[47] From the fifth century BC, the non-possessory ὑποθήκη was the proper security interest for Greek maritime loans. A good example from a much later period (mid-second century AD), which is representative also for earlier periods, is the so-called Muziris papyrus. This document evidences the financing of a round trip from Muziris in India (Malabar coast).[48] The merchant in this transaction did not own the ship, so only the ship's cargo

[43] Rathbone 2003: 213; Schuster 2005: 87. Schuster observes that there is (possibly) evidence of only one maritime loan where the cargo was not pledged to the lender (Dem. 50.17). He also says that in Greek practice it would be rare that cargo *and* ship were pledged. Alternatively, in Greek-Hellenistic practice the borrower's failure to repay the loan was sanctioned by a penalty. This practice was still alive at the end of the Roman Principate. Ulp. D. 13.4.2.8 refers to a maritime loan pursuant to which the debtor owed money 'against a penalty or against pledges' ('*sub poena debebat pecuniam vel sub pignoribus*').

[44] One cannot exclude that occasionally, under maritime loans, the lender would have received a possessory pledge and would take care of the transport, in particular where the lender was a merchant financier who was himself also active in maritime trade. Ulp. D. 4.9.1.7 (discussed later in the chapter) may be an example of such practice.

[45] *Against Lacritus*, 35.10–14. Translated in Bresson 2016: 281–2.

[46] Schuster 2005: 85.

[47] Schuster 2005: 86.

[48] Rathbone 2003: 220. For text and translation of the Muziris papyrus (P. Vindob. G 40822), see De Romanis 2020: 14–30. For a recent discussion, see Harris 2020 (with further references).

was pledged to the financier.[49] This Greek pledge shares many characteristics with the Roman *hypotheca*: it is non-possessory, it concerns future assets (return cargo), it mentions both forfeiture and sale as execution mechanisms, it holds that the debtor shall be liable for any deficit, and it allows the debtor to sell pledged assets free from pledge. These are all characteristics which Greek-Hellenistic pledges already had at an early stage. When from the second century BC the maritime loan was taken over by the Romans, they may have adopted this form of pledge as well.

Reception of the maritime loan in Rome

This Greek commercial and legal institution was adopted by the Romans in the second century BC.[50] The reception of the maritime loan is reflected in Plutarch's account of the maritime loan, which Cato granted to a (large) consortium of shipowners/merchants. In describing how Cato turned from agriculture to more profitable investments, Plutarch says: 'he even practised the most despised form of moneylending, on maritime loans (*nautika*)', and then goes on to give a description of how Cato told fifty merchants and shipowners to form an association.[51] The pledge of the cargoes is not mentioned in Plutarch's account, although it may very well actually have taken place. Almost all the surviving evidence from both the Greek and Roman world concerns maritime loans coupled with a pledge of the cargo and/or the ship and its gear. Maritime loans are also attested in writings from late republican and early classical jurists, Servius Sulpicius Rufus and Labeo.[52] Cato financed a partnership of shipowner-merchants and these individual merchants may have been financed by other lenders as well. This is also reflected in jurists' writings discussing pledges securing maritime loans where multiple lenders or borrowers are involved.[53] Although, in many respects, the structure of commercial finance in Rome was significantly different from that of fourth century BC Greece, the Roman maritime loan was similar to its Greek ancestor.[54] It is therefore possible that already by the first century AD (if not earlier), pledges securing

[49] The document provides, in detail, how the lender can take recourse against the pledged cargo if the maritime loan is not repaid in time.

[50] Rathbone 2003: 212. A comprehensive monograph on the Roman maritime loan is Pontoriero 2011.

[51] See Rathbone 2003: 213–14 (from which the translation is taken).

[52] Ulp. D. 22.2.8; Lab. D. 22.2.9; Pomp. D. 22.2.2.

[53] See Paul. D. 22.2.6 (discussed shortly).

[54] Rathbone 2003: 212.

maritime loans governed by Roman law were either fully evolved non-possessory pledges or at least pledges with a diluted possessory element.

All the direct evidence of Roman maritime loans which were secured by a non-possessory pledge dates from after Julian, when it was generally recognized that pledges could be created *nuda conventione*.[55] However, given that (i) a non-possessory pledge of the financed cargo was a common feature of the Greek maritime loan, and that (ii) the Romans exactly copied this type of transaction already in the last two centuries of the Republic, it is plausible that a pledge with non-possessory features would also be granted in the late republican and early classical Roman periods.

Maritime loans in the Sulpicii archive?

According to Chevreau TPSulp 51 and 52 may have represented the final stage of a maritime loan.[56] We have seen that because of the high degree of risk for the lender, the statutory maximum rate of interest (12 per cent) did not apply to maritime loans. Chevreau points out that the amount of TPSulp 52 (HS 3,000) represents 30 per cent of the amount originally lent pursuant to TPSulp 51 (HS 10,000), which corresponds with a going rate of 30 per cent for this type of loan. Moreover, in Greek-Hellenistic practice it was common to take a pledge over the cargo, with the value of the pledged assets doubling or tripling the amount of the loan. This also is reflected in TPSulp 51 and 52: the borrowed amount is 10,000 sesterces (13,000 including 'interest'), while the value of the pledged assets was around 30,000 sesterces. As soon as the cargo reached its port of destination, the risk of the cargo would transfer to the borrower. Physical control, however, would pass to the lender. This also happened in TPSulp 51 and 52, where the lender took possession of the pledged assets through the rental agreement with the warehouse (TPSulp 45). The debtor then had twenty days to sell the cargo and repay the loan with the proceeds. This could explain—according to Chevreau—why TPSulp 51 and 52 did not include a licence to sell: the debtor, rather than the creditor, was authorized to sell. I am not convinced by this interpretation. Why would the parties take the trouble of casting TPSulp 52 in the form of a loan and why would they have done so several weeks after TPSulp 51 was executed? Is it not far more likely that TPSulp 52 actually is what it appears to be on the face of it: an additional loan coupled with the conversion of a non-possesory into a

55 For example, Scaev. D. 45.1.122.1 discussed later in this chapter.
56 Chevreau 2010: 195–6.

possessory pledge? The original purchase and transport of the wheat from Alexandria to Puteoli could have been financed by a maritime loan, but probably (given the value of the stored grain of 3021,000 sesterces) for a much larger amount than 10,000 sesterces.

Secured maritime loans in the Digest: non-possessory

There is a realistic description of a maritime loan secured by a pledge of the cargo in Scaevola D. 45.1.122.1, which may very well have reflected earlier practices.[57] It deals with a maritime loan financing a voyage from Beirut to Brindisi and back. This maritime loan was secured by a pledge not only on the cargo which the debtor had purchased in Beirut and which was to be carried to Brindisi but also on the goods which the debtor would purchase in Brindisi and which were to be transported back to Beirut. This right of pledge has both possessory and non-possessory elements. The non-possessory element is that the pledged goods were present on a ship rented by the debtor. The possessory element is that the creditor's slave was present on board of the ship, in order to supervise the debtor's dealings with the cargo.[58] However, such a 'supercargo' was not an essential element of maritime loans.[59] In the Muziris papyrus, which does contain elaborate provisions on the pledge of the cargo, the lender did not send a slave to travel with the cargo, because he employed agents in Alexandria, Koptos, and (perhaps) the Red Sea port.[60] At Scaevola's time, the presence of a supercargo as a substitute for *traditio* would not have been necessary, as the purely contractual pledge had already originated.[61]

Secured maritime loans in the Digest: possessory

In maritime loans, the lender's pledge would normally have been a non-possessory one, or at least a possessory pledge with a diluted possessory

[57] For an elaborate analysis of D. 45.1.122.1, see Sirks 2002: 142–9. According to Rathbone (2003: 216) D. 45.1.122.1 discusses a fictionalised test case based on an actual Greek contract. Sirks (2002: 144) holds that '[t]he text is a *responsum*, a legal advice given in an actual case by Scaevola'. See also Sirks 2002: 149. See also Chevreau 2008: 42.

[58] Fuenteseca 2013: 75–6; Rathbone 2003: 213.

[59] In the *Oxford English Dictionary* (online edition), a supercargo (not a Roman term) is defined as follows: 'A representative of the ship's owner on board a merchant ship, responsible for overseeing the cargo and its sale.' In maritime loans the person I call supercargo is a representative of the financier of the cargo.

[60] Rathbone 2003: 220.

[61] Section 6.5.

element (supercargo). There is, however, a late classical legal opinion which—on the face of it—implies that maritime loans were also entered into against pure possessory pledges.

> **D. 4.9.1.7.** *Ulpianus libro 14 ad edictum.* Item Pomponius libro trigensimo quarto scribit parvi referre, res nostras an alienas intulerimus, si tamen nostra intersit salvas esse: etenim nobis magis, quam quorum sunt, debent solvi. Et ideo si pignori merces accepero ob pecuniam nauticam, mihi magis quam debitori nauta tenebitur, si [ante] < a me> eas suscepit.[62]
>
> Likewise, Pomponius, in his thirty-fourth book, writes that it is of little importance whether we bring in our own goods or those of another, provided that it is to our interest that they are safe; for they ought to be returned to us rather than to their owners. Therefore, if I have accepted merchandise as a pledge on account of money lent for a sea voyage, the seaman will be liable to me rather than to the debtor, if he has received the goods from me.

Ulpian says that the shipper (*nauta*) shall be liable towards the lender for the receipt of merchandise which was pledged in order to secure a maritime loan, if he (the shipper) has received it from the lender. This fact pattern corresponds with a possessory pledge, as the merchandise must have been in the factual possession of the lender when the shipper received the pledged goods from him. This would be an exceptional case, as in maritime loans it is the debtor who takes care of the carriage by sea himself (e.g., Scaev. D. 45.1.122.1). D. 4.9.1.7 is, however, suspected of being interpolated, in the sense that '*si ante eas suscepit*' is a post-classical addition.[63] It has also been suggested that the borrower had assigned his claim against the *nauta* to the lender.[64] However, I am not completely convinced by this textual criticism. One cannot exclude the possibility that occasionally, under maritime loans, the lender would have received a possessory pledge and would take care of the transport, in particular where the lender was a merchant financier who was himself also active in maritime trade.

6.4 Early Classical Ancestors of *Hypotheca* in the Digest

In all likelihood the right of *pignus* originated in the early *ius civile* as a form of possessory security.[65] It has been argued, however, that when in the second

[62] Mommsen's emendation of *ante*: *<a me>*. [63] Mentxaka 1986: 268.

[64] Mentxaka 1986: 267–70.

[65] The great majority of modern authors accepts this: see Krämer 2007: 121; De Iuliis 2017. For other interpretations of the early history of *pignus* and *hypotheca*, see Schanbacher 2006; Braukmann 2008.

century BC *pignus* surfaces in Cato and the Comedies, it was in the form of a security interest that could be created by mere agreement and could take the form of a non-possessory pledge.[66] As such, it was a *Fremdkörper* (alien body) in the world of Roman law and must have been a legal transplant from Greece. The Greeks recognized such a purely contractual pledge, and it is from them that it came to Rome.[67] There is an element of speculation in this bold assertion, but it also has a grain of truth. As we can see repeatedly in this chapter (maritime loans) and elsewere in this book (*hypotheca, antichresis,* multiple pledge, fiscal pledge, and conditional sale), Greek-Hellenistic influences cannot be excluded, although perhaps more through transactional practices than by a reception of legal rules or institutions. Moreover, whether or not of Greek extraction, we find ancestors of the *hypotheca* in Roman law from before the age of Julian. Not only are there republican ancestors of *hypotheca* and first-century AD epigraphic sources attesting a non-possessory pledge, there are also several early classical jurists' opinions which appear to be dealing with non-possessory pledges.[68] Although one cannot say that the non-possessory pledge is firmly rooted in surviving pre-Julian jurisprudence, at the same time there are indications in the writings of late republican and early classical jurists making it plausible that non-possessory pledges were recognized by (at least some of) them. These texts were, in any case, all regarded by the *Compilatores* of the *Corpus iuris civilis* as concerning *pignus.*[69]

Alfenus on the pledge of a boat

There is speculation in modern literature that, under republican law, a creditor to whom a pledge had been granted without possession was entitled to *pignoris capio*. Kaser thinks this is an 'old' institution which can be regarded as the 'real' version (execution on a *res*) of the *manus iniectio* (execution on the person of the debtor).[70] This is not the *legis actio per pignoris capionem* which, according to Gaius, was based on statute or custom, but an informal remedy

[66] On the *subsignatio praediorum* as a possible ancestor of *hypotheca,* see section 10.2.

[67] Schanbacher 2010: 404–5. See also Braukmann 2008: 108–12 (with references to Dernburg and other older authors endorsing the same view). De Iuliis 2017: 107–9 considers the Roman pledge as the result of an indigenous development.

[68] For an elaborate discussion of all Digest texts, see Krämer 2007: 211–99. In addition to the texts reviewed below, Krämer discusses Pomp. (Sab.) D. 21.2.34.2; Pomp. (Sab.) D. 46.3.20; Paul. (Plaut.) D. 13.7.37; Cels. D. 46.3.69; Ulp. (Cels.) D. 42.1.4.8; and Marci. (Octav.) D. 20.3.1.2.

[69] They are all included in title 13.7 (*De pigneraticia actione vel contra*) or book 20 (*De pignoribus et hypothecis et qualiter ea contrahantur et de pactis eorum*) of the Digest.

[70] Kaser 1982: 133–4.

which was based on the (express or implied) will of the debtor.[71] It is therefore conceivable that the *conventio pignoris* itself would give the creditor the right to *pignoris capio*, that is to take possession without judicial permission.[72] The case discussed by the late republican jurist Alfenus in D. 13.7.30 may be an example of this.

Alfenus Varus (consul in 39 BC) was the first jurist to write a work with the title *Digesta*, from which Paulus took the fragment which follows.[73] He was one of the most important pupils of Servius Sulpicius Rufus: the '*respondit*' in the text may very well be a reference to Alfenus's master.[74] There is, therefore, a distinct possibility that the text reflects a point of view taken by the possible 'inventer' of the *actio Serviana*.

> **D. 13.7.30.** *Paulus libro quinto epitomarum Alfeni digestorum.* Qui ratiario crediderat, cum ad diem pecunia non solveretur, ratem in flumine sua auctoritate detinuit: postea flumen crevit et ratem abstulit. Si invito ratiario retinuisset, eius periculo ratem fuisse respondit: sed si debitor sua voluntate concessisset, ut retineret, culpam dumtaxat ei praestandam, non vim maiorem.
>
> Someone who lent to a waterman, when the debt was not paid on the day, detained the boat on the river on his own authority. Then, the river rose and swept the boat away. On this, the reply was that if he held the boat against the will of the waterman, the risk of its loss was on him; but if the debtor consented to giving it up to be detained, then the lender was only liable for fault, not for force majeure.[75]

Alfenus (or Servius) distinguishes between two variants of the fact pattern under review, one in which the creditor 'on his own authority' ('*sua auctoritate*') detained the boat against the will of the debtor and another one in which the creditor detained the boat with the consent of the debtor.[76] The *first* variant could be regarded as evidence of the continuing existence of an archaic self-help remedy allowing ordinary (unsecured) creditors to take possession

[71] Kaser 1982: 7. See also Kaser 1982: 133–6. According to Kaser, it is not certain but credible that this private form was also called *pignoris capio*. In a similar sense, Rabel 1971: 230–1; von Lübtow 1957: 311–12. See also the other authors mentioned by Krämer 2007: 218–19 n 26. Against this, Wagner 1968: 63 and Krämer 2007: 218–19 n 26. On the *legis actio per pignoris capionem* as a possible ancestor of *pignus*, see De Iuliis 2017: 19–31.

[72] Kaser 1982: 16–17.

[73] Kunkel 1967: 29; Schiavone 2012: 247.

[74] In Alf. D. 28.5.46 and Alf. D. 33.7.16.1 the text reads '*Servius respondit*'. See Krämer 2007: 212–13. See also Schulz 1953: 205–6; Schiavone 2012: 249.

[75] For an elaborate exegesis of this text, see Krämer 2007: 211–75. See also Bürge 1980.

[76] Krämer 2007: 211–48, 353–4.

of goods belonging to the debtor.[77] In the *second* variant of the fact pattern discussed by Alfenus, the 'consent to giving it up to be detained' could be read as the granting of a right of pledge. The words '*si debitor sua voluntate concessisset, ut retineret*' should then be regarded as equivalent to phrases like '*si debitor pignori dedisset*' or '*si debitor rem suam obligavisset*'. In modern literature this has been interpreted as the granting of a *non-possessory* pledge.[78] This non-possessory pledge would allow the lender to take physical control of the boat when the borrower was in default, in a similar manner as a landlord's *perclusio* pursuant to an urban tenant's pledge. From the late classical period we have evidence of such a self-help remedy available to creditors with a non-possessory pledge. Ulp. D. 47.2.56 says that when a creditor takes the pledged object with him, he is not regarded as wrongfully appropriating it but as 'looking after his pledge' ('*pignori suo incumbere*'). In an imperial constitution from 205 AD by Septimius Severus and Caracalla, reference is made to secured creditors who enforce their pledge by taking possession of the pledged assets when their debtor is in default.[79] According to the constitution they must not be regarded as having used force, although the possession must be gained with the permission of the governor. In another respect too, Alf. D. 13.7.30 aligns with the law on *pignus*. In early classical law the creditor with a possessory pledge would be liable for *culpa*: this is precisely the degree of liability imposed here on the creditor after he has taken possession of the boat.[80]

Cassius on the pledge of (a) wood and a ship

Gaius Cassius Longinus was a great-grandson of Servius Sulpicius Rufus and was a follower of Sabinus.[81] In D. 13.7.18.3, Paul reports an opinion by Cassius on what very well could have been a non-possessory pledge.

> **D. 13.7.18.3.** *Paulus libro vicensimo nono ad edictum.* Si quis caverit, ut silva sibi pignori esset, navem ex ea materia factam non esse pignori Cassius ait, quia aliud sit materia, aliud navis: et ideo nominatim in dando pignore adiciendum esse ait: 'Quaeque ex silva facta natave sint'.

[77] Krämer (2007: 229–30) plausibly argues that this would only allow the creditor to retain the thing as a measure to coerce the debtor into payment.

[78] In particular Krämer 2007: 211–48.

[79] Sev.-Ant. C. 8.13.3.

[80] Zimmermann 1990, 225–7 (with further references).

[81] Schulz 1953: 119.

> If someone provides that wood shall be a pledge for him, Cassius holds that a ship made from this material is not within the scope of the pledge; for the material is one thing and the ship is another. Hence, he holds it necessary to add expressly when the pledge is given: 'whatever things are the creation from or product of the wood'. [82]

When someone has negotiated that '*silva*' shall be pledged to him, a ship built from the wood shall not be subject to the pledge, because the wood and the ship are different materials. In order to achieve that the ship is also charged, Cassius recommends that a clause is included in the pledge agreement which expressly provides that the pledge shall extend to 'whatever things are the creation from and product of the wood'. One thing is clear about this text. *If* it is dealing with a right of *pignus*, this must have been a non-possessory pledge. The ship must have been built by, or on behalf of, the debtor, which presupposes that the pledged material from which it was built was still under his physical control.[83] In several other respects, however, the text is thought to be problematic.[84]

A possible translation of *silva* could be 'coppice': trees which have been felled. This translation solves a problem, which is connected with the fact that if *silva* means woodland or forest it would have been a *res mancipi* (unless it was situated in the provinces). In Cassius's time a *mancipatio* by way of *fiducia cum creditore* would normally be the preferred security interest for *res mancipi*.[85] Nevertheless, I consider it plausible that D. 13.7.18.3 is on *pignus*, even when the pledged object was woodland. There are other early classical Digest texts which may have concerned *pignus* of *res mancipi*.[86] The clause '*quaeque ex silva facta natave sint*' is typical for *pignus* and may have been derived by Cassius from the *formula* of the *interdictum de migrando* ('*ibi nata factave essent*') or from standard form tenant's pledges. It is similar to clauses reported by later jurists in respect of the produce of pledged land. In D. 20.1.32, Scaevola discusses a *conventio pignoris*, which expressly provided that 'whatever was brought on the pledged land or there arose or was produced was to be pledged'. This is, in my view, the clearest indication that we are probably not dealing with *fiducia cum creditore*. Even if the woodland had been

[82] For an elaborate exegesis of this text, see Krämer 2007: 249–75. [83] Krämer 2007: 249.

[84] Krämer 2007: 251–2.

[85] Wagner (1968: 30 n 207) assumes that D. 13.7.18.3 was concerned with *fiducia*. This interpretation is discussed (and rejected) by Krämer 2007: 257–62.

[86] Paul. (Nerv.) D. 20.2.9; Lab. D. 20.1.35; Marci. (Octav.) D. 20.3.1.2; Iav. D. 41.3.16; Pomp. (Sab./Atil.) D. 13.7.6 pr.

mancipated to the creditor, the ship (as *res nec mancipi*) would have had to be charged by way of *pignus* (or separately fiduciarily transferred by way of *in iure cessio*). In theory it would have been possible to add a supplemental *conventio pignoris* to the document recording the *pactum fiduciae*. The clause recommended by Cassius is, however, much more likely to have been part of an independent *conventio pignoris* concerning the wood itself. Another indication is that D. 13.7.18.3 is taken from book 29 of Paul's commentary of the praetor's edict, which was concerned with *pignus*. There is much to be said, therefore, for considering D. 13.7.18.3 as genuinely dealing with *pignus* in the shape of a non-possessory pledge, either on wood or on woodland.

Labeo on the right to sell an apartment building

Marcus Antistius Labeo († 10–21 AD) was the son of a jurist and had been a praetor.[87] His working life as a jurist partly coincided with the reign of emperor Augustus, whose politics he seriously disapproved and whose offer of a consulship he refused.[88] Pomponius's *Enchiridion* says that 'Labeo set out to make a great many innovations on account of the quality of his genius and the trust he had in his own learning which had drawn heavily on other branches of knowledge'.[89] Labeo's most innovative thinking is concerned with the enforceability of *pacta conventa*.[90] He was prepared to grant actions for the enforcement of agreements which were not recognized by the *ius civile* as enforceable contracts. Labeo's opinion in D. 20.1.35, which was apparently considered by the *Compilatores* as dealing with *pignus*, is precisely concerned with such a *pactum conventum*.

D. 20.1.35. *Labeo libro primo pithanon a Paulo epitomarum.* Si insula, quam tibi ex pacto convento licuit vendere, combusta est, deinde a debitore suo restituta, idem in nova insula iuris habes.

If a block which by agreement you had the right to sell is burned down and rebuilt by the debtor at his own expense, you have the same right in the new block.[91]

[87] Kunkel 1967: 114. [88] Schiavone 2012: 311, 319, 339, and 398.
[89] Pomp. D. 1.2.2.47 *in fine*. [90] Gallo 1992: 71–252; Schiavone 2012: 319–33.
[91] For an elaborate exegesis of this text, see Krämer 2007: 276–99.

This fragment may have been concerned with a right of *pignus* created on an appartment block (*insula*) and holds that when the block burned down and was rebuilt by the debtor at his own expense, the creditor shall have the same right in the new block. If dealing with *pignus*, Labeo D. 20.1.35 would—for several reasons—be an important opinion. First of all, it would be an early classical example of a jurist's opinion on a right of *pignus* charged on a *res mancipi*. It would also be an early classical example of a pledge which was to be enforced by selling the pledged property (rather than by way of retention or forfeiture). And finally, Labeo D. 20.1.35 would also be an early classical example of a non-possessory pledge, as the fact that the debtor rebuilt the building presupposes that it was in his full possession.[92]

The words '*ex pacto convento licuit vendere*' are in all likelihood a reference to the *conventio pignoris*, giving the creditor the right to sell the pledged property.[93] These words are hardly different, for instance, from those of Pomp. D. 13.7.8.5: '*cum pignus ex pactione venire potest*'.[94] Here also, an agreement allowing one party to sell his debtor's property is characterized as an agreement to pledge that property. One cannot entirely exclude the possibility that Lab. D. 20.1.35 was concerned with *fiducia cum creditore*, as the charged property was a *res mancipi*.[95] However, I consider it not very likely that where real estate had been mancipated by way of *fiducia*, Labeo would refer to this transaction as *ex pacto convento licuit vendere*. It is true, a *mancipatio fiduciae causa* would have been accompanied by a *pactum fiduciae*, which would have included a licence to sell.[96] However, it would be odd that Labeo would use a clause in this supplemental agreement in order to refer to a *fiducia cum creditore*, rather than to its constitutive acts (*mancipatio* and *pactum fiduciae*). This looks much more like a *conventio pignoris*, which (at Labeo's time) may still have been enforceable on the basis of the *edictum de pactis* or otherwise (separate edict for *actio Serviana*, *actio utilis*, or *actio in factum*).[97] In case of *pignus* the *conventio pignoris* is the constitutive act, so that here a reference to one of its components is less strange. In conclusion, a good case can be made for regarding Lab. D. 20.1.35 as an early classical non-possessory pledge.

[92] Kunkel (1967: 162–5) regards Labeo's text as a description of an early ancestor of the non-possessory pledge, which he calls the 'substitution pledge'. According to Kunkel, this substitution pledge was non-possessory and not enforceable with the *actio Serviana* (whose evolution towards a general pledge remedy had—according to Kunkel—not yet taken place). The creditor merely had a contractual right against the debtor for handing over the pledged thing, in order to exercise his right to sell it to a third party (as contemplated in D. 20.1.35). This interpretation is accepted by Kaser 1982: 18–9, 136–7. See also Kaser, Knütel, and Lohsse 2021: 232. Kunkel's interpretation is rejected by Krämer 2007: 234–6. See also section 5.4.

[93] Kaser 1982: 8.

[94] See also Pap. D. 20.4.3.2.

[95] Krämer 2007: 279.

[96] See section 5.3.

[97] See section 4.5.

6.5 *Hypotheca* Contracted *Nuda Conventione*

A pivotal point in the history of *pignus* is the jurist, Julian. At least, this is the impression one could get after a comprehensive reading of Digest texts on *pignus*. It is Julian who first uses the expression *conventio pignoris*, who first mentions that *hypotheca* could be created by mere agreement (*nuda conventione*), and who may have generalized the *actio Serviana*. Even if all this were true, we would not be dealing with a sudden evolutionary acceleration, a 'punctuated equilibrium'. In several cases (tenant's pledge, warehouse pledge, and pledge and lease-back) the possessory element was already diluted by effectively replacing the *traditio* with other means for exercising control, and in early classical legal opinions traces of non-possessory pledges can be found. In the classical sources the pledge granted *nuda conventione* is often referred to as *hypotheca* and the *actio Serviana* as *actio hypothecaria*.[98] These words, borrowed from Greek, could indicate that there were Greek-Hellenistic influences. Julian's role may have been that he was the first to provide a synthesis of the 'modern' Roman law of pledge.

Pignus, nuda conventione, and *hypotheca*

In the second century AD it came to be recognized that the right of *hypotheca* could be created—as Julian says—merely by means of a contract: '*creditor nuda conventione hypothecam contraxerit*'. The real right of pledge would not require a separate disposition (*traditio*) in addition to the pledge agreement, not even for the pledge of *res mancipi*. It is remarkable that a right *in rem*, which was enforceable against any possessor of the pledged object, could be granted by contract alone. In the case of the transfer of ownership, it was never accepted in classical law that this could take place by agreement only: at the end of the third century AD, Diocletian still ruled that the ownership of goods is transferred through *traditio* and not by 'naked pacts'.[99]

The first jurist in our sources to use the expressions *nuda conventione* and *hypotheca* is Julian.[100] In this fragment we encounter both expressions.

[98] See, for example, the texts quoted in this section. For a complete overview, see Manigk 1916b: 362–3. Manigk has counted the number of references to the noun *hypotheca* (104) and the adjective *hypothecaria* (16) in the Digest. More than half of the references are by Marcian.

[99] Diocl.-Max. C. 2.3.20: '*dominia rerum, non nudis pactis transferuntur*'. Gordon 1970: 1–2 and passim.

[100] The first imperial constitution mentioning *hypotheca* is Sev.-Ant. C. 8.40.2.1 (207 AD).

> **D. 41.3.33.4.** *Iulianus libro quadragensimo quarto digestorum.* Qui pignori rem dat, usucapit, quamdiu res apud creditorem est: si creditor eius possessionem alii tradiderit, interpellabitur usucapio... Plane si creditor nuda conventione hypothecam contraxerit, usucapere debitor perseverabit.
>
> A person giving a thing in pledge usucapts it so long as it is with the creditor; but if the creditor delivers possession of it to someone else, the *usucapio* is stopped... It is evident that if the creditor contracts a hypothec by mere agreement, the debtor will continue to usucapt.

In the first sentence, Julian indicates that the fact that the pledged object is in the hands of the creditor (possessory pledge) does not adversely affect the debtor's *usucapio*. A fortiori, according to Julian, this will also be the case where the debtor has granted a *hypotheca* by mere agreement ('*nuda conventione*'). In D. 41.3.33.4 the term *pignus* is used for a possessory pledge, while *hypotheca* denotes a non-possessory one. In the Digest there is, however, only one text which expressly sets out the difference between *pignus* and *hypotheca*.[101]

> **D. 13.7.9.2.** *Ulpianus libro vigensimo octavo ad edictum.* Proprie pignus dicimus, quod ad creditorem transit, hypothecam, cum non transit nec possessio ad creditorem.
>
> Properly speaking, we use *pignus* for that which transfers to the creditor and *hypotheca* for that in which not even possession transfers to the creditor.

D. 13.7.9.2 has been taken from a commentary on *fiducia* and could have been interpolated. Originally, it could have read: 'Properly speaking, we use *fiducia* for that which transfers to the creditor and *hypotheca* for that in which neither ownership nor possession transfers to the creditor'.[102] Its original purpose would then have been to compare *fiducia* with *hypotheca*: in case of *fiducia* ownership transfers to the creditor, while in case of *hypotheca* neither ownership nor possession transfers to the creditor. However, particularly when Ulp. D. 13.7.9.2 is read in conjunction with a text from Gaius it appears that it may very well be authentic. Gaius D. 50.16.238.2 indicates that the original meaning of *pignus* was possessory pledge. A 'proper' right of pledge ('*pignus proprie*') exclusively concerned something which could be handed

[101] See also Just. *Inst.* 4.6.7.

[102] '*Proprie fiduciam dicimus, quod ad creditorem transit, hypothecam, cum non transit nec dominium nec possessio ad creditorem*'.

over: movable property ('*rei mobilis*'). The '*proprie pignus*' in Ulp. D. 13.7.9.2 is therefore a possessory pledge, which must be distinguished from *hypotheca* (= non-possessory pledge) with a view to possession. In case of *hypotheca* not only does ownership not transfer to the creditor, in contrast with *pignus* not even possession passes to him.[103]

Although the term *hypotheca* is more often used in respect of non-possessory pledges, there are also texts where it is used as a general term for possessory and non-possessory pledges.[104] Kaser was not able to identify texts in which *hypotheca* is used for a possessory pledge only.[105] However, Pap. D. 20.1.1.3 discusses an agreement that if interest is not paid in time, the fruits of the hypothecated goods ('*fructus hypothecarum*') will be set off against the interest. This means that the creditor was capable of harvesting the fruits, so that he must have been in possession of the pledged fruit-yielding property. In the jurists' writings and imperial constitutions there is no consistent and generally accepted terminology for distinguishing possessory from non-possessory pledges.[106] Marcian observes that 'between *pignus* and *hypotheca* only the sound of the name differs'.[107] *Pignus* and *hypotheca* are one species, with basically the same legal consequences. Where Marcian says in D. 20.1.5 pr. that 'property can be given in *hypotheca* for any obligation', this equally applies to possessory and non-posessory pledges.[108] In Marci. D. 20.5.7 pr. the same jurist reports that, according to Julian, where a creditor has sold the pledged property subject to the condition that he may repay the price and take it back, the creditor is liable to assign his actions against the purchaser to the debtor. Marcian adds: 'What Julian writes of *pignus* also applies to *hypotheca*.' In transactional practices, jurists' writings, and imperial constitutions *pignus* and *hypotheca* are often combined.[109]

Hellenistic origin of *hypotheca*

One of the great 'riddles' (Kaser) of modern Romanist research is how and why the word *hypotheca*, borrowed from Greek, was assimilated in Roman

[103] Kaser 1982: 131 n 12.

[104] According to Manigk *hypotheca*, like *pignus*, is also used in order to refer to the pledged object, in particular by Marcian (D. 20.1.16.3.1; D. 20.1.16.6); other references in Manigk 1916b: 344. See also Gai. D. 20.4.11.1; Gai. D. 20.6.7. pr.; Diocl.-Max. C. 8.25.8.

[105] Kaser 1982: 131 n 11. [106] Kaser 1982: 133.

[107] Marci. D. 20.1.5.1 ('*Inter pignus autem et hypothecam tantum nominis sonus differt*').

[108] In Scaev. D. 20.1.34.1 'ὑποθήκη' is called '*pignus*'.

[109] For example, Scaev. D. 45.1.122.1 ('*sub pignoribus et hypothecis mercibus*'); Marci. D. 20.4.12 pr. ('*pignori hypothecaeve*'); Sev.-Ant. C. 8.40.2.1 ('*pignora vel hypothecas*').

legal speech.[110] Is this merely a terminological matter—Greek expressions being used in order to facilitate Greek-speaking communities—or a symptom of a more substantial influence of Greek legal practices? The modern view is that the use of *hypotheca* in the classical sources is a terminological matter rather than evidence of a full-scale legal transplant from Greek-Hellenistic law to Roman law.[111] In my opinion, this does not rule out the possibility that Hellenistic transactional practices did contribute to the origin of new variants of *pignus*. There is a distinct possibility that the Greek loan word *hypotheca* indicates that Hellenistic transactional practices (e.g., maritime loans and ὑποθήκη) did influence the evolution of *pignus* and *hypotheca* to a security right *in rem* that could be created *nuda conventione*. Their knowledge of Hellenistic forms of non-possessory pledges may have contributed to Julian and other jurists taking the relatively small step from possessory pledges with diluted possessory elements to a purely contractual right of pledge.[112] The 'elasticity' of the still-evolving Roman *pignus*, precisely at a time in which cultural and economic exchanges reached a high level in the Mediterranean, would suggest this and the 'singular reception' of Greek terms in the law of security would confirm this presumption.[113]

The term *hypotheca* may have been used specifically for the accomodation of security rights granted pursuant to documents drawn up in accordance with local Hellenistic laws and practices.[114] The word *hypotheca* was frequently used in the Greek-speaking part of the Roman empire and could have entered Roman legal speech via Roman provincial jurisdictions, in order to clarify for a Greek speaking audience which legal institution was covered by the provincial edict.[115] By Scaevola's time, Roman jurists were quite familiar with the Greek/Hellenistic legal contract of ὑποθήκη. In the first century BC, Cicero already referred to ὑποθήκη by means of the Latin transliteration *hypotheca* in a letter he sent to his friend, Q.M. Thermus.[116] This example is taken from the Hellenistic Roman East, where at the time Cicero was proconsul of Cilicia

[110] Kaser 1982: 129. See also Wagner (1968: 24); Fuenteseca 2013: 123–40. See recently also Mauer 2022: 69–93.

[111] Wagner 1968: 22.

[112] For a similar argument, see Kaser 1982: 130.

[113] Kaser 1976: 203. Kaser (1971: 463) observes that there are no 'palpable traces' of an influence of the Greek non-possessory ὑποθήκη and warns that the problem of Greek influences of the Roman law of pledge cannot be solved with certainty '*mit unseren Mitteln*' (Kaser 1976: 203). Braukmann (2008: 58) argues that the Greek ὑποθήκη has at least been an example for overcoming the 'classical' principle of possessory pledge as introduced by Servius Sulpicius Rufus. Schanbacher argues that the Roman pledge was the result of a reception of a Greek legal institution (Schanbacher 2006: 69-70). See also Krämer 2007: 175-6.

[114] Wagner 1968: 21–2. In stronger terms, Braukmann 2008: 58 (example of a deliberate attempt to introduce the purely contractual pledge in Roman law).

[115] Wagner 1968: 20–2; Kaser 1971: 463.

[116] Cic., *Fam.* 13.56.

while Thermus was the propraetor of Asia. This Greek word may even have trickled down to the formal sources of law. Gaius did write a *Liber singularis ad formulam hypothecariam* and from the late classical period there is a monograph by Marcian with the same title. The word *hypotheca* is used consistently by Gaius and Marcian and may be explained by their connections with the eastern part of the Roman empire.[117] They both had studied in Rome but had a Hellenistic background and wrote and taught in the eastern provinces.[118] It is held in modern literature that the terms *hypotheca* and *hypothecaria* were not used in the provincial edict itself, which followed the urban edict closely. These expressions would only be employed in the *responsa* of jurists on rights of pledge granted in a Hellenistic setting.[119] In his commentary on the provincial edict, Gaius refers to 'the *quasi-Serviana*, which is also called *hypothecaria*'.[120] The '*et hypothecaria vocatur*' could suggest that we are dealing with colloquial speech.[121] One cannot, however, exclude the possibility that in its *formula* for the *actio Serviana* the provincial edict may have used the words '*pignus hypothecave*' and in conjunction therewith have referred to '*actio Serviana vel hypothecaria*'.[122] In his monograph Marcian discusses the *exceptio* '*si non mihi ante pignori hypothecaeve sit res obligata*'.[123] Here the word *hypotheca* is used in a procedural device, which may very well indicate that at that time, *hypotheca*, and perhaps even *actio hypothecaria*, had become technical expressions which were included in the provincial edict(s).[124] Also the term '*formula*' in the title of the works of Gaius and Marcian could point in this direction.

Conventio pignoris as 'real' contract (*contractus re*)

Gaius writes in his Institutes that obligations arising out of contract can be divided into four categories. An obligation is contracted through a thing ('*re contrahitur obligatio*'), by words ('*verbis*'), by writing ('*litteris*'), or by agreement ('*consensu*') (Gai. *Inst.* 3.89).[125] Obligations 'contracted through a thing' only arise once the objects in question are handed over from one party to the

117 More than half of the texts using *hypotheca* or *hypothecaria* are from Marcian (*hypotheca*: Gaius 16 and Marcian 64; *hypothecaria*: Gaius 2 and Marcian 8). See Manigk 1916b: 362–3.

118 Liebs 1997: 188, 201.

119 Manigk 1916b: 349.

120 Gai. D. 16.1.13.1 ('*cum quasi serviana quae et hypothecaria vocatur*').

121 Wagner 1968: 23.

122 Kaser 1971: 463. See also Sirks 2019: 330, 332.

123 Marci. D. 20.4.12 pr.

124 On the lack of familiarity with Roman legal terms in the Greek-speaking world of Asia minor, see Huttner 2020.

125 In the same sense Gai. D. 44.7.1.

other. In his Institutes, the only contract referred to by Gaius as giving rise to an obligation *re contrahitur* is *mutuum* (Gai. *Inst.* 3.90).[126] In another work, with respect to *pignus*, Gaius writes: 'Also a creditor who received a thing in pledge is liable through a thing; and he is himself liable for return of the very thing which he received' (D. 44.7.1.6).[127] The characterization of the pledge agreement as 'real', therefore, means nothing more than that the creditor's *obligation* to give back the pledged property arises by operation of law, by the simple fact that physical control has been transferred.[128] This is reflected in the *formula in factum* of the *actio pigneraticia directa*, which expressly states that the creditor has not returned the pledged property after discharge of the secured debt.[129] In other words, a duty to return the charged property did not have to be expressly agreed upon by the parties: it was sufficient that the debtor could demonstrate that property had been handed over by way of pledge to the creditor. This may explain why—in contrast with *fiducia* documents—we do not find contractual provisions on the return of the charged property in the pledge documents which have survived.[130]

When one thinks in terms of 'real contract' it is easy to regard the *conventio pignoris* as an anomaly in so far as it concerns a non-possessory pledge, or to confine the 'real' nature to pledge agreements purporting to create a possessory pledge.[131] This 'real' nature of the *conventio pignoris* could then be used as evidence that originally *pignus* could only exist as a possessory pledge. But if one reads Gaius carefully, one can see that he does not characterize the *conventio pignoris* as a real contract but specifically indicates that the creditor's *obligation* to return the pledged property (after discharge of the secured debt) arises by transferring physical control.[132] It would, therefore, be more accurate to speak of 'real obligations' rather than of 'real contracts'. In other words, when the *conventio pignoris* purports to create a non-possessory pledge it is a valid contract, pursuant to which the parties can contractually agree to create certain rights (e.g., the creditor's right to sell the pledged property in case of default) and obligations (e.g., the debtor's assumption of risk). Only when the physical control of the pledged property is actually transferred to the

[126] Gaius also mentions obligations arising out of transfers made under the mistaken belief that they were indebted (*condictio indebiti*), although he realizes that they are not based on a contract.

[127] '*Creditor quoque, qui pignus accepit, re tenetur: qui et ipse de ea ipsa re quam accepit restituenda tenetur.*'

[128] On *contractus re*, see Wegmann Stockebrand 2017 (*conventio pignoris*: 206–8).

[129] Section 6.6.

[130] Bertoldi (2012: 87) observes that where D. 44.4.4.8 refers to a *pactum* for restitution of the charged property this probably did not concern *pignus*.

[131] Zimmermann 1990: 221.

[132] In a similar sense, Wegmann Stockebrand 2017: 208–25.

creditor—at the beginning or at a later stage—does the 'real' nature of the obligation to restore the property entail that it arises by operation of law.[133] The contract to grant a non-possessory pledge is not an anomaly, nor is Gaius's remark that a creditor who received a thing in pledge is liable 'through a thing' (D. 44.7.1.6) necessarily a remnant of the idea that the right of pledge could originally only exist as a possessory pledge.

6.6 *Actio Serviana* and *Actiones Pigneraticiae in Personam*

From a modern analytical perspective, the *conventio pignoris* is a hybrid institution. It is within the scope of the law of property, because (certainly since Julian) a proprietary right of pledge could be created *nuda conventione*.[134] From Julian onwards, the 'naked' (*nuda*) *conventio pignoris* itself gave rise to an *actio in rem* (*actio Serviana*) that could be instituted against third parties in possession of the pledged property. At the same time the *conventio pignoris* constituted a contractual relationship between the debtor and the creditor, dealing with their rights and obligations *inter se*. This contractual relationship was sanctioned by *actiones pigneraticiae in personam*.[135] The constitutive elements of *pignus* as a legal institution are therefore to be found not only in the *formula* of the *actio Serviana (in rem)* but also in the *formulae* of the *actiones pigneraticiae (in personam)*. For this reason, in this section, I will also take the opportunity to say something about the enforcement of the pledge agreement as a contract with the personal *actiones pigneraticiae*. Like the *actio Serviana* they illustrate how the jurists were ready to adapt Roman law to the needs of the economic environment.

Pledge of *invecta et illata*; *interdictum Salvianum*

The Catonian pledges of *invecta et illata* can already be characterized as representing a preliminary or intermediate stage of a non-possessory

[133] See also Schwarz (1954: 157), who observes that it is obvious that handing over the pledged object was a condition of the *actio pigneraticia directa*, otherwise a *reddere* could not come into question. The concept of a real contract is too narrow here: the *actio pigneraticia contraria* was not only independent from handing over the object, it would also continue to be available to the creditor after the object had been given back to the debtor or sold to a third party (when the object had caused financial damages to the creditor).

[134] Kaser 1982: 23–4.

[135] The *actio Serviana* is sometimes referred to in the sources as *actio pigneraticia (in rem)*: Marcell. D. 44.2.19; Ulp. D. 10.3.7.12; Paul. D. 12.6.13 pr.; Diocl.-Max. C. 8.15.5. Ulp. D. 10.4.3.3 speaks of '*pigneraticia Serviana sive hypothecaria*'.

pledge.[136] In order to strenghten the creditor's position in respect of pledged *invecta et illata*, legal remedies were developed in late republican law.[137] One of these remedies was the *interdictum Salvianum*. This interdict was a prohibitory interdict directed against the tenant, which allowed the landlord to remove pledged assets from the leased farm or land so that they could be sold by way of execution.[138] The landlord would thus be put in the same position as a creditor to whom a straightforward possessory pledge had been granted *ab initio*.[139] This makes it pretty obvious that what were, in effect, non-possessory pledges, already gave rise to legal remedies in pre-classical law. This may not yet have been the full-fledged pledge as a right *in rem* of classical law. At least, this would be the only possible conclusion when one assumes that in late republican law the *interdictum Salvianum*'s only function was to give the landowner a remedy against the tenant (therefore not against third persons).[140] However, probably not long after the introduction of this interdict, the *actio Serviana* was included in the praetor's edict,[141] perhaps originally exclusively for tenant's pledges, so that in the first century BC at least this form of hybrid non-possessory pledge had evolved into a full-fledged right *in rem*.

The *actio Serviana* in the *Edictum perpetuum*

As a general *edictal* action available to all pledge creditors, the *actio Serviana* may have been introduced by Julian in the second century AD, when he drafted the *Edictum perpetuum*.[142] Even if one accepts that it was indeed Julian who did so,[143] the origin of Julian's 'innovation' may lie in the early classical period preceding him. Soon after its introduction in the first century BC the *formula* of this *actio Serviana* may have been adapted to accommodate other creditors than landlords.[144] Out of these incidental grantings of *actiones utiles* an extra-edictal practice may have evolved of granting an adapted *actio*

[136] Giuffré 1992: 117. [137] Kaser 1982: 17. [138] Section 4.4.

[139] Krämer 2007: 198. As such it is the functional equivalent of the self-help remedy of *perclusio* for urban tenancies.

[140] Section 4.4. [141] Section 4.5.

[142] For example, Schulz 1951: 408; Kaser 1971: 472; De Iuliis 2017: 141–54; Kaser, Knütel and Lohsse 2021: 237. Ankum, Van Gessel-de Roo, and Pool (1987: 370) consider it likely that the *actio Serviana* was included in the praetor's edict as a general pledge remedy at the beginning of the classical period.

[143] See section 4.5 for alternative intepretations (Magdelain 1958; Wubbe and Pichonnaz 2003) that from its inception the *actio Serviana* was the general action for pledges.

[144] Kaser 1982: 147, 150–1; Kaser 1986: 322. There are two Digest texts from before Julian who appear to concern an *actio Serviana* granted to other creditors than landlords: Octavenus in Marci. D. 20.3.1.2 and Cels. D. 46.3.69. See Krämer 2007: 291–8.

Serviana to any pledge creditor against possessors of pledged objects.[145] This practice culminated in 131 AD in the inclusion of the generalized *actio Serviana* in the *Edictum perpetuum*. This edictal *actio Serviana* had the *conventio pignoris* as its central element and covered both possessory and non-possessory pledges.

The classical *formula* for the *actio Serviana*—as it was recorded in the *Edictum perpetuum*—has been reconstructed by Lenel as follows:

> Si paret inter Aulum Agerium et Lucium Titium convenisse, ut ea res qua de agitur Aulo Agerio pignori esset propter pecuniam debitam, eamque rem tunc, cum conveniebat, in bonis Lucii Titii fuisse eamque pecuniam neque solutam neque eo nomine satisfactum esse neque per Aulum Agerium stare quo minus solvatur, nisi ea res arbitrio iudicis restituetur, quanti ea res erit, tantam pecuniam iudex Numerium Negidium Aulo Agerio condemnato.[146]
>
> If it appears (a_1) that it had been agreed between Aulus Agerius and Lucius Titius that the object which is at issue would be pledged to Aulus Agerius (a_2) for money owed, (a_3) that that object at the time it was agreed was in the patrimony of Lucius Titius, (a_4) that this money has not been paid nor otherwise satisfaction has been given for this claim and (a_5) it is not because of Aulus Agerius that nothing has been paid, and (a_6) if the object shall not be restored at the award of the judge, (*b*) do you, judge, condemn Numerius Negidius to Aulus Agerius for so much money as the object will be worth?

The forms of action (*formulae*) which were the central element of the formulary procedure were formulated and operated as conditional programs: the *formula* of the *actio Serviana* did have an 'if *a* then *b* structure'. *If* it appears that it had been agreed between a creditor and a debtor that an object was pledged (a_1) and certain other conditions (a_{2-6}) were satisfied, *then* the judge shall condemn the defendant in possession of the pledged object to pay its value to the claimant (*b*).[147] In Lenel's reconstruction of the *formula* of the

[145] Kaser 1982: 150–1.

[146] Lenel 1927: 494–5.

[147] Kaser (1986: 330) has suggested that *in bonis esse* condition (a_3) was originally part of colloquial language, but became a technical expression in classical law. Ankum and Pool (1989: 41) strongly deny this and hold that '[t]he whole *in bonis* terminology should indeed be regarded as a product of the interpretative practice of the jurists'. It would seem that Kaser refers to a different evolutionary stage (origin of *in bonis*) than the much later (classical) stage which Ankum and Pool had in mind. For *in bonis esse* in the *formula* of the *actio Serviana*, see Ankum and Pool 1989; Verhagen 2014; and Sirks 2019. The conditions *pecuniam debitam* and *eamque pecuniam neque solutam neque eo nomine satisfactum esse* (the 'discharge clause') are the foundations of (what we now call) the principle of dependence (accessory nature) and are the subject of the monographs by Out (2005) and Marino (2018). For an elaboration of the condemnation (*b*) of the *actio Serviana*, see the Annex.

actio Serviana the *conventio pignoris* is the central element (*convenisse*, etc.). This may well represent the original text of the form of action, certainly if one accepts that the *actio Serviana* was within the scope of the *edictum de pactis*.[148] However, if the *traditio* originally was an essential element of the granting of the pledge itself, the *actio Serviana*'s *formula* could have reflected this: *Si paret A^m A^m Lucio Titio rem qua de agitur pignori dedisse*...(or *pignoris causa tradisse*). Parallel to *fiducia cum creditore*, the granting of a full-fledged right *in rem* would originally be based on a contractual agreement (*conventio pignoris*) combined with a proprierary disposition (*traditio*). In the hypothetical *formula* reproduced above, this is represented by the phrase *pignori dedisse*. Originally the expression *pignus dare* may have related to possessory pledges and refer to the *traditio* or equivalent acts (e.g., *inductio*) which were necessary to grant a pledge that was enforceable against third parties with the *actio Serviana*.[149]

Debtor's *actio pigneraticia (directa)*

The accessory nature of the right of pledge entailed that upon discharge of the secured debt, it would automatically cease to exist.[150] The debtor could claim restitution of the pledged object with the *rei vindicatio* or the *actio Publiciana*. However, there may have been situations where instituting an ownership-based real action would be of no avail to the debtor, in particular where the creditor was no longer in possession of the pledged object or it had been destroyed. The debtor would originally be granted an *actio in personam*—the *condictio*—against the creditor for the value of the pledged object.[151] This *condictio* may have been the ancestor of a contractual action which was specifically designed and developed by the jurists (formally: the praetor) for

[148] Section 4.5. If the scope of the *actio Serviana* would originally have been confined to tenant's pledges, its *formula* could have read as follows: *Si paret inter A^m.A^m. et Lucium Titium convenisse, ut, quae in eum fundum qua de agitur introducta importata ibi nata factave essent, ea pignori Aulo Agerio pro mercede eius fundi essent*...(If it appears that it had been agreed between Aulus Agerius and Lucius Titius that things introduced or imported into the farm in question, or born or made there, would be pledged to Aulus Agerius for the rent of the farm...). Lenel 1927: 494–5.

[149] Kaser 1982: 5, 132–3. See also Wagner 1967: 182. In Jul. D. 41.3.33.5 the words '*pignori tibi dem*' clearly designate a possessory pledge, which (for the purposes of *ususcapio*) is contrasted with a non-possessory pledge created 'by mere agreement'.

[150] For a detailed reconstruction and interpretation of the *actio pigneraticia (directa)*, see Kaser 1982: 197–207.

[151] Ulp. D. 12.1.4.1 ('*Res pignori data pecunia soluta condici potest*'). Kaser 1982: 93 n 191, 98 n 224.

sanctioning the *conventio pignoris*: the *actio pigneraticia (directa)*.[152] The *formula* of this actio was *in factum concepta*, based on the fact that the debtor had given an object as a pledge to the creditor: *Si rem A^m A^m N^o N^o qua de agitur ob pecuniam debitam pignori dedisse....*[153] The *iudex* would condemn the creditor to pay the monetary value of the pledged object (*quanti ea res erit*).[154] What exactly the creditor's standard of liability was for not returning the pledged property is not entirely clear.[155] Originally this liability may have been confined to cases where the creditor simply refused to return the pledged object or deliberately made this impossible (e.g., by destroying it). Later this liability for *dolus* may have been extended to negligence (*culpa*). Thus, for late classical law Ulpian D. 50.17.23 counts the pledge creditor among those contractual parties who are liable for *dolus* (wilful default) and *culpa* (negligence).[156] In another text, however, the same jurist holds that the pledge creditor is also liable for theft (*custodia*). This extension of liability may have been connected with the origin of a new variant of the *actio pigneraticia*, with a *formula in ius concepta*.

In all likelihood, in the high classical period a second form of action was designed by the jurists for the debtor's contractual action against the creditor. This was an *actio pigneraticia* with a *formula in ius concepta*, which incorporated the concept of *bona fides*.[157] The main advantage of this more flexible *formula*, which may have been the reason for its origin, was that the *ex fide bona* clause allowed the *iudex* to condemn the creditor to return the *superfluum* to the debtor.[158] The phrase '*quanti ea res erit*' of the *actio pigneraticia in factum concepta* may not have allowed for this. The *actio pigneraticia in ius concepta* did not oust *the actio pigneraticia in factum concepta*, which continued to exist alongside the new action. This cannot be explained simply

[152] Kaser notices, however, that the debtor's *actio pigneraticia* has a 'dark prehistory'. Kaser 1982: 229 n 191. Kaser has reconstructed the praetor's edict on the *actio pigneraticia (directa)* as follows: *Quod ob pecuniam debitam pignori datum esse dicetur, de eo iudicium dabo.*

[153] The word *dedisse* in the *actio pigneraticia (directa)* may reflect the original possessory nature of *pignus*, but *pignus dare* could (certainly later) also designate the granting of (possessory and non-possessory) pledges in general. Kaser 1982: 200.

[154] The fact that someone else's property had been pledged also did not prevent that when the secured debt had been discharged, the (non-owning) debtor could institute the *actio pigneraticia* in order to recover the pledged property from the creditor (Ulp. D. 13.7.9.4). In other words, the debtor's (civilian or praetorian) ownership (*in bonis*) of the pledged property was *not* a requirement for a valid and enforceable *conventio pignoris* as a contractual relationship.

[155] Zimmermann 1990: 225–7.

[156] General actions—such as the *actio furti* and the *actio legis aquiliae*—remained available to the pledge debtor, although subject to general principles of concurrent actions. For instance, Gai. D. 13.6.18.1 says that where the creditor has damaged the pledged object the debtor shall either have the *actio pigneraticia (directa)* or the *actio legis aquiliae* against the creditor.

[157] Kaser 1982: 98. [158] Zimmermann 1990: 223.

with reference to Roman traditionalism, which generally preferred the gradual withering away of obsolete institutions above their immediate repeal. The reason for the continuing existence of *the actio pigneraticia in factum concepta* may have been that it sometimes offered certain advantages. The *quanti ea res erit* would condemn the creditor to pay the objective value of the pledged property, even if the actual loss of the debtor was much less (e.g., because he did not own the pledged property).[159] Kaser regards this as a consequence of conservatism, but in a more articulate way. In their consulting practice for private clients and as counsel to praetors and *iudices*, the jurists had elaborated the contractual relationship between debtor and creditor on the basis of the *formula in factum concepta*. This 'rich and dense interlacing of thoughts', which was based on the controversies arising from casuistry, became part of jurisprudence. The jurists held on to this passed-down material, which offered fertile ground for further discussions. They tried to manage with the old form of action and only where this would not be possible would they try to fill gaps with the more elastic and 'modern' *formula in ius concepta*.[160]

Creditor's *actio pigneraticia (contraria)*

For some time during the classical period the *conventio pignoris* did not yet have all the attributes which it had later on. In particular, the creditor may initially not yet have had the *actio pigneraticia contraria* at his disposal. Instead, he would have relied on non-contractual actions (e.g., *actio furti*, *actio ad exhibendum*, *actio de dolo*) and other remedies (e.g., a lien in the form of a defence against the debtor's (personal or real) action for the return of the pledged objects).[161] A striking case discussed by Labeo is recorded in Pomponius's commentary on Sabinus (D. 13.7.3). A creditor visited the debtor (probably) at his home in order to return the pledged asset, expecting to be paid the money owed. Immediately upon having repossessed the pledged object, the debtor hurled it through a window, where it was caught by an accomplice who absconded with it. According to Labeo the creditor could institute both the *actio furti* and the *actio ad exhibendum* against the debtor. According to Pomponius the creditor can also institute the *actio pigneraticia*

[159] Kaser 1982: 230. [160] Kaser 1982: 230–1, whom I have closely followed in the main text.

[161] These remedies would not always be helpful. For instance, a lien (*ius retentionis*) would have been of little help where the creditor had incurred medical expenses for a pledged slave who had died (Zimmermann 1990: 227).

contraria. The fact that Labeo does not mention this (obvious) remedy may be an indication that it did not yet exist in his time.[162] Also, in opinions by late classical jurists (Ulpian and Paul), the debtor is held liable for wrongful behaviour with the *actio pigneratica (contraria)*, while this possibility is not mentioned by the early classical jurists (Sabinus and Cassius) to whom they refer, who instead would grant an *actio furti* or *actio de dolo*.[163] The *actio pigneraticia contraria* would be particularly beneficial to the creditor where the debtor had pledged someone else's property, in the mistaken belief that it was his own. In that event he would not be liable with the *actio de dolo*. The *actio pigneraticia contraria in ius concepta* (with the *bona fides* clause) was much more adapted to cases like this.[164] The debtor's ignorance did not exempt him from this contractual liability.[165] With this action the creditor could claim compensation for the loss of his security interest.[166]

6.7 Continuation of Older Practices

In the Digest and Codex there are a number of texts on a transactional practice pursuant to which the debtor would either rent the pledged object from the creditor or hold it pursuant to *precarium*.[167] This transactional construction is also attested for *fiducia cum creditore* and may have Greek origins.[168] Although from a legal perspective we are still dealing with a possessory pledge—the texts often expressly state that possession is with the creditor—from a practical perspective this pledge was equivalent to non-possessory security: the debtor could continue to use the charged objects. Despite the availability of a more 'modern' alternative (purely contractual pledge), this transactional practice continued to be frequently used until the end of the classical period.

[162] See on Pomp. D. 13.7.3, Kaser 1982: 91–2.

[163] Ulp. D 13.7.36 pr. and Paul. D. 41.3.4.21. See Kaser 1982: 87. More cautiously Schwarz 1954: 136, according to whom one cannot exclude the possibility that Sabinus did not yet know the *actio pigneraticia contraria* in the function of an independent claim for damages.

[164] On this action, see Kaser 1982: 222–34, generally following Schwarz 1954. See also Scheibelreiter 2020: 72–7 (with further references), who considers it 'well defendable' that the contrary action was *in ius concepta* and did have a *bona fides* condition.

[165] See in particular Paul. D. 13.7.16.1. Kaser 1982: 87 n 163, with reference to Schwarz 1954: 142; Scheibelreiter 2020: 70, 89–90.

[166] On the question whether the creditor could sue the debtor for the granting of a substitute right of pledge on property he *did* own, see Scheibelreiter 2020 (who thinks that this reflects Justinian law at most, but certainly not classical law).

[167] See in particular Kaser 1982: 168–83. For convenience's sake I will use 'charge and lease-back' as the generic terms for secured transactions in which the debtor is entitled to use the collateral, pursuant to either a *locatio conductio* or *precarium*, although literally this term only covers the first situation. The expression 'pledge and lease-back' is used for a charge and lease-back involving *pignus*.

[168] Gai. *Inst.* 2.60.

As late as the third century AD Ulpian writes that it is daily ('*cottidie*') practice that pledged assets are left with the debtor pursuant to *precarium*.[169] In this section I will discuss why this practice *originated* and why it *persisted*. One would expect the practice of pledge and lease-back to have been mostly used in respect of farms, houses, and land. Beside the pledge and lease-back, we find in the legal sources another practice in relation to real estate, which continued to exist after the purely contractual pledge was recognized: the granting of pledge by handing over 'title documents'. At the end of this section this practice will be reviewed.

Pledge and lease-back

The point of departure in case of *fiducia cum creditore* must have been that the debtor did not only convey ownership through *mancipatio* but, certainly in case of movable *res mancipi*, would also transfer possession to the creditor.[170] Where possession would return to the debtor before the secured debt was repaid, the creditor would run the risk of losing his security ownership interest through *usureceptio*.[171] This would be different, as Gaius informs us, if the creditor would allow the debtor to use the collateral pursuant to a special legal construction: the debtor is allowed to use the objects serving as collateral pursuant to *locatio conductio* or *precarium*. Exactly the same construction was used in respect of pledged objects. These are three of many jurists' opinions attesting the practice of 'charge and lease-back'.

> **D. 43.26.11.** *Celsus libro septimo digestorum.* Si debitor rem pigneratam precario rogaverit, soluta pecunia precarium solvitur: quippe id actum est, ut usque eo precarium teneret.
>
> If a debtor has asked by precarium for a thing that has been pledged, then when the money is paid off, the precarium is dissolved; for the intention is taken to have been that the precarium would only hold until then.
>
> **D. 41.2.36.** *Iulianus libro tertio decimo digestorum.* Qui pignoris causa creditori tradit, intellegitur possidere. Sed et si eundem precario rogaverit, aeque per diutinam possessionem usucapiet: nam cum possessio creditoris non impediat capionem, longe minus precarii rogatio impedimento esse

[169] Ulp. D. 43.26.6.4. [170] Wubbe 2003: 12. [171] See section 4.6.

non debet, cum plus iuris in possessione habeat qui precario rogaverit quam qui omnino non possidet.

A person delivering land to his creditor by way of pledge is deemed to possess it. Now if he should seek a precarium of it, nevertheless, he can acquire it by long possession; for the creditor's possession is not preventing such acquisition, still less should holding by precarium be an obstacle; for one possessing by precarium has a better possessory title than one who does not possess at all.

D. 13.7.35.1. *Florentinus libro octavo institutionum.* Pignus manente proprietate debitoris solam possessionem transfert ad creditorem: potest tamen et precario et pro conducto debitor re sua uti.

Pignus transfers only possession to the creditor, while ownership remains in the debtor. The debtor, however, can have the use of his property either as precarium or on hire.

Celsus's and Julian's texts have been taken from their treatises on *fiducia*.[172] Nevertheless, their content is in line with opinions (such as Flor. D. 13.7.35.1) which undoubtedly do concern *pignus*.[173] The transfer of ('natural') possession to the creditor presumes that a *traditio* has taken place, while at the same time the debtor can continue to use the pledged object pursuant to *precarium* or a rental agreement. There is, therefore, again a large degree of similarity between both forms of real security, which is caused by their common function as security interest and perhaps even their common origin.[174] Although *usureceptio* finds its origin in archaic law, we do not know when this transactional practice originated in respect of *fiducia*.[175] Given the economic necessity for the debtor to be able to continue to use *res mancipi*, this is likely to have taken place early.[176] In particular, *precarium* is an old institution—originally nothing more than a mere factual surrender—which may have been

[172] Noordraven 1999: 183–4; Bertoldi 2012: 96–8.

[173] According to Noordraven (1999: 198 n 142) D. 43.26.11 was taken from a treatise by Celsus on *fiducia*. Kaser (1982: 329) observes that it cannot be established whether D. 41.2.36 is on *pignus* or *fiducia*. Kunkel (1973: 159) and others hold that the charge and lease-back only was used for *fiducia cum creditore*, so that all texts which were originally on *pignus* and mention this construction are interpolated. Kaser calls this 'intenable interpolation criticism' (Kaser 1982: 169). See also Braukmann 2008: 37.

[174] Kaser 1982: 173–4.

[175] In the course of the third century BC this construction already came to be used in Athens and other Greek cities (Biscardi 1976: 221–2).

[176] See Wubbe 2003: 18, 23–4; Kaser 1982: 169 n 154; Noordraven 1999: 197.

coupled with *fiducia* at an early stage.[177] The same economic necessity would often have been present in case of pledged objects, although in case of *pignus* non-productive assets (e.g., valuables), for which a possessory pledge did not impact the operation of the debtor's farm, business, or profession, may have been more common.

In Roman legal practice, *precarium* and *locatio conductio* were used in order to construct a functional equivalent of a non-possessory pledge. Where an institution fails to perform its functions, the response often is the adaptation of the existing institution rather than the creation of an entirely new one. When this is not possible, existing institutional elements may be used to build a new institution.[178] Such recombination of existing institutional elements (*pignus* and *locatio conductio*/*precarium*) happened here. Where in all likelihood the right of pledge originated as a possessory pledge, some legal basis had to be found for allowing the debtor to continue to use the objects of pledge while still accepting that a *traditio* would be necessary for a fully effective right of pledge.[179] Before Julian, non-possessory security was already created through transactional constructions which were based on *traditio* or equivalents thereof: bringing the pledged objects on the premises (*invecta et illata*), renting storage units in a warehouse (TPSulp 45 and 46), having a slave monitoring pledged cargo (maritime loan). The 'pledge and lease-back' is yet another example of a possessory pledge with a diluted possessory element, by making the debtor a *detentor* for the creditor through *locatio conductio* or *precarium*. We can see this in a text like D. 13.7.37, where Paul says that when a creditor rents out the pledged asset which had been 'delivered' (*traditum*) to him by the debtor, the creditor retains possession. Paul defends this by saying that before he rented the pledged asset, the debtor did not have possession. This may reflect an older practice in which the debtor actually did hand over the pledged object, which the creditor immediately returned to him.[180] This older practice may soon have become obsolete because it would have been a rather silly one. From a legal perspective the result of a pledge and lease-back is the same as an actual *traditio*: the creditor obtains *possessio* of the pledged object for the purposes of the possessory interdicts.

177 Kaser 1971: 388.

178 Greif 2006:194–5; Deakin 2003: 40; Luhmann 2012: 309; Granovetter 2017: 177.

179 Moreover, in early classical law the *actio pigneraticia contraria* and perhaps even the *actio Serviana* may not yet have been available to the creditor, which may also explain why the creditor would wish to have a possessory interdict and a remedy based on *locatio conductio* or *precarium*.

180 Kaser 1982: 180 n 193.

Persistence of pledge and lease-back

Even after it became accepted that a pledge could be granted *nuda conventione* and a *traditio* was no longer necessary, the transactional practice of pledge and lease-back continued to be used. How can this be explained? In all cases (purely possessory pledge, purely contractual pledge, pledge with *locatio conductio*, pledge with *precarium*) the debtor would continue to be the possessor for the purposes of *usucapio*. This, therefore, cannot have been the reason. Krämer has tentatively suggested the following explanation for the combination of *pignus* and *precarium* or *locatio conductio*.[181] The purpose of this construction could have been to prevent that the debtor would after one year reacquire the unencumbered ownership of the object of pledge through *usureceptio*. Krämer relates this to the *exceptio annalis pignoris italici*, a remedy supposedly to have given a defence against the creditor's *actio Serviana* when the pledged object had been in the possession of someone other than the creditor for more than a year.[182] The problem with this explanation is that according to Ulpian this *exceptio* was only available to third parties in possession, and not to the debtor. But Krämer suggests that other jurists may have held a different opinion and the practice of pledge and lease-back may have been a response to this. This practice became obsolete after Papinian unequivocally stated that an object could not be freed from a right of pledge by way of *usucapio* (Pap. D. 20.1.1.2). I find this explanation too speculative and not very convincing. There is no trace in the sources at all of *usureceptio* applying to *pignus*. Moreover, (as we have seen) in the late classical period (therefore: after Papinian) the daily practice still persisted that pledged assets were left with the debtor pursuant to *precarium*. A much more straightforward explanation offers itself. A creditor may have preferred a pledge and lease-back over a pledge granted *nuda conventione* in order to acquire possession of the pledged objects. The relevance of the creditor's possession is that he could invoke the general possessory interdicts against persons interfering with the possession of the pledged objects. In case of a *hypotheca* granted *nuda conventione*, not even 'natural' possession transfers to the creditor.[183] This entails, in particular, that the creditor with such *hypotheca* does not have possession for the purposes of the possessory interdicts. This is different in

[181] Krämer 2007: 373–5.

[182] Ulp. D. 44.3.5.1 and *Ulpiani fragmenta Argentoratensia*, II, IIb (FIRA II: 309–10).

[183] Ulp. D. 13.7.9.2.

case of a pledge and lease-back, whether based on *locatio conductio* or *precarium*. Here the creditor would continue to have possession for the purposes of the possessory interdicts, because the debtor acted as his holder (*detentor*). A creditor may have preferred interdicts over *Serviana* proceedings, because he then did not have to prove that the pledged property had been *in bonis debitoris* at the time the pledge was granted. The interdict procedure may also have been quicker.[184]

What would be the specific advantages of a pledge coupled with *locatio conductio* in comparison with *precarium*? In Marcian. D. 41.2.37 real estate had been pledged and possession had been transferred (*possessione tradita*) to the creditor, and the debtor had subsequently rented the property from the creditor. The debtor must, according to Marcian, be considered as a *colonus* in case of land and as *inquilinus* in the case of buildings. Through these persons the creditor is regarded as possessing the property. This is in line with what we have seen so far for pledge and lease-back generally (including *precarium*). However, from Marcian's express reference to the debtor's position as *colonus* and *inquilinus* it might be inferred that the *invecta et illata* or natural fruits of the pledged real estate would also be pledged to the creditor, also given the fact that in the course of the classical period tenant's pledges (urban real estate) and pledge of crops (rural real estate) no longer had to be expressly agreed, but were implied.[185] The specific remedies attached to tenant's pledges would then also be available to the creditor. The creditor could use the *interdictum Salvianum* in order to obtain actual possession of objects present on the pledged farms and land and would be able to employ the self-help remedy of *perclusio* in respect of objects present in urban properties. In case of a pledge coupled with *precarium* these remedies would not be available. Another reason for preferring *locatio conductio* over *precarium* could have been that the rental agreement would generate extra income for the lender, perhaps to circumvent the statutory maximum interest rate. In case of *precarium* the debtor did not have to reimburse the creditor for the use of the pledged property, which will have been the main motivation for the 'daily practice' mentioned in Ulp. D. 43.26.6.4. In addition, in contrast with a debtor using the property pursuant to *locatio conductio*, the debtor could—as *precario habens*—also invoke the possessory interdicts.

[184] Kaser 1971: 396.

[185] Ner. D. 20.2.4 pr. (urban real estate); Pomp. D. 20.2.7 pr. (rural real estate).

Handing over 'title deeds'

In a constitution from 287 AD, Diocletian rules that where a piece of land had been pledged by way of a chirograph to a (female) creditor, the pledge must be deemed to have been released when she had the chirograph returned.[186] It has been suggested that this practice demonstrates the difficulties in departing from the principle that only possessory pledges could be created.[187] This is, however, not very likely, as by the time of Diocletian the pledge created *nuda conventione* was firmly established. There is also a constitution by Septimius Severus and Caracalla from 207 AD on a case in which the deed of sale of land had been handed over to the secured creditor.[188] The constitution states that when someone has pledged the deed of sale of his land he must have intended to pledge the land itself. The fact that a pledge could be granted by agreement ('*pignus consensu contrahi*') is used as the argument to rule that a person who pledged the deeds of sale of his lands must have intended to pledge these lands. Nevertheless, one cannot rule out that this practice originated in a time in which a *traditio* was still required for a fully effective right of pledge. Giving possession of the title deeds may for the purposes of granting a possessory pledge, perhaps in connection with other outward signs (e.g., presence of the parties on the land), have been treated as equivalent to a *traditio pignoris causa* of the pledged land itself.

The imperial constitutions demonstrate, in any case, that the practice continued long after it had been settled by Julian that a pledge could be created *nuda conventione*. The creditor's possession of the deed of sale certainly could still have practical advantages, one of which could be the protection against false wealth. It could make a prospective secured creditor or purchaser suspicious if the seller would be unable to produce the deed of sale. In addition, as the Severan constitution demonstrates, the handing over of title documents could serve as evidence of the pledge. Moreover, possession of the deed of sale could enable the creditor to sell the property more easily when the debtor was in default. Also, as Scaev. D. 19.1.48 demonstrates, documents concerning real estate were used in order to determine which rights the seller's predecessor had over the property sold: this could also be relevant for the creditor who took security over real estate.

[186] Diocl.-Max. C. 8.25.7. [187] Wagner 1968: 59–60. [188] Sev.-Ant. C. 8.16.2.

7

From Single to Multiple Pledge

7.1 Introduction

The value of certain assets as collateral and borrowers' access to credit could be enhanced if the law would allow security rights to be granted over the same property in favour of several creditors. In particular where the liquidation value of a charged asset considerably exceeds the amount of the original secured debt, there may be sufficient residual value in the collateral for other creditors to be prepared to accept lower-ranking rights of pledge. Here, however, Roman law was rather slow to adapt to the needs of the credit markets. Although there is good reason to assume that non-possessory pledges were recognized relatively early, the recognition of their 'logical sequel'[1]—the multiple pledge—has taken longer. For a considerable time the granting of a pledge would deprive the debtor (during the continuance of the pledge) of the legal power to grant other rights of pledge over the same pledged property (section 7.2). In the second century AD one way was found of getting around this: the pledge of the *superfluum* of the execution of the original pledge. Another was to recognize that subsequent rights of pledge could be granted conditionally (section 7.3). Later in the second century AD it came to be accepted that multiple *unconditional* pledges could coexist over the same property and that each creditor could institute the *actio Serviana* against any possessor of the pledged property (except creditors with a prior pledge). As a corollary of the multiple pledge, the right of lower-ranking creditors to take over the preferential position of higher-ranking creditors (*ius offerendi et succedendi*) originated (section 7.4). A veritable *tour de force* was the extension by the jurists of this *ius offerendi et succedendi* to novation, where a creditor would succeed in his 'own' original ranking. These evolutionary processes took place through trial and error. The persons who drafted the contractual clauses were not always perfectly schooled in the strict legal conceptions of the classical jurists.[2] In the late classical period we even find transactional practices

[1] Kunkel 1973: 155.
[2] Kaser 1976: 201. E.g. Tryph. D. 20.4.20; Marci. D. 20.4.12.8; Pomp. D. 13.7.2.

Security and Credit in Roman Law: The historical evolution of pignus *and* hypotheca. Hendrik L. E. Verhagen, Oxford University Press. DOI: 10.1093/oso/9780199695836.003.0008

associated with earlier periods, which were clumsily drafted (section 7.5). The obstacles for creating multiple layers of security only gradually disappeared, as a result of the constructive manner in which the jurists interpreted transactional practices. The multiple pledge again illustrates that the evolutionary history of *pignus* and *hypotheca* is largely the product of an iterative relationship between practitioners drafting contractual clauses and the jurists accommodating these practices into the Roman legal system.

7.2 Initial Impossibility of Multiple Pledges

For a long time, the evolution towards full-fledged multiple pledges was hampered, possibly by ownership-like characteristics (including forfeiture) which *pignus* continued to have in the early classical period. Ultimately, however, this evolutionary pathway was cleared, still within the classical period of Roman law. Three stages can be discerned in the evolutionary processes which produced the multiple pledge: a first stage in which multiple pledges could not be created; a second—intermediate—stage in which subsequent pledges could be granted conditionally, whether or not coupled with a pledge of the *superfluum*; and a third stage in which multiple pledges could exist simultaneously over the same asset. The different stages overlap, in the sense that transactional practices associated with earlier stages continued to be used in later stages.[3] The Greek-Hellenistic legal institution of multiple pledges has been said to have 'invaded' classical Roman law through the oriental schools of law.[4] The evolutionary sequence discussed in this chapter rather suggests that the multiple pledge is the result of a largely independent legal evolution in the Roman world, but it can certainly not be excluded that certain transactional practices, in particular the *pignoris hyperocha* (pledge of *superfluum*), did have a Hellenistic origin.[5]

First stage: multiple pledges not possible

Parallel evolution of *pignus* and *fiducia*

In case of *fiducia cum creditore*, after the fiduciary transfer by way of *mancipatio*, the debtor would no longer be the owner of the property and would therefore

[3] See in particular Tryph. D. 20.4.20 and Marci. D. 20.4.12.8, both discussed in section 7.5.

[4] Biscardi 1969: 168.

[5] The use of this Greek word by Romans in itself does not provide sufficient evidence for its Greek-Hellenistic origin. See section 6.5 on the use of *hypotheca*.

no longer have the power to transfer it validly as collateral to another creditor. At the beginning of the classical period it was settled that in case of *pignus*, the debtor would remain the owner of the pledged property. The creditor would (in modern terms) only acquire a subordinated real right, an encumbrance, on the pledged property. The debtor's continuing ownership could then (at least in theory) have enabled him to create other rights of pledge over the same asset. Moreover, once a transfer of possession to the creditor is no longer required for the creation of a right of pledge, it becomes much easier to create multiple coexisting rights of pledge over the same object. If the first right of pledge was a possessory pledge, a second right of pledge can easily be created by 'mere agreement' (or vice versa), or one can have multiple non-possessory pledges. Nevertheless, until well into the second half of the second century AD the granting of a pledge would deprive the debtor of his power to grant other pledges over the same property. It seems that for a long time the debtor had only one opportunity to 'split off' a right of pledge from his full right of ownership. This may have been a relic from the past, when *pignus*—like *fiducia*—also was a form of ownership.[6] It may also have been connected with the original nature of *pignus* of a forfeiture. The multiple pledge is difficult to reconcile with the forfeiture pledge, as the pledged asset can be forfeited to one creditor only.[7] The analogous treatment of *fiducia* and *pignus* by the classical jurists may also have contributed to the relatively long persistence of the impossibility of granting multiple pledges.[8]

Pledged property not *in bonis*?

Originally in the first stage of the evolution of the multiple pledge only the first creditor would be able to institute the *actio Serviana*, when the same property had subsequently been pledged to another creditor. How can we explain this in terms of the *formula* of this action? Schanbacher offers an elegant explanation for the debtor's inability to create multiple pledges.[9] If one assumes that the creation of the first pledge would cause the pledged asset no longer to be *in bonis* of the debtor, then it is perfectly logical to deny the *actio Serviana* to the second creditor, because one of the conditions of its *formula* would not be satisfied at the time of the second *conventio pignoris*. Although there are no jurists' opinions expressly stating that pledged assets ceased to be

[6] Kaser 1982: 72-3.

[7] Kaser 1976: 173. One could imagine, however, multiple forfeiture pledges, where forfeiture to the second creditor would be conditional upon termination of the pledge granted to the first creditor.

[8] See Krämer 2007: 370.

[9] Schanbacher 1987: 38–42. In the same sense Gröschler 2014: 362–3. Contra, Ankum and Pool 1989: 19–20; Wacke 1998: 457 n 66; Krämer 2007: 370.

in bonis of the debtor, this is—in terms of the *actio Serviana*—the only conceivable explanation for the non-recognition of multiple pledges. It may very well have been that the initial impossibility of multiple pledges was a side effect of the original nature of *pignus* as a *forfeiture* pledge. The fact that the *datio pignoris* was analogous to, or may actually have been, a *traditio* aimed at the conditional transfer of ownership by way of forfeiture,[10] may have caused the jurists to consider that pledged property was no longer *in bonis* of the debtor. Once it became established that *pignus* was no longer an ownership-based forfeiture pledge but a fully evolved *security interest* giving the creditor an independent power of sale, the coexistence of several rights of pledge on the same object was no longer irreconcilable with the legal nature of *pignus*. There could now be no doubt that after the granting of the first pledge, the pledged property would still be *in bonis* of the debtor. The evolution of *pignus* from a forfeiture pledge to a pledge enforceable by sale may thus have facilitated not only the recognition of the *hypotheca* (*nuda conventione*) but also that of multiple rights of pledge.

Second stage: pledge of surplus and conditional pledge

Two possibilities: Gai. D. 20.1.15.2

From the first half of the second century AD we have evidence of borrowers using the surplus value of collateral in order to attract more credit from other lenders. Apparently in the time of Gaius it had become a settled practice to create several layers of security in respect of the same asset.[11] It must have become so common to do so that it had become customary—as D. 20.1.15.2 indicates ('*solent pati*')—for debtors to disclose earlier pledges to later creditors.[12] The most significant text for this second stage in the evolution of the multiple pledge is taken from Gaius's monograph on the *actio Serviana*.

> **D. 20.1.15.2.** *Gaius libro singulari ad formulam hypothecariam.* Qui res suas iam obligaverint et alii secundo obligant creditori, ut effugiant periculum, quod solent pati qui saepius easdem res obligant, praedicere solent alii nulli rem obligatam quam forte Lucio Titio, ut in id quod excedit priorem

[10] Sections 5.3, 5.6 and 5.7.

[11] When one reads D. 20.1.15.2 one could think that the 'danger' referred to would have been criminal liability (*stellionatus*). However, it seems that *stellionatus* only became a crime at the end of the second century AD, so that this crime was still unknown in Gaius's time. Before that time the 'danger' is that of being condemned with the *actio de dolo* (Kaser 1976: 183), which would lead to *infamia*.

[12] See also Mod. D. 20.6.9.1; Scaev. D. 20.1.34.1. See also FIRA III, no. 91 (*Mancipatio Pompeiana*).

> obligationem res sit obligata, ut sit pignori hypothecaeve id quod pluris est: aut solidum, cum primo debito liberata res fuerit? de quo videndum est, utrum hoc ita se habeat, si et conveniat, an et si simpliciter convenerit de eo quod excedit ut sit hypothecae? et solida res inesse conventioni videtur, cum a primo creditore fuerit liberata, an adhuc pars? sed illud magis est, quod prius diximus.
>
> Those who have already charged their assets and then charge them to a second creditor usually declare, in order to avoid the danger run by those who create multiple charges, that the property is charged to no one except, say, Lucius Titius, to the effect that the asset is charged for the amount exceeding the prior debt, in the sense that the excess is pledged or hypothecated, or for the whole, when the asset is released from the first debt. It must be reviewed whether this is also the position if it is simply agreed that the asset is hypothecated for the excess? When the first creditor is paid off, must the agreement be seen as for the whole or just for the part? But what we have said firstly is better.

Where Gaius refers to the case where 'it is simply agreed that the asset is hypothecated for the excess' this clearly refers to actual transactional practices. These contractual arrangements were agreed for cases where two pledge agreements were entered into, one between the debtor and the first creditor (C1) and another one between the debtor and the second creditor (C2). Although Gaius at the beginning of D. 20.1.15.2 simply refers to 'charge them to a second creditor', it follows from the remainder of the text that it was slightly more complicated than that. Gaius sets out that ideally the debtor and C2 should have provided for a combination of two pledges, one for situations where the first pledge is enforced by execution sale (*pledge of superfluum*) and the other one for situations where the first pledge is discharged by regular payment of the secured debt (*conditional pledge*). Gaius's opinion is that the first arrangement implied the second. Where the parties have only agreed 'that the asset is hypothecated for the excess', there is not only a pledge of the *superfluum* but also a pledge of the charged object itself must be deemed to have been granted, under the condition precedent of termination of the first pledge.

According to Kaser the pledge of the *superfluum* was only possible in combination with a (conditional) pledge of the physical object itself. It rather seems, however, that it was also possible to create a right of pledge on the *superfluum* solely. Although in Gai. D. 20.1.15.2 the words 'the excess is pledged or hypothecated' are interpreted so as to include a conditional pledge of the pledged object itself, a text like Tryph. D. 20.4.20 demonstrates that a separate pledge of the *superfluum* was also possible.[13] We can observe, in any case, that in interpreting standard clauses used in the legal practice of his day, Gaius is willing to go far beyond the actual wording used by the parties, in order to achieve that a poorly drafted pledge agreement would not deprive subsequent creditors of the most adequate form of security available at the time.[14]

Legal construction of the pledge of the surplus

How is the object of a pledge of the surplus defined in the sources? Gaius refers to the transactional practice stating that 'the property is charged' ('*res sit obligata*') for the amount exceeding the prior debt.[15] This seems to express that the physical asset itself is being pledged to the second creditor, for a secured debt equivalent to the surplus value of the pledged property. According to Kaser, this is a manifestation of the somewhat 'vulgar' legal thinking of the scribes, who were guided by the purposes they wanted to achieve rather than by a concern for the correct legal-technical expression thereof.[16] A pledge of the property itself, even if only for an amount equalling its surplus value, would be inconsistent with the still prevailing principle at Gaius's time that the same property cannot be simultaneously charged with more than one right of pledge. This is why the phrase '*res sit obligata*' is recharacterized by Gaius as a pledge of the amount of the surplus: 'the excess is pledged or hypothecated'.[17] However, the jurists apparently also sometimes failed to be legally precise in their description of the object of the pledge. In a late classical text Tryphoninus specifies the object of the pledge as '*pignoris hyperocha*', while Papinian uses the expression '*superfluum pignorum obligare*'.[18] Tryphoninus and Papinian both speak of a pledge of the surplus of the pledged asset rather than the surplus of the proceeds, which (according to Kaser) influenced Tryphoninus to talk of '*quod amplius est in pignore*' rather than *quod amplius est in pretio*.[19]

Typical for the Roman jurists they do not reveal to us a theoretical construction of the 'pledge of the surplus' (they may not even have had one in mind), but are satisfied with making clear that the second creditor shall have

[13] See pp. 241–3. [14] Kaser 1976: 183.

[15] Gai. D. 20.1.15.2. See also the first sentence: 'charge them to a second creditor' ('*alii secundo obligant creditori*').

[16] Kaser 1976: 203. [17] Gai. D. 20.1.15.2 ('*sit pignori hypothecaeve id quod pluris est*').

[18] Tryph. D. 20.4.20; Pap. D. 46.3.96.3. In both texts the inflections of *pignus* refer to the pledged object.

[19] Kaser 1976: 203.

an action with which he can claim the surplus proceeds from the first creditor. One possible construction would be that a 'pledge of the *superfluum*' would actually be a pledge to the second creditor of the debtor's claim against the first creditor for payment of the surplus proceeds. A more plausible interpretation is that a pledge of the *superfluum* would give the second creditor an independent right to the surplus proceeds, which was not a derivative of any entitlement of the debtor to the surplus. A pledge of the surplus would result in the second creditor being granted an adapted *actio in personam* for the surplus proceeds against the first creditor.[20] This is not without parallel: in case of the pledge of claims and antichretic pledges the creditor's adapted *actio Serviana* must also have been an *actio in personam* aimed at payment from the defendant.[21]

7.3 From Conditional to Unconditional Pledge

More than any other variant of the Roman right of pledge, the multiple pledge shows how institutional elements inherited from the past can potentially hamper the adaptation of law to its economic environment.[22] The initial impossibility of creating several charges over the same property is an example of path dependence.[23] It may be a relic of the archaic conception of the creditor's interest as a form of ownership.[24] When it was recognized (perhaps already by Julian) that subsequent rights of pledge could be granted conditionally, the original position that multiple pledges could not simultaneously exist over the same property was still upheld: the coming into existence of the second pledge was contingent upon the termination of the first pledge, so that the same property was never encumbered with more than one pledge at the same time. The transactional practices discussed in the jurists' writings betray the difficulty and uncertainty experienced by the 'juridical apprehension' of this form of pledge.[25] They also illustrate how creative (if not always dogmatically correct) ordinary Roman legal practitioners were and how co-operative and skilled the leading Roman jurists were in overcoming these path dependencies in order to adapt Roman law to the needs of the financial world.

[20] This *actio Serviana utilis* would *not* have been an *actio in rem* aimed at recovery of the actual coins which may have been in C1's possession after the execution sale.

[21] Sections 8.3 and 8.4. [22] Greif 2006: 209. [23] North 2005: 77.

[24] Kaser 1982: 72–3. [25] Manigk 1941: 1279.

Julian on the conditional second pledge

In the construction envisaged in Gai. D. 20.1.15.2, the pledge agreement with the second creditor (C2) is entered into conditionally, subject to the condition that the first right of pledge shall have terminated upon discharge of the secured debt owed to the first creditor (C1).[26] When that condition materializes, the second right of pledge will come into existence automatically, without any further act of the debtor and the second creditor (C2) being necessary. Accordingly, C2 shall then have a right of pledge on the pledged object itself. The second pledge was thus accommodated into the existing legal framework. Formally, the traditional principle that there cannot simultaneously exist multiple rights of pledge on the same property was still upheld. There is a binary mechanism: as long as C1's pledge still exists, C2's right of pledge does not come into existence; when C2's right of pledge comes into existence, C1's right of pledge will have ceased to exist. This construction may already have been in Julian's mind. Julian is the first known jurist who expressly recognized that the pledge could be created *nuda conventione*. It is therefore not so strange that the same jurist would also have accepted that the *conventio pignoris* could be a conditional agreement, with the effect that the right of pledge itself too was conditional. Julian's opinion is to be found in a text from Africanus, in which the latter sets out the opinion of his former master.[27]

> **D. 20.4.9.3.** *Africanus libro octavo quaestionum.* Titia praedium alienum Titio pignori dedit, post Maevio: deinde domina eius pignoris facta marito suo in dotem aestimatum dedit. si Titio soluta sit pecunia, non ideo magis Maevii pignus convalescere placebat. tunc enim priore dimisso sequentis confirmatur pignus, cum res in bonis debitoris inveniatur: in proposito autem maritus emptoris loco est: atque ideo, quia neque tunc cum Maevio obligaretur neque cum Titio solveretur in bonis mulieris fuerit, nullum tempus inveniri, quo pignus Maevii convalescere possit. haec tamen ita, si bona fide in dotem aestimatum praedium maritus accepit, id est si ignoravit Maevio obligatum esse.
>
> Titia pledged land which was not hers to Titius, then to Maevius. Later she became the owner and gave her land to her husband as a dowry at valuation.

[26] See also Marci. D. 20.4.12.8.

[27] In the text '*placebat*', translated in Watson as 'Julian took the view'. Much has been written on this difficult and controversial text. The most convincing interpretation is that of Potjewijd (1998: 97–103), which I largely follow.

> He (Julian) took the view that payment to Titius would not improve the position of Maevius's pledge. The extinction of a prior pledge confirms a later only when the assets are in the debtor's patrimony. In the case put, the husband is like a purchaser. Hence, as the assets were not part of the woman's estate when she gave Maevius a pledge nor when she paid Titius, there was no intermediate point of time at which the pledge to Maevius could become effective. This is the case only if the husband accepted the dowry at valuation in good faith, not knowing it was pledged to Maevius.

Titia had pledged the same piece of land twice, first to Titius (C1) and then to Maevius (C2). At the time she granted these pledges, she did not yet own the land. Later, Titia did acquire ownership of the land, perhaps through inheritance, and conveyed it to her husband as a dowry. It was held by Julian and Africanus that Maevius could not invoke his (second) pledge against the husband, after Titius's (first) pledge was extinguished through discharge. The text strongly suggests that the (second) pledge to Maevius was conditionally granted. For why else would the question be asked whether discharge of Titius would 'improve' Maevius's pledge? The conditional granting of the second pledge is described as 'the extinction of a prior pledge confirms a later pledge'. This is what normally happens when a second pledge is conditionally granted.

It follows from Julian's position that *if* the pledged land had already been *in bonis* of Titia at the time of granting the conditional pledge to Maevius, it could have been invoked against the husband, also where Titius had been discharged after the husband's acquisition of the land.[28] For Julian says that the pledged property should be *in bonis* of the debtor either when the pledge is granted or when the condition materializes. This makes the conditional right of pledge granted to a lower-ranking secured creditor a pretty strong one. Where it is (conditionally) granted by a debtor who owns the pledged property at the time of granting, the second creditor's conditional right will mature into an unconditional right of pledge if and when the condition materializes (i.e., the first pledge is discharged), even if the debtor at that time no longer owns the property. In respect of conditional grantings of rights of pledge the Roman jurists show a tendency to protect the pledge creditor against dispositions made in the period between the conditional grant and the materialization of the condition.[29] This protection was, however, not limitless: if the debtor owned the pledged property neither at the time of the conditional grant nor at the time the condition materialized, the creditor with a conditional second

[28] Ankum and Pool 1989: 19. [29] Potjewijd 1998: 102.

pledge would not be protected. Apparently, Julian could not imagine in these cases that by one act, two rights of pledge would 'convalesce', which had successively been granted by a non-owner over the same land.[30] According to Africanus, however, Maevius's claim against the husband should only be rejected 'if the husband accepted the dowry at valuation in good faith, not knowing it was pledged to Maevius. At face value the text appears to assume as the point of departure that upon Titia's acquisition of the pledged land, not only Titius's right of pledge convalesced but also that of Maevius. Accordingly, Maevius could have instituted the *actio Serviana* (*utilis*) against the husband. This action must be rejected, however, if the husband had been unaware of the pledge granted to Maevius. In this interpretation D. 20.4.9.3 would be an extraordinary fragment: it would accept that a possessor in good faith would be protected against a previously granted security interest of which he was unaware. This would be so extraordinary for Roman law that D. 20.4.9.3 has raised strong interpolation suspicions.[31]

Third stage: coexisting (unconditional) multiple pledges

The conditional pledge was an intermediate stage in the evolution of the multiple pledge. Ulpius Marcellus, *consilium* of Antonius Pius and Marcus Aurelius, is the first jurist from whom an opinion has survived on *unconditional* multiple rights of pledge.[32] The following text is taken from his *Digesta*, which was written between AD 161 and 167.[33]

> **D. 44.2.19.** *Marcellus libro nono decimo digestorum.* Duobus diversis temporibus eandem rem pignori dedit: egit posterior cum priore pigneraticia et optinuit: mox ille agere simili actione instituit: quaesitum est, an exceptio rei iudicatae obstaret. si opposuerat exceptionem rei sibi ante pigneratae et nihil aliud novum et validum adiecerit, sine dubio obstabit: eandem enim quaestionem revocat in iudicium.

[30] For a critical review of D. 20.4.9.3, see Wacke 1997: 457–60.

[31] See in particular Kaser (1976b: 178 n 32), who suggests that the action to which Africanus refers was the *actio de dolo* (rather than the *actio Serviana*) and that references to this action have been clumsily cut away. On the lack of protection of *bona fide* acquirers against unknown pledges see Verhagen 2014 and Verhagen 2020: 135–8.

[32] As Kaser (1976: 186) observes, it cannot be decided whether Marcellus invented the unconditional multiple pledge or relied on precursors.

[33] Kunkel 1973: 213.

A person gave the same property in pledge to two persons at different periods; the latter of the two brought an action on pledge against the former and succeeded; subsequently, he commenced to bring a similar action; the question was raised whether the defence of *res judicata* would avail. If he had pleaded the defence in respect of the property pledged to him and added nothing else which was new and relevant, the defence will without doubt prevail; for he is bringing the same issue to trial.

The *pigneraticia* to which the text refers must have been the *actio pigneraticia in rem*, the *actio Serviana*, since it was instituted by the second creditor (C2) against the first one (C1), so that it could not have been an *actio pigneraticia in personam*. It appears from Marcellus's opinion that C2 does have the *actio Serviana* at his disposal, also where the first pledge still exists. It became accepted that multiple pledges with different rankings could be unconditionally created over the same asset and could simultaneously exist. In procedural terms, both C1 and C2 could institute the *actio Serviana*. The case of D. 44.2.19 is odd, however, in the sense that C2 apparently successfully instituted the *actio Serviana* against a creditor with a prior pledge (C1). We can only guess the reason. C1 may have failed to prove that his right of pledge had been created earlier, since he had raised the defence of a prior pledge (*exceptio rei sibi ante pigneratae*), but apparently to no avail. The praetor may also simply have reached the wrong decision in granting the *actio Serviana* to C2,[34] or the *iudex* may have applied the programme included in the *litis contestatio* mistakenly to the facts of the case. The principle of *ne bis in idem*, in any case, prevented that C1 could subsequently successfully institute the *actio Serviana* against C2.

A more straightforward text from a later period is by Marcian.

D. 20.4.12.7. *Marcianus libro singulari ad formulam hypothecariam.* Si simpliciter convenisset secundus creditor de hypotheca, ab omni possessore eam auferre poterit praeter priorem creditorem et qui ab eo emit.

If the second creditor unconditionally agreed a hypothec, he can take the property from any possessor except the first creditor or a purchaser from him.

[34] There are several texts in the Digest implying that the praetor could make wrong decisions. Thus Ulpian D. 37.10.3.5 speaks of an imaginary 'stupid or unjust praetor' ('*stulti aut iniqui praetoris*'). In D. 1.1.11 Paul contemplates that 'the praetor is also said to render legal right even when he makes a wrongful decree'. See Kelly 1966a: 85.

The meaning of '*simpliciter*' can be derived from the text immediately following D. 20.4.12.7 in the Digest. Marci. D. 20.4.12.8 is concerned with a second pledge which was conditionally granted upon extinction of the first pledge. Thus a pledge granted *simpliciter* is opposed to a conditional pledge, in other words is granted unconditionally.[35] In any case, in D. 20.4.12.7 Marcian expressly restates the general principle for multiple pledges: the second creditor 'can take the property from any possessor except the first creditor or a purchaser from him'. It shows that the *actio Serviana* would be available to C2 in order to recover pledged assets from third parties in possession of the pledged property, but not from C1 or from someone who purchased it from C1 at an execution sale. This extension to purchasers from the first ranking creditor is perfectly sensible. A first ranking pledge would not be of much value if the creditor with a second-ranking pledge could enforce this pledge by successfully recovering the pledged property from someone who had purchased it from the first ranking creditor at execution.

7.4 *Ius Offerendi et Succedendi*

By exercising the *ius offerendi et succedendi* a lower-ranking creditor could take the enforcement of the security in his own hands and use the proceeds of the execution sale, not only for the principal and interest owed to him personally but also for the amount paid by him to the first ranking creditor in order to discharge the first pledge. This made the multiple pledge very effective from an economic perspective. If there was sufficient surplus value in property already pledged, another creditor could safely take a second-ranking right of pledge: such a creditor would not only be entitled to the surplus value but could also establish that he himself could organize the execution sale. Like the multiple pledge itself, this was the outcome of a gradual evolutionary process, triggered by transactional practices which were accommodated by the jurists and the imperial chancery. This has again been a process of trial and error. Several texts in the *Corpus iuris civilis* attest transactions in which the parties failed to meet the legal requirements for achieving that the ranking of a prior pledge would pass to a subsequent one.[36] Typically for their way of thinking, the Roman jurists did not design a theoretical legal framework for explaining the effects of this *ius offerendi et succedendi* but would rather suffice with

[35] Kaser 1976: 205.

[36] For example, the transaction discussed in Paul. (Arist.) D. 20.3.3.

indicating under which circumstances certain powers would transfer from the first ranking creditor to a lower-ranking one.[37] In the late classical period the creditor could achieve that in case of novation the ranking of the original pledge would be preserved, by an analogous application of the *ius offerendi et succedendi*.

Successio hypothecaria

Although the sources on the *ius offerendi et succedendi* are from the late classical period, there are texts from an earlier period which could be regarded as representing a preliminary stage in the evolution of the *ius offerendi et succedendi*.[38] As these texts show, the *ius offerendi et succedendi* has its origin in contractual clauses agreed between debtors and lower-ranking creditors, which provide that the latter shall have the right to offer higher-ranking creditors to take over their rank by paying the original secured debt.[39] An ancestor of the *ius offerendi et succedendi* is the so-called *successio hypothecaria* discussed by Aristo and (later) Gaius.[40]

Paul has recorded an opinion by the jurist Titius Aristo, a member of Hadrian's *consilium* and one of the most prominent jurists of his time.[41]

> **D. 20.3.3.** *Paulus libro tertio quaestionum.* Aristo Neratio Prisco scripsit: etiamsi ita contractum sit, ut antecedens dimitteretur, non aliter in ius pignoris succedet, nisi convenerit, ut sibi eadem res esset obligata: neque enim in ius primi succedere debet, qui ipse nihil convenit de pignore: quo casu emptoris causa melior efficietur.
>
> Writing to Neratius Priscus, Aristo said: Although it is a term of the contract that the first (creditor) shall be discharged, the second (creditor) does not succeed to his right of pledge unless it is agreed that the same property is pledged to him. A person who has not agreed on a pledge cannot succeed to the rights of the first creditor; and in that case, the purchaser of the property prevails.

37 Kaser 1976: 188.

38 Paul. (Arist.) D. 20.3.3; Gai. D. 20.4.11.4.

39 Dernburg 1864: 519–20; Kaser 1976: 188 n 69 (noticing that there are no traces of this in the sources).

40 The expressions *ius offerendi et succedendi* and *successio hypothecaria* are not classical, but first used by the nineteenth-century Pandectists (e.g., Dernburg 1864, 490).

41 Kunkel 1967: 141–4, 318–20.

The debtor had granted a right of pledge to C1. With a third party (C2), the debtor agreed that C1 would be repaid, probably (although the text leaves this open) by the debtor using the money received from C2 in order to pay C1.[42] In the case put before Aristo, the debtor had sold and delivered the pledged property, possibly in another attempt to discharge the debt owed to C1 with the proceeds of the sale.[43] Aristo holds that C2 shall only succeed to C1's pledge if the debtor and C2 have also agreed to a separate pledge for C2.[44] If that has not taken place, C2 shall not be able to recover (with the *actio Serviana*) the pledged property from the purchaser. The mere fact that the debtor and C2 have agreed that C1 shall be repaid with the money borrowed from C2 is not sufficient for C1's right of pledge to pass to C2, neither is it sufficient that C1 is repaid with funds coming from C2 to achieve this.[45] There has to be, according to Aristo, a separate *conventio pignoris* between the debtor and C2. The transaction structure recommended by Aristo fits perfectly in the second stage of the evolution of the multiple pledge.[46] The *conventio pignoris* between the debtor and C2 which Aristo requires must have been conditional upon the discharge of C1's pledge. If the proceeds of C2's loan are used to repay C1, this condition materializes and C2's pledge come into existence as a first ranking pledge.

In D. 20.3.3 we are not yet dealing with the *ius offerendi et succedendi* of late classical law. The 'hypothecary succession' by C2 to C1's pledge in D. 20.3.3 is nothing more than the discharge of C1's original pledge combined with the granting of a fresh one to C2. In this type of succession C2 occupies the position left vacant by the termination of C1's pledge.[47] This vacancy is created by C2 himself, by providing the debtor with the funds to pay the debt owed to C1. Moreover, the *ius offerendi et succedendi* would typically be exercised in

[42] In this sense Schanbacher 2016: 152 and seemingly also Kaser 1976: 174–5.

[43] In this sense Kaser 1976: 174 n 13 and 175 n 23.

[44] In a constitution from Septimius Severus and Caracalla from AD 209 this still needed to be spelt out (Sev.-Ant. *C.* 8.18.1 pr.). This constitution shows not only that transactional practices belonging to a preliminary stage of the evolution of the *ius offerendi et succendi* were still used after this right had fully evolved but also that the same mistakes of law were still made. It also shows that the law was very stable on this issue: the constitution adopts exactly the same approach as Aristo many decades earlier. See Kaser 1976: 175; Emunds and Harke 2015: 18. Other texts in which this requirement of a pledge agreement between the debtor and C2 was satisfied are Pomp. D. 13.7.2; Afr. D. 16.1.17.1; Gai. D. 20.4.11.4; Ulp. D. 27.9.7.5 and Ulp. D. 27.9.7.6. See Schanbacher 2016: 157–60.

[45] See Pomp. D. 13.7.2: at the time the second pledge agreement (debtor C2) was entered into ownership of the pledged property had already been transferred to a purchaser. This meant that the pledged object was no longer *in bonis* of the debtor. The mere fact that the first pledge had been discharged with money coming from C2 did not entail that he would acquire a right of pledge. According to the late classical jurist Marcian (D. 20.6.5.2) C2 could have purchased C1's secured claim, in which case—as Marcian observes—C2's payment to C1 is not a *solutio* of the secured claim (which therefore continues to exist), but a payment of the purchase price for the purchased claim.

[46] Kaser 1976: 175–7.

[47] Schanbacher 2016: 153, 156.

situations where C2 had granted credit to the debtor independently and there was sufficient surplus value in the pledged property to satisfy the debts owed to C1 and C2. Aristo's opinion in D. 20.3.3 seems to be instead concerned with the refinancing of an existing debt. In order to avoid a threatening execution sale or for other reasons (e.g., C2's interest in the continuance of C1's business), C2 is prepared to take over the credit granted by C1, but only if it continues to be secured by the property originally pledged to C1.

Another ancestor: Gai. D. 20.4.11.4

From Gaius we also have an opinion reflecting an earlier stage in the evolution to a full-fledged *ius offerendi et succedendi.*

> **D. 20.4.11.4.** *Gaius libro singulari de formula hypothecaria.* Si paratus est posterior creditor priori creditori solvere quod ei debetur, videndum est, an competat ei hypothecaria actio nolente priore creditore pecuniam accipere. et dicimus priori creditori inutilem esse actionem, cum per eum fiat, ne ei pecunia solvatur.
>
> If the later creditor is willing to pay the earlier his debt, we must ask whether, supposing the earlier refuses to accept payment, the later can bring the *actio hypothecaria.* We are clear that the earlier cannot bring the action, since the non-payment is his fault.

In contrast with Aristo's opinion this text may have been dealing with a case in which—at the time the *successio hypothecaria* was negotiated—C2 had already been granted a right of pledge by the debtor.[48] As recommended in Gai. D. 20.1.15.2, such a second pledge would have been granted conditionally on discharge of the first pledge. In order to make his second (conditional) pledge an unconditional one, C2 declared to be prepared to repay C1, but the latter refused to accept this offer.[49] The question addressed by Gaius is whether the *actio Serviana* is then available to C2. Gaius says only that C1 can no longer institute the *actio Serviana.* The reason behind this is that one of the conditions of its *formula* was no longer met: the absence of creditor's default

[48] Emunds and Harke 2015: 18. Kaser considers it more likely that the second creditor was an (as yet) unsecured creditor, who intended to become a secured creditor by lending the debtor the money to discharge his debt to the first creditor (Kaser 1976: 175 n 23).

[49] See also Pomp. D. 13.7.2; Afr. D. 16.1.17.1; Marci. D. 20.4.12.8. As Kaser (1976: 175) points out, in all these cases C2 was *not* already a creditor with a second-ranking right of pledge exercising the *ius offerendi et succedendi.*

(*mora creditoris*).[50] Although D. 20.4.11.4 does not expressly say so, one would expect that this entails that C1's pledge had ceased to exist and that therefore the *actio Serviana* must now be granted to C2, with which he could recover the pledged property from C1, the debtor, or any third party in possession.[51]

Gai. D. 20.4.11.4 is not yet dealing with the full-fledged *ius offerendi et succedendi*. Like Aristo's opinion it is still within the parameters of the general principles of the law of pledge.[52] Gai. D. 20.4.11.4 says nothing more than that C2 can achieve that his pledge becomes the first one by offering payment to C1, so that the latter's pledge is discharged. The only point of law which Gaius addresses is whether C1's refusal to accept the payment could compromise C2's position. This question is answered negatively, with reference to one of the standard conditions (a_5) of the *actio Serviana*. However, where Aristo in Paul. D. 20.3.3 was concerned with the refinancing of an existing debt, the contractual arrangement of Gai. D. 20.4.11.4 rather appears to belong to the type of transactions for which the *ius offerendi et succedendi* came into existence. C1 and C2 have both granted secured credit to the debtor, with C2 being prepared to pay C1 in order to become the first ranking creditor. Certainly if the debtor and C2 had agreed that the second pledge would secure not only the debt originally owed to C2 but also the amount which C2 was prepared to pay to C1, the end result would be the same as that of the *ius offerendi et succendi*: C2 would have a first ranking right of pledge, which secured both debts.[53]

Ius offerendi et succedendi

For a creditor, it would normally only make sense to accept a right of pledge over property which had already been pledged to another creditor if the

[50] Condition a_5. The negative condition of absence of so-called *mora creditoris* (creditor's default) concerns cases where the right of pledge can no longer be enforced with the *actio Serviana*, because the creditor himself was the cause of the non-discharge of the secured debt. In particular, where the creditor refused to accept repayment of the secured debt, this would have the same legal effect as repayment itself. The creditor could no longer institute the *actio Serviana* against the debtor or third parties, so that the right of pledge had effectively terminated. Strictly speaking this goes against the principle of dependence (accessory nature of the right of pledge), because the secured debt continues to exist. However, it would be too harsh on the debtor if he were forced to hand over the pledged object to the creditor (*actio Serviana*), or could not compel the creditor to give back the pledged object (*actio pigneraticia directa*), where the creditor himself was to blame for the fact that the secured debt was not paid.

[51] The text may have been abbreviated by the compilers of the *Corpus iuris civilis*. Kaser 1976: 175 n 22; Schanbacher 2016: 160.

[52] Emunds and Harke 2015: 22 n 23.

[53] According to Schanbacher (2016: 159), the secured debt would later have been changed by C2 and the debtor, in order to extend it to the amount to be paid by C2 to C1.

surplus value of that property was sufficient to cover the debts owed to both creditors. However, even where there was sufficient surplus value, the second creditor would often like to take matters (in particular: the execution sale) into his own hands, so as to no longer be dependent upon the first creditor. Where the first creditor would sell the pledged property by way of execution, he may not always have been motivated to realizing its market value in full but rather be content with obtaining sufficient execution proceeds for discharging the debt owed to him personally. In late classical law the interest of lower-ranking creditors to take over the execution was recognized.

The final evolutionary step for the *ius offerendi et succedendi* was taken when it came to be accepted that a second-ranking creditor could unilaterally achieve succeeding in the rights of execution attached to the first ranking pledge, to the effect that he would obtain a first priority right of recourse for both the amount paid and the amount owed to him personally.[54] In his commentary on the *actio hypothecaria* Marcian sets out how the *ius offerendi et succedendi* operates.

> **D. 20.4.12.6.** *Marcianus libro singulari ad formulam hypothecariam.* Sciendum est secundo creditori rem teneri etiam invito debitore tam in suum debitum quam in primi creditoris et in usuras suas et quas primo creditori solvit: sed tamen usurarum, quas creditori primo solvit, usuras non consequetur: non enim negotium alterius gessit, sed magis suum. et ita Papinianus libro tertio responsorum scripsit, et verum est.
>
> The property is pledged to the second creditor, even if the debtor does not agree, both for his own debt and interest and for debt and interest paid to the first creditor. He will not, however, obtain interest on interest paid to the first creditor, because he paid it to benefit himself, not another. Papinian, in the third book of his *Replies*, so holds, correctly.

Marcian makes clear, in the first place, that the *ius offerendi et succedendi* is a unilateral right of the second creditor, for which the debtor's consent is not required. More importantly, Marcian holds that the second creditor can enforce his pledge not only for the debt owed to him personally but also for an amount equal to the debt (formerly) owed to the first creditor. It was always clear, in late classical law, that neither the first creditor's secured claim

[54] Payment by C2 has the same legal consequences as payment by third parties generally: extinction of the creditor's claim. We will see later in this chapter that for the amount owed to C2 personally, his ranking only became first because C1's higher-ranking claim was discharged.

nor the right of pledge itself would actually transfer to the succeeding creditor. The personal nature of claims and the accessory nature of the right of pledge continued to prevent this.[55] The relevant right of pledge for the second creditor C2 continued to be the pledge granted to him personally, also after the *ius offerendi et succedendi* had fully evolved. What transferred to C2 was the first priority right to take recourse against the pledged assets which was originally attached to C1's pledge.[56]

Where there were several lower-ranking pledge creditors, each of them did have the *ius offerendi et succedendi*. Thus, where there are three creditors, C3 could exercise the *ius offerendi et succedendi* by paying C1 and thus acquire the right to sell the pledged property. However, C3 would only have first ranking for the amount paid to C1. For his own claim, C3's ranking would stay the same.[57] From the surplus of the execution sale organized by C3, which remained after the debt owed to C1 had been deducted, C2 would have to be paid first. Only if there would still be money left would C3 be entitled to the 'surplus of the surplus'.[58] The only advantage of the *ius offerendi et succendendi* was that it enabled the lower-ranking creditor to organize the execution sale himself: it would not improve the ranking of the pledge for his own claim against the debtor. Where the first creditor had already sold the pledged property by way of execution sale, the *ius offerendi et succedendi* of later creditors ceased to exist and they would at most have a claim for the surplus against the first creditor.[59]

Imperial or jurisprudential innovation?

Can this *ius offerendi et succedendi* be regarded as a logical doctrinal extension of Aristo's and Gaius's hypothecary succession, or must the right to take recourse also for the amount owed to the first creditor be considered as a more radical innovation by the imperial chancery? The words '*sciendum est*', with which Marci. D. 20.4.12.6 opens, presuppose that at the time of this jurist this was already settled law.[60] The immediate origin of the *ius offerendi et succedendi* may lie in the Severan period. In his *Disputationes*, which he wrote during the reign of Caracalla (but was published—at the earliest—during the reign of Alexander Severus),[61] the jurist Tryphoninus takes the position that a

55 Kaser 1976: 189; Out 2005: 94–5. 56 Kaser 1976: 190.

57 Kaser 1976: 189–90; Out 2005: 99–100 (with reference to Marci. D. 20.5.5 pr.; Marci. D. 20.4.12.6; Tryph. D. 49.15.12.12; and Paul. D. 20.4.16).

58 A complicated text, involving three pledge creditors, are Paul. D. 20.4.16 and Marcian D. 20.4.12.8.

59 Pap. D. 20.5.3 pr.

60 Emunds and Harke 2015: 27. 61 Liebs 1997: 126.

creditor who redeemed a ransomed slave who had been pledged to him can take recourse against the proceeds of this slave, not only for the secured debt but also for the amount of the ransom. In D. 49.15.12.12 Tryphoninus advocates an analogous application of an imperial constitution, which grants a lower-ranking creditor a right of recourse for the amount paid to the first ranking creditor 'for the purpose of confirming his pledge' ('*confirmandi sui pignoris causa*'). The imperial constitution to which Tryphoninus refers may very well have been a constitution from AD 197 by Septimius Severus and Caracalla.[62]

> **Sev.-Ant. C. 8.17.1.** Qui pignus secundo loco accepit, ita ius suum confirmare potest, si priori creditori debitam pecuniam solverit aut, cum obtulisset isque accipere noluisset, eam obsignavit et deposuit nec in usus suos convertit.
>
> Someone who has accepted a second-ranking pledge, can strengthen his legal position by paying to the prior in right the amount due to him, or if the amount is offered and not accepted, by sealing and depositing it without turning it to his own use.

On the face of it, C. 8.17.1 only adds to the then existing law (Gai. D. 20.4.11.4) by ruling that in order to 'strengthen' ('*confirmare*') his right of pledge, the second creditor must set apart the money offered to a refusing creditor. Nevertheless, it could have been this constitution which introduced the full-fledged *ius offerendi et succedendi.*[63] Several late classical sources—including another text by Tryphoninus (D. 49.15.12.12)—use (derivations of) *confirmare* (or similar words) in order to express that by exercising his *ius offerendi et succedendi* the second creditor can gain a 'strengthened' right of pledge.[64] This *(con)firmare* entails that the lower-ranking creditor can now institute the *actio Serviana* against anyone (including the first creditor), sell the pledged property, and take recourse against the proceeds, not only for his own secured debt but also for the debt (formerly) owed to the first creditor. Another possibility is that at the time C. 8.17.1 was issued, the *ius offerendi et succedendi* had already been developed by jurisprudence, in particular in Papinian's writings.[65]

[62] See also, e.g., Gai. D. 20.4.11.4; Marci. D. 20.5.5 pr.; Tryph. D. 20.4.20; Alex. C. 8.17.5; Diocl.-Max. C. 8.13.22. The same result could be achieved when a new creditor provided a loan to the debtor, in order to discharge the existing secured debt. See, e.g., Sev.-Ant. C. 8.18.1 and Alex. C. 8.18.3.

[63] Emunds and Harke 2015: 37.

[64] Alex. C. 8.17.5 ('*firmabitur*'). See also Diocl.-Max. C. 8.13.22 ('*confirmat*').

[65] Kaser 190–1.

Papinian as inventor?

During the reign of Septimius Severus and Caracalla as co-emperors Papinian was *procurator a libellis* (later: *praefectus praetorio*).[66] As such, Papinian may have been responsible for drafting C. 8.17.1. At the end of D. 20.4.12.6, Marcian refers to book 3 of Papinian's *Responsa*. There is a text in this very book in which Papinian gives his opinion on the scope of the *ius offerendi et succedendi*.

> **D. 20.5.3 pr.** *Papinianus libro tertio responsorum.* Cum prior creditor pignus iure conventionis vendidit, secundo creditori non superesse ius offerendae pecuniae convenit. **1.** Si tamen debitor non interveniente creditore pignus vendiderit eiusque pretium priori creditori solverit, emptori poterit offerri quod ad alium creditorem de nummis eius pervenit et usurae medii temporis: nihil enim interest, debitor pignus datum vendidit an denuo pignori obliget.
>
> When the first creditor has sold the pledged property pursuant to the terms of the agreement, it is accepted that the second no longer has the right to offer the money. 1. If, however, the debtor without objection from the creditor sells the pledged property and pays the price to the first creditor, it is possible to offer the buyer the money which went from him to the first creditor, together with interest for the intervening period. For it makes no difference whether the debtor sold the pledged property or pledged it a second time.

In D. 20.5.3 pr., Papinian puts first and foremost that the *ius offerendi et succedendi* cannot be exercised when the first ranking creditor (C1) has sold the pledged property by way of execution. This is different, however, where the debtor and C1 have agreed that the secured debt shall be repaid out of the proceeds of a sale by the debtor himself. In D. 20.5.3.1 Papinian holds that the second creditor's (C2's) *ius offerendi et succedendi* can also be exercised against someone who purchased the pledged property from the debtor.[67] By offering to pay the purchaser the amount of the proceeds (increased with interest) which the debtor paid on to C1, C2 can achieve that he succeeds in the rights of execution attached to C1's first ranking pledge. The end result is that C2 can sell the property by way of execution and the purchaser recovers his money.

In book 11 of his *Responsa* (D. 20.4.3.1), Papinian first sets out that the creditor who financed the purchase of the pledged property has priority over the creditor with a prior right of pledge. This is one of the few instances in which Roman law does not determine the ranking of pledges in accordance

[66] Honoré 1994: 190. [67] See also Alex. C. 8.18.3.

with the *prior tempore* principle.[68] The original priority must be restored, however, if 'it happens that the anterior creditor offers to repay him'. Thus, here also the ranking of the pledges can be reversed by the lower-ranking creditor exercising the *ius offerendi et succedendi* vis-à-vis the higher-ranking creditor. It would perhaps go too far to call Papinian, the most brilliant jurist of the Severan period, the inventor of the *ius offerendi et succedendi*, but he has certainly made significant contributions to its elaboration.[69]

Succession in one's own ranking

In Lenel's reconstruction of the *formula* of the *actio Serviana* a negative condition is included: 'that this money has not been paid nor otherwise satisfaction has been given for this claim'. This refers to two categories of events, each of which would effectively terminate the pledge: *solutio* and *satisfactio*.[70] In the course of the classical period the scope of the discharge clause expanded, mostly by the jurists giving an extensive interpretation of the term *satisfactio*.[71] No longer was the granting of alternative (real or personal) security the only way of providing satisfaction to the creditor.[72] *Satisfactio* came to comprise several other legal events that caused the termination of the right of pledge.[73] In D. 13.7.9.3 Ulpian mentions that *satisfactio* will take place by accepting a new debtor ('*reo dato*'). This means that (passive) *novatio* was regarded by the jurists as a case of *satisfactio*. The passive side of debts could be 'transferred' by the creditor allowing the debtor to novate his debt to another debtor. Novation could also take place without changing creditors or debtors but in order to replace an existing contract between the creditor and debtor (as in Pap. D. 20.4.3 pr. discussed shortly). For secured creditors this

[68] See p. 291, 378.

[69] Cf. Pap. D. 20.4.3 pr. discussed below, on the succession in one's own ranking.

[70] I will use the term 'discharge clause' in order to refer to both (negative) conditions relating to the performance by the debtor: *solutio* and *satisfactio*. The discharge clause was mirrored as a positive condition in the *formula* of the *actio pigneraticia directa*, the contractual action with which the debtor could demand the return of the pledged object from the creditor. Therefore, where the secured debt was paid or otherwise discharged, the discharge clause 'switched off' the *actio Serviana* and at the same time 'switched on' the *actio pigneraticia directa*. Because the content of the discharge clause in both actions is exactly the same, the texts on the *actio pigneraticia directa* are also relevant for the *actio Serviana* (e.g., Ulp. D.13.7.9.3) (Out 2005: 163).

[71] Out 2005: 243; Marino 2018: 73–8 and passim.

[72] For example, Cato's pledge templates and Lab. D. 20.6.14. Section 4.3.

[73] Ulp. D. 13.7.9.3 mentions: (passive) novation ('*reo dato*'), transfer in lieu of payment ('*pretio aliquo*') and *satisfactio* 'by mere agreement' ('*nuda conventione*'). In addition, from the classical sources the following instances of *satisfactio* emerge: *acceptilatio* (Jul. D. 12.2.40), *pactum de non petendo* (Marci. D. 20.6.5 pr.), *iusiurandum* (Jul. D. 12.2.40; Tryph. D. 20.6.13; Marci. D. 20.6.5.3), and *compensatio* (Pomp. D. 20.4.4). See in particular Alonso 2007 and Marino 2018.

was not without risks. Paul. D. 46.2.18 restates the classical law of the second and third century AD: a right of pledge which secures a novated debt terminates, but only when the novation was made lawfully.[74] Where the novated obligation was secured by a right of pledge, its extinguishment would cause the right of pledge to terminate, and a new pledge granted in order to secure the novated debt could have a lower rank. In this area the jurists applied their creative skills with great mastery, in order to preserve the ranking of pledges securing novated debts. A veritable intellectual *tour de force* is Papinian's extension of the *ius offerendi et succedendi* to cases of novation where multiple pledges had been granted.

'Repeat the pledging'

Ulpian says in D. 13.7.11.1 that 'through novation the pledge subsides, unless it is agreed that the pledge shall be repeated'.[75] What does '*ut pignus repetatur*' in Ulp. D. 13.7.11.1 mean? Does the original pledge continue to exist or does the expired original pledge have to be granted again?[76] The latter was the case: as the Digest texts reproduced below show, upon novation of the secured debt the creditor would take a new pledge over the same assets. By making his consent to a novation conditional upon an agreement to 'repeat' the pledge, the creditor could achieve the continuation of the security of his debt. Although this goes beyond the jurists' opinions and imperial constitutions that survive, the position may very well have been that rights of pledge would only terminate by novation where there were recognizable indications that the creditor did not want to continue the pledge.[77] Economic rationality, in any case, would entail that the creditor's consent to novation would be given under the condition that the new debt would also be secured by a pledge with the same rank. Papinian's opinion in D. 20.4.3 pr. illustrates how acute the problem was. What probably happened was that creditor C1 had lent money to the debtor, which was secured

[74] Where the novation is made against the *senatus consultum Vellaeianum* (Gai. D. 16.1.13.1), by a minor (Pomp. D. 4.4.50), or is otherwise vitiated (e.g., Paul. D. 49.14.21), it does not discharge the pledge. According to Ankum (1975: 11), followed by Out (2005: 206–7), Gaius and Pomponius represented an older view (novations do not terminate pledges), while late classical jurists like Papinian, Ulpian, Paul, and Marcian endorsed the newer one (novations result in termination). The more plausible interpretation is that the opinions of Gaius and Pomponius are in line with those of the late classical jurists: a right of pledge which secures a novated debt terminates, but only when the novation was made lawfully.

[75] Ulp. D. 13.7.11.1 ('*Novata autem debiti obligatio pignus peremit, nisi convenit, ut pignus repetatur*'). *Repetere* has many meanings in Roman law. Here I follow Wacke's translation of '*ut pignus repetatur*': 'to repeat the pledging' ('*die Verpfändung wiederholen*').

[76] Ankum (1975: 13 n 62) assumes that a new pledge is granted, which has the same rank as the original one. Wacke (2000: 220–1) rather seems to think of a continuation of the original pledge.

[77] Wacke 2000: 230.

by a pledge over certain assets. The same assets were subsequently pledged to another creditor C2. C1 and the debtor then increased the credited amount, by entering into a new stipulation for a higher amount which replaced the original one. Because of his increased exposure, C1 demanded additional security on top of the security already granted. C1's new pledge would normally rank after C2's pledge over the same assets, even for the amount of the original (novated) debt. In order to avoid this result Papinian applies a legal mechanism that had been developed by the jurists (including Papinian himself) for multiple pledges: the *ius offerendi et succedendi*.

> **D. 20.4.3 pr.** *Papinianus libro undecimo responsorum.* Creditor acceptis pignoribus (quae secunda conventione secundus creditor accepit) novatione postea facta pignora prioribus addidit. superioris temporis ordinem manere primo creditori placuit tamquam in suum locum succedenti.
>
> A creditor had accepted a pledge of assets over which a second creditor pursuant to a subsequent agreement also accepted (a pledge), then after novation added further assets to his security. It was held that the first creditor kept his priority in time as if succeeding in his own place.
>
> **D. 20.4.12.5.** *Marcianus libro singulari ad formulam hypothecariam.* Papinianus libro undecimo respondit, si prior creditor postea novatione facta eadem pignora *cum* aliis accepit, in suum locum eum succedere: sed si secundus non offerat pecuniam, posse priorem vendere, ut primam tantum pecuniam expensam ferat, non etiam quam postea credidit, et quod superfluum ex anteriore credito accepit, hoc secundo restituat.
>
> Papinian, in his eleventh book, gave the opinion that if the first creditor makes a novation and takes a pledge of the same assets along with others, he succeeds in his own place. But if the second does not offer to pay off the first, the first can sell the property and keep the amount of the first, not the second loan, and pay the second any surplus over the amount of the first loan.

Although it appears that in Papinian's view the original pledge is terminated by the novation and a new pledge had to be created, this new pledge has the same ranking as the original one. So, for the purpose of ranking, the situation is the same as if the original pledge continued to exist. These texts show how creative the Roman jurists were in reaching this economically efficient result. In a 'slightly artificial' (Ankum) or 'genial' (Wacke) way, Papinian applied the mechanism of the *ius offerendi et succedendi* to novation. The creditor C1 takes over the (original) ranking of the right of pledge which secured the debt originally owed to C1 himself.[78] C1 'succeeds in his own place'. Marcian adopts Papinian's opinion (with express reference to book 11 of the *Responsa*, from which D. 20.4.3 pr. was taken), but adds that C1's first rank is confined to the amount of the original loan. The proceeds remaining after this amount has been deducted from the proceeds of the execution sale must be paid to C2.

7.5 Continuation of older practices

It is remarkable that after it had become settled law that multiple pledges could be granted unconditionally, transactional practices belonging to earlier stages continued to be used. From opinions by late classical jurists we can conclude that in the legal practice of the late Principate pledges which were confined to the surplus value were still created, and that subsequent pledges were still granted conditionally. Kaser rightly regards this as a symptom of the 'dogged clinging of practice to outdated types and forms'.[79] In their interpretations of these transactional practices the jurists are generally guided by the purpose of the parties' agreements rather than by the literal meaning of the contractual clauses.[80] The jurists were even prepared to interpret the wordings chosen by the parties against their literal meaning, in the light of the prevailing construction in their time.

A late classical '*pignoris hyperocha*'

There is one text in the *Corpus iuris civilis* (Tryph. D. 20.2.20) in which the pledge of the surplus is called '*pignoris hyperocha*'.[81] The term '*hyperocha*' (surplus) may very well have come from documentary practices in the eastern provinces of the Roman empire and one cannot exclude the possibility that the Roman transactional practice of pledging the surplus originated there.[82] The express pledge of the surplus continued to be used in late classical practice, even though in this period, as we have seen, multiple pledges could be

[78] Ankum 1975: 10–11. [79] Kaser: 1976, vol II: 187. [80] Kaser 1976: 171.

[81] The author of this text Claudius Tryphoninus, counsel to Septimius Severus, was probably of Greek descent and may have been a Roman official in Syria. Kunkel 1967: 231–3.

[82] See in particular Biscardi 1969: 166–8. See also Kaser 1976: 203. D. 20.4.20 is the only text in the Digest in which the word *hyperocha* occurs. Other texts on the pledge of surplus proceeds are Pap. D. 46.3.96.3 and Paul. D. 22.2.6.

created unconditionally and lower-ranking pledge creditors were, in any event, entitled to the surplus by operation of law.

> **D. 20.4.20.** *Tryphoninus libro octavo disputationum.* Quaerebatur, si post primum contractum tuum, antequam aliam pecuniam tu crederes, eidem debitori Seius credidisset quinquaginta et hyperocham huius rei, quae tibi pignori data esset, debitor obligasset, dehinc tu eidem debitori crederes forte quadraginta: quod plus est in pretio rei quam primo credidisti utrum Seio ob quinquaginta an tibi in quadraginta cederet pignoris hyperocha. finge Seium paratum esse offerre tibi summam primo ordine creditam. dixi consequens esse, ut Seius potior sit in eo quod amplius est in pignore, et oblata ab eo summa primo ordine credita usurarumque eius postponatur primus creditor in summam, quam postea eidem debitori credidit.
>
> You made a first contract with the debtor, then, before you made a second loan, Seius lent him fifty and the debtor charged to Seius the surplus proceeds of the property pledged to you. Then, you lent the same debtor, say, forty. The question put was whether the surplus realized by the pledged property over the first loan went to Seius for fifty or to you for forty. Suppose that Seius was willing to offer you the amount first loaned? I said that it followed that Seius was preferred as regards the surplus, and, if he offered the amount of the first loan and interest, the first creditor was postponed to him as regards the later loan to the same debtor.

The debtor borrowed money from C1 ('you') secured by a right of pledge. The text does not disclose the amount of the first loan, but let us suppose this was 60. The first loan was followed by a loan of 50 by C2 (Seius) to the same debtor, which was secured by a pledge of the *superfluum* of the same property. Then C1 entered into another loan agreement with the debtor for 40. Because the debtor defaulted, C1 enforced the pledge by execution sale for, say, an amount of 100. The question arose who was entitled to the surplus remaining after the original loan was deducted from the proceeds of the execution sale (100 – 60 = 40). The reason why this question was addressed to Tryphoninus must be found in sloppy drafting by the transacting parties or their legal advisers. The parties to the second pledge will still have defined the object of the pledge as: 'the surplus proceeds of the property pledged to you'. Does this refer to the surplus remaining after C1's first loan (60) has been deducted from the sale proceeds, or do both loans granted by C1 first have to be deducted? In other words, would C2 be entitled to 40 (100 – 60) or nothing (100 – (60 + 40))?

Tryphoninus advises that C2's claim for 50 outranks C1's (second) claim for 40, so that C2 would be entitled to the remaining proceeds of 40. This is motivated with a comparison with the *ius offerendi et succedendi*. If C2 would have offered to pay C1's original claim of 60, he would have succeeded C1 as first ranking creditor for this claim. When C2 would then have sold the pledged property by way of execution, he would have been able to apply the proceeds for both C1's original claim (60) and his own claim for 50. Only if the execution proceeds were more than 110 (60 + 50) would there be something left for C1's second claim for 40. Tryphonius's view was that the same result would be justified if not C2 but C1 himself would sell the pledged property by way of execution. Tryphoninus's prefers a restrictive interpretation of the parties' reference to the *superfluum*, because it corresponds with the principle of priority as the central idea for the ranking of secured claims as applied to the *ius offerendi et succedendi*.[83]

A late classical conditional pledge

A text from Marcian illustrates that decades after Gaius's recommendation to take a conditional pledge, this construction was still in use as an alternative to unconditional multiple pledges. Its continuing use caused a problem of interpretation, which again was solved in accordance with the principles governing (the now recognized) unconditional multiple pledges.

D. 20.4.12.8 *Marcianus libro singulari ad formulam hypothecariam*. A Titio mutuatus pactus est cum illo, ut ei praedium suum pignori hypothecaeve esset: deinde mutuatus est pecuniam a Maevio et pactus est cum eo, ut, si Titio desierit praedium teneri, ei teneatur: tertius deinde aliquis dat mutuam pecuniam tibi, ut Titio solveres, et paciscitur tecum, ut idem praedium ei pignori hypothecaeve sit et locum eius subeat: num hic medius tertio potior est, qui pactus est, ut Titio soluta pecunia impleatur condicio, et tertius de sua neglegentia queri debeat? sed tamen et hic tertius creditor secundo praeferendus est.

Someone borrowed from Titius and agreed that his land would be pledged or hypothecated to him. Then, he borrowed from Maevius and agreed that if

[83] Kaser 1976: 200. In Marci. D. 20.4.12.3 the first (secured) creditor had entered into two loan agreements with the borrower, only one of which was concluded before a loan was entered into between the borrower and the second (secured) creditor: the first creditor only ranked ahead of the second (secured) creditor for the first loan.

> the land would no longer be charged to Titius, it would be charged to him (Maevius). Then, a third man lends you money to pay Titius, and agrees with you that the same land should be bound to him by way of pledge or hypothec and that he should take the place of Titius. Is the intermediate man, who agreed that by payment of the money to Titius the condition will materialize, in a stronger position than the third, and should the third be left to regret his carelessness? Even here the third creditor must be preferred to the second.

The debtor successively entered into two loan agreements secured by a pledge over the same piece of land, the first one with Titius (C1), the second one with Maevius (C2). C2's pledge was granted on the condition that C1's pledge would be extinguished. Sometime later, a third party (C3) lent money to the debtor, so that the latter could repay C1. Moreover, it was agreed that the land would be pledged to C3 and that C3 would succeed in C1's (first) rank. The question addressed to Marcian was whose right of recourse prevails, that of C2 or that of C3? This was a question of interpretation of the conditional pledge agreement entered into between the debtor and C2.[84] This question is raised by the drafting of the condition subject to which the pledge to C2 was granted. Strictly interpreted, what had been agreed entailed that upon repayment of C1, C2's pledge would come into existence as a first ranking right of pledge. In this transaction Titius (C1) was repaid, but with the money borrowed by the debtor from C3. Under a literal interpretation this would have caused the automatic termination of C1's pledge, so that the condition pursuant to which C2's pledge was granted materialized.

Marcian is willing to forgive C3 his 'carelessness' in failing to take into account the possible adverse consequences for him of the terms of the pledge conditionally granted to C2. Marcian endorses a more flexible interpretation of the pledge agreement between the debtor and C2. The debtor and C2 must have intended that the second pledge would be conditional upon the *regular* discharge of C1, that is by the debtor repaying the first loan out of his own funds, so that the original pledge and the ensuing rights of recourse are completely extinguished. In other words, the condition subject to which the second pledge was granted to C2 does *not* materialize when a *third party* provides the funds with which C1 is paid, in order to take over his ranking.[85] This interpretation by Marcian reaches the same result as that of multiple unconditional pledges. In that case C3 could have exercised the *ius offerendi et succendi* and succeed in C1's rank for the amount owed to C1.

[84] Kaser 1976: 204. [85] Kaser 1976: 204.

8

Pignus Nominis and *Antichresis*

8.1 Introduction

In economies where debts are valuable and saleable assets, they will also have value as collateral. The first evidence of the pledge of debts (*pignus nominis*) is from the second century AD (Pomponius), but its origins may lie in an earlier period, perhaps even in the Republic.[1] The pledge of claims may have originated as a pledge granted by handing over the documents evidencing the debt to the creditor. This is, however, certainly no longer the case in high and late classical law, where *pignus nominis* (even if accompanied by the delivery of debt instruments) is a variant of a pledge granted *nuda conventione* (section 8.2). The praetor would protect pledge agreements in which the pledged assets were not defined as movable or immovable property but rather as contractual claims owed by third parties to the debtor (section 8.3). In particular where the pledge creditor was entitled to demand payment from the debtor's tenants, *pignus nominis* is not always easy to distinguish from a so-called antichretic pledge of leased real estate.[2] From the third century AD we have evidence that the granting of a pledge could be accompanied by an agreement pursuant to which the creditor was entitled to use the charged property (houses, agricultural land, slaves) and to take its (natural or civil) fruits (section 8.4). The value of the use or the fruits would then serve as payment of principal or interest. This type of arrangement is since the Middle Ages commonly referred to as *antichresis*, although in the *Corpus iuris civilis* itself this term is used only twice.[3] Late classical Roman law knew three variants of *antichresis*: implied, default, and independent *antichresis*.

For both variants of pledge—*pignus nominis* and *antichresis*—the jurists were prepared to introduce drastic innovations in order to give legal effect to a *conventio pignoris*, or an independent *pactum antichreticum*, which allowed

[1] In this chapter (and elsewhere in this book) I will speak interchangeably of the pledge of 'claims', 'debts', or 'receivables'.

[2] See in particular Ulp. D. 20.1.20 (section 8.2).

[3] Marci. D. 13.7.33 and D. 20.1.11.1. For a comparative account of *antichresis* in the papyri of Roman Egypt and in classical Roman law, see Bobbink and Mauer 2019.

Security and Credit in Roman Law: The historical evolution of pignus *and* hypotheca. Hendrik L. E. Verhagen, Oxford University Press. DOI: 10.1093/oso/9780199695836.003.0009

the creditor to demand payment of debts owed to his debtor. The *actio utilis* derived from the *actio Serviana* was an *actio in personam* with which the creditor demanded payment of debts owed to the debtor, despite the fact that the *actio Serviana* itself was an *actio in rem* with which the creditor sought to recover possession of the pledged asset. Moreover, the *formula* of the *actio Serviana* was also adapted in order to make independent *antichresis* enforceable, pursuant to which the creditor was entitled to use property and take its fruits independent of a right of pledge.

8.2 From Tangible to Intangible Collateral: *Pignus Nominis*

The cause of the standard action available to pledge creditors, the *actio Serviana*, was the pledge agreement (*conventio pignoris*), so that in principle any admissible form of property defined therein could be made the object of this action.[4] In classical law (and perhaps already in republican law) it became possible that not only tangible assets were defined as pledged assets but also claims which the debtor had against third parties. This is not so strange, as Gaius observes that everything which can be the object of a sale can also be pledged (D. 20.1.9.1), and already by the time of the late Republic claims could be sold. The first evidence of *pignus nominis* is, however, relatively late: an opinion from the second-century jurist Pomponius reported in a text from the third century AD.[5] After Pomponius, it is not until the third century that in jurists' writings and imperial constitutions we again find texts on *pignus nominis*, or in classical terms, *nomen pignori datum*.[6] The praetor would protect pledge agreements in which the pledged assets were not defined as movable or immovable property but rather as contractual claims owed by third parties to the debtor. It was through the structural coupling of contract that Roman law adapted to the economic reality that claims became valuable assets. The adaptation itself was the work of the jurists, who will have advised litigating parties and the praetor on drafting a form of action which was tailored to the completely different nature of the charged assets.[7] The Roman sources are scarce and only provide a fragmentary picture of the pledge of claims, so that its reconstruction is inevitably, to a large extent, based on hypotheses.[8]

[4] Kaser 1982: 181–2. [5] Marci. D. 20.1.13.2. [6] Marci. D. 20.1.13.2.

[7] Section 8.3. On *pignus nominis* in classical and Justinian Roman law, see Smit 2020 (in Dutch with summary in English).

[8] Kaser 1969: 173. The scarcity of texts on *pignus nominis* could be an indication that this variation of pledge was of less practical relevance than pledges of tangible property. It may, however, also be the

Origin

'In developed economies the bulk of corporate wealth is locked up in debts.'[9] In a market economy it is advantageous that this wealth can be unlocked, by allowing debts to be made liquid by selling them, or by using them as collateral. In the Roman empire, wealth was personal rather than corporate and the bulk of wealth was stored in real estate.[10] But even so, in the Roman economy a great deal of wealth was locked up in debts. Scaevola mentions a banker (*coactor argentarius*) who 'held nearly his entire fortune in debts'.[11] A common attribute of a well-to-do Roman household would be 'a chest containing written instruments and guarantees from debtors'.[12] These debts are most likely to have been contractual debts, arising under loan agreements, stipulations, contracts of sale, and rental agreements.[13] Roman law allowed this wealth to be unlocked. The sale of claims is already attested in an opinion of a republican jurist (Ofilius).[14] In the late Republic the 'transfer' of *nomina* was a method for paying the purchase price for large properties. In one of his letters to Atticus, Cicero writes that he contemplates selling a debt owed by Faberius in order to be able to purchase real estate from Silius.[15] The transferability of debts may even have contributed significantly to Rome's money supply.[16] There is some evidence for the existence of a secondary market for debts in the first century BC.[17] The practice of using claims as collateral may have already arisen during this period.[18] The object of a pledge of claims was a *nomen debitoris*.[19] The term *nomen* was probably influenced by Greek usage and referred to a claim represented by the name of the debtor entered into an account book administered by the creditor of that claim.[20]

result of choices made by the compilers of the *Corpus iuris civilis* in the sixth century AD. Also, the recognition of general pledges may have caused *pignus nominis* to be relatively rare in practice.

[9] Oditah 1991: vii. For Rome see Harris 2011: 230–5, 237, 241–4. See also Dernburg 1860: 461.

[10] The main exception may have been the *societates publicanorum*, which were corporations whose (considerable) wealth was stored in (tax) claims. See Malmendier 2002.

[11] Scaev. D. 40.7.40.8.

[12] Afr. D. 32.64.

[13] Kay (2014: 109) notes that by Cicero's day *nomen* could refer to an entry in an account book in relation to sales, loans, fines, or debts generally.

[14] Ofilius's opinion is to be found in Ulp. D. 44.4.4.6. This opinion is not on a straightforward purchase of debts, but deals with a special situation in which the debtor of the purchased claim had instructed someone else to purchase the claim from his (the debtor's) creditor. In D. 18.4.4 Ulpian records the opinion of Celsus, holding that the seller of a claim does not, unless otherwise agreed, warrant the creditworthiness of the debtor of the sold claim, but only that the debt is owed by that person.

[15] Cic., *Att.* 12.31.2. See Ioannatou 2006: 388–90, 409–12; Kay 2014: 239.

[16] Harris 2011: 225–32.

[17] Kay 2014: 239.

[18] Dernburg 1860: 461.

[19] Paul. D. 13.7.18 pr.; Marci. D. 20.1.13.2; Alex. C. 8.16.4; and Diocl.-Max. C. 4.39.7.

[20] Kaser 1969: 174; Kay 2014: 109.

A constitution by Alexander Severus from 225 AD declares that 'also the claim against a debtor can be pledged, both generally and specifically, as has already earlier been accepted'.[21] But when, exactly, this was accepted cannot be established. The earliest text in the Digest is by Pomponius, a contemporary of Julian and counsel to Hadrian and Antonius Pius.[22] In his commentary on the praetor's edict Pomponius wrote of someone 'whose claim has been pledged'.[23] One does not get the impression that Pomponius was being very innovative when he wrote these words.[24] They suggest that by his time, *pignus nominis* was already a well-settled variation of pledge.

Assignment and pledge

In the nineteenth century Dernburg and other German Pandectists held that *pignus nominis* was a modality of the assignment of claims. According to Dernburg, Roman law never recognized that claims could be the object of real rights. Based on this assumption Dernburg puts forward that essentially *pignus nominis* was a species of the assignment of claims. The powers of the creditor as assignee would have been limited in accordance with the purposes of the pledge agreement, so that they would expire upon discharge of the secured debt.[25] Nowhere in the sources, however, is there any indication that *pignus nominis* was regarded as a modality of assignment. Moreover, as Kaser has elaborated, the actions granted to an assignee would be unsuitable for enforcing a pledge of claims.[26] The pledge creditor's *actio utilis* consisted of not only elements derived from the action for the pledged debt (e.g., *condictio, actio locati*) but also conditions taken from the *actio Serviana* (*conventio pignoris, pecuniam debitam*, etc.).[27] A constitution by Diocletian suggests that the legal practice of granting *actiones utiles* to purchasers and pledge creditors of claims originated more or less at the same time.[28] In respect of granting an *actio utilis* against the debtor of the claim, *pignus* may even have considerably preceded assignment. The opinion by Pomponius (as reported by Marcianus

[21] C. 8.16.4 ('*Nomen quoque debitoris pignerari et generaliter et specialiter posse pridem placuit*').

[22] Von der Fecht (1999: 22) refers to a nineteenth-century view (Fleischmann) that Marcian may have taken 'unhistorical' recourse to Pomponius, in order to strengthen his argument. I find this very unlikely: in those cases where we can check the accuracy of references by one jurist to another (e.g., the reference to Pap. D. 20.4.3 pr. in Marci. D. 20.4.12.5), we find that they generally are accurate. Moreover, where Marcian writes '*cum pignori rem pigneratam accipi posse placuerit*', this indicates that in his time *pignus nominis* was a long-established legal institution. See also Von der Fecht 1999: 22.

[23] Marci. D. 20.1.13.2 ('*cuius nomen pignori datum est*').

[24] Brandsma 2013: 228.

[25] Dernburg 1860: 462.

[26] Kaser 1969: 177–80.

[27] Section 8.3.

[28] Diocl.-Max. C. 4.39.7. See p. 251.

in D. 20.1.13.2) leaves no doubt that by the first half of the second century AD, the pledge creditor of a claim would have his own action against the debtor of the claim. For assignment, it is only in the imperial rescript practice of the third century AD that a tendency develops to grant an *actio utilis* to the assignee of a claim.[29]

Origin in possessory pledge of debt instruments?

The debts which were to serve as collateral would often be evidenced by documents: *chirographa, cautiones, epistulae.*[30] One cannot exclude the possibility that in an earlier period—late republican or early classical—the pledge of debt instruments evolved from the possessory pledge of tangible property. This is speculative, but perhaps the handing over of chirographs (etc.) to a pledge creditor was treated as analogous to a *traditio* of movable property in order to grant a possessory pledge. This is not conclusive, however, as to whether the possessory pledge is the direct ancestor of *pignus nominis*. Much depends on when it was accepted that the *conventio pignoris* (rather than a *traditio* by way of possessory pledge) was the central element of the *actio Serviana*.[31] If it was only Julian who achieved this, then *pignus nominis* may have had its origin in a 'possessory' pledge of debt instruments. If, however, the praetor was prepared—whether or not in the form of *actiones in factum* or *utiles*—to give effect to pledge agreements in an earlier period, then *pignus nominis* may have had its origin as a purely contractual pledge in this earlier period.

In Ulp. D. 20.1.20 a creditor who had lent money for the repair of a rented building and would be repaid out of the rents by way of pledge, was granted adapted actions (*actiones utiles*) against the tenants, on the analogy of a debt instrument (*cautio*) which had been pledged.

D. 20.1.20. *Ulpianus libro sexagesimo tertio ad edictum.* Cum convenit, ut is, qui ad refectionem aedificii credidit, de pensionibus iure pignoris ipse

[29] Gord. C. 4.10.1 (242 AD); Val.-Gal. C. 4.10.2 (260 AD); Diocl.-Max. C. 4.15.5 (294 AD). See Zimmermann 1990: 62; Harke 2008; Kaser, Knütel, and Lohsse 2021: 385–7. These are all constitutions concerning individual dispositions of claims by way of sale, dowry, *datio in solutum*, etc. Ulp. D. 2.14.16 pr. refers to a ruling by Antonius Pius from the second century AD, in which the purchaser from the heirs of a deceased's entire estate is granted an *actio utilis* to enforce a debt owed to the deceased. The inheritance had probably been transferred by way of *in iure cessio*. Harke 2008: 2, 14.

[30] Verhagen 2018: 269–76.

[31] Sections 4.5 and 6.6.

> creditum recipiat, etiam actiones utiles adversus inquilinos accipiet cautionis exemplo, quam debitor creditori pignori dedit.
>
> When it has been agreed that the one who has lent money for the repair of a building should be repaid out of the rents by way of pledge, he also acquires adapted actions against the tenants, on the analogy of a debt instrument which the debtor has given to the creditor in pledge.

From D. 20.1.20, Smits derives that, chronologically, the praetor appears to have first granted an *actio utilis* to the creditor to whom a debt instrument had been pledged.[32] This presumes, according to Smit, that only later an *actio utilis* was granted to the creditor whose *pignus nominis* was granted *nuda conventione*. This is based on the assumption that the arrangement discussed in Ulp. D. 20.1.20 was a pledge of rentals (*pignus nominis*).[33] A more plausible interpretation of this fragment, however, is that it is concerned with an antichretic pledge. Normally, where claims are pledged one would expect that their proceeds would only be applied in order to discharge the secured debt when the debtor is in default.[34] In D. 20.1.20, however, the purpose of the pledge is that from the onset of the transaction the rentals are applied in order to repay the secured debt.[35] This rather points in the direction of an antichretic pledge of the building itself. It is actually a typical case of *antichresis*: the secured debt is paid out of the civil fruits (rentals) of the pledged property.[36] The purpose of the analogy with the pledge of debt instruments (which may have been the most common case of *pignus nominis* in practice) was to support the granting of an adapted *actio Serviana* to the antichretic pledge creditor.[37] In other words, D. 20.1.20 confirms that also the antichretic pledge creditor would have an adapted *actio Serviana* at his disposal, with which he could enforce the leases of the pledged building against the tenants.[38] It is, moreover, rather unlikely that more than a century after Pomponius's casual reference to *pignus nominis*, a late classical jurist would still need the analogy of the 'possessory' pledge of debt instruments in order to

[32] Smits 2020: 152–3.

[33] This is how Kaser (1969: 175 n 10) and Smit (2020: 152–3, 174–5) interpret D. 20.1.20. Manigk 1910 does not mention this text, perhaps also because he does not regard it as a case of *antichresis*.

[34] Section 8.3.

[35] For this reason, even if D. 20.1.20 would be a case of *pignus nominis*, it would then have to be regarded as an antichretic pledge of *claims*.

[36] Section 8.4.

[37] Cf. Marci. D. 20.1.11.1, where independent *antichresis* is treated analogously with *pignus*.

[38] Section 8.4.

reach the conclusion that a pledge of rentals could be enforced against the tenant by the creditor with an adapted action.

Pledging debt instruments in late classical law

A constitution by Diocletian and Maximinian confirms that at the time of the classical jurists ('*responsum est*') it was established practice to pledge *cautiones debitorum*.

> **Diocl.-Max. C. 4.39.7.** Postquam eo decursum est, ut cautiones quoque debitorum pignori darentur, ordinarium visum est, ut post nominis venditionem utiles emptori, sic (ut responsum est) vel ipsi creditori postulanti dandas actiones.
>
> After it has come to the point that even debts instruments were pledged, it has seemed normal that after the sale of a claim analogous actions should be given to the purchaser - as has been provided for in a response - like the ones given to the creditor himself when he demands repayment.

Where the parties had agreed that a chirograph (or *cautio* or other debt instrument) was pledged, this must be understood as that the debt (*nomen*) evidenced by this document had been pledged. In D. 32.59 Julian says that 'it is well-known that we use the word "chirograph" for the action itself, since when a chirograph is sold we understand that the debt has been sold'. D. 32.59 should, however, not be understood as saying that chirographs were negotiable instruments, whose transfer and pledge would be equivalent to the assignment and pledge of the claims they evidenced.[39] For the transfer of debts evidenced by chirographs one would still need to rely on the 'palliatives' (procedural mandate, *novatio*) that classical Roman law offered as alternatives to assignment.[40] D. 32.59 is concerned with the interpretation of contracts: where the parties speak of the sale of a 'chirograph' they must have intended to sell the debt itself. It's the same with the pledge of a 'chirograph': object of the *conventio pignoris* is not the chirograph as such, but the debt itself. Accordingly this *conventio pignoris* would not be enforced with an *actio Serviana* with which the creditor could recover possession of the chirograph,

[39] Sirks 2016 argues that chirographs were like negotiable instruments. For a different interpretation, see Verhagen 2018.

[40] Kaser 1969: 175 n 13. In a similar sense for Hellenistic Egypt Wolff 1978: 167. On these palliatives, see Zimmermann 1990: 58–62.

but (as Diocl.-Max. C. 4.39.7 demonstrates) with an adapted action with which he could demand payment of the claim evidenced by the chirograph.[41]

When it came to be accepted that a right of pledge could be granted *nuda conventione*, the practice of pledging chirographs, although not strictly necessary from a legal perspective, continued. One can easily understand why. Possession of the debt instrument will have facilitated proof by the pledge creditor that the claim evidenced by this instrument was pledged. Moreover, the debtor of the pledged claim would often only be prepared to pay to the pledge creditor if the latter either crossed out the chirograph or gave it back to the debtor, as evidence that the pledged debt had been discharged.[42]

8.3 Execution of *Pignus Nominis*

In modern receivables-based finance transactions, charged claims are almost always claims for the payment of money. The enforcement of these receivables charges is straightforward. The secured creditor notifies the debtor of the charged claim, collects the amount due, and applies the collected proceeds in order to discharge the secured debt. This would have been the same in the Roman credit markets for *pignus nominis*. Paul. D. 13.7.18 pr. states that agreements purporting to pledge claims should be protected by the praetor.[43] Decades earlier, Pomponius had already indicated that where a money claim had been pledged, the pledge creditor could institute an action for payment against the person who owed the money to the pledge debtor. The imperial constitutions of Alexander Severus (C. 8.16.4) and Diocletian (C. 4.39.7) expressly state that this action is an analogous action (*actio utilis*). In case of *pignus nominis* the cause of action (the *factum*) of this *actio utilis* was—like that of the *actio Serviana* itself—the *conventio pignoris*.[44] We will take a closer look at how these adapted actions operated and also pay brief attention to the execution sale of pledged claims (which would have been rare).

Execution of *pignus nominis*: collection of pledged claims

Normally the creditor would enforce his right of pledge by selling the pledged property at auction. In case of a pledge of claims this would be different.

[41] Section 8.3. [42] See also Smit 2020: 153.

[43] '*Si convenerit, ut nomen debitoris mei pignori tibi sit, tuenda est a praetore haec conventio*'.

[44] Kaser 1982: 181–2.

A more convenient way of enforcing the pledge was that the pledge creditor would collect payment from the debtor of the pledged claim and deduct the secured debt from the collected money. The pledge creditor would first notify the debtor of the pledged claim, so that after notification (*denuntiatio*) this debtor would no longer be able to discharge the debt by paying that to the pledge debtor (Alex. C. 8.16.4). The debtor of the pledged claim would be granted an *exceptio* if (after *denuntiatio*) the pledge debtor himself would demand payment of the pledged claim (Paul. D. 13.7.18 pr.). Where the debtor of the pledged claim refused to pay the pledge creditor, the latter could serve an adapted version of the *actio Serviana* against him (which will be elaborated later in this section).[45] Dernburg holds that the pledge creditor could only demand payment of the pledged claim after the pledge debtor had failed to repay the secured debt. This would mean that where the pledged debt was already due and payable but the secured debt was not, the debtor of the pledged claim should have lodged the indebted money.[46]

There is a late classical imperial constitution from AD 225, which indicates how the pledge creditor should take recourse against the proceeds obtained with the adapted action.

> **Alex. C. 8.16.4** Quare si debitor is satis non facit, cui tu credidisti, ille, cuius nomen tibi pignori datum est, nisi ei cui debuit solvit nondum certior a te de obligatione tua factus, utilibus actionibus satis tibi facere usque ad id, quod tibi deberi a creditore eius probaveris, compelletur, quatenus tamen ipse debet.
>
> So if a debtor to whom you have extended credit does not give satisfaction (to you), the person whose account was given to you as a pledge, unless he paid his creditor before learning from you of your obligation (that you had acquired against him), is compelled by analogous action to give satisfaction to you up to the amount that you prove was owed to you by his creditor, but within the amount he himself owes.

This constitution indicates that the pledge creditor's right to demand payment from the debtor of the pledged claim was subject to a double ceiling: it was

[45] Sev. et Ant. C. 8.16.4 says that a claim can be pledged 'generally and specially' (*nomen quoque debitoris pignerari et generaliter et specialiter posse*). Here the pledge creditor would also be granted an adapted *actio Serviana*, except that it would presumably have contained a reference to the general nature of the pledge.

[46] Dernburg 1860: 464–5. If Ulp. D. 20.1.20 was on *pignus nominis*, it would be a case in which the pledge creditor was entitled to institute the adapted *actio Serviana* before there was a default under the secured debt because the parties had expressly agreed that the financier of the repaired building would be repaid out of the rents of this building.

limited not only to the amount of the pledged claim but also by the amount of the secured debt.[47] However, not only Pomponius (in Marci. D. 20.1.13.2) but also Paul (D. 13.7.18 pr.) unequivocally state that the pledge creditor shall deduct the amount of the secured debt from the money received from the debtor of the pledged claim. This rather implies that the pledge creditor could sue the debtor of the pledged claim for the whole amount of this claim and would be under a (contractual or legal) duty to return the surplus to the pledge debtor.[48]

Although there are no texts on the multiple pledge of claims in the *Corpus iuris civilis*, one would expect pledge creditors' rights to take recourse against pledged claims to have been subject to the same principles as would apply to the execution of pledged tangible assets. The first ranking pledge creditor would be exclusively entitled to collect the pledged claims (or sell them) and would be obliged first to pay over the surplus to lower-ranking pledge creditors in accordance with their rank and then pay any remainder to the pledge debtor.[49]

Non-monetary claims

The pledge debtor may also have been a creditor of non-monetary claims. In particular, he may have been a purchaser of tangible property (e.g., real estate, slaves, cattle) which had not yet been transferred to him. The corresponding claim against the seller for conveyance of the sold property could also be pledged and it could then also be enforced by the pledge creditor.[50] Let us suppose that the pledge debtor had purchased land from Negidius, while agreeing that it would be conveyed after six months. The pledge debtor pledged the claim for conveyance against seller Negidius in order to secure a loan obtained from the pledge creditor. When Negidius, after having been sued by the pledge creditor with an adapted *actio Serviana* for conveyance, transferred possession of the land to the pledge creditor, the latter would acquire a possessory pledge of the land.[51] This possessory pledge could in its

[47] See also Dernburg 1860: 466.

[48] Pomponius's works date from before Alexander Severus, but Paul still published under this emperor (Liebs 1997: 151). However, D. 13.7.18 pr. is taken from Paulus's commentary on the praetorian edict, which was written in the 180/190s AD (Liebs 1997: 156), so that C. 8.16.4 may well have changed the law.

[49] Kaser 1969: 186.

[50] Paul. D. 13.7.18 pr.; Marci. D. 20.1.13.2.

[51] One would think that at the same time the pledge debtor would acquire (civil or bonitary) ownership of the purchased object.

turn be executed in accordance with the general execution rules, in particular by auctioning the land.[52] One would expect that if the seller refused to convey the sold property but elected to pay its value instead (*condemnatio pecuniaria*), this would be treated in the same way as if the pledge creditor had collected a pledged monetary claim: the pledge creditor would apply the collected proceeds in order to discharge the secured debt. Finally, it is conceivable that the *conventio pignoris* would allow the pledge debtor to demand conveyance of the purchased property, so that after it had been transferred to the pledge debtor it would be charged with a non-possessory pledge and as such remain in the possession of the pledge debtor.[53]

The adapted action: reconstruction

The actions which pledge creditors could institute in order to demand payment of pledged claims were modelled after the *actio Serviana*. However, they will also have contained elements of the standard contractual actions included in the praetor's edict for the various types of pledged claims (e.g., *condictio, actio ex stipulatu, actio venditi, actio locati*).[54] Thus, for a pledged claim for the payment of 10,000 sesterces arising under a contract of *stipulatio*, the *formula* of this adapted action could hypothetically be reconstructed as follows:

> Si paret inter Aulum Agerium et Lucium Titium convenisse, ut decem, quae Numerium Negidium Lucio Titio dare opportet, Aulo Agerio pignori essent propter pecuniam debitam, eamque pecuniam neque solutam neque eo nomine satisfactum esse neque per Aulum Agerium stare quo minus solvatur, iudex Numerium Negidium Aulo Agerio decem condemnato, si non paret absolvito.
>
> If it appears (a'_1) that it had been agreed between Aulus Agerius and Lucius Titius that the 10,000 sesterces, (a_x) which Numerius Negidius ought to give Lucius Titius, would be pledged to Aulus Agerius (a_2) for money owed, (a_4) that this money has not been paid nor otherwise satisfaction has been given for this claim and it is not because of Aulus Agerius that nothing has been paid, (*b*') do you, judge, condemn Numerius Negidius to Aulus Agerius for 10,000 sesterces; if it does not appear you shall absolve him.[55]

[52] Kaser 1969: 186. [53] Kaser 1969: 187.

[54] See Kaser 1969; Selb 1982: 335; Verhagen 2013a: 60–2; Smit 2020: 258–61.

[55] Reconstruction by Kaser 1969: 181–2. For Smit's reconstruction of the adapted action, see Smit 2020: 259–60 and 328 (in English).

Condition a_1 of the original *formula* has been replaced with condition a'_1, in order to reflect the different content of the pledge agreement. Condition a_3 of the *actio Serviana*, that the pledged property should have been *in bonis* of the debtor, has been deleted from the adapted form of action. The adapted *formula* rather requires, instead, that the money is owed by the debtor of the pledged claim to the pledge debtor (a_x). In addition, the restitution clause (a_6) would be superfluous in this adapted action since it is not aimed at the recovery of possession. The legal consequence (*b*) of the original *formula* has also been changed: the *condemnatio* is no longer for the value of the object of pledge (movable or immovable property) but for the amount of the pledged claim (*b*').

Not only would the pledge creditor Aulus Agerius have to prove that a *conventio pignoris* had been agreed purporting to pledge the claim for 10,000 sesterces which Lucius Titius had against Numerius Negidius pursuant to *stipulatio*. The *formula* would also have to reflect that the defendant (Numerius Negidius) would only be condemned if it appeared that he owed 10,000 sesterces to the pledge debtor Lucius Titius. In other words, the *formula* of the adapted action should not only refer to the *conventio pignoris* and (some of) the other conditions of the *actio Serviana* (secured debt, *solutio, satisfactio*, and *mora creditoris*) but should also be subject to the same condition (*dare opportet*) as would be included if Lucius Titius himself had instituted the *condictio* against Numerius Negidius.[56] This combination of conditions can be called an adapted *actio Serviana*. According to Selb, however, the *actio utilis* granted to a creditor in case of a *pignus nominis* rather is an adaptation of the action with which the pledged claim is enforced (e.g., *condictio*).[57] Also, Smit (elaborately) rejects the characterization of the pledge creditor's action as an adapted *actio Serviana*.[58] What really matters is that this adapted action contains elements of both the *actio Serviana* and the action of the pledged debt (e.g., *condictio*). Whether one calls this action an adapted *actio Serviana* or an adapted *condictio* would be a matter of indifference to the Roman jurists.

[56] Wubbe has suggested in a personal communication to me that the '*dare opportet*' in Kaser's reconstruction is premature, since that would only be the case after Numerius Negidius has been condemned to pay 10,000 sesterces (Verhagen 2013a: 61 n 55). See now also Smit 2020: 232–66. However, we can never be sure how exactly the Roman jurists would have drafted this adapted action. Kaser's reconstruction has the advantage of conciseness and the inclusion of '*dare opportet*' could well have been sufficient for instructing the *iudex* to examine whether Numerius Negidius actually did owe HS 10,000 to Lucius Titius.

[57] Selb 1982: 335.

[58] Smit 2020: 243–57.

Execution sale of pledged claims

Would the pledge creditor have had the power to sell the pledged claims by way of execution sale?[59] The sale itself would not be problematic. We have seen that already in the Republic claims were sold. In one of his letters to Atticus, Cicero mentions *emptio ab hasta* as one of the ways of realizing a claim which was due to him from Caesar.[60] For *pignus in causa iudicati captum* the possibility of selling debtors' claims is confirmed by Ulpian.

> **D. 42.1.15.10.** *Ulpianus libro tertio de officio consulis.* Item quid dicemus? utrum ipsi iudices convenient nomen exigentque id quod debetur et in causa*m* iudicati convertent, an vero vendent nomen, ut pignora corporalia solent? et necesse est, ut quod eis facilius videatur ad rem exsequendam, hoc faciant.
>
> What do we say? Are the judges to enforce the debt and demand what is due to apply it to satisfaction of the judgment, or do they sell the debt as they would sell pledged corporeal things? It must be said that they should adopt the course which, they think, would more easily achieve their object.

Where an attachment has been levied on a claim, the *iudices* assisting the creditor have a choice: they can either demand payment from the debtor of the pledged claim or they can sell it.[61] It is by no means inconceivable that Ulpian's opinion on the execution sale of attached claims served as a precedent for conventional *pignus nominis*, or that they were subject to the same rules. Creditors who by virtue of their (conventional) right of *pignus* were entitled to demand payment of the pledged claim may also have had the option of selling it, in particular where the pledged claim was not yet due and payable.[62]

In comparison with an ordinary sale by the creditor of the sold claim himself, there is an additional complication here.[63] The substitutes for a true assignment—*procuratio in rem suam*, novation, and delegation—would all

[59] According to Dernburg (1860: 469–70), this was possible. Also Kaser (1969: 187) holds that where the pledge agreement contained a right of sale, there is no reason why this should not be possible on the same footing as with tangible property.

[60] Cic., *Att.* 12.3.2. See Ioannatou 2006: 409–12; Kay 2014: 115.

[61] Von der Fecht 1999: 57.

[62] See also Smits 2020: 279–81. Diocl.-Max. *C.* 4.9.1 rules that the imperial treasury has the right to demand payment of debts which are charged by way of fiscal pledge and which are not yet due and payable. This is, however, justified with reference to the public function of the treasury and does not imply a similar right of private pledge creditors.

[63] Ulp. D. 42.1.15.10 seems to imply that the *iudices* also had the power to assign the debts.

require the co-operation of the original creditor as assignor. But when claims are sold by a pledge creditor by way of execution, the pledge debtor may not be willing to co-operate. The pledge creditor could have instituted the *actio pigneraticia contraria* in order to try to compel the pledge debtor to assign the claim to its purchaser at an execution sale. However, this would be time-consuming and ultimately the pledge debtor could only be condemned to pay money, which would not really help where he was insolvent. Perhaps the pledge creditor was authorized to act instead of the pledge debtor, on the analogy of his power of sale where tangible property was sold by way of execution. The purchaser of the pledged claim may also have been granted an *actio utilis* against the debtor of the pledged claim, with which this purchaser himself could demand payment.

8.4 *Antichresis*

Where the creditor was entitled to use the pledged property, gather its fruits, or collect its rents, the question arises whether this would reduce the secured debt or could serve as interest. In many cases, the debtor and creditor would have provided for this in a *pactum antichreticum*.[64] This *pactum antichreticum* was included in, or later added to, the *conventio pignoris*. The late classical jurists accepted that a *pactum antichreticum* could also be implied from the nature of the pledged property. In many antichretic agreements, the creditor's rights to use the pledged property and apply its income by way of principal or interest would be part of the normal settlement of the credit transaction. In the late classical sources, antichretic agreements emerge which were meant as an alternative method of execution. Not only could this 'default *antichresis*' be expressly agreed but it would also sometimes arise by operation of law. The jurists and imperial constitutions even seem to recognize that a *pactum antichreticum* could grant a *sui generis* real right, which could exist independently from a right of *pignus* or *fiducia cum creditore*. The jurists were prepared to adapt the *actio Serviana* in order to grant the creditor an action for the recovery of possession of tangible property (independent *antichresis*), or for the payment of civil fruits (e.g., *antichresis* of rented property). This is yet another example of how the jurists and imperial chancery designed adapted actions in order to uphold agreements with which private parties gave effect to their economic needs.

[64] On *antichresis* in classical and Justinian Roman law, *ius commune*, and modern laws, see Bobbink 2021 (in Dutch with summary in English).

Express, implied, and default *antichresis*

Origin of *antichresis*

Although the earliest Digest and Codex texts on *antichresis* date from the third century AD,[65] it is difficult to imagine that antichretic arrangements were not made earlier. In an agricultural economy which was not fully monetized, the use or natural fruits of farms and land or labour (slaves) served as repayment of loans or as compensation for the granting of credit (interest).[66] Under the archaic legal institution of *nexum* the labour of the charged person (*nexus*) served as repayment of the secured debt.[67] Arrangements pursuant to which the use and/or yields of property were applied in payment of principal and/or interest of loans can be found in many ancient societies. They are recorded in old Babylonian and old Assyrian cuneiform, and in ancient Jewish, Greek, and Greco-Egyptian legal sources.[68] From the kingdom of Arrapha (modern-day Kirkuk, Iraq) more than 300 antichretic loans have been preserved. From Ptolemaic Egypt we have Greek papyri from the third century BC and later documenting antichretic loan agreements.[69] From the early period of Roman Egypt there is papyrological evidence of Romans entering into antichretic loan agreements with local inhabitants.[70] One would think that also in republican and early classical law, where the parties had agreed that the use or the (natural or civil) fruits of the pledged object would serve as repayment of principal or interest, this would be a valid legal arrangement.[71] It is, however, striking that we do not have any evidence of antichretic pledges for the first two centuries of the Principate. For the first century AD this could still be explained by the scantiness of the sources, as relatively few writings from early classical jurists on *pignus* have survived. But for all other variants of *pignus* (*pignus nominis*, multiple pledge, general pledge) there are many jurists' writings and imperial constitutions from the second century AD, while no opinion from that century on *antichresis* has been transmitted.

65 The oldest text is Sev.-Ant. C. 4.24.1 (207 AD).

66 For the Hellenistic legal practice of Roman Egypt in the period 30 BC to 69 AD, Lerouxel 2016 (56–9) has calculated that in 18 per cent. of the loan agreements, interest was paid in kind, while in the registries of the *grapheion* of Tebtynis this percentage is even 34 per cent.

67 For an overview of various credit transactions for which *nexum* could be employed, see Watson 1975: 115–18.

68 Kaser 1982: 206–7. See, e.g., P. Yadin 21 and 22 (130 AD) from the Babatha archive, discussed by Oudshoorn 2007: 168–81; Chiusi 2020: 102–11.

69 Bobbink and Mauer 2019: 3–5.

70 PSI X 1120 (25 BC to 25 AD) and SB XII 11041 (= P. Tebt. II 586)(20–21 AD, Tebtynis). Both papyri are discussed by Bobbink and Mauer 2019: 5–6.

71 In particular in respect of natural fruits this could have been constructed as *datio in solutum*.

The word ἀντίχρησις ('counter-use') appears only twice in the *Corpus iuris civilis*, in two opinions of the late classical jurist Marcian.[72] This word is said to have been derived from χρῆσις ἀντί τινὸς ('use instead of/for something else').[73] The fact that the term *antichresis* appears in two Digest texts (it is absent from the Codex) is too weak a basis to assume that Roman law has been influenced by Greek-Hellenistic laws. Marcian's use of *antichresis* may be explained by his connections with the eastern part of the Roman empire. Marcian had studied in Rome, but had a Hellenistic background and wrote and taught in the eastern provinces.[74] It is by no means inconceivable, however, that the Romans were influenced by Hellenistic transaction practices, which they encountered in Greece or Roman Egypt. In fact, most of the papyri on *antichresis* are from Roman Egypt and date from the first and second century AD.[75] The first texts in the Digest and the Codex date from the beginning of the third century AD, and it may very well be that they were concerned with antichretic pledges which had been agreed in a Hellenistic environment, or which were based on templates (directly or indirectly) derived from Hellenistic originals.[76]

Pactum antichreticum

Antichresis could be agreed upon both in relation to *pignus* and *fiducia*.[77] In relation to *pignus*, the opinions of the jurists refer to this agreement in terms of *pactum*.[78] This *pactum antichreticum* (not a classical term) would normally be included in the *conventio pignoris*, but could also be entered into after the pledge had been granted. In D. 13.7.39 Modestinus gives an example of a *pactum antichreticum* that had been agreed at a later stage: 'Later a pact was made between them that in recompense for his money the creditor should for a given time have possession of the pledge.'[79] This pledge may originally have been a non-possessory pledge, which was later converted into

[72] Marci. D. 13.7.33; Marci. D. 20.1.11.1. In contrast with *hypotheca*, ἀντίχρησις is not latinized by Marcian, but used in Greek. Even in the Greek papyri ἀντίχρησις is only mentioned rarely. One example is Papyrus Groningen 11 (second century AD). See Kupiszewski 1986: 133–4.

[73] It could also have been derived from τί ἀντί χρῆσεως and could thus be understood as the countervalue for the use of capital (Manigk 1910: 14–15; Kupiszewski 1974: 229).

[74] Liebs 1997: 201.

[75] Kupiszewski 1986: 133; Bobbink and Mauer 2019.

[76] Bobbink and Mauer 2019: 28. It seems that in the fifth and sixth centuries AD Roman law influenced legal practices concerning *antichresis* in Egypt, albeit not profoundly (Kupiszewski 1986: 146).

[77] *Fiducia*: PS 2.13.2. Manigk 1910: 59; Erbe 1940: 78; Noordraven 1999: 229; Bobbink and Mauer 2019: 11. For an overview of Roman-Egyptian variants of the *pactum antichreticum*, see Bobbink and Mauer 2019: 14.

[78] Mod. D. 13.7.39; Pap. D. 20.1.1.3.

[79] '*postea pactum inter eos factum est, ut creditor pignus suum in compensationem pecuniae suae certo tempore possideret*'.

a possessory antichretic pledge.[80] The reason for this may have been that the debtor had indicated that he would not be able to pay principal or interest in cash.

In most cases an antichretic pledge would have been a possessory pledge pursuant to which the creditor had direct factual control over the pledged property. The creditor could then use the pledged property himself, for instance by living in the pledged house (Alex. *C.* 4.32.14) or by employing pledged slaves as servants (Diocl.-Max. C. 8.24.2). The *pactum antichreticum* cited above from Mod. D. 13.7.39 appears to refer to an arrangement pursuant to which the value of the factual enjoyment of the charged property is to be deducted from the secured debt.[81] Later in this fragment, however, this agreement is described as 'a pact allowing the creditor to take the fruits for a fixed term'.[82] As we are dealing with a *fundus*, these fruits are likely to have been natural fruits (e.g., olives, grapes, grain), so that this *pactum antichreticum* would allow the creditor to harvest the crops of the pledged land.

Implied *antichresis* and default *antichresis*

In only a small number of texts in the *Corpus iuris civilis* is there an express reference to the *pactum antichreticum*.[83] In many other texts we are dealing with *antichresis* without any mention of the fact that the parties have agreed that the creditor can apply the value of the use of the pledged property or its fruits in (re)payment of principal and/or interest.[84] This does not mean that these texts are all concerned with implied *antichresis*. The texts in the Digest and Codex are often excerpts or abridged and therefore do not reveal all the facts. For some imperial constitutions it can be determined with more certainty that there was no express *pactum antichreticum*: the antichretic nature of the pledge is implied and is even mandatory. A constitution from Septimius Severus and Caracalla from 222 AD (C. 4.24.3) states that a creditor *must* ('*debuit*') deduct the fruits of pledged land from the secured debt, not only the

[80] Manigk 1910: 58–9. A conversion into an antichretic pledge could also take place in case of default under the secured debt: Pap. D. 20.1.1.3 and other texts discussed later in this chapter. Fercia 2012: 39, discusses Mod. D. 13.7.39 as possibly concerning *fiducia*. Noordraven (1999), on the other hand, does not mention D. 13.7.39 as a text on *fiducia*.

[81] Manigk 1910: 58–9; Kaser 1982: 74 n 91, 165 n 134.

[82] '*pactum, ut creditor certi temporis fructus caperet*'.

[83] Marci. D. 13.7.33; Mod. D. 13.7.39; Pap. D. 20.1.1.3; Phil. C. 4.32.17. Bobbink (2021: 32 n 69). Ulp. D. 2.14.52.1 (mentioned by Bobbink) is not concerned with a *pactum antichreticum* between creditor and debtor, but with an agreement between the creditor and a third party, who (apparently acting on the debtor's behalf) had purchased the pledged land.

[84] Bobbink (2021: 32 n 70) mentions nineteen texts, including: Mod. D. 20.1.23 pr.; Paul. D. 20.2.8; Sev.-Ant. C. 4.24.1; Alex. C. 4.24.2; Alex. C. 4.24.3; Alex. C. 4.32.12; Alex. C. 8.27.1; Gord. C. 8.13.9; Diocl.-Max. C. 8.24.2.

fruits which were actually gathered but also those which he should have harvested.[85] Likewise, a constitution from Diocletian from 293 AD (C. 8.24.2) rules that the possessory pledge of slaves implied a duty to use their services and to deduct the value thereof from principal and interest. Therefore, where the nature of the pledged property entailed that it would be used or yielded fruits (living accommodation, slaves, agricultural land) and the creditor was granted possession of it, it would often be presumed not only that the creditor would be entitled to use it but also that the value of the use or fruits would be deducted from the secured debt.[86] Where this loan was interest free, the proceeds of the pledged property would be applied in order to discharge the principal. Where the loan was interest bearing, the fruits would be applied first for the interest and the remainder for the principal.[87]

Sometimes, the creditor's right to use the pledged property and/or take its fruits only arose where the debtor defaulted under the secured debt ('default *antichresis*'). Pap. D. 20.1.1.3 discusses 'an agreement that if interest was not paid in time, fruits of the hypothecated properties should be set off against interest up to the statutory limit'.[88] The text refers to a *pactum* which was specifically related to the failure to pay interest in time. This contractually agreed right of *antichresis* did therefore not arise in case of the late (re)payment of principal. However, where the parties would have agreed so there is no reason why this should not have been legally valid.[89] The *pactum antichreticum* of Pap. D. 20.1.1.3 was probably included in the *conventio pignoris*, because it is framed in a conditional form (*if* interest is not paid in time) and therefore aimed at a potential event of default in the future. This contractual remedy was an alternative to sale by way of execution.[90] A default *antichresis* could also arise by operation of law: the *missio Antoniniana*, introduced by a

[85] See also Sev.-Ant. C. 4.24.1; Alex. C. 4.24.2; Gord. C. 8.13.9; Diocl.-Max. C. 8.24.2. Although the compilation was made in the sixth century AD, it is still remarkable that the first three (Severan) constitutions on the *actio pigneraticia (directa)* in C. 4.24 are all on antichretic pledges. This could indicate that possessory pledges of fruit-yielding property would as a general rule be antichretic.

[86] Manigk 1910: 51–5; Kaser 1982: 208. Manigk (1910: 54) even says that the Roman possessory pledge *is* an antichretic pledge.

[87] Ulp. D. 36.4.5.21, discussed in Kaser 1982: 210 n 301. See also Tryph. D. 20.5.12.1 (Kaser 1982: 210 n 302); Diocl.-Max. C. 8.24.2.

[88] '*Pacto placuit, ut ad diem usuris non solutis fructus hypothecarum usuris compensarentur fini legitimae usurae.*'

[89] Kaser 1982: 211. Manigk (1910: 62–3) and Kaser (1982: 211) consider Paul. D. 20.2.8 as concerning an (implied) *antichresis*, that would only be triggered by the debtor's failure to repay the loan ('default *antichresis*'). See now also Bobbink 2021: 76.

[90] Ulpian D. 36.4.5.21 applies rules on default *antichresis* by way of analogy to a trustee's obligation to pay default interest under a *fideicommissum*. It says that the pledge creditor (in contrast with the beneficiary of a *fideicommissum*) could also sell the pledged assets. Manigk 1910: 61; Kaser 1982: 211.

constitution of Caracalla.[91] The beneficiary of a legacy or *fideicommissum*, who had been put into possession of land which was part of the inheritance, acquired a right of pledge on the land.[92] During the continuance of this possession, the beneficiary should permit the heir to work the land and gather the fruits. However, if the heir failed to do so, the beneficiary was allowed to gather the fruits and store them. Where the nature of the fruits entailed that they were best sold as soon as possible, the beneficiary was allowed to sell them.[93] The value of the fruits would then be deducted from the legacy.[94]

Fruits and their allocation

Civil fruits

Fruits taken in kind were regarded as ('natural') fruits, but so was the rent of leased property ('civil fruits'). For antichretic pledges we have a constitution by Alexander Severus from AD 222, which says that the amount taken 'from the payments of a house which you say is held as a pledge' will reduce the amount of the debt.[95] The language of this constitution suggests that the house was already rented out by the debtor when the right of *antichresis* was agreed.[96] Where the creditor had a right of *antichresis* on land or buildings rented out by the debtor, he would have an adapted action against the tenant. This adapted action was *in personam* and will have combined elements of the *actio Serviana* and the *actio locati*. It will have been similar to the adapted action with which *pignus nominis* could be enforced against the debtor of the pledged claim.[97] The right of *antichresis* could also grant the creditor the right to enter into lease agreements himself with regard to the charged property. Marci. D. 20.1.11.1 was probably concerned with an independent *antichresis* but it also reflects the law on the creditor's right to rent out pledged property.[98] This opinion shows that the right of *antichresis* could either be exercised by the creditor personally taking physical control of the real estate, living there, and

[91] Referred to in Alex. C. 6.54.5. [92] Alex. C. 6.54.5. [93] Ulp. D. 36.4.5.22.

[94] Ulp. D. 36.4.5.21. See Bobbink 2021: 28–30.

[95] Alex. C. 4.24.2 ('*ex pensionibus domus, quam pignori detineri dicis*').

[96] See also Ulp. D. 20.1.20. For a usufruct of already rented property, see Paul. D. 7.1.59.1.

[97] Kaser (1982: 213) has reconstructed the first part of the *formula* of this adapted action as follows: *Si paret inter Aulum Agerium et Lucium Titium convenisse, ut Aulus Agerius possessionem eius fundi (earum aedium) q.d.a. pro usuris eo usque (pignoris loco?) retineat, donec Lucio Titio pecunia debita soluta esset, eamque rem tunc....*

[98] Mod. D. 20.1.23 pr.: pursuant to his right of pledge the creditor can rent out the charged *praedia*. See also Alex. C. 4.32.14: a pact that instead of interest the creditor had the right of habitation implied the right to rent out the property.

taking its natural fruits, or by the creditor letting the property to tenants. In the latter case, the income of the charged property could be collected by the creditor as landlord, if necessary with the *actio locati*.[99] The proceeds could then again be applied by him in order to repay principal or (as in Marci. D. 20.1.11.1) serve as interest. Likewise, the use of pledged slaves could not only consist of the creditor himself making use of their labour or services, but also by letting them out to third parties and collecting the income thus generated.[100] It appears from Ulp. D. 13.7.24.3 that there were certain limits as to the nature of the services (e.g., prostitution) for which pledged slaves could be let to third parties by the creditor.

Amortization, payment of interest, surrogate for interest

There were several ways in which the income produced by the charged property could be allocated between creditor and debtor. The parties could agree that the value of the creditor's use of the property and/or its fruits would be deducted from the debtor's indebtedness to repay the principal amount of a loan ('amortization *antichresis*').[101] More often we find secured interest-bearing loans, where the value of the creditor's use of the property and/or its fruits would be deducted from both principal and interest ('mixed *antichresis*').[102] It may very well have been that generally the allocation of the benefits of *antichresis* was determined by the nature of the secured loan. Where an interest-bearing loan was secured by an antichretic pledge, the value of its use and its fruits would be applied for both principal and interest, first for the interest and the remainder for the principal.[103] Where this loan was interest free, one would expect that the economic benefits of the charged property would be applied in order to discharge principal. Paul. D. 20.2.8,

[99] There would be no need for an adapted *actio Serviana*, which would only be necessary where the creditor would demand payment from lessees under lease agreements entered into *with the debtor*. Here the antichretic creditor himself is a contractual party to the lease agreement and as such is entitled to institute the *actio locati*.

[100] Sev.-Ant. C. 4.24.2.

[101] Mod. D. 13.7.39; Ulpian D. 20.1.20; Alex. C. 8.27.1; Sev.-Ant. C. 4.24.1; Alex. C. 4.24.2; Alex. C. 4.24.3; Diocl.-Max. C. 4.24.12. For *fiducia*, see PS 2.13.2. See also Diocl. C. 8.42.20 on (probably) an independent *antichresis*. See Manigk 1910: 57–8; Kaser 1982: 209.

[102] Diocl.-Max. C. 8.24.2: services provided by pledged slaves must be deducted first from interest and then from the principal amount. Alex. C. 4.24.2 ('*debiti*'), Diocl.-Max. C. 4.24.12 ('*debito*') and Alex. C. 8.27.1 ('*debitum*') all refer to the (secured) debt, which could include both principal and interest.

[103] Ulp. D. 36.4.5.21, which seems to confirm that where the proceeds of the fruits exceeded principal and interest, the creditor was obliged to repay the surplus to the debtor. See also Tryph. D. 20.5.12.1; Diocl.-Max. C. 8.24.2. This allocation of proceeds appears to have taken place in accordance with the rules governing non-antichretic pledges, including fiscal pledges: Flor. D. 13.7.35 pr.; Paul. D. 46.1.68.1.

however, says that where the loan is interest free, the creditor can retain the fruits of the pledged property up to the statutory interest rate, thus effectively turning an interest-free loan into an interest-bearing one.

Antichretic pledges were therefore used where interest had been expressed in monetary terms. Here the monetary value of the use or fruits would determine the time (use) or quantity (fruits) to which the creditor was entitled. Alternatively, the creditor's right to use the pledged property and/or to take its fruits was a *surrogate* for interest payments. The creditor was simply allowed to use the pledged property and/or take its fruits for the term of the loan.[104] Where this had been agreed the parties habitually did not establish a rate of interest. It was agreed that the use of the property and/or its (civil or natural) fruits were compensation for the lender. The economic benefits of the charged property would serve as a surrogate for interest, as the parties themselves often expressed (e.g., *in vicem usurarum*).[105] This means that this form of 'interest *antichresis*' could have a speculative nature.[106] Where the (natural or civil) fruits themselves were the compensation for the granting of credit, the creditor would take the risk that their proceeds were below the market rate of interest, while the debtor ran the risk that they were above market rate.[107] A constitution from Alexander Severus from 234 AD illustrates that surrogate interest was regarded as similar to real interest, but not as identical to it. Alex. C. 4.32.14 provides that the fact that the market value of the creditor's right of habitation would exceed the maximum rate of interest, would not render the pact of *antichresis* illegal. In that case, this constitution says, the rent must be regarded as having been agreed below the going rate for rent, which was permitted. The constitution does, however, give this ruling on the assumption that the creditor did not receive any income by renting out the house. This appears to imply that where the rentals received by the creditor would exceed the maximum interest rate, there might be illegality. In Phil. C. 4.32.17, however, the possibility that the value of the fruits (which served as interest) might exceed the statutory maximum rate of interest did *not* render the agreement illegal: this was justified with reference to the uncertainty of the harvest.

[104] Marci. D. 20.1.11.1; Val.-Gal. C. 4.26.6; Alex. C. 4.32.14; Phil. C. 4.32.17.

[105] Alex. C. 4.32.14 ('*ut vice usurarum inhabitaret*'); Phil. C. 4.32.17 ('*ut fructus in vicem usurarum consequeretur*'); Val.-Gal. C. 4.26.6 ('*in usurarum vicem habitandi facultatem concessit*'); D. 20.1.11.1 ('*cum in usuras fructus percipiat*'). Manigk 1910: 55–6; Kupiszewski 1974: 233–4; Kaser 1982: 212.

[106] So already Manigk 1910: 56.

[107] Manigk 1910: 55–7; Kaser 1982: 209.

Independent antichresis

The right of *antichresis* not only could be granted in relation to *pignus* and *fiducia* but also could be agreed upon independently from these forms of real security.[108] The *Historia Augusta* mentions that in order to enable more Romans of small financial means ('*pauperibus*') to purchase farmland, Alexander Severus granted interest-free loans, which were to be repaid from the fruits of the land. This could very well have been non-possessory and independent rights of *antichresis*.[109] One of the two Digest texts in which the word *antichresis* is used is concerned with such independent *antichresis*.

> **D. 20.1.11.1.** *Marcianus libro singulari ad formulam hypothecariam.* Si ἀντίχρησις facta sit et in fundum aut in aedes aliquis inducatur, eo usque retinet possessionem pignoris loco, donec illi pecunia solvatur, cum in usuras fructus percipiat aut locando aut ipse percipiendo habitandoque: itaque si amiserit possessionem, solet in factum actione uti.
>
> If *antichresis* has been agreed and someone is put in the land or house, the creditor retains possession by way of pledge until the money is paid to him, since he takes fruits as interest, either by letting the property or by living there and taking them himself: so if he loses possession, he can bring an action on the case.

In Marci. D. 20.1.11.1 we are dealing with an arrangement pursuant to which the creditor (i) has a possessory lien (right of retention) for the principal amount of the loan as well as (ii) a right to have the enjoyment of the real estate and its (civil or natural) fruits for interest.[110] This could easily have been set up as a possessory pledge with an antichretic right to take the fruits as interest. That this text nevertheless does not concern a right of *pignus* can be derived from the fact that the creditor is given an *actio in factum* to recover

[108] For a long time in Greek-Hellenistic legal practice, independent *antichresis* was more common than *antichresis* combined with a security interest. Only from the fifth century AD did antichretic security become the rule rather than the exception in Byzantine legal practice. Kupiszewski 1986: 143; Bobbink and Mauer 2019: 14. An example from Roman Egypt is SB XIV 12017 (156 AD, Tebtynis), mentioned by Bobbink and Mauer 2019: 13 (with references to other papyri).

[109] *Hist. Aug.*, Alex. Sev. 21.

[110] The text therefore is a pure interest *antichresis*. One would think that the creditor could also hold back the property until all the agreed fruits were taken by the creditor (Kaser: 1982: 212). Kupiszewski (1974: 234–5) supposes that in contrast with Hellenistic laws, Roman law did not know independent amortization *antichresis*. Kaser (1982: 212 n 311) notes that we cannot know whether its absence is simply due to a matter of lack of sources.

possession of the property rather than the *actio Serviana* itself.[111] The reference to the creditor's lien 'by way of pledge' ('*pignoris loco*') is an analogy. The purpose of this analogy was that the creditor would also be granted an action, which was analogous to the *actio Serviana*, in order to restore his possession. In case of independent *antichresis* the *formula* of the *actio Serviana* needed to be modified, in order to include a reference to the *pactum antichreticum* instead of the *conventio pignoris*. With this adapted *actio Serviana* the creditor could recover possession from any possessor of the land or buildings. Precisely because it could be enforced against third parties in possession, the independent *antichresis* can—in modern terms—be characterized as a real right. However, it was not a security interest: the creditor could not take recourse against the property itself by way of execution sale and did not have preferential rights on its proceeds.[112]

[111] Manigk 1910: 48–9; Kupiszewski 1974: 230–1; Kaser 1982: 85–7; Bobbink and Mauer 2019: 15–16.
[112] Bobbink and Mauer 2019: 15.

9

From Special to General Pledge

9.1 Introduction

Once it was accepted that a pledge could be created *nuda conventione* and over tangible and intangible property, the path was cleared for recognizing a pledge of all the assets which were from time to time part of the debtor's patrimony. Like so many other innovations in the law of pledge, this appears to have taken place in the second half of the second century AD, although the origins of the general pledge may lie in transactional practices of the preceding period. The general pledge could be regarded as incorporating almost all the variations of the conventional pledge. It was a non-possessory pledge (*hypotheca*),[1] the scope of the pledged assets was generically defined (cf. *invecta et illata, taberna, grex*) and was extended to receivables (*pignus nominis*), it allowed the debtor to create other pledges (multiple pledge), and it was a pledge of future assets. It is, therefore, tempting to regard the general pledge as nothing more than a construction made from prefabricated building blocks of earlier periods.[2] There are, however, some difficulties with this interpretation: in particular, the general pledge anticipates (and may even have paved the way for) the special pledge of future assets.

For centuries the general pledge has given rise to two questions (which are still relevant and controversial today): what was its *object* and what were its *legal consequences*?[3] The most plausible answer to the first question is that the general pledge's object was the debtor's entire patrimony rather than a class of assets within that patrimony (generic pledges). As to its legal consequences, controversial in modern literature is the question of whether the debtor could freely dispose of generally pledged assets without the pledge continuing to encumber them. A negative answer to this question would mean that the general pledge could have seriously disrupted commercial intercourse in the

[1] Wagner 1968: 8 n 59.
[2] Cf. Sturm 1993a (for pledge of *taberna*), Daubermann 1993 (for generic pledges), and Van Hoof 2017 (for general pledges).
[3] Wubbe 1960: 224. On the general pledge in classical and Justinian Roman law, *ius commune*, and modern laws, see Van Hoof 2015 (in Dutch with summary in English).

Security and Credit in Roman Law: The historical evolution of pignus *and* hypotheca. Hendrik L. E. Verhagen, Oxford University Press. © Hendrik L. E. Verhagen 2022. DOI: 10.1093/oso/9780199695836.003.0010

Roman empire. If all the debtor's present and future assets were pledged, any purchaser of these assets could be confronted with a secured creditor taking away these assets, even when he could not reasonably have been aware of the pledge.[4] We will see, however, that the general pledge may have created an equilibrium between, on the one hand, the secured creditor's interest of having a preferential right of recourse against the assets comprising, from time to time, the debtor's patrimony, and, on the other hand, purchasers' interests of acquiring assets free from a security interest. This equilibrium is essentially the same as that reached by modern rules allowing debtors to sell charged assets free from the charge in the ordinary course of business. In this chapter we will first look at generic pledges as ancestors of the general pledge (section 9.2). The origin of the general pledge, via the intermediate stage of the so-called *cetera bona* pledge (which was a special pledge combined with a pledge of all the debtor's other assets), will then be examined (section 9.3). In the remaining sections of this chapter the legal consequences of the general pledge will be reviewed (sections 9.4–9.8). It will appear that the Roman general pledge can be regarded as a 'floating' charge of all the assets which were from time to time in the debtor's patrimony.

9.2 Generic Pledges

The first stage in the evolution of the general pledge lies in the Republic. The oldest ancestor of the general pledge is a generic pledge of *invecta et illata*, which we encounter as early as Cato's *De agricultura* in the second century BC.[5] For other generic pledges (*grex*, *taberna*) the evidence is from a much later period. These generic pledges were only encumbering a class of assets within the patrimony of the debtor (although in fact these assets may have been virtually all the debtor's assets). It is not entirely clear whether these generic pledges were regarded by the Roman jurists as being granted *generaliter*, or whether that term was reserved for the pledge of the debtor's entire patrimony. However, what is far more important than terminology is that generic and general pledges share common legal characteristics, which distinguish them from pledges of individually specified assets. For this reason and

[4] This would be the case not only for persons who purchased the property directly from the debtor who had granted the general pledge but even for subsequent purchasers and other acquirers.

[5] Section 4.2.

because they can be regarded as the ancestors of the general pledge, in this section we will first have a closer look at generic pledges.

Invecta et illata

As early as during the Republic we find generic descriptions of the pledged assets in pledge agreements. Cato's pledge templates define the pledged objects as 'all that which is brought on the land' ('*quae in fundo inlata erunt*') and 'all cattle and servants which shall be there' ('*pecus et familia, quae illic erit*').[6] The *formulae* of the *interdictum de migrando* and the *interdictum Salvianum* contain similar generic descriptions of the pledged assets.[7] In the early classical period we encounter more or less the same description of the pledged assets in Labeo's opinion on tenant's pledges,[8] as well as in many later jurists' opinions and imperial constitutions from the Principate.[9] We also have epigraphic sources recording tenant's pledges of *invecta et illata*.[10] Thus the *leges horreorum* use phrasing like '*quae in his horreis invecta inlata importata erunt*'.[11] The tenant's pledge of *invecta et illata* served as a model for other variations of generic pledges. Thus in Scaev. D. 20.1.32, 'whatever was brought on the pledged land or there arose or was produced' ('*quaecumque in praedia pignori data inducta invecta importata ibi nata paratave essent*') was pledged by a landowning farmer to the lender to whom also the land itself had been pledged. In D. 13.7.18.3 the early classical jurist Cassius recommends that in order to achieve that a ship built from the timber of pledged 'wood' ('*silva*') shall also be pledged, it should be expressly provided in the pledge agreement: 'whatever things are the creation from and product of the wood' ('*quaeque ex silva facta natave sint*').

Grex pignori obligatus: pledge of a herd

The herd or flock (*grex*) was of immense importance for the largely agricultural Roman economy. In their treatment of the herd the jurists have tried to adapt

[6] Cato, *Agr.*, c. 146, 149. [7] Section 4.4.
[8] Lab. D. 20.6.14 ('*ut invecta importata pignori essent*').
[9] For example, Nerat. D. 20.2.4 pr.; Pomp. D. 20.2.7.1; Paul. D. 2.14.4 pr.; Ulp. D. 11.7.14.1; Ulp. D. 13.7.11.5; Ulp. D. 20.2.6; Ulp. D. 43.32.1 pr.; Marci. D. 20.2.5.1; Alex. C. 4.65.5.
[10] *Leges horreorum*, FIRA III, no. 145. [11] FIRA III, no. 145c.

the law to the demands of the Roman agricultural economy.[12] Under the influence of Roman agricultural treatises and (perhaps) Stoic philosophy the Roman jurists developed what could be called a 'legal doctrine of the herd'.[13] In the first century AD, Columella writes in his *De re rustica* that the purchase of individual animals entailed the risk that they would not get along with the other animals of the herd.[14] This would often make it more attractive for buyers to purchase a herd as a whole, rather than individual animals from different sellers.[15] This synergistic effect could also benefit the creditor with a right of pledge over the herd where he would sell the entire herd by way of execution. The herd is, moreover, a dynamic aggregate of assets, in the sense that its elements are in a constant flux: old animals die, young animals are born. In accordance with agronomical literature the jurists treated—for some purposes—the herd as such as the object of legal actions and transactions. Thus, as early as in the republican *legisactio* proceedings, the herd as such could be recovered by its owner from its possessor, and for classical law, the 'vindication of a herd' (*vindicatio gregis*) is also attested.[16] The herd as such could also be the object of a right of usufruct and the *vindicatio ususfructus* could be instituted by the ususfructuary in respect of the herd as such. The jurists' treatment of the usufructuary's duty to replace dead, sick, or wounded animals shows a keen awareness of agricultural practices recorded in agronomical literature, and a willingness to take account of economic necessities.[17] Hammerstein's general conclusion is that the views of economic life have had a persistent influence on the formation of the legal rules concerning the *ususfructus gregis*.

This legal doctrine of the herd is also underlying the only known classical text on the pledge of a herd (Marci. D. 20.1.13 pr.), which dates from the third century AD.[18] The granting of a pledge over a 'herd' is regarded as entirely unproblematic.[19] The only question it raises is whether animals born after the pledge was granted are subject to the pledge. That question is answered positively.

> **D. 20.1.13 pr.** *Marcianus libro singulari ad formulam hypothecariam.* Grege pignori obligato quae postea nascuntur tenentur: sed et si prioribus capitibus decedentibus totus grex fuerit renovatus, pignori tenebitur.

[12] Hammerstein 1975: 178–9. See also Van Hoof 2015: 60–1.

[13] Miyasaka 2019: 89–94. According to Hammerstein (1975: 14–21, 179) the influence of Stoic ontology was limited.

[14] Columella, *Rust.* 7.6.5.

[15] Hammerstein 1975: 63–4.

[16] Gai. *Inst.* 4.17; Ulp. (Pomp.) D. 6.1.1.3; Paul. D. 6.1.23.5.

[17] Hammerstein 1975: 79, 136.

[18] The pledge of herds is already attested in Cato's *De agricultura* (c. 149).

[19] Hammerstein 1975: 170–1.

> If a herd has been charged with a pledge, later born animals are included. Indeed, if the whole herd dies and is renewed, it remains subject to the pledge.

The nature of the herd as a dynamic aggregate of assets in particular requires that 'incoming goods' are automatically subject to the pledge. Newly born animals added to the herd would indeed automatically be subject to the pledge, as Marci. D. 20.1.13 pr. confirms. One would also expect, however, that individual animals that were no longer part of the herd, because they were sold and delivered by the owner of the herd, would no longer be subject to the pledge.[20] This is indeed what is assumed in modern literature, although Roman legal sources are lacking. Thus both Wubbe and Hammerstein hold that the debtor could dispose of individual animals free from the pledge. According to Wubbe the pledge of a herd was even regarded by the Roman jurists as the pledge of one single *res*.[21] The individual animals were not pledged but the entire herd as such. In line with this view Wubbe also holds that the creditor could not institute the *actio Serviana* in order to recover individual animals that had been sold and transferred by the debtor. Where the whole herd as such would be sold, the creditor could recover the herd from the purchaser with the *actio Serviana*.[22]

There is, however, an alternative interpretation to the *grex* as a single *res*. Hammerstein has not found any evidence of specific influences of stoic propositions on the legal treatment of the herd. The background of the treatment of the *grex* as one entity and the individual rules of the *usufructus gregis* (which is more elaborated in jurists' writings than the *grex pignori obligatus*) do not lie in philosophical doctrine but in the perception of economic reality.[23] Pomponius, however, endorses a characterization of the nature of the *grex*, which may very well have been influenced by Stoic philosophy.[24] One category of things (*res*) distinguished by Pomponius concerns 'that which is composed of individual entities, subsumed under one designation, such as a nation, a legion, or a herd'.[25] The *grex pignori obligatus* of Marci. D. 20.1.13 pr. could be

[20] Hammerstein 1975: 171–2. See also section 9.6. [21] Wubbe 1960: 236.

[22] Wubbe 1960: 236. Where, however, individual animals were stolen from the herd, there is no reason why the creditor should not be able to institute the *actio Serviana* against thieves, fences, or other possessors of individual animals (Van Hoof 2015: 61).

[23] Hammerstein 1975: 136.

[24] See recently Miyasaka 2019: 89–94, recognizing Stoic influences on the jurists' treatment of the *grex*.

[25] Pomp. D. 41.3.30 pr. ('*quod ex distantibus constat, ut corpora plura non soluta, sed uni nomini subiecta, veluti populus legio grex*').

a pledge of goods belonging to this category of *corpora ex distantibus*.[26] Pomponius considers that, although 'the essence of a herd is such that it subsists through the accretion of animals', there is 'possession of individual animals' and there can be 'no *usucapio* of the herd as such'.[27] According to Pomponius this entails that if there are stolen animals in the herd, they are not usucapted, even though ownership of the remainder of the animals is acquired by way of *usucapio*. Translated to *pignus* this would mean that rights of pledge would encumber individual animals, which were generically designated by the one term *grex* and were from time to time part of the herd.

Pledge of a '*taberna*'

For another important sector of the Roman economy, the retail business, the jurists again adopted a flexible approach and considered it possible to grant a generic pledge over the merchandise located from time to time in a *taberna*. The *taberna* was the 'quintessential commercial facility in the Roman world'.[28] Together with the commercial markets on the *forum* and *macellum*, the *tabernae* 'show a thriving retail economy, with a high degree of specialized trades'.[29] The keepers of *tabernae* would normally finance their business by borrowing from their patrons or from bankers.[30] Where *tabernae* were located on the ground floors of large urban private houses, the owners of these houses may very well not only have let business premises to their freedmen but also may have lent the money to buy merchandise. One would expect that in these cases the parties would expressly agree that the merchandise, stock, tools, and other goods located in the *taberna* would serve as collateral not only for the rent but also for loans provided by the landlord to the tenant of the *taberna*. In other cases, the operation of the shopkeeper's business would be financed by bankers. In the Digest there is an important text on what may have been a banker's loan which was secured by a pledge of the shop's floating stock. From Scaevola we have an opinion on the pledge of a '*taberna*', which (although from an earlier period) is similar to Marci. D. 20.1.13 pr. on the *grex*.

[26] See also Van Hoof 2015: 59–62; Miyasaka 2019: 89–94.

[27] Pomp. D. 41.3.30.2.

[28] Flohr 2013. Mayer (2012: 66) observes: 'This *taberna* economy may only have modestly contributed to Rome's overall GDP, but it changed the socio-economic underpinnings of urban life all across the Roman world and, by extension, allowed for the rise of urban middle classes.' See now also Ellis 2018 and Flohr and Wilson 2017: 12–16. See also section 3.4.

[29] Flohr and Wilson 2017: 13–14.

[30] Ioannatou 2006: 40–1.

> **D. 20.1.34 pr.** *Scaevola libro vicesimo septimo digestorum.* Cum tabernam debitor creditori pignori dederit, quaesitum est, utrum eo facto nihil egerit an tabernae appellatione merces, quae in ea erant, obligasse videatur? et si eas merces per tempora distraxerit et alias comparaverit easque in eam tabernam intulerit et decesserit, an omnia quae ibi deprehenduntur creditor hypothecaria actione petere possit, cum et mercium species mutatae sint et res aliae illatae? respondit: ea, quae mortis tempore debitoris in taberna inventa sunt, pignori obligata esse videntur.
>
> When a debtor pledged a shop to the creditor, the question was put whether this was invalid or whether by 'shop' the merchandise in the shop was to be taken as charged. And if he sold goods from time to time, bought others, brought them into the shop, and then died, could the creditor institute the *actio hypothecaria* for all that was then on the premises, in view of the turnover of stock? Scaevola replied: 'What was in the shop at the debtor's death was subject to the pledge.'

Two questions are raised in this text.[31] The first is whether the pledging of a *taberna* was invalid, or whether it must be understood as a pledge of the merchandise located in the shop. The second question is whether the pledge of floating stock would be effective in the sense that merchandise that was purchased after the pledge had been granted also would be charged. Scaevola appears to answer the second question only, although perhaps his affirmative answer to that question can be read as also affirming the second part of the first one (pledge of '*taberna*' = pledge of merchandise?).

In D. 20.1.34 pr. the pledge of a '*taberna*' is not construed as a pledge of the building structure itself.[32] It gave rise to the question of whether this must be understood as concerning the merchandise (*merces*) which was situated in the *taberna*.[33] At the time of Scaevola it may not have been completely settled

[31] See section 3.4. In addition to the question answered by Scaevola, this text raises other interesting questions as well. In particular, what would be the ranking between the lender's pledge of the merchandise and the pledge of *invecta et illata* to which the person who rented the *taberna* to the shopkeeper would be entitled? From another text by Scaevola it appears that the lender's pledge would prevail over the tenant's pledge (Scaev. D. 20.4.21.1).

[32] Section 3.4.

[33] Wagner (1982: 401) points out that *taberna* does not have this meaning in other classical sources. However, it can be explained by the use of metonymy (Wagner 1982: 401–5). See also Wagner 1982: 405–12 for other 'roots' of the equation of *taberna* and *merces*. There are two other opinions by Scaevola, on legacies, in which movable assets (typically) present in a *taberna* are expressly mentioned by the testator, which suggests that these items were not covered by the term *taberna*: Scaev. D. 33.7.7 and Scaev. D. 31.88.3. Already by the time of Servius Sulpicius Rufus, this interpretation had been adopted (Pomp. D. 33.7.15 pr.). On the legal meaning of *taberna*, see also Dubouloz 2011: 118–24 (who does not mention D. 20.1.34 pr.).

that the single term *taberna* covered the shopkeeper's entire floating stock-in-trade. In the second century AD it may still have been rather bold to designate the merchandise with the word *taberna* because—unlike the herd—it is less clearly one entity.[34] From Scaevola's answer, however, it can be read that there was nothing which could invalidate such a pledge. Scaevola concludes that the merchandise, which was present in the *taberna* at the time of the shopkeeper's death, was subject to the pledge.[35] This implies that the merchandise which entered the *taberna* in the period between the granting of the pledge and the shopkeeper's death would be subject to the pledge. In respect of general pledges, Scaevola himself indicated that the pledged assets did not need to be *in bonis debitoris* at the time of the *conventio pignoris*.[36] However, even if we regard the pledge of a '*taberna*' as a general pledge it is still not without problems. From the jurists' opinions it can be derived that in order for a general pledge to extend to future assets, this normally had to be expressly agreed.[37] If that is so, simply pledging a '*taberna*' might have been insufficient to charge incoming goods. This may have been the reason why Scaevola appears somewhat reluctant to answer the question whether the pledge of a '*taberna*' was valid. In any case, the (second) question, whether a pledge of merchandise encumbers new stock, is expressly (and positively) answered by Scaevola. In this respect the pledge of a *taberna* is treated in the same way as the pledge of a herd. The *merces* located in the *taberna*, however, certainly are not regarded as one *res* with renewable components.[38]

Fundus cum instrumento

Despite its enormous importance for the Roman economy and the treatment of the *fundus cum instrumento* in Roman agricultural literature as one entity, the pledge of a *fundus* was not conceived by the jurists as a charge over an aggregate of economically linked assets.[39] The jurists, although they were familiar with the agronomists' writings and did have knowledge of the operation of agricultural estates, did not recognize the *fundus* as a 'solid legal

[34] Wubbe 1960: 237.

[35] On this fragment, see also Mentxaka 1986: 207–14; Sturm 1993a: 26–54; Daubermann 1993: 116–26.

[36] Scaev. D. 20.1.34.2. See Mauer 2022: 73.

[37] Section 9.4. See Scaev. D. 20.1.34.2 and also Gai. D. 20.1.9 pr. as convincingly emendated ('*in bonis <non> habuit*') and interpreted by Wagner (1968: 127–30).

[38] Sturm (1993a: 38–44) points out that when the present and future merchandise would have been treated as one *res*, the pledge of D. 20.1.34 pr. would also have extended to merchandise arriving at the shop after the shopkeeper's death. See also Daubermann 1993: 24–6.

[39] See also section 3.4.

entity'.[40] They did not attribute legal significance to the connection between farm buildings on different sites as conditioned by their belonging to the same agricultural enterprise.[41] Where several plots of land were used for the operation of the farm, they would be individually specified in the *conventio pignoris*. This is illustrated by the *tabulae alimentariae* from the second century AD, which record the granting of security over real estate in order to secure loans granted by the imperial treasury. In all the recorded transactions several *praedia rustica* are specified (by name, location, and often buildings situated on the land) as properties securing one lending transaction.[42] In these documents, the buildings on the land are also expressly mentioned, although as a consequence of the rule *superficies solo cedit* the charge over the farmland would automatically extend to the buildings on the land.[43]

The agronomists again were largely responsible for the conceptual unification of the notion of *instrumentum*—the range of movable assets which were permanently connected with the operation of a *fundus* as an economic unit.[44] The *fundus cum instrumento* was regarded as a 'separate patrimony' in agricultural literature. For legacies of a *fundus cum instrumento* a large number of legal opinions have been collected in Title 33.7 of the Digest. These texts are part of a rich jurisprudential literature on the interpretation of terms in legacies designating aggregates of things (e.g., a slave's *peculium*, *taberna*, furniture (*suppellex*), and *fundus cum instrumento*).[45] Thus according to Labeo and many other classical jurists it was possible to make a legacy of an operating farm by defining the bequeathed property as '*fundus cum instrumento*' (or '*fundus instructus*').[46] Much casuistry has been preserved in the Digest on which slaves and objects exactly were covered by this concept in individual cases.[47] However, I have not been able to find one text in the Digest or Codex expressly dealing with the granting of a pledge over a *fundus cum instrumento* (or its synonym *fundus instructus*). But that does not necessarily mean that

[40] Steinwenter 1943: 101–3. [41] Steinwenter 1943: 14.

[42] The documents recording the conveyance of land usually contained the name of the plot of land, its extent, the municipality (and sometimes also: *pagus* and *vicus*) in which it was situated, the names of neighbours, natural features of the land, and buildings on the land (Criniti 1991). One can imagine, however, that a generic residual clause would have worked as well, such as 'all other lands used for the farm'.

[43] For example, Tab. Vel., Obl. 2 ('*cum casis (tribus)*'; '*cum casa*'). In Digest texts on dispositions of *fundi*, buildings would sometimes also be separately mentioned (e.g., Scaev. D. 33.7.20.7: '*fundum meum Graecianum cum stabulo et instrumento rustico*'; Scaev. D. 32.35.2: '*fundum Satranum, qui est in regione Niphana, cum taberna*'). The buildings may have been mentioned as one of the markers identifying the land. On *superficies solo cedit*: Gai. *Inst.* 2.73; Ulp. (Lab.) D. 43.17.3.7.

[44] Steinwenter 143: 102. [45] Kaser 1971: 749–50.

[46] Lab. D. 33.7.5; Scaev. D. 32.101 pr.

[47] Title D. 33.7 contains a large number of texts on the accessories of not only bequeathed *fundi* but also *tabernae* and ships. For other expressions, see Steinwenter 1943: 72.

this did not happen in practice: the lack of evidence could be a consequence of failed transmission of jurists' opinions and imperial constitutions. In fact, in one of the few surviving epigraphic sources on charging land we appear to encounter the granting of security over a *fundus cum instrumento* (although another term is used). In the *Formula Baetica* the charged real estate is defined as:

> fundum Baianum, qui est in agro qui Veneriensis vocatur, pago Olbensi, uti optumus maxumusq(ue) esset....[48]
>
> the fundus Baianus, which is located in the territory that is called Veneriensis, in the Olbensis region, in best and fullest condition....

The expression '*uti optimus maximusq(ue)*' is defined by Paul.

> **D. 33.7.22 pr.** *Paulus libro tertio sententiarum.* Fundo legato 'ut optimus maximusque est' retia apraria et cetera venationis instrumenta continebuntur: quod etiam ad instrumenta pertinet, si quaestus fundi ex maxima parte in venationibus consistat.[49]
>
> When a farm is legated 'in best and fullest condition', boar nets and other hunting gear will be included, which also belong to the *instrumentum* if the income of the farm is chiefly derived from hunting.

The phrase '*ut optimus maximusque est*' is equivalent to *instrumentum*. Where a *mancipatio* by way of *fiducia cum creditore* of a *fundus cum instrumento* took place in practice, it is plausible that pledges of a *fundus 'ut optimus maximusque est'* also occurred. Alternatively, the scope of the pledged assets of an operating farm could be defined by making use of the ancient and much-used concept of *invecta et illata*. In Scaev. D. 20.1.32 this concept is given an economically sensible interpretation: not all the slaves who at some time had worked on the land are subject to the pledge but only those slaves who were permanent staff. In Mod. D. 20.1.26.2 the debtor granted a pledge not only over several pieces of land but also over the slaves working on the land from time to time ('*praedia et mancipia quae in praediis erant*').[50] From the second half of the second century AD farms as an economic unit could be pledged by way of a general 'all assets' pledge.

[48] FIRA III, no. 92. [49] PS 3.6.45 is virtually identical. See also Scaev. D. 32.93.4.

[50] In a similar sense Scaev. D. 32.101 pr.; Diocl.-Max. C. 8.14.5. On Mod. 20.1.26.2, see Wagner 1968: 117–20.

9.3 From *Cetera Bona* to Independent General Pledge

The earliest evidence of the second evolutionary stage of the general pledge is Gaius's opinion on a combination of a special pledge and a pledge of the debtor's 'other assets' (*cetera bona*). This was already a general pledge, in the sense of a pledge of *all* the debtor's present and future assets (minus the specially pledged assets). From a few decades later we have the first evidence of the third and final evolutionary stage. In several opinions by Scaevola and Papinianus, later followed by many other jurists' opinions and imperial constitutions, the independent general pledge of all the debtor's present and future assets is recognized.[51] Again, it can be observed that at some stage the praetor responded to a new transactional practice, by extending the existing remedies for *pignus* and *hypotheca* to creditors who had negotiated such wide-ranging security with their debtors. The praetor would accept that the description of the pledged assets required by the *intentio* of the *formula* of the *actio Serviana* was based on the transactional practices discussed by Gaius, Scaevola, Papinian, and other jurists. Moreover, in respect of general pledges, the jurists expressly stated that it was not required that the pledged assets were (as the *formula* of the *actio Serviana* prescribed) *in bonis debitoris* at the time the *conventio pignoris* was entered into.[52]

Cetera bona pledge: Gai. D. 20.1.15.1

The objects of the pledges discussed in the previous section concerned a class of assets within the debtor's patrimony: buildings, tools, inventory, herd, merchandise etc. From the second century AD onwards, we have abundant evidence in the *Corpus iuris civilis* (but not in the epigraphic sources) of general pledges, which were granted over all the debtor's present and future assets. The direct ancestor of this general 'all assets' pledge is the so-called *cetera bona* pledge: the combination of a special pledge over one or more specified assets and a general pledge over all the debtor's (present and future) other assets. Not only is this form of general pledge extremely important from a historical-evolutionary perspective, it is also crucial for solving the main controversy in modern Romanist literature: the question of whether or not the

[51] I call this the 'independent' general pledge because it is not granted in conjunction with a special pledge.

[52] Not only in this section but also in sections 9.4 and 9.6 it will appear that the concept of *in bonis esse* is a fundamental one for the general pledge, not only for the effects on future property (incoming goods) but also for its effects on generally pledged goods which were sold by the debtor (outgoing goods).

general pledge could be objected against subsequent purchasers of generally pledged assets.

From Gaius we have in D. 20.1.15.1 one of the two most important sources of information on the nature and purpose of the general pledge.[53] In his commentary on the *formula hypothecaria*, written somewhere between 153 and 179 AD,[54] Gaius says that the condition of *in bonis esse* must be applied differently to special and general (*cetera bona*) pledges.

> **D. 20.1.15.1.** *Gaius libro singulari ad formulam hypothecariam.* Quod dicitur creditorem probare debere, cum conveniebat, rem in bonis debitoris fuisse, ad eam conventionem pertinet, quae specialiter facta est, non ad illam, quae cottidie inseri solet cautionibus, ut specialiter rebus hypothecae nomine datis cetera etiam bona teneantur debitoris, quae nunc habet et quae postea adquisierit, perinde atque si specialiter hae res fuissent obligatae.
>
> When it is said that the creditor should prove that, when he made the agreement, the thing was in the debtor's patrimony, this applies to that agreement that has been especially made, not to the clause commonly inserted in deeds that beside the property specially hypothecated, the debtor's remaining assets, both those which he now has and those which he will afterwards acquire, will be liable in the same manner as if these things were especially charged.[55]

From a dogmatic perspective Gai. D. 20.1.15.1 is important because it says that in respect of assets not pledged *specialiter*, the condition of the *actio Serviana* that the pledged goods should at the time of the pledge agreement be *in bonis* of the debtor does not apply.[56] From a historical-evolutionary perspective Gai. D. 20.1.15.1 is important, because it is one of the oldest texts on a general pledge, dating from the second half of the second century AD.[57] The '*cetera bona* pledge' is a variant of the pledge created *nuda conventione*. Assuming that it was Julian who introduced this purely contractual right of pledge, it may very well be that this form of a general pledge finds its origin in Julian's time.[58] At the time of the codification of the praetor's edict the general

[53] The other fundamental text is Pap. D. 20.1.1 pr. discussed later in this chapter.

[54] We do not know when exactly Gaius's De *formula hypothecaria liber singularis* was written, but because it refers to Julian's *Digesta* (D. 20.1.15 pr.) this must have been after 153–160 AD (when Julian's work was written (Liebs 1997: 104)). According to Liebs (1997: 188) Gaius wrote from the 140s to around 179 AD.

[55] Wagner 1968: 64–71; Mentxaka 1986: 280–5.

[56] We will return to this in section 9.4.

[57] See also Gai. D. 40.9.29 pr., discussed by Wagner (1967: 163 and 188).

[58] See Paul. (Jul.) D. 47.2.67 pr. (section 9.6). Wagner 1968: 36.

pledge may already have been common practice.[59] Moreover, it shows how again, legal evolution was triggered by transactional practices. Gaius says that *cetera bona* clauses were inserted 'daily' ('*cottidie*').[60] This means that either *cetera bona* pledges were granted on a daily basis, or Roman civilians were familiar with them from their daily experience.[61] In all likelihood the *cetera bona* pledge was developed by transactional lawyers and subsequently commented upon in jurists' writings like Gai. D. 20.1.15.1.

Gaius D. 20.1.15.1 opposes a *conventio* which is *specialiter* made to a pledge agreement in respect of the debtor's *cetera bona*, the latter variant of pledge therefore apparently not being granted *specialiter*. Why would the parties create a special pledge and a general one at the same time? Why would they not simply pledge *all* the debtor's assets? The most plausible explanation is that at the time when this transactional practice originated, the legal status of the general pledge was not yet fully settled. For that reason one or more valuable assets were singled out and specially pledged.[62] What does point in this direction is that the parties considered it necessary to say that generally pledged goods will be treated in the same manner as if they were specially pledged ('*perinde atque si specialiter hae res fuissent obligatae*').[63] The point of reference is still the special pledge and by this analogy, the general pledge is meant to become enforceable.[64] As such, the *cetera bona* pledge could be regarded as a transitory form between the special pledge and the independent general pledge.[65]

Independent general pledge: Pap. D. 20.1.1 pr.

From 206–212 AD, several decades after Gaius, we have the other most important opinion on the (independent) general pledge.[66]

> **D. 20.1.1 pr.** *Papinianus libro undecimo responsorum.* Conventio generalis in pignore dando bonorum vel postea quaesitorum recepta est: in speciem

[59] Wubbe 1960: 224; Wagner 1968: 3.

[60] Wubbe 1960: 224: common appearance in period after the codification in the *Edictum perpetuum*.

[61] See Wubbe 2003: 178.

[62] Wagner 1968: 70–1.

[63] According to Wubbe these words were part of the description of the pledged assets in the pledge agreement and are therefore not part of Gaius's opinion.

[64] Wubbe 2003: 170. See also Ulp. D. 20.2.6, where a tacit agreement ('*tacite... conventum*') to pledge *invecta et illata* is said to have the same legal consequences as a pledge which is 'specially agreed' ('*specialiter convenisset*').

[65] Manigk 1916b.

[66] D. 20.1.1 pr. is taken from a work with the title *Digesta responsa*, which was written by Papinian between 206 and 212 AD (Liebs 1997: 121).

> autem alienae rei collata conventione, si non fuit ei qui pignus dabat debita, postea debitori dominio quaesito difficilius creditori, qui non ignoravit alienum, utilis actio dabitur, sed facilior erit possidenti retentio.
>
> A general agreement to create a pledge is recognised also in respect of those assets that are acquired afterwards. But if the agreement covers specific property of another, which is not then owed to the grantor of the pledge but afterwards has become the ownership of the debtor, the creditor who was not unaware that it was someone else's is not so easily given an *utilis actio* for it, but it is easier for the possessor to retain it.

The gist of this opinion is the same as that of Gai. D. 20.1.15.1: in case of general pledges it is *not* required that the pledged assets were *in bonis debitoris* at the time the pledge was granted. The words '*recepta est*' might indicate that the legal recognition of this type of general pledge had occurred in the recent past, although according to Wubbe they merely indicate that the general pledge was widely recognized, without alluding to its time of origin.[67] From that past we do, in any case, have jurists' opinions on the independent general pledge: the first opinions unequivocally concerning the independent general pledge are by Gaius's younger contemporary Scaevola.[68] These opinions are followed by a long line of jurists' opinions and imperial constitutions confirming that the possibility to grant a pledge over all the debtor's present and future assets had become firmly anchored in classical Roman law.[69]

Later purpose of the *cetera bona* pledge

We also find the *cetera bona* pledge in later fragments, dating from a period in which the general pledge was firmly embedded in Roman private law.[70] This means that uncertainty about the legal status of the general pledge cannot have been the only motive for creating *cetera bona* pledges in the classical period. One must assume that, after the general pledge had been fully

67 Wubbe 1960: 227 n 14. See also Wagner 1968: 6.

68 Scaev. D. 20.4.21 pr. and Scaev. D. 20.1.34.2.

69 Gai. D. 40.9.29 pr.; Scaev. D. 20.1.34.2: Scaev. D. 20.4.21 pr.; Scaev. D. 31.89.4; Pap. D. 20.1.1. pr.; Pap. D. 20.4.2; Pap. D. 20.5.1; Paul. D. 20.1.29 pr.; Paul. D. 20.1.29.3; Ulp. D. 20.4.7.1; Ulp. D. 49.14.28; Ulp. D. 20.1.6–9; Ulp. D. 20.6.4 pr.; Marci. D. 40.8.6; Sev.-Ant. C. 8.16.1; Sev.-Ant. C. 8.13.2; Sev.-Ant. C. 7.8.3; Alex. C. 8.16.4; Alex. C. 8.25.3; 8.33.1; Alex. C. 8.16.5; Val.-Gal. C. 8.17.6; Diocl.-Max. C. 8.13.17; Diocl.-Max. C. 4.10.6; Diocl.-Max. C. 7.72.6; Diocl.-Max. C. 8.27.17. This list is taken from Mentxaka (1986: 279–350), who discusses all these fragments individually.

70 Pap. D. 20.4.2; Pap. D. 20.5.1; Sev.-Ant. C. 8.13.2; Diocl.-Max. C. 8.27.9. See also Paul. D. 20.2.9: combination of a tenant's pledge of *invecta et illata* and an express pledge of a slave.

recognized, the parties who chose to create a *cetera bona* pledge must have intended the special and the general pledge to have different legal consequences.[71] In particular, where the general pledge could *not* be enforced *against certain third parties*, there would be a clear interest for both creditor and debtor for agreeing a special pledge on some assets in combination with a general pledge over the remaining assets. Indeed, as will be elaborated in sections 9.6 to 9.8, the most plausible interpretation is that where a general pledge had been granted, the debtor could freely dispose of generally pledged assets, without the pledge continuing to encumber them. This is where most of the added value of a *cetera bona* pledge lay, after it became settled that the general pledge was valid and enforceable. In addition, in some cases the parties may have specially pledged certain assets, because they would have been excepted from a general pledge, such as slaves to which the debtor was emotionally attached (e.g., concubines, natural children).[72] Another reason for combining a special pledge with a general one could have been that the special pledge was granted for goods which the debtor already owned and the general pledge for assets acquired by him after the pledge was granted.[73] Yet another motive could have been the desire to avoid collective execution proceedings. Where the remaining assets were also pledged to the creditor with a general pledge, the latter could decide to sell only as few assets as would be needed to discharge the (remainder) of the debt. For the creditor this would be more efficient,[74] while for the debtor this had the benefit that he did not lose all his assets. Moreover, this would avoid the great social humiliation attached to the public auction of all the debtor's assets.[75]

Generalis/generaliter

Pap. D. 20.1.1 pr. refers to a '*conventio generalis in pignore dando*': a general agreement to grant a pledge.[76] In modern literature it is held that a distinction

[71] Wubbe 1960: 226; Van Hoof: 2017: 490.

[72] On goods excepted from general pledges, see Wagner 1968: 125–31. Also, goods which as a general rule could not be specially pledged (e.g., *res extra commercium*) could also not be generally pledged. An interesting example is Alex. C. 8.16.5: future awards of athletes cannot be pledged '*privata pactione*': for this reason they can also not be charged by a '*generale pactum*'.

[73] Section 9.4.

[74] This advantage should not be underestimated. According to Haselmann, Pistor, and Vig (2010: 556), for individual creditors real security offers two advantages. Not only are secured creditors privileged over unsecured creditors in the debtor's insolvency but real security also facilitates enforcement against defaulting debtors without having to go through formal insolvency or court-controlled execution proceedings.

[75] Bürge 1980.

[76] *Conventio generalis*: Pap. D. 20.1.1 pr.; Paul. D. 20.1.29 pr.; Sev.-Ant. 8.16.1 Diocl.-Max. C. 8.27.17. See also Ant. C. 7.73.3 ('*pacto universa*'); Alex. C. 8.16.5 ('*generale pactum*'); Ulp. D. 20.1.6 ('*obligatione generali*'); and Ulp. D. 20.1.8 ('*generali obligatione*').

should be made between the manner of granting and the object of the general pledge.[77] The words *generaliter* and *generalis* concern the (generic) nature of the *granting* of the pledge. In this view, whenever the pledged goods are generically defined in the pledge agreement we are dealing with a 'general' pledge. Therefore, in this view, the tenant's pledge, the pledge of a herd, and the pledge of a *taberna*, were all granted *generaliter*. In order to describe the widest possible range of pledged *objects* (i.e., *all* the debtor's present and future assets), the jurists' opinions and imperial constitutions use the nouns 'goods' (*bona*) or 'things' (*res*), often accompanied by the attributive numeral 'all'.[78] Thus, in one of the earliest texts on the independent general pledge, Scaev. D. 20.4.21 pr., the reference is to a charge of 'all his goods which he had and which he would have' ('*omnia bona sua quae habebat quaeque habiturus esset*') and to 'all his things' ('*res suas omnes*').[79] In a number of texts, however, only the words *generaliter* or *generalis* are used, without an express reference to 'all' the debtor's present and future assets. Do these texts also refer to generic pledges, or are they exclusively concerned with 'all assets' pledges, security interests encumbering all the goods from time to time present in the debtor's patrimony?

Although the 'leading' opinions on the general pledge by Gaius (D. 20.1.15.1) and Papinian (D. 20.1.1 pr.) are concerned with all assets pledges,[80] some of the other legal opinions could be interpreted as endorsing the view that also generic pledges (*invecta et illata*, *grex*, *taberna*) were granted *generaliter*. In Gaius D. 20.4.11.2 slaves who were 'specially' (*specialiter*) charged are opposed to slaves who were pledged as *inducta et illata*. The principle exposed by Gaius in D. 20.1.15.1, that in the case of a general pledge agreement (*cetera bona*) the creditor does not have to prove that they were *in bonis* of the debtor at the time the pledge was granted, may have given support to Scaevola's opinion in D. 20.1.34 pr. that the creditor could institute the *actio Serviana* for all that was in the *taberna* 'in view of the turnover of stock'. In other words, Scaevola may have regarded the agreement for the pledge of a *taberna*'s merchandise

[77] Van Hoof 2017: 476.

[78] Scaev. D. 20.4.21 pr. ('*omnia bona sua*', '*res suas omnes*'); Scaev. D. 31.89.4 ('*universa bona patris*'); Sev.-Ant. C. 8.13.2 pr. ('*universa bona*'); Ant. C. C. 7.73.3 ('*pacto universa, quae habet habuitve*'); Alex. C. 8.25.3 ('*universa bona sua*'); Alex. C. 8.16.5 ('*generale pactum de omnibus bonis pignori obligandis*'); Alex. C. 8.33.1 ('*omnia bona debitoris*'). See also Pap. D. 20.5.1; Gai. D. 20.1.15.2.

[79] See also Scaev. D. 20.1.34.2. In a number of texts the terms *generalis* or *generaliter* are coupled with expressions designating the pledged assets, sometimes unequivocally stating that they are all the debtor's present and future assets: Pap. D. 20.1.1 pr. ('*Conventio generalis in pignore dando bonorum vel postea quaesitorum*'); Pap. D. 20.4.2 ('*generaliter bona debitoris pignori accepit*'); Ulp. D. 20.1.6 ('*Obligatione generali rerum*', '*quas quis habuit habiturusve sit*'); Sev.-Ant. C. 8.16.1 ('*generali pacti conventione*', '*quae de bonis tuis facta est*'); Sev.-Ant. C. 8.13.2 pr. ('*universa bona generaliter*'); Alex. C. 8.16.5 ('*generale pactum de omnibus bonis pignori obligandis*'); Val.-Gal. C. 8.17.6 ('*generaliter bona sint obligata*').

[80] See also Scaev. D. 20.1.34.2; Scaev. D. 20.4.21 pr.; and Scaev. D. 31.89.4.

not as 'specially made' but as a pledge agreement that was made *generaliter*. This may explain why he apparently did not consider it necessary to restrict the scope of the pledge to merchandise owned by the debtor when the *conventio pignoris* was concluded, but also considered merchandise subsequently acquired as pledged.[81] It is after Gaius and Scaevola that the meaning of *generaliter/generalis* definitely shifts from the manner of granting to the object of the general pledge (= the debtor's entire patrimony).[82] It is true that neither Papinian D. 20.1.1 pr. ('*[c]onventio generalis in pignore dando bonorum vel postea quaesitorum*') nor Papinian D. 20.4.2 ('*qui generaliter bona debitoris pignori accepit*') expressly indicates (for instance by referring to 'all' the debtor's goods) that the 'general' pledge is a pledge of the debtor's entire patrimony. However, in particular, the context of D. 20.4.2 leaves no doubt that we are dealing with such 'all assets' pledge.[83] During Papinian's lifetime the equation of general pledges with 'all assets' pledges is followed in the imperial constitutions.[84] This line is continued in texts by later jurists and emperors.[85] Several constitutions from Diocletian routinely refer to 'general and special' pledges.[86] Although these sources contain no definition which states that *generalis/generaliter* means that all the debtor's present and future assets are pledged, there is no reason at all to suspect that this was not the case.[87]

9.4 Incoming Goods: Pledge of Future Property

The fundamental difference between a *conventio specialis* and a *conventio generalis* is that in the case of general pledge agreements, the creditor does not have to prove that the pledged assets were *in bonis* of the debtor at the time the agreement was made. Pap. D. 20.1.1 pr. expressly states that also in respect of generally pledged future assets the creditor could institute the *actio Serviana* (*utilis*). It took a long time, however, before it became settled law that all subsequently acquired assets could be validly pledged by way of special pledge.

81 In Lenel's Palingenesia (1889, vol. II: 264) D. 20.1.34 pr. is grouped together with D. 20.1.34.2 (all assets pledge).

82 Wagner 1968: 68–9, 74–5.

83 Wagner (1968: 95) also mentions Ulp. D. 20.6.4 pr. and Ulp. D. 49.14.28 as texts which do not expressly refer to all the debtor's (present and future) goods, but the context indicates that the debtor's entire estate was pledged.

84 Sev.-Ant. C. 8.13.2 pr.; Sev.-Ant. C. 8.16.1; Alex. C. 8.16.5; Alex. C. 8.25.3; Alex. C. 8.33.1. Wagner 1968: 5, 68–9.

85 Paul. D. 20.1.29 pr.; Diocl.-Max. C. 8.27.17. Wagner 1968: 5, 68–9.

86 Diocl.-Max. C. 4.10.6; Diocl.-Max. C. 7.72.6.1; Diocl.-Max. C. 8.27.17.

87 Wagner 1968: 5.

This evolutionary process was not yet completed when Gaius (D. 20.1.15.1) and Papinian (D. 20.1.1 pr.) held that virtually all future assets could be pledged by way of *general* pledge. For a long time, the *special* pledge of a future asset would still only be enforceable with (an adaptation of) the *actio Serviana*, where such asset had its roots in the patrimony of the debtor at the time of the pledge agreement.[88] It is tempting to see the special pledge of future property as an ancestor of the general pledge. We will see, however, that the conditional pledge of future assets did not make the general pledge possible, but that it may instead have been the other way round. It was not until late classical law (Marci. D. 20.1.16.7) that all future goods could be specially pledged by making the granting of the pledge conditional upon their acquisition by the debtor. The general pledge may have opened up the evolutionary pathway towards the full recognition of conditional (special) pledges of future assets.

Special pledges of future property: *invecta et illata*

One of Cato's pledge templates purports to pledge all that which is brought into the estate ('*quae in fundo inlata erunt*').[89] In one of Cato's other pledge templates it is provided that 'all cattle and servants which shall be there shall be pledged' ('*pecus et familia, quae illic erit, pigneri sunto*').[90] More than a century after Cato we encounter more or less the same description of the pledged assets in Labeo's opinion on tenant's pledges (D. 20.6.14). The pledge of *invecta et illata* by definition includes every asset (tools, machinery, furniture, animals, and slaves) which, after the *conventio pignoris* was concluded, were from time to time brought on to the farm(land) or into the house, or born, grown, or manufactured there. For this reason one can consider the pledge of *invecta et illata* as an early manifestation of a pledge of future assets.[91] It could be argued that, on closer inspection, this variation of pledge was not truly a pledge of future goods at all. In D. 20.4.11.2 Gaius observes with respect to the pledge of *invecta et illata* that it is 'not the agreement that created the charge, but the bringing on of the thing'. Therefore, in a sense the tenant's pledge in Gai. D. 20.4.11.2 was a pledge of presently owned assets, if at the time of the *inductio* the object was within the tenant's patrimony. More generally, where for the creation of a right of pledge a *traditio* was still required, the relevant time at which the pledged goods should be *in bonis* could very well

[88] Wubbe 1960: 250.
[89] Cato, *Agr.*, c. 146.
[90] Cato, *Agr.*, c. 149.
[91] Wagner 1968: 9 n 62.

have been the time at which this *traditio* (or equivalent act, such as *inductio*) took place. The condition of the *formula* of the *actio Serviana*, that the pledged assets were '*in bonis*' of the debtor at the time of the *pledge agreement*, may have been an innovation by Julian, inserted in the *formula* when it came to be recognized that *hypotheca* could be granted *nuda conventione*. Perhaps the original *formula* of the *actio Serviana* did state that the pledged assets were *in bonis* at the time of the *inductio* (tenant's pledges) or the *traditio* (other pledges).[92]

Special pledges of future property: fruits, offspring, and products

As we can already observe in Cato's templates, future crops could also be pledged separately, without the creditor being granted a pledge of the land yielding the crops. Likewise also, the future offspring of slaves and the young of animals could be pledged independently from their mother. In all these cases we are dealing with the pledge of future property, in the sense of assets not yet existing at the time the pledge agreement was entered into. In respect of these future assets, the condition that the pledged assets were *in bonis* of the debtor at the time of the *conventio pignoris* was—strictly speaking—not satisfied. They could nevertheless be pledged, as Gai. D. 20.1.15 pr. says: 'future assets can be hypothecated, for example, unharvested crops, offspring of a female slave, and the young of animals once born'.[93]

In D. 20.4.11.3 Gaius holds that where the *conventio pignoris* purports to pledge natural fruits (e.g., crops), it is sufficient that the assets producing these fruits (e.g., agricultural land) are *in bonis* of the debtor at the time it is entered into. Accordingly, where pledged harvested crops were sold and delivered by the debtor to a third party, the creditor to whom they were pledged could recover them with the *actio Serviana*. This would be different, however, when at the time crops were harvested, the land was no longer owned by the debtor. This is confirmed in Pap. D. 20.1.1.2, which also says that if the purchaser in good faith has consumed the pledged fruits then the (analogous) *actio Serviana* cannot be successfully instituted against him.[94] It is not so strange that the Roman jurists saw no difficulty in allowing future crops, newly born animals, and slave children to be pledged in advance. They all have their roots in property to which the debtor (as owner) was entitled at

[92] Section 6.6.

[93] '*Et quae nondum sunt, futura tamen sunt, hypothecae dari possunt, ut fructus pendentes, partus ancillae, fetus pecorum et ea quae nascuntur sint hypothecae obligata*'.

[94] On this difficult and possibly corrupted text, see Wubbe 1960: 250–3.

the time of the *conventio pignoris* and they are owned by no one else.[95] The clause recommended by the early classical jurist Cassius in D. 13.7.18.3, that 'whatever things are the creation from and product of the wood' will be pledged, is based on the same idea. Although these products were not regarded as identical to the pledged wood itself and were not automatically subject to the pledge thereof, they do have their origin in property which was owned by the person who granted the pledge and could, therefore, be pledged.

Special pledges of future property: *res debita*

'Absolute' future property (i.e., assets which do not yet exist) could therefore be pledged if it was generated by assets which were already owned by the debtor. This is different, however, in respect of 'relative' future property. These are assets which physically already exist as separate objects, but which at the time of the pledge agreement are still owned by someone else. When someone else's property had been pledged and the property was afterwards acquired by the debtor (for instance, through purchase or inheritance), a 'convalescence' of the originally imperfect pledge could take place. The creditor would be granted an adapted *actio Serviana* (*utilis*), by means of which the pledged assets could be recovered from possessors.[96] According to Papinian (in D. 20.1.1 pr.) in this adapted action the condition of *in bonis debitoris esse* could only be relaxed (i.e., shifted forward in time) when, at the time of the pledge agreement, the pledged property was already owed to the debtor (*res debita*). When the debtor had concluded a pledge agreement in respect of property which had already been purchased by (but not yet been conveyed to) him, the creditor would upon conveyance by the seller to the debtor automatically acquire an enforceable right of pledge on the property. One could regard this as an extension of the idea behind the pledge of fruits and offspring. Here also the debtor did already have, at the time of the pledge agreement, a legally relevant 'expectation' in respect of the pledged asset. Where the debtor has a claim for its conveyance against a seller, the pledged object is already in the 'run-up of his *in bonis*'.[97] The debtor could have pledged this claim (*pignus nominis*) to the creditor.[98] This claim could then be enforced by the creditor

[95] Wubbe 1960: 250.

[96] On convalescence of rights of pledge see Schanbacher 1987: passim; Potjewijd 1998: 211–308.

[97] Wacke 1997: 451.

[98] According to Potjewijd (1998: 248), this fragment even actually deals with the situation where a pledge had been created over a (e.g., a purchaser's) contractual claim for delivery. There is, however,

against the seller.[99] Upon delivery by the seller to the creditor, the latter would then acquire a possessory pledge of the purchased property.[100] If this were the case, it is only a small step to recognize that also in the absence of a pledge of the claim for conveyance, the pledged property would become charged upon its acquisition by the debtor. Where, however, such expectation of ownership did *not* exist, the creditor would only be protected when in good faith (unaware of the debtor's lack of ownership). The creditor who knew that the property belonged to someone else, while the debtor did not even have a claim for its conveyance, did not deserve to be protected by the (adapted) *actio Serviana*.[101]

General pledges and future property

In all the texts up to and including Papinian recognizing pledges of future property, the debtor already had a legally relevant expectation in respect of the pledged future assets, as fruits or offspring of assets already within the debtor's patrimony, or as things already owed to the debtor (*res debita*). This will have lowered the threshold for accepting that these assets automatically became subject to the pledge once they were acquired by the debtor. The same may have been true for generic pledges, extending to new elements of aggregates of things already owned by the debtor (*invecta et illata*, *grex*, *taberna*). This idea may later have spilled over to general pledges. Moreover, a general pledge is by its very nature geared towards after-acquired property.[102] This may have been the most important reason why it was not even necessary that a legally relevant expectation existed. Originally, however, the scope of the general pledge may have been confined to the assets which the debtor owned at the time of granting the pledge. It has been suggested that, under the influence of Hellenistic practices, transactional practices were only later extended to future goods.[103] The transactional practices on which jurists' opinions were based all expressly mention future goods.[104] Wagner inferred from this that

no indication for this in the text. With regard to a similar fragment on convalescence—Pap. D. 20.4.3.1—also Potjewijd (1998: 117 n 46) admits that only the asset itself had been pledged and not the claim for its delivery.

[99] Paul. D. 13.7.18 pr.; Marci. (Pomp.) D. 20.1.13.2.

[100] Section 8.3.

[101] Wacke 1997: 451.

[102] Wacke 1997: 451–2.

[103] In particular, Frezza 1963: 171. See also Wagner 1968: 6 n 46. Taubenschlag (1955: 125 n 88) refers to the Roman-Egyptian practice of husbands pledging all their—present and future—assets for the obligation to maintain their wives. See also P. Yadin 10 and 17 from the Babatha archive. In Byzantine legal practice we find general pledges drafted in Greek which were strongly influenced by Roman general pledges (Wagner 1968: 6 n 46).

[104] Gai. D. 20.1.15.1 ('*quae nunc habet et quae postea adquisierit*'); Scaev. D. 20.1.34.2 ('*quidquid in bonis habet habiturusve esset*'); Pap. D. 20.1.1 pr. ('*bonorum vel postea quaesitorum recepta est*'); Ulp. D. 20.4.7.1 ('*quae habiturus sum obligaverim*'); Ulp. D. 49.14.28 ('*obligaverat quae habet habiturusque*

originally the agreement to pledge the debtor's entire patrimony would fundamentally not cover the debtor's subsequently acquired property and that later this would (perhaps subject to a limited number of exceptions) require an express agreement.[105] From the jurists' opinions, in any case, it can be derived that in order for the general pledge to extend to future assets, this had to be expressly agreed.[106]

Where the creditor tried to recover possession of assets generally pledged to him, the *demonstratio* in the *formula* of the adapted *actio Serviana* would have been changed. Gaius D. 20.1.15.1 says that in the case of general pledges the creditor did not have to prove that the goods were *in bonis* of the debtor 'when he made the agreement'. This still leaves open the possibility that where the *actio Serviana* was instituted against third parties it was required that the future assets had entered the patrimony of the debtor *after* the pledge was granted. One would indeed expect that the creditor could only recover pledged goods from third parties if, in the period between the conclusion of the *conventio pignoris* and the commencement of the *actio Serviana* proceedings, they would have become part of the debtor's patrimony *(in bonis)*. Only in that event would a right of pledge have come into existence which the creditor could enforce against third parties with the *actio Serviana*.

Pap. D. 20.1.1 pr. and Marci. D. 20.1.16.7

In late classical law it was finally accepted that the creditor and debtor could deliberately grant a special pledge over someone else's property. The right of pledge would be granted 'subject to the condition that it shall have become the debtor's'.[107] It was no longer required that the debtor had—at the time of the pledge agreement—a legally relevant expectation, nor would the creditor's knowing that the debtor did not own the pledged asset be an obstacle to the perfection of a pledge.[108] Pap. D. 20.1.1 pr. and Marci. D. 20.1.16.7 could be

esset'). See also Fragm. de iure fisci 5, FIRA II: 628 ('*non solum ea quae habent, sed et ea quae postea habituri sunt*').

[105] Wagner 1982: 415.

[106] Wagner 1982: 415. See also Gai. D. 20.1.9 pr., as convincingly emendated ('*in bonis <non> habuit*') and interpreted by Wagner 1968: 127–30. In the sixth century AD Justinian considered it still necessary to decree (perhaps in accordance with then prevailing practices) that if the debtor had stated that he pledged 'his assets' without the addition 'both present and future', the general pledge would cover future assets too (Just. C. 8.16.9.1).

[107] Marci. D. 20.1.16.7 ('*sub condicione, si debitoris facta fuerit*'). See also Ulp. (Marcell.) D. 20.4.7.1; Diocl.-Max. C. 8.15.5.

[108] The condition itself would imply such knowledge. Van Hoof considers it odd that the limitation of *res debita* imposed by Pap. D. 20.1.1 pr. could be so easily circumvented, by granting the pledge

reconciled by holding that a *conventio generalis in pignore dando* would by its very nature imply the condition that the right of pledge was conditionally granted in respect of property to be acquired in the future. What is dubious about this assumption is that the first texts on the conditional (special) pledge of future property are from the late classical period.[109] In Ulpian D. 20.4.7.1 the debtor declared: 'I charge in your favour my future assets and also specially charge certain land, should it become mine, in favour of Titius.' This shows that in late classical law the (unconditional) general pledge was still distinguished from the (conditional) special pledge of a future asset. In other words, the general pledge was not regarded as an implied *conditional* pledge.

From a chronological perspective it is therefore questionable to explain the general pledge of future goods in terms of a conditional pledge as later contemplated by Marcian. Future assets which were not rooted in the debtor's patrimony could not yet be specially pledged at the time of Papinian, not even conditionally. They could only be pledged by way of generic or general pledge. Pap. D. 20.1.1 pr. and Marci. D. 20.1.16.7 represent different evolutionary stages of the *special* pledge: while possible only to a limited extent at Papinian's time, Marcian later recognized that all future property could be specially pledged. This principle may have evolved in order to narrow the gap between special and general pledges in this respect. Only under Diocletian, it seems, the imperial chancery did not even require that the granting of the special pledge was framed conditionally by the parties. A constitution from 286 AD rules that the *actio Serviana* itself did not lie where the debtor had pledged an asset of which he became the owner after the pledge was granted. Nevertheless, equity implies that an *actio utilis* is given by analogy with the *actio Serviana*.[110] What this constitution does show, however, is that at the end of the third century AD the special pledge of property subsequently acquired was still regarded as a special problem, which had to be solved by granting the creditor an action on the case on the basis of equity.[111] The general pledge was not a variant of a conditionally granted special pledge of future property but may rather have been one of its ancestors.[112]

conditionally, and therefore argues that Marcianus's conditional pledge was confined to *res debita* (Van Hoof 2017: 480–1). There is no indication for this in the sources.

[109] Wubbe 1960: 227.

[110] Diocl.-Max. C. 8.15.5 ('*sed tamen aequitatem facere, ut facile utilis persecutio exemplo pignoraticiae daretur*').

[111] For example, Marci. D. 22.3.23: the creditor who institutes the *actio Serviana* must not only prove the *conventio pignoris*, but 'he must also show that the property was the debtor's at the time of agreement' ('*illud quoque implere debet rem pertinere ad debitorem eo tempore quo convenit de pignore*').

[112] Wubbe 1960: 227; Wagner 1968: 6.

9.5 General Pledges and Special Pledges: Ranking

The floating charge of the modern common law systems allows the debtor company to deal with its assets freely in the ordinary course of its business so that subsequent dispositions by the company will take place free from the charge, while subsequent grantings of fixed charges will take priority over the floating charge.[113] In Roman law this was certainly different for subsequent special charges. Where the debtor had pledged some of his assets to another creditor, the creditor with an anterior general pledge could recover possession with the *actio Serviana* from that other creditor. Moreover, it was entirely at the discretion of the creditor with the first ranking general pledge against which pledged assets he would first take recourse, including those pledged to others. The ranking of the general (including *cetera bona*) pledge was in classical Roman law subject to the general principle of priority applicable to all types of pledge: the earlier general pledge would rank ahead of subsequent (general or special) pledges granted to other creditors. In this respect the general pledge certainly did have third-party effect. However, also in the absence of an express contractual arrangement to that effect (as in Pap. D. 20.4.2), the creditor with a *cetera bona* pledge would, at the end of the classical period, become obliged by operation of law to firstly execute the specially pledged objects.[114] In classical Roman law the independent general pledge never evolved into a subsidiary security interest. The independent general pledge would only have a subsidiary nature if this had been agreed between the debtor and the creditor.[115]

Prior tempore principle applies

There can be no doubt that where slaves and other assets pledged as *invecta et illata* were also pledged to other creditors, the ranking of the competing pledges would be determined by the *prior tempore* principle.[116] The Roman jurists and the imperial chancery also consistently applied the general principle of priority to the ranking between general pledges and subsequently granted (special and general) pledges over the generally pledged assets.

In one of the first opinions on the general pledge (Scaevola D. 20.4.21 pr.) Titius had pledged all his present and future goods to Seia in order to secure his liability to her as *tutor*. Later, Titius borrowed money from the imperial

[113] Beale et al. 2018: 15.02.
[114] Wagner 1968: 86.
[115] Koops 2010: 46, 48.
[116] For example, Gai. D. 20.4.11.2.

treasury and this time pledged all his present and future goods to the treasury. Scaevola held that Seia's general pledge took preference over the treasury's general pledge.[117] The applicability of the principle of priority to general pledges, also in relation to special pledges, remained firmly entrenched in Roman jurisprudence. In Ulp. D. 20.4.7.1 Marcellus treats the ranking between a general pledge of all the debtor's future assets and a conditional special pledge of land still to be acquired in exactly the same way as where two special pledges were granted in respect of property subsequently acquired.[118] In Pap. D. 20.4.2 Papinian holds that the creditor to whom a general pledge was granted could take recourse against land which the debtor later had specially pledged to another creditor. In Pap. D. 20.5.1 a creditor (C1) had first taken a special pledge of land and later a general pledge of all the debtor's assets. This creditor sold some of the debtor's goods (but not the specially pledged land) to third parties by way of execution sale. This sale was an unauthorised sale, because in respect of the debtor's other assets the (general) pledge granted to another creditor (C2) had been granted earlier than the (general) pledge granted to the selling creditor (C1).[119] The creditor (C2) with the first ranking general pledge over the debtor's other (sold) goods could, according to Papinian, institute the *actio Serviana* against the purchasers of these goods from C1. Indeed, to hold otherwise would have rendered the stronger position of the creditor with the first ranking general pledge illusory. This line of legal opinions is continued by the imperial chancery. A constitution of Alexander Severus from AD 227 (C. 8.25.3) provides that where a debtor had pledged all his goods to creditor C1 and subsequently, without C1's permission or knowledge, entered into a secured loan with another creditor C2, C1's rights shall not be adversely affected.[120] From 260 AD there is a constitution by Valerianus and Galienus (C. 8.17.6) ruling that where goods were charged *generaliter* to C1 and later some of these goods were pledged *specialiter* to C2, the creditor who contracted earlier (C1) shall, pursuant to the general charge, have the stronger position. This rescript was given to someone (Philoxenus) who

[117] This was apparently self-evident to Scaevola. The question put to this jurist was whether a novation of the original debt (by replacing it with a *stipulatio*), which took place after the loan from the treasury, affected the ranking of Seia's pledge. According to Scaevola this was not the case.

[118] The opinion of Marcellus (as restated by Ulpian) is that both rights of pledge did have the same ranking. According to Wubbe (1960: 237–8) the general and special pledge would simultaneously come into existence upon the debtor's acquisition of the land. For a different interpretation, see Potjewijd (1998: 301–2).

[119] The chronological sequence of events was as follows: (1) the debtor grants a special pledge of land to C1; (2) the debtor grants a general pledge to C2; (3) the debtor grants a general pledge to C1; and (4) C1 sells generally pledged assets to purchasers.

[120] The constitution says that this is the case even where C2 is a municipality.

had purchased from the creditor with the general pledge (C1) one of the assets specially pledged to C2. The constitution holds that this purchaser shall not be 'disturbed' by the creditor with the special pledge (C2). In all these legal opinions and constitutions, the creditor with a first priority general pledge can institute the *actio Serviana* against creditors with lower-ranking (general or special) rights of pledge or against purchasers from these creditors. In this respect the general pledge did, without any doubt, have third-party effect.

Subsidiary nature of *cetera bona* pledge: transactional practices

The general rule is that where several goods were (specially or generally) pledged for the same debt, it was completely at the creditor's discretion which of these goods would be sold by way of execution (Mod. D. 20.5.8). The fact that some of the goods were pledged to other creditors did not change this: the creditor was at liberty to take recourse against these assets, even where the debtor still owned assets which were not pledged to others.[121] This would originally also apply to *cetera bona* pledges.[122] The creditor was at liberty to take recourse against other assets of the debtor than those specially pledged to him. This would also be the case where these other assets had in the meantime been (specially or generally) pledged to other creditors. However, the debtor and the creditor could agree that the creditor would only take recourse against the debtor's remaining assets (*cetera bona*) if and to the extent that the proceeds of the specially pledged assets were insufficient to fully discharge the secured debt.[123] Pap. D. 20.4.2 discusses the possibility that the parties voluntarily attribute such a subsidiary nature to the *cetera bona* pledge.[124]

D. 20.4.2. *Papinianus libro tertio responsorum.* Qui generaliter bona debitoris pignori accepit eo potior est, cui postea praedium ex his bonis datur, quamvis ex ceteris pecuniam suam redigere possit. quod si ea conventio prioris fuit, ut ita demum cetera bona pignori haberentur, si pecunia de his, quae <non>

[121] Diocl.-Max. C. 8.13.14. This applies in principle to all pledges, but in sections 9.5–9.7 it will be argued that generally pledged assets were *transferred* free from the pledge.

[122] See Sev.-Ant. C. 8.13.2 later in the chapter.

[123] A similar arrangement concerning maritime loans is discussed in Paul. D. 22.2.6.

[124] For elaborate discussions of this text see Wagner 1968: 75–81, 86, 93, and 95. See also Mentxaka 1986: 300–33.

> generaliter[125] accepit, servari non potuisset, deficiente secunda conventione secundus creditor in pignore postea dato non tam potior quam solus invenietur.
>
> Someone who accepts a general pledge over a debtor's assets has a stronger position than he who subsequently is given a piece of land in pledge from those assets, even if he can recover his debt from other assets. But if the agreement with the first creditor was that the remaining assets were pledged only if the money could not be recovered from those <not> accepted as generally pledged, if the second agreement does not become operative the second creditor is the sole rather than the preferred pledge creditor.

What precisely happened is impossible to reconstruct from this (probably heavily interpolated) text, but there cannot be much doubt about its gist. Papinian's opinion first sets out the principle: where all the debtor's goods are pledged to C1 and subsequently a piece of land is pledged to C2, C1 can take recourse against this land, even though the proceeds of the other assets would have been sufficient. This is different, however, where the debtor and C1 have created a *cetera bona* pledge and have agreed that the debtor's remaining assets shall be conditionally pledged, subject to the condition precedent that the secured debt cannot be recovered from the specially pledged asset. If the proceeds of the specially pledged property are sufficient to satisfy C1, the condition does not materialize, so that the *cetera bona* pledge will not be triggered. Thus, where slave Stichus was specially pledged to C1, whose value would be sufficient to discharge the secured debt, C1 cannot take recourse against the land specially pledged to C2. C1 must first sell Stichus and only when the sale proceeds of this slave are insufficient can he take recourse against the debtor's *cetera bona* (the land) subsequently pledged to C2.

As in the intermediate stage in the evolutionary trajectory of the multiple pledge and the special pledge of future property,[126] the parties use the construction of a conditional pledge in order to realize the desired result. The text appears to indicate, however, that even if the condition materialized, C2's pledge would rank ahead of C1's *cetera bona* pledge. This is because the last sentence of D. 20.4.2 appears to say that *if* the conditional *cetera bona* pledge becomes operative, C2 shall be the preferred ('*potior*') pledge creditor. Could the reasoning behind this have been that the ranking of a conditional pledge

[125] I have followed Mommsen's conjecture. Another proposed conjecture is to replace *generaliter* with *specialiter* (Mentxaka 1986: 303). See also Wagner 1968: 78 (who 'admits' that this conjecture is 'simple and cannot be excluded text-critically'). Wagner himself prefers Lenel's conjecture <*pignori aliter*>. For other difficulties see Wagner 1968: 78–9.

[126] Sections 7.4 (multiple pledge) and 9.4 (future property).

would be determined by the time at which the condition materializes? This is unlikely: it would go against the tendency in Roman jurisprudence that the creditor to whom the pledge has been conditionally granted must be protected against dispositions made in the period between the conditional grant and the materialization of the condition.[127] Moreover, if C2's pledge were to have had priority over C1's conditional pledge, not many creditors with a *cetera bona* pledge would voluntarily have agreed to such a far-reaching form of subsidiarity. The purpose of the agreement discussed by Papinian rather is that C1 has a first priority right of pledge over all the debtor's assets, subject to the proviso that (first priority) recourse can only be taken against the *cetera bona* if and when it appears that the proceeds of the specially pledged property are insufficient.[128]

Subsidiary nature of *cetera bona* pledge: imperial constitutions

A constitution from Septimius Severus and Caracalla from 204 AD rules that the creditor with a *cetera bona* pledge should first sell goods which are specially ('*specialiter*') pledged and the remaining goods shall only be sold if it appears from the first execution sale that there is a deficit. Yet again a transactional practice evolved into a rule of law. The construction, however, is a different one: where in Pap. D. 20.4.2 the *cetera bona* are conditionally pledged, the Severan constitution assumes that all the debtor's assets are unconditionally pledged, but subject to restrictions on enforcement.

> **Sev.-Ant. C. 8.13.2.** Quamvis constet specialiter quaedam et universa bona generaliter adversarium tuum pignori accepisse et aequale ius in omnibus habere, iurisdictio tamen temperanda est. **1.** Ideoque si certum est posse eum ex his, quae nominatim ei pignori obligata sunt, universum redigere debitum, ea, quae postea ex isdem bonis pignori accepisti, interim non auferri praeses iubebit.
>
> Although it is clear that your adversary accepted as a pledge some property specially as well as all his goods generally, and he has an equal right to all of

[127] Potjewijd 1998: 102. See section 7.3 (discussing Afr. D. 20.4.9.3).

[128] The '*potior*' in the last sentence may have been a clumsy insertion by a later editor of the text. It could mirror the '*potior*' in the first sentence, where this word is used in order to indicate that C1 shall be the stronger one of the two competing pledge creditors. The interpolation then somewhat pedantically says in the last sentence that if the condition does not materialize, C2's right of pledge shall not be the stronger one of the two, but the only remaining one. See also Wagner 1968: 80–1.

> it, nevertheless the law should be applied with restraint. 1. So if it is certain that he can collect the entire debt from property pledged to him specially, the governor will order that the property you afterwards received as a pledge from the same goods not be taken from you in the meantime.

This constitution concerns a case where a special pledge has been combined with a general pledge in favour of the same creditor (C1), while some generally pledged assets have subsequently been pledged to another creditor (C2) by way of possessory pledge. The constitution first puts forward the general principle that C1's preferential rights of recourse exist equally in respect of specially and generally pledged assets. Judicial 'temperance', however, requires that this principle sometimes be set aside for the benefit of other creditors. As long as no execution sale of the specially pledged goods has taken place, the creditor with an anterior general pledge cannot recover remaining assets which were subsequently pledged to another creditor.[129] In the period anticipating the execution of the specially pledged goods, creditors with lower-ranking rights of pledge presumably would also not be entitled to take recourse against the debtor's remaining goods. This is only possible after it has become clear that the proceeds of the specially pledged goods are sufficient to discharge the debt owed to the first ranking creditor with a *cetera bona* pledge.[130] Therefore, only if after execution of the specially pledged goods it turns out that there is still a deficit, the creditor with a first ranking *cetera bona* pledge can take possession of (one or more of) the debtor's other assets and sell them by way of execution. The *cetera bona* pledge had become a subsidiary security interest, which cannot be enforced against lower-ranking pledge creditors if the specially pledged assets offer sufficient security to the first ranking creditor. The equitable solution reached for an incidental case in C. 8.13.2, which protected both the debtor and lower-ranking creditors, would because of its economic rationality also be applied in other cases where similar competing rights of pledge existed.[131]

[129] Wagner 1968: 81–6; Koops 2010: 48–50. Diocl.-Max. *C.* 8.27.9, on which Wagner 1968: 87–92. According to Wagner C. 8.27.9 incorporates the same rule as C. 8.13.2. It rather appears that C. 8.27.9 is concerned with a contractual subordination as discussed in Pap. D. 20.4.2. See Koops 2010: 48 n 289.

[130] Wagner 1968: 85.

[131] Wagner 1968: 85–6.

9.6 Outgoing Goods: Dispositions of Generally Pledged Assets

Could the creditor with a general pledge institute the *actio Serviana* against any current possessor who had acquired assets from the debtor in the period after the general pledge was granted? Would such a creditor only need to prove that at some point in time in this period they had been within the patrimony of the debtor? Such right of recovery against purchasers could have paralyzed the debtor's business and disrupted commercial intercourse,[132] also given the facts that general pledges were not publicly registered and that Roman law did not protect a *bona fide* possessor against a pledge unknown to him.[133] In respect of the other variants of pledge the Roman jurists and imperial constitutions generally reach sensible results from an economic perspective.[134] If we assume that the Roman jurists realized that there was a practical necessity that the debtor who had granted a general pledge over all his present and future assets could continue to dispose of his assets free from the pledge, how can this be construed as a matter of Roman law? One possible construction would be to accept that every general pledge implied an authorization of the debtor by the creditor to sell pledged assets freely. There is, however, a plausible alternative for explaining the legal consequences of the general pledge, which reflects the purpose of the parties to create a security interest over circulating assets: a 'floating' charge. In this alternative explanation the concept of *in bonis esse* explains not only the effects of a general pledge agreement on incoming goods (future property) but also those on outgoing goods (disposed property).

Cetera bona pledge

The most compelling argument supporting the hypothesis that generally pledged assets could be disposed of free from the pledge is connected with the continuing use of the *cetera bona* pledge in Roman practice, in a period in which the general pledge was firmly embedded in Roman private law.[135] This

[132] It would have prevented the 'metabolism' of the debtor's patrimony from becoming paralyzed. Wieacker 1939: 232 (for Hellenistic Egypt).

[133] Wubbe 1960: 225. In a similar sense, with respect to the pledge of a *taberna* (see pp. 273–5), Daubermann 1993: 121.

[134] On the economic rationality of the Roman jurists, see section 12.2.

[135] Section 9.3.

shows that uncertainty about the legal status of the general pledge can no longer have been the motive for creating *cetera bona* pledges in the late classical period. In this period the parties who chose to create a *cetera bona* pledge must have intended the special pledge and the general pledge to have different legal consequences, otherwise it would not have made sense for them to differentiate between the two forms of pledge in one security package.[136] In particular, where the general pledge could not be enforced against certain third parties, there would be a clear interest for both creditor and debtor in agreeing a special pledge on some assets in combination with a general pledge over the remaining assets. Thus where the debtor was a merchant or farmer, this would enable him to continue his business and make profits with which the creditor could be paid. The creditor could single out one or more valuable specific assets as constituting the core of his security package. These assets would always be available for recourse, even if they were transferred by the debtor to third parties. In addition, as a fallback for the situation that the execution value of the specially pledged assets was insufficient, the creditor could take preferential recourse against those assets that were in the debtor's patrimony at the time of execution.

This distinction between special and general pledges may be reflected in an opinion of Julian.

> **D. 47.2.67 pr.** *Paulus libro septimo ad Plautium.* Si is, qui rem pignori dedit, vendiderit eam: quamvis dominus sit, furtum facit, sive eam tradiderat creditori sive speciali pactione tantum obligaverat: idque et Iulianus putat.
>
> Even though he owns the thing, if a man sells the thing which he has given in pledge, he commits theft, whether he actually delivered the thing to his creditor or charged it by special pact; and so thinks Julian.

The sale of pledged property by the debtor constitutes theft (*furtum*), according to Julian and Paul, where it was charged by way of special pledge or—which is also a form of special pledge—possessory pledge. This seems to imply that where the debtor had granted a general pledge he could freely (i.e., without committing theft) dispose of his assets.[137] From the late third century AD there are two imperial constitutions from Diocletian, which reflect high and late classical law. One constitution from 293 AD (C. 8.13.14) is an application of the old principle that the right of pledge—as a real right—entailed a right

[136] Wubbe 1960: 226; Van Hoof: 2017: 490. [137] Van Hoof 2022.

to follow (*droit de suite*). Where the debtor had disposed of the pledged property, the creditor not only had a personal action against his contractual counterparty (the debtor) but could also recover possession of the property from a purchaser. The other constitution (Diocl.-Max. C. 8.13.10) could indicate that the recovery of generally pledged assets from purchasers was excepted from this principle. What is particularly interesting about this constitution is that it expressly mentions that (at least according to the creditor) the pledged assets were specified in the deed of pledge ('*quas instrumento specialiter comprehensas*'). Could this be an indication that the creditor would not have such remedy (*actio Serviana*) against a purchaser of a generally pledged asset? One cannot be sure: the reference to '*specialiter*' may also simply have been a restatement of the facts of the case.

Authorization for dispositions in the ordinary course of business

We have a large number of texts on (special) pledges indicating that the creditor's permission to sell the pledged assets would enable the debtor to dispose of the pledged assets free from the pledge.[138] In modern literature it is held that a general pledge over all the debtor's present and future assets would create a presumption that the debtor was authorized to dispose of the pledged assets in the ordinary course of his dealings.[139] There are, however, no jurists' opinions or imperial constitutions in which such an implied authorization is unequivocally confirmed.[140] In modern literature this view is therefore not unanimously endorsed. In his monograph on the herd, Hammerstein notes that the discharge of animals transferred to third parties was not dependent on whether this was a disposition in the ordinary course of business. For third parties this would often be difficult to assess and difficult too for the creditor to monitor.[141] Wagner holds that where Scaevola in D. 20.1.34 pr. only mentions that a pledge of the *taberna* has taken place and is silent on the

[138] See in particular the fragments in D. 20.5, D. 20.6 and C. 8.25.

[139] Sturm 1993a: 42; Van Hoof 2017: 490–1. Wagner assumes that in case of a pledge of the stock of a *taberna* the Roman jurists must have held that the debtor was authorized to sell the goods in the ordinary course of business (Wagner 1982: 85), but denies that such authority existed in case of general pledges (Wagner 1974: 161).

[140] In Pap. D. 20.1.5 the sale of generally pledged assets was an unauthorized execution sale by a lower-ranking creditor. A rescript from Diocletian from 294 AD deals with the situation where a general pledge had been granted to one creditor and another creditor sold one of the debtor's assets (Diocl.-Max. C. 8.27.17). These texts do not concern dispositions *by the debtor* in the ordinary course of his business.

[141] Hammerstein 1975: 171–2.

authorization to sell, one would at least have expected conduct by the creditor from which such authorization could be implied.[142] Wagner's suggestion is that we are dealing with legal interpretation based on the 'nature of things': merchandise as circulating capital.[143] According to Wubbe, the fact that in case of general pledges the pledged assets did not have to be *in bonis* (Gai. D. 20.1.15.1; Pap. D. 20.1.1 pr.) explains why the creditor could not institute the *actio Serviana* against third parties. The creditor could only institute this action against the debtor, in which case it did not matter that the assets were not *in bonis* (Ulp. D. 20.1.21.1). In this view, there is no need to employ the fiction that the creditor impliedly authorized the debtor to dispose freely of generally pledged assets. There is, indeed, a plausible alternative for explaining the legal consequences of the general pledge, which is based on the fundamental legal concept of *in bonis esse*.

A 'unified theory' of general pledge (I)

A sound theory of the general pledge must explain not only why it encumbered goods which at the time of the *conventio pignoris* were not yet *in bonis*. It also has to clarify why the creditor could institute the *actio Serviana* against the debtor and a subsequent pledge creditor, but not against a subsequent purchaser of the debtor's assets. These legal consequences of the general pledge can largely be explained on the basis of the general principles applied by the jurists to the condition of *in bonis esse* to special pledges. Pursuant to these general principles, in a *Serviana* procedure against the debtor the creditor did not have to prove that the pledged property was *in bonis* of the debtor (Ulp. (Jul.) D. 20.1.21.1).[144] In Paul D. 20.4.14 this principle is extended to cases where multiple special pledges were granted by the same debtor. Therefore, where Gai. D. 20.1.15.1 holds that in case of a general pledge the debtor does not have to prove that the pledged assets are *in bonis* of the debtor, this could—in respect of the debtor and other pledge creditors—simply be regarded as an application of a general principle applicable to all (special and general) pledges.[145] Where the creditor with a (special or general) pledge instituted the *actio Serviana* against someone to whom the debtor had sold

[142] Wagner 1982: 414.

[143] But ultimately also Wagner (1982: 417–18) assumes that the pledge of a *taberna* implied a 'tacit' authorization to sell.

[144] See Ankum, van Gessel-de Roo, and Pool 1987: 426; Potjewijd 1998: 38–9, 50.

[145] See also Wubbe 1960: 226.

and transferred one or more of his assets, he did have to demonstrate that they were owned by the debtor at the time the pledge was granted. In this he would fail in respect of those assets which entered the debtor's patrimony after the pledge was granted. This could explain why the general pledge did not give the creditor the right to recover the debtor's assets from third parties, at least in respect of assets acquired after the pledge was granted. In respect of assets which the debtor already owned at the time of the *conventio pignoris*, however, this would not explain why the creditor could not institute the *actio Serviana* against purchasers of pledged assets. These assets would have been *in bonis debitoris* at the time of the pledge agreement, so that all the conditions of the *actio Serviana* were met. Therefore, most but not all of the legal consequences of the general pledge can be explained on the basis of the same principles concerning *in bonis* as were applicable to special pledges. The remaining 'gap' can, however, be closed by adding only one new element to the theory explaining the legal consequences of the general pledge in terms of *in bonis esse*.

A 'unified theory' of general pledge (II)

In case of a special pledge, the pledged object is known and is specially defined by the parties in the pledge agreement.[146] One could say that in case of general pledges the concept of *in bonis esse* takes over the function of a specific definition of the pledged assets in the pledge agreement: the charged assets are defined as all those assets that are or will be in the patrimony of the debtor (*in bonis debitoris*). We find this very clearly in Scaev. D. 20.1.34.2, where the creditor accepted from the debtor 'a pledge of everything which he had or would have in his patrimony' ('*quidquid in bonis habet habiturusve esset*'). As is the case with generic pledges (*invecta et illata*, *grex*, *taberna*), in case of general pledges the charged assets can only be individually identified after the pledge agreement has been concluded: subject to pledge are all those assets that have actually become part of the *bona* of the debtor.[147] Even the principle that the scope of a general pledge was fixed by the debtor's death could be explained in terms of *in bonis debitoris esse*. Once

[146] In case of a possessory pledge, the *traditio* of one or more assets would specify the pledged object(s).

[147] Wagner 1968: 65.

the debtor dies, assets acquired by his heirs are by definition not *in bonis* of the debtor and are therefore not pledged.[148]

The concept of *in bonis esse* would determine not only whether and when an individual object would become charged with a general pledge but also whether and when this object would be discharged from the pledge. The jurists may have interpreted the *conventio pignoris generalis* to the effect that the debtor's assets would only be treated as if they were specially pledged for so long as they were in the debtor's patrimony.[149] The general pledge was a 'floating' charge in the sense that it encumbered the assets which from time to time were within the debtor's patrimony.[150] Thus generally pledged assets which are pledged again to another creditor are still within the patrimony of the debtor and can therefore be recovered by the first creditor with the *actio Serviana*. Generally pledged goods that have in the meantime been disposed of to third parties are no longer *in bonis* and can therefore no longer be recovered with the *actio Serviana*. Where the debtor failed to repay the secured debt in time, the general pledge would 'crystallize' and the creditor could take recourse against those assets which were within the patrimony of the debtor at the time of execution. Where they were already sold and delivered to third parties they could no longer be executed by the creditor with a general pledge. Such a creditor can, however, execute those assets which have been acquired by the debtor with the sales proceeds of the goods sold to third parties. In procedural terms: the *actio Serviana* can be instituted against third parties, for as long as the generally pledged assets are still within the debtor's patrimony.[151]

9.7 Manumission of Pledged Slaves

There is a remarkable difference between the manumission of specially and generally pledged slaves. Slaves who were subject to a general pledge could be manumitted (released from slavery) by the debtor, this in contrast with specially pledged slaves. This would, moreover, also be the case for slaves who were charged by way of a tenant's pledge. How can this differential treatment be explained? Is it a consequence of a statute enacted by Augustus: the *lex Aelia Sentia*? There are problems with explaining this differential treatment wholly in terms of the *lex Aelia Sentia*. Moral considerations too (*favor*

[148] Wubbe 1960: 236–8, with reference to Mod. 20.1.26.2, Paul. D. 20.1.29 pr., and Ulp. D. 20.4.7.1.
[149] Wubbe 1960: 227. [150] Wubbe 2003: 171. [151] Wubbe 1960: 227.

libertatis) may have supported the acceptance of important exceptions to the principle that pledged slaves could not be manumitted by the debtor. There is, moreover, an economic rationale for the differentiation between specially and generally pledged slaves. This rationale is the same for manumissions and dispositions of pledged slaves, which lends support to the idea that both forms of disposition were largely treated analogously by the jurists and in imperial constitutions. A full equivalence, however, of the debtor's power to manumit generally pledged slaves with the power to dispose of generally pledged assets is not supported by the sources, particularly not for *invecta et illata* (which could be manumitted, but not disposed of free from the pledge).

Special, generic (*invecta et illata*), and general pledges

An opinion by the early classical jurist Marcus Cocceius Nerva (consul before 24 AD) on the tenant's right to manumit slaves pledged as *invecta et illata* is recalled in Paul. D. 20.2.9.[152]

> **D. 20.2.9.** *Paulus libro singulari de officio praefecti vigilum.* Est differentia obligatorum propter pensionem et eorum, quae ex conventione manifestari pignoris nomine tenentur, quod manumittere mancipia obligata pignori non possumus, inhabitantes autem manumittimus, scilicet antequam pensionis nomine percludamur: tunc enim pignoris nomine retenta mancipia non liberabimus: et derisus Nerva iuris consultus, qui per fenestram monstraverat servos detentos ob pensionem liberari posse.
>
> There is a difference between assets charged for rent and those which are held as pledge pursuant to an express agreement; we cannot free slaves charged with an (express) pledge, but we can free slaves living on rented premises, until we are locked out for non-payment of rent: after that we cannot effectively free slaves detained by way of pledge. The jurist Nerva was mocked for holding that we can free slaves detained for rent by pointing at them through the window.

The tenant could manumit slaves who were subject to a tenant's pledge, but his power to do so terminated when the landlord exercised his right of lockout for payment default. Nerva was ridiculed ('*derisus*'), according to Paul,

[152] Nerva had a son with the same name who was also a jurist. In the Digest, references to the son are always to *Nerva filius*. See Lenel 1889, vol I: 791.

because he apparently took the view that slaves, who were pledged for rent and were present at the rented premises, could after lock-out still be manumitted by pointing at them. In opinions by Pomponius, Paul, and Ulpian it is also held that the tenant can manumit slaves, unless this was done in order to defraud creditors or after an event of default occurred.[153] These jurists all contrast tenant's pledges with special pledges, in holding that only tenant's pledges entail that the debtor is allowed to 'dispose' of pledged slaves in the form of their manumission. Thus in D. 20.2.6 Ulpian says (with reference to Pomponius) that although in urban tenancies objects brought into the premises are impliedly charged as if this had been specially agreed, such a pledge is no bar to manumission.

When general 'all assets' pledges came to be recognized, the manumission of generally pledged slaves was treated in the same way as slaves subject to tenant's pledges. Two Severan constitutions leave no doubt that in the second half of the second century AD a distinction should be made between the manumission of specially and generally pledged slaves.

> **Sev.-Ant. C. 7.8.2.** Libertas a debitore fisci servo data, qui pignori non est ex conventione speciali, sed tantum privilegio fisci obligatus, non aliter infirmatur, quam si hoc fraudis consilio effectum detegatur.
>
> Liberty bestowed by a debtor of the treasury upon a slave, who is not pledged by special agreement, but who is only charged to the treasury by way of privilege, is not invalid unless it is shown that such liberty was granted with intent to defraud.
>
> **Sev.-Ant. C. 7.8.3.** Ab eo, qui bona sua pignori obligavit, quae habet quaeque habiturus esset, posse servis libertatem dari certum est. non idem iuris est in his servis, qui pignoris iure specialiter traditi vel obligati sunt.
>
> It is certain that liberty can be given to slaves by a master who charges what he has and everything which he will have as a pledge. The law is not the same regarding those slaves who were specially delivered or charged by way of pledge.

According to these constitutions by Septimius Severus and Caracally, generally pledged slaves (including slaves subject to general fiscal pledges or privileges) can be liberated, this in contrast with specially pledged slaves. In C. 7.8.3 (209 AD) it seems likely that the general pledge was a conventional one, while

[153] Du Plessis 2007: 229–30. On D. 20.2.9, see also Wagner 1974: 165–8; Frier 1980: 119–21.

in C. 7.8.2 (without date) the general pledge was a fiscal pledge arising by operation of law (‘*privilegio fisci obligatus*’).

Legal basis for differential treatment: *lex Aelia Sentia*?

In a time where slaves would normally be charged by way of *fiducia cum creditore*, the debtor would no longer have the power to manumit them because ownership of the slaves was now with the creditor.[154] This was not different, however, where slaves were charged with *pignus*. This is remarkable because, in classical law, ownership of pledged slaves remained with the debtor and one of the attributes of the ownership of slaves is the power to liberate them. The debtor’s lack of power to manumit may have been a surviving trait of the ownership-like nature of *pignus* in the law of the Republic, or the result of the analogous treatment of *pignus* and *fiducia* by the jurists.[155] The manumission could also have been treated analogously to later dispositions of pledged property, which could also not adversely affect pre-existing special rights of pledge.[156] According to Dernburg, the debtor’s ownership-based power to liberate pledged slaves, which existed as a matter of *ius civile*, was restricted by legislation. The *lex Aelia Sentia*, enacted *circa* 4 AD by emperor Augustus, invalidated manumissions that would prejudice creditors.[157] More than one hundred and fifty years after its enactment, Gaius still mentions the *lex Aelia Sentia* in an opinion dealing with the manumission of generally pledged slaves.

> **D. 40.9.29 pr.** *Gaius libro primo de manumissionibus.* Generaliter pignori datus servus sine dubio pleno iure debitoris est et iustam libertatem ab eo consequi potest, si lex Aelia Sentia non impediat libertatem, id est si solvendo sit nec ob id creditores videantur fraudari.
>
> It is beyond doubt that a generally pledged slave is, in law, fully the property of the debtor and can obtain lawful freedom from him, if the *lex Aelia Sentia* should not bar freedom, that is, if the debtor be solvent and no evident detriment to the creditors should result.

[154] According to Noordraven (1999: 164), the creditor could manumit slaves who had been mancipated by way of *fiducia cum creditore*. This would, however, have been in breach of his fiduciary duties, certainly where the debtor was not in default.

[155] Kaser 1982: 32. See also Van Hoof 2015: 58.

[156] Kaser 1982: 32.

[157] Dernburg 1864: 12–20, still followed by Van Hoof 2015: 58.

When general pledges came to be recognized, special, generic (*invecta et illata*) and general pledges were subject to the same legal regime (the *lex Aelia Sentia*), although for special pledges this had different consequences than for generic and general pledges. Manumissions of specially pledged slaves (where they took place without the creditor's consent) were irrefutably presumed to be *in fraudem creditoris.*[158] In the case of generic and general pledges, however, an irrebuttable presumption that manumissions would be *in fraudem creditoris* would be much further removed from reality. Here the manumission of a pledged slave would not necessarily affect the creditor's preferential rights of recourse, because there would usually still be many other assets that would be subject to the pledge.

There are texts, however, from which it appears that also manumissions of specially pledged slaves that clearly did not take place *in fraudem creditorum* were nevertheless invalid. Thus Paul. D. 40.1.3 unequivocally states that a slave given in pledge cannot be manumitted, even if the debtor is solvent. In Sev.-Ant. C. 7.8.2 the limitation to manumissions taking place to the fraudulent detriment of creditors is only applied to general pledges. This constitution assumes that specially pledged slaves cannot be liberated at all. The legal position appears to have been that specially pledged slaves could never be manumitted (unless with the creditor's permission), while generally pledged slaves could only not be manumitted when this would be *in fraudem creditoris.* According to Schulz, this means that the *lex Aelia Sentia* cannot have been the cause of the debtor's inability to manumit specially pledged slaves.[159] Let us, therefore, see whether other explanations are plausible for the differential treatment of the manumission of specially and generally pledged slaves.

Power to manumit = power to dispose?

The classical texts on the liberation of slaves pledged by way of tenant's pledges bring Du Plessis to the conclusion that they were 'nothing more than a floating charge'. They would 'float' over the assets from time to time situated at the leased premises and would only 'crystallize' in the event of non-payment of the secured debt.[160] In his dissertation, Wubbe had already taken the position that the pledge of *invecta et illata* was a general pledge, not of all the debtor's assets but of a 'complex of assets'.[161] It was a general pledge of all those assets

[158] Wagner 1974: 175 n 66; Van Hoof 2015: 57.
[159] Schulz 1928: 263–84, followed by Kaser 1982: 32.
[160] Du Plessis 2007: 229. [161] Wubbe 1960: 228.

that were *in bonis* of the debtor (tenant), in so far as they were brought into the rented premises.[162] The texts on the manumission of slaves pledged as *invecta et illata* are regarded by Wubbe as the application of a wider principle governing dispositions by the debtor of his generally pledged assets. A debtor who has pledged his patrimony can liberate his slaves, just as he can sell other objects part of this patrimony, provided that he does not act *in fraudem creditorum*.[163] In a similar manner, Kaser explains the differential treatment of manumission of specially pledged slaves and slaves pledged as *invecta et illata* as a consequence of a 'restrictive interpretation of the pledge agreement, which in this case kept open the debtor's power of liberation'.[164]

But can we draw inferences from texts on the liberation of slaves pledged as *invecta et illata* for the legal treatment of the sale of goods subject to a tenant's pledge? In D. 43.33.1 pr. Julian holds that if a tenant brings a female slave onto the farm by way of pledge and later sells her, the landlord should be granted an *interdictum Salvianum utile* with regard to a child to which she gave birth when with the buyer. This presupposes that a slave who was subject to a tenant's pledge would remain charged when she was sold and delivered to a third party. It is unlikely, therefore, that the tenant could dispose of *invecta et illata* as unencumbered goods, certainly in respect of slaves, equipment, furnishings, and other assets which were destined to remain permanently on the premises. Cato's deportation clause shows already that there was a concern that *invecta et illata* should remain on the premises. There is a distinct possibility that slaves who were destined to stay on the rented premises could not be disposed of free from the charge, while they could be manumitted (until lock-out).[165] Perhaps the tenant's pledge of a farm (or of urban business premises) could—like the *cetera bona* pledge—be regarded as a combination of a 'fixed charge' over certain assets (i.e., slaves and other assets destined to remain on the premises) and a 'floating charge' over others (i.e., goods produced to be sold to third parties). In any case, in respect of slaves pledged as *invecta et illata*, one cannot fully equate the debtor's power of manumission with his power to sell slaves.

Favor libertatis

One cannot exclude that the manumission of slaves was not, or not exclusively, based on legal or commercial considerations but was (wholly or partly)

[162] Wubbe 1960: 232.
[163] Wubbe 1960: 233.
[164] Kaser 1982: 33.
[165] Section 9.6 (generic pledges).

motivated by moral ones. Legal opinions and constitutions on the manumission of generally pledged slaves may be the expression of a *favor libertatis*. In D. 40.1.10 Paul produces an interesting case report of an imperial judgment (*decretum*) by Septimius Severus on the question whether a manumitted slave was still subject to a fiscal general charge (*ius fiscalis*).[166] Aelianus, a debtor of the imperial treasury, had bought Euemeria, subject to the covenant that he was to manumit her. Many years later Aelianus did manumit Euemeria. The *procurator* of the fiscus, after finding that Aelianus's assets did not cover his debts to the treasury and looking for other assets subject to the fiscal charge, commenced legal proceedings on the status of Euemeria (*status quaestio*).[167] The *procurator* may have relied on the rule confirmed in Septimius Severus's and Caracalla's constitution that manumissions carried out with intent to defraud were invalid.[168] The manumission of Euemeria may have taken place at a time when Aelianus's insolvency was imminent.[169] In his *decretum*, Septimius Severus ruled that 'there was no room for the fiscal privilege, whereby all the assets of debtors were treated as pledged to the treasury, since she had been bought subject to the covenant aforesaid, and if she had not been manumitted, she would still have attained freedom under the constitution of the deified Marcus'.[170] Therefore, the manumission had been valid and Euemeria was a freed woman rather than a slave subject to a fiscal pledge. This decision does not appear to be motivated by economic considerations but rather by the *favor libertatis* underlying the constitution by emperor Marcus Aurelius (and Commodus),[171] to which Septimius Severus's judgment refers. Under this constitution, the covenant to manumit functioned like a proprietary encumbrance: even in the absence of an actual manumission by the current owner (Aelianus) Euemeria would have become a free woman on the agreed date and would therefore not be charged in favour of the treasury. The constitution of Marcus Aurelius and Commodus prevailed over the *lex Aelia Sentia*.[172] This would not only be the case in respect

[166] Wagner 1974: 175–7; Daalder 2018: 434–42. As Daalder (2018: 441 n 41) points out, Paul. D. 49.14.45.3 (= PS 5.12.1d) is strikingly similar to D. 40.1.10 and may very well be a restatement of Septimius Severus's judgment in Paul's own words. On fiscal general pledges and 'pledge-like' rights of recourse (privileges), see sections 10.2 and 10.3.

[167] Buckland 1908: 652–6; Kaser 1971: 114–15 and 288–9; Indra 2011.

[168] C. 8.7.2. Wagner 1974: 176–7. Is it too speculative to connect the (probably fictitious) name of debtor Aelianus with the *lex Aelia Sentia*?

[169] Daalder 2018: 440.

[170] '*Placuit non esse iuri fiscali locum, quo omnia bona debitorum iure pignoris tenerentur, quia ea lege empta est, et, si non manumitteretur, ex constitutione divi Marci ad libertatem perveniret.*'

[171] See on this constitution by Marcus Aurelius and Commodus (c. 178 AD), Buckland 1908: 628–36; Finkenauer 2010: 34–44. On the expression *favor libertatis*, see Ankum 2006 and the literature mentioned in Daalder 2018: 441 n 42.

[172] Wagner 1974: 177.

of slaves who were charged in favour of the treasury but also in respect of slaves charged by way of conventional general pledge.[173]

Economic considerations

But let us assume that the differential treatment of specially and generally pledged slaves was also driven by economic considerations: what could they have been? First of all, in the case of manumission of a generally pledged slave there would simply be other assets against which the creditor would have had a preferential right of recourse, while in the case of a fraudulent manumission the creditor would be protected by the *lex Aelia Sentia*.[174] Secondly, manumissions which took place at a relatively young age were frequent and would mostly take place against a negotiated and agreed price.[175] Slaves would 'purchase' their freedom against their market value.[176] From a purely legal perspective this would still have decreased the assets which were part of the debtor's patrimony and which were subject to the general pledge (unless the price for manumission was paid by a third party). The manumitted slave would no longer be owned by the master/debtor and the price for freedom would be paid from the slave's *peculium*, which was legally already owned by his master. Such a formal legal perspective, however, would prevent a good view on economic reality. The anticipated manumission would have been a strong incentive for increased productivity and profitability of slaves' activities and would have reduced supervision costs.[177] Slaves ran their own businesses, often with subslaves, and would purchase stock, produce goods, and lend money to third parties. There is abundant evidence in the Digest of a transactional practice in manumission agreements which made liberation conditional upon the slave rendering a diligent account.[178] This duty to account would generally enhance the possibility that assets which would otherwise remain undisclosed would become available to the master. Moreover, the master would have a stake in future earnings by his former slaves in the form of a legally protected

[173] Marci. D. 40.8.6. Daalder 2018: 441–2.

[174] Wagner 1974: 169–70, 179.

[175] Koops 2020: 41 refers to a hypothetical model by Scheidel, which indicates that roughly 50–75 per cent of the slave population would have been liberated before the age of fifty. There would, of course, also have been manumissions which were not prompted by pecuniary considerations (Koops 2020: 44), such as gratitude, generosity, or love.

[176] Koops 2020: 60–4.

[177] Koops 2020: 46, 65, 71–2.

[178] For example, Labeo in Pomp. D. 40.7.21 pr. Koops (2020: 37) counts approximately seventy instances.

share in his freedmens' inheritance:[179] 'The loss of a slave is sweetened by the acquisition of a freedman.'[180] All this would be beneficial to the 'net worth' of the master and, accordingly, to the value of the assets available to the creditor to whom he had granted a general pledge. In conclusion, from an economic perspective the manumission of generally pledged slaves made sense, in a similar way as other dispositions by debtors of generally pledged assets.

9.8 A Roman 'Floating Charge'

In respect of all the variants of pledge that have been discussed in this book, it can be observed that the Roman jurists and the imperial constitutions generally reach economically sensible results.[181] As soon as they would enter the debtor's patrimony (*in bonis debitoris*), the debtor's goods would automatically be charged. For as long as these assets were in the debtor's patrimony, the creditor could institute the *actio Serviana* not only against the debtor himself but also against any possessor of generally pledged assets (including subsequent pledge creditors). When they were disposed of to third parties these assets would no longer be *in bonis debitoris* and could no longer be recovered with the *actio Serviana*. From an economic perspective, such a general pledge would have many advantages. The debtor could continue to dispose of his assets in the ordinary course of his business and buy new goods with their proceeds. Generally pledged slaves could be manumitted. At the same time, the creditor would have a preferential right of recourse against all the debtor's assets which were part of his patrimony at the time of execution. The general pledge (including the *cetera bona* pledge) would be like what one could call a 'floating' charge over a dynamic fund of assets, pursuant to which incoming goods would be charged and outgoing goods would become free from the charge.[182]

'Things as Thing and Things as Wealth'

There are two different ways of treating things as a matter of law: 'things as things and things as wealth'. In his brilliant essay, Bernard Rudden writes:

[179] Koops 2020: 46, 65, 69. [180] Koops 2020: 65. [181] Section 12.2.

[182] See for Roman law Sturm 1993a: 38–44; Daubermann 1993: 124–6. The fund must not be reified: it is not the fund which is the object of ownership and subordinate real rights (including *pignus* and *hypotheca*), but its component parts. See Verhagen 2013b: 142.

> A thing may be treated for itself and be possessed, used, and disposed of for its own qualities, however banal they be. In this case the legal regime applicable treats the object as unique: it is this house we own and live in, this book we sell and no other. On the other hand every thing may be treated merely as the clothing (in-*vestment*) worn by a certain amount of wealth. In this case the relevant law accords it the modest role of a member of a class, perfectly replaceable and subject to an implacable regime of real subrogation.
>
> The distinction between the uniqueness of things considered for themselves and their total convertibility when treated as wealth does not follow the classic line of fungibility: a pound of flour is unique if its owner wants to make bread with it; a Vermeer in the hands of a pension fund is just another investment.[183]

According to Rudden, the Roman pledge 'seems to be the oldest of the institutions in which a person treats an object only and always in terms of its value'.[184] The creditor is not interested in using the pledged objects (as things), but only in their monetary value (as wealth) if and when an event of default occurs. In that case the creditor becomes obliged to realize the value of the pledged object, by selling and returning the surplus value to the debtor. To the borrower the pledged object is both a thing and realizable wealth: he can both enjoy its use as a thing (*hypotheca*) and call upon its value in order to obtain credit.[185]

The most articulate manifestation of things as wealth is where things are treated predominantly as members of a class: 'as an item in a portfolio every thing can be changed or converted. Nothing is unique'.[186] The Roman general pledge may have operated in this way. Wubbe has put forward that a creditor who accepts a general pledge expects the debtor's patrimony to have a more or less stable value.[187] Where the debtor disposes of an asset, this is generally counterbalanced by the acquisition of another asset, which would then be subject to the general pledge. This process of substitution would normally repeat itself continuously. This idea that the debtor's patrimony is a fluctuating fund with a (more or less) stable value, might explain why the jurists and emperors may have accepted that generally pledged assets could be disposed

[183] Rudden 1994: 83. [184] Rudden 1994: 96–7.

[185] Rudden 1994: 97. Sometimes also a creditor is not only interested in the pledged object as wealth but also as a thing. Pursuant to a *pactum antichreticum* the creditor was entitled to use the pledged property (section 8.4) and pursuant to an (express or constructive) forfeiture clause he could even acquire it as an owner (sections 5.2, 5.6, 11.3, and 11.4). [186] Rudden 1994: 86.

[187] Wubbe 2003: 172.

of free from the pledge. At the same time it would also explain why in situations where this was typically not the case the debtor could not freely dispose of pledged assets.

Pledge of wealth

Not only the general pledge (including the *cetera bona* pledge) but also generic pledges would be like what one could call a 'floating' charge over a dynamic fund of assets. Merchandise in a *taberna* is circulating capital, which is meant to be purchased and sold. If a right of pledge would have the effect that merchandise would be excluded from the circulation of assets, this would entail that it would be stripped of its essential characteristic. A creditor who takes a pledge of the goods of a *taberna* takes a charge of saleable commodities and is aware of the circulation process of money purchasing goods which are then sold for money, and so on.[188] Such a creditor accepts that sold merchandise will no longer be subject to the pledge, while newly purchased merchandise will automatically become pledged. For the creditor, 'each moveable is merely an entirely replaceable element in a portfolio'.[189] Where a marble trader sells a batch of white marble for 100,000 sesterces and purchases black marble with these proceeds, the object of the creditor's general pledge will have changed from the white marble to the black marble. The charged 'thing' has changed but the charged 'wealth' has remained more or less the same. The scope of the pledge of merchandise in a *taberna* was confined to assets that were *in bonis debitoris*, both in respect of incoming and outgoing goods. They would only be charged if they entered the *taberna* (and the debtor's patrimony) and would no longer be charged when they had left it. One piece of collateral would be replaced with another piece, so that the collateral value of the aggregate of assets charged to the creditor would be more or less stable. It is plausible that the pledge of a herd operated in exactly the same manner: individual animals would be pledged from the moment they entered the herd, but would be released from the pledge when the debtor disposed of individual animals.[190] The value of the herd as a whole would be more or less stable and so would be the 'wealth' available as collateral to the creditor to whom it had been pledged. Not only in respect of incoming goods

[188] Wagner 1982: 414. [189] Rudden 1994: 85.

[190] Hammerstein 1975: 172; Wubbe 1960: 236. See also Frezza 1963: 166.

but also in respect of outgoing ones the general pledge, the pledge of the stock-in-trade of a *taberna* and of a herd would have had the same effects.[191]

There may even be a causal relationship between the differential legal treatment of incoming and outgoing goods pledged by way of general and special pledge, respectively. In the case of general pledges, future goods could already at a relatively early stage be pledged without qualification. This may have compensated for the fact that outgoing goods would no longer be pledged. By way of contrast, special pledges would remain attached to outgoing goods, so that there was less need to give the creditor access to the wealth represented by future assets.[192]

Reduction of wealth

There are scenarios in which dispositions by the debtor free from the pledge would reduce the wealth available as collateral to a creditor with a general pledge. Where the debtor would be allowed to create higher-ranking pledges over specific assets, this could seriously damage the position of the creditor with a general pledge. The goods specially pledged to other creditors would no longer be available for recourse by this creditor. It is true that, in theory, the proceeds of the loan provided by another creditor would again be subject to the general pledge and so would any asset purchased with the newly borrowed money. In practice, however, these proceeds would often be used to discharge other creditors, or could even be applied in order to finance more risky investment strategies. The ongoing process of 'conversion' (substitution) would be interrupted. The Roman jurists may have realized this when, in their opinions and in the imperial chancery, they consistently held that a general pledge could be invoked against subsequent pledge creditors.[193] Where the creditor with a general pledge did consent in the granting of security to another creditor, this consent could be given without prejudice to the general right of pledge (which, according to Ulpian, creditors commonly did).[194] One can easily imagine why: the asset pledged to another creditor would otherwise no longer be charged under the general pledge and would not be substituted by another asset.

[191] For tenant's pledges a distinction would have to be made between assets destined to remain on the premises and goods produced to be sold to third parties.

[192] Section 9.4.

[193] Section 9.5.

[194] Ulp. D. 20.6.4.1 ('*nam solent multi salva causa pignoris sui consentire*').

Also where the debtor would sell generally pledged assets, this could sometimes adversely affect the position of the creditor with a general pledge. Wubbe observes that the value of the debtor's entire patrimony will be much higher than the amount of the secured debt, so that small drops in value will not undermine the creditor's security.[195] This is, however, not always true. In particular, where the debtor's patrimony is relatively small, the value of all the debtor's assets and the amount of the secured debt may be more or less equal. A disposition by the debtor could in this case more easily disturb this balance. If the debtor, instead of buying replacement assets, used the money received from the sale of a pledged asset in order to pay other creditors, the position of a creditor with a general pledge would be weakened. The net balance of the debtor's assets and liabilities would remain the same, but for the secured creditor there would be fewer assets available for recourse. It would seem, however, that in the case of the sale of generally pledged assets the creditor was protected against larger transfers of wealth, which could compromise his security, by contractual good faith and rules of fraudulent preferences (*fraus creditorum*).[196] Above all, the creditor could secure his position by singling out one or more valuable assets for a special pledge and take a *cetera bona* pledge over the debtor's other assets.

Return of pledged slave by debtor to seller

A constitution from Diocletian from 294 AD deals with the situation where a general pledge had been granted to one creditor, while another creditor sold one of the debtor's assets (C. 8.27.17). The legal basis of this sale remains unclear. It may have been that this was an execution sale by an ordinary creditor, or that it took place without any legal basis at all. The constitution rules that a secured creditor does not lose his right to recover generally or specially pledged assets, if they were sold by another creditor to whom they were not pledged. A different conclusion would have reduced the wealth available to the creditor with the general pledge: the proceeds of the sale were not paid into the debtor's patrimony, which prevented that they or the assets purchased with these proceeds would be caught by the general pledge.[197] In the *Corpus iuris civilis* there is only one text which deals explicitly with a disposition of (possibly) generally pledged assets by the debtor himself, although *not* as a

[195] Wubbe 2003: 172. [196] Gai. D. 40.9.29 pr. Wubbe 1960: 233.
[197] Wubbe 2003: 174. See also Pap. D. 20.5.1.

seller of generally pledged assets. This text again rather nicely illustrates that where the pledged wealth was in danger of being reduced, the Roman jurists were reluctant to accept that property would be released from the pledge.

> **D. 20.6.4 pr.** *Ulpianus libro septuagesimo tertio ad edictum.* Si debitor, cuius res pignori obligatae erant, servum quem emerat redhibuerit, an desinat Servianae locus esse? et magis est, ne desinat, nisi ex voluntate creditoris hoc factum est.
>
> If a debtor whose assets were pledged returns a slave he has bought, can the Servian action be brought? The better view is that he can, unless the creditor agreed to the return.

The debtor had purchased a slave on a market, who upon delivery was charged by him in favour of one of his creditors. The *aediles currules* were annually elected officials who had jurisdiction over market transactions, among other things. They would (like the praetors) each year promulgate an edict on the remedies they would grant in the exercise of their jurisdiction. This aedilician edict for market sales contained remedies granted to a purchaser where sold slaves were defective or where warranted qualities turned out to be lacking. One of these remedies was the purchaser's right to return the slave and receive back the purchase price (*actio redhibitoria*) from the seller.[198] In the case discussed by Ulpian the debtor/purchaser must have exercised this *actio redhibitoria* and have redelivered the slave to the seller. Because at the time the pledge had been granted the debtor still owned the slave and repudiation of the sale did not have retroactive or proprietary effect, the creditor's right of pledge continued to exist. Therefore, in this particular case the debtor could not freely dispose of generally pledged assets. Although a generally pledged asset had left the debtor's patrimony, it would continue to be charged, unless the creditor would expressly waive his right of pledge.[199]

Wagner and Wubbe consider it inequitable that in this case the creditor could institute the *actio Serviana* against the seller.[200] The purchase price had

[198] The purchaser had the option to either return the slave and receive back the purchase price (*actio redhibitoria*) or demand reduction of the purchase price and keep the slave (*actio quanti minoris*). The content of the aedilician edict is described in Ulp. D. 21.1.1.1. See Kaser, Knütel, and Lohsse 2021: 315–16; Zimmermann 1990: 317–18.

[199] Wubbe 1960: 233. Van Hoof (2017: 487) argues that Ulp. D. 20.6.4 pr. may not concern a general pledge at all, since Ulpian does not express how the pledge was granted (specially or generally). The phrase '*cuius res pignori obligatae erant*' in D. 20.6.4 pr. does, however, rather point towards a general (all assets) pledge. Also Pap. D. 20.5.1 simply speaks of a '*pignorum conventionem ad bona debitoris*'.

[200] Wagner 1968: 106; Wubbe 1960: 233–4; Wubbe 2003:174–5.

been returned to the debtor and would be subject to the general pledge.[201] Wubbe even goes so far as to say that because the result reached in D. 20.6.4 pr. is so blatantly inequitable, this text is implausible.[202] The view endorsed by Ulpian may already have been controversial in antiquity. Ulpian calls it the 'better view' ('*magis est*'), which must mean that there were also jurists who were of the opinion that returned slaves could *not* be recovered from their sellers. However, the result is less inequitable than Wagner and Wubbe believe it to be. It is true that if the coins representing the purchase price would still be in the debtor's coffers when the creditor would execute his general pledge, his position would not have worsened when the slave would no longer be charged in his favour.[203] The same would be true if the debtor had used the purchase price to buy another slave, who would then be subject to the general pledge. There are, however, situations where the outcome of the return of a pledged slave is not 'neutral' for the creditor with a general pledge. Slaves were relatively valuable assets, so it is not completely surprising that their return to the seller would require the pledge creditor's express permission.[204] Besides, it was the seller who sold a deficient slave or warranted certain qualities which proved to be absent. This could have contributed to Ulpian's decision to protect the creditor (for whom there would be no special remedies in the aedilician edict).

[201] See Scaev. D. 20.1.34.2. [202] Wubbe 2003: 175.

[203] In theory, the return of the slave could even have improved the creditor's position. If the slave was defective, or lacked certain qualities which the seller had warranted, the purchase price paid by the debtor may very well have been too high. The cancellation of the sale would accomplish that a slave worth, say, 8,000 sesterces would be replaced by a purchase price of, say, 20,000 sesterces.

[204] Wagner (1968: 105) and Schanbacher (1987: 206) interpret this text as requiring the permission for the return of the slave from the creditor with a general pledge. Van Hoof (2017: 487) holds that such permission was not required.

10

Fiscal Privileges and Title Registries

10.1 Introduction

From the second century AD onwards there is an increasing number of cases in which all of someone's assets would be subject to a general right of pledge arising in favour of the imperial treasury. The origin and evolution of these fiscal general pledges are much disputed in modern Romanist literature. One line of scholars (including Dernburg) considers them to be the result of a purely internal Roman legal evolution, while others think that the origins of fiscal general pledges lie in the Hellenistic world. These fiscal general pledges deserve a new, separate monograph, which would take account of recent research on taxation in the Roman empire and its impact on the Roman economy.[1] However, in this book they cannot be completely ignored. First, fiscal general pledges mostly differed from conventional general pledges in their manner of creation: by operation of law rather than by way of *conventio pignoris*.[2] In most respects the scope and legal consequences of these fiscal general pledges were the same as those of conventional general pledges. Accordingly, available sources on fiscal general pledges can also be used in order to reconstruct the law on conventional general pledges. Secondly, fiscal general pledges are said to have undermined the effectiveness of conventional pledges.[3] Any account of the 'adaptedness' of conventional pledges to their economic environment has to consider the impact of the fiscal pledges on the position of private secured creditors, even where this impact cannot yet be fully assessed. For these reasons, this chapter will give an outline of the origins, scope, and legal nature of fiscal general pledges (sections 10.2, 10.3, and 10.4). We will see that fiscal general pledges may not have undermined the effectiveness of the Roman law of real security at all.

[1] Lenz 1994 gives a detailed legal-historical account in German. On taxation in the ancient world, see Monson and Scheidel 2015.

[2] Wagner 1974: 3. Sometimes rights of pledge arose by operation of law in favour of private individuals. Ulp. D. 27 9.3. pr. discusses a right of pledge on land, which had been purchased by a tutor for one of his pupils with another of his pupil's money.

[3] Thus, for the post-classical period (fourth to the sixth centuries AD), Schulz 1951: 403–4 and Kaser 1975: 313.

Security and Credit in Roman Law: The historical evolution of pignus *and* hypotheca. Hendrik L. E. Verhagen, Oxford University Press. © Hendrik L. E. Verhagen 2022. DOI: 10.1093/oso/9780199695836.003.0011

Not only fiscal general pledges but also the lack of publicity significantly contribute to the negative judgment by modern legal historians on the Roman law of real security (section 10.5). In contrast to most modern Western countries, Rome did not have public mortgage registries for *immovable* property that could be consulted by prospective secured creditors in order to determine whether the debtor was the owner of the property and whether other encumbrances had previously been created over the property. Moreover, again in contrast to modern legal systems, Roman law did not recognize a general principle allowing third parties in good faith to rely on possession of *movable* property. In other words, the adverse consequences of lack of publicity were not compensated for by rules protecting *bona fide* third parties. The oldest right *in rem* (nearly) always prevailed and could not be adversely affected by dispositions made without the consent of the oldest title holder.[4] Here also, however, the adverse consequences may have been less devastating than they are often perceived to be in modern literature.

10.2 Origin of Fiscal Pledges

Ptolemaic Egypt knew the *protopraxia* (*πρωτοπραξία*), a preferential right over all the taxable person's assets in favour of the royal treasury. In the first two centuries AD this preferential right was maintained in the Roman province of Egypt. There is even a provincial edict by a Roman prefect on the enforceability of the *protopraxia*. Wieacker in particular has tried to demonstrate that a number of imperial constitutions which seem to be concerned with Roman fiscal pledges were actually concerned with *protopraxia*.[5] According to other Romanists it cannot be proven, and it is unlikely, that an imperial legal pledge evolved from legal institutions from the eastern Mediterranean (which themselves were derived from Hellenistic examples).[6] There are certainly originally Roman legal institutions which can be regarded as forerunners of the late classical fiscal general pledge, but whether they are really its ancestors cannot be proven. The *direct* ancestor of general pledges arising by operation of law in favour of the treasury appears to be the conventional general pledge.

[4] Verhagen 2014: 982.

[5] Wieacker 1939. For example, Ant. C. 4.46.1; Ant. C. 7.73.4; Ant. C. 8.14.1; Ant. C. 8.14.2; Gord. C. 7.73.6; Diocl.-Max. C. 4.15.4. See also Paul. D. 27.9.2; Paul. D. 46.1.68.1; Marci. (Pap.) D. 49.14.18.10; Paul. D. 49.14.47 pr. Contra Wagner 1974: 119–53.

[6] Wagner 1974: 197.

Purely Roman origins?

There are candidates for indigenous Roman ancestors of the fiscal general pledge. One of these ancestors could perhaps have been the *subsignatio praediorum*. Local magistrates would enter into contracts with citizens on tax farming (*publicani*), concessions (e.g., fishery), and contracts for the building of public works. The amounts to be paid for acquiring these contracts from the municipality were often so large that Roman citizens would form partnerships to exploit these contracts with municipalities. The contract itself would, however, be entered into with one partner only (the so-called *manceps*). The Republican state treasury (*aerarium populi Romani*) or local treasuries could also grant loans to individual citizens.[7] In all these cases the contractual counterparty of the state treasury or municipality would be required to grant security in favour of these public creditors.[8] From Puteoli we have an early—second century BC—reference to this legal institution. A document setting out the terms and conditions for public construction contains the following term:

> Lex parieti faciendo in area quae est ante aedem Serapi trans viam: qui redemerit praedes dato praediaque subsignato duumvirum arbitratu.
>
> Contract for making a wall in the area in front of the temple of Serapis across the road. He who acquires (the contract) shall provide *praedes* and register *praedia* as requested by the duumvirs.[9]

In modern literature this special form of (personal and real) security is often referred to as *cautio praedibus praediisque* or 'praediature'.[10] This was not a private law institution but rather a charge arising under public law.[11] Nevertheless, there is an almost perfect analogy with security subject to

[7] Van Gessel 2003: 97, 98; Biscardi 1983: 143–5.

[8] In some municipal laws (prospective) local magistrates are also required to provide security for the return of 'public, sacred or religious money' belonging to the *municipium*. *Lex Tarent.*, Col. I, 10–11 (Crawford 1996: 304); *Lex Col. Gen.* 91, 3–4 (Crawford 1996: 406).

[9] FIRA III, nr. 153. French translation in Van Gessel 2003: 100. Another document from Puteoli is the *Lex locationis de munere publico libitinario*, reproduced in Van Gessel 2003: 101 (with further references). See also *Lex Malac.* 63 and *Lex Irnit.* 63.

[10] Schulz 1951: 412. According to Lenel (1927: 389–90) it appears from the inscription of Gai. D. 23.3.54 that the praetor's edict contained a '*titulus de praediatoribus*', but he considers it impossible to reconstruct its content.

[11] Kaser 1971: 459–60. This is undisputed for *praedia* granted to the Roman people, but less so for *praedia* granted to *municipia*. Van Gessel 2003: 97. For ancient sources mentioning the public nature, see De Iuliis 2017: 8 n 19.

private law. As in private law there is a clear distinction between personal and real security. In all legislative sources the term *praedes* (sing.: *praes*) refers to the persons engaging themselves for someone else's debts to the state or municipality. In the case of tax farming, building contracts, and other commercial contracts, the partners of the citizen who had contracted with the authorities are likely to have acted as such guarantors.[12] The term *praedium* refers to real security (*subsignatio praediorum*),[13] giving the state special rights of recourse against one or more specific immovable properties of the grantor of this form of security. This form of public real security is—like conventional *pignus*—clearly an encumbrance on the property owned by the grantor of this security interest. Like conventional pledges, it would in practice be enforced by selling the charged property, so that the secured debt could be satisfied out of the proceeds of the sale. The earliest surviving municipal laws which mention this form of public charge date from the first two centuries BC. The institution is, however, said to be rooted in practices which already existed for many centuries and which may go back to the beginnings of the Republic.[14] Its continuing use is attested by the sources until the end of the first century AD.[15]

The grantor of this special security interest would remain in possession of the charged real estate, so that we are dealing with an early manifestation of non-possessory security.[16] Although it is not possible to determine whether this security interest has actually contributed to the recognition of the *hypotheca* as a private non-possessory pledge,[17] the *subsignatio praediorum* might historically be related to *pignus*, *hypotheca*, and *fiducia cum creditore*. According to Biscardi, the 'primordial concept' of *obligatio rei* extended not only to *pignus*, *hypotheca*, and *fiducia cum creditore* but also to *praedia subsignata* and other forms of 'real liability' (such as assets sold subject to *lex commissoria* or slaves encumbered with noxal liability).[18] It expresses that a thing is 'liable' for recourse by a creditor. In a document from the first century AD, recording a *fiducia cum creditore* (TH 65), the debtor swears ('*iuravit*') that the mancipated slave girl is 'neither publicly nor privately charged' ('*in publicum privatumve ob[lig]atam esse*'). This could be a reference to publicly

[12] Von Lübtow 1957: 230, with reference to *Lex Malac.* 65 (*praedes socii*) and Cic., *Dom.* 18.48.

[13] In the this book it will usually be referred to as *subsignatio praediorum*. In the *Lex Irnitana* this form of security is called '*obligatio... praediorum*' and the municipal law of Malaga speaks of '*praedia subdita subsignata obligative*'. *Lex Irnit.* 64; *Lex Malac.* 60 and 63.

[14] Van Gessel 2003: 113–14.

[15] Wagner 1974: 9–13; Wieling 1989: 407.

[16] Van Gessel 2003: 115.

[17] See De Iuliis 2017: 7–9.

[18] Biscardi 1991: 114.

charged slaves who were resident on *praedia obligata*.[19] The praediature was, however, not a *general* charge over all the debtor's present and future assets.[20]

Fragmenta de iure fisci

Another potential ancestor is from the Augustan period.[21] The *Fragmenta de iure fisci* (§ 5) contain the following provision:

> Bona e<orum> qui cum fisco contrahun<t>... <leg>e uacuaria [vicesima] velut <pign>oris iure fisco o<bligan>tur, non solum ea q<uae> habent, sed <et> ea quae postea habituri sunt.[22]
>
> The goods of those who contract with the fiscus by the law regarding the *vacua* [*vicesima*] are charged to the fiscus, as it were by right of pledge, not just those which they have, but also those which they will acquire later.[23]

If the reading of '*lege vicesima*' (emendation by Böcking) is correct, the *lex Iulia de vicesima hereditatum* (6 AD) would have introduced a form of fiscal pledge securing the rent payable by tax farmers (*publicani*) for the right to collect inheritance tax.[24] This tax was introduced for the *aerarium militare*, which functioned as a pension fund for veterans. It has, however, been argued that the fragment actually did read '*lege vacuaria*' (not '*lege vicesima*'), which has been connected with a *lex in vacuum vendendis* as appears in the municipal laws of Irni and Malaca.[25] A sale *in vacuum* by local magistrates could take place under more relaxed rules when an execution sale in accordance with the rules for *praedia obligata* failed to produce a purchaser.[26]

The fragment stems from a work from the late classical period and originally it may not have concerned a pledge of all the debtor's assets at all. Wagner holds that the scope of this fiscal pledge was originally confined to tax

[19] Biscardi (1983: 146) concludes from this that not only land and buildings but also movable property (e.g., slaves) could be charged to public bodies by way of *subsignatio*. According to Van Gessel (2003: 116) only real estate could be charged with this form of security. If that were true, the reference in TH 65 to '*in publicum... ob[lig]atam*' could refer to fiscal pledges arising by operation of law.

[20] In the case of personal security, all the *praes*' present and future assets were liable (Wieling 1989: 405). Wieling interprets this as a right of pledge over the *praes's* entire patrimony, in which case this would have been an early example of a general pledge. However, this is more likely to mean nothing more than that all the *praes*' assets would be available for recourse (without preference) by the public authorities as ordinary (non-preferred) creditors.

[21] For a detailed discussion, see Wagner 1974: 7–69.

[22] *Fragmenta de iure fisci*, Fol. I, nr. 5, FIRA II: 628.

[23] Translation by Koops (2012: 298 n 106) with small changes.

[24] Wagner 1974: 68.

[25] For an extensive discussion, see Koops 2012: 297–301.

[26] Koops 2012: 299–301.

farmers' *praedia* and this Augustan statutory pledge may have partly replaced the *subsignatio praediorum*.[27] Its main significance for the history of fiscal pledges is that it is an early example of a right of pledge arising by operation of law in order to safeguard the payment of debts due to the treasury, although not necessarily a general one. Fiscal pledges evolved into general pledges only after conventional general pledges were recognized. In other words, the present text of § 5 of the *Fragmenta de iure fisci*, which refers to all the debtor's present and future goods, only reflects the law as it stood in the high or late classical period.[28]

Mixed origins

On the basis of a detailed comparison of Egyptian sources with imperial constitutions and jurists' writings Wieacker concludes that they 'add up to a closed picture'. The *privilegium (ius) fisci* of imperial law, pursuant to which the debtor's patrimony is liable 'as if it were a pledge' (*veluti pignoris* or *pignoris vice*), corresponds in its scope, ranking, and realization with the *protopraxia*. *Protopraxia*, *privilegium fisci*, *ius fisci*, *veluti pignoris ius*, and *pignoris vice* all are terms for the same phenomenon.[29] This phenomenon is, according to Wieacker, *not* a variety of *pignus*. The *protopraxia* and its west-Roman equivalents differ from *pignus* and *hypotheca* not only in their creation (by operation of law rather than by agreement) but also in their function and substance.[30] The Roman jurists use the images of *veluti pignoris ius* and *pignoris vice* in order to approximate the legal consequences (enforceability against third parties, execution) of the *protopraxia* in terms of Roman private law, whose forms of thinking they had to apply.[31] The main difference between the *protopraxia* and the fiscal privileges of imperial constitutions is that the *protopraxia* could only be enforced against third parties after it was publicized.[32]

The origins of Roman institutions (e.g., *subsignatio praediorum*) and of the *protopraxia* are not necessarily mutually exclusive, but could be cumulative.[33]

[27] Wagner 1974: 27, 62, 68, 196. [28] Wagner 1974: 197: not earlier than 225 AD.

[29] Wieacker 1939: 254. [30] Wieacker 1939: 254.

[31] Wieacker 1939: 255. According to Coriat (1997: 391) in the third century AD the Hellenistic *protopraxia* was introduced as an implied fiscal pledge in the legislation of the Severan emperors. This was yet another example of a provincial custom which Severan legislation turned into an official institution with general application throughout the Roman empire. See also Lenz 1994: 123–4.

[32] Wieacker 1939: 248–9. However, even in the Western legal sources there are occasional references to publicity. See Ulpian D. 49.14.6 pr. discussed in section 10.5.

[33] Coriat 1997: 392.

The oldest forerunner of the fiscal pledge could have been a Greek-Hellenistic institution, but its reception in general imperial law may have benefited from pre-existing Roman institutions.[34] There is, in any case, a remarkable coincidence between the *subsignatio praediorum* and the *protopraxia*. Under both institutions the state's security is made public and the security cannot be enforced against third parties if the assets have been duly conveyed (i.e., without the intention to defraud the state's right of recourse). This similarity could be a consequence of parallel (analogous) evolution, but Wieling considers Roman influence on the *protopraxia* (rather than vice versa) more likely.[35] In his monograph on general pledges arising by operation of law, Wagner holds that the *protopraxia* is a Greco-Egyptian institution which is never mentioned by the Roman jurists and is unlikely to have been received in Roman law. There was, rather, a parallel evolution between the *protopraxia* and the fiscal *ius pignoris*.[36] In the Sulpicii archive, however, there is a (poorly preserved) document which does refer to *protopraxia*. TPSulp 106 from 57 AD seems to concern the auction in Puteoli of a ship from Sidon (Syria) and/or its cargo, with (presumably) local authorities claiming a preferential right in respect of the proceeds.[37] Because of the fragmentary nature of TPSulp 106 we are left in the dark about the legal background of the auction. The word '*avertisset*' can be clearly read and might point at the embezzlement of cargo or the evasion of harbour taxes or customs duties.[38] The document expressly refers to the '*protopraxia*' to which the Puteolean authorities claimed to be entitled according to 'law and custom' ('*protopraxia [e]t ìure ìpso et consue[tu]dine sibì esset*'). The Greek origins of Puteoli and the presence of a Greek community in this city could explain the presence of the *protopraxia* as a local custom of Greek origin, which was later confirmed by Roman magistrates or the Emperor.[39] In a letter to Trajan from 111 AD Plinius refers to the granting of *protopraxia* to local communities in Pontus and Bithynia by the Roman provincial administration.[40] TSulp 106 may thus provide some

[34] Coriat 1997: 392. [35] Wieling 1989: 409. [36] Wagner 1974: 197.

[37] It is unclear why this document is in the Sulpicii archive: perhaps because they were one of the creditors competing for the proceeds of the ship/cargo with the Puteolean authorities? Terpstra (2013: 64 n 45) points out that the date of TPSulp 106 (22 December 57 AD) is somewhat surprising, as it fell well outside the regular sailing season. Terpstra plausibly suggests that this could indicate that the matter had already been dragging on for several months.

[38] Terpstra 2013: 64, who rightly notes that *avertire* often points in the direction of fraudulent acts and theft (Alf. D. 19.2.31; Ulp. D. 14.4.7.3; Ulp. D. 47.4.1.13; Ulp. D. 47.20.3.1).

[39] Less likely is that a local authority from Sidon exercised in Puteoli a *protopraxia* which originated under local Syrian law.

[40] See Wieacker 1939: 237, who refers to Plin., *Ep.* 10.109. See also, from the late third century (293 AD) a constitution from Diocletian (C. 8.44.23) on what must have been a *protopraxia* for the benefit of the *res publica Thessalonicensium* (Wagner 1974: 85–7) and Pap. D. 42.5.37 on the right of the city of

support to Wieacker's theory that Roman fiscal pledges find their origin in the Hellenistic *protopraxia*. The presence of this fiscal preference on Roman soil may have caused the Roman state or local municipalities to introduce similar local fiscal preferences, which together with indigenous Roman institutions (*subsignatio praediorum* and the statutory pledge of the *Fragmenta de iure fisci*) contributed to the 'gene pool' from which fiscal general pledges evolved.

Fiscal and conventional general pledges

From the second century AD onwards there is an increasing number of cases in which all of someone's assets would be subject to a general right of pledge arising in favour of the imperial treasury.[41] In this century and the next one the *fiscus Caesaris* evolved into a separate bureaucracy,[42] employing many functionaries, who were involved with the extensive financial activities of the Roman state.[43] The public interest was deemed to be best served with granting the treasury preferential rights against the assets of its debtors, both taxable persons and ordinary debtors (e.g. borrowers, tax farmers). There was a close relationship between fiscal and conventional general pledges, and the borderline between the two cannot always be sharply drawn. The general pledges arising by operation of law for the benefit of the imperial treasury appear to have evolved from 'tacit' pledges, which in their turn evolved from express contractual provisions on general pledge. In particular, where the imperial treasury would enter into ordinary contracts (e.g., loan agreements) with citizens, a conventional right of pledge would be granted to the treasury. In one of the first opinions on the general pledge (Scaev. D. 20.4.21 pr.) someone had borrowed money from the imperial treasury and had expressly pledged all his present and future goods to it.[44] In imperial constitutions fiscal pledges were sometimes *deemed* to be granted conventionally. A constitution by Caracalla from 214 AD (C. 8.14.2) deals with a general pledge securing

Antioch to enforce a pledge ('*ius persequendi pignoris*') pursuant to a '*privilegium*' existing under its own law ('*lege sua*') in respect of the assets of a deceased person.

[41] The earliest direct witnesses of fiscal general pledges in the *Corpus iuris civilis* are rescripts from Caracalla (e.g., Ant. C. 8.14.1 (213 AD)) and *responsa* from Papinian (e.g., Ulp. (Pap.) D. 49.14.28). Decisions by Septimius Severus on what must have been fiscal general pledges are reported by Paul, such as 'Moschis's case' (Paul. D. 49.14.47 pr.) discussed later in this chapter.

[42] In addition to the imperial *fiscus*, there were also other fiscs and treasuries (e.g. *aerarium Saturni*). For the purpose of this chapter I will use 'treasury' as the generic term. On the legal personality of the *fiscus Caesaris*, see Lenz 1994: 6–11; Koops 2012: 280.

[43] Lenz 1994: 3–11; Koops 2012: 279–81.

[44] See also Alex. C. 7.73.3. See Wieling 1989: 411.

contracts entered into between the treasury and ordinary citizens.[45] A general right of pledge does arise, according to the constitution, even if it has not been expressly agreed. This suggests that it was deemed to have been impliedly agreed: the general pledge arising in favour of the treasury is constructed as a fictitious conventional general pledge over all the debtor's assets.[46] This implied contract construction may very well have been used with a view to the *actio Serviana*, whose *formula* did, after all, require '*convenisse*'.[47] This does not appear to be, however, an invention by Caracalla's chancery. The words '*certum est*' in C. 8.14.2 could indicate that the implied fiscal pledge was already a settled institution at the time this constitution was issued.[48] The reference in C. 8.14.2 to a pledge which had been expressly granted may also have had a similar function as in Gai. D. 20.1.15.1 for conventional general pledges.[49] There, because the legal status of the general pledge was not yet fully settled, the parties stated that generally pledged goods would be treated in the same manner as specifically pledged goods.[50] Besides, for a general pledge securing contractual debts vis-à-vis the treasury a contractual analogy for the granting of the pledge suggests itself easier than for a tax debt: in Caracalla's constitution from the year before (C. 8.14.1) the fiction of an implied contract is not used for tax debts.[51] One cannot even rule out entirely that fiscal privileges were not descendants of actual rights of *pignus* or *hypotheca* at all, but were rather analogous 'pledge-like' rights of recourse, whose content and enforcement were subject to the same rules as applicable to conventional pledges.[52]

10.3 Fiscal Privileges: Third-party Effect

Legal rules which were developed for the ranking and execution of conventional pledges were applicable—as it were by cross-reference—to pledges or 'pledge-like' rights which arose by operation of law.[53] The fiscal general

[45] Wagner 1974: 76–83.

[46] Wagner 1974: 83, 197; Fuenteseca 2013: 83.

[47] Wagner 1974: 81–3, 197–8.

[48] Wieling argues that the fiscal pledge already had found its place in the *Edictum perpetuum* around 130 AD. According to Wieling (1989, 412) this is 'proven' by the fact that Ulpian refers to fiscal pledges in his commentary on the edict (Ulp. D. 49.14.6).

[49] See p. 280.

[50] For a similar suggestion, see Wagner 1974: 81.

[51] Wagner 1974: 100. Wagner (1974: 92) considers Sev.-Ant. C. 7.8.2 (undated; according to Wagner: 209 AD) as the first imperial constitution on fiscal general pledges arising by operation of law.

[52] Kaser 1971: 468 and Kaser 1975: 316 n 12 speak of a 'pledge-like right of recourse' ('*Pfandähnliches Zugriffsrecht*').

[53] See, for example, the following constitutions by Caracalla: C. 7.73.3 ('*pignoris iure fisco teneantur*'); C. 7.73.4 ('*pignoris iure fisco potuerunt obligari*'); C. 8.14.1 ('*vice pignorum tributis obligata sunt*');

pledges were also in other respects subject to the same principles and rules as conventional general pledges, in particular the enforceability against third parties. A plausible interpretation of the fiscal general pledges appearing in second- and third-century AD imperial constitutions and jurists' writings is that as long as they paid their taxes properly, debtors could freely dispose of their assets.[54] The treasury could only recover assets from third parties which had been transferred by debtors after they ceased to pay taxes when due or in order to defraud the treasury.[55]

Third-party effect in jurisprudence and imperial constitutions

The objects of fiscal general pledges were defined in exactly the same manner as those of conventional pledges: not just those goods which fiscal debtors currently have but also those which they will acquire later. These fiscal general pledges mainly differed from conventional general pledges in their manner of creation: (certainly for tax debts) by operation of law rather than by way of *conventio pignoris*.[56] They were otherwise largely subject to the same principles and rules as conventional general pledges. For example, Pap. D. 50.15.5.2 refers to an execution sale of land for failure to pay direct taxes ('*tributi*'), which takes place pursuant to right of pledge ('*iure pignoris distrahitur*'). In Alex. C. 8.45.1 pr. (223 AD) the emperor rules that where 'my *procurator*', because of debts owed to the treasury, sells land which has been charged ('*praedium obligatum*'), there shall be no liability for eviction. The constitution justifies this on the analogy of an execution sale by a private pledge creditor, who is only liable for eviction where this has been expressly promised by way of stipulation.

A constitution by Caracalla from 215 AD is concerned with the recovery by the treasury from someone who purchased land from the debtor.

C. 8.14.2 ('*veluti pignoris titulo obligari*'). See also: Paul. D. 27.9.2 ('*ius pignoris*'); Paul. D. 40.1.10 ('*iure pignoris*'); Herm. D. 49.14.46.3 ('*ius pignorum*').

[54] Modern literature is divided. Wagner (1974: 161) calls it (with reference to Wubbe) a 'false perception' that objects which the debtor has transferred to third parties are no longer charged in favour of the treasury. Medicus (1976: 429) observes that while for special pledges limitless third-party effects would be acceptable, for general pledges this could hardly be maintained, because it would prevent the debtor from disposing of any of his assets. For this reason, Medicus considers it plausible that—within certain limits (e.g., the ordinary course of business)—the debtor could freely dispose of generally pledged assets which were charged in favour of the treasury.

[55] Paul. D. 49.14.45 pr.

[56] Wagner 1974: 3.

Ant. C. 7.73.4. Si debitor, cuius fundum fuisse et ipse confiteris, prius eum distraxit, quam fisco aliquid debuit, inquietandum te non esse procurator meus cognoscet. nam etsi postea debitor extitit, non ideo tamen ea, quae de dominio eius excesserunt, pignoris iure fisco potuerunt obligari.

If the debtor whose land it was, as you yourself admit, sold it (to you) before he owed anything to the treasury, my procurator will find that you should not be disturbed. For although he became its debtor subsequently, that is no reason why things that had passed from his ownership should have been charged by way of pledge to the treasury.

The constitution rules that land sold and transferred by someone, who at the time of this transaction did not owe anything to the treasury, cannot be recovered for debts incurred afterwards. Although the constitution does not say this in so many words, it would seem to imply that a *fundus* sold and conveyed by someone *after* he had incurred a debt towards the treasury would be charged with a fiscal pledge and could be recovered from the purchaser. This position is taken, in any case, by the imperial chancery under Septimius Severus. The following text is taken from Paul's *Decreta*, a collection of imperial judgments reported by the late classical jurist Paul.[57]

D. 49.14.47 pr. *Paulus libro primo decretorum*. Moschis quaedam, fisci debitrix ex conductione vectigalis, heredes habuerat, a quibus post aditam hereditatem Faria Senilla et alii praedia emerant. cum convenirentur propter Moschidis reliqua et dicebant heredes Moschidis idoneos esse et multos alios ex isdem bonis emisse, aequum putavit imperator prius heredes conveniri debere, in reliquum possessorem omnem: et ita pronuntiavit.

A certain Moschis, who owed money to the imperial treasury arising from the farming of a *vectigal*, had left heirs from whom, after they had entered on their inheritance, Faria Senilla and others had bought landed estates. When they were sued over the arrears left by Moschis, they alleged both that Moschis' heirs were solvent and that many others had bought from the same estate; the emperor thought it right that the heirs ought first to be sued, and thereafter every person in possession for the balance; and he gave judgment accordingly.

[57] See on this important work, Daalder 2018. On D. 49.14.47 pr.—'Moschis's case'—see Koops 2012; Daalder 2018: 519–31.

Moschis had rented the right from the treasury to collect a certain tax (*vectigal*).[58] When she died Moschis still owed money to the treasury pursuant to this tax farming contract. For this the treasury tried to take recourse against pieces of land sold by Moschis's heirs to a woman called Faria Senilla and other purchasers. The emperor ruled that the treasury should first proceed against the heirs of Moschis and that only for the remaining debt recourse could be taken against third parties in possession of property formerly owned by Moschis. This imperial ruling reported by Paul assumes that the treasury did have a general right of pledge (or similar right of recourse), which was enforceable against purchasers of the debtor's property. The interests of third parties in possession ('*omnis possessor*') are taken into account, in the sense that the treasury can only recover the assets from possessors to the extent that the heirs of the treasury's debtor fail to pay the fiscal debt.[59]

Another instance of third-party effect can be found in a constitution from 240 AD by Gordianus. It concerns a case in which a debtor of the treasury had 'given (a) possession' ('*possessionem dedisse*') to his daughter upon her marriage.[60] The constitution holds that in the exercise of the '*ius fisci*' the *procurator* can recover the possession from the daughter. The '*iure pignoris revocare*' is in all likelihood a reference to the *actio Serviana*.[61] This constitution could then be interpreted as ruling that the treasury could enforce its fiscal pledge against someone to whom the debtor had transferred ownership of one of his assets.[62] However, in Gordian C. 7.73.6 the transfer to a third party was one by way of gift. Legal systems (including Roman law) generally are less prone to protect donees than persons who have paid for the acquisition of ownership or a subordinate right *in rem*.[63] Gordian's constitution has been connected in modern literature with his reform of creditors' protection measures. It has also been linked with the idiosyncrasies of proceedings with the *procurator*, who not only was a manager of the treasury's patrimony but could also be a judge in fiscal matters. This could have entailed special legal consequences for the preservation of security rights.[64]

[58] The debtor of the imperial treasury may well have been Numitoria Moschis, whose (second) husband, Lucius Graecius Constans, a tribune in the praetorian guard, erected a memorial for her in a small town near Hadrian's Villa in Tivoli. See the inscription reproduced in CIL XIV, 3626. Koops 2012: 285–7.

[59] Koops 2012: 288–94, who also discusses other interpretations.

[60] Gord. C. 7.73.6.

[61] Wagner 1974: 125.

[62] Wieacker 1939: 243.

[63] See Paul. D. 49.14.45 pr.

[64] Wagner 1974: 127.

Evaluation

Fiscal pledges could therefore—in certain circumstances—be enforced against purchasers of the debtor's assets. It is possible, however, to reconcile Moschis's case with the nature of the general pledge as a 'floating charge', which allowed the debtor to dispose of her assets until an event of default or similar event had occurred. First of all, the sale of Moschis's land took place after she died: it was not the debtor herself who disposed of her assets, but her heirs had sold the land to third parties. The debtor's power to dispose of her assets free from the fiscal charge would, as we have seen in other contexts, meet its natural end upon her death.[65] Secondly, there is a parallel with the termination of the tenant's authority to manumit slaves pledged as *invecta et illata* when the landlord exercises his right of lock-out for payment default.[66] Likewise, only transfers of Moschis's lands which had taken place after she had defaulted in the payment of the rents for the vectigals may have been affected by the treasury's right of recovery. The constitution from Caracalla cited earlier (C. 7.73.4) implies that a fiscal pledge will only come into existence if and when the debtor actually 'owes something to the fiscus'.[67] Two other constitutions from Caracalla—C. 8.14.1 and C. 4.46.1—can be interpreted as reflecting the 'differing intensity' of the fiscal security interest before and after the debtor's payment default of fiscal debts.[68] Before default, the treasury would have a 'latent preferential right of recourse', which would not disrupt the free circulation of goods and would not prevent private creditors from enforcing their rights of pledge.[69] The third-party effect given to a fiscal pledge in Gordian C. 7.73.6 did concern a gift and may also have been linked to the idiosyncrasies of proceedings with the *procurator*.

10.4 Ranking of Fiscal Privileges

The ranking of general pledges arising in favour of the treasury would be determined by the *prior tempore* principle. The priority of both conventional and fiscal general pledges was generally determined with reference to the time at which they came into existence. Nevertheless, if the priority of fiscal pledges would be determined by the first time a person became taxable for the tax

[65] Cf. for generic pledges: Scaev. D. 20.1.34 pr. and Scaev. D. 20.1.32. [66] See section 9.7.
[67] Ant. C. 7.73.4 ('*quam fisco aliquid debuit*'). [68] Klingenberg 1992: 387.
[69] Klingenberg 1992: 387.

concerned—by entry in a *census* register—fiscal pledges would already arise at an early stage and outrank subsequent pledges granted to private creditors. This is particularly relevant for so-called direct taxes (*tributa*). However, there is good evidence supporting the hypothesis that not only for so-called indirect taxes (*vectigalia*) but also for direct taxes the priority would be determined with reference to the time at which the specific tax debt for which the fiscal pledge was enforced actually fell due.[70] To this it can be added that *tributa* would only be levied in the provinces, so that fiscal pledges securing these taxes could not have adversely affected secured finance transactions in important commercial and financial places such as Rome, Puteoli, and Ostia. Most importantly, if Keith Hopkins is right in that even in the late Empire tax pressure was low,[71] fiscal general pledges may not have been seriously disruptive at all. In particular where the fiscal debt was relatively small and there was much surplus value in the charged property, even a second-ranking conventional pledge would have been an attractive option for private creditors. In the late classical period however, the secured position of a private creditor could sometimes have been adversely affected by fiscal pledges arising after the private pledge had been granted.

Fiscal privileges subject to *prior tempore* principle

From a constitution by Caracalla it appears that where a private creditor accepted a pledge of a piece of land which was already pledged to the imperial treasury, the earlier fiscal pledge prevailed over the later conventional pledge.[72] There is, therefore, no doubt that fiscal general pledges could also be invoked against private pledge creditors. The ranking of the fiscal pledge would be determined by the priority principle, which equally applied to fiscal pledges and conventional pledges.[73] There is an (undated) constitution by Caracalla which has been interpreted in modern literature as granting priority to fiscal claims over any claim by (secured and unsecured) private creditors, even claims secured by older rights of pledge.[74]

Ant. C. 4.46.1. Venditionem ob tributorum cessationem factam revocari non oportet neque priore domino pretium offerente neque creditore eius

[70] Ant. C. 4.46.1. [71] Hopkins 1980: 116–20. See more recently Bransbourg 2014.
[72] Ant. C. 7.73.2. [73] Wagner 1974: 202; Wieling 1989: 418.
[74] Frezza 1963: 254; Klingenberg 1992: 386, 391.

> iure hypothecae sive pignoris. potior est enim causa tributorum, quibus priore loco omnia cessantis obligata sunt.
>
> A sale made on account of a failure to pay taxes must not be revoked, either when the previous owner offers the price or when his creditor does so using the right of a hypothec or a pledge. For the claim for the tributes, for which all the property of the person in default has been charged with priority, takes precedence.

The creditor to whom the owner had granted a right of pledge could not recover the property from the purchaser, who had purchased it at an execution sale organized by the treasury.[75] The fiscal privilege prevailed over the conventional pledge, so that also the purchaser's position was stronger.[76] But would this always have been the case? C. 4.46.1 does *not* say, as a general rule, that fiscal privileges always prevail over private security interests. If that had been the intention, the constitution could have sufficed with '*potior est enim causa tributorum*'. The preference of the fiscal privilege is justified by the constitution's subordinate clause: '*quibus priore loco omnia cessantis obligata sunt*'.[77] This indicates that a fiscal pledge only took preference over a conventional pledge of private creditors if the debtor's patrimony was already charged in favour of the treasury when the conventional pledge was granted. In other words, in accordance with the *prior tempore* principle, fiscal pledges were only preferred if they were older than conventional pledges.[78]

In Moschis's case (D. 49.14.47 pr.) it was held that the treasury did have a general right of pledge (or similar right of recourse) against a tax farmer, which was enforceable against subsequent purchasers of that debtor's property.[79] The interests of third parties in possession (which would also include creditors with a possessory pledge) were taken into account, however, in the sense that the treasury should first proceed against the (heirs of the) debtor. Only when the fiscal debt could not be recovered from the debtor's inheritance could the treasury recover assets from third parties. Another example of a mitigation of the consequences of fiscal pledges for creditors with a right of pledge is recorded in Paul. D. 49.14.21. A creditor had to repay a sum of money to the treasury, which had been paid by a debtor of the treasury in order to discharge a debt secured by a right of pledge. Paul agrees with an

[75] According to Wagner (1974: 105–6) '*revocari*' refers to an *actio Serviana* instituted by the ordinary creditor with a conventional right of pledge.

[76] See for conventional pledges Val.-Gal. C. 8.17.6.

[77] Wagner 1974: 103.

[78] Wagner 1974: 103–4. See also Kaser 1971: 466 n 36, 468; Kaser 1975: 231 n 38.

[79] D. 49.14.47 pr. has been discussed in more detail in section 10.3.

opinion by Marcellus that if the treasury recovers what has been paid to a secured creditor, the right of pledge is not extinguished. The secured creditor is not directly safeguarded against the fiscal privilege but is protected in the sense that a vitiated payment of the secured debt does not extinguish his right of pledge.[80]

Prior tempore and fiscal debts

But how did one apply the priority principle to fiscal pledges securing tax debts? Ant. C. 7.73.4 implies that a fiscal pledge will only come into existence if and when the debtor actually 'owes something to the treasury' ('*quam fisco aliquid debuit*'). One possibility would be that the ranking of these fiscal pledges would be determined with reference to the time at which the tax debt actually fell due. This would certainly be the case for so-called indirect taxes (*vectigalia*), such as inheritance tax, manumission tax, and custom duties (*portoria*), which were raised on occasion.[81] In particular in the case of so-called direct taxes (*tributa*), such as land tax (*tributum soli*) and poll tax (*tributum capitis*), this could have been different. These *tributa* were calculated on the basis of *census* lists. There is an imperial constitution of Caracalla, cited earlier, from which it could be deduced that fiscal general pledges securing these direct taxes already came into existence once tax debtors were assessed for taxation.[82] For fiscal pledges securing these direct taxes the priority principle may have entailed that their priority would be determined by the first time a person was registered in a *census* list, rather than with reference to the time at which the specific tax debt for which the fiscal pledge was enforced fell due.[83] This could have adversely affected borrowers' ability to obtain secured credit, as the treasury's security would *de facto* take priority over any security later granted to private creditors. The constitution of Caracalla C. 4.46.1, however, rather suggests that the priority of fiscal pledges securing indirect taxes (*tributa*) would be determined by the point in time at which the taxable person failed to pay them when due ('*tributorum cessationem*').

[80] See for an analysis of D. 49.14.21, Wagner 1974: 127–31; Lenz 1994: 69–71.

[81] Günther 2016. [82] C. 8.14.1 ('*eorum qui censentur*').

[83] Wieling 1989: 428; Klingenberg 1992: 359. Wieling (followed by Klingenberg 1992) sees an analogy with Afr. D. 20.4.9 pr., which says that the priority of a tenant's pledge is determined by the point in time that the lease agreement is entered into, and not by the time the lease rentals actually fall due. Also, the priority of a right of pledge securing future interest payments is determined by the point in time at which the pledge was granted rather than by that at which the interest becomes due and payable (Scaev. D. 20.4.18).

In Scaev. D. 20.4.21 pr. the treasury's pledge was still regarded as being subject to the *prior tempore* principle, but this text concerns two ordinary conventional pledges on all the debtor's assets, the first one granted by him for his obligations as tutor vis-à-vis his pupil and the second one in order to secure a loan received by him from the treasury. In Scaev. D. 20.4.21.1 the lender's right of pledge even prevailed over the treasury's privilege (which may have been a tenant's pledge for the letting of the warehouse), although the fiscal privilege seems to have originated earlier. The priority of the lender may here be explained by the fact that he financed the purchase of the pledged marble slabs. In classical law 'purchase money lenders' had priority over other secured creditors, irrespective of the time at which their security came into existence.[84] In other respects too, fiscal pledges were treated in accordance with the same principles and rules governing conventional pledges. Thus we have seen that in Paul. D. 40.1.10 the manumission of generally pledged slaves could be objected not only against private creditors (e.g., Marci. D. 40.8.6) but also against the treasury.[85] The fact that fiscal pledges originated from conventional pledges may be largely responsible for their equal treatment.[86]

The tide changes

In Marci. D. 42.5.34 the tide appears to have changed. The late classical jurist Marcianus holds that the treasury's preference prevails over the *privilegium* of someone who financed the construction, purchase or equipment of a ship. It is not exactly clear whether the treasury's privilege antedated the financier's privilege, but this may very well have been the case.[87] For purchase money lenders an exception to the *prior tempore* principle would no longer be made: the treasury's privilege would rank ahead of the preferential right of someone who had financed the ship. In addition, in some other cases fiscal pledges prevailed over earlier rights of pledge.[88] Where Scaev. D. 20.4.21 pr. still holds that the (conventional) general pledge which first came into existence

84 Ulp. D. 20.4.5; Ulp. D. 20.4.7. See Frezza 1963: 257–62; Van Hoof 2015: 19–20; Van Hoof 2022. An alternative interpretation is that the lender did have a possessory pledge. The construction of such a possessory pledge may have been the same as the one used in TPSulp 45 and 46: the lender rented the space in the warehouse formerly rented by the debtor. See also Du Plessis 2012: 183–4. This could explain why the lender's pledge prevailed. The marble slabs would then not be *invecta et illata* present in premises rented *by the borrower*.

85 See p. 307–9. Also in other areas (e.g., set-off, liability of sureties) the emperors, the Severi in particular, treated the treasury on the same footing as private creditors. See Daalder 2018: 441–2.

86 Daalder 2018: 441–2.

87 In this sense Wieling 1989: 433.

88 Kaser 1971: 468. See also Kaser 1975: 316 n 1.

prevailed over a more recent fiscal pledge, in Ulp. (Pap.) D. 49.14.28 the imperial treasury's preferential right of recourse over an after-acquired asset was granted preference over an anterior general pledge created by the debtor in favour of a private individual.[89] Another exception to the applicability of the *prior tempore* principle to fiscal pledges was the statutory general pledge against the assets of a *primipilus*. This official had the duty of conveying goods received by way of tax in his province to the treasury for the benefit of the army. In a constitution from 287 AD Diocletian rules that 'the public welfare must take precedence over private contracts'. Therefore, a woman can only claim property pledged to her for her dowry by a *primipilus* if it is determined that the treasury has been satisfied.[90] The potential threat of fiscal privileges to the effectiveness of conventional rights of pledge is illustrated by texts witnessing agreements between debtors and creditors concerning the payment of taxes.[91] The creditor who was liable to pay taxes, or who was confronted with an action for recovery of the pledged land instituted by the treasury, could not invoke the agreement with the debtor as a defence.[92]

10.5 Title Registries

Roman fiscal pledges were not registered in a public register. This increased the chance that ordinary creditors would be granted a pledge on property that was already charged to the treasury. The same lack of publicity was inherent to conventional pledges. Certainly when it was accepted that non-possessory pledges could be granted *nuda conventione*, and later even by way of a general pledge, secured creditors could be confronted with earlier charges. In addition, the risk existed that debtors lacked the power to grant a pledge because they (whether or not fraudulently) charged property they did not own. There was no simple and reliable method available for a creditor in order to check whether the real estate offered by his debtor as security was owned by him and was without previous encumbrances. This was not compensated for by rules protecting *bona fide* third parties. In Roman Egypt a property registry for public and private entitlements did exist. In the western part of the Roman empire, there were criminal sanctions, social norms, and practices

[89] On this interesting text, in which Ulpian restates an opinion by Papinian, see Wieacker 1939: 247; Wagner 1974: 180–92; Wieling 1989: 425–7.

[90] Diocl. C. 12.62.3 ('*Utilitas publica praeferenda est privatorum contractibus*').

[91] For example, Ulp. D. 2.14.52.2.

[92] Pap. D. 2.14.42.

which would in many cases have prevented debtors from granting security over previously charged assets or assets they did not own. For a long time they may have been effective, although the late classical period shows symptoms of them malfunctioning.

Title registries in the Roman empire

In Egypt the Romans introduced in the first century AD a new registration system for the most valuable assets (real estate and slaves): the 'archive of acquisitions' (*βιβλιοθήκη ἐγκτήσεων*).[93] In particular, one concern of the Romans was to prevent that dispositions were made of land, houses, and slaves by persons without title.[94] However, the archive also recorded security interests, so that potential purchasers or secured creditors could see whether the property had been previously charged.[95] Von Woess and more recently Lerouxel have stressed the high quality and accessibility of the archive.[96] Lerouxel even considers the creation of the archive a 'pivotal moment' in the history of the private credit market in Roman Egypt, causing a 'tremendous growth' in the number of secured loans and the amounts loaned out by private parties.[97] The Romans must have been aware—in the first century AD—that the registry they created for Egypt had been very beneficial for the availability of credit. Is it too speculative to conclude from this that they would surely have set up similar registries in the city of Rome if their own law of real security was, because of lack of registries, so poorly adapted to the needs of the financial world? After all, the registration of charges of real estate was not a phenomenon completely unknown to Roman Italy.[98] We have seen that in the Republic when citizens entered into certain contracts with the state treasury or with local municipalities, they might be required to grant a special security interest over real estate in favour of these bodies: *subsignatio*

[93] See in particular Lerouxel 2016: 152–92. See also Pellecchi 2018: 481–2.

[94] Von Woess 1924: 29.

[95] Von Woess 1924: 3–4. A papyrus discovered in Oxyrhynchos records an ordinance dating from 89 AD by Mettius Rufus, prefect of Egypt. One of the provisions of this ordinance reads as follows: 'Therefore I command that all owners shall register their property at the record-office within six months, and all lenders the mortgages that they hold, and other persons the claims which they possess.' FIRA I, nr. 60 (P. Oxy. II 237): translation by Bowman and Wilson 2009: 40.

[96] Von Woess 1924: 31; Lerouxel 2012: 967–8.

[97] Lerouxel 2015: 178.

[98] See also Lerouxel 2016: 279. For a detailed comparison of publicity in Campania and in Roman Egypt, see Lerouxel 2016: 267–89. Lerouxel (2016: 287) concludes that the system of publicity of the archive of acquisition was '*incontestiblement supérieur*' to that of Campania.

praediorum.[99] This form of security was created by a special declaration of the owner of the estate (*subsignatio*), which was registered in the records of the state (*tabulae publicae*) or of the municipality (*tabulae communes*).[100] As Schulz observed, 'whenever we cross the boundary of private law we enter a new world: we find documents, registration and publicity, phenomena which were entirely foreign to classical private law'.[101] Another form of security granted over real estate to public bodies is recorded in the so-called *tabulae alimentariae*.[102] In the second century AD the imperial treasury granted loans secured by a pledge over real estate, with the intention that the interest generated by these loans was for the benefit of children in need. The secured loans were recorded in a document containing the names of the borrowers, descriptions of the real estate, the amounts of the loans, and the rates of interest, all of which were stored in public archives.[103] For taxation purposes, registries of land in the *census* existed from the time of August.[104]

A puzzling question is why the Romans did introduce a property registry for public and private entitlements in Egypt, but failed to do so in their home territory.[105] In Egypt the Romans built upon existing registration systems set up and operated under the Ptolemies.[106] The costs of building upon existing registration systems, including a body of professionals (notaries) experienced in executing and registering transaction documents, may be considerably lower than setting up an entirely new system.[107] Also the Romans' desire to get a grip on property and commercial relationships in their new province may have played a role, in particular with a view to taxation. Another reason, however, is more of a cultural nature and may be that Roman citizens would consider it an unacceptable infringement upon their privacy if third parties could see whether their property had been charged for indebtedness.[108] In the republican period Tiberius Gracchus's attempt to set up land registries was never carried out to completion and (with other archives) were a 'subject of

[99] See also section 10.2. For a comparison of the *subsignatio praediorum* and the archive of acquisitions, see Lerouxel 2016: 272–80.

[100] Crawford 1996: 302. [101] Schulz 1951: 412–13. [102] Criniti 1991.

[103] Wenger 1953: 761–6.

[104] That such registers could also be relevant in property disputes between private parties is demonstrated by Pap. D. 10.1.11, where it is observed that in boundary disputes, when there are no 'old records' ('*vetera monumenta*'), one should follow the most recent registration by the tax authorities (*census*).

[105] According to Arruñada 2020: 262, the costs of archiving should not have been a serious obstacle for creating property registries.

[106] Von Woess 1924: 28.

[107] Lerouxel 2012: 958 writes: '*À l'époque romaine, l'Égypte est donc une grande terre de notariat et elle a atteint un haut degré de culture pratique de l'écrit.*'

[108] Von Woess 1924: 30. See also Moatti 2015: 128–31. For a different view, see Arruñada 2020: 268.

antagonism and altercation.'[109] A lesser degree of social cohesion in Roman Egypt than in Rome may also provide (part of) the explanation. As will be discussed shortly, an important reason why no title registries were set up in Rome and why no principle protecting third parties in good faith evolved in Roman law is likely to have been that in the Republic and for much of the Principate social norms (e.g., *amicitia*) generally provided safeguards against a defrauding debtor who charged someone else's property or failed to disclose an earlier charge.[110] These social norms may not have been as stringently observed in Roman Egypt, where the population was largely non-Roman.[111]

Registration of *protopraxia* and fiscal pledges

An edict promulgated in 68 AD by the prefect of Egypt, Tiberius Alexander, provides that the *protopraxia* can only be enforced against third parties (e.g., purchasers or pledge creditors) if the liability of the debtor's patrimony vis-à-vis the state has been made known to the public.[112] This could take place by public announcement, by entry into the treasury's debtors' register or by entry into the archive of acquisitions (*βιβλιοθήκη ἐγκτήσεων*). In other words, only those third parties who had been warned could be confronted with the state's preferential rights.[113] Tiberius Alexander's edict has been linked to a text by Ulpian.[114] The facts of the case discussed by this late classical jurist were that the treasury had succeeded in a claim which originally belonged to a private creditor. The question whether the treasury for this claim can exercise its *privilegium* is, as Ulpian lets us know, answered differently in rescripts. Ulpian himself is of the opinion that the fiscal privilege only applied from the moment at which the claim is registered in the debtors' register. This in all likelihood was a register kept by the treasury in which (defaulting) debtors were registered and which must have been available for inspection by the

[109] Moatti 2015: 123–4, 131.

[110] For example, Pap. D. 46.3.97: 'Where a debtor under several heads pays money in the absence of any specification, it will be attributed first to the debt due under threat of infamy; then, to that due under penalty; third, to that contracted under hypothec or pledge; after this order of priority, preference is given to one's own debt rather than that contracted for another, for example, as surety. The early jurists so laid down the order because it appeared the probability that a prudent and alert debtor would so have conducted his business.' See also Harris 2011: 230; Ioannatou 2004.

[111] Lerouxel (2012: 946, 967–76) argues that the interaction between the private credit market and the finance of state expenditures may explain why the archive was created. These funding techniques were, however, not unique for Roman Egypt, as Lerouxel also notices.

[112] FIRA I, nr. 58. [113] Wieling 1989: 408. [114] D. 49.14.6 pr.

public.[115] Before the claim transferred to the treasury, any purchaser from the debtor would acquire the purchased property free from the charge (unless it had been conventionally pledged to another creditor). This would be different, however, where at the time of the purchase the treasury was a 'direct' creditor of the seller (e.g., taxes, loan by the treasury). Now all the seller's assets would be subject to a general charge arising by operation of law. This must already have adversely affected commercial intercourse. This would have become even more disrupted if the fiscal preference could also be enforced against third parties for claims which were originated by private creditors and had subsequently been acquired by the treasury, for instance through assignment or inheritance. It appears from Ulpian's opinion that in imperial rescripts different positions had been taken as to whether third parties should be protected. Ulpian's view is that they should be. His position entails that a prospective purchaser can inspect the treasury's debtors' register in order to examine whether the seller is a defaulting debtor of claims owed to the treasury. If the transferred claim is not entered into this register, the purchaser can be sure that the purchased property will not be charged with a fiscal charge on account of claims originated by private creditors which had transferred to the treasury.[116]

Ulpian's opinion could point towards an influence of provincial law (Egypt) on the law of the empire (*Reichsrecht*). It should be noted, however, that this protection of bona fide third parties does not apply to debts originated by the treasury itself (e.g., taxes, loans by the treasury). Unlike under Tiberius Alexander's edict for Roman Egypt, in the western part of the Roman empire publicity was not a general requirement for the third-party effect of fiscal pledges. There is, therefore, a sharp contrast between Tiberius Alexander's general concern that only those third parties who had been warned could be confronted with the state's preferential rights and the incidental protection of third parties in good faith in Ulpian's opinion.[117] In Roman Egypt publicity was adequately taken care of (in particular: registration in the archive of acquisitions), while in Rome publicity would only be relevant in marginal cases. Even for these marginal cases some imperial constitutions must have refused to protect third parties in good faith, as can be inferred from Ulpian's reference to differing rescripts. It is truly remarkable that where in Roman Egypt the public authorities were actively engaged with reforming the

[115] For Roman Egypt (Tib. Alexander's edict), Wieacker 1939: 227. According to Wagner (1974: 118) it cannot be proven that only defaulting debtors were registered.

[116] Wieling 1989: 421–2. [117] Wieling 1989: 408.

institutional framework through publicity measures in order to protect commercial and financial intercourse,[118] this was only of marginal significance for the western part of the Roman empire. Thus, a constitution by Caracalla from 215 AD implies that land sold (and conveyed) by a tax debtor *after* he had incurred a (contractual or tax debt) towards the treasury will be charged with a fiscal pledge and can be recovered from the purchaser. There is no mention at all that recovery by the treasury from purchasers of generally pledged property can only take place when the fiscal pledge has been made public.[119] Perhaps in the third century AD the financial position of the imperial treasury had become so predominant that it should prevail over the interests of commercial intercourse.[120]

Alternative publicity; false wealth

In ancient Athens there was a practice of placing 'mortgage stones' (*horoi*) on mortgaged real estate, indicating the name of the creditor and the amount secured by the mortgage.[121] Even this (simple) practice is not attested for Rome. But this is not to say that Roman legal practice did not have other methods informing third parties or otherwise reducing the risk that secured creditors would be confronted with adverse claims by the real owner or another secured creditor. Thus in Rome creditors used the *columna Maenia* on the *Forum* in order to share information publicly on the solvency and behaviour of their debtors.[122] Where a debtor charged someone else's property, or had failed to disclose already existing charges on newly pledged property, this information may very well have been posted on the *columna Maenia*. Certain types of pledge, in particular tenant's pledges of *invecta et illata*, were so common that prospective creditors and purchasers must have been aware of their existence.[123] For *fiducia cum creditore*, certainly, the *mancipatio* must have offered some compensation for the absence of title registries. The *mancipatio* required the presence of six Roman citizens: five witnesses and a sixth person, the *libripens*, who held a pair of scales. The large number of witnesses not only served to facilitate proof that the *mancipatio* had actually taken place, it also enhanced publicity in the preliminary stage.[124] The *mancipatio* may have served this publicity function well when Rome was a small agrarian

118 Wieacker 1939: 229. 119 Wieacker 1939: 243. 120 Wieling 1989: 421–2.
121 Fine 1951; Finley 1952; Finley 1953: 249–68. 122 Andreau 1999: 12.
123 van den Bergh 2009: 157 n 15.
124 Kaser 1971: 42. See now also Verhagen 2020: 138–41.

community around the Palatine but must have lost much of its effectiveness when Rome developed into a much larger community with hundreds of thousands of inhabitants.[125]

In the European codifications of the nineteenth century the main function of the creditor's possession was that of preventing 'false wealth'.[126] By only allowing possessory pledges, which made it necessary that the pledged assets were removed from the debtor's physical control, situations were avoided in which other creditors would be disappointed where the assets present at the debtor's premises turned out to be charged to a bank or some other secured creditor. In other words, prospective creditors could be sure that the assets which were in possession of debtors were not charged with a security interest. It is unlikely that the desire to prevent false wealth was present with the Roman jurists. We do not find any reference to it in our sources. It is true that as long as a right of pledge could only be granted by a *traditio* to the creditor, any false appearance of wealth would be prevented (because pledged assets would be in the factual possession of the creditor). However, when granting *hypotheca* became common practice in the second century AD and false appearances of wealth could occur, the jurists show no concern at all for this. Even where a pledge had been granted as a possessory pledge, factual control was not required for the entire duration of the pledge, this in contrast with modern codifications.[127] Thus Julian D. 21.1.43.8 says that after his return to the debtor a slave will remain charged with the right of pledge.[128]

Oaths, *infamia* and *stellionatus*

The Campanian *mancipationes* all contain an express 'title warranty'—by way of oath ('*iuravit*')—whose purport it is to guarantee that the security is validly created and first ranking. That title warranties were also used in relation to *pignus* appears from an opinion by Modestinus: '*sua pignora esse quis in instrumento iuravit*' (D. 47.20.4).[129] This opinion by Modestinus could suggest that

[125] Also the fact that the *mancipatio* could only be used by Roman citizens or citizens benefiting from *commercium* may have contributed to this. Sturm (1993b: 349). Another factor contributing to the demise of *mancipatio* was that simpler legal arrangements—in particular the *stipulatio duplae* (undertaking to pay twice the amount of the purchase price)—were available to make a seller liable in case of eviction: Sturm (1993b: 354).

[126] See in particular Hromadka 1971. See also Zwalve 2004: 47–8; Zwalve and Sirks 2012: 438–44, 452, 467–87.

[127] E.g., art. 3:258(1) Dutch civil code.

[128] See also Marcian D. 20.1.13.3.

[129] See also Scaev. D. 20.1.34.2.

these warranties in the form of oaths were included with a view to the *crimen stellionatus*.[130] It was only by the end of the second century AD that imperial constitutions stated that the fraudulent non-disclosure of earlier pledges should be criminally prosecuted, so that it is impossible that the oaths in the first-century documents were made with a view to this crime.[131] Moreover, it appears from several other Digest fragments that the scope of the *crimen* is not confined to oaths. The mere fact that someone knowingly pledged someone else's property or property which had already been charged was sufficient to commit this crime.[132] In addition, where Gai. D. 20.1.15.2 refers to 'the danger run by those who create multiple charges', the 'danger' (*periculum*) referred to could not have been criminal liability for *stellionatus*. Before *stellionatus* became a crime at the end of the second century AD, this 'danger' must have been that of being sued with the *actio de dolo*.[133] A condemnation on the basis of this action would lead to *infamia*. Particularly for Romans belonging to the higher social classes, *infamia* could have serious repercussions: it (*inter alia*) entailed the exclusion from important offices.[134] It can, therefore, reasonably be assumed that for a long time loss of credibility, civil liability, and *infamia* must have had a strong deterrent effect against pledging someone else's property or the failure to disclose already existing charges.[135] But by the end of the second century AD this deterrence apparently was no longer effective, since the fraudulent non-disclosure of earlier pledges came to be criminally prosecuted. The maximum punishment for the *crimen stellionatus* was severe: forced labour for plebeians and banishment or exclusion from their order for members of the higher classes.[136] It must be assumed that this criminal liability served to enhance security of transactions and that it took place in response to abuses that threatened commercial intercourse.[137] It must be doubted, however, whether these criminal sanctions were always an

[130] For a discussion of the 'title warranties' in the epigraphic sources of *fiducia cum creditore*, see Noordraven 1999: 128–30.

[131] See Ulp. D. 13.7.36 pr., referring to the imperial constitutions; Paul. D. 13.7.16.1, expressly mentioning pledging someone else's property and pledging property already pledged to someone else; Phil. C. 9.34.4 pr. When a valuable asset had been pledged for a small debt, granting a second pledge without disclosing the first one was not a *crimen stellionatus* (Ulp. D. 13.7.36.1).

[132] Paul. D. 13.7.16.1; Ulp. D. 13.7.36 pr.; Ulp. D. 13.7.36.1. See Noordraven 1999: 129–30.

[133] Kaser 1976: 183. See also Scaev. D. 20.1.34.1, in which the debtor declares that the creditor must have given credence to the debtor's assurance 'as man of honor' that the pledge was first ranking.

[134] Krämer 2007: 367–8. [135] *Actio empti utilis*: Tryph. D. 20.5.12.1.

[136] Phil. C. 9.34.4 pr.; Ulp. D. 13.7.36.1; Ulp. D. 47.20.3.2. On *stellionatus* from an economic perspective, see Pellecchi 2018: 482–8.

[137] Wacke 1969: 400; Bürge 1979: 128.

effective remedy to ensure a properly functioning law of secured credit.[138] The uncertain legal status of pledged assets, which, despite the newly introduced criminal sanction, apparently remained a problem, is likely to have contributed in the late classical period to the increasing practice of excluding liability for eviction in contracts entered into by creditors enforcing their rights of pledge by selling the pledged assets to third parties.[139] In that case the purchaser could sue the debtor with an adapted version of the action which a purchaser would normally have against the seller.[140] A creditor liable for eviction could assign to the purchaser his contractual action arising against the debtor under the pledge agreement. In both scenarios the purchaser could directly sue the debtor who had pledged someone else's property. This would, however, be of little benefit when the debtor was insolvent, and for this reason the possibility of eviction may have had a depressing effect on prices paid for pledged assets.[141] From D. 13.7.22.4 it appears that in the late classical period it became a customary practice for creditors selling pledged property to enter into a *stipulatio duplae* with purchasers, thus promising twice the amount of the purchase price in the case of eviction. This may have had a positive effect on sales prices realized by creditors enforcing their pledge. At the same time this transactional practice increased risks for secured creditors, which may have resulted in increased interest rates for borrowers.[142]

[138] As Arruñada (2012: 51) observes with respect to the need to rely on criminal law: 'the need to rely on such harsh mechanisms for enforcement provides a glimpse of the opportunity costs caused by lack of proper institutions for conveyancing land and securing credit'.

[139] Pap. D. 21.2.68 pr.; Paul. D. 17.1.59.4. As with so many transactional practices, these clauses may have evolved into a rule of law. From Alex. C. 8.45.1 it appears that the secured creditor—whether a private creditor or the *procurator* of the *fiscus*—is not liable for eviction, unless he has expressly agreed otherwise.

[140] *Actio empti utilis*: Tryph. D. 20.5.12.1.

[141] Bürge 1979: 130–1. Liability for eviction could be a reliable alternative for the secured creditor when creditworthy third parties are liable, such as title insurers (Arruñada 2012: 51). I have not carried out extensive research on this, but although via a *stipulatio* or *fideiussio* (or other form of personal security) such liability was technically possible, I have found no evidence of an established Roman practice of title insurance.

[142] In the classical period the *stipulatio duplae* was broadly used in the context of ordinary sale. In a number of fragments additional remedies are granted to the executing pledge creditor who entered into a *stipulatio duplae*: Pomp. D. 13.7.8.1 (right of retention); Ulp. D. 13.7.22.4; and Tryph. D. 13.7.23 (right of recourse against debtor). See also Ulp. D. 13.7.24: the creditor has an *actio emptio utilis* when evicted after *impetratio dominii*.

11

Late Classical Execution Practices

11.1 Introduction

For a long time, it was purely at the creditor's discretion whether or not recourse would be taken against the charged assets by selling them (at auction or otherwise) and returning any surplus to the debtor. Such a creditor-friendly legal regime could discourage certain persons from borrowing and could thus reduce the demand for credit.[1] The growth of the credit markets and the increasing use of real security may during the course of the Principate have provided stimuli for gradually improving the position of the debtor, in the sense that execution sale would become the general rule and that the creditor became obliged by operation of law to pay the *superfluum* to the debtor.[2] Manigk has observed that in all ancient legal systems this evolution from forfeiture pledge to a pledge enforceable by sale takes place entirely through party autonomy ('*privatautonom*'), and not as a consequence of legislative intervention.[3] In this chapter we will see that for Roman law this is largely, but not completely, true. It was the praetor, who—in accordance with jurisprudence—will at some stage have imposed a mandatory duty upon the creditor to pay the *superfluum* to the debtor and the emperor did intervene by ordering that enforcement should take place by way of execution sale. However, even here it can still be observed that these late classical rules on enforcement find their origin in transactional practices, as we encounter powers of sale coupled with provisions on surplus in documents dating from the first century AD.

This evolution from forfeiture to sale entailed that in high and late classical law forfeiture was no longer the general rule (section 11.2). The secured creditor would normally take recourse by selling the charged property to third parties, but even at the end of the classical period such a sale could also take place to the creditor himself. Where the monetary system itself malfunctions (due to heavy inflation) creditors may be more interested in the physical assets or their products than in realizing their monetary value. In this chapter

[1] Lerouxel 2016: 245. [2] Kaser 1982: 213. [3] Manigk 1941: 1264.

Security and Credit in Roman Law: The historical evolution of pignus *and* hypotheca. Hendrik L. E. Verhagen, Oxford University Press. © Hendrik L. E. Verhagen 2022. DOI: 10.1093/oso/9780199695836.003.0012

we will examine how (express and constructive) forfeiture arrangements—*datio in solutum* (section 11.3) and conditional sale (section 11.4)—can be reconciled with the evolution of *pignus* and *hypotheca* into a security interest, which was enforceable by sale and pursuant to which the creditor could only take recourse for the amount of the secured debt. The conclusion for classical law is that during the entire classical period forfeiture arrangements were deemed legally valid, possibly at first as express forfeiture clauses and over time as constructive forfeiture arrangements. It seems, however, that at the end of the classical period forfeiture arrangements, under which the surplus value accrued to the creditor, became invalid. Under emperor Constantine *leges commissoriae* were expressly declared void in 320 or 326 AD (section 11.5).

11.2 Execution of Charged Property

By the end of the classical period not only were the creditor's power of sale and his duty to repay the surplus attached to the right of pledge by operation of law but enforcement by way of execution sale had become the general rule.[4] *Pignus* and *hypotheca* had evolved into the security interest whose essential traits are still with us today. There is a repeating pattern: a transactional practice, which this time already emerged in the first century AD (and may have republican antecedents),[5] evolved into a mandatory legal arrangement from which the parties could not derogate. This not only protects debtors as structurally weaker parties but certain mandatory execution procedures, in particular public auctions,[6] may have the positive effect of generating the highest possible price for the charged property. This may benefit (in the case of a surplus) not only debtors but also secured creditors and lower-ranking creditors. Thus, rules providing for a compulsory sale of collateral and the return of the *superfluum* to the debtor, as had developed in Rome by the end of the classical period, resulted in an equilibrium in which the interests of creditors and

[4] A similar evolution may have taken place for the execution of fiscal pledges. See Klingenberg 1992: 361, 366–73. For instance, Paul. D. 49.14.45.12 holds that 'if, when the property of a debtor has been sold off by the imperial treasury, a larger sum is obtained, it is both lawful and right to seek its restoration'.

[5] See the late republican jurist Servius Sulpicius Rufus in Ulp. D. 47.10.15.32.

[6] According to Kaser a mandatory duty for the creditor to sell charged assets *in public* (auction), as exists in most modern legal systems, still did not exist at the end of the classical period. See Kaser 1982: 73 n 89, 77. However, a constitution such as Alex. C. 8.27.4, which assumes the public announcement (*proscriptio*) of an execution sale, does suggest otherwise.

debtors were more or less balanced. This equilibrium has proven to be extremely stable over the course of the centuries: one still finds it in Western legal systems today, albeit (as in late classical Roman law) with exceptions.

Realization by sale

In the final stage of the evolution of the execution of real security (*pignus*, *hypotheca*, and *fiducia cum creditore*), the creditor's principal legal right was to sell the charged objects to a third party in the event of default. A constitution by emperor Alexander Severus from AD 222 provides that the agreement to transfer pledged property to the creditor if a loan would not be repaid in time should be read as referring to the right of enforcement granted to the creditor 'at common law', that is to sell the collateral to third parties.[7] This constitution unequivocally indicates that early in the third century AD the sale to a third party had become the ordinary manner of enforcing security.[8] Another constitution by Alexander Severus from AD 225 provides:

> **Alex. C. 8.27.4.** Creditor hypothecas sive pignus cum proscribit, notum debitori facere, si bona fide rem gerit, et quando licet testato dicere debet. si quid itaque per fraudem in pignore villae venditae commissum probare potes, ut inferatur actio, quae eo nomine competit, adi eum cuius de ea re notio est.
>
> When a creditor advertises (the sale of) hypothecs or pledges, if he acts in good faith he should make this known to the debtor, and, if possible, in the presence of witnesses. So if you can prove that anything fraudulent occurred in the pledge of the villa that was sold, go before the person with jurisdiction in order to bring the action that lies on this account.

This constitution assumes that the creditor announces the execution sale to the public (*proscriptio*) and holds that in addition the creditor is obliged by good faith to notify the debtor of the coming sale (*denuntiatio*). The creditor's failure to do so does not invalidate the sale but makes him liable vis-à-vis the

[7] Alex. C. 8.34.1, discussed in section 11.3.

[8] The pledged property could be sold to someone who stood as surety for the secured debt (Paul. D. 17.1.59.1) or to a person who had been ordered by the debtor to purchase it. Scaev. D. 31.89.4 discusses a case in which the heirs had jointly pledged the entire inheritance to a lender in order to refinance the inherited estate's debts. In accordance with a term in the *conventio pignoris*, when the loan was not repaid the lender sold the jointly owned land to one of the heirs.

debtor with the *actio pigneraticia directa*. Yet another constitution from Alexander Severus provides that when, after all the required formalities have been performed, no interested purchasers can be found, the creditor can ask for the emperor's express permission (*impetratio dominii*) to retain ownership of the charged object.[9] The same constitution provides that where a general pledge has been granted the creditor cannot acquire the entire estate of the debtor.

The creditor's power of sale was no longer based upon forfeiture or on an (express or implied) contractual licence to sell[10] but attached to the right of pledge by operation of law. We can see this clearly in a legal opinion by Ulpian which makes clear, first of all, that the creditor not only has the right to sell the property but also a proprietary power to transfer ownership.[11] Secondly, the text shows that a licence to sell no longer has to be agreed but is inherent to the right of pledge.[12] In the absence of a contractual licence to sell the creditor is still entitled to sell and transfer the pledged property, by operation of law ('*iure utimur, ut liceat distrahere*'). This is only different where the debtor and creditor have agreed that the latter shall not sell the property. Like Iavolenus and Pomponius (long) before him, Ulpian says that selling pledged property in violation of an agreement not to sell constitutes theft. But Ulpian also says that such a *pactum de non distrahendo* can effectively be set aside by the creditor giving three notices of default (*denuntiatio*) to the debtor.[13] This is important because it leaves no doubt that the creditor's power of sale is not based on an implied authorization by the debtor but has become attached to the right of pledge by operation of law. This is because not only in the absence of a contractual licence to sell but even in the case of a contractual prohibition to sell, the creditor ultimately does have a power of sale.

Superfluum

When exactly a legal duty to pay the surplus came into being is impossible to indicate, although this may already have been in the second century AD.[14] In the third century AD this duty was firmly entrenched in Roman law. In the

[9] Alex. C. 8.33.1. This constitution concerned *pignus*, but (according to Noordraven 1999: 260) Ulp. D. 13.7.24 pr. provides the same for *fiducia*.

[10] Section 5.7.

[11] Ulp. D. 13.7.4 ('*verum incipit emptor dominium rei habere*').

[12] Kaser 1975: 319; Biscardi 1976: 161.

[13] The last part of D. 13.7.4 has been said to be a post-classical or Byzantine interpolation. See Kaser 1971: 471 n 10. On *denuntiatio*, see Kaser and Hackl 1996: 472–3.

[14] Section 5.7. See also Kaser 1982: 75–8; Noordraven 1999: 247.

Corpus iuris civilis there are, however, only a few late classical texts unequivocally attesting the creditor's obligation to pass on the surplus of execution proceeds to the debtor. There is Papinian's opinion in D. 13.7.42, where he holds that the creditor is liable with the *actio pigneraticia directa* to pay the *superfluum* (and interest thereon) to the debtor. In D. 20.1.21.3 Ulpian says that where in *Serviana* proceedings against a third party in possession the latter is condemned to pay the value of the pledged property, the creditor must return any surplus, which the debtor can claim with the *actio pigneraticia*.[15] Likewise, in D. 13.7.24.2 Ulpian unequivocally provides that the creditor is obliged to pay the *superfluum* to the debtor, but only after he has received the purchase price from the purchaser.[16] Ulpian D. 36.4.5.21 seems to confirm that where, in the case of antichretic pledges, the proceeds of the fruits exceeded the principal and interest, the creditor was obliged to repay the surplus to the debtor. From Marci. D. 20.1.16.9 it could be deduced that a legal duty to pay the surplus existed at the time of emperor Septimius Severus, and also when the pledged property was conditionally sold to the creditor himself.[17] In a constitution from 294 AD Diocletian rules that where a creditor, who had sold pledged objects pursuant to a contractual licence to sell, had purchased a farm with the surplus proceeds, the debtor did not have an *actio in rem* (*rei vindicatio*) in respect of the farm.[18] However, according to the constitution, 'there is an action *in personam*, i.e. on the pledge, for the surplus'.[19] This was in all these texts an *actio pigneraticia* with a *formula in ius concepta*, which incorporated the concept of *bona fides*.[20] The main advantage of this more flexible *formula*, which may have been the reason for its origin, was that the *ex fide bona* clause allowed the *iudex* to condemn the creditor to return the *superfluum* to the debtor.[21]

Redemption

By the end of the classical period the debtor also had a *right of redemption*—the right to recover the charged object by satisfying the secured debt after default.[22] A constitution by emperor Gordian from 239 AD provides that

[15] Ulp. D. 20.1.21.3 is discussed in the Appendix.

[16] According to Noordraven (1999: 245) this text deals with *fiducia*. Also on *fiducia* is PS 2.13.1. In substance these texts are likely to reflect the law on *pignus* and *hypotheca* as well.

[17] Section 11.4. [18] Diocl.-Max. C. 8.27.20. [19] See also Diocl.-Max. C. 8.29.5.

[20] Kaser 1982: 98. [21] Section 6.6.

[22] The *lex portorii provinciae Asiae* (AD 62) provides that the debtor shall have a grace period of thirty days within which he can still pay the tax due. See also Philocles's *hypothekas* (Cic., *Fam.* 131) discussed in section 5.2.

an execution sale is invalid when the creditor refuses to accept the money offered by the debtor before the sale took place.[23] This text must be interpreted as granting the debtor the right of redemption.[24] The constitution from Gordian unequivocally states that the execution sale cannot be revoked when the money was offered to the creditor after the creditor has exercised his power of sale.[25] In case of an execution sale to a purchaser, the debtor could only exercise the right of redemption against the purchaser if such right of redemption had been agreed between the creditor and the purchaser. In D. 13.7.13 pr. Ulpian refers to a written opinion by Julian and an imperial constitution, both saying that as a consequence of such agreement the debtor can institute the *actio pigneraticia (directa)* against the creditor, in order to compel him to assign his action on sale against the purchaser.[26] Alternatively, the debtor can revindicate the pledged property from the purchaser or proceed directly against the purchaser with an *actio in factum*. Finally, the Codex Justinianus contains a regulation by emperor Justinian himself from 530 AD, which refers to the 'ancient law' pursuant to which the debtor still had one year to redeem the property after default.[27] This may have reflected the law of the post-classical period.

The 'watchful eyes of the courts'

From the second century AD onwards we can observe that, although the law of real security does remain by and large creditor-friendly, the imperial chancery intervened in order to provide a considerable degree of protection to debtors. The most fundamental change in favour of debtors was that creditors became obliged by operation of law to sell the pledged object and return the surplus proceeds to the debtor. But in addition to the right of redemption, the debtor's position was also improved in other respects. The sale of pledged property took place 'under the watchful eyes of the courts',[28] but *not* in the

[23] Gord. C. 8.27.8. See also Gord. C. 8.28.2 pr.

[24] The second part of the constitution deals with the case where the debtor offers to pay after the creditor has exercised his power of sale: the latter can only take place when the debtor has defaulted under the loan. It may also be assumed that the first part of the constitution deals with a situation where the debtor has already defaulted. See also Diocl.-Max. C. 8.27.10; Diocl.-Max. C. 8.19.2.

[25] See Felgentraeger 1933: 23.

[26] The constitution mentioned by Ulpian could have been Alex. C. 4.54.2, which is not on pledge but on the case where a farm is sold by its owners subject to the condition that it shall be returned if they or their heirs offer the purchase price to the buyer. Marci. (Jul.) D. 20.5.7 restates the same opinion by Julian.

[27] Just. C. 8.33.3.

[28] Kehoe 2007: 151.

sense that court permission was required for an execution sale or the court actually supervised the sale itself. The supervision would take place retrospectively, by the emperor ruling in favour of the debtor where the latter would institute legal proceedings against the creditor for not abiding by the execution rules laid down in imperial constitutions, or for failing to observe a duty of care.[29] In particular, the Severan (Alexander) '*ius novum*' has many rules on properly conducting the execution of charged assets. In a constitution from 231 AD, Alexander Severus ruled that where a debtor is prepared to pay the remaining part of the secured debt, the provincial governor shall appoint an arbiter who shall determine the exact amount still to be paid.[30] Where the creditor refuses to co-operate, by 'rushing' to sell the pledged property, this improper alienation (*improba alienatio*) shall not deprive the debtor of his ownership. This could not only affect the creditor but also the purchaser of the pledged property. Thus, a constitution by Alexander Severus from 222 AD provides that where the creditor had exercised his power of sale 'in bad faith' ('*dolo malo*'), he must be condemned to pay damages (C. 8.29.1). If such a creditor is insolvent and the purchaser had purchased the pledged *fundus* in bad faith (*mala fide*), the latter must be ordered to give back the land and its fruits. This would only be the case, however, if the debtor offered to pay the purchaser the purchase price plus interest. In other words, even a purchaser who knew that the creditor unlawfully sold the pledged property was protected, in the sense that he would get back the purchase price.[31] Alexander Severus also ruled that a creditor with a possessory pledge of agricultural land was obliged by operation of law to harvest its crops and reduce the secured debt with the value of the crops, including of those crops which he failed to harvest.[32] The same constitution also shows that other protective measures were taken in favour of the grantor of an antichretic pledge, such as granting him a claim for damages caused by deterioration of the land. Likewise, Ulpian writes that the creditor shall be liable if he 'mistreats pledged property or weakens slaves'. Ulpian even holds that the right of pledge will immediately cease to exist if the creditor 'puts a slave-girl to prostitution or compels her to some other disreputable conduct'.[33] A constitution

[29] See Kehoe 2007: 150–5.

[30] Alex. C. 8.27.5.

[31] See also Alex. C. 8.29.2 and Alex. C. 8.29.3. We find similar rulings in later constitutions: Gord. C. 8.29.4 and Diocl.-Max. C. 8.29.5. Gord. C. 8.27.7 rules that where the creditor acted fraudulently, the debtor must proceed not against the purchaser but against the creditor himself.

[32] Alex. Sev. C. 4.24.3. See also Diocl.-Max. C. 8.24.2. See Bobbink and Mauer 2019: 24–6. Other Severan constitutions ruling in favour of debtors are Alex. C. 8.27.1; Alex. C. 8.27.4; Alex. C. 8.27.5; Alex. C. 8.29.1; Alex. C. 8.29.2; Alex. C. 8.29.3. See also Ulp. D. 13.7.25 (p. 354).

[33] Ulp. D. 13.7.24.3.

by Diocletian rules that where the creditor used a 'man of straw' to purchase the pledged property, in order to avoid a sale at arm's length to a third party, the sale would be ineffective.[34]

At the same time, there are still many constitutions and jurists' opinions which can be characterized as creditor-friendly. Where the debtor had provided in his will that none of his *praedia* were to be sold and added as a penalty that they would otherwise be owned by the treasury, Septimius Severus and Caracalla ruled in C. 8.28.1 (AD 207) that this cannot adversely affect the creditor's power to sell *praedia* pledged to him to third parties. In C. 8.27.3 (223 AD) Alexander Severus confirms that the debtor remains liable for any deficit remaining after an execution sale. In C. 8.27.5 (231 AD) Gordian rules that the creditor retains his power of sale even when the major part of the secured debt has already been paid.[35] In classical law the creditor could take physical control of the pledged property when the debtor was in default, in a similar manner as a landlord's *perclusio* pursuant to an urban tenant's pledge.[36] From the late classical period we have evidence of such a self-help remedy available to creditors with a non-possessory pledge. Ulpian D. 47.2.56 says that when a pledge creditor takes the pledged object with him he is not regarded as wrongfully appropriating it but as looking after his pledge ('*pignori suo incumbere*').[37] In an imperial constitution by Septimius Severus and Caracalla, this right to take possession is subjected to judicial control: in Sev.-Ant. C. 8.13.3, reference is made to secured creditors who enforce their pledge by taking possession of the pledged assets when their debtor is in default. According to the constitution, although they must not be regarded as having used force, the possession must be gained with the permission of the governor.

11.3 *Datio in Solutum*

The consequence of late classical constitutions such as Alex. C. 8.34.1, which prescribe an execution sale, was, according to some modern authors, that at this time forfeiture arrangements became invalid.[38] There are, however, quite a few texts on a transfer in lieu of payment (*datio in solutum*) of the pledged

[34] Diocl.-Max. C. 8.27.10.

[35] See also Gord. C. 8.28.2.

[36] See (perhaps)—for early classical law—Alfenus in Paul. D. 13.7.30.

[37] See also Paul. D. 46.1.68.1, on the right of the imperial treasury (*fiscus*) to take possession of assets belonging to a tax debtor (Romulus) 'as if they had been charged to it' ('*bona Romuli fiscus ut obligata sibi occupaverat*').

[38] Noordraven 1999: 259–62.

property to the creditor. They can be regarded as constructive forfeiture arrangements to the extent that at the time they were agreed they purported to effect a *conditional* transfer based on *default*. Like a *lex commissoria*, the debtor's default would trigger a transfer of ownership of the pledged property to the creditor. These conditional transfers in lieu of payment were recognized as valid by the jurists and the imperial chancery for most of the classical period.[39] A number of constitutions and jurists' opinions on *datio in solutum* of pledged property have been interpreted—in particular by Kaser and Peters—as offering protection of the debtor against 'usurious exploitation'.[40] The texts on *datio in solutum* preserved in the *Corpus iuris civilis* contain insufficient proof for the trend observed by Peters and Kaser.[41] This motive can only be reasonably attributed to Alex. C.8.34.1, which dates from the end of the classical period (222 AD).

Alex. C. 8.34.1

The most significant text for the legal validity of a constructive forfeiture arrangement in the form of a *datio in solutum* of pledged property is the constitution of Alexander Severus of 222 AD.

> **Alex. C. 8.34.1.** Qui pactus est, nisi intra certum tempus pecuniam quam mutuam accepit solveret, cessurum creditoribus, hypothecae venditionem non contraxit, sed id comprehendit, quod iure suo creditor in adipiscendo pignore habiturus erat. communi itaque iure creditor hypothecam vendere debet.
>
> A person who agreed that, unless within a fixed time he repaid a loan he received, he would yield (pledges) to his creditors, did not contract the sale of a hypothec, but achieved (only) what the creditor would rightfully have (anyway) in getting the pledge. The creditor, accordingly, should sell the hypothec by the general law (for pledges).

[39] These fragments merely focus on the contractual aspects of the case. It can be assumed that in such cases the acquisition of ownership by the creditor in the event of default was usually based on a *traditio*. As Diocl.-Max. C. 8.13.13 illustrates, in case of a possessory pledge this could be a *traditio brevi manu*. Burdese 1949: 207.

[40] Kaser 1982: 19–20, 73; Peters 1973: 156–61.

[41] Kaser 1982: 19–20, 73; Peters 1973: 161. None of this means that there were no legal remedies in classical law, which allowed the debtor to counter exploitation by the creditor under certain circumstances. If, as a result of undue influence exercised by the creditor, the debtor had agreed to a sale of the charged object to the creditor, *restitutio in integrum* was probably possible. Cf. Peters 1973: 148–9.

In the case giving rise to this constitution, the parties envisaged in all probability a conditional transfer in lieu of payment, although the constitution initially views it as an (invalid) sale of the pledged objects to the creditor. The constitution rules that what the parties had agreed was ineffective: the creditor must sell the pledged property to third parties by way of execution. A constructive forfeiture arrangement in the form of a *datio in solutum* of pledged property to the creditor is recharacterized into a power to sell to third parties. This constitution indicates that at the end of the classical period a constructive forfeiture arrangement in the form of a transfer in lieu of payment based on default was ineffective to transfer ownership to the creditor himself. The reason for this may have been that it is inherent to this type of clause that any surplus value in the pledged property would benefit the creditor rather than the debtor.[42] It is not without reason that this constitution, together with Constantine's prohibition of *leges commissoriae* in C. 8.34.3, was later included in the Codex title on forfeiture clauses.[43]

Protection of the debtor against 'usurious exploitation'?

There is a constitution from Alexander Severus from 230 AD, from which it appears that a sale or *datio in solutum* of the pledged object to the creditor taking place *after* the secured debt became due and payable is perfectly valid.[44] If the creditor and the debtor choose to transfer the pledged property in lieu of payment when the loan becomes payable, no conditional forfeiture arrangement based on default exists. From the legal sources it can be derived that in late classical law an *invalid* forfeiture arrangement is aimed at a default which might possibly occur in the future. If the acquisition of the charged object is the result of an agreement which has been concluded only after the occurrence of the default, then this characteristic is missing and a valid acquisition exists.[45]

In C. 8.13.13, a fragment of the Diocletian era (293 AD), the transfer of pledged property by the debtor in lieu of payment to the creditor is considered entirely valid.

[42] See the discussion of Marci. D. 20.1.16.9 in section 11.4. [43] C. 8.34.

[44] Alex. C. 8.19.1. See Ankum 2007: 496–500, who gives further references. See also the other texts mentioned by Kaser 1982: 20, as supporting the validity of a *datio in solutum* of the pledged object to the creditor; Ulp. D. 46.3.45 pr.; Diocl.-Max. C. 8.13.13; Diocl.-Max. C. 4.51.4.

[45] See the discussion of D. 13.7.34 in section 11.4.

> **Diocl.-Max. C. 8.13.13.** Cum dominam non minorem viginti et quinque annis ea quae obligaverat tibi iure dominii possidere permisisse et in solutum dedisse precibus significes, dominae contractus et voluntas ad firmitatem tibi sufficit.
>
> Since you indicate in your petition that a *sui iuris* woman over age twenty-five allowed you to possess as owner the property that she had pledged to you, and she gave it as payment, the owner's contract and wish provides sufficient confirmation.

According to some modern authors this text serves as an indication that, in the case of a valid forfeiture arrangement, no imperial permission was necessary for appropriation (*impetratio dominii*).[46] While not precluding this interpretation, Peters deems a different explanation to be more plausible. He seeks to explain this by the fact that in this case there is no reason to fear a 'usurious exploitation' of the debtor. The fragment sounds, according to Peters, as if, by way of exception, the debtor was in a stronger position here: it was not the debtor who was concerned about her position but the creditor.[47] I am more inclined to regard the validity of the *datio in solutum* as a consequence of the fact that it took place after the secured debt became due and payable. In later times (and still today) this is considered less onerous than a forfeiture arrangement concluded at the time of granting.[48]

Invalidation for other reasons

There are texts in which a *datio in solutum* of pledged property was considered invalid, but for entirely different reasons than protecting the debtor against 'usurious exploitation'. Ulpian D. 46.3.45 concerns a case where a husband promised his wife that, in the event of dissolution of marriage, he would transfer the pieces of land, which he had pledged for the return of her dowry, in lieu of payment to her. Ulpian advised that if the marriage was dissolved, it sufficed to offer the amount of the dowry. Ulpian interprets the agreement by the parties as leading to a type of alternative obligation: the husband/debtor is obliged to pay the dowry, but has the option to transfer the land instead. This

[46] E.g., Burdese 1949: 126, 207.

[47] Peters 1973: 159. According to Peters, '*domina*' does not mean 'owner' in this context but relates to the (high) social position of the female pledge debtor.

[48] Verhagen 2011b: 127–30 (*Glossa ordinaria* and Jacques de Revigny), 132–3 (Bartolus de Sassoferrato), 137–8 (Charles du Moulin), 140 (Diego de Covarruvias), 142 (Roman-Dutch law).

is not a forfeiture arrangement based on default, and for this reason D. 46.3.45 should not be considered as a text in which the debtor is protected from 'usurious exploitation'.[49] Another text from Ulpian (D. 13.7.25) is concerned with a situation where a debtor might be compelled to 'leave' the pledged property with the creditor, probably in lieu of payment. Ulpian gives the example of a large tract of mountain land, which is charged by way of possessory pledge by a debtor 'who can hardly pay his way let alone do agricultural improvements'. The creditor, however, did bring the land under cultivation and 'made it very valuable'. According to Ulpian, it would not be fair that the debtor should go looking for more lenders, be forced to sell the pledged property or leave it in lieu of payment with the creditor. 'A balance, therefore, must be struck between these considerations by the judge in such a way as to give ear to neither a fussy debtor nor an oppressive creditor.'[50] Here, Ulpian's concern is not so much with the potentially onerous nature of a *datio in solutum* of pledged property but rather with that of the liability of the debtor for reimbursing the creditor for improvements, which could make it difficult for him to discharge the pledge.[51]

In a constitution from 194 AD of Septimius Severus and Caracalla, it is said that a transfer of pledged property in lieu of payment to the creditor does not result in the fulfilment of the debt.[52] Peters and Kaser interpret this text in the context of a prohibited forfeiture arrangement; Kaser with the subtle distinction that this should only apply if the value of the charged object is much higher than the debt.[53] This constitution, however, seems rather to provide a safeguard for the *creditor*: a *unilateral* offer by the debtor to his creditor(s) to transfer the charged object in lieu of payment does not release him. The rationale of this imperial constitution might very well be the same as the one pertaining to provisions found in modern codifications (e.g., § 364 BGB), which provide that the creditor must agree with a transfer in lieu of payment.[54] The debtor should not be able to unilaterally force another performance upon the creditor than the one originally agreed.

[49] Unlike Kaser 1982: 19–20, 73; Peters 1973: 156–61.

[50] '*medie igitur haec a iudice erunt dispicienda, ut neque delicatus debitor neque onerosus creditor audiatur*'.

[51] In Ulp. D. 13.7.24 pr., Ulpian appears to regard the *datio in solutum* of pledged property to the creditor as a normal way of discharging a secured debt. When the creditor is evicted, he shall have an adapted *actio empti* ('*ex empto utilis*') against the debtor.

[52] Sev.-Ant. C. 8.13.1.

[53] Peters 1973: 156–7; Kaser 1982: 20 n 116.

[54] For Roman law, see Zimmermann 1990: 753.

11.4 Conditional Sales

From the high and late classical period, texts have been passed down to us in which—possibly following Hellenistic transactional practices[55]—a sale-based arrangement enabled the creditor to possess pledged property as owner in case of default. In the *Corpus iuris civilis*, we find texts on the validity of a conditional sale of pledged property by the debtor to the creditor, with the failure to discharge the secured debt as the condition triggering the sale. This raises the question whether this type of (what I have called) constructive forfeiture arrangement is reconcilable with late classical enforcement rules, which prescribe the sale of the pledged object to a third party and only allow the creditor to acquire it with the express permission of the emperor (*impetratio dominii*). Over time it became apparent that these conditional sales were legally valid, provided that the purchase price payable by the secured creditor to the debtor reflected the fair market value (*iustum pretium*) of the property, so that when its value exceeded the amount of the secured debt the surplus would go to the debtor.[56]

Pap. FV 9 and Marci. D. 20.1.16.9

We have two fragments from late classical jurists which uphold the validity of a conditional sale of the pledged object by the debtor to the creditor, triggered by a default under the secured debt (loan).

> **FV 9.** *Papinianus.* Creditor a debitore pignus recte emit, siue in exordio contractus ita conuenit siue postea; nec incerti pretii uenditio uidebitur, ut pecunia fenoris non soluta creditor iure empti dominium retineat, cum sortis et usurarum quantitas ad diem soluendae pecuniae praestitutam certa sit.
>
> A creditor lawfully purchases the object of pledge, irrespective of whether this has been agreed at the commencement of the contract or later; it will not be regarded as a sale for an uncertain price if it has been agreed that, on non-payment of the interest charged amount, the creditor may retain the ownership pursuant to his right of purchase, since the amount of principal and interest to be paid at the date of payment is certain.

[55] See also Scaevola D. 18.1.81 pr. Kaser 1982: 20; Schanbacher 2002b: 649.
[56] Marican D. 20.1.16.9.

> **D. 20.1.16.9.** *Marcianus libro singulari ad formulam hypothecariam.* Potest ita fieri pignoris datio hypothecaeve, ut, si intra certum tempus non sit soluta pecunia, iure emptoris possideat rem iusto pretio tunc aestimandam: hoc enim casu videtur quodammodo condicionalis esse venditio. et ita divus Severus et Antoninus rescripserunt.
>
> It can be a term of a *pignus* or *hypotheca* that if the money is not paid by a certain date, the creditor can possess the property as buyer at a fair price then to be assessed. In this case, there is, as it were, a conditional sale, as Severus and Antoninus held in a rescript.

The conditional sales discussed in these texts are in substance forfeiture mechanisms. The debtor and creditor have agreed on 'day 1' of the credit transaction that only in case of a default under the secured debt shall the creditor acquire ownership of the pledged object by way of sale. The effects of Papinian FV 9, in particular, are almost identical to those of an express forfeiture clause. The fact that the purchase price can be set on the principal amount of the loan plus interest means that, where the value of the object of pledge is higher than the amount of the secured debt, the surplus will be for the benefit of the creditor. Marci. D. 20.1.16.9, by way of contrast, expressly states that the purchase price must reflect the *iustum pretium* of the pledged object. The text refers to a rescript by Septimius Severus and Caracalla which considers this constructive forfeiture arrangement as a valid conditional sale of the pledged property. The ruling that the purchase price must reflect the *iustum pretium* of the property means that the secured debt owed to the creditor must be set off against the purchase price owed to the debtor. If the market value exceeds the amount of the secured debt, the balance (which is the surplus value) must be paid by the creditor to the debtor. It is difficult to interpret this text otherwise than that it shows concern for the debtor's position.

Is it possible that Marci. D. 20.1.16.9 really reflects classical notions of fairness,[57] or is the text interpolated? [58] According to Levy, the reference to the 'fair price then to be assessed' ('*iusto pretio tunc aestimandam*') is indeed

[57] According to Levy (1951: 190 n 184) and Feenstra (1957: 514 n 28), '*rem iusto pretio tunc aestimandam*' is an interpolation. Kaser (1975: 320 n 14; 1982: 75–8), on the other hand, does not preclude that the phrase is a result of classical fairness-oriented thinking.

[58] Levy (1951: 190) asserts that the debtor can claim the *superfluum* with the *actio pigneraticia*. In this interpretation, FV 9 and D. 20.1.16.9 would also be consistent. Feenstra (1957: 513–14), however, rightly points out that FV 9 does not mention this at all. In the same sense, Peters 1973: 147. Kaser (1982: 20 n 121) appears to accept the possibility assumed by Levy only in case of an *actio pigneraticia in ius concepta*.

an interpolation, made by the *Compilatores* of the Digest in order to harmonize D. 20.1.16.9 and C. 8.34.3 (Constantine's prohibition of forfeiture clauses).[59] One would think, however, that if at the end of the classical period it was settled that the creditor was obliged by operation of law to refund the surplus to the debtor, the creditor's obligation to pay the fair market value in Marci. D. 20.1.16.9 would be perfectly reconcilable with this. In another opinion, Marcian discusses the practice of the debtor selling the pledged property himself, in order to facilitate him to pay off the secured debt with the proceeds of that sale.[60] Marcian recommends that before the sale actually takes place the creditor shall obtain an undertaking (*cautio*) from the prospective purchaser that the latter shall pay the purchase price *up to the amount of the secured debt* to the creditor. Again, this reflects that the creditor's entitlement to the value of the pledged property is confined to the amount of the secured debt.[61] It is, therefore, not at all impossible that Marci. D. 20.1.16.9 does reflect classical notions of fairness. The rescript of D. 20.1.16.9 is, moreover, not necessarily at odds with the opinion expressed by Papinian in FV 9. The question in dispute in FV 9 only concerned the certainty of the purchase price, which was an essential requirement for a valid contract of sale.[62] The (un)fairness of allowing the creditor to keep the surplus was not at issue. In another fragment of the Digest, reference is made to a rescript, which was rendered by the emperor (who must have been Septimius Severus) at a time 'when Papinian headed the Office of Petitions'. According to this rescript, the creditor could buy the object of pledge from the debtor, since the debtor remained the owner thereof.[63] This rescript probably purported to clarify that, in contrast with a sale of an object of *fiducia*, the sale of an object of pledge was not a disposition to someone already owning the property.[64] Again, the (un)fairness of a sale to the creditor was not at stake. These (and other) constitutions, therefore, were concerned with other issues than whether in case of a conditional sale or *datio in solutum* the surplus must be paid to the debtor.[65]

[59] Levy 1956: 190. See also Feenstra 1957: 514. On Const. C. 8.34.3, see section 11.5.

[60] Marci. D. 20.6.8.10.

[61] Also, in other respects, it came to be recognized that the value of the pledged assets must be shared between the creditor and debtor. Thus, Paul. D. 9.2.30.1 says that if a pledged slave is killed, the creditor can institute the *actio legis aquiliae (utilis)* against the killer for the amount of the secured debt, while the debtor can institute this action for the surplus value (Manigk 1941: 1279).

[62] Zimmermann 1990: 253–5.

[63] Tryph. D. 20.5.12 pr.

[64] Schanbacher 2002a: 642–3.

[65] See Sev.-Ant. C. 8.13.1.

Economic rationale of the '*pactum Marcianum*'

The plague which broke out during Marcus Aurelius's reign in 165 AD and ended in 180 AD was the beginning of one of the most dramatic periods of the whole history of the empire, surpassed in its severity only by the fall of the Western empire in 471 AD.[66] The economy of this period suffered from failing markets and high inflation. In an economy characterized by high inflation it is favourable for creditors of medium- and long-term loans to insist on a forfeiture arrangement. The value of the pledged property will rise in relation to the sum loaned, so that the substitution of the borrowed sum with the charged property will put the creditor in a better position. Let us suppose that a loan of 100,000 sesterces with a term of three years is secured by a pledge of real estate, which at the time of the granting of the pledge has a market value of 120,000 sesterces. In times of hyperinflation (which did occur in the late empire) it may very well be that when, after three years, the loan must be repaid the market value of the property has risen to 500,000 sesterces. If the borrower would fail to repay the loan, forfeiture of the pledged real estate would be favourable for the lender: a claim with a nominal value of 100,000 sesterces would be substituted with real estate with a market value of 500,000 sesterces. The surplus value of 400,000 sesterces could be pocketed by the lender so that the original balance between the amount of the secured debt and the value of the collateral is more or less maintained.

This economic advantage of conditional sales for lenders in times of heavy inflation disappears where they must pay the fair market value (determined at the time of the debtor's failure to pay) of the pledged property to borrowers. Pursuant to the rescript by Septimius Severus and Caracalla, on which Marci. D. 20.1.16.9 is based, the lender must pay to the borrower the balance of the secured debt (100,000 sesterces) and the purchase price (500,000), which is the surplus value of 400,000 sesterces. Would the imperial rescript referred to by Marcian have put an end to the practice of conditional sales? This is by no means certain. Conditional sales of this type can still be an efficient means of taking recourse against charged assets, even when they do not provide protection against inflation. They dispense with the need to auction the property soon after the debtor has defaulted. In a depressed market, the creditor can purchase the pledged property for a low price, has the option to wait for better times for selling the property, or has the opportunity to sell the property outside the framework of an execution sale (which may render a lower price

[66] Giardina 2007: 757.

than an ordinary sale). In modern Italian law, the transactional practice discussed in Marci. D. 20.1.16.9 has never disappeared and is still referred to as '*patto Marciano*'.[67]

Sale to the creditor after the secured debt is due and payable: Marcell. D. 13.7.34

Marci. D. 46.3.44 discusses the case where the debtor sells the pledged property to the creditor in order to discharge the secured debt. The text does not express any reservations (like *iustum pretium* as in Marci. D. 20.1.16.9). However, the crucial difference is that in this text the sale is not conditional upon a future event of default in respect of the secured loan but takes place *after* the secured debt has become due and payable.[68] From an earlier period, the *Corpus iuris civilis* contains a—problematic—text by Marcellus, which from the 'renaissance' of Roman law in the twelfth century until this day has received different interpretations.[69]

> D. 13.7.34. *Marcellus libro singulari responsorum.* Titius cum credidisset pecuniam Sempronio et ob eam pignus accepisset futurumque esset, ut distraheret eam creditor, quia pecunia non solveretur, petit a creditore, ut fundum certo pretio emptum haberet, et cum impetrasset, epistulam, qua se vendidisse fundum creditori significaret, emisit: quaero, an hanc venditionem debitor revocare possit offerendo sortem et usuras quae debentur. Marcellus respondit secundum ea, quae proposita essent, revocare non posse.
>
> Titius lent money to Sempronius and took a pledge against the loan. When sale of the pledge was imminent because the money had not been paid, the debtor asked the lender to buy the estate at a given price. Having succeeded in his request, he sent a letter reciting that he had sold the estate to the lender. Question: Can the debtor set this sale aside on tender of the

[67] In Italian law, the '*patto Marciano*' (whose name is a direct reference to Marci. D. 20.1.16.9) is valid and enforceable without an express statutory basis. See Cass. n. 1625/2015; Cass. n. 844/2020. The Italian legislator recently included the *patto Marciano* in special legislation, see art. 48-*bis* and art. 120-*quinquiesdecies* Testo Unico Bancario and art. 11-*quaterdecies* Law n. 248/2005 (amended by Law n.44/2015).

[68] See also Paul. D. 13.7.20.3 and Tryph. D. 20.5.12 pr. See also Schanbacher 2002a: 642–3.

[69] Verhagen 2011b.

principal and interest which are due? Marcellus's reply was that on the story as set out no revocation was possible.

At first glance the case seems to be a simple one.[70] Creditor Titius informs his debtor Sempronius that he intends to sell the pledged *fundus* to a third party by way of execution. Sempronius then offers Titius the possibility that the *fundus* will remain with Titius by way of purchase. After Titius has accepted the offer, Sempronius gives him a written confirmation. If Sempronius later seeks to redeem the pledged *fundus*, this is no longer possible since it has already been validly sold and delivered to Titius. In this interpretation, a constructive forfeiture arrangement exists: the debtor sells the charged object to the creditor due to default. This, however, involves a forfeiture arrangement that is made only *after* the default has occurred, which in later times was considered less onerous than a forfeiture arrangement concluded at the time of granting the pledge.[71] In my view, it therefore is certainly possible that Marcellus's text does concern the purchase of a charged object by the creditor himself.

The problem with this interpretation is that not Sempronius but Titius appears to be the subject of '*petit a creditore*'.[72] Titius may therefore not be regarded as the creditor to whom the request is made to buy the charged object. According to the greater part of modern literature, there must thus have been a third party in the case of D. 13.7.34.[73] According to Peters and Kaser, Sempronius has granted a right of pledge to Titius as additional security for fulfilling the repayment obligation under a loan provided by Titius with the funds of a third party.[74] When Sempronius later defaulted in repaying the loan, Titius sold the pledged object to this third party and notified Sempronius of this in writing. In this interpretation, there is no purchase by the creditor to whom the purchased property had been pledged.[75] However, might it not be the case that the text was passed down to us in a somewhat corrupted state? In the older Romanist literature, several conjectures have

[70] For a more comprehensive discussion on the interpretations of D. 13.7.34, see Zülch 2001: 63–75.

[71] Verhagen 2011b. See also pp. 352–3.

[72] The other arguments raised against the two-party case are not convincing in my view: see Verhagen 2011b: 119–20.

[73] Amongst others, Peters 1973: 140–2; Noordraven 1999: 264–7; Zülch 2001: 67–75.

[74] Peters 1973: 140–2; Kaser 1982: 74 n 91.

[75] According to Noordraven (1999: 266), the fragment can only be explained if there is a *fiducia cum creditore* between both Sempronius and Titius as well as between Titius and a third party. If Titius is then in default and the third party is preparing to sell the charged property by way of execution, Titius has the power as (fiduciary) owner to transfer the property in lieu of payment to his own creditor (the third party) as part of the second *fiducia*. The 'purchase' to which the fragment refers is, according to Noordraven, in fact a transfer in lieu of payment.

been suggested—for example, that 'Sempronius' should simply be inserted after '*petit a creditore*'.[76] This approach has, in any case, become dominant in the *ius commune*. Starting with Jacques de Revigny, D. 13.7.34 will be used as the main authority for the validity of a forfeiture arrangement that was agreed after the secured debt had fallen due.[77]

Evaluation

Can Marci. D. 20.1.16.9 still be reconciled with the late classical constitutions, which provide that the creditor should sell the pledged object to a third party and only allow him to acquire its ownership with the express permission of the emperor (*impetratio dominii*)? According to some modern authors, it cannot: these constitutions should be interpreted as invalidating forfeiture arrangements (including conditional sales).[78] This would mean that the rescript by Septimius Severus and Caracalla of Marci. D. 20.1.16.9, which allowed forfeiture arrangements based on the collateral's market value, was rendered obsolete by the constitutions of Alexander Severus soon after and again in the next century, by Constantine's unequivocal prohibition of forfeiture clauses. Another interpretation is more plausible.[79] It is clear that at the end of the classical period the creditor was obliged to pay the surplus to the debtor. It would be inconsistent with this that forfeiture arrangements allowing the creditor to purchase the pledged property for the amount of the loan would be valid. If, on the other hand, the parties had agreed that the purchase price would reflect the market value, then the surplus would go to the debtor and there would be no need to invalidate the conditional sale. It is not unlikely that the *Compilatores* endorsed the same interpretation.[80] It may not be a coincidence that, despite Alex. C. 8.34.1 and Const. C. 8.34.3, Marci. D. 20.1.16.9 has been included in the *Corpus iuris civilis*, while Papinian FV 9 has been left out.[81] In this interpretation, only conditional sales of the type described by Papinian FV 9 would be invalid. As to the *impetratio dominii*, this could well only have been necessary where the parties had failed to reach

[76] Proposed by Krüger and Kreller. See Zülch 2001: 61, with references.

[77] Verhagen 2011b: 128–30. [78] Noordraven 1999: 259–62.

[79] See Verhagen 2011b: 114–18, 120–2.

[80] In the medieval *ius commune* C. 8.34(35).1, C. 8.34(35).3, and D. 20.1.16.9 are almost always discussed in connection with each other. The conclusion generally reached by the learned jurists (e.g., Azo, Accursius, Bartolus, Baldus) is that forfeiture clauses are valid, provided the charged object is valued (by an external appraiser or court) at its market price. See Verhagen 2011b.

[81] See Verhagen 2011b: 120–2.

agreement on a sale or *datio in solutum* to the creditor. In other words, the existence of the *impetratio dominii* does not necessarily exclude the validity of forfeiture arrangements in the form of conditional sales or *dationes in solutum*.

The underlying principle which can be distilled from the legal sources is that an invalid forfeiture clause has two elements: if one of these elements is absent, then a *valid* clause has been established. First, it is aimed at a default which might possibly occur in the future. If the acquisition of the charged object is the result of an agreement which has been concluded only after the occurrence of the default, then the first characteristic is missing and a valid acquisition exists.[82] Secondly, the surplus value contained in the charged object accrues to the creditor. If the second characteristic is lacking, because the arrangement by the parties is based on the market value of the charged object and payment of the surplus value to the debtor, then a legally valid clause has been established.[83] This synthesis is not expressed in the *Corpus iuris civilis* itself, not even in Constantine's prohibition. For this, we need to turn to the jurists of the *ius commune*.[84]

11.5 Excursion: Constantine's Prohibition of Forfeiture Clauses

It may be deduced from a number of texts discussed in this chapter that, despite the fact that in the classical period the pledge enforceable by sale eventually evolved into the normal type of pledge, there seemed to have been a need for parties in the high and late classical period to use a forfeiture clause in practice. In the days of Constantine, that must certainly have been the case. The negotiation of a forfeiture clause fits in well with a period that saw high levels of inflation and a shortage of credit.[85] The shortage of credit probably meant that financiers were, in fact, able to impose onerous conditions upon their debtors, such as a forfeiture clause, due to their dominant economic position. With his decree on the annulment of the *lex commissoria*, Constantine intended to put an end to such practices.

[82] D. 13.7.34. A sale or transfer in lieu of payment which is not triggered by default at all can occur for the duration of the pledge (C. 8.13.13; D. 13.7.20.3; D. 20.5.12 pr.).

[83] D. 20.1.16.9.

[84] Verhagen 2011b.

[85] The Roman Empire in the first decade of the fourth century AD saw chronic inflation. See Callu and Barrandon 1986. See also Harper 2017: 177: 'Monetary instability choked credit markets and stifled exchange.'

Constantine's monetary policy

A major factor contributing to rising inflation in the late Roman empire was the monetary policy of successive emperors. The traditional basis of the Roman monetary system was silver coinage.[86] Under Septimius Severus, the silver *denarius* only contained fifty per cent of actual silver. Under subsequent emperors, the debasement of the silver coinage continued, with the effect that at the time of Diocletian the *denarius* had become a coin of silver-plated copper.[87] The tide changed when Constantine realized that it would be impossible to defend the *denarius* and introduced a new monetary system based on the gold *solidus*. The exchange value of the *solidus* was equivalent to its intrinsic value in gold. The introduction of the *solidus* in 309 AD has been labelled as one of the few examples of a monetary reform that was successful.[88] The *solidus* became a stable currency and remained so for centuries. Its stability made it an excellent reference currency for measuring debts and it became standard practice for parties to agree to the *solidus* as the contractual currency of loan agreements.[89] Despite its negative effect of widening the gap between the rich and the poor, the introduction of the *solidus* was, all in all, beneficial to the Roman economy: 'The monetary unity and stability it afforded reinforced the political unity established by Constantine and helped to stabilize long-distance exchange and loans, thereby facilitating commerce.'[90]

C. 8.34.3: Constantine's prohibition of forfeiture

The consequences of Constantine's monetary reform for inflation were ambiguous. For the elite, whose liquidity was expressed in *solidi*, it resulted in a stable currency preserving (or even increasing) their wealth. For the poorer classes, which continued to use the existing silver- (or rather: copper-) based currency, Constantine's monetary reform led to huge increases of prices expressed in bronze and silver-plated coins, and virtually wiped out their purchasing power.[91] This may have caused lenders to insist on the

[86] Giardina 2007: 759. [87] Giardina 2007: 760.

[88] Depeyrot 1988: 237–40: Andreau 1999: 32–3.

[89] Depeyrot 1988: 239. However, one would think that this would primarily be the case for substantial loans and that consumer credit for the lower classes may still have been expressed in the silver and bronze currencies.

[90] Depeyrot 1988: 240. [91] Giardina 2007: 760.

inclusion of forfeiture clauses in pledge agreements, which borrowers in need of credit were forced to accept. It is this practice which Constantine wished to combat. The prohibition by Constantine is formulated as follows:[92]

> **Const. C. 8.34.3.** Quoniam inter alias captiones praecipue commissoriae pignorum legis crescit asperitas, placet infirmari eam et in posterum omnem eius memoriam aboleri. **1.** Si quis igitur tali contractu laborat, hac sanctione respiret, quae cum praeteritis praesentia quoque depellit et futura prohibet. creditores enim re amissa iubemus recuperare quod dederunt.
>
> Since, among other frauds, the harshness of the forfeiture clause for pledges has grown conspicuously, it is held that it is void and that all remembrance of it is permanently abolished. If, therefore, anyone is burdened with such a contract, he may recover his breath through the present enactment which invalidates both current and past (agreements) and prohibits future ones. For We order that creditors lose the property while recovering what they gave.

This constitution is enacted as a general law (*ad populum*) and drafted in a rhetorical style which is typical for many of Constantine's general constitutions.[93] According to Levy, it was part of a much larger legislative reform project.[94] Forfeiture clauses in pledge agreements are declared null and void with retroactive effect: not only are pledge agreements concluded on or after the date of the constitution affected, but also forfeiture clauses included in contracts entered into before that date. The debtor could recover the pledged object from the creditor, even if the creditor had already acquired its ownership through forfeiture.[95] Although Constantine's constitution did provide protection to debtors as structurally weaker parties, it still was rather creditor-friendly. Constantine's decree merely led to partial nullity: only the forfeiture clause itself was null and void. The right of pledge itself continued to be valid, and the creditor could remain in possession of the pledged property. If a debtor who invoked the nullity of a forfeiture clause failed to repay the secured debt, then the creditor did not have to return the pledged object and could sell it to a third party by way of execution.[96] The effect of Constantine's

[92] Constantine's constitution is also included in C.Th. 3.2.1.

[93] Dillon 2012: 65–89. [94] Levy 1956: 191.

[95] According to Levy (1956: 191–2), forfeiture clauses were not void *ab initio*, but voidable. The '*pecuniam revocet*' in C. 8.34.3 means that the debtor (not the creditor) could accelerate the loan, repay the borrowed sum, and thus ensure that the creditor return the pledged property.

[96] Levy 1956: 192.

constitution is similar to that of Alexander Severus's constitution of 222 AD (C. 8.34.1): the creditor's right of forfeiture is replaced with a default-based statutory right to sell the pledged object to third parties.

Justinian law and *ius commune*

Constantine's prohibition has been maintained in the *Corpus iuris civilis*. As such, it has had a major impact on the European *ius commune* and the codifications based thereon.[97] It is remarkable, however, that despite the Constantinian prohibition, the majority of classical texts discussed in this chapter, in particular Marci. D. 20.1.16.9 (purchase at a fair price), have been retained by Justinian. This might be considered an error: the *Compilatores* have overlooked the contradiction. One could also search for an explanation which harmonizes the texts.[98] The elements for what later in the medieval *ius commune* were considered invalid forfeiture clauses, and which are still present in modern codifications,[99] are already found across several fragments in the *Corpus iuris civilis*.[100] The conclusion for classical law is that, during the entire classical period, forfeiture clauses were deemed legally valid, maybe at first as express forfeiture clauses and over time as constructive forfeiture arrangements (conditional sale, transfer in lieu of payment). When it became settled that the creditor was obliged upon execution to pass on the surplus value to the debtor, forfeiture clauses agreed to *at the time of granting the pledge* continued to be valid, provided they entailed that the surplus would indeed go to the debtor.[101] In modern civil law systems, a transfer of charged property to the creditor, which is agreed upon *after* the secured debt has become due, is regarded as valid without qualification. The origins of this principle can be traced back to Jacques de Revigny (ca. 1235–1296), who considered it to be consistent with C. 8.34.3, but it has classical Roman antecedents.[102]

[97] Verhagen 2011b. [98] See also Schanbacher 2002a: 655–7.

[99] For example, § 1149 and 1229 German civil code, art. 2744 Italian civil code, arts 1859 and 1884 Spanish civil code and art. 3:235 Dutch civil code. Pursuant to the original art. 2070(2) of the French *Code civil*, forfeiture clauses were void (see also art. 2088 for *antichrèse*). Since 2006, art. 2348 French civil code does allow forfeiture clauses which are agreed at the time of granting the right of pledge. The value of the property must be determined by an independent expert or by the court, and the surplus must be paid to the debtor.

[100] Section 11.4 (p. 362). [101] Marci. D. 20.1.16.9.

[102] Marcell. D. 13.7.34. For the *ius commune* and the codifications, see Verhagen 2011b: 124–5, 127–30, 132–3, 137–8.

12

Adaptedness of *Pignus* and *Hypotheca*

12.1 Introduction

From the second Punic war until the Antonine plague, the right of pledge evolved from a single possessory pledge over a specific physical thing to a highly versatile security interest that could be granted multiple times over the same asset, as a non-possessory pledge, over receivables, and even over an entire fluctuating patrimony. The evolution of the Roman law of real security was largely triggered by transactional practices, which were accommodated into the existing legal framework by the jurists and supplemented or corrected by the imperial chancery. What was the result, at the end of the Principate, of these evolutionary processes? Did they lead to a law that was adapted to its economic environment?[1] Did the law of real security contribute to economic growth? These questions are not easy to answer for legal historians without a background in economics. What legal historians can do is to examine whether there is enough similarity between contemporary and Roman laws of secured credit in order to make meaningful comparisons. Analytical tools developed by Law and Economics (L&E) and New Institutional Economics (NIE) can be usefully employed to work on Roman legal institutions (section 12.2). We can look, therefore, at what economic analyses of law have to say about the role of the law of secured credit in modern economies, and apply their findings to Roman law (section 12.3). It will appear that classical Roman law of the second and third century AD had all but one (public title registries) of the features which economists consider important for effective collateral laws.[2] The negative effects of the Romans' failure to set up a public register for ownership and security interests in the western part of the empire may for a long time have been neutralized by contractual practices and social norms.[3] This makes it plausible that, for most of the Principate, the Roman law of real security was capable of facilitating credit in a similar manner as its

[1] 'Adaptedness involves the extent to which a social pattern actually benefits the individuals who originated (inherited, borrowed) it' (Sanderson: 2007: 296–7).
[2] For the Roman real security and the economy, see in particular, Pellecchi 2018 and Verhagen 2020.
[3] Pellecchi 2018: 479–88; Verhagen 2020: 138–45.

Security and Credit in Roman Law: The historical evolution of pignus *and* hypotheca. Hendrik L. E. Verhagen, Oxford University Press. © Hendrik L. E. Verhagen 2022. DOI: 10.1093/oso/9780199695836.003.0013

descendants do in modern economies and, therefore, that it did contribute to economic growth in the Principate (section 12.4).

12.2 An Economic Perspective

Legal institutions can be reviewed at two levels: as exogenous and as endogenous variables. When legal institutions are regarded as exogenous variables, the central question is which effects they have on other variables in which economists (or other social scientists) are interested (e.g., economic growth).[4] Legal institutions can also be reviewed at a different level, as endogenous variables that themselves have to be explained. Here, the main purpose is to explain the origin and development of legal institutions.[5] The main strength of economic analyses of law is that they provide the best available methods for analysing the economic effects of legal rules and institutions (exogenous variables).[6] When one is primarily interested in the effects which economic factors have on the evolution of legal institutions (endogenous variables), economic analyses could lead to underestimating the distinctiveness of the legal system and the contribution of factors which are internal to that system.[7] This is, however, not to say that analytical tools developed by L&E and NIE, such as 'bounded rationality', 'path dependence', and 'institutional refinement', cannot be usefully employed to work on institutions as endogenous variables.[8] The motivation of transacting parties, praetors, emperors, and jurists to reach economically sensible solutions was an evolutionary force. The assumption that these persons usually acted rationally can, moreover, help us in trying to reconstruct certain legal consequences on which the legal sources

[4] There are two forms of growth: aggregate (extensive) growth and per capita (intensive) growth. Aggregate growth is simply the result of demographic growth: gross domestic product (GDP) increases merely because there are more people contributing to it. Per capita growth takes place where each worker is producing more, as a result of greater efficiency in production. Per capita growth is generally regarded as the most significant factor for economic progress (Bowman and Wilson 2009: 28.).

[5] Voigt 2019: 20–1.

[6] In their contribution on law and economic institutions, Frier and Kehoe (2007) suggest how the methods developed by L&E and NIE can be applied to examine how economic growth within the ancient world was fostered or impeded by the legal framework. See also Kehoe 2007, Dari-Mattiacci 2015, and other contributions to Kehoe, Ratzan, and Yiftach 2015; Lo Cascio and Mantovani 2018; Willems 2017; and the contributions to Dari-Mattiacci and Kehoe 2020a and 2020b. For a promising approach to legal evolution from the perspective of evolutionary economics, see Eckardt 2011.

[7] Teubner 1988: 222; Luhmann 2004: 63–5; 391–402; Deakin and Carvalho 2011: 112–19; Cotterrell 2006: 6, 18–19.

[8] In the same sense, Frier and Kehoe 2007; Kehoe 2007: 1–52.

are silent.[9] The most important contribution of economic analyses of law for this book, however, is that the economic functions which are attributed to real security can be applied to the Roman law of real security.[10] This can enhance our understanding of whether the Roman law of real security was adapted to its economic environment and contributed positively to economic performance in the Roman empire.

Legal institutions as exogenous variable: measuring economic growth

Measuring growth is the primary task of the *economic* historian.[11] The economic historian's task extends to 'investigating the institutional developments that made it possible to reach a certain level of... capital accumulation': '[r]endering the complexity of this evolution is the key to making sense of the process of growth.'[12] It is the *legal* historian's primary task to render the complexity of *legal* evolution: this task has been performed for *pignus* and *hypotheca* in this book. For investigating how legal institutions may have contributed to economic growth, legal historians are less well equipped. Nevertheless, here also they can contribute to the economic debate. One possible approach in order to measure—in the absence of sufficient statistical data—per capita growth is: 'to identify the existence in antiquity of drivers of economic growth, to demonstrate that the conditions existed which would have made growth possible.'[13] Among the relevant conditions are 'institutional attitudes and stimuli' as appear from 'documentary and epigraphic evidence.'[14] I would think that the existence of a versatile law of secured credit, as appears from the Sulpicii archive and can be reconstructed from the *Corpus iuris civilis*, would count among the conditions which would have made economic growth possible.

In section 12.3 secured credit will be analysed from an economic perspective, not because I regard the drive to minimize transaction costs as the *only*

[9] See for instance my discussions of forfeiture in chapter 5, the determination of the monetary value of *quanti ea res erit* for the *actio Serviana* in the Appendix, and the disposition of generally pledged goods and the manumission of generally pledged slaves in sections 9.6 and 9.7.

[10] Verhagen 2020: 115–21.

[11] Bresson 2016: xxi. On measuring economic growth in the Rome empire, see in particular Bowman and Wilson 2009 and Kay 2014: 269–78.

[12] Bresson 2016: xxii.

[13] Bowman and Wilson 2009: 30.

[14] Bowman and Wilson 2009: 30.

evolutionary force in law,[15] but, rather, in order to review the *adaptedness* of the Roman law of real security to an economic environment in which credit played a significant role. Law and Economics has provided valuable insights into the role of the law of secured credit in modern economies. In my contribution to *Roman Law and Economics*, I have concluded that the economic functions of security identified in economic analyses of secured credit (e.g., risk reduction, reduction of monitoring costs, depersonalizing credit relationships) were also performed by real security in the Roman economy.[16] There is, therefore, enough similarity with the role of the law of secured credit in the Roman empire in order to apply the findings of Law and Economics to it. If the modern laws of real security contribute to economic growth in civil law jurisdictions, then Roman law may very well have had the same effect, since the former is based on (and to a large extent still identical to) the latter.

Economic considerations of the jurists

Gordley argues that Law and Economics is based on a 'fallacy' as it assumes that because a given rule leads to a certain result, and that result furthers someone's interest, the rule was made to promote that interest (efficiency). But the 'rules to which they refer are ancient and framed by jurists who could not possibly have these purposes in mind'.[17] Of course, it is true that the Roman jurists did not ponder the efficiency of a legal rule, as understood by modern Law and Economics. There can be no doubt, however, that the Roman jurists did take (what we call) economic considerations into account when designing or supporting new legal rules.[18] They usually failed to disclose them, or to describe them in a manner which is accessible to us.[19] It is extremely difficult to imagine that legal fields such as the Roman law of contracts, the liability of masters for contracts by their slaves (*actiones adjecticiae qualitatis*), inheritance law, and the law of (personal and real) security were

[15] Luhmann 2004: 266 criticizes the position that 'evolution supports institutions that save transaction and other costs'. I am less sceptical than Luhmann in this respect.

[16] Verhagen 2020: 115–21. See also section 1.5.

[17] Gordley 2019: 766–7. In a similar fashion, Boldizzoni 2011: 84.

[18] In his study on the rules for the liability for defective goods, which were developed by the aediles with jurisdiction over market transactions, Kupisch (2002: 54) suggests examining whether, in certain areas of Roman law, an economic analysis of law *avant la lettre* can be found. For an overview of subsequent research following Kupisch's suggestion, see Willems 2017. See also Kehoe, Ratzan, and Yiftach 2015.

[19] On economic considerations by Roman jurists, see Sirks 2002: 139; Vivenza 2012: 36; and numerous contributions to Lo Cascio and Mantovani 2018 (e.g., Andreau, De Ligt, Pellecchi).

developed by the jurists without regard to the needs of the Roman economy and society in general.[20] Gordley's critique would be justified if the validity of economic analyses of legal change depended on the assumption that, in order for a rule to enhance efficiency, the jurists framing this rule must have intended this. But this assumption is clearly wrong. Just as certain legal rules which were intended to enhance efficiency may fail to achieve this, other rules may turn out to be efficient as an unintended side effect.[21] This useful effect, although not intended, may have contributed to the survival of the rules concerned.[22] This is precisely what is claimed by evolutionary theories of legal and economic change.

There can be no doubt that the Roman jurists *did* take economic considerations into account when dealing with *pignus* and *hypotheca*. It is true, as Schulz observed, that the Roman jurists did not formulate questions like 'What is the economic function of the pledge'.[23] Pellecchi has recently observed that the Roman jurists did not reach their conclusions on the basis of assessments which were conditioned by their economic impact.[24] The 'horizon' of the jurists was essentially defined by the logical structure (legal dogmatics) of the various institutions which the 'polymorphous nature' of the *conventio pignoris* allowed to bring into play.[25] In those few cases where one succeeded in overcoming this fundamental logical structure, this did not happen with the intention to steer the market for secured credit in one or another direction, but simply in order to safeguard, in any case, the choices made by the parties (party autonomy).[26] On this point, I largely but not entirely agree with Pellecchi's (otherwise convincing) account of the economic dimensions of the Roman law of real security. The Roman jurists were frequently prepared to go a long way in order to respect party autonomy and accommodate new variants of *pignus* and *hypotheca* into the system of Roman private law.[27] The *hypotheca* granted *nuda conventione*, the transformation of the *actio Serviana* from an *actio in rem* to an *actio in personam* (*pignus nominis* and *antichresis*), the *ius offerendi et succedendi* and its extension to novation and the general pledge (which most modern civil law jurisdictions still fail to recognize); these are all quite radical innovations, which greatly enhanced the economic adaptedness of the right of pledge. The jurists' main concern, it is true, would normally not be to find the most economically efficient solution, but to find a

[20] Dari-Mattiacci 2015: 275. [21] See also Pellecchi 2018: 480, 488; De Ligt 2020: 96.
[22] Dari-Mattiacci 2015: 276. [23] Schulz 1936: 25. See also Pellecchi 2018: 456.
[24] In the same sense, De Ligt 2020: 96, 104. [25] Pellecchi 2018: 419.
[26] Pellecchi 2018: 490. [27] On Roman party autonomy, see Baldus 2010.

juridically consistent solution for a new problem.[28] The adaptation of an existing form of action by the praetor to a new situation would involve this kind of consistency.[29] But this does not contradict the fact that economic considerations *avant la lettre* did influence the evolution of Roman law. Throughout this book, we have again and again encountered examples of jurists' opinions 'dominated by pecuniary calculation'.[30] We can see this, for instance, in their opinions on the entitlement of lower-ranking pledge creditors to surplus proceeds, the amortization of principal and interest in antichretic pledges, the conditional sale of pledged assets to the creditor for their market value, and in their opinions on whether the secured creditor's interest should be measured in terms of the value of the pledged assets or the amount of the secured debt. The jurists have identified economic issues of collateral which are still relevant today.

Utilitas

According to Watson, the Romans jurists not only failed to give economic motivations, they also rarely justified a rule with reference to known concepts such as *utilitas*. 'Usefulness was not a juristic argument towards a result.'[31] But, frequently, jurists, from Labeo to Ulpian and Paul, did use the concept of 'utility' (*utilitas*) in order to prevent the outcome that a legal rule 'would have led to a result contrary to the needs of legal practice'.[32] A good example from the law of real security is the following statement by Ulpian, on the practice of allowing a debtor to remain in physical control of the object of pledge pursuant to *precarium*: 'And this opinion is most serviceable (*utilissima*), since every day creditors are asked for *precarium* by people for property they have given them in pledge, and *precarium* must apply.'[33] According to Ulpian, daily practice provides the justification for the lawfulness of a legal arrangement chosen by the parties (which was, in effect, a non-possessory pledge), despite the fact that, as a general rule, one cannot hold property one already owns

[28] Pellecchi 2018: 480, 488, and 490. [29] Pellecchi 2018: 480–8, 490.

[30] Hodgson 2001: 351. In a similar sense, with reference to Cato, De Neeve 1984: 95–6; Kay 2014: 152–5. For a good example of economic rationality in respect of real security, see also Pliny's remarks on selling tenants' assets too readily. Plin., *Ep.* 3.19.6.

[31] Watson 2007: 23.

[32] Ankum 2010: 6. Navarra (2002: 12) has identified more than sixty fragments in which a rule is justified by its usefulness (*utilitatis causa, propter utilitatem, utilitatis gratia*). See, recently, also De Ligt 2020: 94–5; Johnston 2022: 34.

[33] Ulp. D. 43.26.6.4.

(as a debtor does in case of *pignus*) pursuant to *precarium*.[34] Another interesting example is Paul's discussion of the opinion of Pomponius, that an agreement to pledge a servitude to a creditor with neighbouring land should be upheld, in the sense that the creditor can exercise the servitude and (after default) sell it to another neighbour. Paul says that Pomponius's opinion should be accepted in view of the benefit to the parties ('*propter utilitatem contrahentium*').[35] The practical advantage of enhancing the debtor's access to credit prevailed over the dogmatic problems of pledging incorporeal assets and selling a servitude independently of the land for whose benefit it was granted.[36] Therefore, although it is certainly true that the highly versatile and effective legal regime of *pignus* and *hypotheca* was not the result of deliberate economic design by praetors, jurists and emperors,[37] this does not rule out that in many instances (what we would now call) economic considerations did support legal solutions.

12.3 Features of a Well-adapted Law of Real Security

The empirical research on the lending behaviour of banks in modern economies demonstrates the importance of the law of real security as a driver for the availability of credit.[38] The research of mid- and eastern European transition economies by Haselmann, Pistor, and Vig shows that 'improvements in collateral law seem to have a statistically significant effect on bank lending'.[39] In a more recent research project on the laws of real security in contemporary economies, Calomoris and his co-researchers have used a cross-country micro-level dataset providing information regarding asset liquidation values in order to examine whether different laws of real security with respect to movable assets and receivables did have an impact on lending by banks in the reviewed countries.[40] Their conclusion was that differences in legal systems' ability to support the use of movable assets and receivables as collateral for bank loans 'substantially affect the ability of borrowers to gain access to credit'. They identified a number of features of laws of real security, each of which they consider important for the ability of debtors to use their movable assets and receivables as collateral and thus to enhance their access to credit.[41]

[34] See also Ulpian D. 13.5.14.1; Mod. D. 41.4.5; Marci. D. 20.1.16.7.
[35] Paul. D. 20.1.12. Pellecchi 2018: 490–7. [36] Ankum 2010: 19.
[37] Pellecchi 2018: 480, 488. [38] Haselmann, Pistor, and Vig 2010: 567–8.
[39] Haselmann, Pistor, and Vig 2010: 550–1. [40] Haselmann, Pistor, and Vig 2010.
[41] Calomiris et al. 2017: 168. See also Deakin, Mollica, and Sarkar 2017: 380.

In this section these requirements for an effective law of security, which are to a large extent a reflection of its economic functions, will be applied (in slightly modified form) to Roman law.[42] It will appear that the classical Roman law of the third century AD satisfies all these requirements, with the exception of one: a collateral registry.

List of features

In their contribution, Calomiris and his co-authors list a number of features of laws of real security enhancing access to credit, which I have adapted in order to reflect the special characteristics of the Roman economy.[43]

1. The law allows a debtor to grant a (possessory or non-possessory) security right in a single category of movable assets, or in substantially all its movable and immovable assets and receivables, without requiring a specific description of the collateral, and (ideally) with a single method of creation. ☑
2. A security right can be given over future or after-acquired movable and immovable assets, and can extend automatically to the products, proceeds, or replacements of the original assets. ☑
3. The law allows the debtor and the creditor to agree who shall have the right to use the collateral, and certain rights to dispose of the collateral can be granted to the creditor or the debtor. ☑
4. A general description of debts is permitted in the collateral agreement and in registration documents. All types of debts can be secured between the parties, and the collateral agreement can include a maximum amount for which the assets are encumbered. ☑
5. Secured creditors are paid first (e.g., before tax claims and employee claims) when a debtor defaults outside an insolvency procedure. ☑
6. A collateral registry or registration institution for security interests over immovable and movable property is in operation, unified geographically and by asset type, and indexed by debtors' names.[44] �
7. The law allows parties to agree in a collateral agreement that the creditor can enforce its security right out of court. ☑

42 See also Pellecchi 2018 and Verhagen 2020.
43 Calomiris et al. 2017: 168.
44 Calomiris et al. 2017: 168, adds that this registry should have an electronic database.

Calomiris and his colleagues oppose the (greater) importance of movable assets and receivables in providing debt capacity for firms to that of real estate. This fits well for modern economies but is less suitable for the Roman empire, where the 'allocation of resources that favor immovable-based production'[45] was much more important.[46] In addition, the protection of debtors is left out of the picture by Calomiris and his co-authors, although a law of real security which is too harsh on security providers may cause them to shy away from credit markets.

Generic and general pledges (1); future assets, fruits, and products (2)

In order to reduce transaction costs, there should be as few formalities for creating security as possible.[47] For the creation of a right of *pignus* or *hypotheca*, no formalities existed. Initially, a full-fledged right *in rem* required that the charged property was somehow brought under the control of the creditor (*traditio, inductio*), but at a later stage non-possessory pledges could be created 'by mere agreement' (*nuda conventione*). In practice, however, the granting of a right of pledge would—for evidentiary purposes—be recorded on writing tablets or papyrus. During the course of the classical period it became standard practice that *res mancipi* were also charged by way of *pignus* or *hypotheca*.[48] Thus, a single method for creating security over all types of asset became available, which, moreover, could also be used for property acquired subsequently.[49] Any *admissible* form of property defined in the pledge agreement could be made the object of a right of pledge.[50] This would include a wide range of assets: movable property, slaves,[51] immovable

[45] Calomiris 2017: 183. [46] See section 3.4.

[47] According to Arruñada (2020: 275 n 36), my positive assessment of the effectiveness of *pignus* and *hypotheca* in Verhagen 2020 is based 'in particular' on Roman law's efficiency in creation (Verhagen 2020: 123–4), which he calls 'at most, a partial and doubtful advantage'. Arruñada reduces my analysis to one element, while in Verhagen 2020 I subject the Roman law of real security to a number of tests (priority and certainty in ranking, comprehensiveness, rights of use, enforcement, and publicity), of which efficiency of creation is only one. Arruñada aims his arrows at the wrong target: the disadvantages connected with efficiency in creation are—according to Arruñada—mainly 'hidden charges and title clouds'. These disadvantages are actually much more connected with lack of registration and the absence of a principle protecting bona fide third parties in Roman law (see pp. 380–1).

[48] *Fiducia cum creditore* had always been possible as a form of non-possessory security. The *mancipatio* did not require an actual transfer of possession. Often, the debtor would rent the property from the creditor or hold it as 'bailee' (*precarium*): Gai. *Inst.* 2.60. See section 6.7.

[49] See also Pellecchi 2018: 479; Verhagen 2020: 123–4. [50] Kaser 1982: 181–2.

[51] For an assessment of the value of slaves as collateral, see Du Plessis 2010: 52–9.

property, and even subordinate real rights (servitudes, usufructs).[52] In addition, the debtor's contractual claims against his debtors could be charged by way of *pignus*. It would also be possible to pledge one's co-ownership interest in property jointly owned with others and commonly owned property.[53] The description of the pledged assets contained in the *conventio pignoris* could be drafted in generic terms, for instance *invecta et illata*, a herd or a shop's inventory, without it being necessary that each individual item be identified and that frequent updates be executed for after-acquired items.[54] From the second century AD, it even became possible to create a 'floating charge' over all the debtor's present and future assets.[55] At an early stage, products from the pledged property could be pledged, provided this was expressly agreed. This is illustrated by the clause recommended by the early classical jurist Cassius in D. 13.7.18.3, that 'whatever things are the creation from and product of the wood' shall be pledged. Gaius (D. 20.1.15.1) and Papinian (D. 20.1.1 pr.) hold that virtually all *future assets* could be pledged by way of general pledge. For special pledges of assets acquired after the pledge was granted, it was originally required that they should have roots in the patrimony of the debtor at the time of the *conventio pignoris*, such as crops, offspring, or land purchased before the granting of the pledge (*res debita*). In late classical law (Marcian), future goods without such roots could be specifically pledged too, by including their acquisition by the debtor as a condition of the granting of the pledge.

Rights of disposition or use (3)

Empirical studies for contemporary economies demonstrate that non-possessory security leads to a greater availability of credit.[56] Charged assets that are essential for the debtor's business should still be able to generate income with which the secured debt can be discharged. By allowing the debtor to remain in possession of the charged assets, he or she will be able to continue using the assets for the exercise of a trade or profession. The archive of the Sulpicii provides epigraphic evidence of a transactional practice of creating non-possessory pledges already in the first century AD. A non-possessory pledge would be even more effective if the debtor were able (with the creditor's

[52] Pellecchi 2018: 488–97.

[53] Ant. C. 8.20.1; Pap. 20.4.3.2; Gai. D. 20.6.7.4; Marci. D. 20.6.8.3. See also Frezza 1963: 148–50.

[54] Lab. D. 20.6.14 (*invecta et illata*); D. 20.1.13 pr. (*grex*); D. 20.1.34 pr. (*taberna*).

[55] For example, Pap. D. 20.1.1. pr. Certain slaves (e.g., the debtor's concubine) or other property would not be subject to a general pledge.

[56] Armour 2008: 19; Calomiris et al. 2017: 165–6.

permission) to dispose of the charged assets in the ordinary course of his or her business. Although originally the debtor could not transfer pledged property, this later changed. With the secured creditor's (express or implied) consent, the debtor could transfer the pledged property without the pledge continuing to attach to it. For general pledges this may have been inherent to the legal nature of this variation of pledge. The logical sequel of the non-possessory pledge is the multiple pledge. In particular, when the (expected) liquidation proceeds of a charged asset exceed the amount of the secured debt, the debtor can optimize the collateral value of the asset if the law enables him or her to create several layers of security in favour of multiple creditors. During the course of classical law, the inability to create multiple pledges over the same assets disappeared, under the influence of transactional practices.

The availability of credit may be further enhanced by giving the *creditor* rights to use the charged assets or even dispose of them. In Roman law, such rights could take several forms. The creditor could use the (natural or civil) fruits of the charged property to discharge the secured debt or to cover the interest (*antichresis*). The creditor could also have the right to charge the collateral for his or her own debts ('rehypothecation').[57] Also, when a creditor assigns a secured claim to another person, that other person (the assignee) should be able to enforce the security when the assigned debt is not properly discharged. Although the assignment of debts was problematic in Roman law, devices were used to achieve the same results, and in those situations the 'assignee' was entitled to enforce the security.[58] One of the ways of 'assigning' the active side of debts was the replacement of the original creditor of the debt with the assignee as the new creditor by way of novation.[59] The replacement of creditors by way of novation was, however, far from efficient. Thus, a constitution by Gordian from 239 AD rules that, where a debt is transferred through novation, the security granted for the original debt should be granted again.[60]

Range of secured obligations (4)

In modern terminology, the classical right of pledge was an accessory right. The whole life of the right of pledge—from its inception to its end—would be

[57] For example, Ulp. D. 36.4.5.21 (fruits); Scaev. D. 44.3.14.3 (rehypothecation). On rehypothecation, see Wubbe 1958.

[58] For example, Paul. D. 18.4.6.

[59] Zimmermann 1990: 60–2.

[60] Gordian C. 8.26.1 pr. For certain cases of passive novation, however, an effective solution was found in the 'succession in one's own rank' (section 7.4).

determined by the existence of the secured debt. The accessory nature of *pignus* and *hypotheca* entailed, first and foremost, that the right of pledge could—in principle—only come into existence when there was a secured debt. Pursuant to the *formula* of the *actio Serviana*, it would come into existence as an actionable real right only 'for money owed', indebted either now or in the future.[61] The interpretation by the jurists of the words '*propter pecuniam debitam*' is a good example of how one condition of the conditional programme comprised in the *actio Serviana*'s form of action formed the basis for a refined set of sub-rules developed by the Roman jurists, which was well adapted to the economy. The principle of dependence (accessory nature of pledge) was not strictly applied by the jurists: pledges could also be granted for conditional and future debts. From Marci. D. 20.1.5 pr. it appears that debts arising under whatever contract (e.g., *mutuum, stipulatio,* sale, rent) or other legal basis (e.g., dowry) could be secured by a right of pledge.[62] The secured debt could not only be an obligation arising pursuant to *ius civile* (e.g., the contracts mentioned above) but could also arise as a matter of *ius honorarium* (e.g., *constitutum debiti*). It would be possible to grant a right of pledge for only part of the debts owed to the creditor (e.g., principal *or* interest, part of the rentals). It would also be possible that a right of pledge would be granted sometime after a loan (or other) agreement had been entered into, for instance because during the term of an unsecured loan the debtor's solvency had deteriorated and the creditor wanted to strengthen his position by taking a pledge. A constitution by Septimius Severus and Caracalla (C. 4.32.4.1) rules that where a pledge had been granted in order to secure interest, but afterwards the debtor promised that he would pay higher interest, the pledge could not be enforced for the higher interest 'since at that time, when the (original) documents were executed there was no agreement that the pledge be bound for such an addition'. This constitution indicates that increased interest would be secured where the pledge agreement had already specifically provided for this. Also, where a banker had provided a 'credit facility' to a client, giving the latter an option to borrow money, a right of pledge could already be granted,

[61] The other main feature of the accessory nature of the right of pledge is that, once the secured debt had been paid or satisfied, or the creditor had failed to accept payment, the *actio Serviana* could no longer be successfully instituted and the right of pledge had effectively ceased to exist. Out 2005; Marino 2018.

[62] The right of pledge could not, however, be used to secure obligations to convey property or to render services (but could presumably secure the expressed monetary value of performances in kind). Kaser 1982: 201, 261; Kaser, Knütel, and Lohse 2021: 232. In the same sense, Lenel 1927: 254, with reference to Ulpian D. 13.7.9 pr.-2; Ulp. D. 12.2.13.5; Pap. D. 3.5.31 pr. For a different view, see Smit 2020: 241–2.

provided that the *conventio pignoris* expressly defined the secured obligations with reference to the future loan.[63]

Ranking (5)

The creditor who was the first in time to take a right of pledge over one or more of the debtor's (or someone else's) assets could be sure that subsequent rights of pledge would not adversely affect his preferential right of recourse.[64] The ranking of multiple pledges over the same property would be determined by the *prior tempore* principle, and only the first ranking pledge creditor would have the right to sell the pledged property (*ius vendendi*).[65] Where the first ranking creditor would actually exercise his right of sale, lower-ranking pledges would be extinguished by operation of law.[66] Lower-ranking secured creditors eventually became as such entitled to the *superfluum*, even in the absence of an express or implied pledge thereof (as still contemplated by Gaius D. 20.1.15.2). When the debt secured by the first ranking pledge was discharged, the second-ranking pledge became a first ranking one, while other lower-ranking pledges would also shift rank correspondingly.[67] A lower-ranking creditor could accelerate this process, by exercising the so-called *ius offerendi et succedendi*. We have seen that the secured debt could be a conditional or future one or could even arise under a contract that still had to be entered into. In most cases, the ranking of the pledge as well as the ability to institute the *actio Serviana* would then still be determined with reference to the time at which the pledge was granted. From several Digest texts the principle emerges that the decisive factor for the priority of a right of pledge is the time at which it is certain that the debtor is bound by the secured debt. In other words, normally the priority and ranking of a right of pledge would be determined with reference to the time it was granted. This would be different, however, where the debtor was still at liberty to decide whether or not the secured debt would arise. The priority of the pledge would then be

[63] In the Digest we find a description of such an arrangement: Paul. D. 20.3.4.

[64] Ulp. D. 42.8.6.6 refers to an opinion by Labeo in which pledges are mentioned as an example of legal acts that are subject to the edict on fraudulent preferences. This principle of voidable or fraudulent preference ('*actio Pauliana*') one also finds—in one form or another—in modern legal systems. The granting of security which takes place at a time at which the debtor is already insolvent (or in certain other circumstances) can be declared null and void at the instigation of other creditors or an insolvency representative.

[65] Pap. D. 20.5.1; Marci. D. 20.5.5 pr.; Alex. C. 8.19.1 pr.; Diocl.-Max. C. 8.17.8. See also Ulp. D 42.1.15.5 on the execution sale of pledged property by way of *pignoris capio*.

[66] Marci. D. 20.4.12.7; Alex. C. 8.19.1 pr.

[67] Marci. D. 20.4.12. pr.

determined by the time the debtor became committed to the secured debt. All the cases discussed by the jurists are based on this principle.[68] Also, the opening of insolvency proceedings did not adversely affect the secured creditor's ability to take recourse against the charged assets. In Roman law, when insolvency proceedings were conducted in respect of the debtor, the secured creditor could still take recourse against the charged property with priority over other creditors. If the creditor was in possession of the charged property, he could sell it to third parties and would only be required to pay the surplus to the person conducting the insolvency proceedings (the *bonorum emptor*). If the pledge was non-possessory, the creditor could institute the *actio Serviana* to recover the pledged property from the person in charge of the relevant stage of the insolvency proceedings.[69] As a matter of Roman law, secured creditors could, therefore, generally be certain that the proceeds of the charged property were exclusively available in order to discharge the secured debt. The ranking of rights of pledge was only rarely reversed by operation of law. This did take place, however, in particular when the money provided by a later secured creditor was used for the benefit of the pledged property, such as the equipment, crew or repair of ships or the storage or transport of merchandise.[70] In an opinion by Papinian (D. 20.4.3.1) and in a constitution from 293 AD by Diocletianus and Maximianus (C. 8.17.7), the pledge over real estate and other goods (e.g., marble plates in Scaev. D. 20.4.21.1) granted to the lender who financed their purchase is considered to have priority over any other (general or special) pledge granted earlier.[71]

From the second century AD onwards, there was an increasing number of cases in which all the debtor's assets would be subject to a right of pledge (or 'pledge-like' privilege) arising by operation of law in favour of the imperial treasury. These fiscal general pledges may not have been as devastating for secured credit as is often assumed in modern literature.[72] In particular, where

[68] For example, Gai. D. 20.4.11 pr.; Gai. D. 20.4.11.1; Afr. D. 20.4.9 pr. For an elaborate analysis, see Out 2005: 72–9.

[69] Kaser and Hackl 1996: 402.

[70] Ulp. D. 20.4.5 and Ulp. D. 20.4.6. For a lucid analysis of texts dealing with credit *ad armandam vel reficiendam navem*, see Pellecchi 2018: 498–504.

[71] Pap. D. 20.2.1 states that by a *senatus consultum* under Marcus Aurelius the pledge of an *insula* granted to the creditor who made a loan for its renovation shall also enure in favour of the person who, at the owner's bidding, actually paid the building contractor. This 'superpriority' of so-called acquisition secured creditors can still be found in modern model laws. See Chapter V, art. 38 of the UNCITRAL Model Law on Secured Transactions (1 July 2016). See also § 9–103 of the United States Uniform Commercial Code (Purchase-money security interest) and Art. IX.—4:102 Draft Common Frame of Reference (Superpriority). Van Hoof 2022.

[72] For example, Kaser (1975: 313) considers it baffling how a collateral system could have existed at all which was so hostile to credit.

general pledges secured debts arising under loans or other contracts entered into between the treasury and citizens, the position would be exactly the same as with conventional pledges granted to private creditors. These general pledges would generally be subject to the *prior tempore* principle, so that they could not adversely affect existing security rights.[73] But, for fiscal preferences too the guiding principle was that imperial procurators, shall in their enforcement, not infringe the rights of prior pledge creditors.[74] They shall only be authorized to sell property charged with anterior pledges where there is a surplus value, and prior creditors shall be paid first.[75] In the late classical period a tendency may have started to grant a special position to the treasury.[76] However, if in the late Empire tax burden was low, as it very well may have been,[77] fiscal general pledges may not have been seriously disruptive at all. The large amount of late classical jurists' opinions and imperial constitutions on *pignus* and *hypotheca*, in any case, do suggest that these security interests continued to be widely used. This could be an indication that fiscal general pledges were not fatal for the effectiveness of real security.

Publicity (6)

For a long time, the combination of social norms, legal rules, and transactional practices must have worked reasonably well to remedy the lack of publicity and the absence of a general principle protecting bona fide third parties.[78] It was only by the end of the second century AD that this combination may have started to become less effective and that pledging someone else's or previously charged property became a serious problem. The case of publicity shows that Hayek's spontaneous orders are not always capable of achieving the most efficient solution (with the lowest transaction costs).[79] Here, the Roman state could have intervened (as it did in Roman Egypt) by setting up public registries in which ownership and other real rights were

[73] Wieacker 1939: 247; Wagner 1974: 158–95, 202; Wieling 1989: 425. Also in other respects fiscal pledges were treated in accordance with the same principles and rules governing conventional pledges. Thus, in Paul. D. 40.1.10 (fiscal pledge) and Marci. D. 40.8.6 (conventional pledge) the manumission of generally pledged slaves could be objected not only against private creditors but also against the treasury. Also, in other respects (set-off, liability of sureties) the treasury is treated on the same footing as ordinary creditors by the emperors, the Severi in particular. See Daalder 2018: 441–2.

[74] Marci. D. 49.14.22.

[75] Klingenberg 1992: 388–9.

[76] Wieling 1989: 426.

[77] Hopkins 1980: 116–20. See more recently, Bransbourg 2014.

[78] Pellecchi 2018: 479–88; Verhagen 2020: 131–49.

[79] Dari-Mattiacci 2015: 285. 'The basic tools of civilization—language, morals, law and money—are all the result of spontaneous growth and not of design, and of the last two organized power has got hold and thoroughly corrupted them' (Hayek 2013: 495).

recorded, but it did not do so.[80] The effects of this were, however, not as devastating as they are professed to be in modern handbooks of Roman law, with the exception perhaps of the end of the Principate.[81]

From a comparative perspective, it is important to note that classical Roman law was not unique in not having title registers for immovable property. English and other modern experiences show that developed credit markets can exist without registration systems for immovable property, and that setting-up and operating such registries is not without difficulties.[82] In respect of movable property, Roman law did not develop a general principle protecting *bona fide* pledge creditors (or purchasers) against lack of title or already-existing charges. Also, this remarkable feature of Roman law can be put in perspective by a comparison with modern laws. In contemporary market economies, contractual claims are valuable assets and therefore an important category of collateral: receivables-based financing is of immense importance for many companies. Nevertheless, as far as the protection against multiple dispositions or unauthorized dispositions of claims is concerned, in many (if not most) civilian jurisdictions (e.g., Germany, the Netherlands, France), the situation is exactly the same as with movable property in classical Roman law. There is neither a public filing system for charges over receivables, nor are there rules on the protection of *bona fide* chargees (or assignees) of receivables.[83] In the credit markets this is no obstacle for taking receivables as collateral, as there are sufficient non-legal incentives which prevent debtors from failing to disclose that their receivables have already been assigned or charged.[84] These non-legal incentives may—at least for many centuries—even have been stronger for all types of assets in ancient Rome.

[80] The function of informing prospective secured lenders can, however, also be carried out by private institutions, such as a network of local notarial archives in sixteenth-century and seventeenth-century Paris (Hoffman, Postel-Vinay, and Rosenthal 2000: 20–1).

[81] For a more detailed discussion, see Pellecchi 2018: 479–88; Verhagen 2020: 138–49; Arruñada 2020: 262–91. See also section 10.5.

[82] According to Arruñada (2012: 233), 'governments have struggled for almost ten centuries to organise reliable registries'.

[83] See, however, art. 1690 section 3 and art. 2075 of the Belgian civil code. For English law, see *Dearle v Hall* (1828) 3 Russ 1. In these jurisdictions, notification fulfils a function for the protection of bona fide assignees against earlier assignments: the assignee who has first given notice of the assignment to the debtor has priority. Oditah (1991: 140) considers it a very poor form of publicity to make the debtor of the assigned claim 'a kind of public register.'

[84] Flessner 2008: 336–49.

Enforcement out of court (7)

In recent historical literature, it is stressed how ineffective the Roman law of civil procedure was in enabling creditors to get what was due to them.[85] This could be an exaggeration. The procedural documents in the archive of the Sulpicii indicate that there were no great obstacles for relatively low placed Romans (freedmen) to have access to justice.[86] The Sulpicii did litigate a lot, and for relatively low amounts, which rather suggests that Roman litigation was overall effective.[87] In any case, *if* litigation was so inefficient, there was all the more reason for creditors for taking real security, because precisely the law of real security enables a secured creditor to take enforcement measures without the need to go to court first.[88] Empirical studies indicate that efficient enforcement mechanisms lead to greater availability of credit, lower interest rates, and less collateral for equivalent levels of borrowing.[89] As early as the first century AD (and perhaps already earlier), creditors would, in practice, take recourse against charged assets by selling them at auction. Auctions were an economically efficient method of selling charged assets.[90] The role of *argentarii* as specializing in giving credit to purchasers at auction further enhanced the importance of credit for the Roman economy.[91] Even where borrowers would default under their loans, lenders could be certain that they would be able to recover their funds quickly through a procedure with which they were well familiar. This probably entailed that lenders were more willing to lend, so that credit was more easily obtainable for borrowers. In his comparative study on the Egyptian and Roman credit markets, Lerouxel therefore concludes that the institution of the auction must have significantly contributed to the number of transactions in the Roman credit market.[92]

The state of the law at the end of the classical period can be summarized as follows.[93]

[85] A recent example is Broekaert 2017 (who completely ignores the Roman law of real security, although his contribution focusses on the archive of the Sulpicii).

[86] Kehoe 2007: 17–25.

[87] See generally on Roman litigation Kelly 1966a and Metzger 2005. For the later Principate Peachin 2016: 173.

[88] Jackson and Kronman 1979: 1143.

[89] Armour 2008: 19.

[90] On the economics of Roman auctions, see García Morcillo 2021.

[91] Lerouxel 2016: 262.

[92] Lerouxel 2016: 266.

[93] This scheme would apply to *pignus*, *hypotheca*, and *fiducia cum creditore*.

1. The creditor must in principle take recourse against the object of security by selling it to a third party (C. 8.34.1), and paying any surplus proceeds to the debtor (D. 13.7.24.2).[94]
2. The creditor can acquire ownership of charged objects in four cases:
   a. the parties have—at the time the security is created—agreed to a conditional sale for the market value (D. 20.1.16.9);
   b. the parties have—after the secured debt has become due and payable—agreed to an unconditional sale or *datio in solutum* (C. 8.19.1.1, D. 13.7.34);
   c. the creditor has obtained imperial permission to appropriate the charged object (*impetratio dominii*; C. 8.33.1);
   d. the parties have agreed that if the secured debt is not paid in time, the creditor shall be entitled to the fruits of the charged property, whose value shall be set off against the secured debt (D. 20.1.1.3).
3. The debtor has a right of redemption, allowing him to recover the charged object by satisfying the secured debt after default, which can be exercised until the enforcement sale takes place (C. 8.27.8).
4. The creditor has a right to withhold redelivery of the charged object until his other, unsecured claims have been discharged (C. 8.26.1.2).

This scheme is strikingly similar to modern execution laws and is, in some respects, more advanced than most contemporary laws. Only recently have several European codifications introduced legislation positively sanctioning the type of agreement discussed in Marci. D. 20.1.16.9 (conditional sale), precisely because it is regarded as an effective security arrangement.[95] Where, indeed, the parties' agreement ensures that the charged property is estimated at its market value at the time of execution and the surplus value is for the benefit of the debtor, there is no need for formal execution proceedings by way of auction. What in the twenty-first century is regarded as 'state of the art' in collateral enforcement was already provided for in the Roman law of the third century AD!

[94] Where for the same debt both personal and real security have been granted, the creditor is at liberty to first proceed against the guarantor (Sev. Ant. C. 8.40.2), unless the suretyship was only assumed for the deficit of the execution sale of the real security (Gord. 8.40.17).

[95] In the revised French civil code a similar arrangement has been positively sanctioned since 2006 (art. 2348 Cc) and in Belgium since 2018 (art. 53 of the 'Act on the pledge of moveable assets' of 11 July 2013). See also Directive 2002/47/EC of the European Parliament and of the Council of 6 June 2002 on financial collateral arrangements, in particular art. 4. On the Italian 'patto Marciano', see p. 359 n 67.

12.4 Legal Evolution and Economic Growth

When we look at the Roman law of real security, is it possible to establish correlations, or even causations, between economic growth and contraction and the emergence, adaptation, or decline of legal institutions? Was the growth of the Roman economy from 200 BC to 200 AD accompanied by an increasing complexity of the Roman law of security? Can the emergence in the third century AD of *antichresis* and of conditional sales of pledged property be seen in the context of credit crises or periods of strong inflation; could legal institutions like this have contributed to economic recovery? Also, did the emergence of general pledges arising by operation of law in order to secure fiscal debts undermine the effectiveness of the Roman law of security? Did these fiscal pledges contribute to the decline of the Roman economy in the third century AD? Many of these questions can be answered affirmatively, some decidedly and others more hesitantly; in respect of fiscal pledges the most plausible answers are negative. The epigraphic and other sources do not provide sufficient data (e.g., on economic growth, size of credit markets, and interest rates) to support a quantitative analysis.[96] Therefore, although it is plausible that there was a correlation between economic growth and contraction and the emergence of certain variants of *pignus* and *hypotheca*, it is impossible to prove 'strong causal links'.[97] Nevertheless, given that: (i) transactional practices usually reflect the economic needs of the parties;[98] (ii) many of these practices were accommodated by the jurists and the imperial chancery into the Roman legal system;[99] and (iii) this resulted in a well-adapted legal framework for secured transactions,[100] it is a plausible inference that the Roman law of real security did adapt to economic needs and contributed to economic growth.

Economic growth and decline and legal evolution

The relatively widely accepted view is that there was major economic (per capita) growth in the second to first century BC, limited growth in the Principate, stagnation or decline after 200 AD, followed by recovery after 300 AD.[101] In recent studies, the period of decline appears to start earlier than 200 AD,

[96] Pellecchi 2018: 466. [97] Gordon 2012: 203. [98] Sections 1.3 and 11.2.
[99] Chapters 4–9, 11. [100] Section 11.3.
[101] Bowman and Wilson 2009: 30, 51–3; Harper 2017: 33.

with the Antonine crisis of 165–180 AD, which was followed by a period of economic recovery.[102] There are various indices which reflect the levels of production, consumption, and economic performance in the Roman empire: shipwrecks, public buildings, housing stock, and ore smelting.[103] The following chart, which is based on levels of lead pollution (caused by emissions from lead–silver mining and smelting) in Greenland icecaps, to a large extent corresponds with what economic historians say about the expansion and decline of the Roman economy.[104]

The chart does support the view that the Antonine crisis was to end a long period of sustained economic growth.[105] During the crisis, imperial silver mining suddenly collapsed, causing a debasement of silver coinage from 164–165 AD and a complete cessation of silver coinage from Alexandria, Palestine, and Syria.[106] Nominal prices for a range of commodities (including

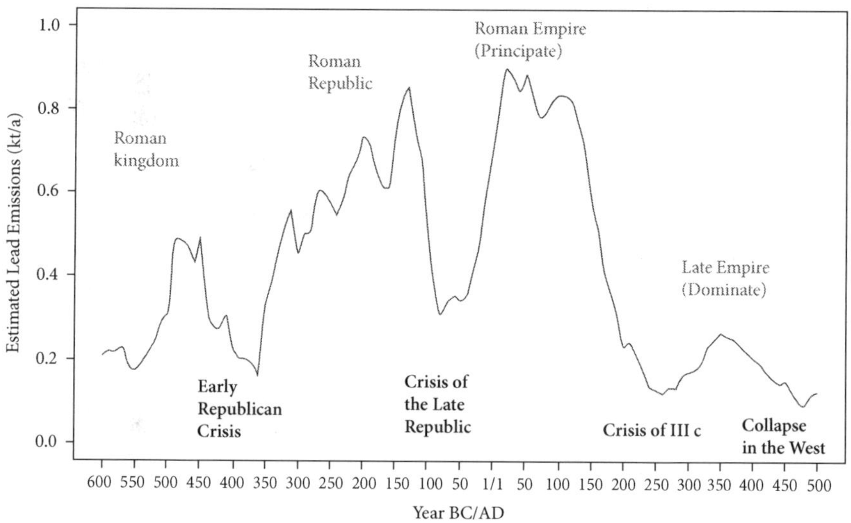

Figure 12.1 'Rome's secular cycles traced by lead pollution in Greenland ice'[107]

[102] Harper 2017: 113–18. See also McConnell et al. 2018. [103] Harper 2017: 33.

[104] On the relationship between silver-mining and the development of trade in the second and first centuries BC, see Kay 2014: 190. For the correlation between the increase in the volume of Roman maritime traffic and the introduction of legal innovations concerning maritime trade, as evidenced by Mediterranean shipwrecks, see Candy 2020.

[105] Harris 2011: 186; Harper 2017: 113–18. [106] Harper 2017:113.

[107] Adapted from a graph developed by Peter Turchin (http://peterturchin.com/cliodynamica/history-is-now-a-quantitative-science/), licensed under the Creative Commons Attribution 2.0 Generic license (https://creativecommons.org/licenses/by/2.0/deed.en). Turchin prepared this graph on the basis of the data produced by McConnell et al. 2018.

wheat) doubled. Real land prices (expressed in wheat) plummeted because demand for land had sharply contracted.[108] Under the reign of Commodus (176–192 AD) the 'sudden burst of inflation' must have hurt creditors seriously.[109]

Not controversial is that, particularly in the third quarter of the third century AD, events occurred which had negative impact on the economy of the whole empire: plague, barbarian invasions, and civil wars led to a significant fall of production and exchanges. The result was a real crisis: desertion of farms, decline of cultivated land, and the paralysis of financial and banking practices caused by heavy inflation.[110] Inflation, although it did not affect ordinary commercial exchanges too seriously, did have a devastating effect on banking activities, lending by private individuals, and on commercial activities dependent upon credit.[111] It even seems that in the second half of the third century AD, professional bankers completely disappear from the scene: about 260 AD *argentarii* disappear from the sources, and after 300 AD *nummularii* as well.[112] It may not be a coincidence that their disappearance coincides with the period of strongest inflation, and their reemergence in the second half of the fourth century AD, with a period in which imperial monetary and economic policies had curbed inflation.[113] Following monetary and other reforms by Diocletian and Constantine, the first half of the third century AD appears to have been a period of economic recovery. The financial sector was revived: the evidence for banking and finance in this period exceeds that for any other period in Roman history.[114]

Economic growth and legal evolution

Alan Watson, like many other important Romanists (e.g., Savigny, Schulz), observes: 'There are no breaks in Roman legal history, only gradual evolution.'[115] The same gradualism is endorsed by mainstream biological Darwinism: *natura non facit saltum*.[116] The evolutionary concept of 'punctuated equilibrium', however, entails that sometimes evolutionary processes dramatically accelerate, causing sudden and radical changes in a system.[117]

108 Harper 2017:113–14.
109 Harris 2011: 251.
110 Andreau 2010: 229–30.
111 Carrié and Rousselle 1999: 578; Harris 2011: 251.
112 Andreau 1999: 33–4; Harris 2011: 251.
113 Carrié and Rousselle 1999: 578; Andreau 2010: 230. See also Silver 2011.
114 Harper 2017:179.
115 Watson 1995: 40–1.
116 For a lucid analysis of the gradualness of biological evolution, see Mayr 2002: 190–204.
117 Mayr 2002: 193; Hodgson and Knudsen 2010: 43.

This also happens in social and legal evolution.[118] There are two periods in which evolutionary accelerations occurred in the Roman law of real security. The first period is the second half of the first century BC, in which almost all the remedies for *pignus* originated: *interdictum de migrando*, *interdictum Salvianum*, *actio pigneratica directa*, and (most importantly) the *actio Serviana*. The practice of pledging *invecta et illata* for farm leases originated in a period in which investment farming became prominent. Likewise, the blooming urban rental markets (in Rome and other cities) for both living accommodation and commercial real estate will have stimulated the evolution of the law on urban rental agreements (including tenant's pledges).[119] There is compelling evidence that in the last one hundred and fifty years of the Republic an economic revolution took place, in which not only agricultural patterns dramatically changed but also trade and finance.[120] The increased inflows of bullion combined with the expansion of available credit produced a large increase in monetary liquidity. In its turn this resulted in 'a major upward inflection in Roman economic activity and the creation both of a more complex system of production and distribution and of an enormous material culture that was to reach its height under the Principate'.[121] In this process, finance played an important role. Kay observes that 'finance in general seems to be viewed by some modern Roman historians more as an arcane offshoot of the Eleusian Mysteries than as a dynamic service industry that can increase the prospects of wealth creation by helping economic agents, such as merchants and farmers, to obtain resources that will allow them to implement ideas for increased production'.[122] *If* (as I think) the *actio Serviana* already originated as a general pledge remedy in the first century BC,[123] this could then be regarded as an adaptation to the growing importance of credit in a commercializing economy.

The second 'punctuated equilibrium' took place in the Nerva–Antonine age, beginning with Hadrian's codification of the praetorian edict.[124] In this period most of the variants of pledge we know today emerged: the *hypotheca* contracted *nuda conventione* (Julian), the multiple pledge (Gaius, Marcellus),

[118] North 2005: 2–3. [119] Sections 3.5 and 4.2–4.4.

[120] Kay 2014. For summary and conclusions, see Kay 2014: 327–34. [121] Kay 2014: 327.

[122] Kay 2014: 6. [123] Section 4.5.

[124] Garnsey and Saller (2014: 82) suggest that during the early Principate there was less need for drastic legal innovations because the most important economic changes had already occurred in the last three centuries of the Republic. De Ligt (2020: 98) considers it significant that 'few entirely new legal remedies seem to have been created during the Principate'. The law of pledge does not entirely correspond to this image of limited legal change in the Principate. It is true, the *interdictum de migrando*, the *interdictum Salvianum*, and the *actio Serviana* were all created in the first century BC. However, the variants of pledge discussed in this book all originated during the Principate. Moreover, the *actio pigneraticia contraria* and the *actio pigneraticia in ius concepta* were also created in the Principate.

the pledge of claims (Pomponius), the floating charge of merchandise in *tabernae* (Scaevola), and the general pledge (Gaius, Scaevola, Papinian). These are all adaptions of the legal system to its economic environment, which in their turn may have fostered further economic growth. These responses did, however, not take place immediately. If the levels of lead pollution do reflect economic growth and contraction in the Principate, the juristic evidence of the emergence of most variants of pledge must be located in a period of economic decline. However, the origins of these variants may very well lie in transactional practices from the preceding period, which was characterized by economic growth. The law often takes time to respond to economic change. Moreover, Roman law of the first century AD already had many of the features for an effective law of secured credit, albeit not always in a fully evolved shape. There were forms of non-possessory security (e.g., tenant's pledges and warehouse pledges) and generic pledges (*invecta et illata*), the products of pledged assets could be pledged, secured creditors could auction (or otherwise sell) the charged assets without court permission, and secured creditors had preferential rights of recourse. The main 'deficiencies' of the Roman law of real security of the first century AD were the absence of multiple pledges and of general pledges.

Crisis

When after the Antonine crisis (or perhaps several decades later) the long period of economic growth was followed by periods of economic contractions and rampant inflation, the law of real security seems to have responded more quickly, by allowing conditional sales and *antichresis*. They are typically forms of security for a subsistence economy and not for a monetized economy. However, where the monetary system itself malfunctions (heavy inflation), creditors may again be more interested in the physical assets or their products themselves than in realizing their monetary value. This could also work for the benefit of debtors, whose lack of cash flow prevented them from paying principal and interest in coin. For instance, the *Historia Augusta* mentions that in order to enable more Romans of small financial means (*pauperibus*) to purchase farmland, Alexander Severus offered interest-free loans which were to be repaid from the fruits of the land.[125] At the same time debtors run the risk of being exploited by their creditors, where the surplus value

[125] *Hist. Aug.*, Alex. Sev. 21.

of the pledged property ends up in the pockets of the creditor (e.g., conditional sales for the amount of the secured debt), or where the value of fruits of the pledged property exceeds the statutory maximum interest rate. In jurists' opinions (e.g., Marci. D. 20.1.16.9) and imperial constitutions of the third century (e.g., Alex. C. 4.24.3) we see, on the one hand, that conditional sales and antichretic pledges are allowed and, on the other hand, that debtors are protected. The popularity of general pledges may also have increased in times characterized by economic crises.

It would be a mistake, however, to associate the law developed in the third century AD by Roman jurisprudence and the imperial chancery exclusively with economic decline. The jurists continued to elaborate and refine the existing body of rules for *pignus* and *hypotheca*. Even after the well of classical jurisprudence had dried up, the classical law of pledge was preserved in the constitutions of third-century emperors and their successors (in particular Diocletian, Gordian, Constantine and Justinian). Constantine's constitution on the *lex commissoria* in pledge agreements even decisively shaped the laws of execution for real security of the European *ius commune* and the modern codifications.[126]

[126] Verhagen 2011b.

APPENDIX

Actio Serviana: Restitution and Valuation (if $a_{1\text{-}6}$, then b)

If the conditions a_1 to a_6 of the *formula* of the *actio Serviana* were met, the judge (*iudex*) was instructed by the praetor (as recorded in the *litis contestatio*) to condemn the defendant to pay 'what the matter will be worth' (b). Where all the requirements for the granting of a valid pledge had been met (a_1 to a_3), the secured debt had not yet been repaid nor any equivalent event (satisfaction, creditor's default) had taken place (a_4 and a_5), the *iudex* would first give the defendant the opportunity to give the pledged object back to the claimant (a_6). For cases where the defendant did not restore the pledged object, the jurists have devised an intricate method for the assessment of the amount which the defendant would be condemned to pay the creditor as claimant. In this appendix we will see that the outcome of this valuation process depended on several factors, in particular whether the pledge was possessory or non-possessory and whether the *actio Serviana* was instituted against the debtor or against a third party in possession of the property. This not always took place on the basis of the pledged object's value (as estimated by the claimant), but would sometimes be determined with reference to the amount of the secured debt. Here, the jurists reached results which reflect the 'economics' of the different fact patterns.

Restitution

Where the judge concluded that the conditions a_1 to a_5 of the *actio Serviana* had been satisfied, pursuant to the clause *nisi restituetur* in the *actio Serviana*'s *formula* he would pronounce an *arbitrium* (a_6) in which he ordered the defendant to restore the pledged object to the claimant. When the defendant complied with this order for restitution and returned the object to the claimant, the procedure would be terminated. A defendant who refused to comply with an order for restitution was referred to with the negative *contumax* (obstinate).[1] The valuation by the claimant (discussed shortly) is in some texts regarded as punishment for the defendant's *contumacia* (Paul. D. 12.3.2; Marcell. D. 12.3.8). All this would put the defendant under pressure to give back the pledged object to the defendant. However, the defendant could not be compelled to surrender the pledged object. He was legally entitled to opt for paying the condemnation and would (if he was a third party in possession of the pledged object) to a considerable degree be protected if the debtor would later institute *rei vindicatio* proceedings against him.[2] We do not know how effective the restitution clause was. There are many cases in the Digest in which the defendant did indeed restore the object, but we also encounter texts in which the defendant decided not to do so.[3] The judge would then have to condemn him to pay an amount representing 'what the matter will be worth' (*quanti ea res erit*). The question then arose how this should be calculated. In case of *actiones in rem*, this amount was normally based on the value of the object (although, as we will see, in case of *pignus* this would sometimes be the amount of the secured debt).

[1] Wubbe 2003: 180. [2] Wubbe 2003: 180. [3] Wubbe 2003: 179–80.

In practice, it was left to the claimant himself to determine the value by a declaration on oath (*iusiurandum in litem*). This would often have provided a stimulus for the defendant to give back the pledged object. Although the average Roman would not commit perjury lightly by excessively overstating the value of the object, a valuation by the claimant himself would often have been on or above the upside of a realistic valuation.[4]

Ulp. D. 20.1.21.3: possessory pledge

There are two texts on the meaning of *quanti ea res erit*—Ulp. D. 20.1.21.3 and Marci. D. 20.1.16.3—which since the *Glossa ordinaria* in the thirteenth century AD have been said to demonstrate that there was an overt difference of opinion between these two jurists. Wubbe (whom I closely follow here),[5] however, has convincingly demonstrated that these texts do not contradict each other, because they are dealing with different situations. Wubbe's point of departure is that the creditor's interest in the pledged property is not in its full value, but rather in its function as collateral for the secured debt. Where the creditor has received the amount of the secured debt, any surplus value of the pledged property is immaterial to him. This is only different when there are special reasons for justifying that the creditor can recover the full value of the pledged property. These special reasons are linked to the special nature of the possessory pledge.[6]

Where a possessory pledge has been created and the creditor has lost possession of the pledged object, the latter can institute the *actio Serviana* against the person in possession. This person (the defendant) can be either the debtor himself or a third party. Ulpian succinctly sets out how the judge should determine the amount due by a defendant who chose not to return the pledged property to the creditor.

> **D. 20.1.21.3.** *Ulpianus libro septuagesimo tertio ad edictum.* Si res pignerata non restituatur, lis adversus possessorem erit aestimanda, sed utique aliter adversus ipsum debitorem, aliter adversus quemvis possessorem: nam adversus debitorem non pluris quam quanti debet, quia non pluris interest, adversus ceteros possessores etiam pluris, et quod amplius debito consecutus creditor fuerit, restituere debet debitori pigneraticia actione.
>
> If the pledged property is not handed over, the amount due from the possessor must be assessed, but differently against the debtor and other possessors: against the debtor for nothing more than what he owes, because the (creditor's) interest is nothing more than that; against others, the assessment can be greater, and if there is a surplus, the creditor must return it to the debtor by the *actio pigneraticia*.

Where the *actio Serviana* has been instituted *against a third party* in possession of the pledged object, the defendant will be condemned to pay the full value of the property. This can be explained with reference to the creditor's liability towards the debtor for *custodia*. This *custodia* liability entailed that the creditor would have to reimburse the debtor for the full value of the pledged property if it could not be returned to the debtor. Only by allowing the creditor to recover the full value of the pledged property from

[4] For example, Paul. D. 12.3.11: it is not readily allowed to inquire into the perjury of someone who has made an oath under the compulsion of law (which concerns the claimant's oath in an *in rem* procedure).

[5] See also Jansen 2017: 31–6.

[6] Wubbe 2003: 183.

a third party in possession will it be prevented that the creditor would suffer a loss as a consequence of the defendant's decision to keep the pledged property. The creditor will receive the full value of the pledged property from the defendant. He can set off his obligation to pass that on to the debtor against the debtor's obligation to pay the secured debt, so that only the amount of the surplus value will have to be actually paid by the creditor. If, however, the value of pledged property turned out to be less than the secured debt, the outcome of the set-off would be that the debtor would be liable to pay the deficit.[7]

All this is different where a possessory pledge has been granted, but full possession of the pledged property has returned to the debtor and the *actio Serviana* has been instituted *against this debtor*. The creditor will no longer be liable for *custodia*, because the property is already with the debtor. Accordingly, in *Serviana* proceedings instituted against him, the debtor will only be condemned to pay the amount of the secured debt.[8] In particular, where there is a surplus value in the pledged property, this would be an economically efficient result. There is no need for the creditor to organize an auction for an execution sale, while the debtor does not afterwards have to sue (with the *actio pigneraticia (directa)*) the creditor for the *superfluum*.

Marci. D. 20.1.16.3: non-possessory pledge

Where the pledge was granted as a non-possessory pledge, the creditor was never liable for *custodia*. His interest in the pledged property is exclusively in its value as collateral. Accordingly, in *Serviana* proceedings against third parties in possession, the creditor can only recover the amount of the secured debt. The seemingly contradictory opinions of Ulpian and Marcianus can thus be reconciled. Marcian does not expressly say that his opinion is on a non-possessory pledge. Wubbe has tried to demonstrate, however, that D. 20.1.16.3 only makes sense if it is so interpreted. In my view, it could also be dealing with situations where the pledge was granted as a possessory pledge, but possession of the pledged object was regained by the debtor before the secured debt was repaid. In particular, section (d) reproduced and discussed later in this Appendix appears to indicate that Marci. D. 20.1.16.3 is not so much exclusively dealing with non-possessory pledges, as with *Serviana* proceedings between creditor and debtor.

This is the opinion of Marcian, which—in imitation of Wubbe—I have subdivided into its successive elements.

D. 20.1.16.3. *Marcianus libro singulari ad formulam hypothecariam.*

(a) In vindicatione pignoris quaeritur, an rem, de qua actum est, possideat is cum quo actum est. nam si non possideat nec dolo fecerit quo minus possideat, absolvi debet:

(b) si vero possideat et aut pecuniam solvat aut rem restituat, aeque absolvendus est: si vero neutrum horum faciat, condemnatio sequetur.

(c) sed si velit restituere nec possit (forte quod res abest et longe est vel in provinciis), solet cautionibus res explicari: nam si caveret se restituturum, absolvitur.

(d) sin vero dolo quidem desiit possidere, summa autem ope nisus non possit rem ipsam restituere, tanti condemnabitur, quanti actor in litem iuraverit, sicut in ceteris

[7] Wubbe 2003: 190–1.

[8] For similar results in respect of the *actio furti* instituted by the pledge creditor, see Paul. D. 47.2.15 pr. and Paul. D. 47.2.88, discussed by Wubbe 1960: 184–5.

> in rem actionibus: nam si tanti condemnatus esset, quantum deberetur, quid proderat in rem actio, cum et in personam agendo idem consequeretur?
>
> (a) In an action for pledged property, the question arises whether the defendant possesses the thing claimed. If he does not possess it and has not dishonestly disposed of it, he should be held not liable,
>
> (b) similarly if he possesses and either pays or hands over the property. If he does neither, he will be held liable.
>
> (c) If he wants to hand the thing over and cannot (for example, because the property is distant or in the provinces), the matter is usually settled by a deed; for if he makes a formal promise to hand over the property, he is held not liable.
>
> (d) If, however, someone has dishonestly lost possession and cannot hand over the property even with the greatest effort, he will be liable for the value assessed by the plaintiff, as in other actions *in rem*. For if judgment were confined to the amount owing, what would be the point of an action *in rem*, since the same result could be achieved by suing *in personam*?

The text begins by indicating in section (a) against whom the *actio Serviana* can be instituted: the actual possessor of the pledged property, which can be either the debtor himself or a third party. Section (a) implies that the *actio Serviana* can also be instituted against a former possessor, if he has disposed of the pledged object in order to escape a condemnation. Section (b) then immediately reaches the heart of the matter. The defendant is presented with a choice: pay the amount of the secured debt (which presupposes that the debtor is the defendant), return the pledged object, or pay the (on account of *contumacia* increased) value of the pledged object.[9] These alternatives were not available where the *actio Serviana* was instituted by a creditor with a possessory pledge against a third party in possession. The creditor would be liable vis-à-vis the debtor for *custodia* and his interest would be in the recovery of the full value of the pledged property. In that event the defendant would be treated the same as in other proceedings *in rem*: either give back the object or pay its value as estimated by the claimant.[10]

If one assumes that the defendant's decision would depend on the economics of the case and would be based on the difference between the pledged object's value and the amount of the debt, then the relevance of section (c) becomes clear. If the value of the pledged property is less than the amount of the secured debt, the most economical option would be for the defendant to give back the property. But what if at the time of the procedure this cannot take place because the object is 'distant or in the provinces'? For this scenario, section (c) says that a *stipulatio* by the defendant, in which he promises to give back the pledged object, is equivalent to actual restitution. This would enable a defendant to opt for restitution and avoid the risk of being 'punished' for *contumacia*. Also, from the perspective of the creditor, this is an economically sensible result. If the pledged object is worth less than the amount of the secured debt, the object will be restored to him. In case of an execution sale, there will be a deficit, but that would have been the case anyhow. If the value of the pledged object exceeds the secured debt and the defendant decides to pay it (rather than restore the pledged object), the creditor is fully satisfied and has no further interest in the pledged property.

Finally, section (d) of Marci. D. 20.1.16.3 deals with an exceptional case and specifies the legal consequences of the fraudulent disposal of the pledged object by the debtor. In this

[9] Wubbe 2003: 187, 191.

[10] Wubbe 2003: 190–1.

situation, the defendant will be liable to pay the value of the pledged property, as declared on oath (*iusiurandum in litem*) by the claimant. This is motivated by Marcian with a rhetorical question: what use would an *actio in rem* (like the *actio Serviana*) have if it would be confined to the amount of the secured debt, given the fact that the same amount could be claimed with a personal action? This personal action would be the creditor's action for payment of the secured debt (e.g., *condictio* pursuant to *mutuum* or *stipulatio*). The answer to that question could simply have been that in the debtor's insolvency the *actio Serviana* would give the creditor a preferential position. According to Wubbe, this passage expresses Marcian's embarrassment caused by an intuitive discomfort with the punitive character of the consequences of the defendant's *contumacia*.[11]

[11] Wubbe 2003: 188–9.

Bibliography

Abatino, B. (2012). '"Pignoris arrabonisve nomine" in TPSulp. 51 (TPN 43) A case of diglossia?' 80 *Legal History Review*, 311–28.

Alonso, J.L. (2007). 'Sull'accessorietà del pegno' in C. Cascione, and C. Masi Doria, eds, *Fides, humanitas, ius: Studi in onore di Luigi Labruna.* Napoli: Editoriale Scientifica, 77–99.

Alonso, J.L. (2020). 'The Constitutio Antoniniana and Private Legal Practice in the Eastern Empire' in Czajkowski and Eckhardt 2020, 44–64.

Amstutz, M. (2001). *Evolutorisches Wirtschaftsrecht: Vorstudien zum Recht und seiner Methode in den Diskurskollisionen der Marktgesellschaft.* Baden-Baden: Nomos.

Amstutz, M. (2002). 'Rechtsgeschichte als Evolutionstheorie. Anmerkungen zum Theorierahmen von Marie Theres Fögens Forschungsprogramm' 1 *Rechtsgeschichte*, 26–31.

Ando, C. (2015). 'Exemplum, Analogy and Precedent in Roman Law' in M. Lowrie and S. Lüdemann, eds, *Between Exemplarity and Singularity: Literature, Philosophy, Law.* New York, NY: Routledge, 111–22.

Andreau, J. (1974). *Les affaires de Monsieur Jucundus*, Rome: École française.

Andreau, J. (1987). *La vie financière dans le monde romain. Les métiers de manieurs d'argent (IVe siècle av. J.-C.-IIIe siècle ap. J.-C.).* Rome: École française.

Andreau, J. (1999). *Banking and Business in the Roman World.* Cambridge: Cambridge University Press.

Andreau, J. (2003). 'Conclusions' in Lo Cascio 2003, 281–8.

Andreau, J. (2010). *L'économie du monde romain.* Paris: Ellipses.

Andreau, J. (2020a). 'Capital and Investment in the Campanian Tablets' in Erdkamp, Verboven, and Zuiderhoek 2020, 417–36.

Andreau, J. (2020b). 'Banking, Money-Lending, and Elite Financial Life in Rome' in Dari-Mattiacci and Kehoe 2020b, 81–111.

Ankum, H. (1972). 'Quelques problèmes concernant les ventes en enchères en droit romain classique' in G. Grosso, ed., *Studi in onore di Gaetano* Scherillo, vol. I. Milano: La Goliardica, 377–93.

Ankum, H. (1975). 'Pignus und novatio im klassischen römischen Recht' in *Festschrift für Erwin Seidl.* Cologne: Hanstein, 1–14.

Ankum, J.A. (1979–1980). 'Furtum pignoris und furtum fiduciae im klassischen römischen Recht' 26 & 27 *Revue internationale des droits de l'antiquité*, 127–61, 95–143.

Ankum, H. (2006). 'Der Ausdruck favor libertatis in den Konstitutionen der römischen Kaiser' in T. Finkenauer, ed., *Sklaverei und Freilassung im römischen Recht. Symposium für Hans Josef Wieling zum 70. Geburtstag.* Berlin and Heidelberg: Springer, 1–17.

Ankum, H. (2007). 'Rescripts of Roman Emperors Promulgated Until the End of the Reign of Diocletian in 305 A.D' in J.E. Spruit, ed., *Extravagantes, Scritti sparsi sul diritto romano.* Naples: Jovene, 491–500.

Ankum, H. (2010). 'The Functions of Expressions with utilitatis causa in the Works of Classical Roman Lawyers' in R. van den Bergh and G. van Nieker, eds, *Libellus ad Thomasium, Essays in Roman Law, Roman-Dutch Law and Legal History in Honour of Philip J Thomas.* Pretoria: Unisa Press, 5–22.

Ankum, H. (2010). 'Spätklassische Problemfälle bezüglich der Verpfändung einer res aliena' in H. Altemeppen et al., eds, *Festschrift für Rolf Knütel zum 70. Geburtstag*. Heidelberg: Müller, 35–44.

Ankum, H., and E. Pool (1989). 'Rem in bonis meis esse and rem in bonis meam esse: Traces of the Development of Roman Double Ownership' in P. Birks, ed., *New Perspectives in the Roman Law of Property*. Oxford: Oxford University Press, 5–41.

Ankum, H., M. van Gessel-de Roo, and E. Pool (1987). 'Die verschiedenen Bedeutungen des Ausdrucks *in bonis alicuius esse/in bonis habere* im klassischen römischen Recht' 104 *Zeitschrift der Savigny-Stiftung für Rechtsgeschichte: Romanistische Abteilung*, 369–436.

Armour, J. (2004). 'The Chequered History of the Floating Charge' 13 *Griffith Law Review*, 25–56.

Armour, J. (2008). 'The Law and Economics Debate about Secured Lending: Lessons for European Lawmaking?' in H. Eidenmüller and E.-M. Kieninger, eds, *The Future of Secured Credit in Europe. European Company and Financial Law Review*, Special Volume 2. Berlin: De Gruyter, 3–29.

Arruñada, B. (2012). *Institutional Foundations of Impersonal Exchange: The Theory and Policy of Contractual Registries*. Chicago, IL: University of Chicago Press.

Arruñada, B. (2020). 'The Institutions of Roman Markets' in Dari-Mattiacci and Kehoe 2020b, 247–98.

Aubert, J.-J. (2016). 'Law, Business Ventures and Trade' in Du Plessis, Ando, and Tuori 2016a, 621–34.

Baldus, Chr. (2010). 'Römische Privatautonomie' 210 *Archiv für die civilistische Praxis*, 2–31.

Balkin, J.M. (1998). *Cultural Software: A Theory of Ideology*. New Haven and London: Yale University Press.

Bang, P.F. (2008). *The Roman Bazaar: a Comparative Study of Trade and Markets in a Tributary Empire*. Cambridge: Cambridge University Press.

Basalla, G. (1988). *The Evolution of Technology*, Cambridge: Cambridge University Press (reprint 1999).

Baxter, H. (1987). 'Autopoiesis and the "Relative Autonomy" of Law' 19 *Cardozo Law Review*, 1987–2090.

Baxter, H. (2013). 'Niklas Luhmann's Theory of Autopoietic Legal Systems' 9 *Annual Review of Law and Social Science*, 167–84.

Beale, H., M.G. Bridge, L. Gullifer, and E. Lomnicka (2018). *The Law of Security and Title-Based Financing*, 3rd Edition. Oxford: Oxford University Press.

Beard, M. (2008). *Pompeii. The Life of a Roman Town*. London: Profile Books.

Behrends, O. (1993). 'Rudolf von Jhering und die Evolutionstheorie des Rechts' in O. Behrends, ed., *Privatrecht heute und Jherings Evolution des Rechtsdenken*. Cologne: Schmidt, 7–36.

Bellocci, N. (1979). *La struttura del negozio della fiducia nell'epoca repubblicana*, vol. I. *Le nuncupationes*. Napoli: Jovene.

Bellocci, N. (1983). *La struttura del negozio della fiducia nell'epoca repubblicana*, vol. II. *Riflessioni intorno alla forma del negozio dall'epoca arcaica all'epoca classica del diritto romano*. Napoli: Jovene.

Bergh van den, R. (2009). 'The Development of the Landlord's Hypothec' 15 *Fundamina: A Journal of Legal History*, 155–67.

Bertoldi. F. (2012). *Il negozio fiduciario nel diritto romano classico*, Modena: Mucchi.

Biscardi, A. (1961). *La lex commissoria nel sistema delle garanzie reali*. Milano: Giuffrè.

Biscardi, A. (1969). 'Die mehrfache Verpfändung einer Sache vom attischen bis zum spätrömischen Recht' 86 *Zeitschrift der Savigny-Stiftung für Rechtsgeschichte: Romanistische Abteilung*, 146–68.

Biscardi, A. (1976). *Appunti sulle garanzie reali in diritto romano*. Milano: La Goliardica.

Biscardi, A. (1983). '*Subsignatio praediorum*' in *Studi in onore di Cesare Sanfilippo*, vol. IV, Milano: Giuffrè, 136–50.

Biscardi, A. (1991). *La dottrina romana dell'obligatio rei*. Milano: Giuffrè.

Biscardi, A. (1992). '"Obligatio personae" et "obligatio rei" dans l'histoire du droit romain' 70 *Revue historique de droit français et étranger*, 187–96.

Bobbink, R. (2021). *Antichresis en pandgebruik. De bevoegdheid van de zekerheidsgerechtigde tot gebruik, beheer en vruchttrekking in rechtshistorisch en rechtsvergelijkend perspectief*. Deventer: Wolters Kluwer.

Bobbink, R., and Q. Mauer (2019). 'Antichresis: a Comparative Study of Classical Roman Law and the Contractual Praxis from Roman Egypt' 87 *The Legal History Review*, 1–28.

Boldizzoni, F. (2011). *The Poverty of Clio: Resurrecting Economic History*. Princeton, NJ: Princeton University Press.

Bowman, A., and A. Wilson, eds. (2009). *Quantifying the Roman Economy. Methods and Problems*. Oxford: Oxford University Press.

Brandsma, F. (2013). 'Pignus nominis: Does the Pledge-Creditor Have a ius in re or a ius in personam?' in V.A. Leontaritou, K.A. Bourdara, and E. Papagianni, eds, *Antecessor: Festschrift für Spyros N. Troianos zum 80. Geburtstag*. Athens: Sakkoulas, 227–36.

Bransbourg, G. (2014). 'Les taux d'intérêt flottants des Sulpicii' in C. Apicella, M.-L. Haack, and F. Lerouxel, eds, *Les Affaires de Monsieur Andreau. Économie et société du monde romain*. Bordeaux: Ausonius, 123–35.

Braukmann, M. (2008). *Pignus: Das Pfandrecht unter dem Einfluß der vorklassischen und klassischen Tradition der römischen Rechtswissenschaft*. Göttingen: Wallstein.

Bresson, A. (2016). *The Making of the Ancient Greek Economy. Institutions, Markets and Growth in the City-States*. Princeton, NJ: Princeton University Press.

Bretone, M. (2006). *Storia del diritto romano*. 20th edn, Roma: Laterza.

Broekaert, W. (2017). 'Conflicts, Contract Enforcement, and Business Communities in the Archive of the Sulpicii' in Flohr and Wilson 2017, 387–416.

Broekaert, W., and A. Zuiderhoek (2020). 'Capital Goods in the Roman Economy' in Erdkamp, Verboven, and Zuiderhoek (2020), 99–146.

Bruns, K.G., and O. Gradenwitz, eds (1912). *Fontes iuris Romani antiqui. Additamentum, Indicem ad fontium Partem Priorem: II. Simulacra*. Tübingen: Mohr.

Buckland, W.V. (1908). *The Roman Law of Slavery*. Cambridge: Cambridge University Press. Reprint 1970.

Burdese, A. (1949). *Lex commissoria e ius vendendi nella fiducia e nel pignus*. Turin: Giappichelli.

Bürge, A. (1979). *Retentio im römischen Sachen-und Obligationenrecht*. Zürich: Schulthess.

Bürge, A. (1980). 'Vertrag und personale Abhängigkeiten im Rom der späten Republik und der frühen Kaiserzeit' 97 *Zeitschrift der Savigny-Stiftung für Rechtsgeschichte. Romanistische Abteilung*, 105–56.

Bürge, A. (1987). 'Fiktion und Wirklichkeit: Soziale und rechtliche Strukturen des römischen Bankwesens' 97 *Zeitschrift der Savigny-Stiftung für Rechtsgeschichte. Romanistische Abteilung*, 465–558.

Bürge, A. (1999). *Römisches Privatrecht. Rechtsdenken und gesellschaftliche Verankerung. Eine Einführung*. Darmstadt: Wissenschaftliche Buchgesellschaft.

Callu, J.-P., and J.-N. Barrandon (1986). 'L'inflazione nel IV secolo (295–361): il contributo delle analisi' in A. Giardina, ed., *Istituzioni, ceti, economie, Società Romana e Impero Tardoantico*. Roma: Laterza, 559–89.

Calomiris, C.W., et al. (2017). 'How Collateral Laws Shape Lending and Sectoral Activity' 123 *Journal of Financial Economics*, 163–88.

Camodeca, G. (1999). *Tabulae Pompeianae Sulpiciorum, Edizione critica dell'archivio puteolano dei Sulpicii*. Rome: Quasar.

Camodeca, G. (2003). 'Il credito negli archivi campani: il caso di Puteoli e di Herculaneum' in Lo Cascio 2003, 69–98.

Camodeca, G. (2017). 'Il latino nei documenti della prassi giuridica campana' in F. Serra, ed., 6 *Linguarum Varietas*. Naples: Università Federico II, 19–37.

Candy, P. (2020). 'Parallel Developments in Roman Law and Maritime Trade During the Late Republic and Early Principate' 33 *Journal of Roman Archaeology*, 53–72.

Capogrossi Colognesi, L. (2012). *Padroni e contadini nell'Italia repubblicana*. Roma: 'L'Erma' di Bretschneider.

Capogrossi Colognesi, L. (2014). *Law and Power in the Making of the Roman Commonwealth*. Cambridge: Cambridge University Press.

Carlà, F., and A. Marcone (2011). *Economia e finanza a Roma*. Bologna: Il Mulino.

Carrié, J.-M., and A. Rousselle (1999). *L'Empire romain en mutation: des Sévères à Constantin, 192–337*. Paris: Seuil.

Cerami, P., and A. Petrucci (2010). *Diritto commerciale romano. Profilo storico*. 3rd edn, Turin: Giappichelli.

Chemain, J.-F. (2015). *L'argent des autres. Le cautionnement dans le monde romain du IIe siècle avant J.-C. au Ier siècle après J.-C.* Versailles: Via Romana.

Chevreau, E. (2008). 'La traiecticia pecunia: un mode de financement du commerce international' 65 *Mémoires de la Société pour l'Histoire du Droit et des Institutions des anciens pays bourguignons, comtois et romands*, 7–47.

Chevreau, E. (2010). 'La pratique du gage dans les *Tabulae Pompeianae Sulpiciorum*' in H. Altemeppen, I. Reichard, and M. Schermaier, eds, *Festschrift für Rolf Knütel zum 70. Geburtstag*. Heidelberg: Müller, 183–96.

Chiusi, T. (2020). 'Legal Interactions in the Archive of Babatha: P. Yadin 21 and 22' in Czajkowski and Eckhardt 2021, 101–14.

Coriat, J.-P. (1997). *Le prince législateur*. Rome: École française.

Costabile, F. (1992). *L'auctio della fiducia e del pignus nelle tabelle dell'agro Murecine*. Soveria Mannelli: Rubbettino.

Cotterrell, R. (2001). 'The Representation of Law's Autonomy in Autopoiesis Theory' in J. Přibáň and D. Nelken, eds, *Law's New Boundaries. The Consequences of Legal Autopoiesis*. Aldershot: Dartmouth/Ashgate, 80–99.

Cotterrell, R. (2006). *Law, Culture and Society. Legal Ideas in the Mirror of Social Theory*. Farnham and Burlington: Ashgate.

Crawford, H. (1996). *Roman Statutes*. 2 vols. London: Institute of Classical Studies.

Criniti, N. (1991). *La tabula alimentaria di Veleia: introduzione storica, edizione critica, traduzione, indici onomastici e toponimici, bibliografia veleiate*. Parma: Deputazione di Storia Patria per le Province Parmensi.

Crook, J.A. (1996). 'Legal History and General History' 41 *Bulletin of the Institute of Classical Studies*, 31–6.

Czajkowski, K., and B. Eckhardt, eds (2020). *Law in the Roman Provinces*. Oxford: Oxford University Press.

Daalder, E.S. (2018). *De rechtspraakverzamelingen van Julius Paulus. Recht en rechtvaardigheid in de rechterlijke uitspraken van keizer Septimius Severus*. The Hague: Boom.

Dari-Mattiacci, G. (2015). 'The Economic Perspective: Demand and Supply in the Reduction of Transaction Costs in the Ancient World' in Kehoe, Ratzan, and Yiftach 2015, 273–92.

Dari-Mattiacci, G., and D.P. Kehoe, eds (2020a). *Roman Law and Economics. Volume I: Institutions and Organizations*. Oxford: Oxford University Press.

Dari-Mattiacci, G., and D.P. Kehoe, eds (2020b). *Roman Law and Economics. Volume II: Exchange, Ownership, and Disputes*. Oxford: Oxford University Press.

Daube, D. (1956). *Forms of Roman Legislation*. Oxford: Clarendon Press.

Daubermann, E.A. (1993). *Die Sachgesamtheit als Gegenstand des klassischen römischen Rechts*. Frankfurt am Main: Lang.

Dawkins, R. (1991). *The Blind Watchmaker*. Reprinted with an Appendix. London: Penguin.

Dawson, J.P. (1968). *The Oracles of the Law*. Ann Arbor, MI: University of Michigan Law School.

Deakin, S. (2003). 'Evolution for Our Time. A Theory of Legal Memetics' 55 *Current Legal Problems*, 1–42.

Deakin, S. (2011). 'Legal Evolution: Integrating Economic and Systemic Approaches' 7 *Review of Law & Economics*, 659–83.

Deakin, S. (2013). 'The Legal Theory of Finance: Implications for Methodology and Empirical Research' 41 *Journal of Comparative Economics*, 338–42.

Deakin, S., and F. Carvalho (2011). 'System and Evolution in Corporate Governance' in P. Zumbansen and G.P. Callies, eds, *Law, Economics and Evolutionary Theory*. Cheltenham: Elgar, 111–30.

Deakin, S., V. Mollica, and P. Sarkar (2017). 'Varieties of Creditor Protection: Insolvency Law Reform and Credit Expansion in Developed Market Economies' 15 *Socio-Economic Review*, 359–84.

De Iuliis, F. (2017). *Studi sul pignus conventum. Le origini. L'interdictum Salvianum*. Turin: Giappichelli.

Dennett, D.C. (1996). *Darwin's Dangerous Idea: Evolution and the Meanings of Life*. London: Penguin.

Dennett, D.C. (2017). *From Bacteria to Bach and Back: The Evolution of Minds*. New York, NY: WW Norton.

Depeyrot, G. (1988). 'Crise économique, formation des prix, et politique monétaire au troisième siècle après J.-C' *Histoire & Mesure*, 235–47.

Dernburg, H. (1860). *Das Pfandrecht nach den Grundsätzen des heutigen römischen Rechts*, vol. I. Leipzig: Hirzel.

Dernburg, H. (1864). *Das Pfandrecht nach den Grundsätzen des heutigen römischen Rechts*, vol. II. Leipzig: Hirzel.

Dillon, J.N. (2012). *The Justice of Constantine: Law, Communication, and Control*. Ann Arbor: University of Michigan Press.

Diósdi, G. (1970). *Ownership in Ancient and Preclassical Roman Law*. Budapest: Akadémiai Kiadó.

Dirix, E. (2013). *De hervorming van de roerende zakelijke zekerheden*. Mechelen: Kluwer.

Dubouloz, J. (2011). *La propriété immobilière à Rome et en Italie (Ier—Ve siècles). Organisation et transmission des praedia urbana*. Rome: École française.

Dunand, J.Ph. (2000). *Le transfert fiduciaire:'donner pour reprendre'. Mancipio dare ut remancipetur. Analyse historique et comparatiste de la fiducie-gestion*. Basel: Helbing & Lichtenhahn.

Eckardt, M. (2011). 'Legal Evolution between Stability and Change' in Zumbansen and Callies 2011, 202–25.

Eckhardt, B. (2020). 'Law, Empire, and Identity Between West and East: The Danubian Provinces' in Czajkowski and Eckhardt 2020, 417–35.

Ehrlich, E. (1913). *Grundlegung der Soziologie des Rechts.* Berlin: Duncker & Humblot.

Ellis, S.J.R. (2018). *The Roman Retail Revolution: the Socio-Economic World of the Taberna.* Oxford: Oxford University Press.

Emunds, Chr., and J.D. Harke. (2015). 'Das ius offerendi et succedendi des nachrangingen Pfandgläubigers' in J.D. Harke, ed., *Facetten des römischen Pfandrechts.* Berlin and Heidelberg: Springer, 15–38.

Erbe, W. (1940). *Die Fiduzia im römischen Recht.* Weimar: Böhlau.

Erdkamp, P., K. Verboven, and A. Zuiderhoek, eds (2020). *Capital, Investment, and Innovation in the Roman World.* Oxford: Oxford University Press.

Fecht von der, W.-R. (1999). *Die Forderungspfändung im römischen Recht: der Vollstreckungszugriff auf Forderungen im Rahmen des pignus in causa iudicati captum und des Fiskalrechts der römischen Kaiserzeit.* Cologne and Vienna: Böhlau.

Feenstra. R. (1957). 'West Roman Vulgar Law' 74 *Zeitschrift der Savigny-Stiftung für Rechtsgeschichte, Romanistische Abteilung,* 502–24.

Felgentraeger, W. (1933). *Antikes Lösungsrecht.* Berlin and Leipzig: De Gruyter.

Fercia, R. (2012). *'Fiduciam contrahere' e 'contractus fiduciae'. Prospettive di diritto romano ed europeo.* Naples: Jovene.

Fine, J.V.A. (1951). *Horoi: Studies in Mortgage, Real Security, and Land Tenure in Ancient Athens.* Athens: American School of Classical Studies.

Finkenauer, T. (2010). *Die Rechtsetzung Mark Aurels zur Sklaverei.* Stuttgart: Steiner.

Finley, M.I. (1952). *Studies in Land and Credit in Ancient Athens, 500–200 BC: The Horos-Inscriptions.* New Brunswick, NJ: Rutgers University Press.

Finley, M.I. (1953). 'Land, Debt, and the Man of Property in Classical Athens' 68 *Political Science Quarterly,* 249–68.

Finley, M.I. (1999). *The Ancient Economy,* updated (2nd edn 1984) with a Foreword by Ian Morris. Berkeley, CA: University of California Press.

Fiori, R. (2014). 'Rise and Fall of the Specificity of Contracts' in B. Sirks, ed., *Nova Ratione. Change of Paradigms in Roman Law.* Wiesbaden: Harrassowitz, 33–49.

Fiori, R. (2016). 'Contract, Commerce and Roman Society' in Du Plessis, Ando, and Tuori 2016a, 581–95.

Fleisig, H. (2008). 'The Economics of Collateral and of Collateral Reform' in F. Dahan and J. Simpson, eds, *Secured Transactions Reform and Access to Credit.* Northampton, MA: Elgar, 81–109.

Flessner, A. (2008). 'Security Interests in Receivables—A European Perspective' in H. Eidenmüller and E.-M. Kieninger, eds, *The Future of Secured Credit in Europe, European Company and Financial Law Review,* Special Vol II. Berlin: De Gruyter, 336–49.

Flohr, M. (2013). 'Building Tabernae - How Commercial Investment Changed the Cities of Roman Italy' 50 *Tijdschrift voor Mediterrane Archeologie,* 84.

Flohr, M., and A. Wilson (2017). *The Economy of Pompeii.* Oxford: Oxford University Press.

Fögen, M.Th. (2003). *Römische Rechtsgeschichten. Über Ursprung und Evolution eines sozialen Systems.* 2nd edn, Göttingen: Vandenhoeck & Ruprecht.

Fögen, M.Th. (2005). 'Zufälle, Fälle und Formeln. Zur Emergenz des synallagmatischen Vertrags' 6 *Rechtsgeschichte,* 84–100.

Fracchia, J., and R.C. Lewontin (1999). 'Does Culture Evolve? 38 *History and* Theory, 52–78.

Fracchia, J., and R.C. Lewontin (2005). 'The Price of Metaphor' 44 *History and Theory,* 14–29.

Frederiksen, M.W. (1975). 'Theory, Evidence and The Ancient Economy' 65 *Journal of Roman Studies*, 164–71.

Frezza, P. (1963). *Le garanzie delle obbligazioni. Corso di diritto Romano*, vol. II. *Le garanzie reali.* Padova: CEDAM.

Frier, B.W. (1978). 'Cicero's Management of his Urban Properties' 74 *The Classical Journal*, 1–6.

Frier, B.W. (1980). *Landlords and Tenants in Imperial Rome.* Princeton, NJ: Princeton University Press.

Frier, B.W. (1985). *The Rise of the Roman Jurists. Studies in Cicero's pro Caecina.* Princeton, NJ: Princeton University Press.

Frier, B.W. (1986). 'Why Law Changes' 86 *Columbia Law Review*, 888–900.

Frier, B.W. (1989). 'Autonomy of Law and the Origins of the Legal Profession' 11 *Cardozo Law Review*, 259–86

Frier, B.W. (2000). 'Roman Law's Descent into History' 13 *Journal of Roman Archaeology*, 446–8.

Frier, B.W. (2016). *The Codex of Justinian*, 3 vols. Cambridge, CUP.

Frier, B.W., and D.P. Kehoe (2007). 'Law and Economic Institutions' in Scheidel, Morris, and Saller 2007, 113–43.

Fuenteseca, M. (2013). *Pignus e hypotheca en su evolución histórica.* Santiago de Compostela: Andavira.

Gallo, F. (1992). *Synallagma e conventio nel contratto: ricerca degli archetipi della categoria contrattuale e spunti per la revisione di impostazioni moderne; corso i diritto romano*, vol. I. Turin: Giappichelli.

García Morcillo, M. (2021). 'Managing Uncertainty and Asymmetric Information in Roman Auctions' in C. Rosillo-López and M. García Morcillo, eds, *Managing Information in the Roman Economy*. London: Palgrave-McMillan, 61–88.

Garnsey, P., and R. Saller (2014). *The Roman Empire.* Oakland, CA: University of California Press.

Gessel van, Chr. (2003). 'Praedes, praedia, cognitores: les suretés réelles et personelles de l'adjudicataire du contrat public en droit romain (textes et réflections)' in J.-J. Aubert, ed., *Tâches publiques et entreprise privée dans le monde romain. Actes du Diplôme d'Etudes Avancées, Universités de Neuchâtel et de Lausanne, 2000–2002.* Geneva: Droz, 95–122.

Giardina, A. (2007), 'The Transition to Late Antiquity' in Scheidel, Morris, and Saller 2007, 743–68.

Giltaij, J. (2016). 'Greek Philosophy and Classical Roman Law: a Brief Overview' in Du Plessis, Ando, and Tuori 2016a, 188–99.

Giuffré, V. (1992). *L'emersione dei' iura in re aliena' ed il dogma del'numero chiuso'.* Napoli: Jovene.

Goldthwaite, R.A. (2009). *The Economy of Renaissance Florence.* Baltimore, MD: JHU Press.

Goody, J. (1986). *The Logic of Writing and the Organization of Society.* Cambridge: Cambridge University Press.

Gordley, J. (2019). 'Comparative Law and Legal History' in M. Reimann and R. Zimmermann, eds, *The Oxford Handbook of Comparative Law.* 2nd edn, Oxford: Oxford University Press, 754–70.

Gordon, W.M. (1970). *Studies in the Transfer of Property by Traditio.* Aberdeen: University Press.

Gordon, R.W. (1984). 'Critical Legal Histories' 36 *Stanford Law Review*, 57–125, reprinted in R.W. Gordon (2017). *Taming the Past. Essays on Law in History and History in Law.* Cambridge: Cambridge University Press, 220–81.

Gordon, R.W. (2012). 'Critical Legal Histories Revisited: A Response' *Law & Social Inquiry* 37, 200–15.

Gordon, W.M., and O.F. Robinson (1997). *The Institutes of Gaius*, 2nd edn, London: Duckworth.

Granovetter, M. (2017). *Society and Economy. Framework and Principles.* Cambridge, MA: Harvard University Press.

Greif, A. (2006). *Institutions and the Path to the Modern Economy: Lessons from Medieval Trade.* Cambridge: Cambridge University Press.

Gröschler, P. (1997). *Die* tabellae-*Urkunden aus den pompejanischen und herkulanensischen Urkundenfunden.* Berlin: Duncker & Humblot.

Gröschler, P. (2008). 'Die Mittel der Kreditsicherung in den tabulae ceratae' in Verboven, Vandorpe, and Chankowski-Sable 2008. Gutenberg: Universität Mainz, 301–19.

Gröschler, P. (2014). 'Pfandrecht und Nießbrauch - Mehrfachbestellung und Konvaleszenz beschränkter dinglicher Rechte im römischen, im gemeinen und im geltenden Recht' in R. van den Bergh et al., eds, *Meditationes de iure et histori: Essays in Honour of Laurens Winkel. Fundamina. Editio specialis.* Pretoria: Unisa Press, 357–70.

Günther, S. (2016). 'Taxation in the Greco-Roman World: The Roman Principate' *Oxford Handbooks Online*. DOI: 10.1093/oxfordhb/9780199935390.013.

Hammerstein, J. (1975). *Die Herde im römischen Recht: grex als rechtliche Sachgesamtheit und Wirtschaftseinheit.* Göttingen: Musterschmidt.

Hanard. G. (1994). 'Interdit salvien et action servienne. La genèse de l'hypothèque romaine' 41 *Revue internationale des droits de l'antiquité*, 239–86.

Harke, J.D. (2008). 'Zum römischen Recht der Forderungsübertragung' 76 *Legal History Review*, 1–18.

Harper, K. (2017). *The Fate of Rome. Climate, Disease, and the End of an Empire.* Princeton, NJ: Princeton University Press.

Harrauer, H., and R. Seider (1979). 'Ein neuer lateinischer Schuldschein P. Vindob. L 135' 36 *Zeitschrift für Papyrologie und Epigraphik*, 109–20.

Harris, R. (2020). 'The Organization of India-to-Rome Trade: Loans and Agents in the Muziris Papyrus' in Dari-Mattiacci and Kehoe 2020a, 163–96.

Harris, W.V. (2011). *Rome's Imperial Economy: Twelve Essays.* Oxford: Oxford University Press.

Haselmann, R., K. Pistor, and V. Vig (2010). 'How Law Affects Lending' 23 *The Review of Financial Studies*, 549–80.

Hayek, F.A. (2013). *Law, Legislation and Liberty. A New Statement of the Liberal Principles of Justice and Political Economy.* London: Routledge (single volume edition of *Rules and Order* (1973), *The Mirage of Social Justice* (1976), and *The Political Order of a Free People* (1979)).

Hodgson, G.M. (2001). *How Economics Forgot History. The Problem of Historical Specificity in Social Science.* London: Routledge.

Hodgson, G.M. (2015). *Conceptualizing Capitalism. Institutions, Evolution. Future.* Chicago and London: University of Chicago Press.

Hodgson, G.M., and T. Knudsen (2010). *Darwin's Conjecture. The Search for General Principles of Social & Economic Evolution.* Chicago, IL: University of Chicago Press.

Hoffman, Ph.T., G. Postel-Vinay, and J.-L. Rosenthal (2000). *Priceless Markets: the Political Economy of Credit in Paris. 1660–1870.* Chicago, IL: University of Chicago Press.

Hofstetter, J. (1999). 'War Atilicinus schuldnerfreundlich?' in J-F. Gerkens et al., eds, *Mélanges Fritz Sturm*, vol. I. Luik, 225–38.

Hollander den, J. (2014). 'The Meaning of Evolution and the Evolution of Meaning' 8 *Journal of the Philosophy of History*, 243–64.

Holleran, C. (2017). 'Finding Commerce: the *taberna* and the Identification of Roman Commercial Space' 85 *Papers of the British School at Rome*, Cambridge: Cambridge University Press, 143–70.

Honoré. T. (1994). *Emperors and Lawyers*, 2nd edn, Oxford: Oxford University Press.

Hoof van, V.J.M. (2015). *Generale zekerheidsrechten in rechtshistorisch perspectief*. Deventer: Wolters Kluwer.

Hoof van, V.J.M. (2017). 'The "generalis hypotheca" and the Sale of Pledged Assets in Roman Law' 85 *Legal History Review*, 474–91.

Hoof van, V.J.M. (2022). 'The Priority of Acquisition Secured Creditors in Classical Roman Law' (forthcoming).

Hopkins, K. (1980). 'Taxes and Trade in the Roman Empire (200 B.C.–A.D. 400)' 70 *Journal of Roman Studies*, 101–25.

Hornblower, S., A. Spawforth, and E. Eidinow (eds) (2012). *The Oxford Classical Dictionary*, 4th edn, Oxford: Oxford University Press.

Hromadka, W. (1971). *Die Entwicklung des Faustpfandprinzips im 18. und 19. Jahrhundert*. Vienna: Böhlau.

Huttner, U. (2020). 'Latin Law in Greek Cities: Knowledge of Law and Latin in Imperial Asia Minor' in Czajkowski and Eckhardt 2020, 137–56.

Indra, M. (2011). *Status quaestio. Studien zum Freiheitsprozess im klassischen römischen Recht*. Berlin: Duncker & Humblot.

Ioannatou, M. (2004). 'Le code de l'honneur des paiements. Créanciers et débiteurs à la fin de la République romaine' in J. Andreau, J. France, and S. Pittia (eds), *Mentalités et choix économiques des Romains*. Paris: De Boccard, 87–107.

Ioannatou, M. (2006). *Affaires d'argent dans la correspondance de Cicéron. L'aristocratie sénatoriale face à ses dettes*. Paris: De Boccard.

Iuliis de, F. (2017). *Studi sul pignus conventum: Le origini. L'interdictum salvianum*. Turin: G. Giappichelli.

Jablonka, É., and M.J. Lamb (2014). *Evolution in Four Dimensions. Genetic, Epigenetic, Behavorial, and Symbolic Variation in the History of Life*, revised edition. Cambridge, MA: MIT Press.

Jackson, Th.H., and A.T. Kronman (1979). 'Secured Financing and Priorities' 88 *Yale Law Review*, 1143–82.

Jakab, É. (2006). 'Vertragsformulare im Imperium Romanum' 123 *Zeitschrift der Savigny-Stiftung für Rechtsgeschichte, Romanistische Abteilung*, 71–101.

Jakab, É. (2014). 'Horrea, sûretés et commerce maritime dans les archives des Sulpicii' in J. Hallebeek et al., eds., *Inter cives necnon peregrinos. Essays in Honour of Boudewijn Sirks*. Göttingen: Vandenhoeck & Ruprecht, 331–50.

Jansen, H. (2010). *Triptiek van de tijd. Geschiedenis in drievoud*. Nijmegen: Vantilt.

Jansen, J.E. (2017). *De actio Serviana en het Nederlandse privaatrecht*. The Hague: Boom.

Jansen, N. (2019). *Recht und gesellschaftliche Differenzierung*. Tübingen: Mohr Siebeck.

Jaschke, K. (2010). *Die Wirtschafts- und Sozialgeschichte des antiken Puteoli*. Rahden: Leidorf.

Johnston, D. (2022). *Roman Law in Context*, 2nd edn, Cambridge: Cambridge University Press.

Jolowicz, H.F., and B. Nicholas (1972). *Historical Introduction to the Study of Roman Law*, 3rd edn, Cambridge: Cambridge University Press.

Jones, D.F. (2006). *The Bankers of Puteoli: Finance, Trade and Industry in the Roman World*. Stroud: Tempus.

Kaser, M. (1950). 'Alberto Burdese, Lex commissoria e ius vendendi nella fiducia e nel pignus' 67 *Zeitschrift der Savigny-Stiftung für Rechtsgeschichte: Romanistische Abteilung*, 557–67.

Kaser, M. (1956). *Eigentum und Besitz im älteren römischen Recht*. Vienna: Böhlau.

Kaser, M. (1961). 'In bonis esse' 78 *Zeitschrift der Savigny-Stiftung für Rechtsgeschichte: Romanistische Abteilung*, 173–220.

Kaser, M. (1969). 'Zum "pignus nominis" ' XX *IVRA*, 172–90.

Kaser, M. (1971). *Das römische Privatrecht*, vol. I. *Das altrömische, das vorklassische und klassische Recht*, 2nd edn, Munich: Beck.

Kaser, M. (1975). *Das römische Privatrecht*, vol. II. *Die nachklassischen Entwicklungen*, 2nd edn, Munich: Beck.

Kaser, M. (1976). *Ausgewählte Schriften*, vol. II. Naples: Jovene.

Kaser, M. (1982). *Studien zum römischen Pfandrecht*. Naples: Jovene.

Kaser, M. (1986). *Römische Rechtsquellen und angewandte Juristenmethode: ausgewählte, zum Teil grundlegend erneuerte Abhandlungen*. Vienna: Böhlau.

Kaser, M., and K. Hackl (1996). *Das römische Zivilprozessrecht*, 2nd edn, Munich: Beck.

Kaser, M., R. Knütel, and S. Lohsse (2021). *Römisches Privatrecht: Ein Studienbuch*, 22nd edn, Munich: Beck.

Kay, Ph. (2014). *Rome's Economic Revolution*. Oxford: Oxford University Press.

Kehoe, D. (2007). *Law and Rural Economy in the Roman Empire*. Ann Arbor, MI: University of Michigan Press.

Kehoe, D., D.M. Ratzan, and U. Yiftach (2015). *Law and Transaction Costs in the Ancient Economy*. Ann Arbor, MI: University of Michigan Press.

Kelly, J.M. (1966a). *Roman Litigation*. Oxford: Clarendon Press.

Kelly, J.M. (1966b). 'The Growth-Pattern of the Praetor's Edict' *Irish Jurist*, 341–55.

Kirov, J. (2005). *Die soziale Logik des Rechts: Recht und Gesellschaft der römischen Republik*. Göttingen: V&R Unipress.

Klinck, F. (2015). 'Verpfändung und Speichermiete in den Tabulae Pompeianae Sulpiciorum' in J.D. Harke, ed., *Facetten des römischen Pfandrechts*. Berlin: Springer, 55–73.

Klingenberg, G. (1992). 'Die venditio ob tributorum cessationem facta' 109 *Zeitschrift der Savigny-Stiftung für Rechtsgeschichte. Romanistische Abteilung*, 350–410.

Koops, E. (2010). *Vormen van subsidiariteit. Een historisch-comparatistische studie naar het subsidiariteitsbeginsel bij pand, hypotheek en borgtocht*. The Hague: Boom.

Koops, E. (2012). ' "Moschis" Case. On the Execution of Fiscal Debts and the beneficium excussionis' 80 *Legal History Review*, 279–310.

Koops, E. (2020). 'The Practice of Manumission Through Negotiated Conditions in Imperial Rome' in Dari-Mattiacci and Kehoe 2020b, 35–77.

Koops, E., and W.J. Zwalve (2013). *Law & Equity: Approaches in Roman Law and Common Law*. Leiden: Martinus Nijhoff/Brill.

Krämer, G. (2007). *Das besitzlose Pfandrecht. Entwicklungen in der römischen Republik und im frühen Prinzipat*. Vienna: Böhlau.

Kreller. H. (1942). 'Formula fiduciae und Pfandedikt' 62 *Zeitschrift der Savigny-Stiftung für Rechtsgeschichte, Romanistische Abteilung*, 143–208.

Krüger, P. (1905), *Corpus iuris civilis. Digesta* (vol. I), *Codex Justinianus* (vol. II). Berlin: Weidmann.

Kunkel, W. (1967). *Herkunft und soziale Stellung der römischen Juristen*. 2nd edn, Vienna, Cologne: Böhlau.

Kunkel, W. (1973). 'Hypothesen zur Geschichte des römischen Pfandrechts' 90 *Zeitschrift der Savigny-Stiftung für Rechtsgeschichte: Romanistische Abteilung*, 15–170.

Kupisch, B. (2002). 'Römische Sachmängelhaftung: Ein Beispiel für die ökonomische Analyse des Rechts?' 70 *Legal History Review*, 21–54.

Kupiszewski, H. (1974). 'Quelques remarques sur les vocabula ἀντιχρησις, ἀρρα, παράφηρνα dans le Digeste' 18 *Journal of Juristic Papyrology*, 227–38.

Kupiszewski, H. (1986). 'Antichrese und Nutzpfand in den Papyri' in H.-P. Benöhr, K. Hackl, R. Knütel, et al. (eds), *Iuris professio. Festgabe für Max Kaser zum 80. Geburtstag*. Vienna: Böhlau, 133–49.

Lambrini, P. (2016). 'Le cause del negozio fiduciario' in I. Piro, ed., *Scritti per Alessandro Corbino*, vol. IV. Tricase: Libellula.

Laor, Y., and E. Jablonka (2013). 'The Evolution and Development of Culture' (review Mesoudi 2011), 52 *History and Theory*, 290–99.

La Rosa, F. (1977). *Ricerche sul 'pignus'*. Catania: [no publisher].

La Rosa, F. (1987). 'La protezione interdittale del pignus e l'actio serviana' in *Studi in onore di Cesare Sanfilippo*, vol. 7. Milano: Giuffrè, 281–317.

Lehne, C. (2014). 'Die Stellung der Juristen im Formularverfahren' 131 *Zeitschrift der Savigny-Stiftung für Rechtsgeschichte, Romanistische Abteilung*, 216–312.

Lempert, R. (1988). 'The Autonomy of Law: Two Visions Compared' in G. Teubner, ed., *Autopoietic Law: A New Approach to Law and Society*. Berlin: De Gruyter, 152–216.

Lenel, O. (1889). *Palingenesia iuris civilis*, 2 vols. Leipzig: Tauchnitz.

Lenel, O. (1927). *Das Edictum perpetuum. Ein Versuch zu seiner Wiederherstellung*, 3rd edn, Leipzig: Tauchnitz.

Lenz, H.M. (1994). *Privilegia fisci*. Pfaffenweiler: Centaurus.

Lerouxel, F. (2008). 'La banque privée romaine et le marché du crédit dans les tablettes de Murécine et les papyrus d'Égypte Romaine' in Verboven, Vandorpe, and Chankowski-Sable 2008, 169–97.

Lerouxel, F. (2012). 'Le marché du crédit privé, la bibliothèque des acquêts et les tâches publiques en Égypte romaine' 67 *Annales. Histoire, Sciences Sociales*, 943–76.

Lerouxel, F. (2015). 'The *βιβλιοθήκη ἐγκτήσεων* and Transaction Costs in the Credit Market of Roman Egypt (30 B.C.E. to ca. 170 C.E.)' in Kehoe, Ratzan, and Yiftach 2015, 162–84.

Lerouxel, F. (2016). *Le marché du crédit dans le monde romain: Egypte et Campanie*. Rome: École française.

Levy, E. (1951). *West Roman Vulgar Law. The Law of Property*. Philadelphia, PA: American Philosophical Society.

Levy, E. (1956). *Weströmisches Vulgarrecht. Das Obligationenrecht*. Weimar: Böhlau.

Lévy, J. Ph. (1987). 'Coup d'oeil historique d'ensemble sur les sûretés réelles' 55 *Legal History Review*, 231–66.

Lewens, T. (2015). *Cultural Evolution. Conceptual Challenges*. Oxford: Oxford University Press.

Liebs, D. (1997). 'Jurisprudenz' in R. Herzog and P. Lebrecht Schmidt, eds, *Handbuch der lateinischen Literatur der Antike, 8. Abt., 4. Band, hrsg. Von Klaus Sallmann. Die Literatur des Umbruchs. Von der römischen zur christlichen Literatur, 117 bis 284 n. Chr.* Munich: Beck, 83–217.

Liebs, D. (2010). *Hofjuristen der römischen Kaiser bis Justinian*. Munich: Beck.

Ligt de, L. (2020). 'Law-Making and Economic Change During the Republic and Early Empire' in Dari-Mattiacci and Kehoe 2020a, 85–108.

Litewski, W. (1994). 'Non numerata pecunia im klassischen römischen Recht' 60 *Studia et documenta historiae et iuris*, 405–56.

Lo Cascio, E., ed. (2003). *Credito e moneta nel mondo romano. Atti degli Incontri capresi di storia dell'economia antica, Capri, 12–14 ottobre 2000*. Bari: Edipuglia.

Lo Cascio, E., and D. Mantovani, eds (2018). *Diritto romano e economia. Due modi di pensare e organizzare il mondo (nei primi tre secoli dell'Impero)*. Pavia: Pavia University Press.

Lübtow von, U. (1957). 'Cato's leges venditioni et locationi dictae' in *Symbolae Raphaeli Taubenschlag dedicatae*, vol. III. Warsaw: Ossolineum, 227–441.

Luhmann, N. (1988). 'The Unity of the Legal System' in G. Teubner, ed, *Autopoietic Law: A New Approach to Law and Society*. Berlin: De Gruyter, 12–35.

Luhmann, N. (1991). 'Operational Closure and Structural Coupling: The Differentiation of the Legal System' 13 *Cardozo Law Review*, 1419–41.

Luhmann, N. (1993). *Das Recht der Gesellschaft*. Frankfurt am Main: Suhrkamp.

Luhmann, N. (2004). *Law as a Social System*. Oxford: Oxford University Press (= translation of Luhmann 1993).

Luhmann, N. (2008). *Ideenevolution. Beiträge zur Wissenssoziologie*. Frankfurt am Main: Suhrkamp.

Luhmann, N. (2012). *Theory of Society*, vol. I. Stanford, CA: Stanford University Press.

Magdelain, A. (1958). *Le consensualisme dans l'édit du préteur*. Paris: Sirey.

Malmendier, U. (2002). *Societas publicanorum: staatliche Wirtschaftsaktivitäten in den Händen privater Unternehmer*. Cologne: Böhlau.

Manigk, A. (1904). *Pfandrechtliche Untersuchungen, I. Heft: Zur Geschichte der römischen Hypothek, Erster Teil: Die pfandrechtliche Terminologie und Literatur der Römer*. Breslau: Marcus.

Manigk, A. (1909). 'Fiducia' in A.F. Pauly and G. Wissowa, eds, *Real-Encyclopädie der classischen Altertumswissenschaft*, vol. VI. Stuttgart: Metzler, 2287–2316.

Manigk, A. (1910). *Gläubigerbefriedigung duch Nutzung. Ein Institut der antiken Rechte*. Berlin: Vahlen.

Manigk, A. (1916). 'Hypotheca' in A.F. Pauly and G. Wissowa, eds, *Real-Encyclopädie der classischen Altertumswissenschaft*, vol. IX. Stuttgart: Metzler, 343–412.

Manigk, A. (1939). 'Privatautonomie' in *Festschrift Paul Koschaker*, vol. 1. Weimar: Böhlau, 266–95.

Manigk, A. (1941). 'Pignus' in A.F. Pauly and G. Wissowa, eds, *Real-Encyclopädie der classischen Altertumswissenschaft*, vol. XX(I). Stuttgart: Metzler, 1239–1284.

Mantovani, D. (2016). 'More than Codes: Roman Ways of Organising and Giving Access to Legal Information' in Du Plessis, Ando, and Tuori 2016a, 23–42.

Marino, S. (2018). *Sull'accessorietà del pegno per la giurisprudenza romana*. Napoli: Jovene.

Marra, P. (2017). 'Un cas particulier de transfert de propriété à titre de garantie: la «Mancipatio Pompeiana»' 64 *Revue internationale des droits de l'antiquité*, 177–200.

Mauer, Q. (2022). *Application, Adaptation and Rejection. The Strategies of Roman Jurists in Responsa concerning Greek Documents*. The Hague: Boom.

Mayer, E. (2012). *The Ancient Middle Classes*. Cambridge, MA: Harvard University Press.

Mayr, E. (2002). *What Evolution Is*. London: Phoenix.

McCall, B. (2009). 'It's Just Secured Credit: a Natural Law Case in Support of Some Forms of Secured Credit' 43 *Indiana Law Review*, 7–44.

McConnell, J.R. et al. (2018). 'Lead Pollution Recorded in Greenland Ice Indicates European Emissions Tracked Plagues, Wars, and Imperial Expansion During Antiquity' 115(22) *Proceedings of the National Academy of Sciences of the United States of America (PNAS)*, 5726–31 <http://www.pnas.org/cgi/doi/10.1073/pnas.1721818115>.

McCormack, G. (2004). *Secured Credit under English and American Law*. Cambridge: Cambridge University Press.

Medicus, D. (1976). Review Wagner 1974 93 *Zeitschrift der Savigny-Stiftung für Rechtsgeschichte: Romanistische Abteilung*, 427–33.

Meissel, F.S. (2004). *Societas. Struktur und Typenvielfalt des römischen Gessellschaftsvertrages*. Frankfurt am Main: Lang.

Meissel, F.S. (2011). 'Vertragspraxis und Privatrechtsdogmatik—Zum Umgang der römischen Juristen mit Vertragsklauseln am Beispiel der societas' in F. Harrer, ed, *Gedächtnisschrift für Theo Mayer-Maly*. Vienna: Springer, 347–62.

Mentxaka, R. (1986). *La pigneracion de colectividades en el derecho romano clásico*. Bilbao: Servicio Editorial de la Universidad del País Vasco.

Mesoudi, A. (2011). *Cultural Evolution. How Darwinian Theory Can Explain Human Culture and Synthesize the Social Sciences*. Chicago, IL: University of Chicago Press.

Metzger, E. (2005). *Litigation in Roman Law*. Oxford: Oxford University Press.

Meyer, E.A. (2004). *Legitimacy and Law in the Roman World. Tabulae in Roman Belief and Practice*. Cambridge: Cambridge University Press.

Mitteis, L. (1891). *Reichsrecht und Volksrecht in den östlichen Provinzen des römischen Kaiserreichs. Mit Beiträgen zur Kenntniss des griechischen Rechts*. Leipzig: Teubner.

Miyasaka, W. (2019). '*Corpus ex distantibus* in Roman Law' in U. Babusiaux and M. Igimi, eds, *'Messages from Antiquity'. Roman Law and Current Legal Debates*. Vienna: Böhlau.

Moatti, C. (1993). *Archives et partage de la terre dans le monde Romain (Iie siècle avant—Ier siècle après J.-C.)*. Rome: École française.

Moatti, C. (2015). *The Birth of Critical Thinking in Republican Rome*. Cambridge: Cambridge University Press.

Mokyr, J. (2017). *A Culture of Growth. The Origins of the Modern Economy*. Princeton, NJ: Princeton University Press.

Mommsen, T., and P.M. Meyer, eds (1962). *Codex Theodosianus*, 3 vols, 3rd edn, Berlin: Weidmann.

Monson, A., and W. Scheidel, eds (2015). *Fiscal Regimes and the Political Economy of Premodern States*. Cambridge: Cambridge University Press.

Morel, J.-P. (2007). 'Early Rome and Italy' in Scheidel, Morris, and Saller 2007, 487–510.

Morin, O. (2016). *How Traditions Live and Die*. Oxford: Oxford University Press.

Morley, N. (2008). 'The Early Roman Empire: Distribution' in Scheidel, Morris, and Saller 2007, 570–91.

Morris, I. (1999). 'Foreword' in Finley 1999, ix–xxxvi.

Morris, I. (2015). *Foragers, Farmers, and Fossil Fuels. How Human Values Evolve*. Princeton, NJ and Oxford: Princeton University Press.

Mouritsen, H. (2016). 'Manumission' in Du Plessis, Ando, and Tuori 2016a, 402–15.

Navarra, M. (2002). *Ricerche sulla utilitas nel pensiero dei giuristi romani*. Turin: Giappichelli.

Neeve de, P.W. (1984a). *Colonus. Private Farm-Tenancy in Roman Italy During the Republic and the Early Principate*. Amsterdam: Gieben.

Neeve de, P.W. (1984b). 'Fundus as Economic Unit' 52 *Legal History Review*, 3–19.

Nicholas, B. (1962). *An Introduction to Roman Law*. Oxford: Oxford University Press (repr. 2010).

Noordraven, B. (1999). *Die Fiduzia im römischen Recht*. Amsterdam: Gieben.

Nörr, D. (2003). *Historiae iuris antiqui: gesammelte Schriften*, 3 vols. Goldbach: Keip.

North, D.C. (2005). *Understanding the Process of Economic Change*. Princeton, NJ: Princeton University Press.

Oditah, F. (1991). *Legal Aspects of Receivables Financing*. London: Sweet & Maxwell.

Oudshoorn, J.G. (2007). *The Relationship Between Roman and Local Law in the Babatha and Salome Komaise Archives. General Analysis and Three Case Studies on Law of Succession, Guardianship and Marriage*. Leiden: Brill.

Out, J.C. (2005). *Vormen van accessoriëteit, een romanistische studie over het verschijnsel accessoriëteit bij het goederenrechtelijke zekerheidsrecht*. Nijmegen: Gerard Noodt Instituut.

Pachtère de, F.G. (1920). *La table hypothécaire de Veleia: étude sur la propriété foncière dans l'Apennin de Plaisance*. Paris: Champion.

Parsons, T., and N. Smelser (1956). *Economy and Society: A Study in the Integration of Economic and Social Theory*. Glencoe: The Free Press.

Peachin, M. (1996). *Iudex vice Caesaris. Deputy Emperors and the Administration of Justice During the Principate*. Stuttgart: Franz Steiner.

Peachin, M. (2016). 'Lawyers in Administration' in Du Plessis, Ando, and Tuori 2016a, 164–75.

Pellecchi, L. (2018). 'Dimensione economica e azione della giurisprudenza: il caso delle garanzie reali' in Lo Cascio and Mantovani 2018, 445–505.

Perani, R. (2021). *Pignus distrahere. La vendita del pegno da parte del creditore pignoratizio*. Milano: Giuffrè.

Peters, F. (1973). 'Der Erwerb des Pfandes durch den Pfandgläubiger im klassischen und im nachklassischen Recht' in D. Medicus and H.H. Seiler, eds, *Studien im Römischen Recht, Max Kaser zum 65. Geburtstag gewidmet von seinen Hamburger Schülern*. Berlin: Duncker & Humblot, 137–68.

Petrucci, A. (2008). 'Riesame del ruolo dei banchieri nelle auctiones private nel diritto classico romano' in Verboven, Vandorpe, and Chankowski-Sable 2008, 277–300.

Plessis du, P.J. (2007). 'The Interdictum de migrando Revisited' 54 *Révue internationale des droits de l'antiquité*, 232–35.

Plessis du, P.J. (2010). 'The Slave in the Window'. *Bulletin of the Institute of Classical Studies. Supplement*, 49–60.

Plessis du, P.J. (2012). *Letting and Hiring in Roman Legal Thought: 27 BCE–284 CE*. Leiden: Brill.

Plessis du, P.J., C. Ando, and K. Tuori, eds (2016a). *The Oxford Handbook of Roman Law and Society*. Oxford: Oxford University Press.

Plessis du, P.J., C. Ando, and K. Tuori (2016b). 'A Word from the Editors' in Du Plessis, Ando, and Tuori 2016a, 3–7.

Pölönen, J. (2016). 'Framing "Law and Society" in the Roman World' in Du Plessis, Ando, and Tuori 2016a, 8–20.

Pontoriero, I. (2011). *Il prestito marittimo in diritto romano*. Bologna: Bononia University Press.

Popper, K.R. (1973). *Objective Knowledge. An Evolutionary Approach*. Oxford: Oxford University Press (reprint with corrections of the first edition 1972).

Potjewijd, G.H. (1998). *Beschikkingsbevoegdheid, bekrachtiging en convalescentie*. Deventer: Kluwer.

Pugliese, G. (1966). 'L'autonomia del diritto rispetto agli altri fenomeni e valori sociali nella giurisprudenza romana' in *La storia del diritto nel quadro delle scienze storiche, Atti del primo congresso internazionale della società italiana di storia del diritto*. Firenze: Olschki, 161–92.

Purcell, N. (1994). 'The City of Rome and the plebs urbana in the Late Republic' in J.A. Crook, Andrew Lintott and Elizabeth Rawson, *The Cambridge Ancient History*, vol. IX. *The Last Age of the Roman Republic. 164–43 BC*. Cambridge: Cambridge University Press, 644–88.

Rabban, D.M. (2013). *Law's History. American Legal Thought and the Transatlantic Turn to History*, New York, NY: Cambridge University Press.

Rabel, E. (1971). 'Nachgeformte Rechtsgeschäfte. Mit Beiträgen zu den Lehren von der Injurezession und vom Pfandrecht' in H.J. Wolff, ed., *Gesammelte Aufsätze*, vol. IV. *Arbeiten zur altgriechischen, hellenistischen und römischen Rechtsgeschichte. 1905–1949*. Tübingen: Mohr (Siebeck), 9–104.

Rathbone, D. (2003). 'The Financing of Maritime Commerce in the Roman Empire, I-II AD' in Lo Cascio 2003, 197–229.

Rathbone, D. (2009). 'Earnings and Costs: Living Standards and the Roman Economy' in Bowman and Wilson 2009, 299–326.

Rathbone, D., and P. Temin (2008). 'Financial Intermediation in First-Century AD Rome and Eighteenth-Century England' in Verboven, Vandorpe, and Chankowski-Sable 2008, 371–419.

Reden von, S. (2010). *Money in Classical Antiquity*. Cambridge: Cambridge University Press.

Renn, J. (2020). *The Evolution of Knowledge. Rethinking Science for the Anthropocene*. Princeton, NJ: Princeton University Press.

Richerson, P.J., and R. Boyd (2005). *Not by Genes Alone. How Culture Transformed Human Evolution*. Chicago, IL: University of Chicago Press.

Rickman, G. (1971). *Roman Granaries and Store Buildings*. Cambridge: Cambridge University Press.

Riggsby, A.M. (2010). *Roman Law and the Legal World of the Romans*. New York, NY: Cambridge University Press.

Robinson, D. (2017). 'Wealthy Entrepreneurs and the Urban Economy: Insula VI 1 in its Wider Economic Contexts' in Flohr and Wilson 2017, 243–62.

Roe, M.J. (1996). 'Chaos and Evolution in Law and Economics' 109 *Harvard Law Review*, 641–68.

Romanis de, F. (2020). *The Indo-Roman Pepper Trade and the Muziris Papyrus*. Oxford: Oxford University Press.

Romeo, S. (2006). 'Fiducia auctionibus vendunda nelle Tabelle Pompeiane. Procedure e modalità di redazione delle testationes nelle auctiones puteolane del 61 d.C.' in *Polis. Studi interdisciplinari sul mondo antico*, 207–58.

Roselaar, S.T. (2010). *Public Land in the Roman Republic: A Social and Economic History of the Ager Publicus in Italy, 396–89 BC*. Oxford: Oxford University Press.

Rostovtzeff, M.I. (1932). Review of J. Hasebroek 'Griechische Wirtschafts- und Gesellschaftsgeschichte' 92 *Zeitschrift für die gesamte Staatswissenschaft*, 333–9.

Rostovtzeff, M.I. (1957). *The Social and Economic History of the Roman Empire*, vol. I. Oxford: Clarendon Press.

Röver, J.-H. (1999). *Vergleichende Prinzipien dinglicher Sicherheiten*. Munich: Beck.

Rubin, P.H., ed. (2007) *The Evolution of Efficient Common Law*. Cheltenham: Elgar.

Rudden, B. (1994). 'Things as Thing and Things as Wealth' 14 *Oxford Journal of Legal Studies*, 81–97.

Rupprecht, H.-A. (2014). 'Real Security' in J.G. Keenan, J.G. Manning, and U. Yiftach-Firanko, eds, *Law and Legal Practice in Egypt from Alexander to the Arab Conquest: A Selection of Papyrological Sources in Translation, with Introductions and Commentary*. Cambridge: Cambridge University Press.

Sanderson, S.K. (2007). *Evolutionism and Its Critics. Deconstructing and Reconstructing an Evolutionary Interpretation of Human Society*. London: Boulder.

Schanbacher, D. (1987). *Die Konvaleszenz von Pfandrechten im klassischen römischen Recht*. Berlin: Duncker & Humblot.

Schanbacher, D. (2002a). 'Die Gegenwart der Geschichte in der Rechtsprechung des Bundesgerichtshofs—BGHZ 130, 101 –' in M.J. Schermaier, J.M. Rainer, and L.C. Winkel, eds, *Iurisprudentia universalis. Festschrift für Theo Mayer-Maly zum 70. Geburtstag*. Cologne: Böhlau, 639–59.

Schanbacher, D. (2002b). 'Romisches internationales Privatrecht in Scaev, 7 Dig (D. 18, 1, 81pr)' 70 *Legal History Review*, 251–64.

Schanbacher, D. (2006). 'Zu Ursprung und Entwicklung des römischen Pfandrechts' 123 *Zeitschrift der Savigny-Stiftung für Rechtsgeschichte, Romanistische Abteilung*, 49–70.

Schanbacher, D. (2010). 'Entwicklungen in der römischen Pfandrechtsdoktrin' in 70 *Ius Romanum Schola Sapientiae*. Trnava: Narodeninám, 401–13.

Schanbacher, D. (2016). 'Hypothekarische Sukzession' 84 *Legal History Review*, 149–64.

Scheibelreiter, Ph. (2020). 'Zum Klagsziel der actio pigneraticia in personam contraria in D. 13, 7, 9 pr' 88 *Legal History Review*, 50–93.

Scheidel, W. (2010). 'Economy and Quality of Life' in A. Barchiesi and W. Scheidel, eds. *The Oxford Handbook of Roman Studies*. Oxford: Oxford University Press.

Scheidel, W. (2012). *The Cambridge Companion to the Roman Economy*. Cambridge: Cambridge University Press.

Scheidel, W., I. Morris, and R.P. Saller, eds (2007). *The Cambridge Economic History of the Greco-Roman World*. Cambridge: Cambridge University Press.

Schiavone, A. (2000). *The End of the Past. Ancient Rome and the Modern West*. Cambridge, MA: Harvard University Press.

Schiavone, A. (2012). *The Invention of Law in the West*. Cambridge, MA: Harvard University Press.

Schiller, A.A. (1978). *Roman Law. Mechanisms of Development*. Berlin: De Gruyter.

Schulz, F. (1928). 'Die fraudatorische Freilassung im klassischen und justinianischen römischen Recht' 48 *Zeitschrift der Savigny-Stiftung für Rechtsgeschichte. Romanistische Abteilung*, 197–284.

Schulz, F. (1936). *Principles of Roman Law*. Oxford: Clarendon Press.

Schulz, F. (1951). *Classical Roman Law*. Oxford: Clarendon Press (reprint 1969).

Schulz, F. (1953). *History of Roman Legal Science*. Oxford: Clarendon Press.

Schuster, S. (2005). *Das Seedarlehen in den Gerichtsreden des Demosthenes: mit einem Ausblick auf die weitere historische Entwicklung des Rechtsinstitutes: dáneion nautikón, fenus nauticum und Bodmerei*. Berlin: Duncker & Humblot.

Schwartz, A. (1984). 'The Continuing Puzzle of Secured Debt' 37 *Vanderbilt Law Review*, 1051–69.

Schwarz, F.V. (1954). 'Die Konträrklagen' 71 *Zeitschrift der Savigny-Stiftung für Rechtsgeschichte. Romanistische Abteilung*, 111–220.

Selb, W. (1982). 'Formulare Analogien in "actiones utiles" und "actiones in factum" am Beispiel Julians' in F. Pastori, ed., *Studi in onore di Arnoldo Biscardi*, vol. III. Milano: La Goliardica, 315–50.

Serrao, F. (2008). *Diritto privato, economia e società nella storia di Roma*, vol. 1. *Dalla società gentilizia alle origini dell'economia schiavistica*. Naples: Jovene (reprint).

Silver, M. (2011). 'Finding the Roman Empire's Disappeared Deposit Bankers' 60 *Historia*, 301–27.

Sirks, B. (2002). 'Sailing in the Off-Season with Reduced Financial Risk' in J-J. Aubert and B. Sirks, eds, *Speculum Iuris. Roman Law as a Reflection of Social and Economic Life in Antiquity*. Ann Arbor, MI: The University of Michigan Press, 134–50.

Sirks, B. (2010). *Food for Rome. The Legal Structure of the Transportation and Processing of Supplies for the Imperial Distributions in Rome and Constantinople*. The Hague (reprint of the original English edition, Amsterdam: Gieben 1991).

Sirks, B. (2016). 'Chirographs: Negotiable Instruments?' 133 *Zeitschrift der Savigny-Stiftung für Rechtsgeschichte, Romanistische Abteilung*, 265–85.

Sirks, B. (2019). 'Die Bedeutung von in bonis in der actio Serviana' 136 *Zeitschrift der Savigny-Stiftung für Rechtsgeschichte, Romanistische Abteilung*, 84–110.

Smit, A.J.H. (2020). *Pignus nominis. De verpanding van vorderingen naar Romeins recht*. The Hague: Boom.

Smith, C.M., L. Gabora, and W. Gardner-O'Keary (2018). 'The Extended Evolutionary Synthesis Paves the Way for a Theory of Cultural Evolution' 9 *Cliodynamics*, 84–107.

Stein, P. (1958). *Fault in the Formation of Contract in Roman Law and Scots Law*, Edinburgh: Oliver and Boyd.

Stein, P. (1980). *Legal Evolution. The Story of an Idea*. Cambridge: Cambridge University Press.

Steinhauer, F. (2007). *Gerechtigkeit als Zufall: zur rhetorischen Evolution des Rechts.* Vienna and New York: Springer.

Steinwenter, A. (1943). *Fundus cum instrumento: ein agrar- und rechtsgeschichtliche Studie.* Vienna: Hölder-Pichler-Tempsky.

Sturm, F. (1993a). 'Die Digestenexegese' in H. Schlosser, F. Sturm, and H. Weber, eds, *Die rechtsgeschichtliche Exegese*, 2nd edn, Munich: Beck, 26–54.

Sturm, F. (1993b). 'Das Absterben der mancipatio' in S. Buchholz et al., eds, *Überlieferung, Bewahrung und Gestaltung in der rechtsgeschichtlichen Forschung.* Paderborn: Schöningh.

Tamahana, B.Z. (2001). *A General Jurisprudence of Law and Society.* Oxford: Oxford University Press.

Tamahana, B.Z. (2017). *A Realistic Theory of Law.* Cambridge: Cambridge University Press.

Taubenschlag, R. (1955). *The Law of Greco-Roman Egypt in the Light of the Papyri. 332 BC –640 AD*, 2nd edn, Warsaw: Państwowe Wydawnictwo Naukowe (PNW).

Temin, P. (2013). *The Roman Market Economy.* Princeton, NJ: Princeton University Press.

Terpstra, T.T. (2008). 'Roman Law, Transaction Costs and the Roman Economy' in Verboven, Vandorpe, and Chankowski-Sable 2008, 345–69.

Terpstra, T.T. (2013). *Trading Communities in the Roman World. A Micro-Economic and Institutional Perspective.* Leiden: Brill.

Teubner, G. (1988). 'Introduction to Autopoietic Law' in G. Teubner, ed, *Autopoietic Law: A New Approach to Law and Society.* Berlin: De Gruyter, 1–11.

Teubner, G. (1993). *Law as an Autopoietic System.* Oxford: Blackwell.

Tomlin, R.S.O. (2016). *Roman London's First Voices. Writing Tablets from the Bloomberg Excavations, 2010–14.* London: Museum of London.

Tuori, K. (2007). *Ancient Roman Lawyers and Modern Legal Ideals. Studies on the Impact of Contemporary Concerns in the Interpretation of Ancient Roman Legal History.* Frankfurt am Main: Klostermann.

Turchin, P., and S.A. Nefedov (2009). *Secular Cycles.* Princeton, NJ: Princeton University Press.

Vaan de, M. (2008). *Etymological Dictionary of Latin and the Other Italic Languages.* Leiden: Brill.

Van Oyen, A. (2020). *The Socio-economics of Roman Storage. Agriculture, Trade, and Family.* Cambridge: Cambridge University Press.

Verboven, K. (2002). *The Economy of Friends. Economic Aspects of Amicitia and Patronage in the Late Republic.* Brussels: Latomus.

Verboven, K. (2008). 'Faeneratores, negotiatores and Financial Intermediation in the Roman World (Late Republic and Early Empire)' in Verboven, Vandorpe, and Chankowski-Sable 2008, 211–29.

Verboven, K., K. Vandorpe, and V. Chankowski-Sable, eds (2008). *Pistoi dia tèn technèn. Bankers, Loans and Archives in the Ancient World, Studies in Honour of Raymond Bogaert.* Leuven: Peeters.

Verhagen, H.L.E. (2011a). 'Das Verfallpfand im frühklassischen römischen Recht' 79 *Legal History Review*, 1–46.

Verhagen, H.L.E. (2011b). 'Die Vereinbarung des Pfandverfalls im ius commune' 19 *Zeitschrift für Europäisches Privatrecht*, 109–44.

Verhagen, H.L.E. (2013a). 'The Evolution of *pignus* in Classical Roman Law' 81 *Legal History Review*, 51–79.

Verhagen, H.L.E. (2013b). 'Ius honorarium, Equity and Real Security. Parallel Lines of Legal Development' in W.J. Zwalve and E. Koops, eds, *Law and Equity. Approaches in Roman Law and Common Law.* The Hague: Martinus Nijhoff, 129–60.

Verhagen, H.L.E. (2014). 'The (Lack of) Protection of Bona Fide Pledge-creditors in Classical Roman Law' in R. van den Bergh et al., eds, *Meditationes de iure et histori: Essays in Honour of Laurens Winkel. Fundamina. Editio specialis.* Pretoria: Unisa Press, 982–92.

Verhagen, H.L.E. (2018). 'Chirographs in Classical Roman Law. Constitutive or Probative?' 65 *Revue internationale des droits de l'antiquité*, 251–306.

Verhagen, H.L.E. (2020). 'Secured Transactions in Roman Law' in Dari-Mattiacci and Kehoe 2020b, 113–56.

Vesting, Th. (2018a). *Legal Theory*. Oxford: Hart.

Vesting, Th. (2018b). *Legal Theory and the Media of Law*. Cheltenham: Elgar.

Veyne, P. (1957). 'La Table des Ligures Baebiani et l'Institution Alimentaire de Trajan' 69 *Mélanges de l'école française de Rome*. Rome: École française, 114–25.

Vivenza, G. (2012). 'Roman Economic Thought' in Scheidel 2012, 25–44.

Voigt, S. (2019). *Institutional Economics. An Introduction*. Cambridge: Cambridge University Press.

Wacke, A. (1969). 'Prozessformel und Beweislast im Pfandrechtsprätendentenstreit' 37 *Legal History Review*, 369–414.

Wacke, A. (1974). *Das Besitzkonstitut als Übergabesurrogat in Rechtsgeschichte und Rechtsdogmatik. Ursprung, Entwicklung und Grenzen des Traditionsprinzips im Mobiliarsachenrecht*. Cologne: Hanstein.

Wacke, A. (1997). 'Die Konvaleszenz der Verfügung eines Nichtberechtigten' 114 *Zeitschrift der Savigny-Stiftung für Rechtsgeschichte, Romanistische Abteilung*, 438–61.

Wacke, A. (1998). 'Max Kasers Lehren zum Ursprung und Wesen des römischen Pfandrechts' 115 *Zeitschrift der Savigny-Stiftung für Rechtsgeschichte, Romanistische Abteilung*, 168–202.

Wacke, A. (2000). 'Erzwingt eine Novation den Verlust bestehender Sicherheiten? – Für eine Forderungsauswechselung auch beim Mobiliarpfand' 6 *Orbis Iuris Romani*, 215–39.

Wagner, H. (1967). 'Zur Freiheitserteilung an den einem Generalpfandnexus unterliegende Sklaven' 33 *Studia et documenta historiae et iuris*, 175–7.

Wagner, H. (1968). *Voraussetzungen, Vorstufen und Anfänge der römischen Generalverpfändung*. Marburg: Elwert.

Wagner, H. (1974). *Die Entwicklung der Legalhypotheken am Schuldnervermögen im römischen Zeit (bis zur Zeit Diokletians)*. Vienna: Böhlau.

Wagner, H. (1982). 'Zur wirtschaftlichen und rechtlichen Bedeutung der Tabernen' in F. Pastori, ed, *Studi in onore di Arnoldo Biscardi*, vol. III. Milano: La Goliardica, 391–422.

Watson, A. (1962). 'The Origins of Fiducia' 79 *Zeitschrift der Savigny-Stiftung für Rechtsgeschichte: Romanistische Abteilung*, 329–34.

Watson, A. (1965). *The Law of Obligations in the Later Roman Republic*. Oxford: Clarendon Press.

Watson, A. (1970). 'The Development of the Praetor's Edict', *Journal of Roman Studies*, 105–119.

Watson, A. (1971). *Roman Private Law Around 200* BC. Edinburgh: Edinburgh University Press.

Watson, A. (1974). *Law Making in the Later Roman Republic*. Oxford: Clarendon Press.

Watson, A. (1975). *Rome of the Twelve Tables. Persons and Property*. Princeton, NJ: Princeton University Press.

Watson, A. (1995). *The Spirit of Roman Law*. Athens, GA: University of Georgia Press.

Watson, A., ed. (1998). *The Digest of Justinian*, 4 vols, Philadelphia, PA: University of Pennsylvania Press.

Watson, A. (2001). *Society and Legal Change*, 2nd edn, Philadelphia, PA: Temple University Press.

Watson, A. (2007). 'Law and Society' in J.W. Cairns and P. du Plessis, eds, *Beyond Dogmatics. Law and Society in the Roman World*. Edinburgh: Edinburgh University Press, 9–35.

Wegmann Stockebrand, A. (2017). *Obligatio re contracta. Ein Beitrag zur sogenannten Kategorie der Realverträge im römischen Recht*. Tübingen: Mohr Siebeck.

Wenger, L. (1953). *Die Quellen des römischen Rechts*. Vienna: Holzhausen.

Wieacker, F. (1939). '"Protopraxie" und "ius pignoris" im klassischen Fiskalrecht' in *Festschrift Paul Koschaker*, vol. I. Weimar: Böhlau, 218–57.

Wieacker, F. (1961). *Vom römischen Recht. Zehn Versuche*, 2nd edn, Stuttgart: Koehler.

Wieacker, F. (1969). 'Zur Verpfändung fremder Sachen' 30 *Legal History Review*, 58–76.

Wieacker, F. (1973). 'Jhering und der Darwinismus' in G. Paulus et al., *Festschrift für Karl Larenz zum 70. Geburtstag*. München: Beck, 63–92.

Wieacker, F. (1977). 'Juristen und Jurisprudenz im Prinzipat' 94 *Zeitschrift der Savigny-Stiftung für Rechtsgeschichte, Romanistische Abteilung*, 319–58.

Wieacker, F. (1988). *Römische Rechtsgeschichte. Quellenkunde, Rechtsbildung, Jurisprudenz und Rechtsliteratur*, vol. I. Munich: Beck.

Wieling, H.J. (1989). 'Privilegium fisci, praediatura und Protopraxie' 106 *Zeitschrift der Savigny-Stiftung für Rechtsgeschichte. Romanistische Abteilung*, 404–33.

Willems, C. (2017). 'Roman Law and Economics. Ökonomische Analysetools als Erweiterung des "klassischen" romanistischen Methodenspektrums' 83 *Studia et documenta historiae et iuris*, 521–37.

Woess von, F. (1924). *Untersuchungen über das Urkundenwesen und den Publizitätsschutz im römischen Ägypten*. Munich: Beck.

Wolf, J.G. (2010). *Aus dem neuen pompejanischen Urkundenfund. Gesammelte Aufsätze*. Berlin: Duncker & Humblot.

Wolf, J.G. (2012). *Neue Rechtsurkunden aus Pompeji, Tabulae Pompeianae Novae*, 2nd edn, Darmstadt: Wissenschaftlichte Buchgesellschaft.

Wolf, J.G. (2013). 'Außerjuristische Wertungen in der Argumentation Papinians' 81 *Legal History Review*, 633–43.

Wolf, J.G. (2015). 'Documents in Roman Practice' in D. Johnston, ed., *The Cambridge Companion to Roman Law*. Cambridge: Cambridge University Press, 61–84.

Wolf, J.G., and J.A. Crook (1989). *Rechtsurkunden in Vulgärlatein aus den Jahren 37–39 n. Chr:* Heidelberg: Winter.

Wolff, H.J. (1978). *Das Recht der griechischen Papyri Ägyptens in der Zeit der Ptolemaeer und des Prinzipat*, vol. II. *Organisation und Kontrolle des privaten Rechtsverkehrs*. Munich: Beck.

Wubbe, F.B.J. (1958). 'Eine Lehre vom *subpignus* im Corpus Iuris Civilis?' 26 *Legal History Review*, 133–94.

Wubbe, F.B.J. (1960). *Res aliena pignori data: de verpanding van andermans zaak in het klassieke Romeinse recht*. Leiden: Universitaire Pers.

Wubbe, F.B.J. (1967). 'Gaius et les contrats réels' 35 *Legal History Review*, 500–25.

Wubbe, F.B.J. (2003). *Ius vigilantibus scriptum, Ausgewählte Schriften/Œuvres choisies*. P. Pichonnaz, ed., Freiburg: Universitätsverlag.

Wubbe, F.B.J., and P. Pichonnaz (2003). 'L'action Servienne dans l'Edit du Préteur' in Wubbe 2003, 203–32 (originally published in M. Humbert and Y. Thomas, eds, *Mélanges à la mémoire de André Magdelain*. Paris 1998: LGDJ, 361–82).

Zimmermann, R. (1990). *The Law of Obligations. Roman Foundations of the Civilian Tradition*. Boston: Kluwer (reprint 1992).

Zülch, C. (2001). *Der liber singularis responsorum des Ulpius Marcellus*. Berlin: Duncker & Humblot.

Zumbansen, P., and G.-P. Calliess (2011). *Law, Economics and Evolutionary Theory*. Cheltenham: Elgar.

Zwalve, W.J. (2004). 'A Labyrinth of Creditors: a Short Introduction to the History of Security Interests in Goods' in E.M. Kieninger, ed., *Security Rights in Movable Property in European Private Law*. Cambridge: Cambridge University Press, 38–53.

Zwalve, W.J., and A.J.B. Sirks (2012). *Grundzüge der europäischen Privatrechtsgeschichte. Einführung und Sachenrecht*. Vienna, Cologne and Weimar: Böhlau.

Zweigert, K., and H. Kötz (1998). *Introduction to Comparative Law*. 3rd edn, Oxford: Clarendon Press, 1998.

Index

For the benefit of digital users, indexed terms that span two pages (e.g., 52–3) may, on occasion, appear on only one of those pages.

Index of Sources

For the benefit of digital users, indexed terms that span two pages (e.g., 52–3) may, on occasion, appear on only one of those pages.

9 780199 695836

Made in the USA
Las Vegas, NV
19 September 2026

d4ce967c-889c-498f-93b7-c971d947d7acR01